STEPHEN CRANE

STEPHEN CRANE

A Life of Fire

PAUL SORRENTINO

THE BELKNAP PRESS OF HARVARD UNIVERSITY PRESS

Cambridge, Massachusetts | London, England 2014

Library of Congress Cataloging-in-Publication Data
Sorrentino, Paul.
Stephen Crane: a Life of Fire / Paul Sorrentino.
pages cm
Includes bibliographical references and index.
ISBN 978-0-674-04953-6 (alk. paper)
1. Crane, Stephen, 1871–1900.   2. Authors, American—19th century—Biography.   I. Title.
PS1449.C85Z866 2014
813'.4—dc23 [B]   2013034237

For Peg

Contents

Part III

FAME, NOTORIETY, AN ALTERED POINT OF VIEW

Part IV

NEW START, OLD HABITS

Part V

SEARCH FOR RESPECTABILITY, COUNTRY SQUIRE

Illustrations follow Chapter 19

STEPHEN
CRANE

Introduction

Problems with Crane Biography

"No one will ever be able to work casually at Crane," wrote the noted American poet John Berryman, "and be certain of anything." Berryman encountered the problems that every other biographer has faced in writing about the most controversial American author of the late nineteenth century: scant primary evidence; garbled chronologies; undated, misdated, and missing correspondence; unverifiable rumors; and contradictory eyewitness accounts. Contemporary newspapers and magazines routinely erred about the year of his birth and the titles of his publications. No other American writer, with the exception of Poe, has left a life record with more opacities and inconsistencies than Crane. His first biographer, Thomas Beer, complained to friends that the "woes of a biographer are crushing me flat"; after finishing *Stephen Crane: A Study in American Letters* (1923), he declared, "Biography is a deadly job and not for a million dollars would I tackle it again." In contrast to the few completed Crane biographies are dozens of discarded attempts to narrate the life of an elusive author who, like the Cheshire Cat, confessed that he could not "help vanishing and disappearing and dissolving. It is my foremost trait."[1]

Beer's book created a major problem in understanding Crane's life and work. Though subsequent biographers, historians, and other scholars questioned its accuracy, they accepted anecdotes, details, and excerpts from Crane's letters found only in Beer's biography; no concrete evidence suggested otherwise. No one knew how damaging the book was to Crane scholarship until Stanley Wertheim and I demonstrated that Beer had suppressed information, altered the chronology of Crane's life, invented anecdotes, created fictional persons, and fabricated virtually all of the letters to and from Stephen and Cora Crane that initially built the foundation for understanding Crane's life.[2] In doing this, Beer so strongly identified with his subject that, as his close friend Ernest Boyd observed, the biography "is, within certain limits, a complete expression of [Beer's] literary personality," which is "stamped as clearly upon his life of Stephen Crane as if it were his own story." Long-time colleague Wilson Follett characterized the identification as pathological: Beer "could quote pages from authors who never wrote any such pages; sometimes from authors who never lived"; and when he encountered "troublesome lacunae in Crane's life he lived through them with that same imagination, quite as if he were Crane; and his imagination could document every happening if he were challenged." Beer's mixture of fact and fiction has, like a computer virus, infected not only Crane scholarship but also literary histories and critical studies of the 1890s. Ironically, the fabricator of Crane's life was himself to become a fabrication in American fiction. A good friend of Thomas Wolfe, Beer is portrayed in Wolfe's *You Can't Go Home Again* and *The Web and the Rock* as Stephen Hook, who lives "almost completely in the lives of others." Whether in the fabricated *Stephen Crane* or in Wolfe's novels, the real Thomas Beer disappears, yet his influence has lived on.[3]

Given the major problems with Beer's biography, there is one inescapable conclusion: "facts" and documents for which he is the only source must be ignored in Crane studies. The implications of this decision are enormous, for countless scholarly books and articles, biographical entries, and popular accounts have relied heavily on him for evidence. Beer invented a number of the most colorful anecdotes in Crane's life—for example, that as a child he repeatedly had nightmares about black riders on black horses emerging from the sea to attack him, that in college he refused to meet Frances Willard because he considered her a fool, and that as an adult he tried to enlist in the Navy. Found only in Beer are some of Crane's most famous "pronouncements," such as that "the root of Bowery life is a sort of cowardice," that he himself was "just a dry twig on the edge of the bonfire," and that Tolstoy's *War and Peace* was too long: "He could have done the whole business in one third of the time and made it just as wonderful. It goes on and on like Texas."[4]

Even after one eliminates Beer's influence, however, other problems remain. Typically a biographer relies upon primary documents—letters, notebooks, diaries, and journals—to understand a subject's thoughts and attitudes. Biographers of Mark Twain, for example, have access to fifty notebooks he kept throughout his life and approximately 28,000 letters to or by him or an immediate family member. In some cases, the wealth of primary material is overwhelming. George Bernard Shaw wrote more than 250,000 letters; Ezra Pound's correspondence consists of 300,000. By comparison, little evidence is available about Crane's life. He did not keep a diary or journal; only one slim notebook survives; and of the 750 or so letters to and from him and Cora, many are mundane; few are richly detailed. Because of the scarcity of biographical documents by and about him, *Stephen Crane: A Life of Fire* situates him within social, political, religious, intellectual, and historical contexts in order to understand his life and significance. Thus, the chapters that follow contain anecdotes, historical details, and observations about such diverse topics as American Methodism, tuberculosis, the 1893 Columbian Exposition, New York City politics, and social customs in Asbury Park and Ocean Grove, New Jersey, in order to recreate the milieu that Crane experienced.

Other important sources are reminiscences by friends, relatives, and professional colleagues about their relationship with Crane. But although an eyewitness account is valuable for reconstructing an author's life, a reminiscence can be as problematic as Beer's biography. How reliable, for example, is a recollection of an event written decades after its occurrence, especially if it uses Beer's fabricated details? In 1903 one of Crane's closest friends, Corwin Knapp Linson, published an account of their relationship. Decades later, he expanded the reminiscence into an extensive memoir based at times solely on Beer. Linson was not above rewriting history himself. A photograph showed Crane smoking a hookah at a party; but before using the photo in the memoir, Linson retouched it so that Crane appeared to be alone, smoking a conventional pipe (see Figures 1 and 2). In other cases, unverifiable assertions in one reminiscence contradict those in another. Following Crane's death, Hamlin Garland published four accounts of their relationship—one in 1900, one in 1914, and two in 1930—that span thirty years and that are the only sources for important events during Crane's time in Asbury Park and New York City; but Garland gave different versions of the same events. Other accounts are equally uncertain. Was Crane fired from the *New York Tribune* after writing a satirical article about a parade in Asbury Park? Some friends insisted yes; others, no. Did Crane write a draft of his first major work, *Maggie: A Girl of the Streets,* in the spring of 1891 at Syracuse University? Classmates staunchly disagreed. Was he short or tall? Yes on both accounts. Color of eyes? Blue to one, deep gray to another.

Besides the reliability or unreliability of memory, a memoirist's rhetorical choices also affect the story. A reminiscence is a biographical sketch, and the more gripping it is, the more it relies on elements of fiction such as plot, setting, dialogue, and characterization. In shaping biographical facts into a narrative, writers emphasize details they recall as significant; but in valuing certain details over others, they interpret events that, viewed by someone else, might assume a different meaning. Among the most vivid—and unreliable—reminiscences are those by two masterful novelists, Willa Cather and Ford Madox Ford. Cather partly fictionalized her historic meeting with Crane during his western trip in 1895. Ford readily acknowledged that he invented details for narrative effect and repeated the same anecdotes throughout his reminiscences, interpreting them differently each time they were told.

Even when writers valued accuracy more than storytelling, they struggled with another potential difficulty. In recounting their memories of Crane, they were also recalling their own lives. Biographical accounts thus became autobiographical as well, as writers recreated earlier versions of themselves. Their reliability, however, depends on how well they recalled details of events as filtered through their own preconceptions. Linson acknowledged this fact by titling his memoir *My Stephen Crane.* Ideally, a biographer should have at least two reliable firsthand accounts to verify facts and events; but with Crane, given the scant evidence and the contradictions within it, this is impossible. Thus, my biography is a narrative of the available documents.

Living what he described as "a life of fire," Crane became an international celebrity by age twenty-four, only to die four-and-a-half years later, burned out from his own intensity. Once he was committed to a writing project, he needed to immerse himself fully in the moment. Dressed as a hobo with only thirty cents in his pocket, he spent four days in New York's Bowery district to experience the life of the homeless for his sketch "An Experiment in Misery." Similarly, from January to March 1894, Crane had a creative burst of energy during which he wrote most, if not all, of the sixty-eight poems in *The Black Riders and Other Lines,* with thirty of them supposedly composed in three days. Though he acknowledged there was "an intensity that the writer [can't] reach every day," he claimed he could "turn the poetic spout on or off."[5]

Crane's distinctive prose style reflected his own personality. Just as his fiction is often disruptive, elliptical, and episodic, his life was fragmented. Within five years he traveled to the American West, Mexico, Cuba, the British Isles, Greece, and the Continent, at times disappearing for weeks from a biographer's view. Likewise, just as his writing yokes together seemingly unrelated images—sleeping men, for example, snore "with tremendous effort, like stabbed fish"—his personality is a yoking together of disparate behaviors.[6] He admired proper military dress but wore dirty, ill-fitting clothes. Variously taciturn and garrulous, confident and insecure, romantic and cynical, steady and mercurial, Crane's conflicting identities masked his true self, a set of irresolvable contradictions that defined him. He rebelled against tradition yet was proud of his family heritage; he acted like a bohemian yet was drawn to social status; he yearned for the romanticized female yet obsessively sought out prostitutes; he fought with a distant God yet wished for His presence.

Often a loner, Crane acknowledged in a poem the "many who went in huddled procession" but identified with the "one who sought a new road" alone. His religious heritage, with its belief that an individual stands alone in a personal relationship with God, deepened his sense of isolation. As a rebel against literary convention, religious orthodoxy, and social convention, he was a fierce individualist; but the source of his isolation was cultural as well. As Alexis de Tocqueville asserted in his classic study of American culture, democracy offers "great benefits" but has "dangerous propensities. It tends to isolate [individuals] from each other, to concentrate every man's attention upon himself." As a result, "it throws him back forever upon himself alone, and threatens in the end to confine him entirely within the solitude of his own heart." Besides Crane, American literature is filled with authors such as Edgar Allan Poe, Emily Dickinson, and Ernest Hemingway who confront their own solitude in their writings. Yet even as Crane was impelled to travel new roads alone, he felt an equally strong urge to be part of community; hence his attraction to sports, parties, and fraternity life. Like Henry Fleming in *The Red Badge of Courage,* he was "doomed, alone, to unwritten responsibilities";

as a survivor of a shipwreck in "The Open Boat," he discovered "the subtle brotherhood of men."[7]

Crane's self-projection complicates a biographer's attempts to achieve psychological accuracy. As one friend quipped about Crane's behavior, "Stevie is just making biography for himself," and his conduct could be frustrating. "I go through the world unexplained," he declared; and after missing a business appointment with his editor, he wrote, "Of course eccentric people are admirably picturesque at a distance but I suppose after your recent close-range experiences with me, you have the usual sense of annoyance." Biographical problems notwithstanding, Crane's allure is inescapable. Despite living only to age twenty-eight, Crane published five novels; two novellas; two collections of poetry; more than two hundred stories, tales, and sketches; and scores of news dispatches. As much as any other American writer in the 1890s, he pioneered narrative and poetic techniques that foreshadow modern American literature. The psychological portrayal of fear in *The Red Badge of Courage* and the stark depiction of slum life in *Maggie: A Girl of the Streets* are groundbreaking; *The Third Violet* is a self-reflexive love story that is a precursor to postmodernism; and the treatment of theme and language in "The Open Boat" has made it a classic short story in world literature. As rich and exciting as Crane's writing is, his life is the stuff of Hollywood adventure. Whether he was experiencing the bohemian life of New York City, surviving a near-death experience at sea, or covering the historic charge up the San Juan hills during the Spanish-American War, his life was front-page news across America. Today, he still captures the public's attention, as seen in Bruce Springsteen's donation of $35,000 to renovate Crane's home in Asbury Park, the use of the expression "red badge of courage" by war correspondents to describe combat troops, and the appearance of his face on the cover of one of the most famous albums in rock music, the Beatles' *Sergeant Pepper's Lonely Hearts Club Band*.[8]

Principles and Practice

For source material I rely heavily on my and Stanley Wertheim's *Correspondence of Stephen Crane* (two volumes), our *Crane Log: A Documentary Life of Stephen Crane, 1871–1900,* and my *Stephen Crane Remembered* because these volumes are more readily available in libraries than the obscure and relatively inaccessible documents cited in them; but I have occasionally cited a document that appears only in an abridged form in *Stephen Crane Remembered*. I have largely avoided using *sic* and square brackets in the text, because they are distracting. I have also silently corrected typographical errors in sources, with one general exception: Crane's letters. Though Crane was a notoriously bad speller and paid little attention to grammar, the errors in his letters often reveal his conflicted psychological nature. He understood that a typist or typesetter needed a clear manuscript to ensure that a text was properly printed; in such contexts his penmanship is legible, and he used typographical symbols such as a circled dot to signify a period. Yet he ignored errors in his correspondence. For example, just as he repeatedly included the apostrophe in "don't" in the manuscript of *The Red Badge of Courage,* he consistently dropped it in his letters. At other times he wrote "F'or" rather than "For."

In narrating a life story, a biographer must make inferences; but as soon as one enters the subject's mind, supposition may be tenuous. Expressions such as "Crane might have done this" or "he probably thought that" can clutter a narrative, but bold assertions such as "Crane hated" or "he feared" may seem mere speculation. Whenever I have inferred something about Crane, I supply evidence for my statement; and whenever I have conjectured, I try to offer a plausible explanation of Crane's psyche based on my overall sense of him.

Throughout the narrative, I paraphrase sources and quote key phrases (mostly by Crane) to capture a person's thought or disposition. Although lengthy quotations can be distracting, the few in the text are important to my interpretation of Crane. For example, his contractual misunderstandings regarding *Wounds in the Rain* and his continual demands for advance payments prompted a reprimand from the publisher Frederick A. Stokes. A significant portion of Stokes's letter and one from Crane's friend Robert Barr about the incident reveal Crane's unbusinesslike behavior. A paraphrase of the two letters would diminish their intensity. Similarly, the death of Dr. John Blair Gibbs in the Spanish-American War tempered Crane's cynicism and irreparably altered his view on war. His little-known graphic account of the incident is memorable.

Following the Prologue, which begins six months before Crane's death, the narrative is generally chronological with one important exception. Chapter 11 covers early 1894 and discusses his ambivalence about women, a theme central to *The Third Violet,* most of which was written in the fall of 1895. To maintain coherence in my analysis of Crane and women, I discuss the novel in Chapter 11. To create immediacy in the narrative, I use dialogue, but I never invent it. When someone speaks, I quote directly from a source, with one minor adjustment: occasionally a source uses phrases (such as "he said") that, if included in my narrative, would sound awkward or be unnecessary; so I have silently revised or deleted them. But I have not changed any quotation in such a way as to alter its meaning.

Although I mention why various works by Crane are important, I avoid extended literary analysis because it can dilute the dramatic tension of the narrative; however, I have made an exception for his acknowledged masterpiece, *The Red Badge of Courage,* to discuss its influence and innovative techniques. Otherwise, I generally discuss a work only to help the reader understand Crane's life. His work is not dependably autobiographical, but at times he encodes a private subtext into a story in order to address personal concerns, thus making the creation of a literary text a form of self-creation as well. For example, I discuss several of the less effective Whilomville stories, in which Crane revisits the setting of his childhood, and a minor novel, *Active Service,* which is based on events in his life and career. More than my readings of any other work discussed in the biography, my analysis of "The Monster" relies heavily on cultural context. The novella is a complex exploration of race, history, and personal identity.

Because pacing is important for a good story, I move quickly through periods in which little is known and slow down for pivotal events in his life. As a fledgling journalist Crane satirically reported on a summer parade, and as a famous author he defended in court and in print an unfairly arrested prostitute. Because these incidents erupted into national controversies and troubled Crane, I spend considerable time narrating them. On another occasion I dramatize his sense of humor. Although literary historians have portrayed Crane as a bleak naturalist, he was often playful, as demonstrated in a little-known encounter with Haitian soldiers in 1898 involving slapstick, merriment, and a military leader he dubbed "Alice-in-Wonderland."

Among the new details about Crane presented in this book are two distressing childhood events (a trip to the New York City slums with his father and a tragic explosion marring a July 4 celebration); anecdotes about Crane's pranks; his synesthesia and its relation to his use of color; his familiarity with *Atwood's Country and Suburban Houses,* by Daniel T. Atwood, and with Beatrice Harraden's *Ships That Pass in the Night;* evidence that *George's Mother* and the Whilomville stories are partly autobiographical; a new explanation for Crane's dismissal from the *New York World* in 1898; and his probable relationships with his uncle Wilbur Fisk Peck and Ernest Hemingway's mother. There are also many new anecdotes about his life. Because so little is known about Crane's early childhood, I have used unpublished letters from the Crane and Peck families to recreate this period. I have also discussed his ancestors and more immediate family members because of their influence on him. Though I mention several of Beer's influential fabrications, I have avoided examining the many differences between previous biographies and mine. John Berryman and R. W. Stallman reawakened scholars to Crane's genius (Melvin H. Schoberlin would have contributed to this renaissance, had he finished his study of Crane); Jean Cazemajou and J. C. Levenson, the latter in his introductions to *The Works of Stephen Crane,* added valuable biographical information; James B. Colvert, Christopher Benfey, and Linda Davis helped introduce him to a larger audience. My biography could not have been written without their important work.

Prologue

Sitting at his desk in his private study at Brede Place, the medieval manor house he lived in for the last part of his life in England, Stephen Crane surrounded himself with mementos of his past—on the wall illustrations from his Whilomville stories based on his youth, on the desk a pistol from his adventures in the West, behind him a bookshelf with his ancestors' theological and historical writings. Outside, across the gently rolling valley, he could see the Brede Church tower, a reminder of the traditional Christianity he had struggled with, and rebelled against, in his life and writings. By age twenty-eight he could look back at a career that had already produced *Maggie,* a defining example of literary determinism in American fiction; *The Red Badge of Courage,* the most important novel about the Civil War; and "The Open Boat," a landmark in world literature. Larger than life, he was as famous—and notorious—as his work. His heroism as a defender of a woman wrongly accused of a crime, as a survivor in a dinghy following a shipwreck, and as a war correspondent on the battlefield had made him an international celebrity. Next to Edgar Allan Poe and Walt Whitman, no other American writer of the nineteenth century was so romanticized in his lifetime.

Crane's life roughly corresponds to the most dramatic period in

American cultural history. The period witnessed such seminal changes as mass immigration, the growth of cities, and the closing of the frontier; advancements in agriculture, transportation, and technology; the rise of industrial capitalism; and the birth of labor unions. By the end of the nineteenth century, America had transformed itself into a leading world power. It was truly a watershed period that closed the gates to a rural, agrarian past with a largely homogeneous population and opened others to an ethnically diverse, urban, industrial future. Similarly, Crane, the most important American writer of his generation, opened the gates to modern American literature. His stark realism anticipated that of Frank Norris, Theodore Dreiser, and James T. Farrell; his imagistic poetry foreshadowed the work of Amy Lowell and Carl Sandburg; and his reliance on personal experience for literary inspiration foreshadowed the fiction of Ernest Hemingway, Sherwood Anderson, and Thomas Wolfe. Just as decisive changes quickly transformed America in the late nineteenth century, Crane raced through his life—as the title of one of his short stories suggests—with "the pace of youth" faltering, yet stripping away human illusion with piercing insight.

Late in January 1900, Crane heard the good news that his brother Edmund's wife, Mary, had given birth to twin sons. Learning that one was named Stephen, Crane sat at his desk and wrote to his namesake:

> My dear Stephen: I need not say to you that I welcomed your advent with joy. You and I will struggle on with the name together and do as best we may. In the meantime, I would remind you to grow up, as much as possible, like your gentle kindly lovable father and please do not repeat the vices and mistakes of
>
> Your devoted uncle,
> Stephen Crane.[1]

Like the Roman god Janus peering simultaneously into the past and future, Crane was looking both back and forward at his family's lineage in America. For two centuries a number of ancestors had borne his name, including one of the founders of the first English settlement in New Jersey in the seventeenth century and one of the colony's representatives to the first Continental Congress in the eighteenth century; and looking forward, Uncle Stephen was advising his nephew to live by

Christian virtues. But Crane was also writing to himself, reflecting on his own past. Though only twenty-eight, he knew he had little time to live: only a month earlier he had suffered a severe tubercular hemorrhage. In looking back at his own life—with the church tower as a visual reminder of spiritual forgiveness—he was acknowledging "vices and mistakes," not only to himself but also to the baby's father, Edmund, the brother Stephen was closest to emotionally, who had become Crane's guardian when their mother died and whose address the peripatetic Stephen often listed as "home." With this letter, the wayward sibling who had rebelled against the traditional Christianity of his parents was beginning to come home. Yet scarcely more than four months after writing it, Crane was dead; he passed away on June 5 in Badenweiler, Germany, where he had sought a cure for his tuberculosis.[2] His body was brought back to London, where friends, paying their last respects at a mortuary, viewed his wracked face behind the glass pane in the coffin lid.

Newspapers around the world immediately reported the death, and journalists in the Society of the Caribbean who had been with Crane during the Spanish-American War adopted a memorial resolution commemorating their lost comrade. On June 17, Cora Crane, accompanied by Stephen's niece Helen Crane and two of his beloved dogs, sailed from England with the body; they arrived in New York City ten days later. On a cold, windy June 28, his colleagues from the Authors Club carried the coffin into the Central Metropolitan Temple, the Methodist Episcopal church on Seventh Avenue, where a scattering of family and friends awaited the service. He was interred in Evergreen Cemetery, Hillside, New Jersey, under a headstone marked "Stephen Crane / Poet—Author / 1871–1900."

Also attending the funeral was Wallace Stevens, a fledgling poet and reporter who covered it for the *New York Tribune*. That night he reflected on the event in his journal:

> The church is a small one and was about third full. Most of the people were of the lower classes and had dropped in apparently to pass away the time. There was a sprinkling of men and women who looked literary, but they were a wretched, rag, tag, and bob-tail. I recognized John Kendrick Bangs. The whole thing was frightful. The prayers were perfunctory, the

choir worse than perfunctory with the exception of its hymn "Nearer My God To Thee" which is the only appropriate hymn for funerals I ever heard. The address was absurd. The man kept me tittering from the time he began till the time he ended. He spoke of Gladstone + Goethe. Then —on the line of premature death—he dragged in Shelley; and speaking of the dead man's later work he referred to Hawthorne. Finally came the Judgement day—and all this with most delicate, sweet, and bursal gestures—when the earth and the sea shall give up their dead. A few of the figures to appear that day flashed through my head—and poor Crane looked ridiculous among them. But he lived a brave, aspiring, hardworking life. Certainly he deserved something better than this absolutely common-place, bare, silly service I have just come from. As the hearse rattled up the street over the cobbles, in the stifling heat of the sun, with not a single person paying the least attention to it and with only four or five carriages behind it at a distance I realized much that I had doubtingly suspected before—There are few hero-worshippers.

★ ★ ★

Therefore, few heroes.

Stevens's commentary is curious, given Crane's stature at the time of his death. Though reviewers had questioned whether he would ever again attain the achievement of *The Red Badge of Courage,* his work was soon flooding bookshops. At the end of June came reprintings of *The Red Badge* and, in England, a reissue of *Maggie* and *George's Mother,* combined as *Bowery Tales.* Later in the year came *Whilomville Stories, Wounds in the Rain,* and the American edition of *Great Battles of the World.* The English editions of *The Monster and Other Stories* and *Great Battles of the World* followed in 1901, with *Last Words* appearing in 1902 and *The O'Ruddy* in 1903. It is easy to forget how much Crane accomplished so quickly. From the minor fictional episodes about New York's Sullivan County in 1892, to the masterful tale "The Open Boat" in 1897, and finally to the innovative "War Memories" and "The Clan of No-Name" in 1899—a span of only seven years—Crane developed his craft more quickly than any other nineteenth-century American writer. Crane had completed *Maggie* and *The Red Badge* before his twenty-third birthday, while Melville did not publish *Moby-Dick* until he was thirty-two. Hawthorne was forty-six when *The Scarlet Letter* appeared, and Twain was forty-nine when he published *Adventures of Huckleberry Finn.* Among the major important writers also born in the 1870s were Theodore Dreiser, Robert Frost, Vachel Lindsay, Frank Norris, Carl Sandburg, Gertrude Stein, and Wallace Stevens, all of whom were indebted to their contemporary. Though one can only guess what direction Crane's work might have taken had he not died at the age of twenty-eight, of all the American writers who died young no one had more potential to become a great writer than Stephen Crane.

Yet Stevens's observation of a listless funeral service ignored by all but a handful prophesied Crane's fate. Alive, Crane was a larger-than-life hero whose exploits were legendary. By 1899 his birthplace had become a hallowed site where admirers paid homage. But in a world with "few hero-worshippers," Stevens realized, heroes like Crane are soon forgotten. Even attempts to memorialize him proved fragile. In the 1920s the Stephen Crane Association championed his work, but it was largely a paper organization run by one person, a Newark high school teacher named Max J. Herzberg, and it was ultimately ineffectual. Despite efforts to preserve Crane's birthplace, the house was torn down and replaced in 1940 with a memorial wall built of bricks from Crane's home, a playground with a bronze plaque commemorating his birthplace, a ceramic plaque bearing his portrait, and thirty-six other plaques depicting scenes from his work. "Could Crane revisit this scene of his birth," read an inscription, "he would rejoice to behold at his earliest home no pomp of monumental stone, but this happy and human rendezvous for children whose laughter illumines a world he found dubious but not without occasion for courage and faith." After many of the plaques were vandalized, the area was fenced off and sold to a private company. In 1997 workers inadvertently bulldozed what was left of the landmark.[3]

Fifteen years after Crane's funeral, Peter Somerville, editor of the *Englishman,* asked Joseph Conrad to write an article about his American friend for the magazine. Conrad replied, "Believe me my dear Sir no paper, no review, would look at anything that I or anybody else could write about Crane. They would laugh at the suggestion. Crane? Who's Crane? Who cares for Crane? . . . Mere literary excellence won't save a man's memory. In fifty years' time some curious literary critic (of the professional scribbler kind) will perhaps rediscover him as a curiosity and write a short paper in order to earn five guineas. . . . Sad but true. I hardly meet anyone now who knows or remembers anything of him. For the youn-ger oncoming writers he does not exist, simply. One or two have heard of the Red Badge and have asked me, 'What sort of thing it is.'"[4]

This biography addresses a similar question: What sort of person was Stephen Crane?

Part I

THE WRENCHES OF CHILDHOOD

1

Roots and Beginnings

1635–1871

STEPHEN CRANE'S BIRTH, on November 1, 1871, in Newark, New Jersey, was greeted with apprehension. At forty-four, Mrs. Crane was well beyond the normal age for childbearing. She had already lost five of her thirteen other children, the last four having died within their first year or so, suffering the fate of their sister Elizabeth Blanche Crane. A healthy baby at age three months, one week later she was dead, her grief-stricken parents suffering "hours of anxiety." Despite assertions to his father-in-law that "the Lord is good," Reverend Crane cloaked his pain by tersely writing, "I need not comment."[1]

Nonetheless, the family celebrated the arrival of another of God's holy children. His birth in the red-brick, three-story parsonage at 14 Mulberry Place gave neighbors a rare chance to visit the Cranes, whose church duties kept them preoccupied. That evening, a proud father wrote in his diary that the baby would be named after two other Stephen Cranes. Reverend and Mrs. Crane had long stressed their pride of heritage by identifying their children with previous namesakes. Although family tradition held that the first Stephen Crane had traveled from England to Massachusetts in 1635 and that his son Stephen had later moved to Connecticut, the direct line of Reverend Crane's ancestry was rooted in New Jersey, for as his youngest son later wrote, "The family is founded deep in Jersey soil (since the birth of Newark), and I am about as much of a Jerseyman as you can find." Jasper and Azariah Crane founded Cranetown (later renamed Montclair), and Jasper helped to settle Newark. The new baby's first namesake (1640?–1710?) emigrated from England or Wales and was one of the sixty-five "Associates" who founded Elizabethtown, the first English settlement in New Jersey, in 1665–1666. Prominent in the community, he swore allegiance to King Charles II, but rebelled against Governor Philip Carteret because of an illegal land deal involving one of the governor's political allies. His grandson, the baby's second namesake (1709–1780), served as a sheriff, judge, mayor, and trustee of the First Presbyterian Church in Elizabethtown. A patriot of the American Revolution, he was Speaker of the New Jersey Assembly, president of the two Colonial Assemblies in New York, and a delegate to the Continental Congress. Had he not been called home in June 1776 to help settle a political crisis involving Tories in the New Jersey legislature, he would have been in Philadelphia to sign the Declaration of Independence. Eventually captured by the British in June 1780, he died of bayonet wounds.[2]

The latter's sons also valiantly aided the cause of colonial America. Jonathan was executed after refusing to reveal the location of General Washington's army to the enemy; one brother rose to senior commodore in the Navy; and William, the oldest son, commanded the 6th Regiment of New Jersey Infantry during the American Revolution, was wounded during the advance on Quebec, and was ultimately promoted to major general. His son William later won fame as a naval commander during the War of 1812 and against the Barbary pirates in 1815. Still other family members were imprisoned on British ships in New York harbor during the Revolution. To later generations of Cranes, their ancestors were courageous patriots defending their unalienable rights. Not surprisingly, Reverend and Mrs. Crane's youngest child was raised with anti-British sentiments because of the fate his ancestors had suffered at the hands of the enemy, and as an adult he angrily asserted, "Our family has little cause to love the gentle Britisher."[3]

Stephen's maternal ancestry, also firmly rooted in American soil, was descended from Henry Peck, a founder of New Haven, Connecticut. Corporal Jesse Peck and his five sons served in the Connecticut militia during the Revolution; later family members proudly joined the Sons of the American Revolution and Daughters of the American Revolution. By the nineteenth century, a number of the Pecks were spreading the Good News of God across America as Methodist ministers. "Upon my mother's side," as Stephen recalled, "everybody as soon as he could walk, became a Methodist clergyman—of the old ambling-nag, saddle-bag, exhorting kind."[4]

Crane was proud of his ancestry. Later generations of the family thought that the Revolutionary Stephen Crane had offered the opening prayer at the First Continental Congress in 1774 (they were mistaken) and had signed the Declaration of Independence. In 1895, when Stephen visited Carpenters' Hall in Philadelphia with his friend Frederic M. Lawrence, he proudly pointed out Crane's portrait among the portraits of other delegates to the Congress. In 1896 Stephen joined the Sons of the American Revolution, and in 1899 planned to commemorate his ancestry in a novel about the American Revolution. To his mind, his ancestors had assumed responsibility for their actions without self-pity or self-congratulation, a code of behavior against which he would later judge his fictional characters. "I swear by the real aristocrat," he declared. "The man whose forefathers were men of courage, sympathy and wisdom, is usually one who will stand the strain whatever it may be. He is like a thorough-bred horse. His nerves may be high and he will do a lot of jumping often but in the crises he settles down and becomes the most reliable and enduring of created things."[5]

Crane's ancestors imbued him with military pride, but he also inherited a strong religious background. However much he rebelled against it in later years, it always informed his personality and the themes and style of his writing. In the only surviving portrait of his father (see Figure 3), a stern gaze reveals the judgmental attitude of a minister whose religious tracts condemned idle amusements like smoking, drinking, and gambling, all of which Stephen reveled in. Yet Reverend Crane was also a loving, caring father with a strong sense of independence, tenacity, and fortitude—traits that his youngest son would inherit. Despite obvious differences between father and son, they were uncannily similar in upbringing, personality, and disposition. Both were the youngest sibling in a large family, and both lost a father early on: Jonathan was almost eleven; Stephen, eight. Father and son were each partly raised by, and relied upon, an older sister named Agnes. As young adults, both rebelled against some form of Christianity: the father, against Presbyterianism; the son, Methodism. And both used the power of the written word to criticize and satirize human foibles.

Jonathan Townley Crane was born near Elizabethtown in Connecticut Farms (today part of Union), New Jersey, on June 19, 1819, the youngest of six children of William and Sarah (Townley) Crane. He was raised a strict Presbyterian, with a Calvinist emphasis on predestination and infant damnation.[6] After his father's death and his mother's death from cholera two years later, he and his sister Agnes lived with an aunt in New Providence. To support himself, Jonathan became an apprentice to Smith Halsey, a Newark trunk maker who became a surrogate father to him. Proud of his work, Jonathan kept until his death several of the trunks he had made. At age eighteen, he dramatically changed his vocation while living with his aunt, whose home was a haven for Methodist ministers, one of whom, the Reverend Curtis Talley, had married Agnes. After attending a revival at his brother-in-law's church, Jonathan converted to Methodism and decided to become a preacher. To help him achieve his goal, his brother Richard paid Halsey the remaining part of the indenture. In 1841, at the age of twenty-one, Jonathan used the money he had earned as a trunk maker and as a teacher in local schools, supplemented by a modest inheritance from his father's estate, to enroll in the College of New Jersey (later Princeton University).[7]

Because Jonathan had read widely and studied on his own, he was given advance standing as a second-term sophomore and excelled as a student and writer in a liberal curriculum grounded in the classics. In his senior year, he was elected president of the Cliosophic Society, one of the school's two literary societies; was awarded a prize for English composition; and wrote essays under the pen name "Theodorus" for the *Nassau Monthly,* Princeton's literary magazine. Curiously, the essays anticipated the thinking later displayed by his son Stephen. In a witty and ironic essay titled "The Fiction of Our Popular Magazines," Theodorus criticized sentimental literature, as Stephen later did in such works as *Maggie: A Girl of the Streets* and "The Blue Hotel," because it misled naïve readers into confusing their own mundane lives with those of heroes and heroines in melodramatic adventures. Similarly, Theodorus's "English Strictures on American Slavery" and Stephen's college sketch "A Foreign Policy in Three Glimpses" censured British imperialism.

After graduating from college in 1843, Reverend Crane became an exhorter in the Methodist Church and was soon licensed to preach. Because itinerant Methodist ministers stayed in an assigned circuit no more than three years, he was repeatedly reassigned. Of his first five appointments, two lasted for a mere six months, two for one year each, and the last for about two years. Traveling with only a horse and a few religious texts, he spread God's Word throughout New Jersey and New York. During his ministry, his self-deprecating sense of humor prompted friends and family to consider publishing a collection of anecdotes about him. He could quip about how his undelivered mail had "disappeared mysteriously, vanished into thin air, à la mode de Virgil," and how a church member swore that Reverend Crane's sermon on dancing was "the most ridiculous piece of nonsense he ever heard." Once, when he absentmindedly began repeating a sermon he had already given to the same congregation, he jested, "Well, we have another barrel load along with us, and we'll see what we can do with another text." Yet at times he feared that his "preaching was doing no good"; and when crises arrived unexpectedly—"storms, sickness, & absences grown-out of our bereavements"—life became "a troubled dream."[8]

Reverend Crane was as much a writer as he was a preacher committed to spreading Methodism. A prolific author of books and essays on religious and social issues, he was well known for polemical tracts like *An Essay on Dancing* (1849), *Popular Amusements* (1869), and *Arts of Intoxication: The Aim and the Results* (1870). These tracts were more than simply diatribes against social practices. He readily acknowledged that dancing was an important social ritual in certain cultures, and to those who criticized his attack on dancing because he was "wholly unacquainted, *experimentally,* with his theme," he wittily responded that he was "in the honourable companionship of the gentlemen who have penned learned disquisitions upon *Capital Punishment.* It is not needful, either to dance, or to be hung, in order to be able to come to a conclusion touching the expediency of the performance." Similarly, in *Popular Amusements* he condemned such pastimes as the theater and the idle reading of fiction, but he carefully made distinctions. Novels, for example, were in his view not inherently good or bad. The criteria should be whether "the portraiture be true, and there be a good reason for the portrayal." He tried his hand at writing a novella, *The Lawyer and His Family: A Temperance Story for Youth* (1845); and though he criticized sentimental romances, he recommended that people read "*the best works of fiction*" by such authors as Dickens, Trollope, and Thackeray. When parents in the Methodist community worried that Sunday-school libraries were being packed with "worldly literature," he calmly explained that educated children needed to supplement their religious reading with books from a "secular list" of worthwhile literature. In addition to his own appreciation of classical literature, Crane read widely among dramatists like Aristophanes and Shakespeare and poets like Byron, Shelley, and Poe. Like his father, Stephen parodied sentimental fiction and insisted that fiction approximate reality.[9]

Reverend Crane married Mary Helen Peck in 1848. Born in Wilkes-Barre, Pennsylvania, on April 10, 1827, to the Reverend George and Mary Helen (Myers) Peck, Mary Helen was the middle child and only daughter among their five children and grew up thoroughly immersed in Methodism. Her father, author of religious and historical works and editor of the *Methodist Quarterly Review* and the *Christian Advocate and Journal,* shaped the direction of Methodism in nineteenth-century America. Born in a log cabin, he embodied the rugged individualism of early America as he spread the Gospel to the frontier. He ended his distinguished career as pastor and presiding elder of the Wyoming Conference in Pennsylvania. Among his four brothers, all of whom were Methodist ministers, was Mary Helen's equally influential uncle Jesse Truesdell Peck, later a bishop and cofounder of Syracuse University. Mary Helen attended the Young Ladies Institute of Brooklyn, New York, was teaching in the Sabbath school at the Pacific Street Church in Brooklyn, New York, by 1845, and graduated from the Rutgers Female Institute in 1847.[10]

A complex personality in whom straitlaced orthodoxy battled with a restless, creative spirit, Mrs. Crane spent much of her early married life caring for an ever-growing household; but later, driven by a persistent determination and religious fervor, she became a prominent figure in the Woman's Christian Temperance Union. As president of two WCTU chapters in New Jersey (Asbury Park and Ocean Grove) and one in New

York (Port Jervis), and as state superintendent of press for the WCTU in New Jersey, she lectured on social vices like alcohol and gambling. She also lobbied for women's rights and suffrage and published newspaper articles on religious and reform issues. But she also composed sketches and paintings, carefully crafted wax figures, and wrote short fiction, humorous letters, and moralistic fables that dramatized her family memories and political leanings. In her story "Thanksgiving or Christmas, *Which?*" she depicts a fatherless son, Little Zekey (affectionately called "Stevie"); in her letters, she evokes the imaginary local communities of Sandune Park and Scrub Oak Grove (Asbury Park and Ocean Grove); and in one particular fictional letter ("Jerusha Ann Stubbs to Cousin Abigail Jane"), she portrays a woman married to a man named Jonathan for forty years—the number of years that Jonathan Townley and Mary Helen Crane would have been married in 1888, the year she published the letter, had he not died in 1880. In her best work, she satirized a patriarchal society that denied women suffrage and equal rights. In "Jerusha Ann's Third Letter," the appropriately named "Deekin Uriah Blatherskite," whose blustering attitude hypocritically undercuts his professed Christian sensibility, complains about "radikel wimmin folks who went rampagin round the country a preechin and lecturin and meddlin with polyticks, and upsetting all the fundymental institushuns of government, and was rapidly a usurpin the divine prerogytives of men folks." Ironically, Mrs. Crane was also criticized for constantly traveling to lecture on church business rather than staying home with her children. Nonetheless, after her husband's death she was devoted to Stephen, though in later years, despite his love for her, he was surprised, according to a niece, that someone so educated and imaginative "could have wrapped herself so completely in the 'vacuous, futile, psalm-singing that passed for worship' in those days." Crane eventually portrayed his mother ambivalently as Mrs. Kelsey, the overbearing, indefatigable mother and religious zealot in *George's Mother.*[11]

Moving from New York to the small village of Belvidere in New Jersey later in 1848, following her marriage, Mary Helen had little in common with neighbors who identified her as "from *the city*," and her husband's frequent travels left her feeling "something of a *baby*—I can hardly help feeling lonely when left alone." Yet the couple had a loving relationship; and as a symbol of their firm commitment to their children, they saved a portion of their wedding cake for their offspring to unpack years later.[12] She playfully rebelled against her mother's admonition that she address her husband formally as "Mr. Crane," instead calling him "Jounty," her fond, playful compression of "Jonathan" and "Townley." A sentimental dreamer, she wondered whether they would grow old together like Darby and Joan, the elderly, devoted married couple in Henry Woodfall's immensely popular ballad "The Joys of Love Never Forgot: A Song" (1735).[13]

Desiring to settle down and raise a family, Reverend Crane gladly accepted the appointment as principal of Pennington Seminary, in Pennington, New Jersey—a school sponsored by the New Jersey Conference of the Methodist Episcopal Church—in 1849. Though the seminary was suffering from declining enrollment and financial difficulties, he reinvigorated it and developed a reputation as a caring, disciplined educator whose actions reflected his words. When a bully tried to incite a rebellion among his peers against the new principal's rules, Reverend Crane quickly lectured him on insubordination. By the next morning, the disgruntled student was gone. On another occasion a father insisted that the school prevent his son from smoking, even "if you have to break his neck!" But when the father put a cigar in his mouth and told his son to find a match, Reverend Crane, disturbed by the parent's double standard, "inwardly determined that if John's neck was to be broken for following his father's example, the father himself must do the deed."[14]

Under Reverend Crane's leadership, enrollment increased with the admission of women, the New Jersey Conference purchased the school, and students regularly experienced the " 'power' of the old-time Methodism" during religious revivals.[15] As Reverend Crane's fame as an educator spread throughout the state, he frequently lectured on subjects like temperance and women's suffrage. In 1849 Dickinson College, where Jesse Peck had been president from 1848 to 1852, made him an honorary member of its Belles Lettres Literary Society, and in 1856 it conferred upon him the degree of Doctor of Divinity.

Reverend Crane was a tireless scholar thirsting for knowledge; yet despite his academic and administrative accomplishments at Pennington, he was reassigned to the circuit, first to Jersey City (1858–1859), next to Haverstraw, New York (1860–1861), then back to New Jersey in Newark (1862–1864) and Morristown (1864–1866), leaving his family in "a per petual whirl" without a permanent sense of home.[16] When the Cranes abruptly moved to Bound Brook, New Jersey, in 1874, Agnes could only dread living in such "a horrid, stupid, old place" where she did "not know a soul": "I hate it and everyone in it."[17] Angry and alone, she retreated into the fictional world of her diary to talk with her alter ego, "Samantha." Her brother Stephen would never fully recover from the psychic dislocation of family and place. In 1881 he acquired a copy of *Atwood's Country and Suburban Houses,* one of the most popular "house pattern books" in the nineteenth century.[18] Besides offering practical ways to design homes for the middle class, the book was a metaphor for domesticity and "our united American civilization," as its author, Daniel T. Atwood, proclaimed.[19] For Stephen the book took on additional meaning. Throughout his adult life, he struggled with his own rootlessness and his longing to create the home he had never had. Although he was careless with his possessions, he kept the book till his death to remind him of that goal.

Such was the stress of continual moving that when the position of editor of the *Christian Advocate* became available, Reverend Crane dreamed of being offered it and settling in New York City. Despite his rural upbringing, he, like his wife, preferred urban settings, as he confided to Reverend George Peck. Nonetheless, he suspected that he would never receive the position, because he was "not in the 'Ring'"; his acute sense of being an outsider was a feeling that Stephen would share. "We smaller fig," the reverend had written earlier to his father-in-law, "must stand aside . . . tho' I must confess that I think it unfair that episcopal pets, if such things exist, should ride over the rest of the preachers." But from his perspective, bishops did favor certain ministers. With the exception of his nine years at Pennington, the Crane family had relocated constantly. As the family grew, the moves became increasingly difficult, so that by 1863 there were "nine reasons for disliking perpetual moving." When in 1867 he was assigned to Centenary Collegiate Institute (now Centenary College), a high school in Hackettstown, New Jersey, that he had helped to found for Methodist children, he hoped the family would regain the stable sense of place they had once had at Pennington. Yet twelve months later, despite his protest, the local bishop pressured him to accept yet another position: Presiding Elder of the Newark District. Besides often preaching three times daily, he supervised thirty-six ministers and managed the activities of forty churches. The enormous responsibilities of the job and the thought of the sixth move in ten years left Mary Helen, she confessed, "all unstrung from the anxiety."[20]

Despite uncertainties and anguish created by itinerancy, Reverend and Mrs. Crane educated their children on how to live righteously in a sinful world. He, as well as his wife's father and her Uncle Jesse, had already published advice on raising God-fearing children. Rather than filling their minds with "a tangle of metaphysical subtleties," Reverend Crane advised, religion should be taught as a set of simple, practical truths, and he believed that even though a loving father might chastise his children, he must treat them fairly.[21] He also rejected the widely held notion, popularized in Thomas Hughes's novel *Tom Brown at Rugby,* that fighting developed courage and heroism rather than "milksops and 'missies.'"[22] Yet as the Civil War had shown, Reverend Crane asserted, the best soldiers were not ruffians but "men of principle, quiet citizens, who, perhaps, had never before struck a man in anger in all their lives."[23] Years later his youngest son, Stephen, would explore the problematic nature of courage in his war stories.[24] Similarly, Jesse Peck's *God in Education: A Discourse to the Graduating Class of Dickinson College, July 1852* and George Peck's *Formation of a Manly Character: A Series of Lectures to Young Men* (1854) were popular Methodist manuals for the development of Christian character, and Stephen heeded their advice. Jesse Peck's insistence that the truth about human nature is "found not chiefly in books, but in men; not mainly in facts, but in general principles; not so much in the sayings as in the doings of the race" explains Stephen's predilection for life experience rather than formal education as a means of acquiring knowledge.[25] And George Peck's dictum that "to feel sympathy for the suffering, we must put ourselves into their circumstances" describes why Crane became a tramp to understand Bowery life in New York City for his autobiographical sketch "An Experiment in Misery."[26]

Crane, however, struggled with his Methodist heritage. Throughout much of his life, he rebelled against the kind of narrow orthodoxy epitomized in Jesse Peck's tract on human depravity and divine retribution, *What Must I Do To Be Saved?* (1858). Stephen received a copy in 1881 and was expected to obey Bishop Peck's teachings: "You alone must suffer for your own obstinate rebellion." Though Stephen would soon reject the dogmatism of his ancestors, it shaped his mind and imagination. Much of his prose and poetry depicts a postlapsarian battleground in which vain, deluded humans struggle against a hostile, animistic nature; and an inscrutable God—if He does exist—is variously compassionate toward, angry with, or indifferent to humanity.

Crane's anxiety exemplified late nineteenth-century America's spiritual disorientation as scientific advances and a growing sense of the frailty of human institutions undermined traditional faith. Crane never resolved his own spiritual angst, captured poignantly in "The Open Boat," in which the correspondent, Crane's persona, confronts a godless universe indifferent to the plight of humanity. Missing in the world are "bricks" to hurl at "temples"—Crane's image of dissent against outmoded social and religious institutions—because there are "no bricks and no temples": once-rational actions and traditions have become meaningless.[27] Crane rejected the teachings in *What Must I Do To Be Saved?* but the book became, like *Atwood's Country and Suburban Houses,* a vade mecum that he kept throughout his life as he searched for an earthly and spiritual home.

2

Childhood

1871–1884

NONE OF BABY Stephen's eight siblings was remotely near his age, the closest being the eight-year-old George. Stephen was essentially raised as an only child. Before he was one, he had begun walking by pushing a chair around the parsonage, but his health soon became a concern. Though he was thriving in September 1873, a month later he was so sick that the family feared for his well-being. In the earliest-known photograph of him, taken around 1873, a toddler stares wistfully from the frame as if already aware of life's uncertainty (Figure 6).[1]

Signs of the boy's intelligence were soon evident. Before age two, Stephen was writing letters to his "ganma" and spelling and pronouncing words of five and six syllables, with the help of his brother Edmund. By three he had taught himself to read; a year later he was reading the novels of James Fenimore Cooper. His precociousness did not surprise the family. By age three, Mary Helen, the oldest child, knew her alphabet and spoke in complete sentences; a year later she was sewing and reading. William ("Willie") was amusing his family with "certain baby witticisms" before age two; and Luther taught himself to read by age five and a half. Agnes was walking at eight months, sooner than any of her siblings, and by adolescence was reading incessantly, a trait that her parents feared would impair her health.[2]

Intensely imaginative and drawn to language and role playing as early as two and a half, Stephen was fascinated by the pattern on his dinner plate—letters of the alphabet encircling a peacock in a garden—and changed his name from "Tevie" to "Pe-pop-ty," a fictional persona that befuddled the family but that became an affectionate nickname. At age three, when he learned that his grandparents had sent him their love, he pointed to words in their letter: "Is that the love?" Upon his father's saying yes, the child studied the letter, turned it over, and asked, "Whose love is it on this side?" One time, Stephen imitated his brother Townley, a fledgling journalist who had asked their mother the correct spelling of a word. Pretending to be a reporter, Stevie scribbled on a piece of paper and when stumped by a word asked, "Ma, how do you spell 'O'?"— in hindsight, a humorously ironic question from a child who became one of the worst spellers in American literature. He frequently invented games and adventures for his friends to play; and when he was alone, buttons became soldiers whose elaborate battle maneuvers he spent hours enacting on the floor. But his imagination could get him into trouble. When he was about seven, according to his niece Alice, he shot an arrow into a painting by his mother that showed hunters shooting ducks. Though there is no record of her reaction to his pretending to be a hunter, she might not have spared the rod.[3]

In May 1877, Reverend Crane most likely took his youngest son to "Children's Day," an annual celebration sponsored by the American Sunday-School Union and held in Brooklyn, New York, thirty miles from the family home in Paterson, New Jersey. Reverend Crane was a leading voice in the Union and had written articles for its *Sunday-School Times;* five-year-old Stephen would have looked forward to the festivities—exciting games, street vendors, a parade—designed specifically for the more than 50,000 children at the celebration. Seeing the delight in the children's faces during the celebration reminded Reverend Crane of New York's indigent children; and before returning home, he walked through the slums on the Lower East Side of Manhattan, immediately struck by the painful contrast between playful children marching through the streets of Brooklyn and forlorn waifs in the tenement dis-

trict a mile away. He was committed to the growing Social Gospel movement, whose Christianity had an ethical and religious imperative to address economic inequality through social action. He soon published an
article in the *Sunday-School Times* that criticized unrealistic depictions of
children as innocent angels. Had Jesus been in New York City in May
1877, Reverend Crane implied, He would have been not at the festival
in Brooklyn but in the slums helping ragged street urchins. Reverend
Crane also admonished sentimental philanthropists who professed Christian love but avoided the tenements, and he chided officials for ignoring
urban poverty.[4]

If Stephen attended Children's Day, he would also have been in the
Lower East Side and would have noticed the stark contrast between the
children at the festival and those in the slums. Years later, the painful experience of seeing other children in dirty, tattered rags surely remained
in his mind as he depicted them in *Maggie: A Girl of the Streets.* Unlike his
father, however, Crane showed little interest in humanitarian causes and
didactic reform literature, and he generally avoided advocating moral
positions. *Maggie* is no advertisement for the Social Gospel movement,
yet, like his father, Crane criticized social hypocrisy and empathized with
the downtrodden and outcast. In chapter sixteen of *Maggie,* the minister
who avoids contact with Maggie to protect his respectability exemplifies
the hypocritical philanthropist whom Reverend Crane had seen pointing from afar at the urban poor on the Lower East Side.

Early on, Stephen's siblings recognized his determination as well as his
frail health. Barely more than a toddler, he swam with his brothers in
New Jersey's Raritan River while holding on to the collar of Solomon,
the family's Newfoundland retriever. Unafraid of the river's depth, he
announced that he would "fim" on his own to "Wee-Wee" (William)
and was rescued by Edmund only at the last minute, gasping but fearless,
just as he was sinking. "We boys," Edmund proudly recalled, "were natu-
rally delighted with his grit." In 1879, at the age of seven, he nearly died
from a poisonous snakebite on a camping trip, and survived only because Wilbur treated the wound until a doctor could cauterize it. Crane
faced a snake in another camping trip, in 1894, and recreated both experiences in "The Snake," wherein a rattlesnake and a young man—with
"all the wild strength of the terror of his ancestors, of his race, of his
kind"—instinctively react with fear and hatred during a primal confron-

tation. Written in 1894, the story was a template for Crane's later stories depicting his confrontation with irrational forces on the frontier in Mexico or the American West, at sea stranded with three other men in a ten-foot dinghy, and on the battlefield witnessing tragic loss. In each case Crane searched for the significance of experience in an indifferent universe.[5]

On another, less dramatic occasion six-year-old Stephen and his mother traveled to the Wyoming Valley of Pennsylvania in July 1878 to visit family in nearby Scranton and to hear Frances E. Willard, national secretary of the recently formed (1874) Woman's Christian Temperance Union, speak on the evils of alcohol and recruit new members to the "blue-ribbon army," the informal label for America's Gospel Temperance Movement. Willard recounted a dramatic story about how alcohol had driven a youth to commit murder. Condemned to hang, he escaped death when the trap door sprang and the rope broke; but he was hanged again. Forced to attend the speech were Stephen and his friend Post Wheeler, whose fathers were Methodist ministers and whose mothers were active in the temperance movement. Though the audience cried for the youth's lost soul, the two little boys were entranced more by the drama and excitement of Willard's cautionary tale than by its moral message.[6] The following day, July 3, they attended the centenary commemoration of the Wyoming Valley massacre, an episode in which British troops and Indian warriors had attacked nearby Forty Fort in Wyoming, Pennsylvania, patriots had been tortured and murdered, their homes had been razed, and Iroquois villages had been destroyed throughout upstate New York in retaliation.

With peddlers hawking food, balloons, and other trinkets and a Scottish Highlander in costume playing a bagpipe for stray coins, the event gave Stephen and Post a taste of drama and exploration. With twenty-five cents each and freedom to roam the grounds, they were enthralled. The independence allowed Stephen to experience firsthand the demon drink that Frances E. Willard had vilified the day before. Seeing a sign that read "Beer 10 cents," he gave the vendor money. When the vendor tried to keep it without providing the drink, the strong-minded Stephen demanded, "You gimme a beer or gimme back my dime!" And when the vendor tried to give him a glass half-filled with foam, Stephen erupted angrily, "That ain't half full! . . . You fill it up." The taste, however, was unimpressive. "Tain't any better'n ginger ale," he told Post, who was surprised by his friend's boldness. Post had recently taken a pledge of temperance and proudly wore a blue ribbon, though he was at least partly motivated by the expectation that the beautiful girl handing out the ribbons would kiss him for his decision. He could only ask Stephen, "How'd you dast do it?" "Pshaw!" Stephen replied. "Beer ain't nothing at all. . . . How was I going to know what it tasted like less'n I tasted it? How you going to know about things at all less'n you *do* 'em?" Post's dismay was short-lived. Impressed with his friend's logic—and unimpressed with the girl, who did not kiss him—he removed his ribbon.[7] For Stephen, the incident typified his ongoing need to experience life directly rather than vicariously. Whether he was drinking beer while his mother listened to a temperance lecture, spending a night in a New York City flophouse to understand the urban poor, or facing enemy fire during combat in Cuba to know the possibility of imminent death, Crane was convinced that honest art must be rooted in the intensity of personal experience.

Young Stephen was molded by his own firsthand experience as well as his siblings' influence. Little is known about their childhood, but it seems to have been marked by imaginative playfulness and peculiar conduct. Despite the high moral standards of their parents, the Crane children's behavior produced unexpected amusement in otherwise solemn situations. Reverend Crane once set a trap in his church in order to catch a rat. Unexpectedly, two of his offspring interrupted a service by proudly marching down the aisle with rat and trap in hand, proclaiming, "Here it is, Father. You said to bring it to you as soon as we found it." On another occasion, during a sermon, he reached into his pocket for his handkerchief, only to discover an infant's undershirt. At Pennington, one of his sons was playing happily in the sand. That evening after saying his prayers, however, he became concerned about whether God protected people "down here" or only "up yonder." To ease his anxiety, his mother assured him that God cares for everyone in both places. Would he like to go to Heaven and "be a little Angel," she asked? Musing on the uncertainty of playgrounds in Heaven versus their certainty on earth, he replied that he preferred just being "a little Angel down here in the dirt."[8]

As young adults, the children were rebellious, even eccentric, at times. Sixteen-year-old Townley appalled his matronly grandmother Peck with his taunting attitude. Despite his request that she "excuse all Peaf Steaks in writing and spelling" in a letter to her, she would have been distressed by his intentionally egregious misspellings, including that of her last name as "Pek"; by his wanting grandfather "to look for my duch pipe"; and by his secretly writing the letter during school. Townley mocked his father and his sister Agnes by scribbling answers to preprinted questions in her memory book. Writing as "J. Townley Frane, Jr.," he sarcastically claimed that Julie P. Smith, popular writer of romances for young ladies, was his favorite novelist; that his favorite nonreligious book was his father's *Popular Amusements;* and that he would like to be pope. There must have been turmoil in the parsonage after the discovery by Reverend Crane, who had denounced Romanism and idle amusements like sentimental romances, of Townley's outlandish behavior and his invasion of Agnes's privacy.[9]

Equally outrageous was his brother Wilbur, who attended the College of Physicians and Surgeons in New York City. Repeatedly failing the course on anatomy, he smuggled the lower half of a corpse of a forty-five-year-old woman and secretly stored it in a barrel on the roof of his apartment building. Although he intended to boil the corpse and mount the skeleton for study, sickness and a cold spell that kept water in the barrel frozen prevented him from completing his project. When local neighbors became suspicious of Wilbur's nighttime activities on the roof, they investigated and found a foot, a pelvis, and other body parts in the barrel, leading one neighbor to insist she would be sleepless for months because "all sorts of ghosts and bugaboos were about to visit her." After police confiscated the body parts and concluded that they had not been stolen from a local cemetery, Wilbur, undaunted, asked that the body parts be returned to him. Though the county physician agreed with the request, Wilbur's medical skills were not as strong as his persuasive ability: he never passed anatomy.[10] After struggling in the classroom for five years and having his thesis on typhoid fever rejected twice, he left medical school without a degree.

As adults, most of the Crane siblings had respectable careers. Mary Helen ("Nellie") taught painting in Newark and Asbury Park; Agnes was a schoolteacher; George and Edmund were laborers; William practiced law and became president of the American Lithia and Chemical Company. Tragedy plagued other Crane siblings. Luther Peck Crane, a rail-

road brakeman, nearly died in 1884 from an accidental overdose of lau-
danum for illness. He passed away two years later at age twenty-three,
when he slipped and crushed his arm while coupling cars. Wilbur's life
ended sadly as well. After losing hope of becoming a doctor, he moved
back to the family home at Asbury Park. He worked for two years gathering shore news for local newspapers and the *New York Tribune,* then
alienated family members when he married William's servant. Just when
he was beginning to succeed modestly as a businessman, however, his
wife took their children and left him. Grief-stricken, he escaped to
Georgia, where he died during the flu epidemic of 1918.

The most tragic story, though, was that of Jonathan Townley, who
might have become a significant figure in American journalism and who,
after Stephen, was the most talented writer among his siblings. He ap-
prenticed as a correspondent for the *Newark Advertiser,* established a news
bureau on the New Jersey coast for the Associated Press and *New York
Tribune* in 1880, and served as editor of the *Asbury Park Shore Press* in
1882–1883. Known as the "Shore Fiend" because of his ability to locate
stories, he was a curious blend of contradictions and eccentric behavior.
On the job, he dressed shirtless year round and wore a dirty hat, a ban-
danna knotted around his neck, and a long coat with the collar turned
up, yet at New York's theaters he sported a finely cropped beard, walking
cane, silk hat, and immaculate suit always two sizes too large. He loved
displaying his collection of oddities, which included an ancient pottery
lamp from Cyprus, a stool made from a whale's backbone, and what he
called his "'crazy' quilt." Ever playful and whimsical, he signed a news
dispatch "Enarc" ("Crane" backwards); and when General Wanton S.
Webb brought his promotional exhibit "Florida on Wheels" to Asbury
Park, Townley gave him a seashell decorated with two Cranes in a web, as
a gift from him and his wife. When he discussed the upcoming annual
baseball game between the *Shore Press* and its rival, the *Asbury Park Daily
Spray,* he joked: "The 'typos' of the *Daily Spray* are practicing with ball
and bat both night and day in anticipation of 'laying out' the *Shore Press*
nine" in their upcoming "celebrated match game," though the *Spray's*
editor, Billy Devereaux, "has secured the services of a Trenton ambulance, which he has ordered to be in readiness to carry him off the ball
ground. . . . In his position as pitcher of the *Spray* nine he expects to be
under the necessity of 'tumbling' to numerous 'hot balls.'" Verbal playful-

ness among local journalists extended toward Townley, in turn. When news reached Asbury Park that heirs to Lord Townley's estate in England, valued at $100 million, were still being tracked down after more than fifty years, a local paper jested that it now knew why "our young friend, Mr. J. Townley Crane, splits his name in the middle. He has always been very proud of his name, and no doubt when the family comes into possession of its millions Townley will remember us all in a fitting manner."[11]

Throughout much of his career, Townley was a well-known journalist respected in political and newspaper circles and a popular speaker on newspaper work. He served as secretary of the New York Press Club and as league historian of the National League of Baseball, and he staunchly advocated women's rights. When the Asbury Park school system had financial problems, he recommended a woman for election to the board of education, arguing that women deserved greater rights, were more fiscally responsible than men, and would ensure that expenditures did not exceed the budget. Against considerable opposition, he ultimately persuaded school officials to elect the woman. Though a talented speaker and journalist, Townley suffered great misfortune in his life and career. His first wife, his childhood sweetheart, died in 1883 at age twenty-nine after five years of marriage, during which they lost two children. Within two years after he remarried in 1890, his second wife was committed to an insane asylum and died shortly thereafter. Townley married his third wife in 1893, but they divorced in 1900. A chronically ill alcoholic, he eventually could not work and lived periodically with his brother Wilbur and sister-in-law in Binghamton, New York, starting in the late 1890s; when he became violent, he was temporarily confined to the Binghamton Hospital for the Chronic Insane at least twice. Apparently, he returned to Port Jervis and became superintendent of streets, but died indigent in the New York State Hospital in Binghamton in either 1908 or 1909, depending on whether one trusts the death certificate or the tombstone. To fellow journalist Post Wheeler, the once-talented Townley devolved into a "physical derelict" who "needed only a crossbow and a dead albatross slung about his neck to be [Gustave] Doré's ideal model for the Ancient Mariner."[12]

Equally sad was the fate of Stephen's uncle Wilbur Fisk Peck, whose troubled life as a lonely outsider seeking the absent father foreshadowed the tribulations of his nephew Stephen and may have helped to shape his psyche. The striking similarities in their emotional makeup may have been evident to Crane. Both were wayward sons, isolated in life, yearning for a missing father; both confronted their doubts and anxieties through poetry; and both knew of the tragic irony of war at the 1863 Battle of Chancellorsville, in which sacrifice seemed ultimately futile.

Believing himself to be the "the prodigal who wasted his substance in riotous living," Wilbur had been struggling since childhood with personal disappointment, self-doubt, and spiritual anguish. In letters he wrote to his parents from school, the teenage Wilbur apologized for "all the unnecessary trouble that I have occasioned you" because of "my weakness and many failings." In contrast to his anxiety over having disappointed his parents was his muted frustration—perhaps even anger—concerning a father whose stern parenting and itinerant religious activities frequently kept them apart geographically and emotionally. He could apologize for offending his father, but, feeling abandoned, quickly retort that his father upset him as well. Dispirited, Wilbur confessed he had become "broken down in body and mind."[13]

Fearing he could never please his father by matching the accomplishments of his two brothers or those of his namesake—the prominent American clergyman, educator, and theologian Wilbur Fisk—Wilbur chose not to pursue the ministry. He knew that his decision would raise questions in a family in which his father, two brothers, four uncles, and numerous cousins had become Methodist ministers. Instead, he attended medical school at the University of the City of New York. In November 1862, after graduation, he was quickly commissioned as an assistant surgeon with the 178th Pennsylvania Infantry, and by June of the following year was in charge of the Union hospital at Yorktown. The horror of surgery under primitive conditions traumatized him. Writing his father a month after the Battle of Chancellorsville, one of the bloodiest in the Civil War, he struggled to cope with his own demons. He still feared that he might "write anything or do anything to injure your feelings" and labored "to trouble you no more." Haunted with "depressed spirits" and feeling completely "*alone,*" he pleaded with his father: "I wish no letters from home unless they can be happy in tone. I wish not to allude to the past again."[14]

The precise details about Wilbur's earlier relationship with his father are unknown; but by October 1872, he was battling alcoholism. Believing that he could handle the problem alone, he vowed privately to abstain from liquor; but the thought of total abstinence overwhelmed him, and his pledge was short-lived. By June of the next year, he was vowing again, but this time there was a notable difference. With his father and brother-in-law Jonathan Townley Crane as witnesses, he pledged abstinence for three years: he could handle his problem only by confronting it piecemeal.

A year later, his marriage in crisis, Wilbur turned to Jonathan for help. Fourteen years older, Crane was the trusted mentor who had known his brother-in-law since their days at Pennington, where Wilbur had been a student. Distraught, he asked Crane for guidance. Keep your "courage up," Crane advised; do not "get in despair, & throw one's self away"; and "let your wife see that you can do better, in every respect, without her, than with her." During crises in the past, Wilbur had relied on poetry as catharsis. While struggling with the emotional separation from his father, he had written a poem expressing anguish at being separated from a loved one. This time was no different: he wrote poetry to ease his mind about marriage. "Your theme, the 'Argument of Love,'" Crane reassured him, "is certainly a popular one, judging by the style of the numberless weeklies, & Monthlies, which are filled with it. I certainly see no harm in your spending your leisure hours thus; & good may come out of it." Unfortunately, Wilbur's life did not improve. When his father died in 1876, an obituary praised three of the late Reverend Peck's children: two sons were "efficient and devoted ministers"; his daughter was "accomplished" in her endeavors. Wilbur was simply listed as "a physician."[15]

It is unknown how well Stephen knew his Uncle Wilbur, but the close friendship between Stephen's father and uncle suggests that Wilbur was a welcome family member in the Crane household. In later years Wilbur lived in northeastern Pennsylvania, near Orange and Sullivan counties, where his nephew spent much time. Crane proudly kept and wore his uncle's Civil War sword while a member of the corps of cadets at Claverack College and Hudson River Institute, near Albany, New York, in 1888–1890.[16] Wilbur may have been the source for one of Crane's best short stories, "An Episode of War," in which a sword is a prominent symbol and a wounded officer's arm is amputated in a field hospital. The original title, "The Loss of an Arm" (with "An Episode of War" as a possible subtitle), shifts the focus to the task of a surgeon. Because Crane said the story was based on an actual person and event, he might have recreated one of his uncle's distressing experiences at Yorktown.[17]

Of all the Crane and Peck family members, no one had as great a positive influence on Stephen's early life as his sister Agnes ("Aggie") Elizabeth. "Have come to the conclusion," she wrote in her diary in 1874, "that the 'Doctor's Daughter' although fascinating is not a criterion for *me*. Am going to be a 'D. D.' of another type just as good if I can't be pretty or preternaturally smart."[18] An aspiring author with a burning passion to write, an advocate of women's rights, and a tomboy with an insatiable thirst for science and literature, she was equally comfortable watching a baseball game, darning socks, or reading Virgil. Like Stephen, Agnes had a conflicted sensibility. A woman who wanted to please her parents by striving to be a proper lady and better Christian, she nevertheless rejected her father's condemnation of unrealistic fiction and secretly read popular sentimental romances; a trusting church member guided by her faith, she tired of facing life alone when "storms sweep o'er and o'er" her, "making a sad shipwreck of life"; a mature ironist aware of the vagaries of life, she yearned to see things "through the rose tinted, trusting glasses of ignorant youth." Yet the rose symbolized her own longings. Pinned in her diary was a rose named after Thomas Moore's sentimental poem "The Last Rose of Summer" (1805). Like the rose "blooming alone" in Moore's "bleak world," she too was the lonely outsider searching for her soul mate, the "flower of her kindred." Unlike Agnes, Stephen was rarely sentimental, and he questioned in one of his poems those who "don green spectacles before you look at roses." Yet her independent, ironic, rebellious, sensitive personality influenced his mind and art.[19]

A brilliant student, Agnes won awards for her writing and language skills as a junior at Centenary Collegiate Institute and graduated as class valedictorian in June 1880. In November she was working as a governess, but was ill suited for the task of educating an unruly child and maintaining a sense of propriety. By 1882 (or possibly 1881), she was teaching at the Mountain House School in Port Jervis, New York. Repeatedly harassed by disruptive boys, she resigned in December, despite the local board of education's attempt to persuade her to remain. The following April, she was applying for a teaching position in Paterson, but by fall was employed at the Asbury Park School in Asbury Park, New Jersey. Fifteen when her youngest brother was born, she assumed much of the responsibility for raising him because their parents were frequently away on church business. Before he was three, she began taking him to Sunday school, where he delighted in receiving a religious lithograph as a reward for weekly attendance; she included him in her taffy-pull parties, where he shared freshly made candy with his other trusted companion, Solomon the dog; and, most important of all, she became the compassionate surrogate mother who protected him from the anxiety of loneliness. Family and friends recalled one incident when Agnes literally supported him. In August 1878 the Crane family built a summer shack, which Agnes playfully named "Saint's Rest," near the falls of the Mongaup River in Sullivan County's dense forest. Because the shack was small, she arranged for Stephen to sleep in a hammock directly above her. When it broke, he landed on his sister, who lamented that "his bones were not sufficiently upholstered to make it anything but an unpleasant experience."[20]

Despite her mother's assurances that she would transform herself into a swan, the self-described "ugly duckling" of the family reimagined herself in her fiction as a heroine surrounded by admiring gentlemen. In "A Victorious Defeat," an attractive, rebellious girl is surprised to learn that the farmer she has fallen in love with is actually editor of the *New York Beacon,* a happy turn of events for an aspiring author like Agnes. In "The Result of an Experiment," an ugly schoolteacher named Avis (Latin for "bird," an appropriate name for a Crane) wins the heart of the hero. In "Laurel Camp, and What Came of It," which transforms the setting of Saint's Rest into Laurel Camp, a rebellious Bess Fleming learns "a new sweet light of self-revelation." It may be coincidence that Crane's most famous character, Henry Fleming in *The Red Badge of Courage,* has the same last name and struggles with his own self-revelation, but Stephen clearly shared his sister's ironic sensibility throughout much of his work.[21]

Recognizing Stephen's talent, Agnes encouraged him to write. At age eight he composed a now-lost story about a child named Little Goodie Brighteyes.[22] Agnes did, however, preserve his earliest surviving piece of literature, the poem "I'd rather have—," written shortly after his eighth birthday. Remarkable for its rhythm, humor, and irony, it captures a

child's Christmas wish for a dog. But more than expressing Crane's lifelong love of animals, it depicts a lonely child searching for companionship. He found it with Agnes, his closest friend, mentor, and surrogate
mother, whom he suddenly lost when she died from cerebrospinal men-
ingitis on June 10, 1884, at the age of twenty-eight. Brothers William and
Edmund honored her by naming daughters Agnes, and Stephen memorialized her as the beautiful twenty-eight-year-old Sarah Bottomley Perkins in "Uncle Jake and the Bell-Handle" (1885).[23] Her death, however, abruptly ended his innocence. On the cusp of adolescence at the
age of twelve—with Agnes, his anchor, now gone—he felt abandoned
and alone, drifting emotionally, intellectually, and psychologically on an
ocean he later described as "Superlative in vacancy / Upon which nevertheless at fateful time, / Was written / The grim hatred of nature." With
an irony that Stephen and Agnes would have recognized, his journey
would last as long as that of his anchor: twenty-eight years.[24]

3

The *Holiness* Controversy

1874–1879

THE FOURTEEN METHODIST ministers and their families who met at the quinquennial Peck family reunion in 1874 had much to talk about and celebrate.[1] In the spring, the Cranes had moved to Bound Brook, New Jersey; and since the previous reunion four years earlier, Stephen's grand-uncle Jesse Peck had become a bishop (1872) and his grandfather's auto-biography, *The Life and Times of Rev. George Peck, D.D.*, had appeared (1874). Reverend Crane had published *Holiness the Birthright of All God's Children* and was at the height of his influence in the Methodist church in America. No one at the reunion had an inkling that he would soon be publicly attacked over a heated theological issue and forced to return to itinerant ministry at a lower salary. The incident would leave the Cranes shaken and embarrassed.

Before the Civil War, itinerant preachers like the "Methodist bulldog" Peter Cartwright had blazed across the American frontier with their "Primitive Methodism." Though many of them could not "conjugate a verb or parse a sentence, and murdered the king's English almost every lick," Cartwright insisted that they did not need formal theological training—indeed, he scorned it—if they "could mount a stump, a block, or old log, stand in the bed of a wagon, and without note or manuscript, quote, expound, and apply the word of God to the hearts and consciences of the people." No religious group was more successful than the Methodist Church in converting settlers on the American frontier, and by the 1840s Methodism had become the largest religious denomination in America. As Peter Cartwright boasted, "Illiterate Methodist preachers actually set the world on fire" while educated ministers from other faiths "were lighting their matches!"[2]

By the end of the Civil War, the Methodist Church in America had established twenty-three colleges, three theological schools, and eighty-four seminaries or academies; it published nine newspapers, including one for children, as well as the *Methodist Quarterly Review;* and it conducted a major book-publishing business in seven cities. One publishing house alone printed more than a dozen books a minute every working day for a year. In 1866, the church celebrated the centennial of its birth. But because officials feared that the church had slipped into a spiritual malaise, they used the occasion to reflect upon their previous accomplishments and future goals. As recognition of Reverend Crane's influence within the community, he was chosen to deliver the centenary sermon before the Newark Conference. Selecting the biblical metaphor of the fruitful vine as family tree, he recounted how the church "began to take root, and spread its green leaves over the land," so that "watered by the dews of heaven, the vine grew." Although Methodists were proud of their "great numerical strength," he feared that "a blight and a mildew" of complacency would destroy the vine: "Ceasing to be holy, we shall cease to be safe." Crane's admonition was more than a clichéd response to a church lacking the zeal of first-generation leaders like Peter Cartwright. In order to revitalize the roots of American Methodism, ministers met the following year in the appropriately named town of Vineland, New Jersey, to form the National Association for the Promotion of Holiness. The movement condemned anything that interfered with an individual's unmediated relationship with God—for example, the artifice of Gothic churches, the ornate quality of modern hymns, and the literary and academic style of many sermons—and advocated a return to that old-time frontier religion in which souls were won on the battlegrounds at camp revivals.[3]

As pastor of the Methodist church in Morristown (1864–1866), Reverend Crane had been directly involved in the future growth and revitalization of the country's Methodist Church. He oversaw a revival that re-invigorated church membership and in 1866 laid the cornerstone for a new church in Morristown.[4] By 1874 he had already distinguished himself as a preacher, teacher, and scholar; had been chosen four times to represent the Newark Conference in the church's General Conference; and had served as presiding elder of the Newark District (1868–1872) and Elizabeth District (1872–1876). But as one of a new breed of Methodist ministers who were better read and better educated than their forebears, he was soon to be attacked by more traditional clergy.

Reverend Crane generally supported the Holiness Movement, but he struggled with the widely held belief that although one can experience a conversion that frees one from previous sins (justification), a second conversion (sanctification) was needed to eliminate every trace of depravity.[5] This view, he concluded, diminished the significance of the first experience and returned to the strict Calvinism he had rejected as a teenager. Struggling to clarify his own position, he challenged himself to "read aright" the major texts on the subject; and after writing a defense of his position, he showed the manuscript to George Peck for comments. Though his father-in-law was a leading advocate for the more orthodox view that insisted upon justification and sanctification for total conversion, he respected Crane's right to disagree. By the middle of 1874, Crane had published *Holiness the Birthright of All God's Children,* in which he rejected the idea that sin remained after the first conversion experience. Justification, he believed, could cleanse one's sins; and although sanctification was desirable, it was not necessary for salvation.[6]

The response to *Holiness* was swift. The book proved more controversial than any other religious tract recently sanctioned by the Methodist Book Concern, which oversaw the printing and publishing of Methodist literature in America. Although some reviewers praised it as "an important contribution" to the ongoing debate regarding conversion and as "one of the most suggestive books we have ever read," the attacks were devastating. Previously, the Book Concern had supported the publication of controversial religious tracts, with a clear understanding that the views of a particular author did not necessarily reflect those of the publisher or the Methodist Church. With the publication of *Holiness,* however, Crane was vilified for "inimical" and "revolutionary" views that threatened the governing principles of Methodism and "would necessitate great changes in our Discipline, hymn book, biographies, standard and current literature, and in the pastoral addresses of our Bishops, and general and annual conferences." Critics charged that not only was it disgraceful for people to read the anti-Wesleyan writings of "a man holding official position in the Church, placed there by the appointing power"; but the fact that a respectable Methodist publisher had printed those writings was "a still greater outrage." They demanded that "such want of official integrity should not be allowed to pass unnoticed" and that church leaders prevent future "outrages." One reader solved the problem simply: "I felt so cheated by the book that after a careful reading, I put it into the stove, where I was sure it would do no harm."[7]

Ad hominem attacks on Crane became vitriolic. In a book-length assault titled *The Abiding Comforter,* Reverend Anthony Atwood, a founder of the National Association for the Promotion of Holiness, denounced the "so called" Doctor of Divinity and his "absurdities"—"the most dangerous to the stability of faith, in those recently born of God, of any that could be uttered"—which, if adopted, would ruin Methodism.[8] Atwood tried to force the church hierarchy to choose sides in the battle. "What say the leading authorities? . . . What say the fathers in the Church, the leading writers and leading names of the most deeply devoted to God, men who have been taught of the Spirit in the deep things of God?" Then, with a warning that clearly alluded to Crane, Atwood admonished "all our bishops" with "a word of counsel: . . . be careful whom we appoint to the office of presiding elder of a district." Readers of the book would have noticed the admonition not to reappoint Crane as a presiding elder. The matter worsened when Atwood tried to alienate him from George Peck by emphasizing that Crane's theological position contradicted Peck's own writings. Sanctimoniously alluding to Luke 12:53— "the father would be against the son, and the son against the father"— Atwood also urged the recently appointed Bishop Jesse Peck to assert his authority by announcing his position on the matter "to the world and the church."[9] An even more acerbic critic identified Crane with pure evil. *Holiness* was "a horrid carcass" and "a poisonous reptile" that threatened the foundations of the church: "If a snake should stealthily glide into our house, would we not make short work with him on discovery? Would we not bruise his head, and cast his horrid carcass into the street?" No respectable Methodist would have missed the allusion to the bibli-

cal prophecy in Genesis 3:15 of the ultimate conquest of good over evil
—and the further implication that church officials needed to "bruise"
the evil force that had placed the serpent in the house of Methodism.
Church leaders were urged "to personally victimize Dr. Crane" in order
to "put [him] down reputationally and officially" and to destroy "all his
hopes of ecclesiastical preferment." But Reverend Daniel Wheadon, editor of the *Methodist Quarterly Review* and one of Crane's few public supporters, protested "so evident a scheme of proscription" and reassured
churchgoers there was no need to establish a list of forbidden books—an
"*Index Expurgatorius*"—to protect church orthodoxy.[10]

Throughout the ordeal, Reverend Crane remained above the conflict.
As he privately confided to his father-in-law, "In regard to the 'Holy
War,' I feel as you do. If we can not discuss the subject of holiness without showing unholy temper, injustice & unfairness, it is clear that we
don't know much about it practically: & if we profess to enjoy it, we
show the possibility of self deception. I have not written a line in reply
to the attacks made on me, nor do I mean to do it. At the same time, I
consider every thing that is said by all parties, & learn all I can." More
intimately, he confided to his wife that the ordeal had been painful.
Shaken by virulent attacks, he immediately began revising *Holiness,* a
process he continued until his death, in order to clarify his position.
Within months a second edition appeared, reaffirming his position.[11]

A man of principle and integrity who followed his conscience even
when it butted against tradition and authority, Reverend Crane praised
America's Methodist Church in his next book, *Methodism and Its Methods,* yet proposed ways to correct what he considered its weaknesses.
Beneath his self-assurance, however, was a hidden anxiety concerning
his own future churchly role. Crane readily acknowledged that officials
might differ on church matters, but hoped that if they, like the biblical
Paul and Barnabus on their joint ministry to spread the Good News,
parted ways over differences, they would not become embittered. He
recognized the painful similarity between their situation and his own
and prayed that the animosity toward him would soon subside. The timing of *Methodism and Its Methods* made him even more apprehensive.
Published in the fall of 1875, the book appeared only months before the
1876 General Conference, during which ministers would be reassigned
and staff members elected. Scheduled for discussion at the conference

was whether presiding elders should also be elected. The idea had been hotly debated earlier in the century—so much so, that it helped to divide the Methodist Church—but had lain dormant for decades.[12]

No direct evidence suggests that the growing case against Reverend Crane precipitated the renewed interest in the question. Church policy dictated that an elder be appointed for a term of four years, after which he was returned to the itinerancy, although a bishop could arrange for a minister to serve a second term by assigning him to another district, as was the case with Reverend Crane. His health may also have been a factor: in 1876 he was listed as a "supernumerary minister," a title for clergy whose physical condition temporarily prevented them from carrying out their ecclesiastical duties. In fact, from late 1873 to early 1874, ill health had made it difficult for Reverend Crane to fulfill his responsibilities. Nonetheless, he worried about political in-fighting and those with "scheming ambition" who "rise to high places more by maneuvering than by merit." Though apparently no formal charges were filed against him, hostile published comments and the concerns of his parishioners in the Elizabeth District, who were anxious about the impact of the *Holiness* controversy on their spiritual community and confused about the meaning of their own conversion experience, forced the church hierarchy to act. By spring, Crane knew he would no longer be a presiding elder and was being reassigned to the itinerancy. Exhausted by the ordeal, he once again had to move his family—this time to Paterson, New Jersey, where he assumed duties as pastor of the Cross Street Church. With his father-in-law's death on May 20, days after the end of the General Conference, he lost his most powerful ally in the Methodist Church and probably much hope of regaining his standing in it. As a result of the controversy, Crane, once a leading voice in the ministry, had been silenced. Having written six books on important religious issues between 1848 and 1875, during the last four years of his life he would primarily write only short notes and articles on minor church matters.[13]

The *Holiness* controversy embarrassed the Cranes publicly and wounded them emotionally. They were a respected Methodist family, but the attempt to pit Reverend Crane against his wife's father and uncle and to insinuate that he aimed at subverting church dogma must have disrupted the children's sense of their father as protector. Moving from one parsonage to another forced repeated separations from friends and schoolmates. Stephen, two and a half at the start of the furor, would have been unaware of its immediate effect on his family; but growing up, he must have sensed the impact of the controversy on his parents and siblings. A photograph taken around 1879, showing him alone, dressed in a sailor's outfit, and posed next to a rowboat (see Figure 7), foreshadowed his future lonely journey on life's turbulent sea. In the meantime, as traumatic as the *Holiness* incident was for the Cranes, a more devastating one was less than two years away.

4

Onward to Port Jervis

MARCH 1878–FEBRUARY 1880

REVEREND CRANE HAD HOPED to stay in Paterson; but when the Cross
Street Church needed to reduce operating costs, he reluctantly resigned
in March 1878 so that the church could engage a minister willing to accept a lower salary. Reassigned again, he was appointed pastor of Drew
Methodist Church in Port Jervis, New York. Near the junction of three
states—New York, New Jersey, and Pennsylvania—and known as the
"River City" because it is bounded by the Delaware and Neversink rivers, the once-rural canal community was rapidly becoming a thriving
railroad and business center of ten thousand people. By 1878, Port Jervis
already had its first telephone—only one year after the White House got
one. Within little more than a decade, the town would have a sewage
system, arc street lighting, and homes illuminated with electricity rather
than gas.[1]

Ever hopeful, Reverend Crane accepted his new assignment because
the town and congregation "strike me v. favorably"; but his first sermon,
based on Matthew 6:34—"So do not worry about tomorrow, for to-
morrow will bring worries of its own; today's trouble is enough for today"—suggested a deep-rooted anxiety about what to expect from yet
another congregation.[2] He had not known what his new assignment

would be until ten days before arriving in Port Jervis on April 6. As he continued to revise *Holiness the Birthright of All God's Children,* he worried about how the controversy surrounding his book might hamper his ministerial effectiveness.

His own hardships notwithstanding, Reverend Crane had always advanced social causes, especially relating to another contentious issue among American Methodists. Since the eighteenth century, they had been divided on slavery and the role of African Americans in the church. Because of forced segregation, blacks had formed their own denomination, the African Methodist Episcopal Church, in 1816; but because their departure had not solved the problem of segregation, the Methodist Episcopal Church split into Northern and Southern denominations in 1844. Crane had written a college essay at Princeton about "the accursed system" of slavery; and as pastor of a Methodist church in Jersey City, New Jersey, he had denounced it in 1859 in "Christian Duty in Regard to American Slavery," an influential sermon published and disseminated the following year. Though slavery had ended, its ugly legacy had not. Illiteracy and poverty were widespread problems among blacks. To address these issues, Reverend and Mrs. Crane quickly established the Mission Sunday School for local blacks and the Drew Mission and Industrial School for black women and children. After organizing a clothing drive and fundraising concert supported by local women, Mrs. Crane was commended for her efforts to improve the condition of African Americans. Years later, Stephen recalled these "lady philanthropists," who after donating clothing and other domestic items "came away poorer in goods but rich in complacence."[3]

To raise money for the parsonage and their causes, the Cranes charged adults a dime and children a nickel to attend a varied series of lectures. Included among Reverend Crane's presentations were discussions on astronomy, the nature of truth, a scientific explanation for the inevitable destruction of the universe, and "trashy literature."[4] Mrs. Crane's included "the false religions of India" and "China and its people"; she almost certainly dragooned a shy six-year-old Stephen into being one of the children dressed in Chinese garb. A dramatic speaker, she also electrified standing-room-only audiences as she urged them to take the temperance pledge. With crayon illustrations that she and her daughter Nellie had made, Mrs. Crane depicted the effect of alcohol on the brain with an experiment in which egg white mixed with alcohol quickly congealed as though it had been cooked. An indefatigable crusader, Mrs. Crane vowed to fight until all of the almost eighty saloons in Port Jervis were closed.

On September 2, 1878, Stephen started attending the Main Street School, and by March was on the honor roll; but after getting ill, as he frequently did in his early years, he dropped out. Later he enrolled in the Mountain House School to be closer to his sister Agnes, who taught there. With the exception of three months in Roseville, New Jersey, he attended school in Port Jervis from age six to eleven.

Each morning as Crane left the parsonage on East Broome Street for school, he gazed upon the most dramatic natural feature in Port Jervis: the sheer cliffs of Twin Mountain Tract, Point Peter and Mount William, spiraling above and looming over the city. Local children personified the peaks as bald-headed Pete and Bill, and hikers regularly climbed them for a scenic, bird's-eye view of the city; but for Stephen the stark contrast in perspective between the grandeur of a mountain and the smallness of people seen below revealed a harsh truth about reality that became central to his fiction and poetry. Crane often uses an ironic double perspective that emphasizes the distance between characters trapped by their egos and prejudices and a narrator who recognizes their folly and insignificance. Viewed from the mountaintop, human vanity is nothing more than an illusory self-image. In one form or another, the image of a mountain appears repeatedly in Crane's work as an indifferent force, sometimes associated with a plea for an answer from an inscrutable God. In a poem inspired by the local setting and at first variously titled "The Prayer of the Peaks" and "The Prayer of the Mountains," the narrator sadly concedes, "In the night / Grey heavy clouds muffled the valleys, / And the peaks looked toward God, alone." As omniscient narrator in the poem, Crane distanced himself from characters with an inflated sense of self-importance, but he never resolved his own battle with guilt, hubris, and spiritual uncertainty. Whereas he was "fairly dazzled by the size" of his ego—"The Matterhorn could be no more than a ten-pin to it"—he soon confessed to his own "unworthiness" and acknowledged that his "fight was not going to be with the world but with myself." A six-year-old Stephen would not have understood an ironic perspective on humanity, but the daily sight of peaks soaring above Port Jervis prepared him for future battles and would become an important image in his work.[5]

Stephen struggled with his family's need to move frequently and years later worked through his sense of displacement in children's stories called the Whilomville tales. In "The Fight," which is based on a confrontation between a twelve-year-old bully and a nine-year-old Stephen that became "historic in the family," Stephen's alter ego concludes that "this whole business of changing schools was a complete torture" because it forced him to go "alone . . . among a new people, a new tribe. . . . He was a stranger cast away upon the moon. None knew him, understood him, felt for him." Struggling with the social codes of his peers, Stephen was, like a child in another Whilomville story, "the exile" and "social leper" barely surviving in "the jungles of childhood." Essentially an only child, with siblings considerably older and parents frequently preoccupied with church business, he was often alone. When Agnes's failing health prevented her from helping to raise Stephen after the family moved to Asbury Park, he roamed the neighborhood in search of mothering. Kindhearted women would feed him and mend his garments, and in exchange he would tell stories to their children. Meddling church ladies delighted in gossiping about Mrs. Crane's casual housekeeping habits and informed her that she should travel less and spend more time raising her family. But even though she was absent, Stephen continued to draw inspiration from her remembered oratory and was learning the power of storytelling: a form of enchantment as well as a marketable commodity exchangeable for food and clothing.[6]

Stephen also wrestled with a lifelong anxiety over public speaking. Reverend Crane took pride in his children's ability to declaim, working directly with them as "Professor of Rhetoric & Elocution to the whole posse" in preparation for exercises in oratory. Stephen, however, was terrified by the thought of speaking formally to peers. In the nineteenth century every schoolchild practiced declamation to prepare for adulthood, and McGuffey Readers, the most widely used textbooks at the time, contained poetry to be memorized for recitation. Among the popular poems were Caroline E. S. Norton's sentimental "Bingen on the Rhine" and Tennyson's "Charge of the Light Brigade." Years later in "The Open Boat," Crane remembered the "dinning" of "myriads of his school-fellows" forced to mindlessly recite "Bingen." In the Whilomville story "Making an Orator," he satirized an educational requirement that "operated mainly to antagonize many children permanently against arising to speak their thoughts to fellow-creatures." At first Jimmie Trescott, Crane's persona, skips school by pretending to be sick; but eventually he is forced to return to "the place of torture," where he promptly forgets almost all of the few lines of Tennyson's poem he had memorized. "On this day," Crane was to learn, "there had been laid for him the foundation of a finished incapacity for public speaking which would be his until he died."[7]

Growing up in Port Jervis, Stephen lived in an area steeped in legend and tall tales. In the eighteenth century, Orange and nearby Sullivan counties were part of the American frontier, and local histories were packed with legends of local folk heroes and dramatic events. In July 1879 Stephen, like any other adventurous child drawn to pageantry, probably attended the unveiling of a monument commemorating the hundredth anniversary of the Battle of Minisink. The ceremony honored the fallen patriots who had risked their lives for freedom when a party of Indians and Tories, led by the warrior Joseph Brant, ransacked settlements in the area's only major skirmish during the American Revolution. Crane developed a lifelong interest in history and the American Revolution and as an adult revisited the battlefield for his sketch "A Reminiscence of Indian War" honoring the patriots, "that bronzed and sturdy race who were hewing their way through the matted forests and making homes in the dense jungles of an American wilderness."[8]

The commemoration of another Revolutionary event in July horrified Stephen. Like other towns across America on July 4, Port Jervis annually celebrated the country's birth with a public reading of the Declaration of Independence. The plan for the 1879 festivities was to be no different. The day would begin with the firing of a cannon and the ringing of church bells, followed by a parade comprising a band, military organizations, and every fire company in the town. After the parade reached Orange Square, which was adjacent to the parsonage, Reverend Crane was scheduled to give the blessing before the reading of the Declaration. Other festivities were planned, culminating with fireworks in the square. No one would have missed the music, the pageantry, and the largest parade ever in Port Jervis, especially young Stephen, who lived across the street from the square and whose father was a major participant in the activities. The day, however, began tragically. As Samuel Hasbrouck and Theodore Jarvis, two veterans from the U.S. Colored Volunteer Heavy Artillery, were loading a cannon, it exploded prematurely, hurling both men a considerable distance. The accident maimed their bodies and horribly burned their faces. Jarvis, blinded by the incident, apparently soon died. A doctor saved Hasbrouck, who lost an eye and died in 1913 after a long illness perhaps partly caused by the accident. Despite the tragedy, the scheduled July 4 events, including the reading of the Declaration, continued as planned. Yet there must have been shock and disbelief in the Crane household, especially for Stephen. The terrifying image of a faceless, one-eyed African American saved by a doctor remained associated with July 4 and the Declaration of Independence in Stephen's mind until it resurfaced in his harrowing classic "The Monster."[9]

Within months, another tragedy devastated Stephen. On December 31, his father preached on Genesis 47:8, Pharaoh's question to an aged Jacob: "How many are the years of your life?" But in exploring the question with his congregation on the last day of the year, Reverend Crane reflected on his own life. On Christmas Day he had written a brief autobiographical sketch for a Methodist publication, and in the previous few weeks he had been facing his own mortality as he became increasingly ill from cholera. Hoarse and physically exhausted, he could barely talk by the end of his sermon. Three weeks later he was, as he wrote in his diary, "home all day, again, which is a rarity for me, unless a storm prevails." As his condition worsened, Mrs. Crane, as if troubled by a dire premonition, became "tortured all day by nervous headache."[10]

Pondering the ultimate question of life, he ended his diary entry on Saturday, February 14, with "his Maker."[11] On Monday morning, after preaching vigorously the day before, he was climbing the stairs to his study when he experienced chest pains. When mustard plasters on his chest and feet and a touch of brandy and morphine failed to ease the pain, Mrs. Crane called for a doctor; but within thirty minutes of the attack, her husband, age sixty, was dead.

Reverend Crane's death shocked the community; and with 1,400 mourners, more than twice the size of his congregation, his funeral was the largest that Port Jervis had ever seen. An even larger service, presided over by a dozen ministers with about a hundred others in attendance, was conducted in Elizabeth, New Jersey, before interment in the family plot in Hillside's Evergreen Cemetery. Within days, bereaved friends and parishioners were buying memorial photos of Reverend Crane, and later a stained-glass window in Drew Methodist Church was dedicated to him.[12]

The death disrupted the Crane household.[13] Before the end of February, the Cranes were forced to leave the parsonage and moved to Roseville, near Newark, for three months. With the family's economic future uncertain, Edmund, Wilbur, and Luther dropped out of Centenary Collegiate Institute to help support the family, and Edmund and Stephen were sent to live with relatives, the family of H. W. Van Sycle (also spelled "Van Sickle"), on a farm in Sussex County. To help pay for their room and board, Edmund became a schoolteacher.

Grief-stricken, Mrs. Crane struggled with the anguish of her fatherless children. In all likelihood, the most distressed was young Stephen. At age eight, he had never witnessed the death of a loved one, but now in the parlor of the parsonage, as was the custom for a wake in the nineteenth century, the casket was on display. In later years he said practically nothing about his father in letters or conversation—only that "he was a great, fine, simple mind"—but fathers are often missing from his work. The pattern was unmistakable. The suddenly absent father, the grieving, struggling mother, and the child alone in the world captured the traumatic loss of home and family that Stephen had experienced.[14]

5

Schooling at Asbury Park, Pennington, Claverack

MARCH 1880–SPRING 1890

IN JUNE 1880, after being temporarily dislocated for three months, the Cranes returned to Port Jervis to live with Stephen's brother William at 21 Brooklyn Street in the "Brooklyn" area of town, so they could save money. Searching for a location suited to her social standing and religious beliefs, Mrs. Crane moved to 508 Fourth Avenue in Asbury Park, New Jersey, in June 1883; by 1885 she was living in Arbutus Cottage at 605 East Fourth Avenue. Asbury Park and nearby Ocean Grove were well established as Methodist strongholds in Monmouth County. Historically, the area had its roots in the camp-meeting movement, which was especially popular on the American frontier in the first half of the nineteenth century as a way to encourage new converts during what Francis Asbury called "harvest time." Later in the century, campsites moved near rail lines for easier access, and permanent communities of cottages and auditoriums replaced makeshift tent grounds.

In 1869 the Methodist Camp Meeting Association established a permanent campground on the New Jersey coast that the members named "Ocean Grove" and began selling lots for summer vacations and religious fellowship. An artesian well was named Beersheba; there were a Pilgrim Pathway and a Mt. Tabor Way; and two bordering lakes, Wesley

Lake on the north side and Fletcher Lake on the south, were named after Methodists John Wesley and John William Fletcher. Advertising itself as "The Summer Mecca of American Methodism" where, according to the *New York Tribune,* "the soul hungry for intellectual pabulum can feast to its fulness," Ocean Grove soon became a popular destination for Methodist families. Not surprisingly, the town enforced stringent regulations that reflected beliefs of the community. Perhaps the most conspicuous of these (enforced until 1977) was the banning of vehicles within town limits, from 12:01 A.M. Saturday night to 11:59 P.M. Sunday evening. No one was exempted. In 1875, when Ulysses S. Grant came to Ocean Grove on a Sunday to speak to five thousand campers and Civil War veterans, the president had to leave his horses and carriage outside the chained gates and walk a half-mile to the auditorium.[1]

The sale of novels and liquor was also prohibited within city limits, and on Sundays soda, candy, and newspapers could not be purchased. The title deeds of plots stipulated that if alcohol was ever sold on the premises, the property would revert to the original owner. When hundreds of empty beer bottles were found littering the streets outside cottages, the bottles were collected and washed, covered with a label that bore a printed sermon on the evils of alcohol, then returned to their owners to remind them of their sinful ways—and possible loss of property. Local businesses, however, circumvented the policing by the local Law and Order League. Rolling wagons amusingly called "arks" dispensed beer throughout Asbury Park, and "speak-easies" catered to customers with a secret password: "sea foam" for beer and "cold tea" for whiskey. Despite objections to the sale of tobacco on Sunday, physicians using the alias "Dr. Jekyll" wrote pseudo-scientific prescriptions for a "q.s." (medical abbreviation for "a sufficient quantity") of "Tabaci Foliumm" with instructions to "use as directed."[2]

Of all the local inhabitants, none was more famous than James A. Bradley, who bought the first lot sold in Ocean Grove in 1870 and a year later purchased 500 acres of land nearby that he developed into an oceanside resort community. Named after Methodist bishop Francis Asbury, Asbury Park became a major summer family attraction on the East Coast in the nineteenth century. The town's leading citizen, "Founder" Bradley owned the boardwalk, beach, and most of the real estate and imposed his prudish morality on the community. Aphorisms dotted the boardwalk: "Modesty of apparel is just as becoming to a lady in bathing costume as in silks and satins," declared one sign; "As a rule respectable people retire from the beach at 10 P.M.," proclaimed another. Crane later satirized a community where visitors needed "no guide-book nor policemen" to show them how to behave, because they have "signs confronting them, at all points, under their feet, over their heads and before their noses. 'Thou shalt not' do this, nor that, nor the other."[3]

Mrs. Crane was already familiar with Monmouth County, having visited Ocean Grove several times since 1872, when Jonathan bought a lot at the Ocean Grove Camp Ground. Besides Stephen, two of her other children came to the area. Townley had assumed charge of the Long Branch departments of the *New York Tribune* and the Associated Press in 1880, and Agnes had been hired to teach at Asbury Park School starting in the fall of 1883. Like Asbury Park and Ocean Grove, the county was also a Methodist stronghold, and regional papers such as the *New Jersey Tribune* and *Monmouth Tribune* vigorously supported prohibition. In one year alone, according to the minutes of a WCTU convention, Mrs. Crane wrote twenty-five columns for a local paper and apparently more than 150 dispatches for the Associated Press, the *New York Tribune,* and other New York newspapers.[4] By 1889 her newspaper work was being acclaimed and reprinted nationally.[5] In September 1883 she became president of the WCTU of Asbury Park and Ocean Grove and was reelected annually until failing health forced her resignation in January 1891. During her tenure she represented the local WCTU chapter at conventions in St. Louis, Salem (New Jersey), Nashville, Atlanta, and Boston; served as the WCTU's superintendent of the press in New Jersey; and chaired the organization's national Committee on Juvenile Work.[6] To supplement her income from temperance work, Mrs. Crane relied on dividends from inherited shares in coal mines in Kingston, Pennsylvania; but when the Panic of 1884 led to strikes in the Pennsylvania mines, she lost income, forcing her to rent rooms in Arbutus Cottage to summer visitors. The coal crisis became personal for the family as well. In March 1884 at the Wyoming Methodist Conference in Scranton, she formally charged her brother the Reverend George M. Peck with dishonest management of the family's share of the mines. Though Reverend Peck was found innocent, the court concluded that he had exceeded his authority.[7] The trial also shamed the Crane and Peck families. Allegations of jealousy, involvement of prominent clergy, and Mrs. Crane's breakdown under cross-examination made front-page news. Nothing is known of her youngest son's reaction, but at twelve years old he would have been disturbed by the incident. His father had been debilitated by spiteful attacks from fellow ministers; his mother, from intra-family warfare.

Stephen enrolled in the sixth grade at Asbury Park School in September 1883 and did well in his first year, but after two years he transferred to Pennington Seminary. He joined the literary Philomathean Society and probably enrolled in the literary curriculum (classical and scientific programs were also available), but the school's strict rules proved confining. Students were required to attend two religious services daily in the seminary chapel, a prayer meeting Wednesday evening, Sunday service at either the local Methodist or Presbyterian church, and Bible class in the afternoon back in the chapel; secular amusements were strictly monitored and on Sunday were prohibited. Imprisoned in an authoritarian system, Stephen desperately sought an escape. In the fall of 1887, when he was charged with being involved in a hazing incident, he denied the accusation; but after a professor accused him of lying, Crane angrily packed his trunk, returned to Asbury Park, and told his family that "as the Professor called me a liar there was not room in Pennington for us both, so I came home."[8]

Instead of pursuing the ministry—the goal of many students at Pennington—Stephen wanted to attend a school that prepared him to enter West Point and pursue his dream of a military career. Such a school was Claverack College and Hudson River Institute, a coeducational, semi-military high school and junior college about thirty miles south of Albany in Columbia County, New York.[9] Like Pennington, the school had a Methodist affiliation, required chapel attendance, and banned social activities such as dancing and gambling, but it was more cosmopolitan. Students from fourteen states and as far away as Central America enrolled, especially in its renowned musical program that annually featured prominent singers and musicians from New York City.

When Stephen insisted on leaving Pennington, Mrs. Crane struggled with his decision because of the family's connection with the school. As principal, her husband had rebuilt it financially and academically after it had almost collapsed; but when the family could not convince Stephen to return, she allowed him to transfer to Claverack in January 1888 after she learned that his board and tuition would be only $160 (the rate for a minister's son) instead of $225 and that her instructions to the school would be followed: he was to have a studious roommate and carefully structured academic program. He hoped to bring along his horse for companionship. When P. T. Barnum's circus abandoned a pony with poor eyesight, a young Stephen, identifying with another outcast, adopted it. The pony delighted in performing tricks for its new owner, and together they frolicked along the Asbury Park shore. Claverack policy, however, prohibited students from bringing a horse to school. Because the livery was attached to a hotel, the school was concerned that the hotel might lead students astray.[10]

Crane was assigned to a third-floor cubicle on "Flack Alley," a corridor in the dormitory named after the Reverend Arthur H. Flack, who had succeeded his father as president of the school. Stephen quickly befriended fellow "tough devils," who secretly reveled in earthly delights condemned at home. Whatever hope Mrs. Crane had that her son's roommate would influence Stephen positively was for naught. As soon as he arrived at Claverack, Stephen and his roommate, Earl Reeves, began knocking on cubicle doors: "We're taking up a collection of tobacco."[11]

Mornings were spent sleeping late and being tardy for class, and his studies were eclectic. Although he initially enrolled in the Classical curriculum, he later switched to the Academic, which emphasized composition, science, history, mathematics, and the Bible. Students in both programs were typically prepared to enter the third year of college; but he was an unorthodox student, for when he entered Lafayette College in the fall of 1890, having completed two and a half years at Claverack, he was still only a freshman. He enjoyed history and literature, but disliked grammar because of its emphasis on rules and denounced narrowly defined academic programs: "There is nothing; save opinion—and opinion be damned."[12] Yet he identified with texts that spoke to him personally. He memorized passages from Tennyson's "In Memoriam" and William Cullen Bryant's "Thanatopsis," both of which deal with loss, doubt, and loneliness during a spiritual crisis. The sudden death of Arthur Hallam at age twenty-two deprived Tennyson of his closest friend, who had counseled and guided him, and Bryant, writing at age eighteen, sought a way to explain the significance of death. Both poems resonated with Crane, whose early years were filled with reminders of sudden loss. By the time he arrived at Claverack at age sixteen, Crane had lost his father (age sixty), sister Agnes (twenty-eight), brother Luther (twenty-three), his brother Townley's wife Fannie (twenty-nine), and their two babies.

Crane also socialized with girls in the art and music programs at Claverack. Phebe English gave him several paintings that he later hung on his walls at Syracuse University and in New York City. Knowing his interest in the military, she also gave him one titled *War and Peace,* which patriotically depicted the American flag. Like his male friends, he often romanticized his relationships with girls. He fell in love with Jennie Pierce, "madly, in the headlong way of seventeen. Jennie was clever. With only half an effort she made my life so very miserable." Following his short-lived romance with red-headed Harriet Mattison, his peers quipped: "Stephen was the first martyr. He seems also to be the last. Anyway, these red sunsets must be very Harrying." When his colleagues described a local belle, he predicted, "My God, what a lot of harm she is going to do before she dies!" And when he and other students, neatly dressed in their military uniforms and ruffled dresses, ventured out on a group date, their trip ended abruptly when they quarreled over the destination. Exasperated, the boys fled together. Soon afterward, they formed a secret society of misogynists, the "S. S. T. Girlum," with initials reminiscent of the rallying cry *Sic semper tyrannis.*[13]

Crane's membership in the society was short-lived. One day, fellow student Harvey Wickham secretly played matchmaker: he arranged a rehearsal for a music recital but invited only two people. When Crane arrived, he was dismayed to find that Harriet was also there. "Damn you, Wickham," Crane cursed, as his colleague left the two estranged lovers alone together. But soon thereafter, Crane thanked Wickham for arranging the tryst. Crane's reputation as a lover spread rapidly among his peers. Armistead Borland, fourteen, idealized the older Crane as a hero and claimed to have learned much about poker and seduction from him. A few years later, Crane acknowledged that during his flirtations he "was such an ass, such a pure complete ass," but the emotion of his "schoolboy dreams . . . was probably higher, finer, than anything of my afterlife."[14]

Crane played tennis, was the catcher for the school's baseball team, and rose rapidly in rank in the military program. In his second year he was first lieutenant of Company C in the student battalion and adjutant of the corps and was promoted to captain for the following year. Whether in sports or military exercises, Crane firmly believed in the importance of team precision and honorable deportment. When one student challenged another to a fight, Crane insisted that they adhere to the commonly accepted Marquess of Queensberry rules for amateur boxing. Wickham recalled Crane's "perfectly hen-like attitude" while training fellow cadets for the Prize Drill, an annual competition among the military companies. When Wickham accidentally dropped his rifle during competition, Crane stormed, "Idiot! Imbecile! . . . You were fairly decent up to the last minute. And then to drop your gun! Such a thing was never heard of. Do you think *order arms* means to drop your gun?" Crane's assertiveness paid off, for Company C won the prize in 1890. On another occasion, when Wickham and a friend lampooned the pomp of military spectacle by parading with their jackets turned inside out, Crane exclaimed, "So! You're a professional damn fool. That is it."[15]

Crane's rebellion against school and church rules and his rigid adherence to military rules on the drill field reveal his conflicted personality. He seemed a loner, an outsider whose raw experience belied his age and set him apart from his peers. An inveterate poker player, he hid behind the mask of his cards, knowing that in life, as in poker, one concealed one's feelings in order to succeed. Unable to penetrate his diffidence, students joked that he was "the Stephen cranium." He smoked and gambled, skipped classes, escaped at night to Mrs. Myers's local shop for coffee and dessert, and pumped the church organ to avoid being forced to sit in a pew and listen to a sermon; yet he disdained what he considered childish pranks such as breaking into a student's cubicle and upsetting furniture, going on a nighttime raid in an apple orchard, or tying up a grocer while he slept. He often identified with the school's "social outcasts," Cuban students marginalized by their American peers. Yet as his inscription in a friend's autograph album revealed—with specific mention of a particular card game, his name, and his place of origin—he also sought peer acceptance:

Whist
Very Sincerely
Your F'riend
S. T. Crane
New York City
C.C.&H.R.I. March 27, 1888

Unlike poker, in which individuals were pitted against each other, whist was a game for four players in two teams; you needed the partnership of "Your F'riend." Crane identified himself as a resident of cosmopolitan New York City, rather than of Methodist-dominated Asbury Park, to establish his worldliness in the eyes of peers. He also gave himself a middle initial. Middle names became popular in the United States and Great Britain at the end of the eighteenth century, and by the end of the nineteenth century most Americans had one; but of the fourteen Crane children, he alone lacked a middle name. Later, when he enrolled at Claverack, he signed his name with the added "T"—a likely choice, given that his father, brother Jonathan, and sister Elizabeth had the same middle initial, which stood for "Townley."[16]

The happiest period in Crane's life consisted of "the sunny irresponsible days at Claverack, when all the earth was a green field and all the sky was a rainless blue." The school's literary societies, weekly music recitals, guest lecturers, and student magazine, *The Vidette,* stimulated him culturally. Although he never read deeply or widely, those years were his most intense period of exposure to the classics and contemporary literature. Plutarch's *Lives,* with its spirited historical descriptions of Greece and Rome and its biographies of classical statesmen and generals, was the model for a class assignment that became his earliest known signed publication, "Henry M. Stanley," a biographical and historical commentary about the African explorer and journalist, published in the February 1890 issue of *The Vidette.* It illustrates young Crane's admiration for adventurous correspondents.[17]

During the 1890 spring term, he was expecting to return to school in the fall, for he had recently been elected captain of the baseball team and promoted to captain of his company. He was also excited about applying to West Point, especially after reading the January 1890 issue of *The Vidette,* which carried an essay on the physical and academic requirements for admission to the academy. His brother William, however, urged him to reconsider. An amateur Civil War historian, William had once regaled a young Stephen with tales about the battles of Chancellorsville and Gettysburg that had fueled his brother's longing to be a professional soldier; but William was now convinced that no war would be fought during Stephen's lifetime and thus there was little chance for military glory. Instead he urged his youngest brother to pursue a more practical profession. The decision must have been difficult. To a seventeen-year-old, the thought of being paid $540 annually as a cadet and, upon graduation as a second lieutenant, receiving a starting salary of $1,500 was enormously appealing; that choice would have ensured him financial stability for at least the minimum of eight years of service required of academy graduates. He also wanted to preserve the tradition of his patriotic, military ancestors. As a military career began to look increasingly like a dream, he found himself suddenly adrift as a student, for his desultory course of study had prepared him for little else. Because the family owned stock in coal mines in nearby Kingston, Pennsylvania, some-one—in all likelihood William, the most practical member of the family—suggested that Stephen apply to Lafayette College's mining-engineering program. Crane eventually agreed, and knowing that he would be leaving Claverack, declined the position of captain on the baseball team. But he left the school reluctantly. Shortly after arriving at Lafayette, he wrote to a Claverack classmate: "So you are not having a hell of a time at C. C., eh? Well, you had better have it now because, mark my words, you will always regret the day you leave old C. C. . . . I have still left a big slice of my heart up among the pumpkin seeds and farmers of Columbia Co." If a piece of his heart lay behind, the challenge of maturity lay ahead.[18]

6

College at Lafayette and Syracuse

SEPTEMBER 1890–MAY 1891

ADMINISTERED BY THE Presbyterian Synod of Pennsylvania, Lafayette College, in the town of Easton, had a rigidly structured curriculum that prohibited electives during the four-year program. All students were required to study the Bible and attend chapel daily, and all classes, as the school's catalogue proudly asserted, were framed within a "systematic and thorough study of the Word of God," with "special attention . . . given to the harmony of Science with Revealed Religion."[1]

After paying the fifteen-dollar tuition for the fall semester, Crane enrolled on September 12, 1890, and saved money by moving into Room 170 in East Hall, where accommodations were cheaper because of the hall's distance from classrooms.[2] A week later he pledged to Delta Upsilon.[3] Part of the initiation was a trek up Mount Paxinosa. Deep in thought, Crane hiked the trail alone, smoking silently as he gazed at Easton and the Delaware River in the distance. Stuck emotionally in the past, he missed his Claverack friends and realized that his fledgling military career had abruptly ended. Gone was the chance that he might emulate Paxinosa, the Shawnee warrior whose heroic exploits in colonial New York and the Wyoming Valley of Pennsylvania had captured the imagination of local youngsters; and gone, too, was paternal protection ever since the death of his father, a strong family man like Paxinosa.[4] As Crane had done while hiking the mountains overlooking Port Jervis, he recalled how insensible nature was to humanity. The reassurance of an all-pervasive God promised by his religious upbringing offered little solace in an indifferent universe.

Crane enrolled in seven required courses—Bible, French, algebra, chemistry, industrial drawing, elocution, and theme writing—and failed five of them primarily because of poor attendance. His highest grade was 92, in elocution; the lowest, a zero, in theme writing, which he despised because it was taught by engineering faculty who forced students to write on technical subjects using specialized jargon.[5] Ironically, the future writer terrified of public speaking received his lowest grade in a writing course and his highest in elocution. Despite his poor performance, he was not expelled. Because of low enrollments, Lafayette reclassified weak students and allowed them to take fewer courses. Crane's negligent behavior was by no means unique. Only about 50 percent of the Class of '94 left school without censure before graduating.

Crane was interested more in extracurricular activities than in his studies. Besides joining a fraternity, he played intramural baseball and participated in the college's Washington Literary Society and its rival Franklin Literary Society, both of which maintained libraries and sponsored lectures and debates. He also joined the Campus Club, a student-run organization that provided meals at a lower cost than the university's plan.

Lafayette had a reputation for rowdy students. On Halloween 1870, during an event known as a "horn spree" because of the ruckus created from horns and tin pans, students had painted and tarred the chapel, destroyed classrooms, and burned down outhouses. By the late 1880s, vandals were tearing out cistern pumps, dragging a horse into a campus building, and causing a gas explosion in another. Other schools were prone to childish behavior as well, and Stephen's family knew about Reverend Jesse Truesdell Peck's problems while president of Dickinson College (1848–1852). When Reverend Peck had tried to instill a strict moral code, students had lured him into a freight car, locked him in, and rolled it to a different part of town; another time, they had concocted a scheme to detain him in an insane asylum. After they had shot his dog, emptied washbasins from windows onto Mrs. Peck, and torched his privy, Peck, convinced that he was unsuited for college administration, had resigned in 1852.[6]

Crane helped to defend the honor of the freshman class. During the annual Banner Scrap, freshmen protected a banner hanging ten to twelve feet off the ground on the corner of a building. Sophomores dumped bags filled with flour on them, often followed by water, then tried to capture the banner, which they could reach only by standing on the bodies of freshmen. A battered Crane defended the banner and later re-captured the scrap in his novel *Active Service,* wherein freshmen and sophomores clashed to uphold "the honor of their classes," displaying "an energy" that a professor could "not detect in the classroom." As Crane wrote to a Claverack schoolmate, "fellows here raise more hell than any college in the country."[7]

One event during class rivalry almost irreparably altered Crane's future. Hazing had become a major problem on campuses throughout the country, and at Lafayette police occasionally arrested marauding students fighting in the streets of Easton. The college was still recovering from an incident during the winter of 1885–1886. When a freshman had refused to admit sophomores into his room, they had battered down his door and broken his windows to gain entrance. After someone fired a pistol twice, students had panicked and fled. Thirteen students had been suspended. A similar incident occurred shortly after Crane's arrival in September 1890. Sophomores broke into the room of two freshmen, one of whom, defending himself with a baseball bat, fractured the skull of an assailant. Two weeks later, marauding sophomores demanded that Crane open his door. After he refused, they broke in. An ashen Crane was standing in a corner holding a pistol, the entire scene dimly lit by a flickering oil lamp. Everyone was horrified, and as Crane wilted, the pistol slipped out of his hand. Crane never spoke about the incident, and only draconian measures prevented other near-fatal pranks. In September 1891, on the night before Dr. Ethelbert Dudley Warfield assumed the presidency of Lafayette, sophomores stormed into the freshman rooms. During Dr. Warfield's inaugural address, he condemned hazing at Lafayette and promised to stop it immediately. Within hours, ten sophomores were suspended. Newspapers around the country applauded Dr. Warfield's stance, and the townspeople of Easton held a banquet in his honor.[8]

Before the semester had ended, Crane decided that mining engineering was "not at all to my taste," but hesitated telling his mother because she had been worrying about his desultory academic record.[9] Instead he asked his brother Edmund to intercede for him. With the exception of Agnes, none of his siblings understood him better than Edmund. When Stephen had been farmed out as a child following their father's death, Edmund had acted as a caretaker; and when their mother died, Stephen chose Edmund as his guardian. In later years the peripatetic Crane repeatedly listed Edmund's home in Hartwood, New York, as his permanent address.

Crane wanted to leave Lafayette. Although he was becoming interested in a literary career, Lafayette's English program, which was as rigid as its other programs, would have been a disastrous choice. The courses required no writing and emphasized philology rather than literature. "English should be studied like Greek," proudly asserted Francis A. March, the first professor of English at an American college; students, he believed, should study classic texts "dwelling line by line and word by word upon worthy passages." For Crane, teachers like March resembled "that incoherent mass of stage drivers and baggagemen" badgering guests outside resorts, "roaring and gesticulating, as unintelligible always as a row of Homeric experts." The feeling among members of the Lafayette faculty was mutual: the young upstart should seek his education elsewhere.[10]

After less than four months in Easton, Crane packed his bags and left for home with little more than a piece of a Lafayette pennant to show for his stay. By chance, another student with the surname "Crane" also left before graduation, prompting playful classmates to remember "Our Departed" in the school's yearbook:

> Funny fowls were these two Cranes,
> Steve had wit and Dwight had brains,
> Dwight was short and Steve was tall,
> One had grit, the other gall.[11]

Wit and grit Stephen had—the genius and fortitude to travel the uncertain road to success. But he also had gall: the rebellious confidence to challenge established tradition.

Hoping to find another institution for her son, Mrs. Crane arranged a transfer to Methodist-affiliated Syracuse University, which—she was assured by the school's bulletin—was far from "a saloon or any social evils that shock the moral sense" and had never had "a moral aberration between the sexes, or a cause, because of these associations, to bring anxiety or trouble to a parent's heart."[12] Under the leadership of its chancellor, the Reverend Charles N. Sims, the school touted the high moral standards of its founders, one of whom was Stephen's grand-uncle Bishop Jesse T. Peck. In all likelihood, Stephen accepted his mother's decision that he attend Syracuse because it had a good baseball team.

To lower costs, Mrs. Crane arranged for Stephen to live with Bishop Peck's wife. Because of the family connection, Mrs. Crane apparently convinced university officials to grant her son a scholarship. His admission was simplified because he had attended Claverack, one of Syracuse University's recognized gymnasia—secondary schools designed to prepare students for college; but one prerequisite for admission was waived. According to university policy, the only gymnasium students admitted "without further examination" were those who could submit "certificates of having satisfactorily accomplished the required preparatory studies." Crane's academic record at Claverack hardly met the criterion. After enrolling on January 6, he stayed with Widow Peck to please his mother; but within a few days, having offended his great-aunt with his bohemian ways, he moved briefly to a boardinghouse and then settled in to the Delta Upsilon house. He arrived, a friend recalled, "in a cab and a cloud of tobacco smoke."[13]

Though glad to be free of Mrs. Peck's strictures, Crane was apprehensive about the move. Living alone at Lafayette, he had not needed to share space with a roommate; now he feared that many DU brothers who were studying for the ministry at Syracuse might frown on his lifestyle. Upon arriving at his room, however, he was relieved to see that his new roommate, Clarence N. Goodwin, had a large, well-used tobacco pipe plainly in view. He soon met other like-minded renegades—Mansfield J. French, Frederic M. Lawrence, Frank W. Noxon, and Clarence Loomis Peaslee—who enjoyed freedom from parental control.[14] They often gathered in Stephen and Clarence's room, which was strewn with clothing, sports gear, books, news clippings, and piles of paper; the walls were likewise cluttered with Stephen's favorite drawings and pictures. When other students complained that smoke from the room constantly permeated the house, Stephen and his fellow smokers escaped to the unheated cupola, where they fashioned an Arabian parlor complete with a Turkish pipe. They spent many a cold hour there, wrapped in coats, mittens, and ear muffs, smoking and playing cards, singing bawdy drinking songs, and engaging in the banter of hearty comrades. Once, Goodwin took Crane's Syracuse pennant to an intercollegiate sporting event without telling him. When Goodwin pretended that someone else had borrowed but not returned it, Crane joked that the charade reminded him of someone who, cooking steaks for himself and his roommate, insisted, "your beef-steak fell in the fire." All would have distinguished careers: Goodwin and Peaslee as lawyers; French as a civil engineer and architect; Lawrence as a physician; Noxon as an author, journalist, and businessman; and Crane as the most controversial American writer of the 1890s.[15]

Nothing about Crane's coursework or behavior in class, however, could have predicted his future. Because the curriculum at Syracuse was more liberal than the one at Lafayette, Crane registered as a nondegree student and thus had complete freedom in the choice of courses. Since he was interested in literature and history, he enrolled in an English-literature course taught by Chancellor Sims, and attended—possibly enrolled in as well—Professor Charles J. Little's history course, but he frequently slept late and skipped class, which began at 7:45 A.M.[16] He hated carrying around his hefty literature textbook, Alfred H. Welsh's *Development of English Literature and Language,* which he mocked as being full of "sentences, ponderous, solemn and endless, in which wandered multitudes of homeless and friendless prepositions, adjectives looking for a parent, and quarrelling nouns, sentences which no longer symbolized the language form of thought but which had about them a quaint aroma from the dens of long-dead scholars." One day, Professor Sims became exasperated by Crane's arguing in class and retorted with an appeal to Scripture: "Tut, tut—what does St. Paul say, Mr. Crane, what does St. Paul say?" To which Crane arrogantly replied, "I know what St. Paul says . . . but I disagree with St. Paul." Other authority figures witnessed his combativeness as well. Once, while sharpening silverware, his fraternity's house steward, a senior, shouted, "I want a freshie to turn grindstone; come on, Crane!" Unwilling to be bullied, Stephen snapped back that he "never had and never would turn grindstone for anybody." He was, as one friend observed, "a reproach to the industrious, anathema to the pious and a joy to the un-Godly."[17]

Aware of her son's penchant for rebellion, Mrs. Crane wrote several letters to Frank Smalley, professor of Latin, expressing her anxiety about Stephen's academic future and requesting that Professor Smalley, a fellow DU brother, urge Stephen to study. Early in the semester, Smalley invited Stephen to his home for conversation. Though he recognized Crane's brilliance, he quickly realized that his guest "would not be cramped by following a course of study he did not care for." Other professors were more blunt. "Crane, you'll never amount to anything. Why don't you let up on writing and pay a little more attention to conic sections?" It was no secret on campus that he scoffed at scholarly rigor and despised academic tradition. In a student publication that highlighted "grinds" (industrious students), his name was listed among those of other freshmen, along with a passage from Samuel Rogers's sentimental poem about a teardrop, "On a Tear":

> Sweet drop of pure and pearly light,
> In thee the rays of virtue shine,
> More calmly clear, more mildly bright
> Than any gem that gilds the mine.

No one on campus would have missed the ironic humor of identifying Crane as a "pure" beacon of "virtue." His salty language was legendary among his peers. "Wait until you hear Steve swear," his friends would often say.[18]

Crane readily acknowledged that he preferred baseball to classwork. Soon after he arrived at Syracuse, the school's head coach asked him, "What can you do?" "Not much," replied Crane coolly, puffing on his pipe.

> "Can you row?"
> "Nop."
> "Jump?"
> "Nop."
> "Swim?"
> "Nop."

"Throw the hammer?"

"Nop."

"Play football?"

"A little."

"Humph! A little. That won't do here. Can you play baseball?"

"Betcher life!"

"What can you play best?"

"Catcher."

Within an hour he was on the field, impressing even jaded seniors with his skill. Later, he was encouraged to play professionally.[19]

Unlike Easton, the city of Syracuse had a minor-league team, the Syracuse Stars, which turned professional in 1890. When the team folded after one year in the American Association league, it sold its uniforms to the university's team, and players combined the garments with their own clothing. Wearing a crimson sweater, beige trousers, black stockings, and patent-leather shoes, Crane was proud of being the youngest team captain in American college baseball, and played tenaciously. Normally quiet and reserved off the field, he immersed himself in the game, praising teammates for good plays but sarcastically criticizing them for careless mistakes. He was variously a loner and joiner, a garrulous talker and laconic observer, a taciturn individual and self-confident nonconformist.[20]

The team's best all-around player, Crane was a good batter; but because he was not physically strong, he rarely hit more than a single and sometimes strained his arm throwing to second base. At times playing without a glove, he stoically coated his hands with iodine and witch hazel to disinfect wounds and toughen the skin. Though occasionally assigned to short stop, he was the team's catcher, a position glorified in the hugely successful and influential guidebook *Base-Ball: How to Become a Player* (1888), by John Montgomery Ward, one of the most popular ball players in the nineteenth century. Ward had riveted the imagination of boys around the country with his advice on how best to play the game. An inveterate lover of baseball, Crane would most certainly have read the book and identified with Ward's depiction of the ideal catcher: "Were it not for the extreme liability to injury, the position of catcher would be the most desirable on the field; he has plenty of work of the prettiest kind to do, is given many opportunities for the employment of judgment and skill, and, what is clearer than all to the heart of every true ball player, he is always in the thickest of the fight." Despite Crane's physical limitations—he was 125 pounds, barely five feet seven inches, and of average strength and throwing ability—Ward's book assured him that ultimately "the size of the candidate seems not to be of vital importance." At least as important were the player's "pluck and stamina" and his "quick wit," especially if he wanted to be a professional catcher: "He loses no time in deciding upon a play, he is never 'rattled' in any emergency, he gives and receives signals, and, in short, plays all the points of his position, and accomplishes much that a player of less ready perception would lose entirely." Of all the players on the team, "the catcher has almost complete control of his own play, he is dependent upon no one but himself, and, in spite of everything and everybody, the nature of his work remains the same."[21] The book would have given Crane a credo for his own performance on and off the field. The catcher was part of a team working to overcome opposition, but he also confronted his fate alone. Ward's description prefigures the stoical, self-reliant behavior that Crane would dramatize in his Cuban war stories and news dispatches and that he would admire and emulate on the battlefield in Cuba. The self-reliance of the catcher, his steadfastness in the face of possible injury, and his willingness to confront his fate alone were a model for the kind of life that Crane admired.

Crane participated in numerous other extracurricular activities. He served as secretary-treasurer of Claverack's alumni association; joined the Tooth Pick Club (an eating club); served as captain of his fraternity's Cricket Club; and was a member of the Nut-Brown Maiden Sledding Club (named after a popular college song). During the literary segment of DU meetings, he read his own stories and essays for comment and engaged in "optionals," impromptu presentations on any subject. He also frequented Thomas W. Durston's bookstore in the city. Among his most valued purchases was *The Poetical Works of John Keats, with a Life,* which he inscribed "Stephen Crane / Syracuse NY / Jan 18th / 91."[22] Crane rarely wrote his name in a book and only when he planned to keep it.[23] He also discovered Tolstoy's *Anna Karenina* and *War and Peace,* as well as Goethe's *Faust,* and Durston apparently introduced him to Goethe's *Farbenlehre* in Sir Charles Eastlake's 1840 translation: *Theory of Colors.* Goethe's discussion of how colors produce specific physiological effects and his association of color with moral and emotional states of mind influenced Crane's symbolic use of color, most notably in *The Red Badge of Courage*. Later, Stephen enjoyed Emile Zola's novel *Le Ventre de Paris* (translated as *The Fat and the Thin*), telling friends in 1896 that he wished he could have written the last chapter.[24] Although he feared that too much reading might hamper the development of his own individual style, he could immerse himself totally in a story. As a youngster, when he had first discovered the popular genre of Western dime novels, filled with sensational tales of adventure, he would sit on his windowsill, chewing tobacco and glancing darkly at a deck of cards on the table. Whenever someone was shot in a novel, he would fire his pistol and punctuate the sound with a loud whoop. As an adult Crane delighted in telling an anecdote about someone whose pistol had accidentally exploded, saying he "never saw a boy scatter so," with perhaps a hint of self-deprecation.[25]

Crane met "some dam pretty girls" in Syracuse; he pronounced it a "dandy city at least and I expect to see some fun here." Among his favorite haunts were the local theaters and the Music Hall on North Salina Street, infamous among college students for its scantily clad singers and dancers. Crane also enjoyed pranks. He and his college friend William McMahon would discuss contemporary art, much of which McMahon considered affectation. Several of their friends were aspiring artists whose drawings, music, and writing were, to McMahon, incomprehensible. Crane had once teased McMahon by trying to pass off as serious work a poem about Pearl, who was an artist and Crane's girlfriend:

> Pearl, coming in Ethiope night
> With straw upon her head
> And gray ashes on her yellow glove
> She was not buried
> But dead.

McMahon recognized it as drivel.[26]

One night, at a party with their friends, McMahon proposed to Crane a practical joke ridiculing pretentious art. After guests had politely listened to an hour-long recital by two piano students, then admired Pearl's supposedly innovative artwork, McMahon announced that Crane, besides being a poet, was an accomplished pianist. Asked to play, he feigned modesty, then acquiesced to their encouraging applause. Momentarily collecting his thoughts, he pounded the keys cacophonously. When a guest whispered something, he punctuated his glower at her with an interminably long beating of a single key with one finger, then ended his performance with a loud bang on the piano. Awed by what they assumed was a prodigy's avant-garde composition, the audience applauded wildly. A servant at the party, however, was not bamboozled by the joke. Privately she whispered to Crane, "Mistah, I think you'd better give up yo music and stick to yo poems."[27]

Despite his antics at the party, Crane loved music. He played the guitar, flute, and melodeon and liked to accompany his brother Edmund in L. F. Brackett's popular duet "In Meadows Green."[28] On Sunday evenings, he and Frank Noxon would sometimes attend recitals at St. Paul's, the local Episcopal cathedral distinguished by its towering spire, stained-glass windows, and imposing Gothic Revival architecture. Since the late 1880s, the introduction of boy choirs had reinvigorated liturgical music in American Episcopal churches. Sitting in the last pew to avoid being ostentatious, Frank and Stephen would sing along with the choir. Though Crane rebelled against institutionalized religion, he was drawn to its mystery and ritual. His father had instilled in him a love of singing. "The words which are sung, Sabbath after Sabbath," Reverend Crane wrote, "sink into the memories and hearts of the children." In Crane's poem "Each small gleam was a voice" (1895), the memory of his father and of St. Paul's, its interior painted with light streaming through stained-glass windows and filled with the sound of boy choirs, evoked "little priests, little holy fathers," whose "good ballads of God" were "little songs of carmine, violet, green, gold." The rebel found momentary affirmation in a choir's praise of God.[29]

On the surface, Crane was an unremarkable freshman drifting with little direction, yet he yearned to become a writer and experimented with literary techniques. During a DU chapter meeting at the end of January 1891, he read his political commentary on imperialism that evolved into his dramatized essay "A Foreign Policy in Three Glimpses." In May, he delivered another piece—probably "The King's Favor," a humorous blend of fiction and journalism about an African chief who tries to give one of his wives to a New York tenor in appreciation of his singing. With its appearance in the college's *University Herald* (owned and produced by the DU fraternity) during the same month, it became his first published signed short story. "Greed Rampant," a dramatic skit possibly written around this time, satirizes avaricious Jews and Gentiles trying to enter Heaven, identified as "Paradise, New Jersey"; its anti-Semitism reflected the racial and religious stereotypes then popular in America. Crane was hoping that he could publish a story in a national magazine. In March, when Thomas Durston received a thousand free copies of the popular children's magazine *St. Nicholas* for distribution, Crane most likely got a copy, then wrote "Jack," a tragic story about a dog's defense of a boy after a bear attacks him on a hunting trip.[30] Though the magazine rejected the submission because it had a surfeit of dog stories, a disappointed Crane nonetheless appreciated the editor's favorable comments. Regardless of what he was writing at the time, the legibility of his penmanship and the use of compositor's symbols demonstrated his commitment to publication. He knew that compositors were paid by the speed at which they could set type and that the process relied on their ability to read an author's handwriting.

Ironically, Crane's recalcitrance in the classroom and his increasing need to write brought a major turning point in his professional career. After he did poorly on exams and complained that the history textbook was inaccurate, an exasperated Professor Little asked, "Mr. Crane, what are you in this university for?" "Professor," he responded, "that is a question I have been asking myself for some time." When Little then asked what especially interested him, Crane said, "Journalism." "If that is the case, my neighbor, Eggleston, is editor of the *Syracuse Standard* and I should be very glad to ask him to give you a reporter's job, for until you get knocked about through contact with life, you will be wasting yourself at the university."[31]

Professor Little's offer led to Crane's being hired by Willis Fletcher Johnson as the Syracuse correspondent for the *New York Tribune*. Johnson was the day editor of the newspaper and a longtime friend of the Crane family through a mutual connection with Pennington Seminary. He had graduated from the school in 1875 and later had become president of the alumni association. He was already familiar with Crane's ability, since the days when Stephen had been a stringer for his brother Townley's news agency in Asbury Park. When Crane read that a swarm of caterpillars on railroad tracks had delayed a train in Minnesota, he immediately devised a two-part journalistic spoof of science and technology in the American tradition of the tall tale. According to a drunken "wild-eyed man in overalls," a railroad track in New York's Onondaga County was covered with huge bugs, which, a local "erudite recluse" concluded, were a species of rare predatory mollusk. Published on June 1, 1891, in the *Syracuse Daily Standard* as "Huge Electric Light Bugs" and in the *New York Tribune* as "Great Bugs in Onondaga," the literary hoax occasioned a tongue-in-cheek editorial the next day, probably written by Johnson with help from Crane. Crane's rollicking satire exemplified his playfulness, and the metaphors foreshadowed a dominant theme in his work: life as war. Bugs with "armor" were "pickets or skirmishers" that died "with a crackling sound like the successive explosions of toy torpedoes" in a battle with a train, the "iron monster" of technology. For Crane, humanity was continually in conflict with a merciless God, indifferent nature, and a bitter fate.

Little's admonition that Crane was wasting his time at Syracuse did not change Crane's life, because he was already planning on a writing career; but the advice that he needed to experience life directly began to shape his "creed of conduct," as well as his approach to journalism and literature. Crane's nascent talent as an observer of life's vagaries was becoming increasingly astute, and Syracuse presented a world he had never seen before. Pennington and Claverack were situated in rural villages; Easton, being larger, had more of the amenities of a town; but none of the places compared to urban Syracuse. The New York Central line, the primary means of access to the city, came in on Railroad Street (now Washington Street), which was lined on both sides with bordellos euphemistically called "parlor houses." As a reporter for the *Tribune,* Crane frequented the police court, entertainment halls, and tenement districts searching for stories about the underbelly of Syracuse. With a childlike quest for adventure, which he would never lose, he interviewed prostitutes in the city's police court and roamed through dark thoroughfares, seeking out tramps, waifs, and the downtrodden lurking in deserted streets. From this experience came a draft of his groundbreaking novella *Maggie: A Girl of the Streets,* an early version written at the DU house. One weekend, while Crane was away, a member of the fraternity read the manuscript, "which was saturated with obscenity and profanity," to his housemates. Amid "great hilarity," they pronounced it "crazy stuff."[32]

Though Crane was not expelled from Syracuse University, the dean repeatedly admonished him for his apathy toward his studies, and by the end of the semester was urging him to leave unless he changed his attitude. Crane, however, was already finished with formal education. He never graduated from any school. "College life is a waste of time," he complained, because it interfered with his plan to be a reporter: "Not that I disliked books, but the cut-and-dried curriculum of the college did not appeal to me. Humanity was a much more interesting study. When I ought to have been at recitations I was studying faces on the streets, and when I ought to have been studying my next day's lessons I was watching the trains roll in and out of the Central Station. So, you see, I had, first of all, to recover from college." Nonetheless, Crane left with fond memories of his friends at Syracuse. During the winter of 1892–1893, he returned to see them at the annual fraternity reception. Like a doting older brother, he punched holes in their stiff dress shirts so they could wear the studs he had brought along and impress the coeds with their proper attire. His visit to campus, however, did not instill in him a desire to return to the classroom. Once he left school for good, he never doubted his decision. One night in May 1891, he burned an inscription into the east wall of the DU cupola:

Sunset—1891—May

Steph Crane

He thus marked the moment at which the sun set on his journey through education, as he pondered the dawn of a new career in the journalistic haunts of New York City.[33]

Part II

LEARNING THE CRAFT

7

Fledgling Writer

1887–DECEMBER 1891

IN THE 1890S, aspiring young writers and artists read Rudyard Kipling's immensely popular novel *The Light That Failed* (1890), about a rebellious young Impressionist painter and war correspondent named Dick Heldar, who believes that deprivation stimulates creativity. He leads a bohemian life of poverty in the slums of London, seeking raw truth there and later on the battlefield. As a painter, Heldar uses color to convey emotional responses and believes that the only valid source for art is one's personal experience, even if it is ugly or unpleasant.

Although Crane never mentioned *The Light That Failed* by name, there is a striking similarity between the theme it embodies and the artistic credo that he was developing in the early 1890s, a period during which he was enthusiastic about Kipling's work. Like Heldar, Crane concluded that "the most artistic and the most enduring literature was that which reflected life accurately," as based on the artist's own experience of it. In all likelihood, Crane read *The Light That Failed* when it appeared in *Lippincott's Monthly Magazine* in January 1891.[1] The following year, he was already living as a poor bohemian in New York City. He would soon move in with other artists while experimenting with color imagery in his own work and developing an impressionistic, painterly prose style; a few years later, he would be serving as a war correspondent in Greece and Cuba, like Dick Heldar. Crane's impoverished lifestyle led his family to wonder why he put himself through hardship when he was always welcome to live more comfortably with siblings. Crane and Heldar were convinced, however, that their way was the only true path to legitimate art. Just as Heldar asserted that "there are few things more edifying unto Art than the actual belly-pinch of hunger," Crane declared: "It seems a pity . . . that art should be a child of suffering; and yet such seems to be the case. Of course there are fine writers who have good incomes and live comfortably and contentedly; but if the conditions of their lives were harder, I believe that their work would be better." Crane maintained a lifelong fidelity to observed experience as the basis for art, and, like Heldar, employed color imagery. Crane was already familiar with the basics of painting, having known artists: his mother, his sister Mary Helen ("Nellie"), and two of his girlfriends, Phebe English at Claverack and Pearl at Syracuse. Nonetheless, Kipling's imagery inspired Crane, especially in the Sullivan County tales and sketches of 1892, and the later explosion of color imagery in *The Red Badge of Courage*. *The Light That Failed* gave Crane a set of artistic beliefs and a plan for carrying them out. He soon rejected what he called his "clever Rudyard-Kipling style," with its glib humor and contrived prose; but he never lost his love for Kipling, whom he met on April 25, 1896, in New York. He had thirteen volumes of Kipling's works in his library at Brede Place in England, more than those of any other author.[2]

As exciting as the idea of emulating Dick Heldar was, Crane believed —probably even before reading *The Light That Failed*—that he was beginning "with no talent, but an ardent admiration and desire" to write. His brother Townley, despite his idiosyncrasies and self-destructive behavior, was already an established professional journalist who served early on as a mentor. Together they represented a new breed of journalists. The previous generation of writers in America disliked journalism and considered it beneath serious art. Among them, William Dean Howells and Henry James had had distressing experiences as news reporters early in their careers, and later, in their fiction, portrayed journalists as loathsome and amoral. Subsequent generations, however, saw the profession of journalism not as a threat to literature but as a serious career and a respectable training ground for writers of fiction.[3]

Townley's summer bureau on the New Jersey shore was part of an extensive network of agencies that gathered news from July to September at resorts like Saratoga Springs (New York), Newport (Rhode Island), and Nahant (Massachusetts). Throughout much of the nineteenth century, only the wealthy could afford to vacation at summer resorts; but by the latter part of the century, this began to change as the middle class expanded. Daily excursions from New York, New Jersey, and Pennsylvania transported vacationers to Asbury Park and Ocean Grove. Nearby was Long Branch, a popular destination since 1869, when President Grant had made it the nation's "Summer Capital," a custom repeated by Presidents Hayes, Garfield, Arthur, Harrison, McKinley, and Wilson. As the "Monte Carlo of America," it lured dreamers to its fabled gambling tables and racetrack, while celebrities like Jim Fisk, Diamond Jim Brady, and Lillian Russell mingled in the town with political and military leaders such as Winfield Scott, George Meade, and Philip Sheridan. Crane began working at Townley's bureau in Asbury Park as a stringer during the summer of 1888 (or possibly 1887) scouring hotel registers for names of newly arrived guests, gathering current news, and excerpting what local reporters called "the usual Sunday gabble" for the *New York Tribune*. Following a standard format, news releases praised resorts for their distinctive qualities, summarized local events, and listed where recent arrivals were staying. Stephen's news reports from 1887 to 1891 were so inconsequential that Townley simply incorporated them into his own news releases for the *Tribune,* collecting a standard space-rate for them and paying Stephen out of pocket. Though the younger brother's work was generally indistinguishable from that of other local reporters, a precocious Stephen may have flexed his literary muscles in an early piece of particular note. In July 1887 the *Philadelphia Press* published a fictional sketch submitted by Townley's news agency, "Asbury's New Move," about an attempt by the puritanical Superintendent Snedeker to thwart a public flirtation between two young lovers, "a pair of those tender seaside doves who have been so numerous at Asbury Park." Though "young people" considered him "hardhearted," he was convinced that by preventing "these demonstrations of the nilly-noodles in loud costumes," he would "receive the plaudits of sensible folks everywhere." The sketch clearly satirized founder James Bradley's efforts to legislate morality in Asbury Park; and though it was unsigned, its irony, distinctive prose, and idiosyncratic style were characteristic traits in what may well have been Crane's first known publication—at age fifteen.[4]

By 1890 Crane's contributions to his brother's news agency had increased to the point where Townley informed the *Tribune* that he was employing him and listed him on a prospectus as secretary of "Crane's New Jersey Coast News Bureau, Sandy Hook to Barnegat Bay." During the day, Stevie, as he was affectionately called by fellow journalists, rode his bicycle around Avon, Asbury Park, and Ocean Grove searching for newsworthy material. In the evening, he often met with other cub reporters—some of whom, like Ralph Paine and Post Wheeler, would remain lifelong friends—to enjoy beer and clams, swap stories, and compose news dispatches to be wired from the Postal Telegraph Office.[5]

One particular news assignment became a seminal moment in Crane's literary career. In August 1891, Hamlin Garland, an innovative new writer and critic who was redefining the practice and study of American literature, was delivering a series titled "Lecture-Studies in American Literature and Expressive Art" for the Seaside Assembly in Avon-by-the-Sea, New Jersey. On August 17, Crane covered Garland's lecture on William Dean Howells, the most powerful literary voice in the country at the time, for the *Tribune*.[6] Afterward, Crane shyly introduced himself to Garland and asked if he could borrow his lecture notes in order to write his newspaper report. Garland casually gave them to him without thinking much about the matter and promptly forgot Crane's name. The report, which was published the next day, consisted mostly of extensive quotation from Garland's notes, with an emphasis on Howells's belief that a novelist must render experience subjectively and "be true to himself and to things as he sees them."[7] The appearance of the report prompted Garland to inquire about the reporter, and over the next few days they discussed literature and shared another interest: their love of baseball. Garland had been a pitcher in his youth and evidently enjoyed discussing the intricacies of a curve ball with the former catcher.

The timing of their meeting proved auspicious for the fledgling writer, since at this point Crane had no definite professional plans, no artistic vision, no voice or subject. As he later told his friend Corwin Knapp Linson, when he first began writing he could barely think of anything to write about. Garland proved to be a good role model. His recently published groundbreaking collection of short stories, *Main-Travelled Roads*

(1891), was widely praised for its honest portrayal of character, dialect, and setting on the western prairies; his seaside lectures, espousing a new theory of fiction, appeared in two crusading journals, the *Arena* and the *Forum,* and would later be collected in *Crumbling Idols* (1894). Like Ralph Waldo Emerson's essay "The American Scholar" and Walt Whitman's first preface to *Leaves of Grass, Crumbling Idols* was a literary manifesto that championed individual experience as a source of knowledge and guide to action and called passionately for a new literature that would free writers from the chains imposed by literary tradition. Dedicating his book "to the men and women of America who have the courage to be artists," Garland encouraged them to pursue their own creative impulses and discouraged them from acquiring their education solely from schools, which emphasized the past. For too long, those "bulwarks of tradition" had forced aspiring essayists to imitate Joseph Addison; aspiring novelists, Sir Walter Scott or Charles Dickens; aspiring dramatists, William Shakespeare. Like other long-revered literary masters, these idols were now crumbling. It was time, Garland exhorted his followers, to defy conformity with "rebellious art." "Write of those things of which you know most," Garland urged in a separate essay, "and for which you care most. By so doing you will be true to yourself, true to your locality, and true to your time."[8]

Though there is no evidence that Crane read *Crumbling Idols,* Garland's 1891 lectures in Asbury Park almost certainly contained the spirit —if not the wording—of the published essays. Crane typically disregarded theories, but Garland clearly articulated vague ideas he had been grappling with. For a struggling writer who had rejected college and had been challenging established beliefs and institutions, Garland's advice was inspiring. Interviewed for a news article in 1894, Crane echoed Garland's sentiments: "The curse of our literature, the reason why we have done so little to create a genuine literature of our own in this country, is that our writers have imitated other writers of other countries instead of saying what they had to say in their own way of putting themselves into their work."[9] The pupil in search of direction had found his teacher.

Crane ended the summer of 1891 the way he had begun it: with an escape into the wilderness. In mid-June he had joined three friends— Louis E. Carr, Jr., Frederic M. Lawrence, and Louis C. Senger, Jr.—on a hunting, fishing, and camping trip in Sullivan County near Port Jervis. It was the first of several invigorating summer trips they made there and to Twin Lakes in Pike County, Pennsylvania, within the next four or five years. During the day they read books or roamed through the wilderness, and Crane's skin became ruddy and tanned in stark contrast to his fair hair. After supper they smoked, talked, and played cards around a blazing campfire until late into the night. Only inclement weather dampened their youthful spirit. When they planned another camping trip in Sullivan County in the spring of 1892, they ignored the fact that it was still the rainy season. As soon as they pitched their tent, a biting, cold storm settled in. Unable to find dry firewood and keep warm in a soaked tent, they suffered for four days till the storm cleared. Before leaving, Crane memorialized the trip by carving into a tree: "Allah il Allah! And it rained forty days and forty nights." Though Crane disparaged religion, its language and imagery—whether in God's prediction to Noah or the muezzin's call to prayer—provided a lens that focused his ironic depiction of reality.[10]

The trips into the wilderness energized Crane's imagination, as had the American frontier for so many other American writers, from Captain John Smith, Governor William Bradford, and William Byrd II to Thoreau and Mark Twain. One night, the four campers discussed their future careers. Lawrence talked about following in his father's footsteps and becoming a doctor; likewise Senger, whose father was a lawyer. When they asked Crane about his plans, he answered succinctly: "You know what I am going to do." He was right. None of them questioned his ability to pursue what they considered "the most difficult of all professions."[11]

Following the camping trip and the close of Asbury Park's 1891 summer resort season on Labor Day, Stephen moved to his brother Edmund's home in Lake View (now part of Clifton but then a suburb of Paterson), New Jersey, to continue his writing. During the fall and winter of 1891–1892, he explored New York's tenement districts for background material to use in writing *Maggie,* a novel that would revolutionize American urban fiction. While working on it, he was also transforming his camping experiences in Sullivan County into nineteen tales and sketches that he called his "first work in fiction." In several of the sketches, "wonderful yarn-spinners" recount local legends and folklore about a seasoned hunter's tracking a "wounded wild hog for 200 miles," the "siren voice" of a panther that enticed people from their homes and into the woods by imitating the sound of a crying baby, and "a very reckless and distracted giant who . . . carelessly pelted trees and boulders" at the land and "set off several earthquakes under it," thus creating the county. Other sketches dramatize the extraordinary experiences of four city men in the wilderness. Generally identified only by their epithets, the "little man," "tall man," "pudgy man," and "quiet man" battle with their own fear, conceit, and insecurity, as well as with a hostile, animistic nature filled with man-eating bears, gaping caves, glowering mountains, and dark forests. The sketches also show Crane confronting his own isolation. In "The Octopush," four fishermen stranded on tree stumps in a pond are "alone, separated from humanity by impassable gulfs"; in "A Ghoul's Accountant," "the music of the wind in the trees is songs of loneliness, hymns of abandonment"—an obsessive, haunting reminder of young Stephen's isolation and sense of abandonment following the unexpected deaths of his father and his sister Agnes, and an eerie precursor of his experience being stranded at sea five years later. Highly imitative, the sketches recall Edgar Allan Poe's macabre treatment of a nightmarish world and Mark Twain's comical handling of the tall tale, but their impressionistic use of color, startling metaphors, and ironic deflation of pompous characters foreshadow distinctive traits that would define Crane's mature style.[12]

At the end of September, Crane returned to Sullivan County, along with three of his brothers—Townley, William, and Edmund—and their mother, to visit the clubhouse at the Hartwood Park Association. The Crane family had been camping in the county since 1878; and in 1889, William, along with friends and relatives, had begun acquiring local land, part of which they sold to the association. In 1893 the association was incorporated as the Hartwood Club, a private resort with a hunting and fishing preserve. With William as its first president, it would later become an idyllic setting for Crane. On September 30, 1891, Crane recorded in the clubhouse register the arrival of "a flock of Cranes," whose "mother bird had considerable difficulty in keeping her children quiet and in making them retire for the night." The Cranes fished for pickerel, but the family had more than pickerel on their mind. Five months after marrying Townley in June 1890, his wife, Anna, had begun to experience physical and mental problems. By the following September, two weeks

before the family trip to the Hartwood clubhouse, Anna had been declared insane and had been committed to the Trenton Asylum in New
Jersey. Two months later, on November 16, she died.[13]

Anna's death depressed Mrs. Crane, who was already in failing health.
She had a history of neuralgia and had suffered a nervous breakdown in
1885–1886; after that, she had recuperated. By November, however, ill
from a carbuncle on her neck and from a severe cold contracted in Boston while attending the first world convention of the Woman's Christian
Temperance Union, she was bedridden in a hospital in Paterson, with
Stephen and other family members at her side. On December 7, three
weeks after Anna's death, she died at the age of sixty-four.[14]

As with the deaths of his father and his sister Agnes, Stephen was silent
about his mother's passing. It is clear that she was fond of her youngest
child. Though her will stipulated that her belongings be divided among
her seven surviving children, she made special provisions for him. Her
library was to remain intact until he was twenty-one, at which point he
could then choose one-quarter of the books as well as those in which
she had written his name, among which was his father's Bible. To help
Stephen receive "as liberal an education as he is able to take, having a
due regard to his health and to his own wishes in the matter," up to $300
was to be set aside annually until he was twenty-five so that he could
complete a four-year college program.[15] When the will was drawn up in
1885, Mrs. Crane had tried to ensure Stephen's physical, intellectual, and
spiritual well-being. By the time of her death, however, he had already
rejected formal education and institutionalized religion, and his lifestyle
was beginning to weaken his body.

Because Crane had dropped out of college, he received no money
from his mother's estate, but he supplemented his meager income by
selling his Sullivan County tales and sketches to the *New York Tribune*.
During the summer of 1891, Townley told Willis Fletcher Johnson, who
was vacationing in Asbury Park, that his kid brother wanted to show
Johnson two stories he had written but was too shy to approach him directly. Although Stephen had previously submitted news dispatches to
Johnson from Syracuse, he had never met him, and with the exception of
his journalistic spoof "Great Bugs in Onondaga," these submissions had
been routine reports. Johnson reached out to Stephen, reminding him of
his longtime friendship with the Crane family, and offered to help with

his writing. As soon as Johnson read what he later called Crane's "fantas-tic and impressionistic fiction sketches," he accepted them for publica-tion. After readers responded favorably to their appearance in the *New York Tribune* in February 1892, he bought twelve more, which appeared in July and August 1892. Encouraged by Johnson's support, Stephen also showed him an early draft of *Maggie* sometime during the summer of 1891 or 1892. Johnson was impressed with its mastery of language, char-acterization, and graphic depiction of urban slums. As Stephen recovered from his college experience and learned the rigors of narrative writing, he rapidly developed an awareness of the distinction between what he called the "clever school" of popular fiction as a marketable commodity and fiction as serious art.[16]

8

Satirist in Asbury Park

SUMMER 1892

DURING THE SPRING OF 1892, Crane stayed at William's house in Port Jervis while continuing to write sketches about Sullivan County. On May 28, he left for Asbury Park to resume work as a *New York Tribune* shore correspondent, missing by five days an event that shook Port Jervis. On June 2, a black man wrongfully charged with raping a woman was twice hanged from a tree across the street from the house. William was among the few townsfolk who tried unsuccessfully to prevent a mob of about two thousand from lynching the man and gave a deposition at the inquest. Although Stephen did not witness the tragedy, he would have learned about it from his brother and from detailed accounts in the *Tribune*. Five years later, he transformed the prejudice, fear, and violence of Port Jervis into his story "The Monster."[1]

The Sullivan County tales and sketches mixed humor and improbable events for the diversion of idle Sunday readers. Crane realized that those stories were often contrived, artificial, and derivative; years later, he remarked, "How I wish I had dropped them into the waste basket!" Since the previous August, he had been thinking about Garland's insistence that authors adhere to their own personal vision and write about what they know and care about. Increasingly he was becoming convinced that good writing, whether fiction or journalism, should be based on an honest depiction of what one sees. Returning to Townley's news agency for another summer of resort reporting, he knew he would not be satisfied simply reporting trivial facts. One day during that summer, he and Arthur Oliver, his classmate at Lafayette and a fellow New Jersey journalist, were sitting on the beach discussing the difficulty of using language to transform one's personal experiences into art. "Somehow I can't get down to the real thing," Oliver lamented. "I know I have something unusual to tell, but I get all tangled up with different notions of how it ought to be told." In response, Stephen tossed a handful of sand into the wind. "Treat your notions like that," he asserted. "Forget what you think about it and tell how you feel about it. Make the other fellow realize you are just as human as he is. That's the big secret of story-telling. Away with literary cads and canons. Be yourself!" By the end of the summer, Crane's views would unalterably shape his private life and public career.[2]

In late June, while working out of Townley's office in the Lake Avenue Hotel, Stephen met Alice Augusta Brandon Munroe, nicknamed "Lily." With her teenage sister Dorothy ("Dottie") and her mother-in-law, she was staying at the hotel. Lily had had a wealthy upbringing—early years in England followed by public and private schooling in New York City. Married in 1891, she was now estranged from her husband, Hersey Munroe, who frequently traveled for the U.S. Geological Survey as a topographer. During the summer, Stephen and Lily fell in love; they spent hours riding the carousel at Asbury Park's Hippodrome and walking along the beach and boardwalk. Older and more prudent, Lily could tell that Stephen was a restless spirit who cared little for his health and appearance. He was constantly coughing because of incessant smoking, and he wrote notes to himself on his shirt cuffs. Impoverished and insecure, he became upset when her singing attracted other admirers, and he skipped buying ice cream for himself—he actually disliked it—so that he could treat her to a scoop at Day's in Ocean Grove, where the Victorian porches and courtyard garden of the ice cream parlor created a romantic haven. Her father, a respected businessman, disapproved of Crane's bohemianism and discouraged their relationship. When Crane was invited to dine with the Brandons in New York City, he tried to impress them by speaking briefly in French to Lily's father, who, Crane knew, was multilingual. In response, Mr. Brandon curtly chided him: "My daughter does not speak French, Mr. Crane."[3]

Despite differences in temperament, Lily and Stephen loved each other. She recognized his intelligence, sincerity, and curious blend of contradictions. He was not handsome, yet she was struck by the intensity of his gray, almond-shaped eyes; he was prudish about women's bathing suits and self-conscious when dancing with her, but he delighted in shocking straitlaced matrons who judged other vacationers; he expected to die young, yet he had an intense desire to be happy. His occasionally taciturn demeanor belied a playful, kindhearted spirit. He treated Dottie affectionately, as though she were a niece, and bet her a necklet that his brother Townley would never remarry (a bet he lost).[4] An impulsive romantic, Crane once asked Lily to light a candle in her window in New York so that he could see her as she walked around the room. When it began to rain, she assumed that he had left and blew out the candle, only to learn later that he had stayed, hoping that she would relight it, and had caught a devastating cold. Stephen had once jokingly told his nieces that if he ever met a woman with hair as golden as theirs, he would marry her instantly.[5] Lily became this woman. Before the summer had ended, she was seriously considering his plea that they elope.

At the height of their relationship, Stephen entrusted Lily with copies of his stories, including the manuscript of *Maggie,* and he arranged for his friend David Ericson to paint her portrait (it was never completed). Crane idealized her in two short stories. "The Captain," an amusing sketch written during the summer of 1892, describes a boat excursion and involves wordplay about courtship, a "'smart young man' from nowhere," and three young city women—a composite portrayal of Lily. One woman, ostensibly talking about the trip, hopes "we can go out again to-morrow." When another asks what she might catch if she went fishing, the captain quips, "You might catch some of those young men." The following spring Crane composed "The Pace of Youth," a fictional billet-doux that recounts the love affair between a young man and woman who work at her father's carousel in the amusement park at Asbury Park. The young man's desire for marriage is complicated by her indecision, his insecurity about a possible rival suitor, and the father's resistance to their romance. Eventually they elope in a carriage drawn by "a young and modern" horse, while the father vainly tries to catch them in an "old vehicle" drawn by "its drowsy horse and its dusty-eyed and tranquil driver." Crane recreated his own situation in the story. Playing with his surname, he was the young man, who, bird-like, gets "a good view from his perch" at the carousel and who, along with Lizzie (a name similar to Lily) escapes along "the trail of birds." Stimson, the authoritarian father, who is estranged from his wife, represents Lily's father and husband, Mr. Brandon and Mr. Munroe. The iron and brass rings that the young man puts on a wooden arm for riders on the carousel to grab symbolize matrimonial rings, and the fleeing carriage on the road of life is "youth, with youth's pace . . . swift-flying with the hope of dreams." With the pace of youth, Crane told Lily via the short story, they could escape their past and start life anew.[6]

A romantic dreamer, Crane knew he lacked direction and needed to prove his worth. He avoided seeing Lily for several months until he felt "worthy to have you think of me"; then, in April 1893, following the publication of his first novel, he began a series of impassioned love letters, chronicling "how much I have changed." He was now on the road to "my success" as a writer. With the publication of *Maggie,* he bragged that "Hamlin Garland was the first to over-whelm me with all manner of extraordinary language. The book has made me a powerful friend in W. D. Howells. B. O. Flower of the '*Arena*' has practically offered me the benefits of his publishing company for all that I may in future write. Albert Shaw of the 'Review of Reviews' wrote me congratulations this morning and to-morrow I dine with the editor of the 'Forum.'" While Lily had become "the shadow and the light of my life;—the whole of it," Crane knew that her marriage—"the present griefs which are to me tragic, because they say they are engraven for life"—inhibited their relationship.[7] For her part, Lily sensed the difficulties involved in eloping with an impetuous youth and stopped answering his letters. When her husband, whom she eventually divorced in 1897, discovered their secret relationship, he destroyed Lily's mementoes of Stephen: his letters (somehow four survived), photos, and the manuscript of *Maggie.*

Though Stephen's dispatches from Townley's bureau to the *New York Tribune* were still unsigned in 1892, they were unmistakably his, marked by his biting, sardonic style. The diction, imagery, and characterization were so distinctive that, had Stephen developed no further as a writer, he would have been assured a successful career as a journalist. His ironic sensibility was suited for skewering the social and cultural pretensions of vacationers, as well as the smug complacency of civic and religious leaders who legislated their own ethical and religious values. Crane also lampooned the carnival-like atmosphere of the beach resorts. Photographers convinced tourists to have their "features libelled" by posing with dogs and babies; fair maidens—"a bit of interesting tinsel flashing near the sombre hued waves"—were pursued by their beaux, whose "rose-tint and gilt-edge" demeanor as they strutted in their "somewhat false hues" belied their normally levelheaded behavior; and the most daring visitors enjoyed "contrivances to tumble-bumble the soul and gain possession of nickels" so long as each amusement ride was "of course, a moral machine" that provided respectable pleasure. Seekers of culture attended classes at the Seaside Assembly in Avon-by-the-Sea, where "art students . . . chatter and paint and paint and chatter," while others inspected exotic sea-growths and chased "June-bugs around the block on warm nights."[8]

At times, Crane's feigned seriousness hid his tongue-in-cheek sense of humor. In "Joys of Seaside Life" an androgynous "Greek dancer, or whatever it is," combined the "grin of the successful midnight assassin and the smile of the coquette." Bedecked in jewelry and "impossible apparel" consisting of "a chromatic delirium of red, black, green, pink, blue, yellow, purple, white and other shades of colors not known," "he, or she"—a verbal construction repeated fourteen times in various forms in one paragraph—performed so bizarrely that initially "there was a panic. Brave men shrunk," but not so much as to discourage the performer from passing around a tambourine to collect tips. Similarly, "The Seaside Hotel Hop" is a comic tour-de-force about the typical Saturday-night dance at a shore hotel. In the 1890s, youth became increasingly enamored of dancing. The summer season at ocean resorts typically began with a grand ball followed by weekly hops. Crane satirizes avaricious hotel owners, judgmental spinsters, young men acting aloof, and a daring girl whose dress, cut lower than her bathing suit, makes her appear like a bronze-headed porcelain doll. By the end of the evening, when the dull music has finally ceased and everyone has retired, the silence is broken only by babies howling "their midnight chorus, or the fat man with the thirty-two-foot diapason snore."[9]

Although Crane avoided espousing a political agenda, his sardonic eye exposed social hypocrisy among vacationers. On July 20, 1892, Jacob Riis gave an illustrated lecture in Avon-by-the-Sea on the plight of the poor who inhabited tenement houses. In his sociological studies in *Scribner's Magazine* (1889), *How the Other Half Lives: Studies among the Tenements of New York* (1890), and *Children of the Poor* (1892), Riis criticized the growing economic inequality in America and worked to eliminate poverty, strengthen the family unit, and improve urban housing. Riis had come to Avon to raise money for the King's Daughters, an organization of Episcopal church women in New York City dedicated to improving tenement life. Listening to the lecture, Crane immediately noticed the contrast between middle-class vacationers enjoying gentle sea breezes and the urban poor suffering stifling conditions in crowded tenements. Though vacationers contributed a modest amount of money to help give children a temporary respite in the country, Crane's sarcastic statement that they were "not entirely forgetful of the unfortunates" implied that their flight from the city was also an escape from any sense of moral obligation.[10]

In contrast to the vacationers were the religious teachers and preachers, the "sombre-hued gentlemen" who arrived "in solemn procession, with black valises in their hands and rebukes to frivolity in their eyes." Self-righteous and intellectually arrogant, these staid pillars of religious respectability sat in "noiseless gloom" to "discuss their pet tried and untried theories"; they complained about the noise from the Observation Wheel, an early version of the Ferris wheel, because it disturbed "their pious meditations on the evils of the world." They condemned dancers at a hop for their vanity, yet silently concluded that if they themselves were dancers—only in theory, of course—they would be better than those frivolous sinners because they would simply apply "certain little geometric calculations" that would allow them to "waltz in such a scientific manner, with such an application of the laws of motion, that the best dancers would, indeed, be surprised." Whether the target was mindless spectators, hypocritical vacationers, or self-righteous ministers, Crane's satire repeatedly hit straight and center.[11]

Of all Crane's news reports, none had as devastating an impact on his early newspaper career as his coverage of the Junior Order of United

American Mechanics, which held an annual "American Day" parade in Asbury Park. A patriotic, nativist organization of workingmen, the JOUAM advocated the restriction of immigration, promotion of American business over foreign competition, and inclusion of the Bible in public education. Townley, having reported on the parade the previous two years without fanfare, assigned the task to his brother and went fishing. On August 17, fifteen bands and three thousand JOUAM members marched in what would soon be called "the parade that made Stevie Crane famous." As Arthur Oliver remarked, Crane positioned himself leaning against the door jamb of a local business, his cigar gripped firmly between his teeth "with the half-amused, half-quizzical expression of one who looks into a kaleidoscope." Rather than report events objectively, he often used them to frame social commentary based on shifting perspectives. He admired the honesty and dignity of the marchers; but from the point of view of someone who had respected military drill at Claverack, he criticized their strident music, ill-fitting clothes, and sloppy marching. His bitter satire, however, was aimed elsewhere. Smug, elitist summer visitors observing the parade wore "summer gowns, lace parasols, tennis trousers, straw hats and indifferent smiles," while self-serving local businessmen were blinded by avarice: "The bona fide Asbury Parker is a man to whom a dollar, when held close to his eye, often shuts out any impression he may have had that other people possess rights. He is apt to consider that men and women, especially city men and women, were created to be mulcted by him." Crane's parade report thus framed a biting social commentary on those observing the marchers.[12]

Before leaving town, Townley asked another newspaperman, William K. Devereaux, to peruse Stephen's submission for any obvious problems. Devereux was amused by it and forwarded it to the *Tribune,* even though he expected that the newspaper's staid editors would reject it. Because the *Tribune* building was being remodeled, however, the editorial offices were temporarily disorganized, and as a result Crane's article slipped through and appeared unsigned on August 21 in the series "On the New-Jersey Coast."

The furor generated by the article was immediate, but ironically it did not come from the focus of Crane's satire—Asbury Park visitors and businessmen—because the sale of newspapers was prohibited there on

Sundays and thus unavailable for them to read. Instead, it came from members of JOUAM, who felt that the article derided their patriotism: on August 23 they formally complained about its "un-American" criticism. The next day the *Tribune* printed JOUAM's letter, along with a retraction praising the Junior Order and deploring the inadvertent printing of such a repulsive column. The crisis was compounded by the fact that Whitelaw Reid, owner of the *Tribune,* had resigned as U.S. ambassador to France in the spring to enter politics and was the Republican nominee for vice-president on Benjamin Harrison's ticket against Grover Cleveland and Adlai Stevenson. Because the race was especially close at that time, both parties were courting the labor vote. Republicans found themselves in an especially tenuous situation. Only weeks earlier, strikes at the silver mine in Coeur d'Alene, Idaho, and at the Homestead Steel Works near Pittsburgh, Pennsylvania, had ended violently and had incited labor opposition to the incumbent Republican administration. As soon as Crane's article appeared, Reid's political opponents attacked him as anti-labor. When criticism of Reid increased, the *Tribune* issued another retraction on August 28; it tried to distance Reid from the debacle by pointing out that he had not been directly involved in the daily operation of the newspaper since 1889 (the year he became ambassador to France) and that he could not have approved of the dispatch because he was in the Midwest campaigning. Nonetheless, JOUAM blamed Reid for the article, opposed his candidacy, and formally passed resolutions at the local, state, and national levels of JOUAM condemning him.[13]

Legend has it that upon hearing of the incident, Reid wired, "Discharge every man connected with that parade story." The details of what actually happened are vague, but both Crane brothers were instantly fired. Meanwhile, Asbury Park was abuzz with gossip about how, as Billy Devereux commented, "Stevie . . . toyed with a boomerang." Without identifying his brother by name, Townley immediately declared publicly that correspondents should not be denounced or discharged for stating their opinion: "Some people here . . . claim that the correspondents have no right to say anything about the town excepting in the way of praise and when articles are published that they do not like they are very bitter in remarks about the writers. . . . I have been reviled like a pickpocket over an alleged Associated Press dispatch that was never seen by any person in the employ of the great news gathering corporation until it was published. . . . When the editors are not suited with their reporters' work they discharge them." One local paper, however, took a less generous view. The *Asbury Park Journal* decried the article as a "studied insult" and "gross affront," maintaining that its author "has a hankering for razzle-dazzle style, and has a great future before him if, like the good, he fails to die young."[14]

Crane reacted with bemusement at having written a story that made a difference. At first agitated over the controversy, he asked for advice from Willis Fletcher Johnson, who reminded him "that ordinary news reporting was not a good place for subtle rhetorical devices"; an author with his ability "ought not to waste his time reporting that 'The Flunkey-Smiths of Squedunk are at the Gilded Pazaza Hotel for the season.'" When Crane discussed the incident with Garland, Garland respected the reporter's intellectual honesty but was amused by his naïveté concerning his dismissal from the *Tribune:* "What did you expect from your journal—a medal?" To which Crane bitterly responded, "I guess I didn't stop to consider that. I was so hot at the sight of those poor, misshapen fools shouting for monopoly that I gave no thought to its effect upon my own fortunes. I don't know that it would have made much difference if I had. I wanted to say those things anyway." The incident made Townley as "glum as a king who had lost his crown," according to Oliver, but Stephen wore the "saintly smile he always had ready for every disaster" and was tickled by his own notoriety. "You'd hardly think a little innocent chap like me could have stirred up such a row in American politics," he said to Oliver. "It shows what innocence can do if it has the opportunity!"[15]

Despite Crane's amusement about the incident, Oliver wondered whether Crane no longer believed what he had said on the beach about the need for writers to believe in "the real thing." "No!" Stephen insisted. "You've got to feel the things you write if you want to make an impact on the world." When Oliver reminded him that he had indeed made an impact, Crane put his hand on his friend's shoulder and quietly replied, "That bears out just what I said." Nonetheless, when Crane realized that his local reputation had been tarnished, he applied for a position with the American Press Association, proposing a trip to the South and West during which he would write feature articles. Despite his claim that he was an experienced journalist whose "articles had been appearing in newspapers for years," the APA shied away from hiring a renegade writer steeped in controversy.[16]

Townley's immediate future was more promising. In the fall he became associate editor of the *Asbury Park Shore Press,* and later, with the help of Reid, was reinstated as a reporter for the *Tribune.* After discovering that Townley had not written the article, Reid wrote him that he admired his literary and journalistic skills.[17] As late as 1898, Townley was still with the *Tribune.*[18] Years later, Reid joked that he would have been elected vice-president had the article not appeared: Stephen Crane "was the man who beat me for vice-president. I don't know whether Grover Cleveland ever knew how much he owed him."[19] In truth, it is difficult to say what impact Crane's article had on the outcome of the election. Harrison and Reid did lose two important states directly connected to the JOUAM incident, New Jersey (site of the parade) and New York (site of the *Tribune*); and the popular vote was close, 43 percent for the Republicans and 46 percent for the Democrats. But the Democrats outdistanced the Republicans in electoral votes, 277 to 145. Still, the perception among many, including Stephen, was that the article had seriously damaged the Republicans and irreparably changed the young journalist's career.[20] Although three reports from Asbury Park possibly by Crane appeared in the *Tribune* shortly after the JOUAM incident, they may have been written earlier. After they were published, the *Tribune* never printed another piece by Crane and mostly vilified his work in scathing book reviews. Even after his death, the newspaper continued to denigrate his character and achievement.

Crane had the last word in the uproar over the parade article. In 1896, the *New York Journal* approached the celebrated author of *The Red Badge of Courage,* offering him the chance to write a feature article on any subject for a Sunday edition of the newspaper. Crane hesitated at first, because of other professional commitments, but the offer of $50 for a quick piece of writing was too powerful an enticement. Because he had been thinking about returning to Asbury Park, where he had not been since the uproar about his article in the *New York Tribune,* he made the visit itself the subject of his article. On August 16, 1896, exactly four years after the date of the parade, the *New York Journal,* a rival of the *Tribune,* published what would be Crane's final commentary on Asbury Park. Crane depicts rapacious hackmen, young men and women with an inflated sense of self-importance, and James A. Bradley, whose moral aphorisms "define virtue as a physical inertia and a mental death."[21] The irony and satire are vintage Crane, but even more notable is the inclusion of his name in the title of the article: "Asbury Park as Seen by Stephen Crane." The reporter who had lost his job for being sarcastic had become famous enough to be newsworthy himself.

9

Maggie

BETWEEN CRANE'S INITIAL forays into New York in the fall of 1891 and his move to the city a year later, he began writing an allegory about Little Mary Laughter, who, like Alice in Wonderland, dreams of an anthropomorphic world. The ground and trees are made of paper, the water is ink, and a poet who serves as her guide is "fantastically clothed in the paper leaves of magazines and newspapers." The country is overpopulated with "Rhymers and Writers" traveling to "the East" to present their manuscripts to King Publico. "Bring Me Poetry!" he demands. "Bring me Rhymes! Bring Me Prose and Everything! I want to have some Fun, and also I want to learn Something." The Critical Guards, however, harass and beat the authors, while "a great Litterateur Who thought He knew a Lot" charges that the poetry of "the Young Man" is so clearly derivative from other writers that it amounts to plagiarism. Crane's inability to finish the allegory reflected the same anxiety he had expressed earlier that year in "The Way in Sullivan County," which dealt with the profession of authorship in late nineteenth-century America. Writers had long struggled with the tension between striving for what they considered serious art and giving the public sentimental romances and action-packed adventures that treated reading as a diversion. With leisure time increasing among the middle class after the Civil War, publishing syndicates catered to readers' tastes by encouraging authors to produce a marketable product and by selling a slew of melodramatic stories to national magazines and newspapers. In Crane's allegory, influential New York City editors (the Critical Guard in the East) ensured that the reading public (King Publico) got what it expected: a safe blend of news and articles that were entertaining and occasionally educational. The dilemma for a serious artist (the Young Man) was how to meet the demands of the public without compromising one's artistic integrity. Crane struggled with this problem for the rest of his life.

Despite anxiety created by the commercialization of art, New York City was the ideal place for an aspiring journalist and author running at the pace of youth. Earlier in the century, Boston had been the bastion of literary publishing and culture in America, and William Dean Howells, editor of the *Atlantic Monthly* until 1881, was its most influential representative; but with his move to New York City to become associate editor of *Harper's New Monthly Magazine* in 1886, the center shifted. By 1893, nineteen English-language dailies and a score of foreign-language newspapers were being printed in New York City. A testament to the importance of New York as the leader in journalism was "Newspaper Row," a series of skyscrapers on Lower Manhattan's Park Row that included the Times Building, with its level of arcaded arches; the Tribune Building, with its ornate clock tower and spire; and the gold-domed World Building, the tallest building on earth when it was completed in 1890. Increasingly, journalism was becoming a legitimate training ground for young writers of realistic fiction. James L. Ford, influential managing editor of *Truth* magazine, encouraged any young journalist who wanted to write "the enduring novel of New York" to immerse himself in "the great east side" and be "so full of his subject, so thoroughly in sympathy with his characters—no matter whether he takes them from an opium joint in Mott Street or a ball at Delmonico's—and so familiar with the various influences which have shaped their destinies, that he will set about his task with the firm conviction that he has a story to tell to the world."[1]

In September–October 1892, Crane may have worked briefly for the *Newark Daily Advertiser,* where Townley had been employed as a cub reporter. In late October he moved into a boardinghouse at 1064 Avenue

A (formerly Eastern Boulevard and now the site of Sutton Place) in Manhattan, the first of his many residences during four years in New York City. He shared a room with his Delta Upsilon brother Fred Lawrence, who, along with other boarders, was attending medical school. All had come to New York City to find their fortune. Crane captured the moment by sardonically naming the house "The Pendennis Club" after William Makepeace Thackeray's *Pendennis,* a satirical novel about a youth who ventures from the country to London in order to seek his place in life and society.[2] Crane identified with the fatherless main character, who, finding college not to his liking, becomes a poet, novelist, and journalist.

No other metropolis in America could have offered the roommates as much cultural diversity and worldly pleasure as New York City. By the last decade of the nineteenth century, its Italian population was the size of Naples; its German population, the size of Hamburg; and its Irish population, twice the size of Dublin. By 1890, 330,000 Jewish immigrants were living in one square mile on the Lower East Side. Nearby was the Bowery district; its thoroughfare, also known as the Bowery, was the oldest in Manhattan and the only major street in the city never to have had a church on it. "It was the opinion of the most observant traveler," a journalist noted, "that no city in Christendom possesses a street comparable" to it. Crane and his roommates explored the Bowery, where theaters, beer gardens, and music halls offered every sort of entertainment, from variety shows to classical operettas.[3] For the adventurous, there was Carmencita, a scandalous belly dancer later immortalized in Thomas Edison's short film *Carmencita Dancing;* and Loie Fuller, a star with the Folies Bergère, who revolutionized dance by experimenting with electric light, mirrors, and silk to portray things in nature and who later became the personification of Art Nouveau. The cheapest and most popular places were the dime museums, which offered entertainment for the working class. Glib barkers guided visitors through the Curio Hall, with its mummy mermaids, exotic antiques, and wax figures of notorious criminals; the Hall of Human Curiosities, with its bearded lady, turtle boy, and dog-faced man; and for an additional five cents, the theater, where "The heroine she'll thwart her foes,/ Shoot the villain, and goodness knows/ She'll prove her lover guiltless of crime." Two of the most famous attractions at the dime museum were the so-called Missing Link, a human with a tapered head known as "Zip, What is It?" and a tableau that depicted "The Downward Path; or, How Girls Go Wrong." Crane parodied the tableau's melodramatic portrayal of the fallen woman in *Maggie: A Girl of the Streets* and alluded to Zip in "The Monster."[4]

When Crane was not immersing himself in city life, he was slowly and methodically working on the manuscript of *Maggie*. First he would compose a sentence in his head, then carefully transcribe it. Rarely did he correct a text, and never did he ask for suggestions. On rare occasions he would ask someone to read a manuscript, but only to check on factual accuracy and to see the effect his writing had on readers. Whenever he lacked inspiration, he would repeatedly sing the same verse from a song until he could write, or he would read from books in his room.[5] At least three of them are likely to have inspired his writing of *Maggie:* Voltaire's *Candide* parodied romance clichés and satirized an inexperienced youth's naïve optimism; a collection of Guy de Maupassant's short stories demonstrated techniques for a realistic depiction of human behavior; and Emile Zola's *Pot-bouille* presented slum life naturalistically. Voltaire's parody, Maupassant's realism, and Zola's naturalism resurfaced in Crane's bleak portrayal of a naïve, sentimental girl in the tenements of New York.

In Asbury Park the previous August, Crane had shown an earlier version of the manuscript to Hamlin Garland, who was so impressed that he wrote a note of introduction to Richard Watson Gilder, editor of *Century Magazine:* "Dear Gilder: I want you to read a *great* M.S. of Stephen Crane's making. I think him an astonishing fellow. And have advised him to bring the M.S. to you." Before doing so, however, Crane revised the manuscript based on his own experiences in the city and added a second subtitle, *A Story of New York*. A stone-throwing fight he had witnessed in the neighborhood became the opening scene, and the Brooklyn suburb of Williamsburg, the Central Park Menagerie, the Metropolitan Museum of Art, and Blackwell's Island (now Roosevelt Island), which he could see from his apartment overlooking the East River, became part of the setting. By the time he had finished the manuscript, it differed drastically from the version Garland and Willis Fletcher Johnson had seen. It was now a brutal depiction of an amoral universe in which a girl living in the slums is driven to prostitution. Before he took the revised manuscript to Gilder, in the winter of 1892–1893, he penciled across the bottom of Garland's note, "This is not the MS spoken of. This is a different one."[6]

Even without Garland's endorsement, Crane would have sought out Gilder, the son of a Methodist minister who had occasionally visited the Crane household during Stephen's childhood. Gilder championed tenement reform and published moralistic essays condemning urban squalor, but he considered the manuscript too harsh for the straitlaced audience of the *Century*. Crane took it to Ripley Hitchcock, literary advisor of D. Appleton and Company, at Johnson's suggestion. "That boy has the real stuff in him," Hitchcock told Johnson, but he, too, feared that it was not commercial enough to sell. Other publishers urged Crane to delete the foul language; but he insisted, "I can't, as that is how such men talk."[7]

Despite claiming to be open-minded, leaders of the American literary establishment preferred tradition over innovation, decorum over impropriety, idealized depiction over reality. As self-proclaimed arbiters of taste, they protected the reading public from indecency. Clearly missing from *Maggie* was the sentimentalizing and moralizing prevalent in other treatments of tenement life. Americans were developing a growing fascination with, and fear of, slum life in urban tenements, as reflected in such sociological studies as Reverend Thomas DeWitt Talmage's *The Night Side of City Life* (1878) and Jacob Riis's *How the Other Half Lives* (1890) and in the popularity of sentimental, melodramatic fiction about urban slums—novels such as *The Detective's Ward; or, The Fortunes of a Bowery Girl* (1871) and *Orphan Nell, the Orange Girl; or, the Lost Heir* (1880). A dominant theme in slum fiction was the rags-to-riches story, a perennial cliché. In Edward Townsend's tale *A Daughter of the Tenements* (1895), the heroine, despite the foils of a villain and her impoverished life selling fruit on the streets, becomes a successful ballerina, inherits a fortune, and lives happily ever after with her husband. When a slum novel ended tragically—as with the seduction, betrayal, and death of the heroine in Edgar Fawcett's *The Evil That Men Do* (1889)—the ethical consequences of improper behavior were obvious. Crane, however, was not interested in analyzing the causes of, or offering solutions for, urban poverty; instead he offered a stark, unsentimental portrayal of slum life.

Unable to find a publisher, Crane reluctantly decided to finance the book himself. In January 1893, he sold his share of his mother's house in Asbury Park and his stock in the coal mines of Kingston, Pennsylvania, to William, who may have lent him the rest of the money needed for publication. Around January 18, Crane submitted his copyright application to the Library of Congress by sending one dollar and a typewritten title page that read "A Girl of the Streets, / A Story of New York. / — By— / Stephen Crane"; but he could not include the required two copies of the book, because it had not yet been typeset and bound. Within the next month or so he added the name "Maggie" to the title, and he changed the name of the author. Crane was concerned that the publication of a controversial book might embarrass his prudish family; and when friends had said that he might get arrested for breaking the vice laws by writing such a strong book, he had joked about using a pseudonym. Then he had searched the New York City telephone directory and learned that the two most common names were "Johnson" and "Smith." He added a "t" to the first one to make it sound more aristocratic. Thus was born "Johnston Smith." "Commonest name I could think of," he told a friend. "I had an editor friend named Johnson, and put in the 't,' and no one could find me in the mob of Smiths." The printer, known as a publisher of religious books, also preferred anonymity; and though it gladly accepted Crane's money, it refused to let its imprint appear on the title page. The book was printed privately in New York sometime in late February or early March 1893 and sold for fifty cents, an unusually high price at a time when paperbacks by established authors were selling for ten to twenty-five cents. Its yellow binding and repeated use of the word "yellow" in the text reflected the growing popularity of the color as a challenge to the norm during a decade known as the "Yellow Nineties." Oscar Wilde replaced the green carnation he wore in his buttonhole with a yellow sunflower, and English and French publishers bound novels in yellow to alert readers to their lewd content. When Wilde was arrested in 1895 on the charge of "gross indecency," the headline of one newspaper proclaimed "Arrest of Oscar Wilde / Yellow Book Under His Arm."[8]

Maggie is the first significant example of literary determinism in American literature. In a violent, chaotic world, children and adults battle for survival. Unlike the popular sentimental fiction of the day, *Maggie* does not offer Christianity as a haven from a war-torn jungle. At its best, Christian practice is ineffectual; at its worst, hypocritical. The poor are shunned by the wealthy and condemned as sinners by preachers. Throughout, characters mask their hypocrisy with the appearance of respectability. When Maggie's brother hits her in public, their father angrily tells him to leave his "sister alone on the street," implying that he can hit her at home, where no one can see them. Maggie envisions her boyfriend as a knight who will rescue her from a bleak existence; but after he seduces her, her presence threatens his respectability. Distraught, Maggie approaches a minister whose "eyes shone good-will"; but instead of trying "to save a soul," he, too, shuns her to protect his respectability.[9]

Rejected by her family, her vulgar boyfriend, and a church official, Maggie turns to prostitution for survival. In the famous Chapter 17, Crane compresses several months of her life as a prostitute into a single evening. As she walks from the theater district to the river, the imagery and the descriptions of her ten potential clients rehearse her deterioration and eventual death. By the end of the chapter, the radiant electric lights and excited conversation of theatergoers are replaced with darkness and silence, as her clients devolve from a well-dressed gentleman to a drifter in torn, greasy rags. In a bitterly ironic conclusion to the story, Maggie's mother, upon learning of the death of her daughter, cries out, "Oh, yes, I'll fergive her! I'll fergive her!"[10] Although the novella emphasizes a Darwinian struggle for survival in a society in which family and church are meaningless institutions, Crane's use of irony throughout keeps the story from devolving into the pure naturalism of Zola or the cheap melodrama of countless stories of innocent girls seduced and ruined by villains. Repeatedly, characters shield themselves from reality by embracing hypocritical moral codes that pass as middle-class values. A prose style replete with jarring diction and sensory impressions renders character, theme, and setting. Seemingly incongruous adjectives—as in "ignorant stables," "passive tugboat," and "violated flowers"—suggest feelings and perceptions.[11] Imagery describing a tenement building evokes the sight of swirling, yellow dust, the sound of women screaming and gossiping, the smell of cooking food, and the feel of a quivering, overcrowded building, thus creating a world of moral and physical degradation. With its candid treatment of squalor, relentless irony, episodic structure, and impressionistic depiction of reality, *Maggie* was radically innovative and opened the literary gates for American experimental fiction in the twentieth century.

In celebration of the book's appearance, Crane's friends, the "Committee for the Advancement and Preservation of *Maggie*," printed formal invitations for a party at the Pendennis Club. With a hammer in one

hand and a copy of *Maggie* in the other, John Henry Dick urged each arriving guest to buy the book and toast Stephen's success. After several
hours of toasts, drinking, and ever-louder singing accompanied by Stephen on banjo, neighbors were in an uproar, and the "dragon," Stephen's
playful nickname for the landlady, came to the door to complain that she
"rented rooms to gentlemen, not animals." Crane frantically waved his
hand at the revelers to "Cheese it!" (street boy's slang for a warning),
opened the door a crack, and told her, "The animals apologize and will
return to their cages at once!"[12] Despite occasional tension between him
and the "dragon," they liked each other. In 1896 he began writing a story
about a boardinghouse run by a landlady and her beautiful daughter, but
other projects kept him from completing it. The two women never forgot him and were among the few to attend his funeral in New York City.

To encourage sales, Crane hired four men to sit and read the book on
New York's elevated train, one in back of the other, to convince passersby that "the whole metropolis was *Maggie*-mad." He also sought out
Garland's advice for promoting it. Since seeing Garland the previous
summer, Crane had stayed in touch: "Things go pretty slow with me, but
I manage to live." As soon as the book was printed, Crane sent him a
copy with an inscription justifying literary realism:

> It is inevitable that you be greatly shocked by this book but continue,
> please, with all possible courage to the end. F'or it tries to show that envi-
> ronment is a tremendous thing in the world and frequently shapes lives
> regardless. If one proves that theory, one makes room in Heaven for all
> sorts of souls (notably an occasional street girl) who are not confidently
> expected to be there by many excellent people.
>
>   It is probable that the reader of this small thing may consider The
> Author to be a bad man, but, obviously, this is a matter of small conse-
> quence to
>   The Author

Though Crane did not sign his name, Garland knew the true identity of
the author from having read an early version of the manuscript and invited the young writer to visit him at his brother Franklin's apartment in
New York. "I hardly dare tell you how good that story is," he said enthu-

siastically, and urged Crane to send review copies to influential friends, ministers, and critics.[13]

Among them was William Dean Howells, the most powerful literary critic in America and, as Theodore Dreiser once described him, the "lookout on the watch-tower, straining for a first glimpse of approaching genius." Garland met with Howells to discuss the new author; but when Crane did not hear from Howells after about three weeks, he wrote him a melancholy letter, concluding that Howells must have found the book "a wretched thing." In fact, Howells had been busy with other matters; as soon as he read the novella, he invited Crane to his home in Manhattan for tea to discuss it in early April. Crane was ecstatic about visiting the dean of American letters. In his coverage of Garland's lecture on Howells in Asbury Park in 1891, he had reported: "No man stands for a more vital principle than does Mr. Howells. He stands for modern-spirit, sympathy and truth." Anxious about his tattered clothing, he borrowed pants and an overcoat from a friend for his meeting with Howells. Their lively discussion lasted well into the evening. Howells immediately recognized in *Maggie* the kind of literary realism he had been espousing, and "thoroughly respected" Crane's "literary conscience" and "literary skill." When Crane returned to the Pendennis Club late that night, his friends were excited to hear details about the meeting, especially since he had told them little about his earlier meeting with Garland. Overwhelmed by the experience, Crane said little; but a day or so later, he was filled with an "illumination of countenance and exaltation of spirit," as Johnson recalled, to have the support of two such important writers.[14]

Yet Garland and Howells tempered their enthusiasm because of the book's unrelenting pessimism. When Garland published a review in the *Arena,* a crusading reform magazine devoted to social amelioration, he praised the novella because "it voices the blind rebellion of Rum Alley and Devil's Row" and "creates the atmosphere of the jungles"; but he insisted that realistic writing should allow for moral improvement. The novella lacked "rounded completeness. It is only a fragment. It is typical only of the worst elements of the alley. The author should delineate the families living on the next street, who live lives of heroic purity and hopeless hardship." Likewise, Howells feared that Crane's coarse language "would shock the public from him." When Howells asked Crane whether he

had considered more conventional language, he retorted, "No, . . . that is
the way they *talk*. I have thought of that, and whether I ought to leave
such things out, but if I do I am not giving the thing as I *know* it."[15]

The concerns of Garland and Howells foreshadowed the literary establishment's shunning of the novella. Only two reviews appeared in
1893, the one written by Garland and another published in Crane's
hometown newspaper the *Port Jervis Union*. After reading a review copy,
John D. Barry, assistant editor of *Forum* magazine, wrote Crane to say that
although he did "really believe that the lesson of your story is good . . .
you have driven that lesson too hard. There must be moderation even in
well-doing; excess of enthusiasm in reform is apt to be dangerous." Barry
advised Crane that "mere brooding upon evil conditions . . . is the most
dangerous and the most sentimental of all brooding, and I don't think
that it often moves to action, to actual reform work." To Barry's credit,
he genuinely wanted to help Crane's literary career and invited him to
the *Forum* office to discuss *Maggie*. Crane listened eagerly as Barry explained the art of storytelling and how dialogue reveals character: "Talk
reveals, it lightens narrative." Despite this advice, Crane was disappointed,
having spent two years on what he had hoped would be his first major
piece of fiction. Barry's concern typified the attitude of reform-minded
editors who encouraged realistic portrayals of life, but were unprepared
to accept coarse language or depictions of social problems without sentimental pleas for reform. When Rudyard Kipling referred to a character's
drinking brandy and soda in a novel being serialized in the *Ladies Home
Journal,* Edward Bok, the *Journal's* editor, insisted that the beverage be
changed. Kipling curtly replied by alluding to a popular concentrated
milk for babies: "Make it Mellins-food." After Bok's autobiography,
The Americanization of Edward Bok, was published in 1920, the managing
editor of the *Ladies Home Journal* quipped that the book should have
been titled *The Bokization of America.* Her caustic remark led to Bok's firing her.[16]

Maggie went practically unnoticed in America and, from Crane's point
of view, was often misread by the few who bothered to look at it.[17] Crane
complained to Corwin Knapp Linson: "No one would sell it, not even
the jays who otherwise would sell their souls for a nickel. I sent copies to
some preachers who were maniacs for reform—not a word from one of
'em. . . . You'd think the book came straight from hell and they smelled

the smoke." The commercial failure of the book was his "first great disappointment." He had excitedly anticipated the impact that its publication would have, but it "fell flat. . . . Poor Maggie! she was one of my first
loves." Looking back at the book in 1924, the noted critic Carl Van
Doren identified its significance: "Modern American literature may be
said, accurately enough, to have begun with Stephen Crane thirty years
ago."[18]

Crane's life was anything but ordinary. By the time he was twenty-
one, he had proposed to a married woman, created a national furor over
a news article, and written a groundbreaking novella. Despite his great
disappointment over *Maggie,* Crane maintained a sense of humor. In
March, having just written a bleak narrative about slum life, he published
"Why Did the Young Clerk Swear? Or, the Unsatisfactory French," the
first of four sketches he published in the humor magazine *Truth* in 1893–
1894. It is a hilarious parody of the French Naturalism that influenced
Maggie. When he learned that a copy of the book was one of the few
items intact after a fire in a studio, he assumed "a caricatured posture of
importance," according to his artist friend Henry McBride, and joked,
"Who knows, maybe in the years to come that may be considered the
most valuable item to have been rescued from your fire." Around the
same time, Crane met William Francis ("Frank") Ver Beck, an illustrator
living in New York City, and Phil May, a popular British artist and illustrator of books and magazines who had come to America to attend the
1893 Chicago World's Fair and to illustrate articles about it for England's
Daily Graphic. Frigid night air kept them in Frank's apartment; when
Phil and Stephen decided to stroll up Broadway, they borrowed Frank's
tiger skin to wrap around themselves to keep warm. Seeing what appeared to be a large animal traipsing along the thoroughfare at 3:30 A.M.,
an officer hauled them down to the Tenderloin district's police station;
he eventually released them, but kept the tiger skin. Unable to return
home with the skin, the two nightwalkers sent Frank a note playfully
hiding their identity:

> Dear Verby: Your tiger-skin got loose last night and did great damage
> along Broadway. Finally captured and taken to the Tenderloin station.
> Steve May.
> Phil Crane.

Ironically, *Maggie,* Crane's first love, would increase in value and continue to be notorious well into the twentieth century. In 1893, a copy of the book was worthless; in 1917, it brought a mere $7.50 at auction. With the renewed interest in Crane in the 1920s, however, bibliophiles eagerly searched for it. When William Howe Crane's daughters stumbled upon a barrel of copies of the book, they sold one or two, then burned the rest to maintain its resale value. And when Stephen's sister Mary Helen was offered $750 for her inscribed copy, she initially became excited because she and her husband, a Methodist minister, desperately needed money for house repairs. However, they considered the book immoral and feared it would be turned into a sensationalized film that would entice people to read it. She solved her dilemma by likewise burning the book. Today, fewer than forty copies exist.[19]

Crane would have been delighted with the sale of one particular copy. In 1930, Garland needed money to help finance his new home in Los Angeles and sold his inscribed copy of *Maggie* for $2,100.[20] Garland had been crucial in the establishment of Crane's career, especially as it related to the writing of a new kind of fiction that challenged the crumbling idols of literary tradition, and now his most famous pupil had paid him back.

10

Genesis of *The Red Badge of Courage*

1893–FEBRUARY 1894

IN JANUARY 1893, a major snowstorm blanketed New York City and turned an art studio at Broadway and 30th Street into a warm haven for three frozen souls. Louis Senger had arranged the intimate gathering: he wanted to introduce Crane to his cousin Corwin Knapp Linson, a painter and illustrator who had spent part of his childhood in Port Jervis and Sullivan County and who had been trained at the Académie Julian and the Ecole des Beaux-Arts in Paris. Crane's taciturn nature made it difficult for him to form new relationships; and after Linson showed Senger and Crane his paintings and they exchanged pleasantries, there was little to say. Stephen sat awkwardly on the divan, nervously laughing at Louis's droll remarks and incessantly smoking cigarettes, his fingers yellowed from nicotine.

Noticing the discomfort, Louis mentioned that Stephen had just published "A Tent in Agony," his first story in a commercial magazine, and then handed to CK (Corwin's nickname, pronounced "Ceek") a copy of the December 1892 *Cosmopolitan,* which he had brought with him. Crane, feeling self-conscious, slid to the end of the divan, but his anxiety faded as he explained how the magazine had bought the story. One morning he had walked into the office of John Brisben Walker, owner of

Cosmopolitan, and nervously handed him a manuscript: "This is a fish story. I will be here in a week." As promised, Crane returned the following week. "I know, I know," he said to Walker, expecting to be rebuffed. "Let me have it back." Unbeknownst to Crane, however, Walker had decided to give him $150 for the story and had already commissioned Dan Beard, who had recently illustrated Mark Twain's novel *A Connecticut Yankee in King Arthur's Court* (1889), to illustrate the story. As soon as Walker showed him Beard's drawings, Crane was delighted. "He has put a fork on the devil's tail. That is right. . . . You ought to have seen the fun catching that bear with the tent wrapped around him! . . . It is all a little too good to be true." CK liked the story, as well as its author. Later, when Stephen was leaving, he said, "See you again soon"; to which CK replied, "Come and sleep here if you want to, the joint is open house."[1]

Over the next two years, Crane would often take Linson up on his invitation, staying there and at other friends' lodgings in New York. After the Pendennis Club disbanded in mid-April, he followed his landlady to another boardinghouse on West 15th Street and occasionally shared a loft with artists and illustrators on East 23rd Street. For a while he also shared a loft on William Street with Hamilton King, who was then drawing a series of East Side studies for a local newspaper and who later achieved fame as one of America's leading illustrators. He may also have lived briefly in a boardinghouse at 61 Washington Square South, which would become known as the House of Genius because of the number of future great artists—among them Frank Norris, Theodore Dreiser, Eugene O'Neill, and O. Henry—who lived there at different times. Madame Catherine R. Branchard, the much-loved and generous landlady, rented only to artists even though they were often late in paying rent. At her eightieth-birthday celebration, she captured the spirit of the house: "Art is grand and literature is wonderful. But what a pity it is that it takes so many barrels of liquor to produce them. Why, this is not a house; it's an aquarium."[2]

Though Crane lived at various residences, Linson's studio stood at the center of the city's excitement. For about twenty hours a day, starting at four in the morning, the streets outside were a welter of horse-drawn cars, fire engines, and passersby as the city rumbled with humanity. During evenings, Crane and Linson climbed the ladder to the flat roof and listened to a distinguished cast led by Ada Rehan performing Shake-

speare's comedies at Daly's Theater around the corner, after which hawk-
ers bellowed through megaphones for cars to take theatergoers home.
New York "roars always like ten thousand devils," Crane later wrote,
and its intensity was warlike. He took the Staten Island Ferry to Fort
Wadsworth, the oldest continuously operated military installation in
America, to watch warships entering the harbor. Back in Linson's studio,
he saw Emile Stangé's sketch of a cruiser anchored in the Hudson River
with the cityscape in the background and named the drawing "The
Sense of a City Is War." He had used similar tropes in *Maggie:* a mother
tosses "her arms about her head as if in combat"; street toughs move
"like frigates contemplating battle"; a thrown beer glass bursts "like a
bomb."[3]

Just as intense as the city's excitement were Crane's poverty and im-
pulsiveness. Having spent nearly all his money on the ill-fated *Maggie,* he
remained impoverished until the success of *The Red Badge of Courage.* At
times, he could afford little more than potato salad for days on end; at
other times, he ate nothing. When he occasionally sold an article, he
would join friends on Saturday nights at the Boeuf-à-la-Mode, a cheap
Sixth Avenue dive they renamed "The Buffalo Mud," where, as Linson
recalled, "anything was permitted that would not bring the police." Amid
frenetic waiters scurrying wildly between crowded tables, diners periodically banged spoons against bottles and glasses while singing "A Hot
Time in the Old Town Tonight." Self-absorbed and undisciplined about
money, Crane lived in the moment. After a dinner left him and Phil May
with only pennies, Crane blithely assumed that he could borrow money
from one of their friends. But his optimism proved misguided; and when
a beggar approached him, Crane bantered half-jokingly, "You get over
on the other side of the street—we're working this side!" On another
occasion, after getting paid for an article, Crane treated his artist friend
David Ericson to dinner. Shortly after arriving at the restaurant, Crane
was inspired to write another article. Immediately he got out his ever-
present pad and pencil, began writing, and said little for the rest of the
meal. After eating, he left the restaurant, forgetting that he had promised
to pay for his friend's meal. Yet, as Fred Lawrence noted, he could also be
magnanimous: money "always slipped through his fingers without leaving a trace." After Crane lent Post Wheeler twenty dollars, his friend
asked if he needed repayment quickly. "Good heavens! Forget all about

it! Don't ever mention it!" After he received fifteen dollars for "Why Did the Young Clerk Swear? Or, the Unsatisfactory French," he splurged by treating friends to a champagne dinner. The next morning, he was again penniless. Often broke, he amused himself by writing "Ah, haggard purse, why ope thy mouth," a humorous poem in a venerable literary tradition: the poet's lament to his empty purse. When the purse reproaches him with its "empty stomach," Crane replies, "I'd sell my steps to the grave / If t'were but honestie." Impulsively, he crumpled up the paper and tossed it into a wastebasket, only to have it rescued by Linson.[4]

Crane's poverty was made more tolerable by the praise he received for *Maggie* from Garland, Howells, Albert Shaw, editor of the American edition of *Review of Reviews,* and Benjamin Orange Flower, editor of the *Arena*. That spring, their encouragement prompted him to brag to Lily of his accomplishment and to write "The Pace of Youth," his fantasy about elopement. "A bird of a story," Linson declared, but he wondered how Crane could recall so many details about people in Asbury Park whom he hadn't seen in months. Stephen replied, "Can't you make sketches from memory? Of course. Well, haven't I known these types since I was a kid? Certainly." When Linson saw Crane with a wet towel wrapped around his head and asked him about it, Crane explained that the story "got me going and I couldn't sleep, so I got up. Been at it all night. A wet towel cools the machinery all right. And I work better at night. I'm all alone in the world. It's great!"[5] The response illustrates Crane's intense, spontaneous work habit and reveals his habitual sense of himself as a loner.

Undaunted by the failure of *Maggie,* Crane wanted to write another novella about New York City. Heeding advice from Garland, Howells, and Barry that he depict the slums less starkly, he began *George's Mother* in late March as a companion work to *Maggie,* but set it aside when he worried that it would be unsalable. "If I had a new suit of clothes, I'd feel my grip tighten on the future—it's ridiculous but it doesn't make me laugh," he lamented to Linson. Frustrated, he decided to write a potboiler, a story written hastily and only to make easy money. Crane knew that formulaic hack writing sold better than literary fiction. After reading such a piece, he joked with Linson: "It seems that my opinions and the opinions of the powers that pay for this stuff are not in agreement. Else I would be asking you out to dinner at the Astor House." On another occasion, he became so disgusted after reading a trite war story that he flung the magazine aside with a loud "Huh!" "What's the matter, Steve?" a friend asked. "I've just read a battle story in that magazine," he replied, "and I was thinking I could write a better one myself." "Why don't you, then?" Crane paused for a moment, then exclaimed, "By jove! I believe I will."[6]

Thus was born *The Red Badge of Courage*. As Crane told Louis Senger, "I deliberately started in to do a pot-boiler . . . something that would take the boarding-school element—you know the kind." Crane was alluding to the rash of immensely popular Civil War novels by such writers as Horatio Alger, Jr., Oliver Optic (pen name of William Taylor Adams), and Henry Castlemon (Charles Austin Fosdick) that dramatized exciting adventures of young recruits who matured as they fought chivalrously on the battlefield. A descendant of American patriots, Crane had long been fascinated with the military, and as a child had imagined martial campaigns. His success in the military program at Claverack, his desire to attend West Point, and his passion for football—"that's great. That's bully! That's like war!"—revealed his patriotic enthusiasm for the armed services. Although Civil War fiction had been popular during and immediately following the deadliest conflict in the nation's history, interest had waned in the 1870s as people tired of war accounts; but that changed dramatically in the 1880s and 1890s, when aging veterans swelled the ranks of the Northern organization the Grand Army of the Republic (GAR) and reminisced about the war. Articles in newspapers and magazines focused on military topics such as weaponry, troop numbers, and battle locations, and personal accounts depicted raw recruits maturing into seasoned veterans. No publication was more influential than the immensely popular series of articles "Battles and Leaders of the Civil War," which appeared in *Century* magazine (November 1884–November 1887) and was reprinted as a four-volume set with additional articles, maps, and other explanatory material.[7]

As an illustrator, Linson collected the *Century* and other magazines in order to study work by other artists. Flipping through the *Century,* Crane discovered "Battles and Leaders of the Civil War." Although it included graphic accounts of the Battle of Chancellorsville and a series titled "Recollections of a Private," most of the articles were written by Union and Confederate officers who emphasized the facts and events of the

Civil War, rather than its effect on individuals. Heedless of the mess he was making as he littered the floor with magazines, he searched for a depiction of human emotion amid the morass of details about combat. "I wonder that some of those fellows don't tell how they *felt* in those scraps. They spout enough of what they *did,* but they're as emotionless as rocks." Though dissatisfied with his search, he thanked CK for his patience and departed hastily, leaving the mess on the floor. Crane could be impulsive and irresponsible; and forty years later Linson still recalled that he was "a most uncertain and self-interested Indian at times, but he also had his moments of ample generosities."[8]

In June, Crane declined Linson's invitation to join Emile Stangé and CK on a camping trip for several months in the Ramapo Hills of New Jersey. He needed a more stable environment while he drafted an early version of his war story, and furthermore he could not afford the trip. By mid-June, he had moved back to Edmund's house in Lake View. Edmund never expected his youngest brother to pay for lodging, but Stephen was always embarrassed about relying financially on his family. When he had first moved to New York City in the fall of 1892, he had sought to change his ways. "Ed, if ever I come into your place and ask for a nickel, don't give me more than that." Within days, however, he had returned, forlorn and disheveled, sheepishly asking for a nickel to ease his hunger. Silently Ed had given him the money.[9] It would be one of many times that Ed and William rescued their brother from poverty.

Edmund's home—with its sense of structure, protection, and domesticity—ensured Crane an ideal work setting and the emotional stability missing among the studios of anxious artists struggling to survive in frenetic New York City. During the day, Crane immersed himself in recreational activities. His interest in football, a college sport that was becoming increasingly popular off campus, led to his organizing the first football teams in Lake View for local youth. He never lost his sense of childhood and often played war games with his nieces. Sitting in a corner barricaded with chairs, he defended himself as they stormed his makeshift fort and clubbed him with rolled-up newspapers.[10] In the evening, he enjoyed singing around the piano and visiting friends. After everyone had retired, Crane would retreat to the garret to write undisturbed. Sleeping till late morning, he would eat breakfast at noon, then repeat the cycle.

　　While developing his war novel, Crane turned to shorter pieces for quick money, but only a satirical playlet, "At Clancy's Wake," appeared during the summer of 1893. His other attempt quickly devolved into a frustrating comedy of errors. In the spring he wrote "The Reluctant Voyagers," a six-chapter story about two men in silly bathing suits who fall asleep on a raft, drift out to sea, and eventually end up in New York City. Linson's attempt to illustrate the story met with one problem after another. When they searched the docks for a suitable model for the sea captain, they found only "ocean kings. Too high-toned for us," Crane complained. When they stood on a hot tin roof under a blazing sun and posed for a photograph as the reluctant voyagers, Crane yelled impatiently, "Hurry up there! . . . Gosh! You can brown wheats on this tin!" After submitting the story for publication, a magazine held it for six months, then requested revisions. When he resubmitted it, the magazine lost the illustrations and failed to publish the story. It did not appear in print until February 1900, after he had recycled it in a desperate attempt to earn money. The incident typified Crane's proclivity for reusing material. A few weeks after he had written "The Reluctant Voyagers," hoping to salvage something from his failed, first novella, he returned to Tommie Johnson, Maggie's brother who had died in infancy, and resurrected him in three slum stories. Written early in the summer of 1893, the stories made him no money immediately. Because he was convinced that the theme of economic inequality in "An Ominous Baby" would make it more marketable during a period of labor unrest in America, he became impatient when Linson was slow in completing the illustrations for it. It was not published until May 1894. The other two stories fared worse. "A Great Mistake" did not appear until March 1896; "A Dark-Brown Dog," not until March 1901.

　　By September 1893, Crane, fearing he might continue to be a financial burden on his brother, moved back to New York City, seeking work. In mid-September or early October, he and three budding artists—William Waring Carroll, Nelson Greene, and R. G. Vosburgh—moved into a large studio in the old Needham building on East 23rd Street, recently abandoned by the Art Students League, and lived there intermittently until the spring of 1895. With its "slumberous corridors rambling in puzzling turns and curves," wrote Crane, the building was filled with the creative energy of writers, artists, and musicians.[11] An epigraph chalked on a wooden beam in one of the studios read, "Congratulate yourselves if you have done something strange and extravagant and broken the monotony of a decorous age." This sentence, a slightly altered quotation from Emerson's essay "Heroism," captured the iconoclasm of youthful bohemians striving to define the hopes of their generation.

It was a time of poverty for Crane and his friends. Despite repeated loans of five dollars from William, the months following the loss of money on the printing of *Maggie* were the lowest point economically in Crane's life. The four roommates were supposed to split the monthly rent of fourteen dollars, but Stephen rarely could afford his share. When he arrived at the Needham building in the fall, he was wearing rubber boots because he had no shoes. Perpetual hunger made him, as a friend noted, "thin—almost cadaverous." At night, after playing poker amid lively discussions about art, literature, politics, and religion, three of the roommates would cram into the same bed, with the fourth sleeping in a coal box. During the day, they would swap clothes, depending on who had a job prospect or the energy to seek employment. One dreary day during the winter of 1893–1894, Crane spent his last five cents—in all likelihood borrowed—for carfare to meet with Edward Marshall, Sunday editor of the *New York Press*. He hoped that his letter of introduction, probably from Howells, would help him to get hired as a reporter. Marshall recognized Crane's extraordinary talent but did not hire him, because he sensed that Crane lacked the discipline for the hectic pace of newspaper work. Instead he offered to buy tales and sketches for the paper's Sunday supplements. At the end of the meeting, Crane, too proud to ask Marshall to lend him five cents for carfare, walked two and a half miles from the *Press* building to 23rd Street in freezing rain without a coat. The ordeal landed him in bed for a week.[12]

Garland, like Howells, was constantly looking for employment for Crane, and in the winter recommended that he write an article about America's growing economic disparity. A year earlier, an impending fiscal disaster had seemed unlikely: the World's Columbian Exposition had opened in Chicago on May 1, 1893, to celebrate the four-hundredth anniversary of Columbus's discovery of the New World and the subsequent progress in science, culture, and technology. Visitors rode on George Ferris's giant wheel, watched Eadweard Muybridge's moving pictures in the first commercial movie theater, ogled Little Egypt dancing the hoochee-coochee, and marveled at exhibits in the Manufactures and Liberal Arts Building, the largest building in the world, covering more than eleven acres and soaring to more than nineteen stories. For the first time, Americans sampled Juicy Fruit gum, Quaker Oats, Shredded Wheat, hamburgers, and diet carbonated soda. On opening day, President Grover Cleveland proudly announced, "I cherish the thought that America stands on the threshold of a great awakening. The impulse with which this Phantom City could rise in our midst is proof that the spirit is with us." The fair's electrically lit white stucco buildings, known as the White City, inspired the "alabaster cities" in the nation's most beloved song, Katherine Lee Bates's "America the Beautiful." "Sell the cook stove if necessary and come," Hamlin Garland urged his parents. "You *must* see this fair." Within days of the fair's opening, however, the nation was hit with a four-year financial crisis that would be the worst depression until the 1930s. By October, more than eight thousand commercial institutions, with liabilities of almost $285 million, had failed. Striking silk weavers in New Jersey, steelworkers in Pennsylvania, coal miners in West Virginia, and trainmen in the West rioted, demanding higher wages. In April 1894, Coxey's Army, a throng of unemployed workers galvanized by populist Jacob Coxey, marched to Washington insisting that Congress authorize public-works programs to create jobs; its Western contingent was Kelly's Army, whose ranks included an unknown young writer named Jack London.[13]

During the economic crisis, New York newspapers had been providing lurid coverage of the distribution of loaves to masses of shivering men huddled at midnight hoping for a piece of bread and admittance into a flophouse. Though Howells had originally encouraged Garland to write about the homeless, Garland was convinced that Crane would do a better job. Crane was excited by the task because he enjoyed investigative journalism and was familiar with the underbelly of the city. On February 26, 1894, he ventured down to the Bowery during a horrible blizzard. Almost eighteen inches of snow fell in thirty hours, accompanied by a steady wind of forty miles an hour. Though worn out from the ordeal, he stayed up all night to record his impressions. The next day, Linson found Crane in bed exhausted. Why hadn't he protected himself with warmer clothing? Crane's response typified his reluctance to en-

gage in idle speculation and his belief in pursuing an honest interpretation of reality: "How would I know how those poor devils felt if I was
warm myself?"[14]

Like Whitman earlier and Hemingway later, Crane valued unmediated, personal experience over abstractions as a way to confront life. If
the sentence from Emerson's "Heroism" resonated in Crane, the next
one in the essay would have done so as well: "Always do what you are
afraid to do." Characters in his fiction, most notably Henry Fleming
in *The Red Badge of Courage,* constantly encounter primal fears. How
they respond demonstrates who they are. The same was true for Crane,
who immersed himself in the extremes of living. Not until 1899 would
Theodore Roosevelt make famous the phrase "the strenuous life," but
the concept permeated the 1890s. In reaction to a genteel, increasingly
mechanized culture, men turned to outdoor activities like camping and
hunting—and competitive sports like boxing and football—to test their
limits and to assert their manhood. Crane's immersion in the slums of
New York was his way to understand what books could not teach him.

The result of Crane's Bowery experience during a blizzard was "The
Men in the Storm," a powerful depiction of homeless men huddled in
the frigid night air waiting for admittance into a five-cent flophouse.
The topic was not new. Other contemporary writers had written about
economic disparity and moralized about the need to address poverty,
unemployment, and homelessness; but Crane's approach was radically
different. He generally avoided social commentary and considered his
Bowery tales and sketches to be works of art that realistically portrayed
human frailty. Crane empathized with social outcasts and exposed the
horrors endured by the homeless, many of whom had come to New
York City seeking their fortune but who "were trying to perceive where
they had failed, what they had lacked, to be thus vanquished in the race."
Yet he never theorized on the causes of social injustice or sentimental-
ized his depiction, because he considered preaching "fatal to art in literature." His aesthetic aim was to set forth reality as he perceived it. As he
wrote to Lily in March–April 1894, writers "are the most successful in
art when we approach the nearest to nature and truth."[15]

Despite physical exhaustion from his ordeal, the experience energized
Crane. "I have enough ideas to keep me busy the next two years," he said
excitedly, and within a few days Garland and Howells had convinced the

Bacheller and Johnson syndicate to commission him to write about the flophouses in the city. To gather material for the article, Crane and one of his roommates, William Waring Carroll, dressed as tramps and explored the Bowery with only thirty cents in their pockets. Four days and three nights later, they resurfaced in tattered clothes, drenched from freezing rain, minus their overcoats, their toes sticking out of holes in their shoes. "My lord! has it come to this?" one of their friends exclaimed. Carroll was shaken by the ordeal, but Crane, though weakened by a hacking cough, grinned because he knew he had gotten excellent material for what would become one of his most moving journalistic sketches, "An Experiment in Misery."[16]

Crane was not the first journalist to disguise himself in order to gather material for a story. By the time he began exploring the Bowery, the device had been used widely. In 1887 the *New York World*'s Nellie Bly (whose real name was Elizabeth Cochrane) exposed mismanagement in an asylum by pretending to be insane and getting herself committed; and by 1894, the *World* was publishing articles almost weekly describing one or another reporter's personal account of having briefly been a tramp, lion tamer, or fire fighter. For younger writers, direct, personal experience became the basis for not only journalism but fiction as well, while the more traditional voices in literature found the method extreme. The popular humor magazine *Judge* ridiculed authors who strove to write only about what they had experienced. In a sketch in the magazine, a novelist sits by a fire until he perspires, then sits in the snow for ninety minutes, in order to write about a character who is ill. "Was this man insane?" the magazine responded. "He was not. He was an author who had observed with surprise and envy the phenomenal success of the pulmonary novel, the dyspeptic novel, the paretic novel, and the appendicitis novel, and who had determined to get himself into proper condition for writing a pneumoniac novel."[17]

Ironically, while Crane was exploring immersion as the basis for his art, he was continuing to imagine and write about a war that had ended more than six years before his birth. As he had done at Lake View, each night he worked four to five hours starting around midnight, then slept till late morning. It is unclear how quickly he conceived and revised the manuscript of his war novel. The first title—*Private Fleming / His Various Battles*—suggests Crane's intention to imitate the pattern in other novels and first-hand accounts, in which a new recruit tested in combat becomes a seasoned veteran. Typically the fictional versions also included a sentimental subplot with a love interest and a mother acting as the hero's moral guide. Chapter 1 of his novel, with its schoolgirls and Fleming's mother, contains remnants of an intended subplot. About a third of the way through, he abandoned the draft begun at Lake View because it was no longer a potboiler but had become a strikingly original dramatization of a terrified youth in his first battle. As he told Louis Senger, "Well, I got interested in the thing in spite of myself, and I couldn't, I couldn't. I *had* to do it my own way." One day, sensing that a recently written passage was exceptional, he exclaimed, "That is great!" At first, his apparent conceit bothered David Ericson; but after Crane read the passage aloud, Ericson realized how right his friend was. He was not so much arrogant as confident that he was doing what the "Battles and Leaders" writers had not: capturing the feelings, not just the actions, of the recruit.[18]

11

Struggling Artist, Poet at Work

FEBRUARY–MARCH 1894

From January to March 1984, while Crane was working on *The Red Badge of Courage,* a burst of energy resulted in a number of poems in free verse, which, as he explained to Willis Brooks Hawkins, "just seemed to be the perfectly obvious way of expressing what I felt at the moment." Crane was convinced that he could not have expressed the same feelings in prose any more than he "could have chewed up green paper and spit out ten dollar bills." In mid-February he visited Corwin Knapp Linson in his new studio on West 22nd Street, where Crane found him quietly working on a drawing. "What do you think I have been doing, CK?" he asked with "a sphinx-like smile," dropping a manuscript on top of Linson's work. Crane stood by silently as Linson began to read, but his anxiety intensified his impatience. CK had barely scanned the first few poems when Stephen exclaimed,

"What do you think?"
"I haven't had time to think! I'm seeing pictures."
"What do you mean?"
"Just what I said. They make me see pictures. How did you think of them?"

Crane's finger passed across his forehead: "They came, and I wrote them, that's all."[1]

Linson liked Crane's imagery, but was puzzled by the striking disregard for traditional literary conventions—rhyme, rhythm, and form—that he expected in poetry. "That's all right," Crane assured his friend. "If you can see them like that it's all I want." Then he chanted lines from the comic opera *Robin Hood:* "It takes nine tailors to make one man, / And a ninth of a man is he." The legend of Robin Hood had become increasingly popular in the nineteenth century, and Howard Pyle's illustrations and adaptation of the legend in his classic novel *The Merry Adventures of Robin Hood* (1883) had become the quintessential beloved work read by every schoolboy in Crane's generation. Crane often sang casually to relieve anxiety and calm his mind. At such moments, he was another of Robin's convivial outlaws: a musical Alan-a-Dale, a jovial Friar Tuck.[2]

But not all of Crane's friends appreciated his poetry. After an acquaintance curtly dismissed his poems, Crane privately complained, "CK! I know everyone can't like them, but I hate to give a man a chance to hit me in the back of the neck with an ax." Even his roommates mocked him by pinning on the wall a caricature of him and a parody of his poetry: "See what they do to me. They think I'm a joke, the Indians! They pin up these slams when I'm out. They make me ill! The mutts yowl like bobcats when I try to write, but I'll get my innings. I'll put 'em in a book"—and he did in *The Third Violet*.[3]

Crane found greater support for his poetry from Garland, who in late December 1893 had moved into an apartment in Harlem with his brother Franklin, then appearing in James A. Herne's melodrama *Shore Acres* at Daly's Theater. When Crane needed a haven from the frenetic pace of life among artists at East 23rd Street, he visited the Garland brothers. Franklin was an excellent cook, and Hamlin had become a mentor to Stephen after their first meeting in Asbury Park, in 1891; he had inscribed *Prairie Songs,* his recently published collection of poems, to "Stephen Crane / A genius."[4] Stephen, often gaunt and depressed when he arrived at the Harlem apartment, would become more relaxed in the brothers' presence, yet he habitually withheld a great deal even from his friends. Crane was self-absorbed, like "one remote from the practical business of living," and said so little about his personal life that Garland incorrectly assumed he was estranged from his family.[5] Though not lazy by nature, Crane never helped wash the dishes after a meal simply because he never thought of it. Ever impulsive, he responded solely to whatever thoughts captured his inquisitive mind at the moment.

One day in March, Crane arrived at Garland's apartment with a number of poems. In the past he had shown drafts of his writing to friends, family, and roommates for their immediate reaction, rather than for their critical commentary; but with Garland it was different. A successful professional author and influential critic, Garland was someone whose opinion mattered a great deal to Crane. Feeling as though he might be intruding on Garland, he gave him the manuscript "with pretended indifference" and chatted idly with Franklin. Garland was immediately struck by the astonishing originality of the poems, written cleanly without any sign of revision. "Have you any more?" he asked excitedly. Crane, pointing to his temple, replied, "I have four or five up here . . . all in a little row. . . . That's the way they come—in little rows, all ready to be put down on paper."[6]

In all likelihood, Garland was looking at fair copies of poems that had already been rewritten; this would explain the apparent lack of revision. But Crane's assertion, according to one of Garland's inconsistent reminiscences, that he did not need to arrange words in his head before transcribing them made his creative process sound like automatic writing, a form of composition conducted without conscious thought or deliberation and often attributed to paranormal phenomena. In the nineteenth century, the rise of interest in spiritualism had made automatic writing a popular subject, sometimes with humorous results. When one medium claimed that she was conveying messages from Mars, critics noted that her so-called Martian language sounded very much like her native French. Garland was intrigued by Crane's method of composition, and as president of the American Psychical Society he accepted psychic explanations. Only a few months earlier, he had arranged for a Los Angeles psychic to have her supposed paranormal abilities tested in Boston for five weeks.[7] With this in mind, he tested Crane by having him write a new poem on the spot. Without hesitation, out came the memorable "God fashioned the ship of the world," a bitter parody of Genesis in which "at fateful time" humanity was doomed to drift "forever rudderless" while "many in the sky / . . . laughed at this thing." Crane's ironic despair foreshadowed the pessimism of contemporaries such as Frank Norris and Theodore Dreiser. Startled by the poem, Garland now possessed white-hot evidence of Crane's brilliance: Crane was exactly the kind of new writer he had championed in *Crumbling Idols.* Here, Garland was convinced, was an original poet.

Garland insisted that Crane show the poems to William Dean Howells, who already knew of Crane's interest in poetry from their meeting a year earlier, when Crane had been impressed with Emily Dickinson's creativity as Howells read her poetry to him. Howells, however, had reservations about Crane's poems. Though he advocated stylistic experimentation, he disliked free verse and concluded that Crane's rejection of traditional versification made his poems formless and "too orphic": "It is a pity for you to do them, for you can do things solid and real, so superbly."[8] Howells admired Dickinson's innovative approach to versification; unlike Crane, she did not totally abandon conventional form. Yet Howells was struck by the freshness and originality of Crane's poems and believed, like Garland, that they should be published. He tried unsuccessfully to convince Henry Mills Alden, editor of *Harper's Magazine,* to do so.

John D. Barry, who also admired the poems, was better at marketing them. In April he recommended them to the Boston publisher Copeland and Day and arranged for Crane to attend a formal gathering of the Uncut Leaves Society at the elite Sherry's restaurant on April 14. The honored guest, Frances Hodgson Burnett, and other distinguished authors were scheduled to read from their work. Among those attending were novelist Gilbert Parker, poet and critic Henry Stoddard, and children's writer and editor Mary Mapes Dodge, all of whom were influential voices. Wishing to introduce them to a new star in the literary firmament, Barry encouraged Crane to read his poetry at the event. Crane was flattered by the offer, and his friends became excited about a possible breakthrough in his career. Fred Lawrence and Louis Senger came down from Port Jervis to attend the affair, along with Linson and Lucius L. Button, another of the medical students at the Pendennis Club. But Crane was uneasy at the thought of being the center of attention, even briefly, and attempts to persuade him to attend the event failed. When he told Barry that he would "rather die than do it," Barry offered simply to introduce Crane to the other guests, then read the poems himself; yet

Crane was adamant. Attempts by his friends failed as well. "No one will see you!" they said. "Say, don't you want to hear Barry give 'em Stephen Crane, the new poet?" "Come on, Steve, they're lions, we want to hear 'em roar!"[9]

Being the center of attention was always "a social crisis" for Crane, because it left him "witless and gibbering" and "as cold as iced cucumbers." Rather than attend the society's banquet, he stayed at his new apartment on 111 West 33rd Street, where he had moved in early April to escape the noise and ridicule at the Art Students League. Not until the last year of his life did he overcome shyness about hearing his own markedly slow speaking style. He was also uncomfortable with the emphasis on appearance at formal affairs. "Evening dress; Ladies are requested not to wear bonnets," announced the invitation. One news account of the event focused more on what the guest of honor wore—"beautifully dressed in white silk, garnished with mousseline-de-soie, and a corsage bunch of violets"—than on what she read at her first reading in New York City. Crane enjoyed the proper attire of his peers at the annual fraternity receptions, but he was never drawn to the glamour of associating with dignitaries. He also seemed anxious about the way his iconoclastic poems would be received. He valued his poetry above his fiction, but he feared the poems might be misunderstood and dismissed, as *Maggie* had been. More than anything he had written so far, they exposed deep-rooted religious conflicts as he struggled to understand the human condition, the meaning of truth, and the nature of God—if there was one. He was so steeped in his Methodist past, as Amy Lowell astutely commented years later, "that he could not get it out of his head. He disbelieved it and he hated it, but he could not free himself from it." Crane told a friend that he had written the poems in nontraditional style because "no one would print a line of mine, and I had to do something odd to attract attention." In truth, however, the poems were a form of catharsis: he had to write them in order to purge deep-rooted resentment against his religious upbringing.[10]

Barry's reading at the Uncut Leaves Society banquet started inauspiciously. Because a reception was planned for Mrs. Burnett that evening, the scheduled list of readings had been shortened, but Barry persuaded the organizers to add him to the list. When he announced that he wanted to read the poems of a new poet, some attendees whispered, "Who is

Stephen Crane?" By the end of the reading, the question had been answered, and Crane's friends raced to tell him the good news. The audience had concluded that his was an important new voice in American poetry. At first, Crane thought that his friends were exaggerating to ease his apprehensions; but as they related the details of the evening, he gradually believed them. That night, he slept happily for the first time since coming to New York.[11] Only days earlier, Crane had been so dejected that he had considered changing careers. He had gone to see Elisha J. Edwards, a *New York Press* reporter who had occasionally provided him with a place to sleep in his room on West 27th Street during 1892–1893 and who had read an early version of the manuscript of *The Red Badge of Courage* in the spring of 1893. "I am going to chuck the whole thing," Crane lamented. "I have worked two years, living with tramps in the tenements on the East Side so that I could get to know those people as they are, and what is the use? In all that time I have received only $25 for my work. I can't starve even to carry on this work, and I'm going home to my brother in New Jersey and perhaps learn the boot and shoe trade."[12] So far, Crane had published only one New York City sketch: "The Broken-Down Van" in July 1892.

The day after the Uncut Leaves Society affair, Crane received more good news. In an interview that Howells granted to the *New York Press,* the "Greatest Living American Writer" announced that Crane "promises splendid things" and that *Maggie* was "a remarkable book." The newspaper also printed excerpts from the novel and added additional commentary most likely written by Edward Marshall, the interviewer: "There is unquestionably truth in it; the kind of truth that no American has ever had the courage (or is it bravado?) to put between book covers before." Excited by the prospect of finally earning money as a writer, he sent Garland a copy of the *Press* articles. "People can come to see me now," he excitedly wrote, and they "say that I am a great writer. Counting five that are sold, four that are unsold, and six that are mapped out, I have fifteen short stories in my head and out of it. They'll make a book."[13]

Now that Howells had praised *Maggie* and its author's literary potential, Crane, who hadn't contacted Lily for months, immediately wrote to impress her with his achievements. He proudly told her that during the past two years he had independently developed a "little creed of art"—

the same theory of literary realism advocated by his "literary fathers," Howells and Garland—and that he had two books coming out in the spring. Crane believed that the road to success had been "more of a battle than a journey" and was convinced that initially Garland and "that terrible, young radical" (Crane himself) had struggled to publish in mainstream magazines because editors preferred light, sentimental fiction rather than realistic, sometimes depressing stories. "Howells, of course," had been "too powerful" for those editors, and, Crane boasted, he likewise had "proved too formidable for them."[14] Crane's assertions, though, were the posturing of an insecure youth wooing his lover. The claim that he had been independently developing a literary theory since 1892 ignored the fact that he had learned about the theories of Howells and Garland in 1891 in Asbury Park during Garland's lectures. His approach to writing was less a formal theory than an intuitive grasp of how best to translate his sensory impressions into words. He was also overly optimistic about forthcoming work. The anticipated reissue of *Maggie* by the Arena Company never occurred, and publication of *The Black Riders,* his first collection of poetry, was delayed for almost a year because Crane and the publisher disagreed over the book's contents.

Shortly after writing the letter about his literary creed, Crane and Linson apparently visited Lily at the residence of her wealthy parents in New York. Years later Linson remembered a visit uptown, and although he had forgotten the name of the woman they visited, it was most likely Lily. At some point they discussed *Maggie*. When Stephen and Lily got into a spirited debate about whether fiction should be didactic, he declared: "You can't find preaching on any page of *Maggie!* An artist has no business to preach. . . . A story must have a reason, but art is—oh, well, not a pulpit." The discussion confirmed their fondness for each other. In all likelihood he wanted her to read the book; but hoping to sell the few copies he had left, he instead gave her the manuscript. Heading home after the visit, a jovial Crane asked Linson, "Didn't you like it? I don't know anything finer than the natural talk of a nice girl with brains in her head." Lily was the love of Crane's life. She had been raised in an educated family well established in social circles. Though he rebelled against social norms, he yearned for the respectability that she had.[15]

The two sketches he soon published—"A Night at the Millionaire's Club" on April 21 and "An Experiment in Luxury" on April 29—

seemed partly inspired by one or more visits to the Brandon home. In the latter, a youth visits his friend Jack in the Fifth Avenue home of Jack's millionaire father; its high ceilings and stained glass evoke Linson's description of the Brandon residence that he and Crane had visited. Insofar as the youth is investigating the "eternal mystery of social condition" during his visit, the sketch complemented "An Experiment in Misery," published a week earlier; but its unflattering portrait of a prosaic father, socially conscious mother, and insipid daughters suggest Crane's ambivalence about the Brandon family, who had questioned his relationship with Lily and his ability to care financially for her and her son, born in 1893. If Crane disdained the Brandons' materialism, his aversion may have appeared in "A Night at the Millionaire's Club" under the guise of a club member named Chauncey Depew, a transparent allusion to Chauncey M. Depew, at the time president of the New York Central Railroad and later a United States senator whose rise to wealth and power typified the growing economic inequality that Crane had addressed in "An Experiment in Misery." The disdain that Depew and his fellow club members feel for literature and history, two of Crane's passions, becomes overt in the story when Ralph Waldo Emerson, Nathaniel Hawthorne, George Washington, and Alexander Hamilton attempt to visit the club. Ignorant of who they are, club members demand, "Don't let 'em in here!" "Throw 'em out!" "Kill 'em!" It would be wrong to reduce the two sketches to autobiography. Crane was fond of Lily's two sisters, Dot and Stella, and their mother's dedication to suffragism would have limited frivolous social concerns. Crane likely used his experience with the Brandon family as background for larger issues. Clearly, though, he perceived himself as an outsider looking in on a privileged world that he simultaneously hated and wished to join.[16]

Crane's concern over the growing inequality of social conditions affected his feelings about the Brandon family, prompting his artist friend Nelson Greene to claim that "Stevey was an avowed Socialist."[17] Crane may have briefly flirted with socialism, and his depictions of poverty in "The Men in the Storm" and "An Experiment in Misery," and of a rich, acquisitive society in "An Experiment in Luxury" and "A Night at the Millionaire's Club," are striking; but he avoided economics in his works and letters, and "An Experiment in Misery," like most of his best fiction, ends on a note of ambivalence. Though its young protagonist (Crane's persona) has become more aware of social inequality in urban America and feels guilt concerning his privileged position, he does not pity the downtrodden and does not conclude that they are simply victims of an environment beyond their control. Crane was also ambivalent about politics. In October 1895, he asked a friend to vote for his brother William in an upcoming election; two days later he wrote, "I hate to monkey about politics." Yet within a few months, he was in Washington, D.C., thinking about writing a political novel. Adding to his ambivalence was his distrust of institutions and easy solutions: he was aware that socialist reformers like Daniel De Leon could be as intolerant as the leaders they criticized. In 1890 De Leon joined the Socialist Labor Party, but five years later established his own organization, the Socialist Trade and Labor Alliance, because he could not compromise with other union leaders.[18]

Crane's relationship with Lily, complicated by the fact that he associated the Brandons with a materialistic society, was marked by his ambivalence about women as well. A confident analyst of people and their behavior in his writing, Crane was deeply insecure around women. "If the five of us started out and gathered in four girls," he joked with colleagues, "I'd be the odd man ten times out of ten." John Northern Hilliard claimed that Stephen "took up with many a drab, and was not overly particular as to her age, race or color." When Crane learned in 1892 that a Claverack schoolmate "lack[ed] females of the white persuasion," he advised him: "Just read these next few lines in a whisper:—I—I think black is quite good—if—if its yellow and young." In October 1895, after a poker game in Crane's loft, a player noticed a woman sleeping in the bedroom. "Gosh!" Crane said. "I didn't hear her come in Teasingly, his companions asked whether she had inspired *Maggie*. "Some of her," he replied. Yet Nelson Greene asserted that he never saw Stephen with a prostitute, because he was "a fellow of remarkably clean mind and speech," and other friends attested to his gentlemanly, even chivalrous behavior. One evening, during the winter of 1897, a young prostitute passed Crane and Robert H. Davis, a reporter for the *New York Journal,* as they were walking along the street. Crane placed a hand on his heart, removed his hat, bowed gallantly, and offered to help show her "the way out" of prostitution. "You shouldn't hang out here, kid," she advised him, then turned away. "This is a long cañon," he told Davis. "I wonder if there *is* a way out." Naïvely imagining that she was seeking redemption,

Crane had offered to rescue her, but his gallant effort was misguided. Though Davis calls her "Maggie" in his account of the incident, she is not like the docile eponymous character in *Maggie: A Girl of the Streets,* but more like her foil, the audacious streetwalker Nell, who has learned to manipulate men. In a reversal of roles, Maggie, not Crane, was the seasoned advisor.[19]

Ambivalence about relationships comes from a fear of intimacy, which is typically rooted in a childhood fear of rejection and abandonment. It often surfaces in adulthood and leads to the avoidance of close emotional ties; to codependent relationships, in which one seeks to rescue another; and to low self-esteem, which causes one to be embarrassed by praise and recognition. Crane's life fits the pattern, starting with the abrupt departure of caregivers: the loss of his father and his sister Agnes, the forced separation from his family after his father's death, and the absent mother away on church duties. The pattern is apparent in Crane's fiction as well. A crude bartender deserts his girlfriend; an immature recruit abandons a dying comrade; terrified parents fleeing during a war forget to take their child. Rather than risk emotional pain from intimacy, Crane compartmentalized his relationships and hid behind various masks, a trait that explains why contemporaries gave disparate accounts of his personality. It is also the source of his fondness for a staid maiden like Nellie Crouse, whom he would start to pursue at the end of 1895, and his obsessive attraction to, even preference for, prostitutes. Neither kind of woman required emotional closeness. In the world of socialites, where proper behavior has been codified, the investment is shallow; in that of the streetwalker, it is financial. Ambivalence also surfaces in Crane's fiction. Whereas Pete views Maggie as a sexual object ("I'm stuck on yer shape. It's outa sight"), George Kelcey envisions her as the "dream-girl, the goddess" on a pedestal, and hopes to "get a chance to rescue her from something." Crane wanted both.[20]

Crane dramatized his conflict about women in *The Third Violet,* a novel written in the fall of 1895 and focusing on the life of artists in the old Art Students League building. Billie Hawker, a fictionalized Crane, is attracted to two women, the bohemian Florinda O'Connor and a wealthy, aristocratic socialite named Grace Fanhall; but by the end of the novel, his conflict over them remains unresolved. Whereas Florinda was based on Gertrude Selene—a studio model for Nelson Greene, who later became an artist—two other women were the inspiration for Grace.[21] While writing the novel, Crane was undoubtedly thinking about Lily, who loved violets. He had met her while she was vacationing at an Asbury Park hotel during the summer; likewise, Hawker meets Grace during her summer vacation at a Sullivan County Inn. And Grace's New York home, like Lily's, is the height of opulence. Just as Hawker has a rival suitor in Jem Oglethorpe, Lily's husband, Hersey Munroe, was Crane's rival. Stephen's assertion to Lily that he had "renounced the clever school in literature" resurfaces in Billie and Grace's discussion about people who attempt to be verbally "clever."

More provocative, though, is the other prototype for Grace Fanhall. In late September 1895, Grace Hall, a woman from a respectable, wealthy Midwestern family, moved into the American Fine Arts building on West 57th Street. She had come to New York City to study voice and pursue a career in opera. Although Crane was sharing a loft with Post Wheeler at 165 West 23rd Street at the time, and in mid-October moved back temporarily to Edmund's house in Hartwood to work quietly on *The Third Violet,* he would have met her on his frequent visits to friends in the Art Students League who were living in her building. She was soon offered a contract with the Metropolitan Opera and made her debut at Madison Square Garden, but her promising career ended abruptly. A childhood illness, which had left her temporarily blind for several months, made her eyes especially sensitive to stage lights. Her passion for opera helps to explain the use of the plot, theme, and imagery of Verdi's *La Traviata* and *Il Trovatore* throughout *The Third Violet.* Six months after coming to New York, she returned to Oak Park, Illinois, to marry her fiancé, Dr. Clarence Hemingway. Their first son, Ernest, grew up reading Crane's children's stories in *Harper's* and *The Red Badge of Courage;* he became a renowned journalist and author whose writing, career, and philosophical outlook on life were remarkably similar to those of Crane. It is almost as though he grew up to *be* Stephen Crane. After achieving his success, he ranked Crane, Henry James, and Mark Twain as the three "good writers" in American literature and praised *The Red Badge* as a "great boy's dream of war . . . one of the finest books in our literature." Might Ernest Hemingway have first begun to admire his literary father after hearing about the famous author his mother had known, and perhaps fallen in love with, in New York City?[22]

12

Frustrated Artist

APRIL–DECEMBER 1894

AROUND THE THIRD week in April 1894, Crane appeared at Hamlin Garland's apartment, a huge manuscript stuffed in a pocket of his ulster. As with his sheaf of poems in March, he hesitated to hand over the pages. There was a "seeming reluctance," Garland recalled, but Crane's "queer, self-derisive smile" indicated his desire for the opinion of the established author. After reading the manuscript, Garland was amazed anew at Crane's talent. How could someone who in conversation was "disjointed and quaint rather than copious or composed" write so well about a war he had never experienced? Was Crane channeling the spirit of a Civil War veteran like a medium? Garland was surprised when Crane responded that his knowledge of battle had come from playing football: "The psychology is the same. The opposite team is an enemy tribe!" On another occasion he said, "I got my sense of the rage of conflict on the football field."[1]

The second half of the *Red Badge* manuscript was missing because Crane could not pay the fifteen-dollar typing fee.[2] He had asked Nelson Greene for a loan to cover the cost, but Greene was similarly poor. In desperation, Crane had even considered pawning one of his two treasured Civil War swords, which had belonged to his father and his Uncle

Wilbur. Finally, Garland's brother, Franklin, lent him the fifteen dollars. Crane returned with the rest of the manuscript on April 24, just before Garland's departure for Chicago the next day. Crane was depressed by his inability to support himself financially as a writer. The euphoria he had experienced from Howells's praise only a few days earlier had already worn off. "You'll be rich and famous in a year or two. Successful authors always look back with a smile on their hard times," said Garland encouragingly. "You may be right," Crane replied, "but it's no joke now. I'd trade my entire future for twenty-three dollars in cash." After sixteen months of broken shoes, tattered clothing, and empty pockets, he could not smile about his prospects.[3]

Garland urged the publishers S. S. McClure and Irving Bacheller to hire Crane as a writer and mailed two of his sketches—most likely "An Ominous Baby" and "The Men in the Storm"—to Benjamin Orange Flower at the *Arena,* adding that "the author is hungry." By the end of April, Crane had revised his manuscript partly in response to Garland's suggestions. Then, with a letter of recommendation from Garland, he submitted it in early May to McClure for publication in either the McClure Newspaper Features Syndicate, founded in 1884, or in *McClure's Magazine,* which had just been established in 1893. McClure was a likely choice for Crane. Magazines paid quickly and provided an avenue for republication of material in book form. The timing was fortuitous for Crane because the magazine industry was on the verge of a major breakthrough in terms of cost, production, and circulation. In 1885 the four leading magazines—*Century, Harper's, Scribner's,* and the *Atlantic*—sold for twenty-five to thirty-five cents and were geared to middle- and upper-class readers. With improved technology for reproducing illustrations, a decrease in postage rates, and an increase in advertising, publishers began producing cheaper magazines for a wider audience. In 1885 there were 3,100 magazines in America; a decade later there were more than 5,100. After selling the first issue of *McClure's Magazine* for fifteen cents, McClure announced in the second issue, "More good reading than any other magazine—the price will be ten cents—and the publishers will make money."[4]

Among McClure's interests was investigative reporting, and in subsequent years his muckraking staff produced a rash of exposés, the most famous being Ida M. Tarbell's history of the Standard Oil Company, featured in the magazine from 1902 to 1904. The June 1894 issue carried Garland's "Homestead and Its Perilous Trades," based on his visit to Homestead, Pennsylvania, a year after the town was the scene of a violent clash between management and steelworkers. On Garland's recommendation, McClure commissioned Crane to research and write a piece on coalfields, then hired Linson to illustrate the article. In mid-May they visited a mine near Scranton, Pennsylvania; but because McClure's policy was to pay only after the job was completed, they had to cover their expenses up front. Penniless, Crane borrowed fifty dollars from Linson, but never paid it back. His frequent failure to repay loans was not an effort to take advantage of family and friends; he simply never placed a high value on money.[5]

Crane and Linson spent a night at the Valley House in Scranton, then another at the home of painter John Willard Raught in Dunmore, while working on what became "In the Depths of a Coal Mine," Crane's harsh critique of the exploitation of boys and draft animals in the mines and the devastating effect of black-lung disease. Although he normally remained detached and ambivalent about social and political theories and movements, he was outraged by the working conditions imposed upon miners and the contrast between their lives and those of the robber barons who owned the mines. It was an ironic turn of events, given that his family had owned stock in the Pennsylvania mines and he himself had inherited some of it. Crane and Linson also visited one of Crane's uncles, Reverend Luther W. Peck. Despite Crane's outspoken rebellion against his religious heritage, he loved his relatives and stayed in touch with them. A free spirit, he nevertheless yearned for the stability of family roots.

In June, Crane returned to Port Jervis for the summer, optimistically telling family and friends that his war novel and collection of poetry would be published within a few months. It would be one of many examples of his misunderstanding of the literary marketplace. Convinced he had nothing to worry about, he lounged around William's and Wilbur's homes, though his newly acquired Bowery demeanor offended some of the more staid townspeople. He had no desire for polite conversation or adherence to social conventions; and with his urban slum accent, he ruffled them with stories about getting a black eye in a grand brawl in the Bowery and seeing a Chinaman murdered on Mott Street.[6]

Crane's tales about his experiences in the New York slums were more than idle chatter, for he was writing his second novella about life in the city's grimy tenement districts. After finishing *The Red Badge* in late April, Crane returned to *George's Mother* and finished it in November, confidently telling Garland that it left *Maggie* "at the post"; but he did not submit it to a publisher until the success of the war novel assured him of a readership. At first, Crane had intended it to be a companion piece to his other East Side novella. George Kelcey and his mother live in the same tenement building as the Johnsons, and George is smitten with Maggie; but the restrained style, tighter plot, and more psychologically complex treatment of character in *George's Mother* reveal that Crane had taken the advice to move beyond crude language and the brutal, melodramatic treatment of the slums in *Maggie*.[7]

In *George's Mother*, Crane confronted anxieties about rebelling against his religious heritage. Before moving to New York City, George lives in rural Handyville near Bill Sickle's home. The last of five siblings, he loses his father early on and becomes "a wild son" who rejects the straight and narrow religious path of his mother. The pattern is unmistakably autobiographical. Rural Handyville is a fictional representation of rural Hurleyville in Sullivan County, and the Cranes' youngest child, who lived with the Van Sycle family following his father's death, rebelled against authority. When Mrs. Kelcey forces George to attend church, he hears fervent professions of faith from the congregation and a homily on damnation from a "pulpit swathed in gloom, solemn and mystic as a bier." The traumatic experience leaves him feeling "completely alone and isolated" in "the mists of his shame and humiliation." In creating a fictional rebellious son, Crane was recalling his own struggles with isolation and religious guilt.[8] As much as he professed a radical independence, he craved the emotional protection of traditional family values. But George is not a projection of Stephen alone; another "wild son" was Townley, whose alcoholism exacerbated his physical and mental problems. While working for the *Asbury Park Shore Press*, Townley must have been tempted more than once to slip into the saloon next door run by William B. Kelsey. The alcoholic son in Kelsey's saloon lent some of his traits to the wild son George Kelcey.[9]

The behavior of Townley and Stephen worried their mother, who resembled the resolute, moralizing Mrs. Kelcey.[10] Like Mrs. Crane, Mrs.

Kelcey is a widow and a staunch supporter of the church who travels extensively as a speaker for the Woman's Christian Temperance Union; she has a mental breakdown; and she dies after a long period of suffering. She proudly sings Isaac Watts's "Holy Fortitude; or, The Christian Soldier," a hymn popular among Methodists and temperance workers, which suggests that she, like Mrs. Crane, is a Methodist who sees herself as battling against evil in the army of the Lord.[11] Mrs. Kelcey, too, is determined that her sons not stray from the church and become alcoholics. Yet in the end, George becomes a derelict; she dies in a delirium, believing she is back in peaceful Handyville with her husband; and George, like the insane narrator in Charlotte Perkins Gilman's unforgettable short story "The Yellow Wallpaper," can only stare at the "clusters of brown roses" on the wallpaper and see "hideous crabs crawling on his brain."[12]

What are readers to make of Crane's fictionalized struggle with his occasionally dysfunctional family in *George's Mother*? Ostensibly, he stopped working on the book to write a potboiler about the Civil War; but in fact, the initial experience of confronting his past was too painful. At the beginning of the story, Charley Jones "regarded himself in the mirror that multiplied the bottles on the shelf back of the bar." The image of proliferating bottles captures the self-destructive cycle in which one drink leads to another, and the reflection of Charley implies that his drinking partner, George Kelcey, is looking at himself as well. Indeed, the verb "to reflect" is used several times to convey George's state of mind. Yet the reader is never told explicitly that George is looking at himself— an appropriate elision, since Crane likewise could not look into the mirror of his own soul. The original title of the book was *A Woman Without Weapons,* suggesting that it was going to focus on a mother who could not be an effective Christian soldier in God's army. The final title, however, highlights the psychological portrayal of an unresolved mother-son conflict in which neither character fully understands the other. Like George Kelcey, Crane finally recognized that his "mother took pride in him in quite a different way from that in which he took pride in himself."[13]

Haunted by his own demons, Crane sought solace at Edmund's new home in Hartwood, New York. Edmund had moved there in mid-May, 1894, to become custodian of a 3,600-acre tract of land owned by

William; according to Stephen, he served as "postmaster, justice-of-the-peace, ice-man, farmer, millwright, blue stone man, lumberman, station agent on the P.J.M. and N.Y.R.R, and many other things which I now forget." Edmund was the sibling Stephen felt closest to, and he became Stephen's guardian following their mother's death. Shortly after Edmund's move, Stephen stored all his furniture at Edmund's home. Despite his peripatetic lifestyle, he identified Hartwood as home on his passport. A bucolic hamlet with only three houses, Hartwood became a psychic refuge from the vagaries of life and a portal to nature's comforts. Crane enjoyed horseback riding through "the blessed quiet hills of Hartwood," as well as sailing alone on Hartwood Lake or on the millpond near Edmund's home in a boat he and his brother had built. Sitting indoors by the front window, Crane worked on his manuscripts, stopping only when an opportune breeze prompted an escape to the sailboat for a peaceful outing on what they had christened "Stephen Crane's Pond."[14]

At the end of July, Crane and about two dozen friends stayed for almost a month at "Camp Interlaken," their name for a site located on a narrow strip of land between two lakes at Twin Lakes in Pike County, Pennsylvania. The trip was organized by Fred Lawrence's mother to celebrate the completion of his internship and staff appointment at Philadelphia's Hahnemann Medical College. For the first time in months, Crane felt good about his future, believing that his war novel and collection of poetry would soon be out. As always, he found the outdoors exhilarating, swimming in the lakes, playing baseball, and roaming through the woods—"as happy there," Linson recalled, "as a colt let loose in pasture."[15]

Campers at Twin Lakes typically commemorated their experience with a memento. One year it was a group photograph; another time, a humorous poetic account of the camping trip. That August, with help from Louis Senger, Crane celebrated the experience by designing and writing a four-page burlesque newspaper, the *Pike County Puzzle*. Filled with inside jokes, it captured the joy and friendship of the campers and revealed the self-deprecating humor of Crane's aliases, "Pan-cake Pete" and "Signor Pancako." Teasing him about his penchant for elaborate pronouncements on life and literature, the newspaper commented on "the cloud-capped pinnacle of his thoughts," from which "he fell and was grievously injured"; and regarding his limited singing ability, the paper recommended that he should "plough with it, but after corn ripens you will have to seek employment in the blue-stone works. We have seen voices like yours used effectively for cider presses." Crane also satirized the newspaper business. Unlike the *Pike County Puzzle,* he claimed, "rival" newspapers like the *Misleading Record* and the *Curry Ear-Trumpet* got the facts wrong because they "follow the vagaries and falsehoods of modern newspapers." In contrast, the *Puzzle,* one "of the most advanced and exasperating types of rural journalism," had additional benefits: cows given a bran made of milk and "our clever sheet" were kept healthy, and a "well-known forger" would have frozen to death had he not burned copies of the *Puzzle* to keep warm.[16]

Underneath the playfulness in the *Pike County Puzzle* was Crane's growing suspicion of misguided journalism. In his poem "A newspaper is a collection of half-injustices" (written the same year as the *Puzzle*), he bitterly criticized the profession of newspaper reporting. This was the age of "yellow journalism," in which mass marketing, intense competition, and distortion of facts were used to spread innuendo and sensationalism. Howells, in *A Modern Instance* (1881), and Henry James, in *The Bostonians* (1886), depict the danger that the new journalism posed to honest reporting. For Crane, a newspaper "is a court / Where every one is kindly and unfairly tried / By a squalor of honest men"; it is a marketplace "Where wisdom sells its freedom"; and it is "A Collection of loud tales / Concentrating eternal stupidities." Ever since being fired by the *New York Tribune* in 1892, Crane had been leery of journalism. As a result of the JOUAM incident, he had been unfairly tried in the marketplace; in two years, after publicly defending a wrongly arrested prostitute, he would again be unfairly tried and would see his career as an investigative journalist end abruptly.

Crane was also learning that an author had limited ability to control the fate of his publications. When his article "In the Depths of a Coal Mine" was syndicated in late July and published the next month in *McClure's Magazine,* Crane discovered that McClure had deleted passages that rebuked coal brokers "who make neat livings by fiddling with the market" and mine owners who "get so much" while "miners, swallowed by the grim black mouths of the earth day after day get proportionately so little." After reading the article, Crane angrily tossed it aside: "The birds didn't want the truth after all. Why the hell did they send me up there then? Do they want the public to think the coal mines gilded ball-rooms with the miners eating ice-cream in boiled shirt-fronts?" Despite the excisions, the article was one of Crane's most trenchant pieces of journalism and foreshadowed *McClure's* later muckraking.[17]

Crane had more influence regarding the publication of his first collection of poems, but his relationship with the publisher was equally tense. Crane—or possibly John D. Barry—had submitted them to Copeland and Day in the spring; but when months passed without any response, Crane inquired about the status of his manuscript in late August. He was excited about the possibility of their publishing it. Founded by Herbert Copeland and Fred Holland Day the year before, the firm specialized in well-crafted books in the tradition of fine printing then being revived by private English presses such as Kelmscott, Ashendene, and Doves. It was developing an avant-garde reputation in America by publishing such authors as Dante Gabriel Rossetti and Oscar Wilde, as well as by issuing the British magazine *The Yellow Book,* which epitomized the Decadent movement of the 1890s.

Crane's letter prompted Fred Day, managing editor of the firm, to ask his poetry editor, Louise Imogen Guiney, to evaluate Crane's manuscript. A poet and essayist widely regarded in literary circles for her critical insight, she recommended publication, but agreed with Day that a number of inferior poems should be omitted. When Crane received the list of excisions, he wrote one of his most adamant letters:

> We disagree on a multitude of points. In the first place I should absolutely refuse to have my poems printed without many of those which you just as absolutely mark "No." It seems to me that you cut all the ethical sense out of the book. All the anarchy, perhaps. It is the anarchy which I particularly insist upon. From the poems which you keep you could produce what might be termed a "nice little volume of verse by Stephen Crane" but for me there would be no satisfaction. The ones which refer to God, I believe you condemn altogether. I am obliged to have them in when my book is printed. There are some which I believe unworthy of print. These I herewith enclose. As for the others, I cannot give them up—in the book.
>
> In the second matter, you wish I would write a few score more. It is utterly impossible to me. We would be obliged to come to an agreement upon those that are written.

If my position is impossible to you, I would not be offended at the
sending of all the retained lines to the enclosed address.

For a little-known author who had yet to sign a contract for a book,
Crane's insistence on his iconoclastic views exemplified what he had already told Lily: that his career had been "more of a battle than a journey."
He acknowledged his own "literary prejudices" and, like Day, thought
that some readers would dislike the poems, but he preferred to have his
unpublished manuscript returned rather than have it bowdlerized.[18]

Whereas Crane saw his poetry as serious work full of "anarchy,"
Guiney considered it youthful posturing by a talented though not strikingly original author who took "himself too seriously." "S. Crane is ex-
travagantly young," she told Day, "and will outgrow his saucy little 'ethical meanings.' The stuff is good stuff, as literature, on a second reading as
on the first. . . . The book will be interesting, for it is all thought-stuff.
There is no great variety. Like so much atheism of the sort, it is, at bottom, not anti-Christian, not opposed at all to the true spirit of religion,
but only to the cants and shams and ignoble interpretations of 'Christian'
men." Twelve years older than Crane, she had already experienced her
own youthful phase of religious doubt and was now amused by his adolescent swagger. "Humor him in everything," she advised Day. His poetry
"is no great affair. His fashion of printing prose as poetry is sensational,
but this is a flashy age, so 'tis!"[19]

Initially, Day agreed to include the poems marked "No" and offered
Crane a contract for 10 percent of the sales; yet three weeks later, in October, Crane was surprised when Day sent him a new list consisting of
seven poems, three of which he now refused to publish and four he
urged Crane to omit. Because none of the seven poems appeared in *The
Black Riders and Other Lines,* Crane must have acquiesced to the cuts; but
in doing so, he had not tired of the "battle" to protect the "ethical sense"
of his book. Even without these seven, *The Black Riders* still depicts a
malicious Nature and an inscrutable God. In all likelihood, Crane agreed
to delete the seven poems because he felt the book still manifested "anarchy." For Day, *The Black Riders and Other Lines* typified the kind of
avant-garde work he was seeking and captured the *fin-de-siècle* mood. In
short, neither side fully capitulated, and both sides won.

In mid-September, Crane returned to New York City. By early October, he had moved back into the old Needham building on East 23rd Street, supplementing his meager income with occasional newspaper work. Optimism about his literary future had been tempered by reality. Though his collection of poems was scheduled to appear the following year, he could not expect a huge amount of money from sales, for the policy of Copeland and Day was to produce limited editions. He also found it difficult to get steady work and had heard nothing from S. S. McClure about *The Red Badge of Courage*. When he wrote to Hamlin Garland in November, he had "just crawled out of the fifty-third ditch into which I have been cast. . . . McClure was a Beast about the war-novel and that has been the thing that put me in one of the ditches. He kept it for six months until I was near mad. Oh, yes, he was going to use it but—." Crane already had reason to be annoyed with McClure. In late December 1893, he had approached the publisher for work, but had been forced to cool his heels for an hour in what Garland called Mc-Clure's "pen for culprits." He was also still upset with the bowdlerization of "In the Depths of a Coal Mine."[20]

From Crane's point of view, McClure's indecisiveness about *The Red Badge* was inexcusable. McClure, though, lacked the money to buy the story. He had invested heavily in his new magazine during an economic recession; and with the first issue in June 1893, he was already near bankruptcy because of the financial panic. A year later, he was still struggling financially and devising novel ways to get money—schemes such as borrowing it from his authors or convincing his wife's doctor to invest four hundred dollars in the magazine. Even if he had had the money to buy Crane's manuscript, he was preoccupied with the magazine's first major serial, Ida Tarbell's history of Napoleon Bonaparte, which was scheduled to begin in November 1894.[21]

Unaware of all this, Crane was dissatisfied with McClure's inaction. In October, Edward Marshall suggested he take the manuscript to Irving Bacheller, who had joined with James W. Johnson in 1884 to form a press syndicate similar to McClure's. In all likelihood, Crane did not show him the typescript that Garland had helped to pay for; the manuscript had been substantially revised. Crane had become so disenchanted with the repeated rejection of his war novel that he decided to burn the manuscript if it was turned down one more time. Fate decreed otherwise: Bacheller and his wife stayed up much of the night reading the manuscript to each other, thrilled by the story, and the next morning he told Crane he wanted to publish it. After Crane borrowed fifteen dollars from his fraternity brother John Henry Dick to have another typescript made, Bacheller paid Crane ninety dollars for the serial rights.[22]

Bacheller planned to use the novel in the syndicate's new "Six Day Serial Service," which was scheduled to begin at the end of the month and which would supply newspapers around the country with stories of 4,000 to 15,000 words. Yet there was a problem. His contract with the newspapers stated that no serial would run more than six installments and that each installment would range from 2,000 to 2,500 words. The stipulated length of the stories was simply based on the amount of time that editors assumed readers would spend on reading an installment. If each installment was too long and the story ran for too many issues, newspaper editors feared that the public would stop reading. Because Crane's manuscript contained about 50,000 words, it was clearly too long as stated in the contract. At 2,500 words per installment, it would have taken a newspaper twenty days to publish the novel. Bacheller nevertheless convinced editors to publish the complete manuscript, but they reconsidered their position before publication. The novel appeared in a condensed and truncated version of about 15,000 words. Though it is unclear whether Crane, Bacheller, or both cut and edited the text, Crane felt that the syndicated version of his novel was "much worse than its original form."[23]

Despite Crane's reservations, the syndication of the novel in six installments on December 3–8, 1894, drew immediate praise. Writing as "Holland" in the *Philadelphia Press,* Elisha J. Edwards called it "perhaps the most graphic and truthful" portrayal of the Civil War and predicted that Crane would likely become "the most powerful of American tellers of tales." Within days of publication, Bacheller took "Stevey"—as the avuncular Bacheller called him—to Philadelphia to meet the staff of the *Press.* "Word flew from cellar to roof that the great Stephen Crane was in the office," Bacheller recalled. "Editors, reporters, compositors, proof-readers crowded around him shaking his hand. It was a revelation of the commanding power of genius." Waiting to meet his admirers, Crane was anxious about their intentions. All he could think of was Kipling's poem "The Young British Soldier," a grimly humorous lesson about the need for fatalistic resignation to one's duty even in the face of death. Crane repeated the lines obsessively to Bacheller:

> When you're wounded and left on Afghanistan's plains,
> And the women come out to cut up what remains,
> Jest roll to your rifle and blow out your brains
> An' go to your Gawd like a soldier.

Crane enjoyed his instant stardom, but questioned at what price glory. Editors, like ruthless Afghan women, "cut up" a manuscript, leaving it, like the syndicated *Red Badge,* "much worse than its original form." They were also capricious. Editors "who would not have wiped their old shoes on him before then" suddenly wanted to meet him. When the editor of a well-known magazine told Crane that he wished he could have published *The Red Badge,* Crane was silently amused: the magazine had actually rejected it. Now, however, his name alone was drawing attention. As a practical joke, Crane wrote a story and asked a friend to submit it for publication under his own name. When it was rejected, Crane resubmitted it to the same magazine, but this time under his own name.[24]

It was immediately accepted.[25]

13

On the Verge of Celebrity

JANUARY–OCTOBER 1895

IN EARLY 1895, after the success of the newspaper version of *The Red Badge of Courage,* Irving Bacheller hired Crane to travel to the West and South, then to Mexico, on what Crane called "a very long and circuitous newspaper trip" to write feature articles for the newly formed Bacheller, Johnson, and Bacheller syndicate. Before leaving, he tried to ensure additional work. After being lauded in the editorial offices of the *Philadelphia Press,* Crane returned to New York City and visited Ripley Hitchcock at D. Appleton and Company, bringing with him a letter of introduction, probably from Garland or Howells, and two newspaper stories as examples of his work. Crane was hoping to publish a collection of his stories; but when he mentioned the serialized *Red Badge,* Hitchcock asked to see it, and Crane mailed him newspaper clippings of the novel. In early February, Appleton accepted the novel for publication, though Crane did not sign a contract until mid-June, a month after returning from his trip. Unfortunately he was not a businessman. Although the contract stipulated that he would earn a royalty of 10 percent of annual sales, he would receive nothing from foreign-rights sales and no money until Appleton had recovered its total publication costs.[1]

Before heading west in late January, Crane gave Hitchcock the complete text of the novel. Exactly what it included has led to much debate about whether Hitchcock saw the original manuscript or a carbon copy of the revised version that had been typed for Bacheller's serialization.[2] The answer is important because vast differences exist between the manuscript of the novel (55,000 words) and the published Appleton book version (46,000). Portions of three chapters and a complete chapter were deleted from the manuscript and are not in the book version, but in other cases passages included in the manuscript are likewise missing from the book. Equally confusing is the source for the last sentence in the book, which does not appear in the manuscript. Unfortunately, the typescript (or typescripts) used by Appleton to prepare the novel for publication has been lost, and there is no documentary evidence to show conclusively whether Crane made these changes on his own or Hitchcock imposed them on him.

Hitchcock was an aggressive editor. In 1896 he insisted that Crane delete profanity and obscenity from *Maggie: A Girl of the Streets* before Appleton would publish it, and later he shaped Theodore Dreiser's *Jennie Gerhardt* (1911). Most famously, he transformed Edward Noyes Westcott's disorganized manuscript of *David Harum* (1898) into an enormously successful novel. Hitchcock was, as Post Wheeler described him, "the cleverest book-doctor of his time." Most likely, Crane gave Hitchcock not the original manuscript of 55,000 words but a revision in the form of either another manuscript or a carbon copy of the typescript originally prepared for Bacheller. While Crane was traveling, Hitchcock took the revised version, prepared another typescript, and sent it along with suggested revisions by express mail to Crane, who then made a number of corrections based on things he and Hitchcock had noticed in the text. Unfortunately, only one of Hitchcock's recommendations can be inferred with certainty: when he suggested that the title was too long, Crane proposed deleting the word "red." Clearly, however, Crane dictated the title, and this suggests that he had some control over the final contents of his novel, which he finished revising after returning from his trip in May. Although his professional relationship with Hitchcock seems to have been amicable, he was occasionally annoyed with other editors. He had already fought with Copeland and Day regarding the contents of *The Black Riders* and later objected to editorial revisions to his stories in the *Century* and *Saturday Evening Post*. As one literary agent explained to

Richard Watson Gilder, editor of the *Century,* "Of course you know how sensitive authors are about their literary children, and how much they dislike making any changes in them."[3]

At the end of January, Crane headed west "en route to kill Indians," as he joked to his friend Lucius L. Button.[4] He understood the Western myth of cowboys, renegades, and shoot-outs that was popularized in dime novels well known to every schoolboy. Yet he was also aware of the passing of the frontier. When the 1890 Census revealed that there was no longer a contiguous frontier line—that is, an area beyond which there were fewer than two people per square mile—the U.S. Census Bureau officially announced that the frontier was closed. Three years later, at the Columbian Exposition in Chicago, Frederick Jackson Turner examined the impact of the West on the American psyche in his famous speech, "The Significance of the Frontier in American History." Like an ocean wave, civilization had swept westward across the continent in the nineteenth century. Turner imaged the West as a "sea of grass" that pioneers had first sailed on in prairie schooners and later in trains, characterized by *Harper's Weekly* as "The Modern Ship of the Plains"; but he realized that with the disappearance of the frontier came industrial and social forces of a capitalistic system that would transform the land. Crane had already written about the West.[5] In May 1894, he had published "Billie Atkins Went to Omaha" (later retitled "An Excursion Ticket"), a minor story about a Bowery tramp's journey from Denver to Omaha on freight trains, and in October a burlesque sketch, "In a Park Row Restaurant," about the Wild West as a distinctly American concept. In January 1895 came his second Western story, "A Christmas Dinner Won in Battle," in which the "wave of progress" precipitated by the coming of the railroad changes a prairie town into an industrialized city.[6]

Crane's Western trip was a turning point in his personal outlook and professional career. Until 1895, his travels had been mostly limited to the area around Port Jervis, Asbury Park, and New York City. The West transformed him. Passing through Philadelphia and St. Louis, he headed for Lincoln, Nebraska, to cover a story that had been receiving national attention. Drought and windstorms during the previous summer and the frigid winter of 1894–1895 had impoverished the state. The devastating loss of crops and livestock had forced many families to flee; those who remained desperately needed assistance. The disaster was worsened by greed and corruption over shipments of food, supplies, and coal for indigent farmers, as well as by a growing perception among Nebraskans that businesses would avoid investing in the state. After arriving in Lincoln on February 1, Crane interviewed officials, then for three days traveled through the heart of the stricken area in the northern part of the state, where he interviewed farmers and huddled in an unheated hotel room while a snowstorm brought sixty-mile-an-hour winds and temperatures of fourteen to eighteen degrees below zero. The experience led to his first report on the trip, "Nebraska's Bitter Fight for Life," an encomium to farmers who relied "upon their endurance, their capacity to help each other, and their steadfast and unyielding courage."[7] Only months earlier, Crane had been questioning the nature of courage in his Civil War novel, but now his eyewitness experience of human dignity under siege by natural forces was tempering his cynicism.

During his stay in Lincoln, Crane visited the office of the *Nebraska State Journal* and met Willa Cather, a senior at the University of Nebraska, years away from becoming a major American author. In December she had copyedited the newspaper version of *The Red Badge of Courage* for the *Journal,* where she worked part time. She was struck by the disheveled clothing and gaunt appearance of the writer, whose melancholy eyes "seemed to be burning themselves out" and who "went about with the tense, preoccupied, self-centered air of a man who is brooding over some impending disaster." An aspiring author who skipped classes to see Crane, she wanted to learn about his method of composition and views on literature. At first, protective of his own thoughts and feelings, he responded frivolously to her questions. When she said that she admired Guy de Maupassant's short stories, he replied, "Oh, you're Moping, are you?" Eventually drawing him out, she expressed interest in what she called his "double literary life: writing in the first place the matter that pleased himself, and doing it very slowly; in the second place, any sort of stuff that would sell." He had realized, he told her, that he needed to support himself by writing marketable fluff because writing serious fiction was a painstaking process: "The detail of a thing has to filter through my blood, and then it comes out like a native product, but it takes forever." Cather then described a class she had recently taken, taught by Professor Lucius Sherman, head of the English Department at the University of Nebraska, whose book *Analytics of Literature: A Manual for the Objective Study of English Prose and Poetry* (1893) involved counting words and phrases. Cather rejected the technique; and when she mentioned it to Crane, he quickly responded, "Where did you get all that rot? Yarns aren't done by mathematics. You can't do it by rule any more than you can dance by rule. You have to have the itch of the thing in your fingers."[8]

Cather's partly fictionalized account of Crane, published after his death under the pseudonym "Henry Nicklemann," may describe her creative process more accurately than his, and her statements that he carried a volume of Poe in his back pocket and had hands resembling those of Aubrey Beardsley offer a romanticized portrait. Her brief encounter with him, however, remains the only eyewitness account of Crane's Western trip. Though her later comments about his work were occasionally bitter, she remained fascinated by him, concluding after his death that "all his life was a preparation for sudden departure."[9]

By the middle of February, Crane had left Lincoln and stopped briefly in Hot Springs, Arkansas, to report on the mineral baths. A self-described "youthful stranger with . . . blonde and innocent hair," he prided himself on having avoided being swindled in a barroom con game, though ironically he may have fallen for a popular scam later in Mexico City, where street vendors passed off cheap opals as expensive gems. Other unscrupulous vendors would fill birds with buckshot, to ensure that they would remain perched on an outstretched finger. Inevitably, the birds would die shortly after unsuspecting tourists had purchased them. Crane offered four rules of advice to unsuspecting travelers, the first and last being, "Do not buy anything at all from street vendors."[10]

On February 16, Crane arrived in New Orleans, where he attended the opera and enjoyed Mardi Gras. Finding the city exhilarating, he wrote Linson a letter in playfully fragmented French and mock German, telling him, "Friedweller die schonenberger je suis dans New Orleans." By the middle of March, he had visited Galveston and San Antonio, his experiences in both confirming that the Old West existed only in the romanticized vision of "travellers tumbling over each other in their haste to trumpet the radical differences between Eastern and Western life." Modernization's "sweeping march of the West," however, had erased many of the dissimilarities: "an illustration of Galveston streets can easily be obtained in Maine," and "the Gulf of Mexico could be mistaken for

the Atlantic Ocean." Crane criticized romantic depictions of the West
that were designed to lure tourists. Whereas a guidebook depicted San
Antonio as "three old ruins and a row of Mexicans sitting in the sun," it
was actually "a totally modern" city with "rows of handsome business
blocks."[11]

In *The Red Badge of Courage,* Crane had imagined a world in which
courage, honor, and bravery seemed mere abstractions; yet on his trip to
the West, he discovered the stoic endurance of Nebraskans and the heroic struggle of two hundred Texans who, in 1836, against insurmount-
able odds, withstood Santa Anna's army for twelve days. An admirer of
selfless actions, Crane declared, "The Alamo remains the greatest memorial to courage which civilization has allowed to stand." Unlike his earlier
journalism in Asbury Park and New York City, Crane's Western newspaper reports reveal his belief in the need for moral courage and the stoic
acceptance of one's duty under pressure. After his trip, Crane remarked
that he had

> always believed the western people to be much truer than the eastern
> people. We in the east are overcome a good deal by a detestable superficial
> culture which I think is the real barbarism. Culture in it's true sense, I take
> it, is a comprehension of the man at one's shoulder. It has nothing to do
> with an adoration for effete jugs and old kettles. This latter is merely an
> amusement and we live for amusement in the east. Damn the east! I fell
> in love with the straight out-and-out, sometimes-hideous, often-braggart
> westerners because I thought them to be the truer men and, by the living
> piper, we will see in the next fifty years what the west will do. They are
> serious, those fellows. When they are born they take one big gulp of wind
> and then they live.

Unlike Easterners, with their distorted values and artificial social con-
ventions, Westerners embraced self-reliance and rugged individualism.
Hamlin Garland, having grown up on farms in Wisconsin, Iowa, and the
Dakota Territory, epitomized these virtues. "To Hamlin Garland / of the
great honest West," wrote his disciple in a copy of *George's Mother,* "From
Stephen Crane / of the false East."[12]

In San Antonio, Crane took in the night life. On one occasion Frank
Bushick, editor of the *San Antonio Express,* took Crane to see the Chili

Queens, colorfully dressed women who enticed passersby to their open-air stands in the plazas to buy food that, according to Crane, tasted "exactly like pounded fire-brick from hades." Troubadours serenaded customers, while the Queens charmed them with their banter. Calling Crane a "goodlookin' compañero," Martha, one of the most famous Queens, asked him playfully, "Does your mother know you're out?" "Yes," he replied, "I've heard a lot about you and that's why I came around to see you." "Oh, my!" she joked, "You're a big kidder too," then pinned a rose on his coat as a sign of her affection.[13]

Crane arrived in Mexico City on March 19, 1895, and remained in Mexico for nine weeks. In "Stephen Crane in Mexico (II)," his account of the two-and-a-half-day, thousand-mile train trip from San Antonio, he was an "archaeologist from Boston" who had once attended a Northern school with Cubans (Crane's allusion to his Eastern roots and his experience with Cubans at Claverack) and who was traveling with a "capitalist from Chicago." Crane contrasted the ways in which he and the capitalist responded to "these black curtains of darkness which intervened between them and the new and strange life" they encountered in Mexico. The capitalist bragged about his children and his personal wealth; in a country with an exchange rate of two-to-one in favor of the American dollar, he "jingled his coin with glee" and boasted, "Doubled my money!" In contrast, Crane the archaeologist unearthed the cultural heritage of Mexico for his American readers. As he had been doing throughout the trip, he immersed himself in the local culture. He climbed the mile-high Popocatépetl, joking beforehand that whether he would "be well afterward is a matter of speculation," and attended such popular entertainments as the circus, which he loved, and bullfighting, which he disliked because of the "cold, sinister, merciless" bullfighter, who was little more than "an executioner, a kind of moral assassin." Given Crane's love of horses, he was especially disturbed by their frequent maiming during the spectacle.[14]

Although Crane's newspaper dispatches treated the local residents humorously, he tried to understand and empathize with their culture. Among the dispatches, an untitled essay, sometimes referred to as "Above All Things" or "The Mexican Lower Classes," remained unpublished in his lifetime, perhaps because Bacheller found it too controversial. The piece explores the difficulty of writing about a culture that one is not thoroughly familiar with and about arrogant travelers who judge foreigners by their own standards: "It perhaps might be said—if any one dared—that the most worthless literature of the world has been that which has been written by the men of one nation concerning the men of another." Crane was impressed with the ability of Mexicans, despite their poverty, to accept their fate serenely and be "exceedingly devout, worshipping with a blind faith," unlike the urban poor Crane had depicted in his New York City sketches. Although Crane did not sentimentalize the plight of Mexicans—"I even refuse to pity them"—he disapproved of economic injustice whether he encountered it in Mexico or New York or Pennsylvania. Crane rarely used the first-person pronoun in his writings, but in that essay it occurs repeatedly and as many as five times in a short paragraph of three sentences, suggesting the deeply personal nature of the dispatch. When he discouraged writers from sitting "in literary judgment on this or that manner of the people," he was acknowledging his own difficulty in understanding, and empathizing with, a "new point of view."[15]

As soon as Crane returned from Mexico in mid-May, he gave Bacheller an itemized list of expenses, which included the cost of a revolver, one of the items he had supposedly bought for the trip. For the first time in his life, Crane had had an expense account, though his handling of it revealed his occasionally unethical behavior. Nelson Greene had come along on the excursion; and as soon as he saw the revolver, he mentioned that it looked like one he had seen before, but Crane quickly dismissed the similarity. When alone with Greene, however, he chided him for being a "damned fool. Why did you want to try to queer me like that. I borrowed the gun . . . to pad out my expense account."[16] It would not be the last time he acted dishonorably.

Finishing his business, Crane fled to Hartwood to recuperate from the trip.[17] Although it had been exhausting, he returned with fond memories and an altered point of view and spoke excitedly about his adventures to family and friends. "Magnificent! Magnificent!" was the way he described a religious procession in Mexico; and when he visited Linson, there "was a riot of talk. For once his tongue found freedom."[18] For the rest of his life, he would proudly display the pistol, serape, and riding gear he had acquired on the trip, and would value them more than his fourteen newspaper dispatches, which Bacheller considered "vivid."[19] Later he would often allude to his Western experience in conversation and in writing, as in the 1898 war dispatch "Grand Rapids and Ponce." And it would inspire him to write several Western short stories that include two of his most famous tales, "The Bride Comes to Yellow Sky" and "The Blue Hotel," which dramatize—one comically, the other tragically—the natural consequences of the Easternization of the American West.

When Crane returned from his trip, in May, Copeland and Day had just published *The Black Riders and Other Lines.* The book had a distinctive interior design: untitled poems appeared in all capital letters, preceded by roman numerals, and each poem was placed at the top of a separate page. Although Crane seemed pleased with the design, he had not collaborated with the publisher on the book's production and cared little about the matter. The manuscripts of Crane's poems reveal no special regard for layout and a completely conventional use of capitalization. When Copeland and Day told him that they planned to print the book in a format "more severely classic than any book ever yet issued in America," he misunderstood the statement to mean that they wanted to use "old English type" and was worried because "some of my recent encounters with it have made me think I was working out a puzzle." When they clarified the matter by sending him a sample page, he accepted their choices for layout and typography. He also quickly accepted the Copeland and Day's standardization of his idiosyncratic punctuation and their rejection of the initial cover design, which Crane had liked and which had been done by his friend Frederick C. Gordon. Although Crane read the page proofs, he was not interested in seeing corrected proofs. (He took the same approach with *The Red Badge of Courage.*) He did object to the poems' being "paragraphed"— his word for "separated into stanzas"—but this was not a major issue for him.[20]

Crane insisted, however, on calling his poems "lines" to emphasize his break with literary tradition, and he became "enraged at the word 'poet' which continually reminds me of long-hair and seems to me to be a most detestable form of insult." Written in free verse, the lines are short, pithy explorations of cosmic issues about the nature of God and existence. Unlike the conventional, genteel poetry popular at the time, the lines dramatize a stark internal monologue in which Crane explores love, war, religion, and morality and confronts the spiritual beliefs of his ancestors. With the exception of articles, prepositions, and conjunctions, the most frequently repeated words in *The Black Riders* are "I" (200 times), its variations—"he" (102), "my" (95), "me" (89), and "you" (84)—and "God" (82). Crane later said in 1896 that it was his most autobiographical work. Though he had rejected the image of an unforgiving, wrathful God as portrayed by the ministers George and Jesse Peck, it haunted him throughout his life as he struggled with his own psychological and religious identity.

> "Think as I think," said a man,
> "Or you are abominably wicked;
> "You are a toad."

To which Crane's inner voice replies:

> "I will, then, be a toad."

Nowhere was the rebellion more acute than in the poem that begins with an epigraph from Exodus 20:5—"And the sins of the fathers shall be visited upon the heads of the children, even unto the third and fourth generation of them that hate me." Against this, Crane lashes out:

> Well, then, I hate Thee, unrighteous picture;
> Wicked image, I hate Thee. . . .

Repudiating the idols of religious and literary tradition, Crane dedicated *The Black Riders and Other Lines* to Garland, whose similarly iconoclastic *Crumbling Idols* gave his literary son permission to break away from tradition. Yet despite defying a wrathful God and even questioning His existence, Crane sensed

> . . . another god,—
> The god of his inner thoughts.
> And this one looked at him
> With soft eyes
> Lit with infinite comprehension,
> And said, "My poor child!"

The search for "The god of his inner thoughts"—one that also "whispers in the heart / So softly"—was what Emerson called the need for each individual to establish an "original relation to the universe." For Crane, as for Emerson, religious authority was indwelling. Crane rebelled against doctrinaire orthodoxy, but he sought reassurance from a lost father, a safe haven within one's own uncertainties, a spiritual refuge away from the darkness and into the marvelous light.[21]

Crane valued *The Black Riders and Other Lines* more than *The Red Badge of Courage* because "the former is the more ambitious effort. In it I aim to give my ideas of life as a whole, so far as I know it, and the latter is a mere episode,—an amplification."[22] His poetic style reveals these ideas. The structure of the lines is based on allegory and parable, literary forms traditionally used to dramatize the significance of events and moral principles. In *The Black Riders* a question is often asked, its traditional answer is rejected, and a new answer—or no answer—is the result. Because the meaning of Crane's lines is implicit, they can be interpreted in various ways, thus creating confusion, the way the parables of Jesus confused his disciples—a point that Crane would have remembered while writing his verse. Meaning thus becomes problematic in *The Black Riders:* the diction is sparse, settings lack detail, and statements or situations are often connected with the word "then," which merely introduces additional information in a time sequence. Syntax—or more broadly language itself—does not convey ultimate meaning. Instead, one is left with the indeterminate nature of Truth, Reality, and God and the insignificance of human actions. Just as Crane's lines are gnomic, so too is Existence.[23]

Upon publication, *The Black Riders* created an immediate stir. Although some reviewers dismissed the collection as "slovenly work" and "poetic lunacy," others compared Crane to Whitman and Dickinson, proclaimed him "the Aubrey Beardsley of Poetry," and pronounced it "the most notable contribution to literature to which the present year has given birth." Crane's distinctive poetic style prompted a number of parodies, which Post Wheeler dubbed "stephencranelets." Parody was a popular genre in late nineteenth-century literature, and no other American writer was more frequently parodied at the time than Crane following the publication of *The Black Riders.* In one parody, "After Stephen Crane," his poem "I have heard the sunset song of the birches" finds its counterpart in "I have smelled the sunset song of the lobsters"; in another, "After the Manner of Mr. Steamin' Stork," "I saw a man pursuing the horizon" is recast as "I saw a man making a fool of himself." Crane laughed at the parodies of *The Black Riders,* though when reviewers ridiculed the book's design, he reassured Copeland and Day that he supported their decisions about it: "I see they have been pounding the wide margins, the capitals and all that but I think it great." Howells had taught him to discount reviews. Once, Crane had complained about reviewers who wanted to read only "beautiful stories." Amused, Howells had advised him not to take them seriously: "Most of these reviews were written by young girls or boys. Whoever is available at the hand of the Editor gets to write a review."[24]

Curiously *The Black Riders* caught the attention of two then-unknown American writers. In 1899, Jack London sent a poem imitating Crane's style to his friend Cloudsley Johns and introduced him to "as strange a volume as has been put out in many a day—O, it's already old."[25] Years later, Carl Sandburg praised Crane's poetry as "terribly serious work in libertarian rhythms" and composed "Letters to Dead Imagists" in honor of Crane and Dickinson.[26] Sandburg identified with both of them; and when he struggled with publishing his own poetry, he tried an experiment. Along with several of his poems that had been rejected by editors, he included two from *The Black Riders* and one poem from Dickinson, without identifying their source, and gave the packet to three well-established readers. Although one reader stated that a couple of the poems (Crane's) were publishable, the other two readers rejected all of them and, quipped Sandburg, "threw Crane and Emily Dickinson into the discard along with Sandburg."[27]

Shortly after returning to New York City, Crane attended meetings of the Lantern (variously spelled "Lanthorn" or "Lanthorne") Club, which Irving Bacheller (the permanent president), Willis Brooks Hawkins, Edward and I. D. Marshall, Charles W. Hooke (a.k.a. "Howard Fielding"), and Crane had formed in December 1894.[28] After an initial fee of twenty dollars, members paid two dollars in monthly dues.[29] The club first met on Monkey Hill on William Street, near the Brooklyn Bridge and the newspaper buildings of Park Row in lower Manhattan; but it soon moved to 126 William Street into what was reputedly the oldest house in the city—the former home of Captain Kidd and later a refuge for George Washington and other generals during the American Revolution. Located in a shanty on the roof of the house, with a lantern and an antique key above the entrance, the club room was decorated as a ship's cabin.[30] Prominent on its walls was a horse's skull found near Sleepy Hollow, New York. Taking advantage of the fact that Washington Irving had been born and had lived nearby on William Street, club members joked that the skull came from Ichabod Crane's horse, Gunpowder, in Irving's "The Legend of Sleepy Hollow." At the entrance hung a sign that read, "No games of chance," prompting one journalist, upon leaving, to joke, "That's right. You haven't a chance."[31]

Letting "their hair grow long and their minds grow high," as Bacheller remarked, members prohibited a dress code and the title "Mr." A cook prepared lunch daily and dinner on Saturday evenings. Every other Saturday, a member read a draft of one of his new poems or short stories; then colleagues discussed only its weaknesses, not its strengths. Applause was likewise forbidden, so the highest praise an author got was complete silence in response to his draft. Crane said little at the gatherings, but eventually read "The Wise Men," an unexceptional short story that, as its subtitle suggests, was little more than "A Detail of American Life in Mexico." It is unknown what comments the story elicited from club members; but because Crane apparently did not try to publish it immediately, he must have recognized that it was undistinguished. Ironically, H. G. Wells later considered it "a perfect thing. . . . I cannot imagine how it could possibly have been better told," and it helped the club raise money to pay rent and other expenses. Facing financial problems in 1898, the club printed and sold autographed copies of *The Lanthorn Book: Being a Small Collection of Tales and Verses Read at the Sign o' the Lanthorn, 126 William Street, New York.* The opening piece, the longest in the book, was "The Wise Men."[32]

In another attempt to raise money, Bacheller suggested that club members start a children's newspaper and argued that, by giving watches and other prizes to children who solicited subscriptions, they could build a substantial circulation. Crane and Albert Bigelow Paine were among those interested in pursuing the project; and as they left the club one evening, one of them noticed a line of tramps outside a bakery awaiting a free loaf of bread: "A year from tonight we will come here and give a dollar bill to each of the men on the line." Although the paper was founded, it never generated enough subscriptions to compete against the more popular *St. Nicholas Magazine* and the *Youth's Companion,* which in the 1890s had a circulation of half a million. Paine dramatized the club's failed attempt to start a successful paper in his novel *The Bread Line: A Story of a Paper* (1900), which ends with the members, who have lost everything in their venture, standing together in the same breadline.[33]

Occasionally the club invited distinguished guests such as Stanford White, Ethel Barrymore, and Theodore Roosevelt to join them, making only one request: that they write something on the burlap-covered walls before leaving. Julian Hawthorne, Nathaniel's son, wrote, "The best thing in the world is a good man—but a good woman is better"; Howells stumbled with "I can't think of anything to save me"; and novelist Edward Eggleston, parodying Crane's poetry, inscribed:

Lines by a prose writer

_____

_____

_____

_____

Among the most memorable celebrities that Crane would have met at the club was Samuel Langhorne Clemens, who was fifty-nine years old at the time. Linson recalled that Crane liked Clemens but that he considered most of his writing, with the exception of *Life on the Mississippi,* unrealistic:

"This whoop over his stuff contaminates the air."

"Now, Steve, you don't mean all that. Of course, anybody can shoot holes in anybody. Mark's all right."

"I didn't say HIM, I said his *stuff.* Sam Clemens is all right, but Mark Twain—."[34]

Clemens and Crane knew each other, even if only casually. Clemens apparently wrote at least one letter to him, visited the Lantern Club several times, and was the guest of honor at a luncheon in July 1895.[35] Crane would almost certainly have been there. After returning to New York City in mid-May from his trip out west, he ate lunch regularly at the club, used it as his mailing address, and even occasionally slept there.[36]

Although he already knew at least two other important American writers—Garland and Howells—this may have been the first time he had
met a truly international celebrity. Crane was probably asked if he was
related to Clemens's brother-in-law, Theodore Crane, though this was
unlikely. Of the five colonial ancestors of the Cranes, the Stephen Crane
who had helped to found Elizabethtown, New Jersey, was the origin
of Stephen's line; Theodore's began with another of those progenitors.
Yet in reply to Clemens's question, Crane might have said yes. Confused
about his own genealogy, he wrongly believed that his Revolutionary
namesake Stephen Crane was the son of Jasper Crane, a founder of Newark, New Jersey. He also believed that Jasper Crane and the Stephen
Crane who had helped to found Elizabethtown were related. Despite
Stephen's confusion, the belief that he was related to Clemens's brother-
in-law may have prompted conversation between the two authors.[37]

Crane would also have been interested in hearing about Clemens's
brief Civil War experience, recounted in the semi-autobiographical short
story "The Private History of a Campaign That Failed" (1885), which
had been written for the *Century*'s "Battles and Leaders of the Civil War"
series. Of the more than one hundred writers in the series, only Clemens
described his feelings. Crane would have noticed the contrast between
the dry accounts of military details elsewhere in the series and Clemens's
dramatic portrayal of a youth whose desertion on the battlefield initiates
him into the realities of war. Because Crane had recently written his
own account of the private history of another Civil War youth, he would
have been keen on discovering whether Twain had read *The Red Badge of
Courage.*[38]

During the next few months, Crane floundered in his attempt to market himself and his work. He arranged for a copy of *The Black Riders*
to be sent to Karl Knortz, an author and educator who had translated
Henry Wadsworth Longfellow and John Greenleaf Whittier into German and had done much to introduce American literature to his native
Prussia. Only *Maggie* was translated into German during Crane's lifetime.
Apparently, Crane also discussed with Copeland and Day the possibility
of reprinting *Maggie;* but when he could not locate a copy—Crane routinely misplaced manuscripts and books—he offered them "eight little
grotesque tales of the woods which I wrote when I was clever."[39] But
after he could not find copies of the Sullivan County tales and sketches,

the deal fell through. He also submitted *A Woman Without Weapons,* the original title of *George's Mother,* to an unknown publisher; it did not appear until a year later, which suggests that it might have been initially rejected. In September he thought he had been hired as a drama critic for the *Philadelphia Press,* but the offer was rescinded. Crane was inept at business negotiations; and had he not had the assistance of influential professionals like Garland, Howells, and Bacheller writing him letters of support and introducing him to the right people, he might never have become famous.

By August, Crane was back in Pike County for another summer camping trip and was looking at page proofs of *The Red Badge,* though he did not "care much to see" them because he had grown tired of the project. Since completing the book in the spring of 1894, he had finished *George's Mother,* established his reputation as a journalist, and published *The Black Riders,* and was already thinking about his next novel. In October, he moved in with Edmund's family in Hartwood. As much as he enjoyed city life, he needed regularly to escape from it. In Pike County he was "cruising around the woods. . . . I have lots of fun getting healthy. Feel great"—a sobering reminder that his frail constitution benefited from clean mountain air. Hartwood was just as energizing. What could be "finer than a fine frosty morning, a runaway horse, and only the still hills to watch. Lord, I do love a crazy horse with just a little pig-skin between him and me." He also enjoyed the freedom from constant deadlines "I am working pretty well here. Better than in New York."—and he was comfortable with setting his own pace: "I haven't written a line yet. Dont intend to for some time." Crane also brought to Hartwood his few items of furniture and other belongings, including a cloisonné teapot and plaster wall plaques of Mozart and Beethoven, evidence of his appreciation for exceptional music and craftsmanship. "If I don't come back," he told Edmund's wife, "these things are yours." One might ask: Back from where? Some future trip? Or was he alluding to life itself? Crane was convinced he would not live long and valued only a handful of material objects, such as his Civil War swords and the riding gear from his Western trip.[40]

Crane's frail body, constant cough, and sallow complexion suggested that he had contracted tuberculosis in childhood, as had other family members. His Aunt Agnes and his brother William suffered from bleeding lungs, and she died from the condition. His brother George, gaunt even as a child, had a chronic cough, and his sister Nellie was forced to leave home to recover from a serious illness, in all likelihood tuberculosis. Long considered a hereditary disease, its infectious nature was not established until the late nineteenth century. Crane would have been exposed to it during his investigations of New York City's tenement districts. At the time, the city had one of the highest rates of tuberculosis in the world, and nowhere was it more prevalent than in the crowded Bowery slums.[41]

So numerous were the artists who contracted tuberculosis—Chopin, Mozart, Keats, and Poe among them—that it became known as a "romantic disease" that could bestow the aura of genius. "I should like to die of consumption," wrote Lord Byron in 1828. "The ladies would all say, 'Look at that poor Byron, how interesting he looks in dying!'" Crane would soon begin writing his novel *The Third Violet,* in which he paid homage to Giuseppe Verdi's opera *La Traviata,* one of the century's great works dramatizing the impact of tuberculosis. Like Verdi's heroine, Violetta, exhausted by her restless life, Crane was convinced that he would not live long. His wall plaque of Mozart, who died at age thirty-five, reminded him of that. In 1895, before Crane became famous, he had told Willa Cather that he was uncertain about his professional and financial future. When she had said that he would probably be famous in ten years, he had quickly replied, "I can't wait ten years, I haven't time." Crane's realization from childhood that he would most likely die young explains his almost obsessive need to take risks and test his limits—for example, when he spent four days and three nights dressed as a tramp in freezing weather in order to experience poverty firsthand in the slums of New York City; or when he later stood up in the line of fire during the Spanish-American War in order to experience what Hemingway would later call "grace under pressure." Of the few books he kept in college, none was more cherished than *The Poetical Works of John Keats,* which included a biographical introduction by James Russell Lowell. In reading Lowell's description of a poet who had lived briefly but intensely, Crane saw his own life. "We were designed in the cradle, perhaps earlier," wrote Lowell, "and it is in finding out this design, and shaping ourselves to it, that our years are spent wisely." Keats had found his design; so, too, had Crane.[42]

Part III

FAME, NOTORIETY,
AN ALTERED POINT OF VIEW

14

International Fame

IN PORT JERVIS, New York, on July 5, 1886, ten thousand people watched a three-mile-long parade that culminated at Orange Square for the dedication of a monument to Civil War veterans. A local newspaper touted the celebration as the city's finest day.[1] Several years later, at the site of the monument (across the street from where Crane had lived in Port Jervis), the aspiring novelist most likely talked with veterans of the 124th New York State Volunteer Regiment, known as the Orange Blossoms, who had initially seen combat at the Battle of Chancellorsville, fought in late April–early May 1863. *The Red Badge of Courage* is based on the battle, and the 124th became the model for Crane's fictional 304th Regiment. In all likelihood, veterans' reminiscences about the realities of combat tempered whatever enthusiasm Crane initially had to write a potboiler depicting war romantically. More than any other battle during the Civil War, the Battle of Chancellorsville revealed the tragic irony of combat. Although Robert E. Lee won the battle, it was a Pyrrhic victory. The Confederate Army suffered enormous casualties and lost its brilliant General "Stonewall" Jackson, who was accidentally wounded by his own men during the battle and died shortly thereafter.

Besides listening to veterans and perusing the "Battles and Leaders,"

Crane might have read any of the published personal narratives written by Civil War veterans, as well as nineteenth-century war fiction such as Stendhal's *Charterhouse of Parma* (1839), Tolstoy's *Sebastopol* (1855), and Zola's *La Débâcle* (1892). He probably had no single source, but was writing within a tradition of unromanticized art, photographs, and first-hand accounts depicting the loneliness, terror, and confusion of the common soldier during the Civil War. Crane's desire to break literary rules is clear if one compares *The Red Badge of Courage* with other war fiction of the nineteenth century. Heavily influenced by Sir Walter Scott, novelists treated war as a romantic adventure involving patriotic heroes who fought chivalrously for honorable causes. The plots of the novels were melodramatic and often had a domestic love story. Although a few of Crane's contemporaries wrote realistically about war, none of them succeeded as well as he did in capturing the intensity of combat and parodying romantic treatments of war. At the outset of *The Red Badge,* when Henry Fleming complains that the tall soldier's description of a rumored imminent battle will be incorrect like so many other rumors—"like as not this story'll turn out jest like them others did"—Crane is also alerting the reader to his own intention: his story will differ from the usual war fiction.[2]

None of Crane's other works would be as pioneering and influential as his Civil War novel. In changing the title from *Private Fleming: His Various Battles* to *The Red Badge of Courage: An Episode of the American Civil War,* Crane signaled that the real struggle in his novel is internal, not external. With the exception of passing references to Washington, Richmond, and the Rappahannock River, he avoided all social, political, and historical markers connected with the war.[3] Rather than concentrating on details such as weaponry, battlefield tactics, and other military issues, Crane examined the workings of the youth's ever-changing emotional state and attitude toward bravery and war. Throughout the book, the focus is on Henry's fragmented, disconnected experiences over two days. He knows little about what is going on around him. Often he hears only rumors; and when he tries to see clearly, he is stymied by darkness, smoke, and gunfire. Readers are provided only an inexperienced recruit's subjective impressions, conveyed through striking imagery and metaphors. No other American novel relies so heavily on color as *The Red Badge.* Like Impressionist painters, Crane recreated the sensory impressions that color and light have on the eye. The focus was on the individual's fleeting, subjective perception of reality rather than on an attempt to recreate reality objectively. Clouds are "sorry blue," a blue uniform has "faded to a melancholy shade of green," and Fleming's romantic illusions about warfare are deflated with a "yellow light thrown upon the color of his ambitions."[4]

Structurally and thematically, *The Red Badge of Courage* deals with Fleming's rites of passage. On the first day, he flees from the battlefield and deserts his comrades. Variously justifying his actions and feeling guilty about them, he longs for a wound, a symbol of bravery, to offset his cowardice. He soon receives it, not from the front end of a Confederate's rifle, but from the butt end of the rifle of a frightened, retreating Northern soldier. The next day Henry is reunited with his comrades, who believe that his wound is a "red badge of courage." He fights valorously and carries the regiment's flag, even though doing so makes him an easy target. By the end of the novel, he feels "a quiet man-hood." Whether he has indeed become a mature hero or is still the victim of his own romantic illusions at the end of the story has been a hotly debated issue. Given Henry's constant shifts between smug confidence and self-doubt, some readers find it difficult to accept that a youth could suddenly gain maturity after only two days. The ambiguous conclusion, however, exemplifies Crane's commitment to psychological realism. Henry has learned about the nature of fear and courage and is proud of his accomplishments on the second day of battle, but he is bothered by his desertion of his unit and of the tattered soldier. He feels concern, however, not out of moral compunction but out of fear of being exposed as a coward. He has matured in terms of knowledge and experience, but he still rationalizes away the ethical consequences of his behavior. The image in the last sentence of the novel—an observation by the narrator, not Henry—reiterates the ambivalence: "Over the river a golden ray of sun came through the hosts of leaden rain clouds." Just as there can be sun and rain, so can Henry be socially, but not ethically, mature.[5]

Henry's uneven development occurs in a world where nature is indifferent and human actions seem insignificant. Communication is ineffectual, as troops "stuttered and stammered" and are "blubbering" and "babbling." In combat, they "dropped here and there like bundles." Officers act foolishly. One "raged" like "a spoiled child"; another "was galloping about bawling." At the end of the story, the Union troops end up at the same location they started from, as though nothing had been accomplished. In the midst of the action, nature, with its "deep aversion to tragedy," ignores the horror of war. As the battle rages on, "a cloud of dark smoke as from smoldering ruins went up toward the sun now bright and gay in the blue, enamelled sky." Though Henry momentarily believes that the landscape offers him a "religion of peace," with its chapel-like "high, arching boughs," he is terrified to find a decaying corpse, suggesting there is no harmony between nature and humanity. In the original manuscript of *The Red Badge,* Henry's mother gives him a Bible; but in revision, Crane deleted the passage because he believed that traditional religion was insufficient as a guide through late nineteenth-century America's spiritual crises.[6]

The Red Badge of Courage redefined American war fiction and has become the touchstone against which other war novels are judged. An immediate bestseller, it went through two, possibly three, printings in 1895 and perhaps a dozen more in America in 1896 and has never been out of print.[7] H. L. Mencken, whose discovery of the new author's work in the 1890s helped convince him to pursue a career in journalism, recalled that the publication of *The Red Badge* was "like a flash of lightning out of a clear winter sky; it was at once unprecedented and irresistible."[8] Ernest Hemingway believed that with one exception (*Miss Ravenal's Conversion from Secession to Loyalty,* by John William DeForest) there was no "real literature of our Civil War" until Crane's novel. William Faulkner considered it "the only good war story I know." And F. Scott Fitzgerald, criticizing Hollywood for its unrealistic treatments of the Civil War, encouraged filmmakers to read the book.[9]

From the outset, the book has been at the center of two controversies: Which country, the United States or Great Britain, first recognized Crane's genius, and did the book constitute unpatriotic criticism of American soldiers? Though American reviewers quickly praised the book's literary style, psychological realism, and ironic treatment of war—topics that today are still widely discussed—English reviewers were generally more incisive. George Wyndham, the most perceptive critic of *The Red Badge* during Crane's life, was an army veteran, politician, and literary scholar whose review influenced the favorable response to it in England and is still one of the best introductions to the book. Crane's portrayal of war, he thought, was "more complete than Tolstoi's, more true than Zola's." Wyndham distinguished between war accounts written by "gallant soldiers" interested "in strategy and tactics"—articles of the sort found in "Battles and Leaders of the Civil War"—and Crane's strikingly original, limited perspective on a recruit's struggles with fear, indecision, and warring emotions. Crane typically ignored reviews: "There is only one person in the world who knows less than the average reader. He is the average reviewer." But he admired Wyndham, who "has reproduced in a large measure my own hopeful thoughts of the book when it was still for the most part in my head."[10]

Amid the widespread praise in England and America, the book was also criticized, most notably in the American magazine the *Dial*. The associate editor, William Morton Payne, dismissed it in a perfunctory review, and the magazine's owner, Civil War veteran General Alexander C. McClurg, denounced the book as "a vicious satire upon American soldiers and American armies." Incorrectly assuming that it had first been published in England, General McClurg condemned it as an English attempt to embarrass American soldiers by dismissing them as either cowardly or ineffectual. Responses from supporters and critics were immediate. Agreeing with McClurg, J. L. Onderdonk, a newspaper editor from Idaho, ridiculed the book as a "literary absurdity. . . . If this work is realism, it is realism run mad, rioting in all that is revolting to man's best instincts, and utterly false to nature and to life." But in letters to the *Dial*, Ripley Hitchcock provided background on the publication of *The Red Badge* and cited favorable reviews; and British journalist Sydney Brooks criticized McClurg for his "misjudged patriotism and bad criticism."[11]

Of all the reviews, the one by Howells may have troubled Crane the most. In June 1895, Howells praised *Maggie* for its realistic use of dialect. Despite its profanity, violence, and melodrama, it became his favorite work by Crane. But in October he was ambivalent about *The Red Badge*: it could have been more concise and realistic in its depiction of war, he thought. And although "the psychological side" of the book was worthwhile, its primary significance was that it suggested "the greater things that we may hope from a new talent working upon a high level, not quite clearly as yet, but strenuously." Howells was lukewarm about *The Red Badge* and *The Black Riders* because he did not consider them serious literature.[12]

Crane felt that he had disappointed one of his literary mentors. After Garland had introduced him to Howells's work in 1891, Crane had begun reading extensively and formulating a literary credo: "I decided that the nearer a writer gets to life the greater he becomes as an artist, and most of my prose writings have been toward the goal partially described by that misunderstood and abused word, realism. Tolstoi is the writer I admire most of all." Crane's admiration for realism and for the literary ideals of Tolstoy reiterated Howells's position in his popular introduction to a fine 1888 translation of Tolstoy's war novel *Sebastopol* (1855), which Crane had probably read in Asbury Park around 1891–1892. He waited, though, until August 1896 to inscribe a copy of *The Red Badge* for Howells, proffering thanks from himself, in the third person, "for many things he has learned of the common man and, above all, for a certain readjustment of his point of view victoriously concluded some time in 1892." But Crane never sent the book to Howells, possibly because he reconsidered the validity of the inscription. In fact, Crane's war novel did not reflect an adjusted point of view: it was purely an imaginative construction, rather than an accurate, realistic depiction of life based on observation and experience—the type of fiction advocated by Howells. Realizing that the novel avoided Howellsian realism, Crane was not proclaiming "triumphant shouts" over its success, because he feared that doing so might "turn me ever so slightly from what I believe to be the pursuit of truth."[13]

Regardless of the mixed response that Howells gave to Crane's writings, Crane remained indebted to him for the "interest which you have shown in my work." Along with Garland, Howells helped Crane to understand another battle: the one in the literary marketplace between realistic and romantic writers. Realists like Garland and Howells criticized romantic stories—which relied on action rather than character development, on predictable clichés, and on melodramatic treatments of love, adventure, and combat—because the true purpose of such tales was to offer an escape from the daily realities of life. Instead, realists strove to represent accurately the speech, settings, and circumstances of ordinary people, in ordinary situations, facing complex ethical choices. F. Marion Crawford, one of the most popular nineteenth-century writers of romantic fiction, distinguished romantic fiction, intended "to amuse and interest the reader," from that "odious thing, a 'purpose-novel'": "A man buys what purports to be a work of fiction, a romance, a novel, a story of adventure, pays his money, takes his book home, prepares to enjoy it at his ease, and discovers that he has paid a dollar for somebody's views on socialism, religion, or the divorce laws." As Crawford stated bluntly, the profession of storytelling involved the practical matter of how to sell one's commodity. The titles of melodramatic fiction by two Chicago writers and publishers, Paul James Duff and William Wilson Knott, exemplified the attempt to market books so as to lure readers of romance as well as realism. Duff's books included *Tessie's Temptation: A Realistic Story of Woman's Love and Man's Weakness* (ca. 1895) and *Rosa's Confession: A Realistic Romance of Love and Adventure* (1897), while Knott penned *Forbidden Fruit: A Story with a Purpose* (ca. 1893) and *His Fatal Wager: A Highly Sensational and Realistic Novel* (ca. 1894). By 1894, romantic writers were winning the battle for readership with popular novels like *Trilby,* George Du Maurier's sinister tale of romance and sentimentality, and *The Prisoner of Zenda,* Anthony Hope's story of political intrigue.[14]

Crane's syndicated interview with Howells, "Howells Fears the Realists Must Wait," in October 1894, expressed their joint concern that the popularity of romantic fiction would delay the acceptance of realism. Just as Garland's *Crumbling Idols* had shaped Crane's literary views, so too did Howells's theoretical statements in *Criticism and Fiction* (1891), which were summarized in the interview. Romantic novels were unrealistic, Howells insisted, because they equated life with "love and courtship": "Life began when the hero saw a certain girl, and it ended abruptly when he married her." A realistic novel, however, kept love and courtship in perspective and saw them not as the whole of life but simply as part of it.[15]

Recognizing that he risked losing income if he ignored popular taste, Crane speculated in the interview whether realistic novels would be "a profitable investment" in an age when readers preferred romance to the accurate portrayal of daily life. If fiction was a commodity to be bought by a publisher and sold to a consumer, then one's stock would be bullish or bearish on the literary stock market, depending on public acceptance. Though Howells encouraged every realistic writer to remain "true to his conscience," he acknowledged that the battle between private vision and public demand would be "a long serious conflict." Because the fate of American fiction was partly being decided by popular taste, realists faced a dilemma: Should they strive for an honest interpretation of reality, or should they simply cater to the public demand for romance and become, as Howells called them, "public fools" acting like a "trained bear" in a circus or sideshow? Or could they write in both worlds without discrediting their goals?[16]

By refusing to be a trained bear in his pursuit of the writer's profession, Crane recognized the difficulty of his position. In his short career, he had been repeatedly frustrated by publishers. In 1893, when no one would publish *Maggie,* he had printed it at his own expense. In 1894, he had battled with two publishers: negotiations over the publication of *The Black Riders and Other Lines* had temporarily stalled because Crane disagreed with Copeland and Day; and he had become convinced that S. S. McClure had treated him poorly by holding on to the manuscript of *The Red Badge of Courage* for six months without taking action. By the time of the interview with Howells in October 1894, professional setbacks had strained Crane's patience; and although he was only two months away from national recognition with the newspaper publication of *The Red Badge,* he was still a year away from commercial success and international acclaim with the book publication.

In the fall of 1895, Crane fictionalized these issues in *The Third Violet,* a novel set at a country resort and in New York City. Its genesis was a series of vignettes written a year earlier—"Stories Told by an Artist," "The Silver Pageant," and "In a Park Row Restaurant"—about bohemian life in the old Art Students League building, experiences that he drew upon for half of the novel. Beginning it in mid-October, Crane "adopted such a 'quick' style for the story" that by the time he had finished it in late December, he concluded that it was "pretty rotten work." After letting Edmund read part of the manuscript, Crane summarized his brother's response: the tale's "style wouldn't be used by the devil to patch his trousers with." Later, Crane described the novel as "serious work," but reviewers disagreed. Serialized in newspapers during October–November 1896 and published by Appleton in May 1897, it was quickly dismissed as a "vacuous trifle."[17]

On the surface, *The Third Violet* exemplifies what Howells had criticized in the interview: a typical romance in which boy meets and pursues girl and they live happily ever after. In fact, it is Crane's most autobiographical novel. Billie Hawker, a painter, and George Hollanden, a writer, incorporate different aspects of Crane's own inner conflict—the serious artist struggling with the need to earn a living by catering to popular tastes—and Hawker's other friends are based on Crane's New York roommates in 1893–1895. The novel also parodies the literary conventions of romantic novels and examines the nature of the arts, specifically writing and painting, in the marketplace. Much of the dialogue focuses on the difficulties that authors and painters face in striving to balance popular taste and personal vision. Like Crane just before publication of *The Red Badge,* Hawker is on the verge of fame, but he struggles with the debate between Jem Oglethorpe, a rich rival who contends that the best artists are those who earn the most money, and Hollanden, who says they are the worst. After studying art in Paris, Hawker returns to America but finds that in order to survive, he must cater to the marketplace by painting designs for mass-produced tomato cans. Though forced to equate art with advertising, he privately adheres to the realist credo of painting "the ordinary thing," and his discomfort about his demeaning work intensifies his social awkwardness. As Hawker gets off the train in the opening scene, he accidentally hits the nephew of Grace Fanhall in the head with an easel, a symbol of his profession; Hawker's clumsiness foreshadows his awkwardness with Grace and his own difficulty in accommodating his profession in social contexts. His anxiety mars his work and affects his relationships with other artists. He gets upset while "discussing art with some pot-boiler" who, like Oglethorpe, defines art solely by its commercial success, and he approaches his craft violently. Painting "with a wild face like a man who is killing," Hawker envisions a "burning" sky colored with "powder smoke" as though a weapon had been fired. When Hollanden questions the accuracy of Hawker's depiction of the setting, Hawker screams, "Shut up or I'll smash you with the easel"! Associating artistic creation with violence suggests Hawker's internal battle concerning his professional future: Should he pursue his personal vision of truth, or should he be content to continually replicate the same images on cans, just as trained bears mass-produce romances by replicating the same literary form? In Chapter 1, when Hawker rides in a carriage to his parents' farm, he gets off at a crossroad that represents the metaphorical crossroad in his professional development. He could follow the path of Purple Sanderson, who has struggled before achieving fame and wealth as an artist, or he could follow that of

Hollanden, who has begun his writing career "with a determination to be a prophet" but has devolved into "being an acrobat, a trained bear of the magazines, and a juggler of comic paragraphs" whose livelihood depends solely on public acceptance.[18]

Crane reached his own crossroad while writing *The Third Violet* in the fall of 1895. A celebrity after the publication of *The Red Badge of Courage,* he struggled with the conflict between commitment to a vision and the lure of widespread acclaim. On the one hand, he was delighted with the "passionately enthusiastic" reviews of his war novel, yet he feared becoming a trained bear because of the public's obsession with the "damned" *Red Badge* and worried that instant fame might "turn me ever so slightly from what I believe to be the pursuit of truth." Now that the book had been critically acclaimed, he told a magazine editor, "I suppose I ought to be satisfied, but somehow I am not as happy as I was in the uncertain, happy-go-lucky newspaper-writing days. I used to dream continually of success then. Now that I have achieved it in some measure it seems like mere flimsy paper." Just as he had learned during his interview with Howells a year earlier, the anticipation of success could easily erode one's artistic vision. For Crane, however, the real danger in the pursuit of a vision was ultimately "not the world . . . but man's own colossal impulses more strong than chains." He knew that the pursuit of fame for its own sake—an "appetite for victory, as victory is defined by the mob"—could sidetrack him from "a sincere, desperate, lonely battle to remain true to my conception of my life and the way it should be lived."[19]

Elbert Hubbard, the self-proclaimed "ex-officio General Inspector of the Universe," attempted to transform Crane's fame into a marketable commodity and display him like a trained bear. After working successfully as general manager of a leading manufacturer and distributor of soap products, Hubbard became the central figure in a group of artists and craftsmen—the Roycrofters, in East Aurora, New York—who championed the arts-and-crafts movement in America. In 1895, Hubbard founded Roycroft Press in order to emulate the finely printed books of William Morris's Kelmscott Press in England; and he cofounded with Harry P. Taber *The Philistine: A Periodical of Protest,* which criticized the Eastern literary establishment and orthodox thought in general. With a circulation of 225,000, it was the longest-lived and best-loved journal of literary resistance during the 1890s.[20]

Crane published his poetry in the *Philistine* and in Hubbard's two other magazines, the *Roycroft Quarterly* and the *Fra;* and Hubbard prominently displayed caricatures of him by W. W. Denslow, later the illustrator of *The Wonderful Wizard of Oz,* on the Roycrofters' shop walls. "The Charge of the Rough Writers" depicted authors on hobbyhorses galloping madly toward the public; and in an untitled caricature, Crane, decked out in a suit and diamonds, greeted "His Satanic Majesty" (presumably Hubbard). Hubbard's promotion of his star contributor, however, worked to Crane's disadvantage. Hubbard refused to pay for submissions because of what Frank Noxon sarcastically called a "democratic prejudice against royalties" and instead offered to advertise the book publication of *The Red Badge of Courage,* but he never did. As Amy Lowell put it, it "was difficult for the world to believe that a man championed by the arch-poser, Elbert Hubbard, could have merit. . . . It was a thousand pities that poems such as [Crane's] should appear under the aegis of the Roycrofters." Hubbard praised Crane's work, but his jests about contemporary poets were occasionally caustic: "Why Bliss Carman and Stephen Crane do not write for *Lippincott's* has long been a mystery to me. Some of their verse is bad enough. But the secret is out. They have only two names apiece."[21]

With his penchant for self-promotion, Hubbard created a paper organization called the Society of the Philistines, which formally invited Crane to a banquet commemorating his "merit as a man and your genius as a poet."[22] The iconoclastic *Black Riders* had already demonstrated that Crane was the kind of radical new voice the society was promoting. Upon receiving the invitation in Hartwood, though, he was shocked— "You could have knocked me down with a gas-pipe when I got their bid" and his first instinct was to decline the offer. His shyness and his embarrassment at not having suitable clothing prompted him to ask Willis Brooks Hawkins for help: "My dress suit took to the woods long ago and my 1895 overcoat is not due until 1896. I have not owned a pair of patent leather shoes in three years. Write me at once and tell me how to get out of the thing. Of course I am dead sore but I think if you will invent for me a very decent form of refusal, I will still be happy up here with my woods." After Hawkins promised that Crane would be helped with the proper attire and that he had nothing to fear, Crane accepted the invitation; but neither of them anticipated Hubbard's self-serving plan for the event. A master of advertising, Hubbard released Crane's letter of acceptance to the Buffalo newspapers without his permission and printed three pamphlets to publicize the event. The first was an eight-page invitation from "The Members of the Society" inviting guests to join Crane for dinner on December 19 in East Aurora (the site was later changed to the Genesee House in Buffalo). He mailed the invitation to seven hundred people he hoped would not attend, just to get their comments on the occasion. The second pamphlet, a souvenir menu titled "'The Time Has Come,' the Walrus Said, 'To Talk of Many Things,'" included responses from about three dozen invited guests who declined to attend and a cover design caricaturing the title of *The Black Riders:* a man (presumably Crane) pursues the horizon while four black riders on rocking horses descend from the rays of the setting sun. After the banquet, Hubbard reprinted their regrets along with additional ones, newspaper reviews of the banquet, his essay on Crane, and some of Crane's work in *A Souvenir and a Medley.* The more that people knew of the banquet, thought Hubbard, the better-known he and his own endeavors would be. Several of Crane's friends, including Irving Bacheller, Hamlin Garland, and Ripley Hitchcock, did not attend, perhaps sensing that the invitations were ultimately a way of publicizing not only the honored guest but the publicity agent as well. As Harry Taber said, Hubbard had little to do with the banquet "except to talk somewhat discursively upon his favorite topic: Love and Himself."[23]

As December 19 approached, Crane's fear and shyness made him increasingly ambivalent about the banquet. Although he told Hawkins that it would be "probably the greatest pleasure of my life, I feel as if I were astride of your shoulders. And if I could stop the thing now I would." On the night of the banquet, Crane's anxiety proved prophetic. Hubbard had assured him that the occasion would be more than "a pleasant meeting and dinner" because "you represent a 'cause' and we wish in a dignified, public (and at the same time) elegant manner to recognize that cause." Though embarrassed by the praise, Crane at times seemed to be enjoying himself, but the event devolved into a drunken roast of the guest of honor; as Claude Bragdon declared, Crane was a "young ox led to the slaughter." He and other speakers were heckled and ridiculed by "freaks and near-freaks," as Noxon characterized them; and at least one guest threatened to leave in protest. When a story in the *Buffalo Evening News* the following day depicted the banquet as a respectable affair, Crane sent the clipping to an acquaintance and wrote, "This is not at all what happened."[24]

Hubbard bragged that the "banquet started Stevie Crane on the road to fame—there's no doubt about that!" Several months later in 1896, according to the *Lotus,* a rival of the *Philistine,* Hubbard, the "self-appointed manager of Stephen Crane," was planning another banquet for "his protégé," though this was being done without Crane's approval, as was the case with another event. In November, Hubbard announced that the Society of the Philistines was planning a banquet for the Japanese poet Yone Noguchi, who was living in San Francisco. When reminded that Noguchi had not been invited, Hubbard lashed back, "If Mr. Noguchi does not care to be present on the occasion he can stay away and be damned." Hubbard's publicity stunts did little to advance Crane's reputation, yet Crane did not blame him for the fiasco at the December 19 banquet, and they remained friends until Crane's death. When he received a copy of Hubbard's *A Souvenir and a Medley,* which reprinted regrets from those unable to attend the Philistines banquet, he laughed uncontrollably at Charles F. Lummis's pun on the title of one of Longfellow's popular poems: "I am sorry that I cannot assist at the Hanging of the Crane, but I trust Justice may be done."[25]

Although Crane put on a brave face after the banquet, he undoubtedly realized that Hubbard had used him. A "panic-stricken" Crane was "in a blue funk," Hawkins recalled, dispirited and disillusioned by what he had thought was going to be an honest tribute to his literary achievements. Fame had brought him to East Aurora, named after the mythological goddess of dawn, where he had become enlightened about the price of celebrity. But fame had come too quickly for the diffident Crane, and his attempt to understand it is revealed in his letters to Nellie Janes Crouse, a wealthy socialite from Akron, Ohio.[26]

Before heading on his Western trip, Crane had met Nellie, who was visiting a sister in New York City, through a mutual friend, Lucius L.

Button, at a tea party in January 1895. Despite his disdain for the artifice of social events—"Teas bore me . . . because all the girls gibber"—Crane cornered Nellie for almost four hours after he discovered that she had been reading the syndicated *Red Badge of Courage*. She found him egotistical, unattractive, and unwilling to share her with anyone else.[27] Uneasy and awkward, Crane must have struggled to make conversation. Having attended Syracuse University, he probably inquired if she was related to John R. Crouse, a wealthy banker who had funded construction of the school's Crouse College, then asked about her father's experience during the Civil War as a common soldier.[28] Almost a year after the tea party, Crane claimed that he had abruptly ended his trip west in May 1895 and returned to New York after he saw an American woman in Mexico who reminded him of Nellie; but when he went to see Nellie, she had already returned to Akron. On December 31, days after finishing *The Third Violet*, Crane began an intensive correspondence with Nellie that ended after about three months when she apparently stopped writing.[29] Her letters have not survived, but his seven fervent letters are satirical, melodramatic, and bitterly ironic as he struggled with the conventions of courtship, with the tension between the personal integrity of the artist and the demands of the literary marketplace, and with the international acclaim that followed the book publication of *The Red Badge of Courage*—topics central to *The Third Violet*. Like Hawker in the novel, Crane assumed poses that variously revealed and hid his true feelings. When Crouse disapproved of his calling himself a "wild shaggy barbarian," as well as a "chump" and "blockhead"—the latter two epithets are also used for Hawker—he quickly became a refined critic with "a considerable liking for the man of fashion if he does it well." Similarly, he reversed his position on one of his own short stories, "A Gray Sleeve," in response to her comments. Written in May around the time that he tried to see Nellie a second time, it is a sentimental, melodramatic story about a Union officer and Confederate woman who fall in love after seeing each other only once. The officer, with "his reddish, bronze complexion, his yellow hair," and his "dusty" uniform was clearly a blond version of Stephen, deeply tanned from his Western trip, in his typically tattered clothing. After writing half of the story, he had had trouble completing it. "I'm all written out, my mind's a blank," he had lamented to Nelson Greene. "I

can't write any more. I don't believe I'll ever write again. I'm through."
He realized that "A Gray Sleeve" was not serious art, but romantic fluff
written by "a trained bear of the magazines." And in writing Nellie and
himself into the story, he struggled with its ending. In the final scene, as
rain from "the leaden sky" falls "with a mournful patter," there is only
hope, not certainty, that they will be reunited. Crane sent Nellie "A Gray
Sleeve" in January 1896. Anxious about her response, he first called it
"not in any sense a good story," but quickly labeled it "charming" after
she said she liked it. Crane's shifting positions and his self-effacing, ingra-
tiating comments revealed his insecurity and low self-esteem as he tried
to court a beautiful, intelligent socialite. Crane waited till he was famous
before writing to her and included in his first letter a clipping from the
Buffalo Evening News highlighting the Philistines banquet to validate his
success as a writer.[30]

A habitually shy bohemian rebel who restrained his emotions, Crane
seemingly revealed his soul to a woman with whom he had spent only a
few hours at a public event. According to one of her daughters, Crane
visited Nellie in Akron before her marriage in 1897, and her children
were "brought up on Crane's love for her." But the only evidence of
their relationship is in his letters, which reveal a divided mind trying to
understand the nature of his fame, prompted by his reaction to the banquet. On December 31, Crane wrote Nellie a satirical letter about the
banquet, but on the same day, lacking self-assurance, he asked Hawkins
for his opinion: "I am very anxious to hear wether you are satisfied with
the dinner. I did not drink much but the excitement soon turned everything into a grey haze for me and I am not sure that I came off decently."
The banquet was the first public event honoring his fame as an author.
Crane wanted the adulation that success brought, for it proved that the
family's black sheep was not so black after all; but he also recognized the
evanescent nature of celebrity and the danger of becoming a trained
bear in the literary marketplace. "So you think I am successful?" he asked
Nellie. "Well I dont know. Most people consider me successful. At least,
they seem to so think."[31]

Begun on the last day of the year, the letters also read like a New Year's
resolution to find a confidante who, like him, "had lived a long time" in
terms of experience and to whom he could say what "no woman has

heard . . . until now."[32] Yet for all his emotional outpouring, Crane, like the Player Queen in *Hamlet,* "doth protest too much, methinks." He is variously despondent:

> I am simply a man struggling with a life that is no more than a mouthful of dust to him.

full of self-pity:

> The storm-beaten little robin who has no place to lay his head, does not feel so badly as do I.

or maudlin:

> I will be glad if I can feel on my death-bed that my life has been just and kind according to my ability and that every particle of my little ridiculous stock of eloquence and wisdom has been applied for the benefit of my kind. From this moment to that deathbed may be a short time or a long one but at any rate it means a life of labor and sorrow. I do not confront it blithely. I confront it with desperate resolution.[33]

Taken as a whole, his attempts to court her soon ran thin. Within the first two weeks, he wrote her three times; during the next four, three times; and during the last five, once, in a letter composed at two different times after she had rejected him.

Despite Crane's assertion that he was "quite honest and simple," the letters were full of stilted posturing as he attempted to portray himself as a respectable, ambitious young man of virtue and principle. Yet while he was confessing gloom and despair to Nellie, he was joking with Viola Allen, a Claverack schoolmate, about his boyhood romance with one of their friends and was telling another admirer that "I am a good deal of a rascal, sometimes a bore, often dishonest."[34] Setting aside schoolboy flirtations that may have occasionally been more than casual, Crane's love relationships before meeting Nellie had been mainly with prostitutes, chorus girls, and an older married woman, Lily Brandon Munroe. Insecure about his own identity, he never resolved his ambivalence about women. They were either the dark temptress or the fair maiden, and only Lily came close to embodying both aspects. Crane roamed through urban dives and untamed wilderness, reveling in boyish adventures; he proclaimed his bohemian rejection of stifling orthodoxy; yet he sought respectability and acceptance from the society he had abandoned.

Within a year, the man who had proudly declared his affinity for the outcast state would be cast out from that society.

15

Price of Fame

JANUARY–SEPTEMBER 1896

AFTER THE FIRST TWO cantos of *Childe Harold's Pilgrimage* appeared in 1812, Lord Byron announced, "I awoke one morning and found myself famous." The shy poet was immediately sought after and lionized, admired by women, and discussed in literary circles throughout London. After the publication of *The Red Badge of Courage* in October 1895, Crane said to his friend Tom Masson, literary and managing editor of *Life* magazine, "I know now how Byron felt, when he awoke one day to discover himself famous." Crane suddenly had become the darling of the literary world, receiving requests for submissions and answering correspondence that had "reached mighty proportions," including at least one letter from a female admirer offering to send a photograph of herself to her new hero. While in New York on business in late January 1896, he found the public adulation so overwhelming that the "damned city tore my heart out by the roots and flung it under the heels of it's noise. Indeed it did. I couldnt breathe in that accursed tumult." "I had grown used to being called a damned ass," he told Hitchcock, "but this sudden new admiration of my friends has made a gibbering idiot of me. I shall stick to my hills"—and he did, leaving the city abruptly at the end of the month for Hartwood.[1]

His sudden fame, however, trapped him in the exhausting limelight of celebrity over the next several months. Journalists interviewed him so frequently for feature articles that he repeated or paraphrased himself about his literary beliefs and his ancestral and literary antecedents. He was proud of his namesakes who had served patriotically in colonial America, and he strove to write realistically and accurately without being didactic. "Preaching is fatal to art in literature." If there is a moral, "let the reader find it for himself." Paraphrasing a passage in Emerson's essay "Intellect," Crane declared that there "should be a long logic beneath the story, but it should be kept carefully out of sight." When asked about the sale of his war novel, he replied, "Oh, of course, I should be glad if everybody, Canadians, Feejees, Hottentots, wild men of Borneo, would buy 'The Red Badge'—four copies of it—but they won't; so what's the use of thinking of the reader? If what you write is worthy, somebody will find it out some time. Meanwhile that is not one of the problems that interests me." But he also questioned people's ability to be astute readers: "Trust their imaginations? Why, they haven't got any! They are used to having everything detailed for them. Our imaginations are defunct for lack of use, like our noses. So whether I say a thing or suggest it, I try to put it in the most forcible way." Yet he struggled throughout his career with the battle between public demand and artistic vision, the conflict described in "Howells Fears the Realists Must Wait."[2]

Despite posing as a bohemian nonconformist, Crane was attracted to the social status that fame accorded because it confirmed his accomplishments. When poor and unknown in the fall of 1892, he had sarcastically labeled his boardinghouse the Pendennis Club, but he relished his association with clubs. Already a member of the Hartwood Club and the Lantern Club, he joined or attended functions at the Authors Club, Players Club, and Union League Club in New York City in 1896 and later at the Savage Club in London.[3] In the spring, he was delighted upon being accepted into the Sons of the American Revolution. Clubs were frequently recognizing his distinction, though for Crane, who had barely survived Hubbard's raucous banquet in Buffalo, a "dinner scheme mingles my emotions. In one sense, it portends an Ordeal but in the larger sense it overwhelms me in pride and arrogance to think that I have such friends."[4] In early January, Ripley Hitchcock began planning a dinner for him at the Authors Club, and later in the month Irving Bacheller toasted him at a dinner at the Lantern Club.[5] In April the Lantern Club hosted a banquet honoring him again, with Howells as principal speaker praising the young author; and in July the Kauai Kodak Club tried to entice him to visit Hawaii by making him an honorary member.

Despite the acclaim that greeted *The Red Badge of Courage,* Crane was ready to write about a new subject because he had exhausted "the sum of my invention in regard to war." Publishers, however, wanted to benefit from his popularity by encouraging him to write short war pieces that could be quickly published. When John S. Phillips, cofounder of *McClure's Magazine,* asked him in December to write a series of sketches about Civil War battlefields for the magazine or the McClure syndicate, Crane initially hesitated because he had "a good many orders and requests, and I am busy at them." But he might also have been recalling McClure's ill treatment of him in 1894, when McClure had held the manuscript of *The Red Badge* without publishing it; the battlefield sketches might be held indefinitely as well. Yet Crane hesitated to reject an assignment because of his difficulty in getting work only months earlier. As a compromise, he proposed that he begin the project in the spring, after he had met his other commitments, and that he visit battlefields during the season when the battles had occurred so that "the color of things there now would be the very same color of things of the days the battle was fought." Though he was expected to rely on biographical, geographical, and military facts associated with each battle, he envisioned the articles as an impressionistic account of his experience of the settings. His association of color with battle—or more specifically with the sights and sounds of battle—was more than a literary technique. As Willis Brooks Hawkins discovered, Crane was endowed with synesthesia, the subjective response of a sense (such as vision) other than the one (such as hearing) being stimulated. One evening in Brooklyn, while they were watching nearby ships, a vessel almost hit the pier; just in time, a seaman yelled the order to veer away. "Great heavens! What a green voice!" exclaimed Crane. When Hawkins asked him whether he associated colors with sounds for "poetic effect," he replied, "Certainly not," and explained that every sound evoked in him the sight of a color. He was surprised that Hawkins and other people did not automatically associate color with sound. Crane's synesthesia partly explains his repeated use of color to evoke mood and sensory details in such works as *The Black Riders,*

"The Blue Hotel," "The Bride Comes to Yellow Sky," and most famously *The Red Badge of Courage.*[6]

Had Crane left in the spring, the points on his itinerary would probably have been Shiloh in Tennessee (where a battle had been fought on April 6–7, 1862) and Chancellorsville, Virginia (April 30–May 6, 1863). The latter was closer to New York City, and Crane was already familiar with the battle there, since he had made it the focus of *The Red Badge.* Phillips, however, persuaded him to reconsider his schedule. Crane traveled in mid-January to Fredericksburg, Virginia, site of a major battle in December 1862. Besides touring the battlefield, Crane interviewed Confederate veterans and consulted written reports and accounts of the events. The battle had been a devastating loss for the North. Although the South had established a well-fortified line of defense on hills overlooking Fredericksburg, the North had valiantly but hopelessly attacked, suffering almost thirteen thousand casualties. The loss had demoralized the North; and its leader, General Ambrose E. Burnside, had been relieved of command at his own request. Considering it the most dramatic battle of the Civil War, Crane planned on contrasting its ineffectual leaders with the heroic fighters of the 69th New York Infantry Regiment, which had been decimated during the battle.

Crane eventually dropped the project. Battlefield sketches required such a level of historical accuracy that if he "did not place the only original crown of pure gold on the heads of at least twelve generals," he complained to Phillips, "they would arise and say: 'This damned young fool was not there. I was however. And this is how it happened.'" He was, moreover, busy writing Civil War short stories for McClure. These had become "a daily battle with a tangle of facts and emotions," and at least one of them—a fictional story about the Battle of Fredericksburg, "The Little Regiment"—was "awfully hard" and kept him "in internal despair." Feeling that he was "often inexpressibly dull and uncreative," he hoped that McClure would suggest a new topic to write about, for Crane was realizing that any future Civil War stories would inevitably be compared to *The Red Badge of Courage* and found lacking. Because "I used myself up in the accursed 'Red Badge,'" he declared that readers "may just as well discover now that the high dramatic key of *The Red Badge* cannot be sustained."[7]

In November, three Civil War stories that Crane had written for Mc-

Clure and three that he had written for Bacheller's syndicate were collected in *The Little Regiment and Other Episodes of the American Civil War,* published by Appleton in the United States and by Heinemann in England. Mixed reviews reflected the uneven quality of the stories. Whereas one critic thought they exhibited "extraordinary power of imagination," to another critic they were "hasty and careless work." After completing them, Crane asserted that they would be "positively my last thing dealing with battle." Ironically, he would still be writing about war in his dying days.[8]

Wanting to capitalize on the immediate success of *The Red Badge,* Appleton offered to reprint *Maggie* if Crane would work with Hitchcock to revise the text. Crane had already developed a good working relationship with his editor during the publication of *The Red Badge;* and when he submitted *The Third Violet* to Appleton in December 1895, Hitchcock accepted it immediately. Though he had reservations about the dialogue and character development, he admired Crane's talent and clarified his own constraints as an editor: "I should make any suggestions with the greatest diffidence." Whatever suggestions he offered, he apparently deferred to Crane's judgment. If Crane did make any changes, they must have been minor because a month after submitting the manuscript, in the midst of other writing projects, he told Hitchcock that he was finished: "*The Third Violet* is a quiet little story but then it is serious work and I should say let it go."[9]

Finishing the war stories for *The Little Regiment* in February, Crane started working immediately on *Maggie.* Like his contemporaries Frank Norris and Theodore Dreiser, Crane was often careless about spelling, punctuation, and grammar and expected an editor to correct his mistakes, but he specifically addressed Hitchcock's objection to the rough language in the book, undoubtedly a reason that publishers had rejected it initially. Crane deleted blasphemous oaths and profanity—what he called "words which hurt"—converting "damn" and "hell" to "d—m" and "h—l" or "h—ll." He made other stylistic and substantive changes, the most important being the deletion of the penultimate paragraph in Chapter 17, in which Maggie is followed by a fat, greasy man with "brown, disordered teeth" whose body "shook like that of a dead jelly fish." The passage, which demonstrates how desperate Maggie has become as a prostitute, was apparently too graphic for Hitchcock. Yet despite his concern about language, he and Crane worked together well. Crane would mail him reworked chapters "to see if they suit"—a sign that Crane was receptive to additional revision—and Hitchcock accepted Crane's insistence that the book not have chapter titles. By the last week in March, Crane was reading page proofs, but he quickly grew tired of the project and could not finish writing a preface to the book. "The proofs make me ill," he complained to Hitchcock. "I am too jaded with Maggie to be able to see it." He was more blunt with *Maggie*'s English publisher, William Heinemann: "I hate the book."[10]

Crane never had the patience to proofread a text closely, and he was ready to move beyond the book he had started five years earlier. He also sensed there were problems with it. "Seems to me the book wears quite a new aspect from very slight omissions," he told Hitchcock, then reminded him that the book was "very short." Concern about length was nothing new for either of them. When Crane had brought some stories to Appleton in December 1894, Hitchcock had asked if he had a longer manuscript that could be published as a book; the request had prompted him to submit *The Red Badge of Courage*. Later, when Crane had submitted *The Third Violet*, Hitchcock had gladly accepted it, though its length made him unsure about which of Appleton's book series was appropriate for it: it was too short for the "Town and Country Library," too long for the "75-cent series." Crane's concern regarding length also implied that he thought the revisions compromised the book's artistic integrity. He was right. Though Hitchcock was not interested in changing the novella's basic plot or themes, the result was a bowdlerized, incoherent text. "In the new edition," a reviewer wrote, "one notes many revisions, all of them unimportant and almost all of them ill-advised."[11]

Crane acknowledged that his eccentricity might have annoyed his editor, for it was "my foremost trait." He was notorious for suddenly appearing at one's doorstep, then just as abruptly leaving. He did not, however, admit that he could be deceptive in his dealings with publishers. One incident strained his cordial relationship with Hitchcock. Though Appleton contracts did not require authors to submit their subsequent books to them, the conventional business practice was to do so. With the publication of *The Red Badge* and acceptance of *The Third Violet* before it had been put into final production, Hitchcock assumed that Crane was an Appleton author. In March, however, he was surprised to discover that the Anglo-American firm Edward Arnold was publishing Crane's next novella, *George's Mother.* In a curious apology, Crane claimed that Harry Thompson, a former Claverack schoolmate and now American manager for Edward Arnold, had "appealed to my avarice and failing appealed to my humanity." Crane acknowledged that he had "violated certain business courtesies" by giving a satirical voyage fantasy titled *Dan Emmonds* to Edward Arnold, but he avoided telling Hitchcock that he had also given the firm *George's Mother.* Though *Dan Emmonds* was advertised as forthcoming in November, it never appeared because Crane wrote only ten pages of the projected novel; instead, Edward Arnold published *George's Mother* in America in May and in England the following month. It was the first time Hitchcock had heard of the book, and it caused consternation, for Appleton had an arrangement with Heinemann concerning English publication rights to Crane's works. In July, Crane was forced to assure his American publisher that he would not again violate business convention, as he had done with *George's Mother,* and that he had written to Edward Arnold saying that he would honor Appleton's arrangement with Heinemann. Accepting Crane's promise, Hitchcock continued to work with him and oversaw the publication of *The Little Regiment* later in the year.[12]

Because Crane's novellas about the New York slums were released around the same time—*George's Mother* in late May and *Maggie* in early June—they were frequently reviewed together, with widely varying notices. *Maggie,* which appeared on *Bookman*'s bestseller list, "has rendered the seamy side of modern existence, the real life of the slums, with a force and actuality of description that has not been equaled by any depiction of low life," and the verisimilitude of *George's Mother* was the work of "an artist's hand." Yet *Maggie* was also seen as evidence that Crane's talents were "in a process of degeneration" (a verdict based on the mistaken assumption that it had been written after *The Red Badge*), and *George's Mother* was considered nothing more than a potboiler "with a succession of dull and uninteresting events. The book means nothing."[13]

Of all the reviews, none was more significant than Howells's influential essay "New York Low Life in Fiction" in July. Howells praised *Maggie* for its "quality of fatal necessity which dominates Greek tragedy" and *George's Mother* for its "mastery" and "extraordinary insight." He compared Crane with Abraham Cahan, the Lithuanian-born editor of the Yiddish daily newspaper *Forverts,* and a prominent writer of fiction about Jewish life on the Lower East Side, whose novel *Yekl: A Tale of the New York Ghetto* had just been published. Howells praised both writers for their realistic depiction of the slum environment. As soon as Crane read the essay, he told Howells that it was, "of course, the best word that has been said of me" and that he wanted to meet Cahan, whose book he had been reading. Howells arranged for a meeting at his summer home in Far Rockaway, New York, on August 25; and on September 22 Crane and Cahan, along with Garland, were honored at a dinner at the Lantern Club as outstanding exponents of realism in fiction. A few days later, Crane and Cahan spent an evening together on the East Side. It would be the last time they met, but years later Cahan still recalled how pale, thin, and weak his companion had been.[14]

In early March 1896, Crane was in Washington studying political life for a projected novel for McClure. Again, he said nothing to Hitchcock about a possible deal with McClure, going so far as to ask Hitchcock for help in making contacts in Washington. He roamed throughout Congress and met influential politicians, including "those long-whiskered devils from the West"; but of all his contacts, he most wanted to meet Senator Matthew Quay from Pennsylvania, former chairman of the Republican National Committee and one of the most powerful members of Congress. Like Crane, Quay was the son of a minister and had won the Congressional Medal of Honor at the Battle of Fredericksburg during the Civil War. For years his name was synonymous with Pennsylvania politics. A master of the political system who manipulated patronage, Senator Quay would have been an excellent prototype of a complex American titan for the novel; but Crane, after becoming frustrated by his inability to get beyond public deeds and unveil the personalities of congressmen, stopped trying to write a political novel: "These men pose so hard that it would take a double-barreled shotgun to disclose their inward feelings and I despair of knowing them." Renowned for his astutely laconic style, Quay knew, as one person observed, "how to keep silent in fifteen languages."[15]

At the beginning of April, Crane moved back into the studio apartment he had shared with Post Wheeler at 165 West 23rd Street in New York. During the next several months, he wrote stories and articles for the Bacheller and McClure syndicates. His articles on city life ranged from humorous observations about bicycles and cable cars to poignant treatments of opium addiction and a confused old lady's desperate attempt to find work. Escaping to Hartwood in June and July, he wrote three stories inspired by his Western trip the previous year, and in September began a series of feature articles for William Randolph Hearst's *New York Journal*. Crane was one of several bright stars in the journalistic galaxy that Hearst hired after buying the *Morning Journal* in 1895 (he established the *Evening Journal* in 1896). In a bitter circulation war with Joseph Pulitzer, Hearst lured away members of the *New York World*'s Sunday staff—writers such as Arthur Brisbane, whom Damon Runyon later described as the "all-time No. 1 genius" of journalism, and Richard F. Outcault, who had created the Yellow Kid, a cartoon character who wore a yellow nightshirt and was the central figure in one of Pulitzer's most popular strips.[16] In retaliation, Pulitzer hired another cartoonist to draw the same character. The war between the two publishers devolved into "Yellow Kid Journalism," which got shortened to "yellow journalism." Other acclaimed writers hired by Hearst included Julian Hawthorne, James Creelman, and Richard Harding Davis.

To sell more papers, both publishers relied on sensational headlines, lurid stories, photographs, and cartoons to attract readers. When Alan Dale, the *New York Journal*'s drama critic, interviewed the risqué stage actress Anna Held, the headline read "Mlle. Anna Held Receives Alan Dale Attired in a Nightie" and included sketches of her dressed accordingly; a column written by a "sob sister," the generic pseudonym of any female reporter who wrote sentimental stories, was labeled "Why Young Girls Kill Themselves"; *The Other House* was serialized as "Henry James' New Novel of Immorality and Crime; The Surprising Plunge of the Great Novelist into the Field of Sensational Fiction." The atmosphere in the *Journal* newsroom was often frenetic, yet productive. When a story broke, S. S. Chamberlain, the paper's managing editor, bellowed commands, and a mass exodus of reporters, the self-described "wrecking crew," rushed to the scene. In Crane's opinion, one had to be drunk, crazy, or Sam Chamberlain to run the *New York Journal*.[17]

By the summer of 1896, Crane was, like Byron, an international celebrity fêted by the literary world; and as with Byron, who permanently left England following charges of sexual misconduct, scandal would soon damage Crane's career, leading eventually to self-imposed exile from America. In 1892, his life had been disrupted by his report on the JOUAM parade in Asbury Park; likewise, his career as a professional journalist would be transformed by a chain of events involving police corruption, the wrongful arrest of a prostitute, and defamation of character. No incident in Crane's life was more richly detailed and disturbingly recorded than the aftermath of his investigation of New York City's Tenderloin district.

For decades, the Democratic political machine in New York State and New York City had exercised tremendous power in the daily running of politics. Popularly known as "Tammany Hall," the name of its headquarters building at 331 Madison Avenue, the machine had acquired a reputation for corruption and political scandal, the most famous being the arrest of William M. "Boss" Tweed and the "Tweed Ring" in 1871 for defrauding the city of millions of dollars. By the time of the 1894 election, the Republican Party, with help from the city's Good Government organizations (derisively called "Goo-Goos" by Tammany Hall), had amassed enough strength to oust the Democrats. Suddenly the state had a Republican governor; and New York City, a Republican mayor.

One of the most corrupt organizations controlled by Tammany Hall had been the New York City Police Department. Following the 1894 election, a six-member Board of Commissioners, with Theodore Roosevelt serving as its president, was set up to reform the department. In the same year, the New York State Senate set up a committee chaired by Clarence L. Lexow (R) to investigate charges of widespread police brutality and corruption. In 1895 their massive report—more than ten thousand pages—recommended that the whole Police Department be indicted.[18] The task was especially difficult in the Tenderloin district, a sprawling amusement area lying roughly between Fifth and Ninth avenues, from Madison Square to 19th Street. When Police Captain (later Inspector) Alexander "Clubber" Williams had been transferred from a quiet precinct to this graft-ridden center of vice in 1876, he had supposedly quipped, "For some time now I've had to be content with the cheaper cuts of meat, like round steak. From now on, I'm sure I'll have a more generous diet of thick, juicy tenderloin."[19] During the Lexow Committee's investigation, Williams claimed that although his police income had been modest, he had saved enough money to buy a home and property in New York City; a waterfront home complete with a yacht in Cos Cob, Connecticut; and real estate in Japan. Though he denied any wrongdoing, he resigned a few months later. In an ironic twist on the American dream, he invested the more than $300,000 he had earned from graft and became a multimillionaire.[20]

In addition to the theaters, trendy bars, restaurants, and hotels on the main thoroughfares, the side streets in the Tenderloin were lined with saloons, bordellos, opium dens, and gambling parlors. The saloons were so busy on Sunday, the only day most workers had off, that bartenders worked in four consecutive shifts. When the Board of Commissioners attempted to enforce the Raines Law (1896), which permitted only hotels with at least ten bedrooms to sell liquor on Sunday, "Raines Law Hotels"—saloons that had turned makeshift spaces into bedrooms— suddenly sprang up in the city. Though the law allowed people to drink with their meals, a magistrate ruled that one pretzel and seventeen beers constituted a Sunday meal.[21] Attempts to clean up the area were compromised by a thoroughly entrenched system of widespread bribery that, although operating more covertly since the 1894 election, still assured police protection for illicit activity.

Recognizing Crane's drawing power as a journalist, Hearst asked him in early August 1896 to write feature articles about the Tenderloin for the *New York Journal*.[22] On August 12, Crane went to Madison Square Garden to cover William Jennings Bryan's acceptance speech for the Democratic Party's nomination for president. Bryan's fame as an eloquent orator, demonstrated only weeks earlier in Chicago at the Democratic National Convention during his "Cross of Gold" speech, guaranteed a huge crowd.[23] Concerned about crowd control, Roosevelt assigned one thousand police officers to monitor the forty thousand people who showed up for the twelve thousand seats in the Garden. It soon became clear that Roosevelt had not assigned enough police to monitor the crowds. Tempers flared as police admitted gate crashers but turned away ticket holders. Crowds broke through police ranks twice; and although only one injury was reported, most certainly others were hurt as well. A record heat wave shortened tempers, with the thermometer hovering around ninety degrees in the Garden. An impatient crowd became even more restless following an interminably long introduction by William J. Stone, governor of Missouri, and a lackluster speech by

Bryan. Fearing that he might be misquoted in the press, Bryan chose not to rely on his oratorical skill as a seemingly improvisational speaker and instead read a logically organized paper that lacked the emotional power and verbal fireworks he was famous for. Within minutes, people began to leave the Garden; and by the time Bryan finished his speech almost two hours later, more than half of the audience had gone. The problem with crowd control outside the Garden continued into the evening. When it was announced that Bryan would speak from his hotel window, police could not stop the ten thousand people who, according to a reporter, "rushed on, stopping the cable cars and carriages, falling over each other in their mad flight."[24]

The next day, local newspapers condemned "Teddy's Recruits" for their inept handling of the crowds, and soon thereafter Crane wrote Roosevelt to complain about the matter.[25] They had been friends since S. S. McClure had introduced them earlier in the summer, when he was considering asking Crane to write an article about the police force. On July 20 at the police court, Roosevelt had granted Crane an interview during which the commissioner had "much to discuss . . . about 'Madge,'" his word for *Maggie*. Despite the incident at the Garden, Crane wanted to trust Roosevelt's judgment in general about police management; along with his letter, he included an inscribed copy of *George's Mother* and a typescript of the Western tale "A Man and Some Others." Because of Roosevelt's devotion to the American West, Crane was hoping for his comments on the short story.[26] Roosevelt already admired Crane's work, especially *The Red Badge of Courage;* and over dinner with Jacob Riis, the three of them had discussed social conditions in New York City. Roosevelt defended the police, saying that controlling huge crowds in tense situations was difficult, and Crane was confident that Roosevelt would enforce ethical behavior among members of the force. Although no one had filed an official complaint of police brutality on the night of Bryan's speech, Roosevelt told Crane he would observe their conduct at the Garden on the evening of August 18, at the speech of Bourke Cockran, an influential New York Democrat opposed to Bryan's nomination.

Still, Crane was incensed by the behavior of the police. Realizing that harsh criticism in his Tenderloin articles for the *New York Journal* might tax his relationship with Roosevelt, he attacked the police and, indirectly,

Roosevelt's management of them in three articles in late August–early September in the *Port Jervis Evening Gazette,* cloaking his identity by using only his initials as a byline. Although he was under contract to write for the *New York Journal,* Crane occasionally bypassed professional obligations to suit his own purposes. Written hastily for quick money, the articles recycled material he had already published. Their publication in a small-town newspaper almost guaranteed that New Yorkers would not see them, but Crane, knowing that Roosevelt was heading west on a trip, wanted to be certain he would not read them. Roosevelt left New York on August 21 for three weeks; the articles appeared, one per week, while he was away.

Had Roosevelt seen them, he would have been incensed by Crane's accusations. The "wretched mismanagement . . . brutality and unnecessary harshness" of the police in their handling of the crowd at the Garden was "simply shameful" and would not have occurred had Thomas F. Byrnes still been Superintendent of Police. After Roosevelt became president of the Board of Commissioners, he had forced Byrnes to resign. Byrnes was known for his autocratic style, but Roosevelt's decision had nevertheless been controversial. What had been "gained in official honesty through administrative reform," Crane charged, was "more than counter-balanced by the effects of official incapacity and inexperience." In addition, the harassment of shopkeepers by the enforcement of "an obnoxious sanction of the blue laws" and the "systematic police persecution" of prostitutes for alleged solicitation were evidence that the culture of enforcement needed to be reconsidered. Concerned for his own reputation, Crane hoped that his harshest criticisms of the police would remain buried and eventually forgotten in Port Jervis.[27]

The titles and organization of the three articles, however, suggest that Crane may have grown increasingly anxious about the intensity of his censure. The first article—"Poor Police Arrangements at the Bryan Meeting: A Brutality and Harshness That Was Not Possible under the Byrnes Regime"—begins by attacking the police. The title of the second article—"What an Observant Correspondent Sees Worth Noting" —is strikingly neutral, and its criticisms are tucked away amid discussions of such topics as delicatessens, hoopskirts, and puns. With an even more generic title—"An Interesting Letter from Our Correspondent"—the third article surrounds its mild disapproval of the Raines Law with mundane news. Though the newspaper editor may have supplied the titles, Crane buried his criticisms more deeply in the second and third articles. Fearing a possible backlash from Roosevelt after the blatant attack against the police in the first article, he apparently became ambivalent about a journalist's moral obligation to voice his objections and downplayed them in the next two articles.

After returning to New York on September 11, Roosevelt invited Crane, Hamlin Garland, Jacob Riis, and big-game hunter William Chanler to lunch. While Roosevelt spoke freely with Garland about Western fiction, with Chanler about hunting in Africa, and with Riis about East Side parks, Crane sat silently, looking, as Garland recalled, "like a man in trouble," for in front of him was the man responsible for the police administration he had just vilified in print.[28] Up to this point in Crane's career, little of his writing had focused on social critique; and when it did—as in "A Foreign Policy in Three Glimpses," "In the Depths of a Coal Mine," and "An Experiment in Luxury"—the attacks were generally focused on abstractions such as imperialism, stereotypes such as greedy coal barons, or vague commentary about social conditions. With the three articles in the *Port Jervis Evening Gazette,* however, he was talking about specific, recent events in New York City that had been sanctioned by a specific person, Theodore Roosevelt. Crane was defending "the rights of the humble citizen" against "over zealous policemen."[29] In less than a month, his words would prove directly relevant to himself.

16

The Dora Clark Incident

FALL 1896

BY THE MIDDLE OF September, Crane was investigating the Tenderloin for Hearst. He observed the proceedings at Jefferson Market Police Court, then concluded that he needed to study court victims firsthand.[1] Crane's decision began a series of events that would end in disaster. In an article titled "Adventures of a Novelist," Crane portrayed himself as a gentleman who had resolved an ethical dilemma and protected an innocent victim against an abuse of power; in a courtroom drama, he became the protagonist who suffered from the consequences of his choices. No other event in Crane's life revealed more clearly the devastating cost of his conflicted personality.

Crane states in "Adventures of a Novelist" that late on September 15 he was interviewing two chorus girls at a Broadway resort. Before they left at 2 A.M., a streetwalker named Dora Clark joined them. As Crane escorted one of the chorus girls to a nearby trolley car, a plainclothes policeman named Charles Becker arrested the other women for allegedly soliciting two men who had merely walked by. Terrified, they cried hysterically, and the other chorus girl, pointing at Crane, screamed, "He's my husband!" Surprised, Crane said nothing at first; but when he confirmed her statement, Becker reluctantly let her go. Despite Crane's assertion that Clark was also innocent, Becker did not believe him. "Do you know this woman?" he challenged Crane, who said he did not. "Well, she's a common prostitute," retorted Becker. "And if you people don't want to get pinched too, you had better not be seen with her." He took Dora Clark to the 19th Precinct station house to be charged with solicitation.[2]

Concerned for her safety, Crane and the chorus girl followed them. The scene at the station grew chaotic. The chorus girl sobbed incessantly, and Clark demanded to be given a court hearing in the morning to file charges against Becker, claiming that the arrest was part of an ongoing attempt to harass her because of an incident three weeks earlier. She had been accosted on a poorly lit block of Broadway by a dark-skinned man she thought was black. When she had chastised him for his behavior, he had become angry, revealed that he was a plainclothes policeman named Rosenberg, and arrested her. During the earlier hearing, concerning her arrest by Rosenberg, Clark's account of mistaking his race had provoked laughter at his expense; and though she had been found innocent, he had whispered to her that he and other policemen in the 19th Precinct would seek revenge against her. Becker's confrontation with Clark in the early-morning hours of September 16 was the fourth time she had been arrested for solicitation since the incident with Rosenberg.

After Dora Clark was locked up, Crane walked the chorus girl home. Sensing that he was hesitant to get involved with Clark's case, she urged that he do so. "By George! I cannot," he exclaimed. "I can't afford to do that sort of thing. I—I—." Fearing damage to his reputation, he was speechless and defenseless. According to "Adventures of a Novelist," Crane returned to his apartment and began justifying his actions to himself. Like Mark Twain's Huckleberry Finn after he writes a note to Miss Phelps saying where Jim, the runaway slave, is hiding, Crane felt momentarily cleansed of his guilt; and also like Huck, he acknowledged his true feelings when they were awakened by his moral sense. Initially, he struggled with the decision to defend Dora Clark in court and to criticize the police in a major New York City newspaper. In "Adventures" Crane refers to himself twenty-five times as the "reluctant witness." About one-third of the article is an internal monologue in which Crane debates the implications of his actions:

> All that I value may be chanced in this affair. Shall I take this risk for the
> benefit of a girl of the streets? . . . Have I a duty as a citizen, or do citizens

have duty, as a citizen, or do citizens have no duties? Is it a mere myth that there was at one time a man who possessed a consciousness of civic responsibility, or has it become a distinction of our municipal civilization that men of this character shall be licensed to deprecate in such a manner upon those who are completely at their mercy?

Crane believed that Clark had been unlawfully arrested. What would other "men of character" do in such a situation? "Do these reputable citizens interfere? No, they go home and thank God that they can still attend piously to their own affairs."[3]

Home was more than a physical location; it represented the comfort accompanying the fame and success Crane had worked so hard to achieve during the previous several years. Now that he was an international celebrity, in the vanguard of a new era in American literature, it seemed senseless to risk everything for a common streetwalker. It was the same question that a minister in *Maggie: A Girl of the Streets* faces when Maggie approaches him for comfort and protection; rather than risk losing his respectability, he avoids her. Crane's ironic treatment of the story of the Good Samaritan in his first novella had returned to haunt him. If he simply dismissed Clark as "a girl of the streets," he would be ignoring someone to shield his reputation. He must have realized that he had done something like this with his three articles in the *Port Jervis Evening Gazette.* Rather than publicly condemn the New York police in a metropolitan newspaper, he had protected his reputation and sidestepped the issue by going home to Port Jervis and publishing them there. If he felt duty-bound to expose an arrogant police force, he had to accept the consequences of his actions. With the publication of "Adventures of a Novelist" in the *New York Journal,* he acknowledged his own struggle with respectability and his ultimate acceptance of a moral obligation.

Crane rushed to the police station to help Dora, but the desk sergeant advised him to leave: "If you monkey with this case, you are pretty sure to come out with mud all over you." Though he returned to his apartment, Crane was determined to rescue her and set his alarm clock so that he could be in court by 8:30 A.M. Intellectually, Crane knew he was doing the right thing, but he still had conflicting emotions, as revealed in his story "In the Tenderloin: A Duel between an Alarm Clock and a Suicidal Purpose," published only a few days later on October 1. A man known as Swift Doyer and an unnamed girl, in all likelihood a prostitute, quarrel because she has lied to him; he strikes her on the head with an alarm clock. She then confesses that she has taken a fatal dose of morphine and begins falling into a stupor, but he resuscitates her. She tries to revive a fly she has accidentally killed. Eventually they fall asleep at a table, her fingers entwined in his hair. This sordid depiction of Tenderloin life seemingly has no direct connection with Crane's dilemma, yet the story is about anger, regret, and rescue. Crane's anger and frustration toward Dora, as well as his anger toward himself for getting involved with her, are displaced onto Doyer. (Though the name could derive from Doyer Street in New York's Chinatown, it may be more than a coincidence that "Dora" and "Doyer" sound alike.) The "woefully pale" and "nerve-weak" Doyer might conceivably be a portrait of Crane racked by the evening's events. Just as Doyer concludes that "strange things invariably come into a man's head at the wrong time," Crane felt inconvenienced by his moral qualms. Like Doyer, he regretted his hasty actions. And just as Doyer rescues the girl from death in the wake of their quarrel, Crane, after distancing himself from Dora, rescued her with his testimony. Ultimately, "In the Tenderloin" deals with Crane's own potential social and professional suicide resulting from his defense of Dora Clark.[4]

Because Crane knew that his physical appearance might affect his credibility, he did his best to look respectable. He donned a suit and combed his long hair before showing up for the hearing. After the magistrate heard Clark's version of her arrest the night before, he asked Becker: "Is there any doubt in this case, officer?" "None at all," the policeman replied. "She's an old hand and always lies about it." Hearing no evidence to counter Becker's claim, the magistrate was about to pronounce Clark guilty and fine her, when Crane, who had been sitting silently, jumped up and exclaimed, "Your honor, I know the girl to be innocent." "And who are you?" asked the startled magistrate. "I am Stephen Crane the novelist." After Crane had confirmed Dora's story, the magistrate found her innocent.

Crane's fame guaranteed that his involvement with Dora Clark would be newsworthy. Only hours after her acquittal, he admitted to a *New York Journal* reporter that he had felt as scared as Henry Fleming in *The Red Badge of Courage*:

> "I was badly frightened, I admit, and would gladly have run away, could I have done so with honor."

"And now that it is over, I presume you are also like your hero, in being ready to face a sword ordeal without a tremor?"

"No, no! I differ from my own hero, for I would be just as frightened the next time!"[5]

Within days, newspapers throughout the country were depicting the Dora Clark affair as a tense, romantic melodrama in which Crane emerged a "champion" "as brave as his hero" in *The Red Badge,* who had come to Dora's "rescue": "He Wore No Red Badge of Courage, but Pluckily Saved a Girl from the Law."[6] Regardless of how newspapers treated the incident, the focus was on Crane himself—not on his reporting about the Tenderloin district, not on Dora Clark, and not on her charge of police harassment.

With the publication of "Adventures of a Novelist" in the *New York Journal* on September 20, 1896, Crane hoped that the melodrama would end, but it soon became a tragedy in which personal misfortune resulted from a flaw in the hero himself. Crane was the scion of a religious family with an esteemed ancestry, and his impulse to defend Dora was at least partly motivated by his sense of justice; but the champion who needed to maintain respectability also compulsively sought out the urban underworld and empathized with its denizens. It was "more than a place," he felt. "It is an emotion."[7] Crane secretly led a double life, and his flaw was a personality at odds with itself.

In "Adventures of a Novelist," Crane suppressed damaging details that were subsequently exposed in newspaper reports and court testimony, and he lied about his knowledge of Dora Clark. He had arranged to meet the two "chorus girls" (street argot for "prostitutes") at a Turkish smoking parlor, one of the five hundred or so drug dens in New York City, called "Turkish" because hashish was the cheapest and most available drug. The so-called resort where they met Clark was the Broadway Garden, a notorious hangout for prostitutes, which, as one newspaper reported, was routinely "crowded with rum-befuddled patrons" and with women, "mostly outcasts," who "go in without escorts, but rarely leave alone." Crane also pretended in "Adventures" that he had known nothing about Clark until the September 15 incident; but he had alluded to Rosenberg's arrest of her in the second article in the *Port Jervis Evening Gazette* and had most likely attended at least one of her four arraignments at the Jefferson Market Court during the previous three weeks. Later he had claimed: "[She] may be nothing but a prostitute. I know nothing whatever as to that. I have no information on that subject." Crane's deception would soon unravel.[8]

With funds from two charitable organizations, Clark hired a lawyer and filed charges on October 2 against Charles Becker and Patrolman Martin Conway, who had recently arrested her.[9] Though Crane declined to file charges against Becker, he offered to testify in her behalf. Clark's insistence on vindication prompted a violent response from the police.[10] Becker tracked her down two days later and brutally beat her. Crane, hoping to escape interviews, fled from New York.[11] Previously, whenever he had felt overwhelmed by the city, he headed for Port Jervis or Hartwood; but this time, he worried that his association with a prostitute would embarrass his straitlaced family, so he hid out with Fred Lawrence in Philadelphia.[12] Still, he trusted Roosevelt to treat everyone fairly and telegraphed him that he would testify at Becker's trial.[13]

Once Crane returned to New York, however, it became clear that the police were attempting to frighten him away from testifying. While he'd been out of town, they had raided his apartment and had found an opium layout tacked up on his wall, a souvenir from his research for "Opium's Varied Dreams"—a graphic account of opium use in Chinatown and the Tenderloin widely syndicated the previous May. They threatened to arrest him for maintaining an opium den and spread rumors that he had consorted with prostitutes, taken money from them, and left the city to avoid being subpoenaed. Crane's faith in Roosevelt and other police administrators was wrongly placed: they were skeptical of Dora Clark's assertions and of the accuracy of Crane's testimony. Roosevelt tried to persuade him not to testify because it would damage Crane's reputation, yet the would-be white knight insisted on doing so. The incident ended their relationship.[14]

On October 15, the date of the hearing into Clark's charges against Conway and Becker, Crane arrived at police headquarters on Mulberry Street at 3 P.M.; but because of the number of cases scheduled, the hearing did not begin until 9 P.M. and lasted till almost 3 A.M. It would be recorded as the longest trial ever held at the headquarters. Because there were a half-dozen cases ahead of Clark's, dozens of witnesses were crammed into the waiting room—twenty for her case alone. Witnesses sneered and pointed at Crane, whispering to people sitting nearby about the famous author forced to mingle with commoners like them. Discomfited by their behavior, he wandered nervously up and down the hallway, smoking constantly, and only left the building for food during a thirty-minute recess at 11 P.M.

After waiting for almost eleven hours, an emotionally and physically exhausted Crane, the last scheduled witness, entered the courtroom close to 2 A.M. If anyone present had thought that the Board of Commissioners had eliminated police corruption and that this would be a fair trial, their hopes would already have been dashed by the sight of a courtroom packed with policemen and by the barrage of witnesses called in behalf of Becker. Habitués of the Tenderloin had been threatened or bribed to testify that Dora Clark had solicited two men and that Crane had not been with her. One streetwalker who had entered the building as a witness for the prosecution had mysteriously become a witness for the defense by the time she entered the courtroom: "Big Chicago May," as she was known, claimed that Clark had offered her twenty-five dollars to testify falsely against Becker and had tried to rally fellow streetwalkers. "We must protect ourselves," Clark had supposedly said. "Becker is persecuting us. We must break him. Then I'm going to Europe."[15]

After Crane took the stand, Becker's attorney accused him of having eavesdropped on the proceedings so far, thus setting the tone for a grueling, aggressive cross-examination. Crane reiterated his September 16 deposition maintaining Clark's innocence, but the defense ruthlessly attempted to discredit him. Though this particular court had been set up specifically to try cases against policemen accused of misconduct (not private citizens), Crane was repeatedly asked about his private life. The magistrate upheld objections to the line of questioning and ordered that part of it be stricken from the record, but the focus of the trial quickly shifted from Clark and Becker to Crane.[16]

During cross-examination, Crane refused to answer questions about whether he had smoked opium and consorted with prostitutes, such as the well-known Sadie Traphagen. Overwhelmed, he covered his face with his hands to prevent the unrelenting barrage of questions from scorching his brain.[17] Eventually, however, he admitted that during the previous summer he had visited 121 West 27th Street, the home of Sadie's sister, a prostitute who used the pseudonym "Amy Leslie."[18] The address was on a block between Sixth and Seventh avenues that had long been notorious for its brothels and opium dens. West 27th Street was so jammed with prostitutes that it was, as Reverend Charles Parkhurst complained to the Board of Police Commissioners, "almost impossible to go through . . . especially in the late evening unless you are satisfied to turn into the middle of the street."[19]

After the magistrate had adjourned the hearing, the defense asked that one more witness be allowed, a janitor in the 27th Street house. The janitor testified that the building was a brothel where clients were often robbed and that Crane had lived there with a woman for six weeks during the summer. When the prosecution objected to the last-minute testimony, the magistrate excluded it, but the damage against Crane had already been done: now everyone knew that he had been living with Amy Leslie in a house of prostitution. With Crane's testimony discredited, the court found Becker innocent, concluding that although he may have been overzealous in his pursuit and detainment of Dora Clark, he had acted in good conscience and had done nothing illegal.[20] In contrast, Crane's career as an investigative reporter had been ruined. The gallant knight who had defended an innocent Dora Clark had been exposed as a seedy habitué of the Tenderloin.

Newspaper headlines sensationalized the trial. The *New York World* recounted a "racy story" about Crane's living "with a Tenderloin girl" and being involved in "an opium smoking episode," while a headline in the *New York News* flatly announced: "Woman's Arrest Justifiable." Other newspapers were outraged by the court's decision. The *Brooklyn Daily Eagle* bluntly criticized Crane's trial, in which a defense attorney was allowed "to worry, confuse, bully and insult citizens" while protecting a police organization that had been condemned as "one of the most corrupt, brutal, incompetent organizations in the world." The *New York Journal* defended Crane as "an honorable gentleman who had the courage to protect an unfortunate woman." The "simply outrageous" attack on him "was part of a deliberate and despicable scheme of police intimidation."[21]

Yet Crane's character was permanently damaged. Even decades after his death, false rumors that he was an opium addict darkened his reputation. The incident made him *persona non grata* to the police. Friends like Frederic Lawrence, Corwin Knapp Linson, and Edward Marshall supported him during the ordeal, but the incident strained his relationship with others. Roosevelt told Garland that he had "tried to save Crane from press comment, but as he insisted on testifying, I could only let the law take its course." Though Garland sympathized with Crane's desire to maintain a set of core principles, he concluded that Crane's "stubborn resolve" to defend Dora Clark was "quixotic" behavior: "The shady side of his bohemian life was turned to the light." Seeing Crane in McClure's office one day, Garland offered him fatherly advice: "Why don't you cut loose from your associations here? Go to your brother's farm in Sullivan County and get back your tone. You don't look well. Settle down to the writing of a single big book up there, and take your time to do it." Crane quickly responded, "I'll do it," but he was telling a white lie. If he had been unable to go home to his family in Sullivan County before the trial, he undoubtedly could not do so now, with the added embarrassment and humiliation resulting from it.[22]

His reputation tarnished and his friendship with Roosevelt severed, Crane still believed that he had made the right decision in defending Clark. As he wrote to William, "You must always remember that your brother in that case acted like a man of honor and a gentleman and you need not fear to hold your head up to anybody and defend his name. All that I said in my own article in the *Journal* is absolutely true, and for my part I see no reason why, if I should live a thousand years, I should be ever ashamed or humiliated by my course in the matter."[23] Crane had bravely defended an innocent person and was outraged by police graft and corruption, but calling "Adventures of a Novelist" "absolutely true" was disingenuous. The article portrayed an honorable Stephen; the trial revealed his feet of clay.

Whatever principles Crane had fought for in his defense of Clark dissolved in November when the Democratic-controlled Tammany Hall was voted back into office. Party loyalists chanted, "Well, well, well, reform has gone to hell"; and soon after, the notoriously corrupt Captain William Devery, whom reformers only a few years earlier had tried to imprison, became the city's chief of police. Crane knew that his career as an investigative journalist in New York was over and that he had to leave the city. Although he had been planning to go to England since at least September because the British had given such a favorable reception to *The Red Badge,* he was certain that the embarrassing details of the Dora Clark affair would precede him. When the Bacheller syndicate offered to send him to Cuba to report on the growing insurrection against Spain, he immediately accepted. While waiting for news that a boat was available to take him to Cuba, he wrote three Tenderloin sketches for the *New York Journal* and twice visited Cambridge, Massachusetts, to report on Harvard football games. After several false reports about transportation to Cuba, he suddenly received official notice at the end of November that a boat was available, and within hours he was gone.[24]

The stories about Dora Clark and Charles Becker, however, continued. In early December, she rented a room in a boardinghouse; but when other boarders complained about her late-night activities, she was evicted. Seeking revenge, Clark broke into the landlady's room, woke everyone up by banging out "Coming through the Rye" on a piano, shredded the curtains, and scattered ink all over the carpet and rugs. On her way out, she smacked the landlady with a satchel. Despite a warrant for her arrest, she was last seen cavorting nightly with affluent boys in Broadway's roof-garden dance halls.[25]

Becker's fate was more dramatic. Like Crane, he had roots in Sullivan County (his birthplace), had come to New York City in his late teens, had worked at a number of odd jobs, and in November 1893 had been sworn in as a police officer, having saved up the two hundred fifty dollars Tammany Hall extorted from police candidates. Becker had been assigned to the 29th Precinct, where he worked under Inspector Alexander "Clubber" Williams. Following the November 1896 election, the return of corruption to the Tenderloin allowed him to thrive. He was promoted to sergeant in 1907 and a year or two later, when department ranks were reorganized, he automatically became a lieutenant. On the surface, Becker thus seemed the victor in the Dora Clark affair, yet Crane had the last word. A few days after Becker's trial, Crane visited Sing Sing prison in Ossining, New York, for an article on the electric chair and the convicts' graveyard. That "throne of death"—situated in the execution chamber, "the place for the coronation of crime"—"waits in silence and loneliness, and waits and waits and waits" for "its next stained and sallow prince" to be crowned. On July 30, 1915, after being found guilty of conspiring to murder his gambling partner, Charles Becker became the first policeman in America to be given a coronation on the throne of death.[26]

17

Jacksonville

NOVEMBER–DECEMBER 1896

IRVING BACHELLER SENT Crane to Florida, hoping that his "last, great, shining star" could help his modest syndicate struggle against the mighty Pulitzer and Hearst conglomerates. When *The Little Regiment* was published in November 1896, Crane was reminded that his war stories were not based on personal experience, and he decided that a clandestine operation into Cuba would provide a fine opportunity to experience conflict directly. Tempering his sense of adventure was his recognition that this might bring tragic consequences. So he returned to Port Jervis to get William's legal assistance in drawing up his will, and he reminded Edmund's wife that if he did not return, she was to have the furniture and other possessions he had moved to Hartwood in the fall of 1895. Back in New York he applied for a passport, then on November 27 he headed south for the next phase of his career.[1]

Cuba and Puerto Rico were Spain's only remaining colonies in the New World after 1865. Occupied and settled by Spaniards in 1511, Cuba had used the labor of African slaves—430,000 by 1840—to become the world's leading sugar producer. As the colonial government became increasingly despotic, calls for freedom and independence had intensified, and a grueling ten-year war had begun in 1868. A truce signed in 1878 had led to Cuban representation in Spain's parliament and the eventual abolition of slavery, but the war had destroyed the sugar industry, ended the fight for independence, and killed 250,000 Cubans. As the Cuban economy weakened, the United States had invested capital and technology to keep the sugar mills competitive with European mills; by 1894, 90 percent of Cuban exports were going to America. With tension between Spain and Cuba continuing, poet and journalist José Martí renewed the cry for independence, and in 1895 fighting had erupted again.

On June 12, 1895, President Grover Cleveland had declared America's neutrality. Though he criticized Spain's oppression of Cuba and Americans supported Cuban independence, the United States was selling munitions to Spain and prohibiting their shipment to Cuban insurgents. To get around this prohibition, some Americans engaged in "filibustering" (from the Spanish *filibustero,* meaning "freebooter") — that is, smuggling arms to the insurgents. The smugglers called their vessels "filibusters." In particular, they used three small boats, known as the "Cuban fleet" or "Cuban navy": a fishing steamer named the *Commodore* and two tugs, the *Dauntless* and the *Three Friends.* Of the approximately seventy expeditions attempted by 1897, twenty-seven reached Cuba. Much of this activity had been organized by the Cuban Junta, a national organization that was based in New York City and that had been set up to raise funds and aid the independence movement.[2]

The major embarkation point for Cuba was Jacksonville, Florida. A seaport and popular winter resort, it had the largest and most elegant hotel in the South, the St. James, which accommodated five hundred people and offered filtered table water, steam heat, and other luxuries. Despite having a population of only twenty-eight thousand people, Jacksonville offered activities for everyone. Families attended performances at the Park Opera House and Wild West shows at the Base Ball Park, while the more adventurous could visit dozens of saloons and gambling dens throughout the city, as well as brothels on "the line" on Ward Street.

Jacksonville was also the most exciting place for the Junta's quasi-clandestine filibustering. Operating out of a cigar store, Cuban nationalists planned filibustering expeditions and supplied misinformation about the boats in order to deceive the U.S. government, Spanish authorities, and Pinkerton spies hired by the Spanish consul to investigate anyone suspected of filibustering. Various ruses were developed to smuggle munitions into Cuba. Ships with cargo for any Cuban port were required on their return trip to carry clearance papers from the town where they had docked; if the shipowners had no reasonable explanation for the trip, they were subject to a fine of five thousand dollars and the loss of their boat. During the previous summer, the *Commodore* had sailed repeatedly from Charleston, South Carolina, and stopped at Cuba; but when it had reached its destination of Tampa, Florida, it had been empty of cargo. Each time, the captain claimed that a storm had forced him to throw the cargo overboard to save the steamer. On another occasion, when the *Three Friends* had sailed for Cuba carrying an illicit cargo of men, munitions, and correspondents, the *Commodore* had warded off spies and local authorities by displaying a sign reading "Positively No Admittance" and posting a guard to prevent anyone from boarding.[3]

To many young men, filibustering offered sheer adventure. As a child, Crane had read Charles Kingsley's popular historical novel *Westward Ho!* (1855) about Captain Francis Drake and other heroic Elizabethan sailors seeking gold in the Caribbean, lured to sea by romance and patriotism. The book title also became the nickname of Emanuel Leutze's famous representation of Manifest Destiny in his painting *Westward the Course of Empire Takes Its Way* (1861). Crane, on his Western trip in 1895, had traversed the region that Leutze depicted and that earlier adventurers had sailed across in their prairie schooners. Now he was embarking on a trip that would capture the spirit of Kingsley's novel: "Filibustering is as near, perhaps, to the times celebrated by Charles Kingsley as we get in this day of other predominant ideals. The romance of it catches the heart of the lad. The same lad who longs to fight Indians and to be a pirate on his own account longs to embark secretly at midnight on one of these dangerous trips to the Cuban coast." By sneaking into Cuba as a war correspondent, Crane was living a version of the games he and his boyhood friends had played as cowboys and pirates, of his bohemian adventures with other "Indians" during his literary apprenticeship in New York, and of his explorations during his Western trip. The appeal of venturing "to some quarter of the world where mail is uncertain" and the allure of an ocean adventure were irresistible. From his early years swimming in rivers, sailing on lakes, and riding horseback on the New Jersey coast, Crane was drawn to water, a symbol of freedom, cleansing, and unlimited expanse.[4]

As resistance to Spanish rule increased on the island, journalists seeking fame and glory hastened to Florida, hoping to secure passage on a filibustering boat, evade Spanish patrols, and reach the insurgents in Cuba. The mission, however, was fraught with problems and danger. When journalists in Jacksonville tried to arrange passage on a filibuster, they immediately aroused suspicion because two steamer lines already made regular trips from Florida to Havana. Spanish gunboats routinely attempted to capture or destroy filibustering boats, and the Spanish considered American journalists to be spies. Shortly after arriving in Cuba on the *Three Friends* in July, Charles Govin, a twenty-three-year-old reporter for the *Key West Equator-Democrat,* was bound to a tree, shot repeatedly, and hacked to pieces with machetes by Spanish guerrillas. He was a horrific reminder to other young reporters, like the twenty-five-year-old Crane, of the fragility of life and the terror of war.

Crane arrived in Jacksonville on November 28, 1896. To maintain his anonymity, a special concern given his fame and notoriety following the Becker trial a month earlier, he registered at the St. James Hotel as "Samuel Carleton," a pseudonym associating him with one of America's most popular poets at the time, Will Carleton, whose poem "Cuba to Columbia," published in April, had captured the country's increasing sympathy for an embattled neighbor pleading for assistance: "Fairest of Freedom's daughters, / Have you no help for me?"[5]

Unlike other journalists frequenting the hotels and popular restaurants around Jacksonville, Crane fled to a dockside saloon, where (as a fellow journalist remarked) his name was unlikely to be familiar to "oilers, deck hands, sponge fishermen, wharf-rats and dock thieves, and all the rest of the human flotsam." But in a town crawling with spies and intrigue, an alias did not ensure anonymity. Within days of arriving in Jacksonville, Samuel Carleton was rumored to be a syndicate journalist heading for Cuba or an army veteran planning military tactics "We are troubled occasionally by Spanish spies," Crane remarked. "They follow us a good deal but they seem very harmless."[6]

On November 29, expecting that a filibustering ship would take him to Cuba within a day, Crane put his life in order by composing a series of detailed letters. Though he had written his will, Crane had characteristically lost it. Attempting to reconstruct the document from memory, he dictated its contents to a stenographer-typist in a letter to his brother

William. William would be the executor of the estate, with one-third going to him and another one-third to Edmund, both of whom had been giving their brother lodging for years; his two other brothers, George and Townley, would get one-sixth each. Other family members would get various items "as mementoes of me." To manage his publications, he appointed William Dean Howells, Hamlin Garland, Willis Brooks Hawkins, and Ripley Hitchcock as his literary executors and proposed that two collections of his stories and sketches be published as separate books: the first would consist of adventure stories (such as "One Dash—Horses," "The Wise Men," "The Snake," "A Man and Some Others") and the second would gather his *New York Press* sketches of city life, to be collectively titled "Midnight Sketches."[7] Finally, he ensured that his horse would be cared for until it died. In April 1896, having money for the first time in his life, he had bought a horse from Elbert Hubbard for sixty dollars, as well as a new Mexican saddle and expensive riding gear. Smart, playful, and unpredictable like its master, Peanuts (a.k.a. Monkeyshines, because of its mischievous nature) proved that "a good saddle-horse is the one blessing of life."[8]

Also on Crane's mind was Amy Leslie. Distraught at his sudden departure for Jacksonville, she accompanied him on the train as far as Washington, then most likely returned the same day. Their traveling together partway implies there was much unfinished business before Crane left on his trip. Their last moments together, he said, were "the most painful of my life and if I live a hundred years I know I can never forget them." Trying to comfort Amy, her "old hubber" wrote several letters on November 29 and another on December 12 to express "all the love in the world" for her and his sadness over their "temporary separation."[9]

"Positively frightened for the girl at the moment of parting," Crane wrote a grief-filled letter to Hawkins, asking that he help Amy "in what is now really a great trouble." Apparently, she had told Crane she was pregnant, with the hope that he would propose marriage or help her pay for an abortion, though in all likelihood she said nothing about her other sexual involvement (with a man named Isidor Siesfeld). Shortly before leaving for Jacksonville, Crane asked Hawkins to manage his financial affairs while he was away and wrote him a check for five hundred dollars to be disbursed in smaller amounts to himself for business expenses and to Amy for medical and living expenses. The source of the money is murky and complicated. It seems that Amy had already given Crane eight hundred dollars on November 1, his birthday, though it is unclear why. He did not need a loan, because for the first (and only) time in his life he was affluent, earning royalties from his five books in print. She later claimed that she had expected Crane to deposit the money in a bank for her. On November 5, he deposited six hundred dollars into his own account, ostensibly keeping two hundred of Amy's eight hundred. By the end of the month, when Crane wrote Hawkins a check, there was $776.50 in the account, though part or all of this could have come from royalties. During the next several months, confusion about the money would worry Crane.[10]

Unable to leave quickly for Cuba, Crane relieved the tedium by reading the recent reissue of the bestseller *Under Two Flags* (1867, 1896), a romantic adventure novel by Marie Louise de la Ramée, who used the pen name Ouida. The gallant nobleman Bertie Cecil chooses to save a woman's honor rather than defend himself against a false charge of forgery, and the spirited gamine Cigarette, whose love for Bertie is unreciprocated, saves him by throwing herself in front of his firing squad. Crane had read the book as a child, but eventually realized that "most of us forget Ouida" because her novels are full of clichéd plots, stereotyped characters, rambling speeches (Cigarette's dying farewell takes five pages), and extraneous details that reveal more about Ouida's knowledge than about the story itself. In all likelihood, Crane reread the book only because the journal *Book Buyer* asked him to review it, for he normally ridiculed sentimental characters who, like those in *Under Two Flags,* "abandon themselves to virtue and heroism as the martyrs abandoned themselves to flames." But this time, he was struck by their personal integrity and sense of sacrifice.[11]

More surprising was Crane's self-revelation in his review. With the exception of a few interviews he gave earlier in 1896 following the success of *The Red Badge of Courage,* he rarely spoke publicly about himself and literature, but on this occasion he did. Praising the book for "the gospel of life it preaches"—a curious statement for someone who believed that didactic literature was not art—he alluded to the Realism War that he and other authors had been fighting under the leadership of Howells. What was popular at the time, he implied, was an idealized form of romantic storytelling in which authors "sing of portières and champagne and gowns," as well as "Beauty's perfections." In contrast were realistic stories depicting "profane and human" characters with "imperfections" and "doleful flaws." The review also suggested Crane's hidden anxieties and human frailties. Only about five hundred words long, it includes almost two dozen personal pronouns ("I," "me," the collective "we") with constructions like "I had outgrown," "I often find," "we men of doleful flaws," "affected me," and "I confess"—expressions that reveal Crane's innermost thoughts and self-examination.

Read within the context of the recent Dora Clark incident, Crane's response to Ouida's novel was revealing. Here was a story of characters sacrificing themselves out of principle in order to save someone else. Bertie Cecil risks his reputation to defend a woman's honor; Cigarette protects him by becoming a martyr. From Crane's point of view, he had risked his own personal and professional standing for Dora. He had no illusion that he inhabited the kind of fantasy world that Ouida portrayed in *Under Two Flags,* in which Bertie regains his title and reputation and marries a princess. Nevertheless, he identified with a world in which "pain, death, dishonor is counted of no moment so long as the quality of personal integrity is defended and preserved."

Yet Crane's reading of Ouida's romantic novel also reminded him of flawed, "profane and human" characters in literature—and in love affairs. Crane's letters to Amy are unique in his correspondence with women. Unlike his letters to Lily Brandon Munroe and Nellie Crouse, which are full of adolescent posturing and self-promotion, these begin with salutations to "My Blessed Girl," "My dearest," "My own Sweetheart," and "My Beloved" and intimately confess an impassioned love for her. The most that Lily ever got was "Dearest L.B."; Nellie, a mere "Dear Miss Crouse." Equally significant, he avoided addressing Amy by name and signed his letters cryptically with only "Your lover," "S," or "C," thus hiding his association with her in case someone else read the letters. It is impossible to know how deeply Crane cared for Amy; but having had his reputation tarnished only weeks earlier, he was particularly fearful of losing even more of the celebrity he had struggled so long to achieve. The presumed intimacy in the letters to his "blessed sweetheart" Amy may have been at least partly a way to calm a woman troubled by a possible pregnancy and a sense of abandonment. Crane the caretaker would have wanted to rescue and protect her as much as he had Dora, but Crane the rascal easily strayed from his ideals. Despite assurances of devotion and loyalty to Amy, he could not resist the attraction of another free spirit. His life was once again about to change, as he entered Jacksonville's Hotel de Dreme, a house of assignation with "a 'Class A' rating" owned by a woman who called herself Cora E. Taylor.[12]

Cora had been born as Cora Ethel Eaton Howorth in Boston in 1865. Her father, John Howorth, was an artist, and her paternal great-grandfather, George Howorth, had been a wealthy art dealer in Boston who specialized in restoring oil paintings. Less is known about her mother, though her maternal grandfather, Charles Holder, had manufactured pianos in New York City. After Cora's father died when she was six years old, her mother had remarried and moved to New York. Apparently, her mother had died soon thereafter, and Cora had been raised by George Howorth, until he died when she was fifteen. In his will he left her an inheritance but did not name a guardian.[13]

Around the age of seventeen, she had begun a four-year relationship as the mistress of Jerome Stivers, a notorious playboy and heir to a successful New York carriage-manufacturing business started by his father. During this time, they apparently lived at the London Club, a popular gambling parlor at 6 West 29th Street, where Cora served as the hostess. The street was notorious for prostitution; and though most of the solicitation occurred west of 6th Avenue, near the house where Crane had lived with Amy Leslie on 27th Street, the address of the London Club put it between Fifth and Sixth avenues in the heart of the Tenderloin. As was the case at the time, gambling parlors—whether in New York, Jacksonville, or elsewhere—invariably served more than one purpose. In all likelihood, Stivers had not allowed his mistress to be a prostitute, but Cora surely learned the business skills she needed later to run her own establishment in Jacksonville.[14]

In 1886, at the age of twenty-one, Cora had married a wealthy dry-goods businessman named Thomas Vinton Murphy, whose father had been a controversial figure as collector of revenues for the Port of New York; but in less than two years the marriage had ended. Cora's second marriage—to an English aristocrat named Captain Donald William Stewart in London in 1889—had quickly faltered. By early 1892, she was back in New York and the mistress of another wealthy playboy, Ferris S. Thompson, whose father had been a founder of the First National Bank of the City of New York and later of the Chase National Bank. Identifying herself as "Lady" Stewart, she and Ferris had lived lavishly and traveled widely, throughout Europe and as far east as Constantinople on the Orient Express. Their relationship had ended when Cora stabbed him in the arm after he left her for an actress in Paris. Cora's estranged husband, Captain Stewart, had tried to sue Thompson in 1895 for alienating her affections, but the suit had been dismissed.

By 1895, Cora was in Jacksonville as "Cora Taylor." She leased a boardinghouse called the Hotel de Dreme—named after its former proprietor, Ethel Dreme—and bought its contents, then converted it into one of Jacksonville's most fashionable houses of assignation, a thinly disguised brothel that also featured gambling and other amusements. Sometime before December 4, 1896, Crane met Cora at the hotel. At thirty-one, she was the older by six years. According to Ernest W. McCready, correspondent for the *New York Herald,* Crane discovered a copy of one of his books, possibly *The Little Regiment,* in the living room of the Hotel de Dreme and later saw Cora reading it.[15] They had much in common. Both had come from respectable families and had lost their fathers early on, Cora at age six and Stephen at age eight. Both had been raised as an only child, Cora literally and Stephen figuratively (there was a significant age difference between him and his next-oldest sibling). Both had already traveled—Crane to the West and Mexico, and Cora to England and the Continent—and unbeknownst to them, fate had already brought them near each other. Monmouth County in New Jersey, with its horseracing and with Phil Daly's famous gambling casino, the Pennsylvania Clubhouse in Long Branch, attracted the rich and famous to the shore. From 1886 to 1888, while Stephen was reporting local news in Asbury Park, Cora and her first husband frequented the family horse farm in Deal, a mile away, and nearby Monmouth Park racetrack. Crane later reminisced about the way Phil Daly and the Monmouth Park Racing Association had popularized Long Branch, which prospered until the New Jersey legislature shut down horseracing in 1893.[16]

On December 4, as a sign of their friendship, Crane gave Cora a copy of Rudyard Kipling's novel *The Seven Seas* (1896),[17] a copy of *George's*

Mother inscribed to "an unnamed sweetheart,"[18] and an unidentified book inscribed:

> To C. E. S.
>
>   Brevity is an element that enters importantly into all pleasures of life and this is what makes pleasure sad and so there is no pleasure but only sadness.
> Stephen Crane
> Jacksonville, Fla
> Nov [for December] 4th, 1896.[19]

Crane created a playful sense of mystery in calling Cora "an unnamed sweetheart," and his longer inscription revealed that C. E. S. (Cora Ethel Stewart) had confided to Crane the truth about her marital status.[20] Knowing that he had become smitten with a twice-married woman and was soon leaving for Cuba, Crane expected that their relationship would be short-lived. Only weeks earlier, he had published "I explain the silvered passing of a ship at night," a mournful poem about fleeting relationships in which lovers, like ships passing in the night, drift past each other only to reach "waste," "loneliness," and "sadness."[21]

Crane planned to travel to Cuba with Sylvester Scovel, head of the *New York World*'s correspondents in Jacksonville, who tried to rent the *Commodore*. An extremely fast steamer, it could outrun the revenue cutter *Boutwell,* which patrolled the shores for violations of neutrality laws, and had already attempted to reach Cuba four times. When negotiations between Scovel and the boat's owners broke down, the *New York World* quickly sent a yacht, the *No. 83,* to Jacksonville; but Scovel found it unsuitable and returned to New York City to find another boat.

In the meantime, the *Commodore* was cleared by the secretary of the treasury to sail to Cuba so long as it did not violate U.S. neutrality laws. The issue soon became complicated. A lawyer for the Cubans argued that the decision about a ship's cargo and the decision about its destination were separate issues. If the Treasury Department cleared a ship to sail to Cuba, it should not "matter whether she had on board arms or sausages." Only if a ship's manifest exceeded "the number necessary to man the vessel" could it be called "an armed expedition."[22] Although the official position of neutrality was generally enforced, the number of crew members considered excessive was conveniently left undecided, and filibustering expeditions often sailed with fanfare and publicity in response to Americans' widespread support for the insurgency.

As the steamer prepared to leave port on December 31, no one doubted its purpose, for a local newspaper had reported details about its cargo of munitions. Pedro Solis, the Spanish consul in Florida, formally complained about the cargo; but when asked whether he knew the purpose of the weapons, he coyly responded, "I don't know. They may be for the Spanish army." Solis's disingenuousness belied his true feelings about the *Commodore.* He was required to approve the papers of any ship heading for a Spanish port; but when asked if he would do so knowing that munitions were intended for the insurgents, he quickly replied, "Certainly I will . . . just the same as if the cargo were potatoes for the Spanish army." Loyalty to Spain was less important than his own greed: he collected a fee based on the ship's tonnage. The heavier the cargo, the more money he made.[23]

The *Commodore* sailed from Jacksonville at approximately 8:00 P.M. on New Year's Eve with forty boxes of rifles, a thousand pounds of gunpowder, more than 200,000 cartridges, three hundred machetes, and a crew of twenty-seven or twenty-eight men, with Crane listed as a seaman earning twenty dollars a month. Trouble with the boat began quickly. In a dense fog on the St. John's River, less than two miles from port, the *Commodore* struck a sandbar off Commodore's Point; the *Boutwell* towed it back to port at dawn on January 1. In a tragic error, perhaps because Captain Edward Murphy and the two engineers were on board the *Commodore* for the first time, no one checked to see whether the hull had been damaged by the grounding. In a second attempt to get to sea, it beached at Mayport with the *Boutwell* nearby. Reversing its engines, the *Commodore* freed itself from the sandbar.[24]

These difficulties boded ill. Just about the only sailors not sick from the rough sea were Crane and the captain, who smoked and swapped tales in the pilot house. When a leak was discovered in the engine room at about 10 P.M., the pumps failed to remove the water. Crane immediately set up a line of men with buckets to bail water from the room. With unbearable heat and faint streaks of lighting that cast "mystic and grewsome shadows," as Crane recalled, the room resembled "the middle kitchen of hades" with "soapish sea water swirling and sweeping and swishing among machinery that roared and banged and clattered and steamed."[25] Crane must have remembered words spoken only hours earlier. Before crossing the bar, Captain Kilgore of the *Boutwell* had cried out, "Are you fellows going to sea to-day?" When Captain Murphy had replied yes and his steamer whistled a salute to the *Boutwell,* Kilgore had removed his cap: "Well, gentlemen, I hope you have a pleasant cruise."

18

The *Commodore* Incident

JANUARY 1897

ABOUT SIXTEEN MILES from Mosquito Inlet (today called Ponce de Leon Inlet) and a hundred miles from Jacksonville, the *Commodore* lost power and came to a standstill. Crew members panicked.[1] One covered himself in life preservers; another pleaded to be thrown overboard rather than wait for a harrowing death; another begged the captain to blow up the ship with dynamite; still another climbed the rigging and tried to stand on his head. Valiantly, Crane helped to calm the crew and kept watch on the bridge with binoculars, searching the horizon for land. When he began slipping on the uneven deck, he removed his new shoes, threw them overboard, and said, "Well, Captain, I guess I won't need them if we have to swim."[2]

Attempts to restart the engine failed, and in the early-morning hours of January 2 Captain Murphy ordered everyone to abandon ship. Crane's initial reaction revealed his conflicted behavior. According to one account, upon hearing the captain say there was little chance of survival, Crane strapped on a belt equipped with two revolvers and a bowie knife because he wanted to look like a warrior if his body washed ashore. There was a tinge of romanticized affectation in his self-image, but he remained resolute in his actions. When the scene became extremely cha-

otic, Crane restrained a Cuban who was ineptly trying to launch a lifeboat. In contrast to Crane's steadfastness was the cowardice of Paul E. F.
Rojo, agent for the boat's owners and commandant of the Cubans on
board. Instead of looking after his men, he quickly grabbed his extra
clothing and two valises, one of which was "about as large as a hotel,"
and made sure he was the first person in a lifeboat. "He reminded me of
George Washington." Crane quipped. "First in war, first in peace—and in
the lifeboat."[3]

After three lifeboats were launched, the final four crew members—
Captain Edward Murphy; William Higgins, an oiler; Charles B. Montgomery, the steward; and Crane—crowded into a ten-foot dinghy. When
the third lifeboat quickly foundered, its seven men returned to the *Commodore* to build makeshift rafts. One of the men, believing that the attempt was futile, jumped into the sea without a life jacket; three others
got stranded on the ship when it sank at 7 A.M. The men in the dinghy
attempted to use a line to tow the remaining three crew members on
their rafts; but when the turbulent sea made the task impossible, one of
the crew began to rein in the line and attempted to board the dinghy.
Knowing that it could not support the weight of a fifth man, the men in
the dinghy released the rope, dooming the crew members.

The fate of the dinghy likewise seemed hopeless. The four exhausted
men barely had strength to row, and the captain, who had broken his
arm, could not help. Any sudden movement was dangerous because the
dinghy's gunwales were barely six inches above the waterline. By 4 P.M.
the men were a quarter-mile from shore, a few miles south of Daytona.
Seeing people on the beach, they fired a pistol and waved a flag of distress, but their actions were misinterpreted as mere playfulness. Because
of the strong wind, current, and surf, they knew that the dinghy would
most likely capsize if they attempted to reach land. Staying beyond the
breakers, Crane and Higgins took turns rowing. By morning, the dinghy
had drifted north of Daytona.

After about six hours, the first lifeboat reached shore with twelve
Cubans, including Rojo. Immediately, he wired the Junta in Jacksonville
with news of the disaster and arranged for a sailboat to take the twelve
men to New Smyrna, Florida.[4] Shortly after a second lifeboat with four
more Cubans landed, newspapers across the country began reporting the
disaster. Rumors quickly spread regarding the fate of the ship and its

crew: "Filibuster Sunk—Crane Missing," "Twelve Men Lost Through Treachery," "The *Commodore* Was Scuttled."[5] Ships at sea, and bicyclists ranging over the seventy miles of coast between St. Augustine and New Smyrna Beach, desperately searched for survivors.[6] Back in Jacksonville, Cora was distraught. When an empty lifeboat washed ashore, a friend's lament echoed her thoughts: "God save Crane if he is still alive."[7]

Having been afloat for almost thirty hours and seeing no sign of rescue, the four men in the dinghy risked heading in to shore through rough surf on the morning of January 3. With only two life preservers available, the captain insisted that these be given to the inexperienced seamen—Montgomery, who could not swim, and Crane. Higgins was an excellent swimmer, and the injured captain had little faith in his own chances of survival. Though the dinghy capsized in the breakers at Daytona Beach, a resident passing by jumped into the water to rescue them. Within minutes, other residents arrived with coffee, blankets, and clothing for the weary survivors. Unfortunately, the strongest swimmer, Billie Higgins, drowned, having apparently been struck in the head by the dinghy when it overturned in the surf.

Hearing that Crane was alive, Cora cabled him on January 3: "Thank God your safe have been almost crazy." Then, in an impulsive decision that typified her improvident attitude toward money, she immediately sent another telegram entreating him to catch a special train to Jacksonville—"never mind overcharges."[8] Because it was Sunday, however, no regular trains ran south of St. Augustine, and the earliest he could have gotten back to Jacksonville was Monday evening. In any case, his first instinct was not to return immediately to Cora. Unwilling to leave until after Higgins had been buried in a local cemetery,[9] he spent the night in Daytona Beach. Following the funeral, he hoped to take a train south. He was determined to find passage to Cuba, yet he also seemed to be running away from Cora.[10]

Unwilling to wait until Monday evening to be reunited with Crane, Cora caught the first morning train and arrived in Daytona Beach about noon on Monday.[11] While they waited for a return train, she and Stephen sought privacy in a corner of the station and embraced. Greeting them at the Jacksonville station later that day were other *Commodore* survivors and more than a hundred Cubans. Despite the adulation that they showered on the world-famous author, Crane remained humble and appreciative. Earlier, while at the St. James Hotel, Miss Lillian Barrett, a nine-year-old vacationing with her family in Jacksonville who later achieved fame as a novelist and playwright *(The Dice of the Gods),* had heard that a famous author was staying at her hotel. She had become fixated on Cuban independence and had heard lurid stories of the dire plight of insurgents. In response, she published in a local newspaper a melodramatic poem about "Little Cuba," depicting its "blood-red" streets with families "shrieking for food" and "babies all nude." Identifying Crane "as the divinely appointed savior" of the island, she was determined to add his signature to her autograph album, which already contained signatures from William Jennings Bryan, champion boxer John L. Sullivan, and Richard K. Fox, owner of the *National Police Gazette.* She had been unable to corner Crane before he had sailed, and now she excitedly greeted him in the hotel lobby when he returned from Daytona. Though exhausted from his experience and wearing ill-fitting garments that had shrunk to half their size during his ordeal, he waved her over. "Where's that album?" She retrieved it from the clerk's desk, where she kept it for easy access, and he wrote: "Stephen Crane, Able Seaman, S S Commodore. January 4, 1897."[12]

Immediately following the *Commodore* disaster, newspapers printed stories of possible sabotage, suggesting that someone opposed to the Cuban insurrection had tampered with the pumps. A representative of the Junta quickly blamed the accident on mechanical failure and human error, for treachery implied dissension within the Cuban community in Jacksonville. Paul Rojo also denied the charge and accused Chief Engineer Redigan of being drunk and ignoring the pumps. Crane and Murphy defended Redigan and dismissed the accusation of treachery; but Murphy was already a potentially unreliable witness, for he denied that the *Commodore* had run aground, despite clear evidence that it had done so twice. Only Montgomery claimed treachery, based on cryptic remarks made to him. A Spanish sympathizer watching sailors load cargo onto the ship had warned, "Load up with your guns, but you will never get them to Cuba in that old tub." And minutes before sailing, another Spaniard had pleaded with Montgomery to stay on land: "My God, Charlie! Don't go on that ship. You risk your life." After the boat had run aground twice, Montgomery, sensing disaster, had told Crane, "God, I don't feel right about this ship, somehow. It strikes me that something is going to happen to us. I don't know what it is, but the old ship is going to get it in the neck, I think." To which Crane had replied sarcastically, "Are any of us going to get out, prophet?"[13]

For several days Cora nursed a bedridden Crane, who was physically and emotionally exhausted from the ordeal. In the past, he had always been indifferent to danger and had fatalistically accepted the consequences of his actions. As a child, he had impressed his brothers with his perseverance while learning to swim; he had acted bravely in defending Dora Clark; and as a survivor of a harrowing experience on the Atlantic Ocean, he was still, according to the captain, "the spunkiest fellow out . . . a thoroughbred . . . and a brave man, too, with plenty of grit."[14] But now, more than at any other time in his life, he needed writing as catharsis and as a way to understand his experience. At first, he was "unable to write a thing," as he told the *New York World*. And he declined an offer from another paper—one thousand dollars for a thousand words about the incident—in order to honor his commitment to the Bacheller syndicate. By January 6 he sent Bacheller "Stephen Crane's Own Story," an account of the sinking of the *Commodore,* but the piece clearly betrays the struggle he went through to write it. The point of view shifts abruptly from first person to third, the narrator confesses that he has "forgotten to mention" a particular fact earlier in the report, and the ending reveals Crane's difficulty in understanding the sinking of the boat and the drowning of sailors on the rafts:

> We rowed around to see if we could not get a line from the chief engineer, and all this time, mind you, there were no shrieks, no groans, but silence, silence and silence, and then the *Commodore* sank. She lurched to windward, then swung afar back, righted and dove into the sea, and the rafts were suddenly swallowed by this frightful maw of the ocean. And then by the men on the ten-foot dingy were words said that were still not words, something far beyond words.

This is a powerful description, but the repetition of the conjunction "and" six times in a short paragraph bespeaks Crane's inability to get beyond merely stringing details together rather than interpreting them. The speech of the men in the dinghy was less an attempt at meaningful utterance than a visceral response to tragedy. Crane wanted to tell the complete story, but he could not: "The history of life in an open boat for thirty hours would no doubt be instructive for the young, but none is to be told here and now"—instructive for the young indeed, Crane included.[15]

In mid-January Crane returned to New York for about three weeks and was formally honored for his heroism at the Lantern Club. When asked by newspapers to discuss the incident, he could say no more than what he had written in his report. Needing first to talk out his anxiety, he escaped to the safety of Hartwood, where, around the warmth and comfort of a crackling fire in Edmund's stove, he developed a more carefully crafted version of the incident. He recited it almost completely before writing it down. By early February he was back in Jacksonville, dining with Captain Murphy at the Hotel de Dreme and reading him a first draft:

> "Listen, Ed, I want to have this *right*, from your point of view. How does it sound so far?"
>
> "You've got it, Steve. That is just how it happened, and how we felt."

The story is called "The Open Boat," and in it Crane finally captured the broad social and metaphysical significance of their experience. Its subtitle plainly states its purpose: "A Tale Intended To Be after the Fact—Being the Experience of Four Men from the Sunk Steamer *Commodore*." Previously, Crane's fiction had focused largely on characters isolated in a society fragmented by human indifference and lack of communication. Henry Fleming abandons the tenuous community of his fellow soldiers and wanders aimlessly through the smoke and fog of a battlefield; Maggie is rejected by family, church, and society; homeless men huddle in a breadline under the falling snow before retiring to a flophouse. Because Crane had always felt a sense of cosmic isolation in a cold, amoral universe where individuals battle for survival, it is not surprising that his persona in "The Open Boat," a correspondent, has "been taught to be cynical of men"; but writing a tale after the fact changed this view. Crane acknowledged that humanity's limited perception of reality prevented attempts at finding order in random, chaotic events—assuming that some sort of order did exist—and that family, church, and conventional society seemed at best outmoded trappings offering a veneer of hope and stability. Yet the experience in an open boat had taught him the efficacy of a "subtle brotherhood of men" bonded as a community while facing imminent death.[16]

The captain asked Crane how he planned to end the story: "How do you wind it up, when poor old Billie was floating face down and all those people came running down to pull us out of the breakers?" Crane read him the concluding paragraphs.

> "Do you like it or not, Ed?"
> "It's good, Steve. Poor old Billie! Too bad he had to drown. He was a damn good oiler."

As the best swimmer in the group, Billie would have survived in a rational universe; his death affirmed the tragic limitations of humanity's attempt to control its own destiny. Crane gave him a form of immortality—the oiler is the only character in the story who has a name—and honored his companions in his dedication to the collected volume, *The Open Boat and Other Tales of Adventure* (1898): "To / The Late William Higgins / and to / Captain Edward Murphy and Steward C. B. Montgomery / of the Sunk Steamer Commodore."[17]

"The Open Boat" has remained one of the greatest short stories in Anglo-American literature. "No living English prose writer of his years approaches his wonderful gift of original and penetrating observation," said Harold Frederic, and H. G. Wells called it "the crown of all his work." Despite achieving some level of catharsis by writing it, Crane remained haunted by his experiences. Following its completion, he wrote a shipwreck story in March to cash in on his sudden fame as a seaman. In "Flanagan and His Filibustering Adventure," the captain of the *Foundling* signs on for a filibustering expedition "just for fun, mostly" and drowns when his ship sinks during a storm. The story lacks the greatness of "The Open Boat," but suggests Crane's residual pain as one of four foundlings from the mother ship adrift in "a great wind-crossed void." Like Flanagan, Crane had gone to sea partly for heroic adventure—the kind that Kingsley had promised in *Westward Ho!* to romantic dreamers; but as a result of his ordeal, he now "understood doom and its weight and complexion." "The Filibustering Industry," written around the time of "Flanagan," was ostensibly about the business of smuggling arms into Cuba, but it dealt more with Crane's conflicted obligations to employers, confidants, readers, and himself: "Responsibility is so arranged upon the shoulders of the average correspondent that it is more cruel than kind to burden him with facts of vast political significance." The burden extended to his own anxiety about the perceived abandonment of the seven crewmen lost at sea. When the *Commodore* had run aground in mud, the *Boutwell* had towed her to safety with a line; but when the men in the open boat had attempted to tow a makeshift raft, they had been forced to let go of the line to save their own lives. Logically, Crane knew there had been no other choice; but emotionally, the anguish was unbearable. "Death and the Child," written later in 1897, captured the turmoil of the Greco-Turkish War, and its reliance on nautical imagery to describe battles on land indicated Crane's obsessive need to work through his pain. Combat, to him, was like "the sea during a storm," with its "cold and tumultuous billows"; the babble of fleeing peasants was like that of "men drowning"; and a character's movement was like that of "a corpse walking on the bottom of the sea." By the end of the story, another foundling, a child forgotten and abandoned by his terrified parents, envisions the landscape as "a colossal wave" flecked with the "foam which one sees on the slant of a rough sea." That sense of abandonment reflected Crane's own guilt over the men left behind on rafts and on the *Commodore*. In "The Open Boat," he alluded only briefly to the "seven turned faces"; but in one of his finest poems, "A man adrift on a slim spar," he captured the harrowing memory of the "weary slow sway" of a sailor's "lost hand" as the man is swept into "the sea, the moving sea, the sea."[18]

Crane's near-death experience also prompted him to reconsider his budding relationship with Cora. Within days of the *Commodore*'s sinking in January 1897, Crane inscribed an unidentified book to her:

> To C. E. S
>
> Love comes like the tall swift shadow of a ship at night. There is for a moment, the music of the water's turmoil, a bell, perhaps, a man's shout, a row of gleaming yellow lights. Then the slow sinking of this mystic shape. Then silence and a bitter silence—the silence of the sea at night.
>
> Stephen Crane[19]

The inscription paraphrased Crane's poem about ships passing in the night, and, more important, it referred to a novel that he and Cora had read: Beatrice Harraden's *Ships That Pass in the Night.* Published in 1893, it was reprinted at least eleven times in its first year, sold more than one million copies, and became one of the most popular books of the 1890s. After reading it during the summer of 1896, Crane told Richard Senger, a brother of his friend Louis Senger, that he had enjoyed the book. Cora liked it too, having read it sometime after 1894, and copied excerpts and its epigraph into her notebooks.[20] The transcriptions reveal much about her frame of mind. The epigraph consists of lines from Longfellow's *Tales of a Wayside Inn:* "Ships that pass in the night, and speak each other in passing, / Only a signal shown, and a distant voice in the darkness, / So, on the ocean of life, we pass and speak one another, / Only a look and a voice, then darkness again and a silence." The excerpts she copied read:

> Everyone is lonely, but everyone does not know it. But now and then the knowledge comes like a revelation, and we realize that we stand practically alone, out of anyone's reach for help or comfort.

> When we come to think about it seriously, it is rather absurd for anyone to expect to have uninterrupted stretches of happiness. Happiness falls to our share in separate detached bits, and those of us who are wise, content ourselves with these broken fragments.[21]

Longfellow's and Harraden's lines capture the sense of isolation, sadness, and uncertainty that Cora expresses throughout her notebooks and reflect Crane's psyche as well. Since Cora and Stephen knew that happiness was ephemeral, they lived intensely in the broken fragment of the moment. Soon after their first meeting at the Hotel de Dreme, they might well have wondered whether two such lonely ships would do more than merely pass in the night.

Having read *Ships That Pass in the Night,* they knew one possible answer. The novel recounts the tragic love story of Bernardine Holme and Robert Allitsen. Whereas Robert struggles with commitment and inaction, Bernardine is a self-reliant New Woman who is a teacher, journalist, and political activist. They meet at a sanatorium in Petershof, Switzerland, where they have both sought treatment for tuberculosis. Bernardine recovers and returns to England to work in her uncle's bookstore; Robert writes her a love letter, but tears it up before mailing it. When he inherits money following his mother's death, he tracks down Bernardine to express his love in person; but soon thereafter, she dies in a wagon accident. Robert then realizes the mistake he has made in not seizing the moment earlier to express his feelings. Heartbroken, he returns to the sanatorium, awaiting his death from tuberculosis. The title of the novel quickly became a catchphrase for an ephemeral love affair, and its plot dramatized the consequences of inaction.

Almost three years before meeting Cora in late 1896, Crane acknowledged his tuberculosis and described the life he wanted to live:

> There was a man who lived a life of fire.
> Even upon the fabric of time,
> Where purple becomes orange
> And orange purple,
> This life glowed,
> A dire red stain, indelible;
> Yet when he was dead,
> He saw that he had not lived.

Crane "lived a life of fire," and the "dire red stain" was another kind of red badge: the blood in his lungs, "indelible" because his illness was incurable. Crane was determined not to be like the man in the poem, who, at the end of life, "saw that he had not lived." This is the mistake that Robert makes. By alluding to Harraden's novel in his inscription to Cora, Crane acknowledged that she, like Bernardine Holme, was a New Woman and that they needed to live fully in the moment. Only a few days before writing that inscription about ships that pass in the night, he had been reminded of his own frailty and the mutability of life.

19

The Greco-Turkish War

JANUARY–MAY 1897

DESPITE THE ORDEAL at sea, Crane was determined to work as a foreign correspondent for Bacheller. While in New York City in January 1897, he applied for a passport to travel to Cuba, Mexico, and the West Indies. He was back in Florida by the middle of February, hoping to sail to Cuba along with fellow correspondent Charles Michelson aboard the *Buccaneer,* another Hearst yacht that doubled as a dispatch boat trying to evade the U.S. blockade aimed at enforcing neutrality laws. When the plan failed, Crane left Jacksonville and headed south for the swamp country around Indian River. Looking for another filibuster headed for Cuba and "wading miserably to and fro," he complained to William about the "attempt to avoid our derned U.S. navy. And it cant be done."[1] Following the widespread news about the sinking of the *Commodore,* the navy had intensified its antifilibuster patrols. Crane was convinced that he could not get to Cuba soon. He changed his plans abruptly and was back in New York City by the middle of March, hastily arranging for employment.

Crane was a poor businessman with bad luck, questionable ethics, and incessant financial problems. In September 1896, he had begun a profes-

sional relationship with Paul Revere Reynolds, America's first professional literary agent, whom he had met earlier in the year at the Lantern Club. Acting as the business representative of authors, Reynolds
would sell their manuscripts to magazines and publishers in exchange for
a commission. His relationship with Crane, lasting almost three years,
would periodically become strained; his client's unprofessional behavior
often tested the trust and patience of editors and publishers. In September, Crane asked Reynolds to sell "A Man and Some Others," one of the
three Western tales he had recently written, but urged him not to approach Bacheller or McClure. Unknown to Reynolds, Crane was apparently using him to get more money by breaking prior agreements with
publishers to whom he was financially indebted. Reynolds sold the story
to *Century Magazine* the following month, but found himself forced to
negotiate between Crane and the editors regarding offensive language in
the story. Although Crane deleted one phrase, an editor was still concerned about the swearing that remained. "It is hardly necessary to say
that Mr. Crane will not like the excisions in his Ms.," Reynolds told the
editor. "It is pretty safe to say that an author does not like to see the child
of his brain cut or in any way changed." In October, Crane again avoided
his obligation to McClure by urging Reynolds to sell the serial rights to
The Third Violet directly to the *New York World*.[2]

Money problems followed Crane to Florida. Before he had left for
Jacksonville the previous November, Bacheller had advanced him seven
hundred dollars in Spanish gold for expenses. Crane had either thrown
the money overboard because of its weight before abandoning the *Commodore* or had lost it after the dinghy capsized in the surf. In late February, writing from Jacksonville, he urged Hitchcock to send him payment
from the Heinemann editions of *Maggie* and *The Little Regiment* to cover
mounting expenses—"very important," he insisted.[3] He had hoped that
the sale of "The Open Boat" would help him immensely, but Reynolds
could not convince *Scribner's Magazine* to pay more than three hundred
dollars. While in New York in March, Crane became a correspondent
for Hearst's *New York Journal* to report on the impending Greco-Turkish
War and negotiated an independent contract with the McClure syndicate, which sold his dispatches to other American newspapers and to the
Westminster Gazette in London. In exchange for a loan of some six or

seven hundred dollars, he agreed to give S. S. McClure first option on serial publication of his next stories and first option on his next book, a group of stories centered on "The Open Boat."

Crane did not anticipate how the arrangement might work against him. If McClure published Crane's next stories, the price would be deducted from the loan; but if he did not publish them, he could hold them for collateral. The arrangement posed little risk for McClure and put the burden on Crane to produce publishable work. McClure also expected Crane to begin working off his debt immediately; this may well be the reason Crane wrote "Flanagan and His Short Filibustering Adventure" so quickly, before he sailed for Europe. He had hoped to relax with his family in Port Jervis and Hartwood before leaving, but he needed to stay in New York to finish the story. This became the first stage of an increasingly frenetic lifestyle in which Crane would sacrifice his art and his health in order to pay his debts. Within a few months, Crane realized his mistake in asking McClure for a loan instead of an advance on royalties. Stuck in the "ardent grasp" of a publisher who refused to advance him any money, he was forced to borrow from other sources to defray his bills. As he confided to William, "I am not sure that I am not in trouble over it."[4]

Before the trip to Europe, Crane continued to be plagued by the police and the financial arrangement with Amy Leslie. On January 19 he was an honored guest at the French Ball given by the Cercle Français de l'Harmonie in Madison Square Garden. An annual event, the ball would begin respectably but occasionally devolved into lewd and outrageous behavior as prostitutes circulated among masqueraders, well-heeled gentlemen brawled in the street, and drunken attendees slid down banisters and attempted to dance on champagne bottles. With a crowd of seven thousand, extra police under Captain Chapman, who had been Patrolman Becker's superior officer during the Dora Clark incident, were assigned to maintain order. Carolina Otero ("La Belle Otero"), the Spanish dancer whose affairs with numerous members of royalty had made her the most sought-after courtesan in Europe, was among the celebrities that night; but when Little Egypt—whose "hoochee-coochee" dancing at the "Street in Cairo" exhibit at the 1893 World's Columbian Exposition in Chicago appalled and delighted fairgoers—tried to attend the French Ball, Captain Chapman, dubbed the "police apostle of purity" by one newspaper, denied her entrance. He could not, however, stop the free-flowing wine that "made men jump up and down" and "maul and kiss the young women."[5]

Crane seemed bemused by the event, and when asked for his impressions, replied, "There is the reflection of the light upon the white shirt bosoms of the men. That is about all I can see." But as the defender of a prostitute in a recent incident that had embarrassed the New York City police force, Crane was bound to be harassed. When he left the ball, police tried to arrest him for drunkenness. A day or so later, while he was walking along Madison Avenue with journalist James L. Ford, they again attempted to arrest him on trumped-up charges. He had clearly become a target for their anger.[6]

Crane was also increasingly concerned about what he cryptically referred to as Amy Leslie's "mental condition." Hawkins continued to give her money from the fund Crane had set up before leaving for Jacksonville in November, and he arranged a job for her as a model for Crane's friend, artist and photographer F. H. King; but by March, Hawkins, besieged by her frequent letters and visits pestering him for money, had grown weary of acting as the middleman between a constantly vanishing author and his increasingly shrill lover. In April, Crane sent two checks (one for a hundred dollars; another, twenty-five pounds) for Amy, but she never got the money: the first, sent to her, went to the wrong address; Hawkins, disgusted by the ordeal, returned the second one to Crane. After a series of misunderstandings among Hawkins, Leslie, and her attorney, George Mabon, over the next several months, Amy concluded that Hawkins was embezzling her money. After Mabon threatened him with arrest in November, Hawkins refused to act further on Crane's behalf. Amy then quickly sued Crane, insisting that it had taken "two stormy interviews" with him just to get two hundred fifty of the eight hundred dollars she claimed she had originally given him to deposit in the bank. On January 3, 1898, her attorney obtained a warrant of attachment against Crane's property from the Supreme Court of the State of New York; the warrant, for five hundred fifty dollars, froze his royalties at Appleton. Though the suit was eventually settled out of court with legal help from William, it left Crane embittered by "that black-mail at Appleton's."[7]

Crane's relationship with Amy was inconsistent. Shortly after he arrived in Jacksonville in November, her "poor, forlorn boy" was writing impassioned love letters to his "sweetheart," declaring that he thought of her "night and day," asking her to remember him "even in her dreams," and imploring her to "be good and wait for me." But there is a hollow ring to later urgings that she trust his "faith and . . . honesty," since at that time he was with Cora Taylor. Crane was fond of Amy; but trapped as a caretaker in their relationship, he longed for the fierce independence and intellectual companionship that Cora offered. Widely read, Cora exemplified the New Woman the way the semiliterate Amy could not. For all his posing as a bohemian rebel, Crane behaved the same way in uncomfortable social situations: he hid emotionally, sometimes literally. He had shrunk from attending the reading of his poems at the Uncut Leaves Society; he had cornered Nellie Crouse for hours at a tea party to avoid mingling with strangers; and he had needed to be coerced into attending the Society of the Philistines banquet honoring him. His struggle with formal events and close relationships with women stemmed from his inability to deal comfortably with social mores and to resolve conflict maturely. By April 1897, Amy, perhaps hearing rumors about Crane's relationship with Cora, was feeling bitter and abandoned. Crane later apologized—if he had offended her, "it was more by fate or chance than from any desire of mine"—and vowed to help her always. Offering to send more money, however, was merely a way of assuaging his guilt and denying responsibility for the consequences of their affair.[8]

Crane's inconsistency toward Amy typified his mercurial, occasionally irresponsible, behavior. One evening before leaving for Europe, he showed up unexpectedly at Linson's door after not seeing him for several months. Now that Crane was famous, he played, according to Linson, the part of "a rather dandified" celebrity who, in contrast to the unkempt, bohemian Crane, was neatly attired and well groomed, and sat properly instead of slouching on the sofa. He wanted to have a farewell dinner with his old friend and to ask him about Greece, where Linson had been in 1896 illustrating the first modern Olympic games for *Scribner's Magazine*. "Willie Hearst is sending me for the war," he announced. "What I'll do among those Dagoes I don't know. What are they like, CK? How did you chin their lingo?" Crane also complained about the "mountain of lies" regarding his involvement in the Dora Clark affair, and casually mentioned that he had met a woman in Jacksonville who would travel with him and whom he would marry in England. But he feared that their presence on the same steamer would only exacerbate rumors about him: "The weasels would draw blood anyhow." Crane said nothing more about the unnamed Cora or the other woman—Amy Leslie—to whom he was still professing love. The staid Linson, who would become increasingly religious in later years, knew nothing about Crane's penchant for unconventional behavior. His assertion that Crane's "appreciation of the charm and frankness of true womanhood, and the innocence of young girlhood, was chivalry itself" revealed once again Crane's guarded personality, which compartmentalized his behavior around friends and family.[9]

Because Crane's hastily arranged trip to Europe meant there was no time to visit his family before leaving, Edmund rushed to New York to see his brother off. As a parting gift, Crane gave him a copy of Charles King's recent novel, *An Army Wife* (1895). A military veteran who served in the West and befriended William F. "Buffalo Bill" Cody (and later wrote scripts for Cody's silent films), King was a popular and prolific novelist whose sentimental adventure stories dramatized army life on the frontier. The thought of living in the wilderness appealed to Crane, who had long been attracted to the American West and whose favorite years had been spent at a military school. Crane had been reading *An Army Wife* while waiting to set sail for Europe. On March 20, he and Cora departed for Liverpool aboard the Cunard liner *Etruria*. Before joining him for the voyage, Cora had left Jacksonville without paying all her bills.[10] On March 22 a warrant for nonpayment of debts was issued against her, and furniture from the Hotel de Dreme was seized as security. Instead of settling her debts, she had likely used whatever money she had to finance her trip.

By the end of the month, Crane was in London, where the English literary world eagerly awaited him. Despite the recent assertion by W. Robertson Nicoll, influential founding editor of the London *Bookman*, that America lacked any significant young writers, the *London Daily Chronicle* pronounced Crane "the one young writer of genius that America possesses." Shortly after the U.S. book publication of *The Red Badge of Courage*, Sidney Pawling, editor and partner in the firm of William F. Heinemann, had written him to say: "We think so highly of your work —of its actuality—virility & literary distinction that we have been very pleased to take special pains to place it prominently before the British public." Within hours of arriving in London, Crane visited Pawling and Heinemann and remarked that he was headed for Crete because, having been acclaimed as a war writer, it was time he saw some actual fighting. Besides Crane's self-deprecatory sense of humor, Londoners found his modesty refreshing at a time when so many other famous novelists seemed intent on self-promotion.[11]

Richard Harding Davis, a colorful American reporter en route to the Greco-Turkish War for the *London Times,* hosted a formal luncheon for Crane at the luxurious Savoy Hotel. Davis had earlier told his brother that *The Red Badge of Courage* was "the last word as far as battles or fighting is concerned," and he was eager to meet its author. Crane accepted Davis's luncheon invitation at once; and though he had told Nellie Crouse that Davis was a "stuffed parrot" with "the intelligence of the average saw-log," his sarcasm reflected anxiety that she might prefer a suitor like Davis. Clean cut, straitlaced, and a self-styled soldier of fortune, he was already famous as a journalist and as the author of *Van Bibber and Others* (1892), a popular collection of amusing stories about a young socialite. He later became Charles Dana Gibson's model for the handsome gentleman who always escorted the Gibson Girl—the celebrated personification of the feminine ideal—and was characterized in Sinclair Lewis's *Dodsworth* as an adventure-seeking hero. During Crane's poverty-stricken days in New York City, when he could barely find work, he had bolstered himself with Garland's reassurance that he was a better writer than Davis. Yet Crane and Davis had more in common than he knew. Both came from respectable families, with parents who had been writers and journalists; both were proud of their heritage and joined the Sons of the American Revolution; both were athletic but struggled academically and dropped out of college; both represented the new breed of writers whose journalism influenced their fiction.[12]

Among those invited to the luncheon were Anthony Hope, whose novel of political intrigue, *The Prisoner of Zenda* (1894), had made him an international celebrity; Justin Huntly McCarthy, who had been in the House of Commons and was an Irish Nationalist author; J. M. Barrie, who would create Peter Pan; and Harold Frederic, London correspondent for the *New York Times* and author of *The Damnation of Theron Ware* (1896), who had earlier praised Crane's war novel. Davis told his mother, the noted author Rebecca Harding Davis, that the luncheon had gone well and that Crane was "very modest sturdy and shy. Quite unlike I imagined." The event was best remembered for an unexpected announcement. During the festivities, a lance sergeant on horseback suddenly arrived at the Savoy with a huge envelope intended for Davis and marked "On Her Majesty's Service." The stunned crowd assumed that war had just broken out between Greece and Turkey and that Davis was being sent to the front—but the message was merely from General Evelyn Wood, sending his regrets about the luncheon because he had been detained at the War Office. Crane, who loved horses and adventure, reveled in the humor of the event and accepted Wood's letter as a souvenir from Davis.[13]

Davis, however, quickly expressed some reservations about Crane. On April 1, 1897, they left for Greece, but parted in Paris because Davis was planning a brief side trip to Florence, Italy, where his brother was the American consul. While they were waiting in the London station for the train that was to take them to Dover for passage to France, Davis saw that "a bi-roxide blonde" was accompanying Crane and tending to his luggage. This was Cora, who had been discreetly staying in London while her lover was being lionized as America's new literary star. They were planning to travel on the same train but in different compartments.

On April 3, Stephen and Cora sailed from Marseilles aboard the *Guadiana*. Five days later they arrived at Piraeus, the port of Athens, to report on the impending Greco-Turkish War. Greece had become concerned about the growing tension between Christians and Muslims on Turkish-ruled Crete. Following a rebellion by Christians in 1896, Greece had begun supplying arms to the rebels, and by February it had invaded the island, proclaiming that Crete was now united with Greece. Fearing that the trouble might spread to the Balkans, the five European countries that were party to the "Concert of Europe" (which Crane called the "Concert of Powers"), a nineteenth-century agreement to act together on mutual concerns, sent a formidable array of allied warships to blockade Greece from further assisting the rebels.

When Turkey declared war on Greece on April 17, Crane was outside the royal palace on Constitution Square in Athens, observing the enthusiastic crowd that had gathered to support the Cretan rebellion against Turkey. The subsequent thirty-day struggle consisted mainly of retreats and rear-guard actions by the Greeks, who were unprepared for war and were overwhelmed by a better-trained army. Following a three-day bombardment of Arta by the Turks and the disastrous retreat by panic-stricken Greek soldiers on April 29, the European powers forced the humiliated Greeks to withdraw from Crete and accept an armistice on May 20. Disillusioned Greek soldiers felt betrayed by their foreign-born king, who had yielded to pressure from the European alliance, and by their commander-in-chief, Crown Prince Constantine, who lacked military experience and who had been given orders to retreat whenever he was close to victory.

Crane's hopes for his involvement in the war were unrealistic. Discovering that his reputation as a famous author of war fiction had preceded him, he was convinced that he would be asked to be a member of Prince Constantine's staff. "Wont that be great?" he wrote William elatedly. "I am so happy over it I can hardly breathe. I shall try—I shall try like blazes to get a decoration out of the thing but that depends on good fortune and is between you and I and God." Without military experience, however, he was unlikely to be assigned to a combat position in a foreign army, and his cynical view of heroism, apparent in his stories about the Civil War, undermined his yearning for a medal for bravery. In a dispatch written three weeks later ridiculing American and English war correspondents, Crane portrayed himself as "the wild ass of the desert who wanted a decoration" and who had made the king leery of granting journalists an interview. In fact, he was still struggling with the embarrassment resulting from the Becker trial. He wanted to ingratiate himself with his much older brother, a judge and respected community leader who was the paterfamilias of the Cranes. Coming from an ancestry rooted in the soil of American patriotism, he wanted to prove that the bohemian rebel could become an honorable member of society. All he had to do, he naïvely thought, was earn a medal.[14]

Fate decreed otherwise. Before leaving for the battlefield on April 18, Crane mailed Amy Leslie a hundred dollars; but she never received it because she had moved to a different address in New York City. He traveled to Epirus, a region in northwestern Greece, where he witnessed skirmishes between Greek guerrillas and Turkish troops near Janina. He left before the Greek retreat when he learned of more intense fighting in Thessaly. By the end of the month, he was back in Athens, where he witnessed public outrage and rioting following the news of Greek reverses in Thessaly. "Why was Greece shamed? Whose fault was it?" demanded an Athenian journalist. When he insisted on answers from the king, the journalist was snubbed by a servant at the palace door: "The King does not receive to-day."[15]

On April 30, Crane, Richard Harding Davis, and John Bass, head of the *New York Journal* staff, left Athens for Thessaly, the central region of mainland Greece, traveling first by steamer to Stylis, then hiring carriages to take them to Lamia. Arriving there at midnight on May 1, Crane and the other journalists were forced to sleep on a hotel floor in a town crowded with soldiers. Accompanying the American journalists was Cora, who, as "Imogene Carter," had been hired as a war correspondent by the *New York Journal* at Crane's request.[16] Though Carter has occasionally been called the first woman war correspondent, Harriet Boyd, a graduate student at the American School of Classical Studies in Athens and a volunteer nurse and relief worker in Thessaly, was also writing for the *Journal;* later she became a famed archaeologist. Davis was shocked to learn, as he told his family, that Carter was actually "a Lady Stewart who has run away from her husband to follow Crane." "She is a commonplace dull woman old enough to have been his mother and with dyed yellow hair. He seems a genius with no responsibilities of any sort to anyone."[17]

En route to Pharsala early the next day, the journalists ran into countless Greek civilians fleeing the advancing Turks. When stopped by sentries at the outskirts of the city, Bass and Davis headed for Velestino, soon to be the site of a major battle; Crane went to Volo, a seaport village twelve miles east of Velestino, overlooking a harbor where English, French, and Italian warships were massed. Cora stayed in Pharsala and spent the night sleeping on a billiard table in a coffeehouse. With a letter of introduction from the U.S. minister, Eben Alexander, she was hoping to interview the crown prince at Greek headquarters the next day; but when he hastily departed after ordering another retreat, a disappointed Cora headed for Volo to join Crane.

On May 4, the Turks launched a major attack at Velestino, having failed a week earlier on three separate days to dislodge the Greek forces there. Sick from dysentery, Crane disguised his illness by claiming it was a toothache, but it forced him to miss the first day of the second battle of Velestino. Determined that for the first time in his life he would witness a significant battle rather than mere skirmishes, he rode on horseback with Cora to Velestino the next day, arriving at a mountain battery overlooking Greek forces below and shelling the Turkish army in the distance.

Also on the scene were Davis and Bass. Davis, sensing a professional rivalry with Crane, seemed delighted to have arrived there before him, but blamed Cora for Crane's lateness. If he "had not had that woman with him," Davis confided to his family, "he would have been with us and not at Volo and could have seen the show toothache or no toothache." But he also denigrated Crane's behavior: "There was nothing to be said about what Crane did except that he ought to be ashamed of himself"—possibly an allusion to the recent exposure of the seamy side of Crane's character. Crane's traveling with a married woman also upset Davis's sense of propriety and morality.[18] Though he admired Crane's literary skills, he could not accept his bohemian disregard of manners. Davis later satirized Crane as an irresponsible correspondent in the short story "A Derelict" (1901).[19] Yet Sylvester Scovel, fellow war correspondent in Greece, thought differently about Cora. "I was afraid that she would ruin him," he wrote to his wife, "but really her influence has, so far, been the reverse." He believed that Cora's presence was what inspired Crane to write "such good work."[20]

Unlike Davis, Bass tolerated Crane's behavior and admired his cool head. When heavy bombardment began, Bass quickly took shelter in a trench, while Crane, pushing himself to the margins of experience, calmly sat on an ammunition box, lit a cigarette, and brushed the hair back from his eyes with his hat. Crane observed the artillerymen's precision in firing a cannon; they acted not as individuals but as a team. When Bass asked what impressed Crane most about the battle scene, he replied that it was "the mental attitude of the men. The Greeks I can see and understand, but the Turks seem unreal. They are shadows on the plain— vague figures in black, indications of a mysterious force." His response reflected his own ongoing personal battle—in the Sullivan County tales and sketches, *The Black Riders,* and *The Red Badge of Courage,* for example—between an individual's limited understanding of reality and an inscrutable force in nature. Like black riders of the sea, these black "vague figures" symbolized unsolvable mysteries in a disjointed universe. Witnessing at Velestino his first major battle, Crane internalized two perspectives. As a naïve observer philosophizing on the excitement of war, he was exhilarated by its din: "a beautiful sound—beautiful as I had never dreamed. It was more impressive than the roar of Niagara and finer than thunder or avalanche—because it had the wonder of human tragedy in it. It was the most beautiful sound of my experience, barring no symphony. The crash of it was ideal." "This is one point of view," he added. "Another might be taken from the men who died there." Crane had learned firsthand what Henry Fleming had found difficult to accept: the illusion that war was a heroic struggle for honor.[21]

Crane's descriptive essay "A Fragment of Velestino," his most subjective account of his first experience of combat, revisits the imagery, characterization, and theme of *The Red Badge of Courage*. Both portray a calm, indifferent nature; both ignore larger social and political contexts; and both treat war as a machine churning out unnecessary casualties. At first, Crane the "Westerner" is disoriented by the rocky, barren setting unlike any other place he has seen.[22] His literal and figurative points of view are shifting and limited, and he realizes that his account is only a fragment of the reality. The structure of the essay, like that of *The Red Badge,* is episodic, as though the disjointed, sometimes absurd nature of experience revealed the insignificance of war. A bandage wrapped around a bloody face evokes a domestic image in which a grandmother attempts to treat a boy's toothache; artillery shells seem like flying empty beer bottles; a soldier misunderstands an officer's order that he retrieve a pair of field glasses and returns with a bottle of wine. The most poignant episode is Crane's discovery of a corpse, identified with the same epithet associated with Henry: "the youth." Spurred on by patriotism, the Greek commoner had evidently purchased his own equipment and rushed into battle still wearing street clothes. If there is ambivalence at the end of *The Red Badge of Courage* regarding Henry's maturity, there is none for this other youth: his initiation into war brings death.

On May 6, apparently on the verge of a Greek victory, Crown Prince Constantine inexplicably ordered another retreat. Colonel Constantine Smolenski, commander of the Greek forces at Velestino, was enraged at the prince's incompetence, but obeyed the order. Amid the shelling from Turkish artillery, Crane and Cora caught the last train from Velestino; and just as the advancing Turks reached the hills overlooking Volo, the two were among the chaotic mass of refugees who crowded onto every available ship and fishing boat in the harbor. Crane was incensed that nearby foreign ships refused to help with the evacuation and that an English Red Cross ship could not be used because a surgeon following "some rules—God knows what they were" was "the accursed idiot who, by devil's luck, was in charge."[23] On the drill field at Claverack, Crane had vociferously taught the rules of conduct; on the battlefield in Greece, he learned lessons of life.

By the second week in May, Crane and Cora were back in Athens. They rested for a few days, then headed back north on May 17 on a dispatch boat to observe the Greek resistance at Domoko. There they discovered that Prince Constantine had ordered his troops to abandon Domoko and retreat to Thermopylae. The following day Crane helped to evacuate refugees from Stylidia, after which he and Cora boarded an ambulance ship crammed with wounded soldiers returning to Athens. Following the signing of an armistice on May 20, he and Cora rested from their ordeal and went sightseeing. Curiously, Crane, who was interested in history, did not appreciate classical antiquity. "Athens is not much ruins, you know," he wrote William. "It is mostly adobe creations like Mexico although the Acropolis sticks up in the air precisely like it does in the pictures."[24] His commentary was odd because although the phrase "adobe creations" probably referred to the ubiquitous houses with terra-cotta roofs in Athens, by 1897 decades of excavation and preservation on the Acropolis and at surrounding sites had already uncovered many classical structures, and in 1896 the first modern Olympic games had helped to renovate the city.

Crane occasionally jested about his Greek experience. After observing a skirmish in which Turkish troops fled, he submitted his dispatch to the Turkish censor. "This will have to be toned down," he said gravely. Where Crane had said that the Turks "fled," the censor insisted that the wording be changed to "retired in good order"; "turned tail" became "had fallen back steadily." When the censor came across the term "routed," he struggled to find a euphemistic synonym. "I can't think of a milder expression than this one here—'the Turks were routed.' Can you help me? You are a writer." Imitating the censor's grave tone, Crane replied, "If I were you I'd simply say that the indomitable Turks changed front and advanced."[25]

Crane had gone to Greece partly to test his own manhood and partly to see if he had captured the essence of combat in his war fiction. He had wanted to stop writing about war more than a year earlier and had declared that *The Little Regiment and Other Episodes of the American Civil War* would be his last work dealing with battle. As magazine editors hounded him for more war stories, however, he realized that *The Red Badge* had become an albatross around his neck. He dismissed it as "a mere episode," reassuring readers and himself that he remained committed to a core tenet of realism: "The nearer a writer gets to life the greater he becomes as an artist."[26]

As much as Crane struggled to move beyond the Civil War as a subject, he could never escape his own internal war. And he continued to ponder the individual's struggles against forces of fate or chance. The battles he witnessed in Greece confirmed what he had imagined about the terror and ultimate futility of war in *The Red Badge of Courage*. As he later told Joseph Conrad, his experience there convinced him that his war novel was "all right."[27]

Yet the sight of homeless, starving women and children, hideously wounded soldiers, and fields of corpses robbed him of creativity. "Words are not adequate to describe" the experience. In one month he had seen the carnage of war: a soldier shot through the neck while rolling a cigarette; another whose face had been disfigured by a bullet that had passed through both cheeks; a wounded soldier decapitated after being captured. "There is more of this sort of thing in war," Crane concluded, "than glory and heroic death, flags, banners, shouting and victory." In the past, Crane had transformed his daily experiences into fiction—as in the Sullivan County tales and sketches, "The Pace of Youth," and *The Third Violet*—but out of the Greco-Turkish War ultimately came only two stories. As with his experiences following the sinking of the *Commodore,* he had to reconcile himself to the horror of what he had seen.

It took Crane almost six months to transform his Velestino dispatches into "Death and the Child," his first war story after witnessing combat. War, the story demonstrates, could no longer be envisioned as a potential means of growth and maturation. About two years after the Greco-Turkish War, he wrote the novel *Active Service,* but there the war is merely the setting for a comical love story. Crane had been deeply moved at seeing waifs in New York's slums following a children's celebration, veterans tragically disfigured during a July 4 celebration, and the corpse of a father who had unexpectedly died. The Greco-Turkish War affected him just as deeply. In *The Red Badge of Courage,* he had astutely imagined, as an outsider, a youth's struggle to mature psychologically and morally and to experience combat for the first time. Now, in "Death and the Child" —which ends with the twice-posed question "Are you a man?"—Crane was Peza, the war correspondent appalled by the sight of brutal death and acutely aware of his own insignificance. Peza's egotism regarding his presumed importance in the universe recalls Crane's earlier self-admonishment about how "fairly dazzled he was by the size of" his own ego at age twenty-one. "The Matterhorn could be no more than a ten-pin to it," he had told Nellie Crouse. Occasionally one needs "to trample upon one's own egotism." He was reminded of this fact in Greece; and as a result of events that occurred between the fall of 1896 and the spring of 1897, involving public humiliation in New York, a crisis at sea, and terror on the battlefield, Crane had become a changed man.[28]

By the end of the month, Stephen and Cora had left Athens, most likely together, and sailed for Marseilles. Accompanying them were two Greek servants, the twin brothers Adoni and Constantin Ptolemy, and a puppy that Crane had rescued and named "Velestino, the Journal dog."[29] Before heading for England, they spent almost two weeks in Paris, where Crane was charged a hundred pounds after Velestino chewed up the carpet and draperies in a hotel room.[30] Despite the financial burden of the damage, Crane could never forget the joys that dogs had brought him throughout his life; and when Velestino died two months later after "a fine manly fight"[31] against distemper, Crane wrote an emotional letter to Sylvester Scovel saying that Velestino would be buried wearing a collar that Scovel had given him as a present.

Crane had not only become a man—he had deepened his humanity.

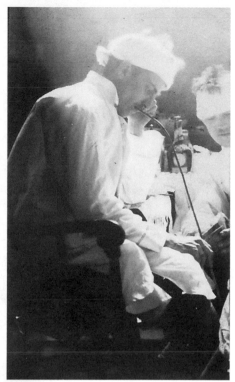

Figure 1. Stephen Crane smoking a hookah at a party. He and a friend are dressed in medical-school clothing.
STEPHEN CRANE COLLECTION, SPECIAL
COLLECTIONS RESEARCH CENTER,
SYRACUSE UNIVERSITY LIBRARIES.

Figure 2. C. K. Linson retouched the photo of Crane shown in Figure 1, and titled it "Vignette—when writing 'The Pace of Youth.'"
STEPHEN CRANE COLLECTION, SPECIAL
COLLECTIONS RESEARCH CENTER,
SYRACUSE UNIVERSITY LIBRARIES.

Figure 3. Jonathan Townley Crane.
STEPHEN CRANE COLLECTION, SPECIAL
COLLECTIONS RESEARCH CENTER,
SYRACUSE UNIVERSITY LIBRARIES.

Figure 4. Mary Helen Peck Crane.
STEPHEN CRANE COLLECTION, SPECIAL
COLLECTIONS RESEARCH CENTER,
SYRACUSE UNIVERSITY LIBRARIES.

Figure 5. Stephen Crane's birthplace, 14 Mulberry Place, Newark, New Jersey.
STEPHEN CRANE COLLECTION, SPECIAL COLLECTIONS RESEARCH CENTER, SYRACUSE UNIVERSITY LIBRARIES.

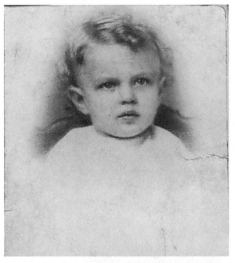

Figure 6. Stephen Crane, around 1873.

Figure 7. Crane on the New Jersey coast, around 1879.

Figure 8. Stephen Crane as a lieutenant in the Claverack College and Hudson River Institute cadet corps, 1889 or 1890.

Figure 9.   Syracuse University baseball team, spring 1891. Crane is seated in the middle of the first row.
STEPHEN CRANE COLLECTION, SPECIAL COLLECTIONS RESEARCH CENTER, SYRACUSE UNIVERSITY LIBRARIES.

Figure 10.   Lily Brandon Munroe and her husband, Hersey Munroe.
STEPHEN CRANE COLLECTION, CLIFTON WALLER BARRETT LIBRARY OF AMERICAN LITERATURE, ALBERT AND SHIRLEY SMALL SPECIAL COLLECTIONS LIBRARY, UNIVERSITY OF VIRGINIA.

Figure 11. Party at the Pendennis Club to celebrate the publication of *Maggie,* March 1893. Crane is seated with a banjo.

Figure 12. Nellie Crouse, winter 1896.

Figure 13. Cora Crane, probably
taken about the time of her marriage
to Captain Donald William Stewart in
1889 and inscribed later to a niece.
STEPHEN CRANE COLLECTION, SPECIAL
COLLECTIONS RESEARCH CENTER,
SYRACUSE UNIVERSITY LIBRARIES.

Figure 14. Stephen Crane in Athens,
Greece, May 1897.
STEPHEN CRANE COLLECTION, CLIFTON
WALLER BARRETT LIBRARY OF AMERICAN
LITERATURE, ALBERT AND SHIRLEY SMALL
SPECIAL COLLECTIONS LIBRARY, UNIVERSITY
OF VIRGINIA.

Figure 15.   Cora Crane in Athens, Greece, May 1897, in the uniform of a war correspondent. Inscribed to Stephen Crane with her pen name, "Imogene Carter."

Figure 16.   Crane in his study at Ravensbrook with mementos of his western trip on the desk and walls, 1897–1898.
STEPHEN CRANE COLLECTION, CLIFTON WALLER BARRETT LIBRARY OF AMERICAN LITERATURE, ALBERT AND SHIRLEY SMALL SPECIAL COLLECTIONS LIBRARY, UNIVERSITY OF VIRGINIA.

Figure 17.   Stephen Crane aboard the *Three Friends* during the Spanish-American War, May 1898.
STEPHEN CRANE COLLECTION, CLIFTON WALLER BARRETT LIBRARY OF AMERICAN LITERATURE, ALBERT AND SHIRLEY SMALL SPECIAL COLLECTIONS LIBRARY, UNIVERSITY OF VIRGINIA.

Figure 18.   Crane in his study at Brede Place, September 1899.

Last photo taken of Stephen Crane with his dog "Spongie"—

Figure 19. Stephen Crane at Brede Place, 1900. The inscription is in the hand of Cora Crane.

Figure 20. Villa Eberhardt, Badenweiler, Germany, the house in which Stephen Crane died.

Part IV

NEW START, OLD HABITS

20

Ravensbrook, Harold Frederic, Joseph Conrad

JUNE–OCTOBER 1897

STEPHEN AND CORA'S DECISION to settle in England in June 1897 was an act not of expatriation but of exile. As one observer noted, Crane had become "the most thoroughly abused writing man between the Atlantic and Pacific." "Idiocy, garbage, rot, bombast, drivel, indecent, besotted, opium-laden, fustian, bluster, balderdash, stupid, swell-head stuff were but a few of the mildest adjectives" flung at one book alone, *The Black Riders.* Police would have harassed him in New York City, and the strait-laced residents of Hartwood and Port Jervis would have shunned the former "hostess" of a Jacksonville pleasure resort. Cora's hasty departure from Jacksonville with unpaid bills also made her return difficult. England seemed a favorable place to relocate. Cora knew the culture from having lived there earlier, and Stephen was already a celebrity in the country. He asked Edmund to ship the rugs and other household articles he had stored at Hartwood. Stephen and Cora could now make a new start.[1]

The move to England, though, entailed a major problem. Only a few years earlier, Cora had been well known in British society as "Lady Stewart." Married to Donald William Stewart in 1889, she had lived with him until 1892 in the townhouse of her father-in-law, Sir Donald Martin

Stewart, commander-in-chief of British forces in India. She no doubt had dined in the finest restaurants and been invited to formal receptions at the royal court. When she first returned to England with Stephen, she asked her brother-in-law, Sir Norman Robert Stewart, to help persuade her estranged husband to divorce her. Recently divorced himself and remarried, Sir Norman sympathized with the request but cautioned Cora that if she had already married Crane, "you ought to be very careful of your secret for a very large circle of your friends must only know you as Mrs. Stewart."[2]

Arriving in England sometime before June 10 with their servants, Stephen and Cora briefly stayed in furnished rooms in Limpsfield, Surrey, then lived for ten months in Ravensbrook Villa, a pretentiously named, plain brick-and-tile house that Harold Frederic had found for them in the neighboring town of Oxted, within commuting distance of London.[3] Situated in a damp area at the bottom of a hill, the house was anything but ideal for Stephen's ailing lungs.

The area attracted a literary colony that was a precursor to the Bloomsbury group and the Parisian expatriates of the 1920s. Frederic, Edward Garnett and his wife, Constance (an esteemed translator of Russian literature), Ford Madox Ford (then known by his given name, Ford Hueffer), Robert Barr, and Edward R. Pease were neighbors in the area of Romney Marsh, close to London. Farther down, in Rye, Sussex, lived Henry James, and nearby in Essex were Joseph and Jessie Conrad. The proximity energized the writers, as they sought comments on their manuscripts, argued about literary perspectives, and shared their homes. "We lived rather in each other's pockets and interested ourselves rather in each other's affairs," recalled Ford. The familiarity could, however, devolve into unpleasantry, as it did years later when H. G. Wells characterized James's often complicated prose style, with its "vast paragraphs" that "sweat and struggle," as the work of a hippopotamus trying to pick up a pea.[4]

Though Stephen and Cora never officially married because Captain Stewart refused to divorce her, they presented themselves publicly as Mr. and Mrs. Crane. There was actually no need to hide their marital status from their literary neighbors, who were quite liberal about nontraditional relationships. Frederic, Ford, and Wells (whom Crane did not meet until 1899) lived with women who were not their wives, and Henry

James tolerated deviations from Victorian morality—an attitude that tended to be true of Britons in general. As a child, Crane had scorned the British, but in later years he came to appreciate their sensibility. "Over here," he wrote John Northern Hilliard in America, "happily, they don't treat you as if you were a dog, but give every one an honest measure of praise or blame. There are no disgusting personalities."[5]

The Oxted-Limpsfield area was also known as a center of radical politics. Founded in 1884, the socialist Fabian Society was named after Roman general Quintus Fabius Maximus, whose military strategy had been to wear down opponents through attrition rather than direct confrontation in battle. The Fabians—whose members included Wells, George Bernard Shaw, and, later, Leonard and Virginia Woolf—wanted to foster democratic socialism by transforming society gradually rather than through revolutionary means. The secretary of the group was Edward Pease, who considered Crane an elitist for occasionally preferring to be shaved by a servant.[6] More radical were the Russian exiles, led by the anarchist Prince Peter Kropotkin, who were awaiting the overthrow of czarist Russia. To David Garnett, son of David and Constance, the writers, freethinkers, and nontraditionalists in the area were "the heretics who first colonized the pineclad wastes of Surrey"—people like his parents, who "did not wish to fit into the Victorian social hierarchy."[7]

Although Crane knew members of the Fabian Society, it is difficult to say how much contact he had with them because the only source of information is Ford Madox Ford, whose reminiscences are unreliable. Ford tells the same anecdotes repeatedly and each time changes significant details. He claims, for example, that he first saw Crane at a Fabian Society meeting at Edward and Margery Pease's house, where, "looking young, pained, and dictatorial," Crane lectured on the use of flags to send Morse code.[8] When Ford first tells the anecdote, he expresses dislike for Crane's arrogance; yet when he recounts it again, he claims that he liked Crane immediately. In all likelihood, the incident never occurred. Crane hated public speaking and did not learn about flag signaling until he was with the Marines in Cuba in 1898. Similarly, a number of Ford's other assertions about Crane—for instance, that he disliked Robert Louis Stevenson, that he mistook a pile of stones for the remnant of an ancient fortress, that he enjoyed swatting flies with his pistol—are false, or colorful exaggerations at best. Ford alleges that Crane could assume the slang of a Bowery street tough ("he was a fly-guy that was wise to all the all-night pushes of the world") as easily as he could mimic the speech of a Western frontiersman, and that his behavior variously amused, puzzled, and embarrassed friends.[9] Ford readily acknowledged the fictional bent of his reminiscences: "Where it has seemed expedient to me I have altered episodes that I have witnessed but I have been careful never to distort the character of the episode. The accuracies I deal in are the accuracies of my own impressions."[10] A brilliant narrator, Ford Madox Ford never let facts get in the way of a good story.

Yet there is an element of truth beneath the invented surface of Ford's characterization. Crane was a loner, but yearned for the comradeship of fraternity brothers; an outsider indifferent to everything but his own concerns, yet a patrician proud of his colonial roots; a bohemian rebel who had written about, and preferred, prostitutes, but who had wooed from afar a perfectly respectable woman he had met only once at a tea party in New York City. To some acquaintances, his divided self was a source of delight and frustration; to others, his rebellion was more of a pose than a commitment. Role playing was often an enjoyable form of self-deprecation for Crane, as in an anecdote recorded by the novelist and critic Edwin Pugh:

> "Say, when I planted these hoofs of mine on Greek soil I felt like the hull [whole?] of Greek literature, like one gone over to the goldarned majority. I'd a great idea of Greece. . . . So I said to the chocolate-box general of the Greek army: 'Can I go into the fighting line?' And he says to me . . . 'Not in those trousers, sonny.' So I got back at him with: 'How near may I get to the fighting line, then?' And he says in his eloquent way, 'Not less than two miles.'" Then Stevie paused, filled, drained his glass, and said very solemnly in that extravagant Yankee accent which he affected when he was telling a story: "That commanding officer was right for sure. I never was within two miles of the fighting line. But I was mostly two miles nearer the Turks than the Greek army was. Bekase they ran like rabbits."[11]

Crane is obviously a master storyteller shaping his narrative for dramatic impact. There is the exaggerated Yankee dialect, the changing of details for comic effect (Crane had actually been at "the fighting line"), the use of the glass as a prop, the pause before the final punch line. Here again is evidence of a divided self. Crane disliked speaking formally in settings over which he had little control; but in small gatherings of friends, where he felt safe, he was a delightful raconteur.

Harold Frederic was Crane's first important friend in England. After starting his literary career as a journalist and editor in Utica, New York, he had become London correspondent for the *New York Times.* Married with four children (two others had died in infancy), he had established another household with Kate Lyon, with whom he had three more children, eventually moving with them to Homefield in Kenley, Surrey. Remarkably, he maintained frequent contact with his wife and their children, sometimes spending as much as two weeks with them. Despite his controversial life, Frederic was popular socially and active politically as an advocate of home rule for Ireland. A year before he and Crane met, he had published his most famous novel, *The Damnation of Theron Ware* (published in England as *Illumination*). A realistic portrayal of a young Methodist minister whose faith is challenged by science, religion, and sexuality, it outsold *The Red Badge of Courage* in 1896.[12]

Crane and Frederic had a common background. Both had grown up in a strict Methodist family, had begun their careers as journalists, and had become celebrated authors. Before meeting Crane, Frederic had already praised "the mysteriously unknown youth" who had written the "extraordinary" *Red Badge,* and Crane later admired his friend's skill as a storyteller and his ability to balance a cosmopolitan demeanor with his simple upbringing in rural New York State. "No gilding, no varnish," Crane said of Frederic's personality. "A great reminiscent panorama of the Mohawk Valley!" There was a connection between them even before they had met. In 1873, the Northern New York Annual Conference of the Methodist Episcopal Church had been held in Frederic's hometown, Utica. Local families happily provided accommodations for visiting church clergy, and Frederic's mother and grandmother had been excited that the presiding bishop and his wife would be staying with them. Frederic would have been in the congregation at the conference when the bishop had announced the new pastoral appointments at the closing session; later, he would recreate the session and depict the bishop as the "slow, near-sighted old gentleman" in the opening chapter of *Theron Ware.* Crane recognized the artistry of the novel, declaring, "Here is a writer!" Would he also have recognized the bishop that Frederic described? It was Stephen's granduncle Jesse Truesdell Peck. Frederic had fictionalized Stephen's ancestor in his novel.[13]

One and possibly two of the more amusing anecdotes about Crane's time in London in 1897 involved Frederic. Soon after they met, Crane wanted to express his admiration for Frederic's literary talent by treating him to a snack at a pub. Short on cash, Crane first borrowed a sovereign from a fellow newspaperman, planning to spend part of it on food and the rest apparently on personal items. After Crane paid the bill, the barmaid laid down the change in front of Frederic, who, deep in conversation, mechanically picked it up and put it in his pocket. Crane's respect for his new friend was so profound that he said nothing rather than embarrass him, prompting Crane to sheepishly ask the newspaperman to lend him another sovereign. On another occasion, Crane was startled by what seemed to be a mirage. S. S. McClure was in London with his two brothers, and all of them—with their distinctive features, fair hair, and mustaches—looked identical. "I've had a terrible shock," he said to a friend, possibly Frederic. "I was coming through the Strand just now and I saw three S. S. McClures standing at the corner of Bedford Street."[14]

In August, while driving to visit Frederic on his birthday at Homefield, Kenley, Stephen and Cora were injured in a carriage accident when a poorly harnessed horse broke away, overturning the trap. Both were badly shaken, and Crane broke his nose and injured his knee.[15] Kate and Harold nursed them for a week at Homefield while they recuperated. Cora tried to sue for damages, but wound up only with frustration. She was "disgusted," she later told a friend, "with the English justice shown Americans": owners of a livery stable could "take mild Americans out in their traps which they can, without fear of punishment, turn upside down and dump the passengers out on the road, ruin their clothes and scar them for life. So I never want to see another lawyer if I can avoid it."[16]

To help the Cranes recover, the Frederics invited them on a three-week vacation in Ireland, where a wealthy admirer had lent Harold a house in the village of Ahakista, on Dunmanus Bay. Here Crane finished "The Monster" and collected material for his "Irish Notes," five travel sketches published later in the year. The vacation was a pleasure for both couples. But tension developed between them early the next year when a well-intentioned proposal went awry. To save on living expenses, Frederic proposed that both families move to Dunmanus Bay and share a seaside mansion complete with seven bedrooms, hot and cold tap water, and two boats. "My Dear Boy," he wrote to Crane, "We can work as well as loaf." Yet when Harold and Cora argued about the details of the household arrangement, he regretted "the unhappy blunder of making the proposition." Within days of the argument, he wrote Cora an anguished letter apologizing for his behavior: "I take all the blame upon myself for not having realized that under the changed conditions, the things that we had so pleasantly in a community of comradeship would recede into the background, and that our points of difference would rise up and rush forward to monopolize attention." The precise nature of the "changed conditions" was unclear; Frederic merely acknowledged that "since last Autumn Ravensbrook has defined for itself a system and routine of its own—quite distinct, as is natural, from the system of Homefield—and that an effort to put these two side by side under one roof would necessarily come to grief." As a way to make amends, he invited the Cranes to visit the Frederics in Ireland for three weeks in the spring of 1898.[17]

Despite a genuinely close friendship between the two families, Frederic saw that their daily lifestyles might clash. Even more likely to cause conflict were the similarities and differences between the personalities of the two authors. At age forty, Frederic was around fifteen years older than Crane. Whereas Crane had been famous for barely two years, Frederic had already been editor of two newspapers, had been the *New York Times* correspondent in London since 1884, had developed an international reputation as a journalist, and, as a member of the National Liberal Club, was close friends with leading British and Irish statesmen and members of Parliament. The gregarious Frederic enjoyed the formality of the social gatherings that Crane always wanted to flee. In November, Frederic introduced him to the Australian author George Lewis Becke (who used the pen name Louis Becke) and invited them to his home for roast suckling pig on November 19. Crane was also Frederic's guest at the club on December 11 and met William Pritchard Morgan, a prominent liberal member of Parliament. Crane, habitually taciturn in public gatherings, listened quietly to lively discussions about social reform; his sagging mustache (an observer noted) concealed "a set sneer" that exemplified his wariness of any national organization offering panaceas and a far-reaching agenda. As Crane later wrote to George Wyndham, the British undersecretary of state for war, "I am no believer in your general charities. A general charity is about as useful as a wormeaten blanket for two men. Someone should get some warmth out of it. Usually everybody gets a little irritation. Hope is the most vacuous emotion of mankind."[18]

Frederic was secure with his lifestyle and open about his relationship with Kate Lyon; in contrast, Crane never reconciled the opposing forces in his personality. Shunning convention, he nonetheless sought respectability with Cora as they started their lives anew by presenting themselves as a married couple. Unlike Kate and Harold, Cora and Stephen could never publicly acknowledge their deception. At times, Crane must have been terrified that his respectable family back home would discover his sham. At war with his own divided self, he was occasionally irritable even around his closest friends.

In some ways, Harold and Stephen were too much alike. Both lived recklessly and were constantly in debt because of excessive spending; they wrote incessantly to pay bills; they badgered agents and publishers for advances on royalties and on work they had merely outlined. They saw in each other the frailties they chose not to acknowledge in themselves.[19] Though Cora stated, perhaps a bit defensively, that Crane "never got in childish rages with people because they did not consider his work as good as he, himself considered it," Crane admitted that he annoyed people with his eccentric way of suddenly disappearing. He praised Frederic's American fiction; at the same time, he irritated Frederic by criticizing his friend's decision to turn to British subjects in his fiction. As Frederic revised the manuscript of his novel *Gloria Mundi* (1898), it is perhaps no coincidence that the main character's interest in prostitutes and his penchant for fleeing came to reflect the personality of Frederic's new literary friend.[20]

Crane had a more significant literary relationship with Joseph Conrad, who had read *The Red Badge of Courage* and immediately recognized Crane's "gift for rendering the significant on the surface of things and with an incomparable insight into primitive emotions." This was what he himself was trying to do in *The Nigger of the "Narcissus."* Crane had just begun reading Conrad's novel, which was being serialized in Heinemann's *New Review,* and wanted to meet the author, who had composed his sea tale on a theme common in Crane's work: isolation versus solidarity. Sidney Pawling, Heinemann's partner, arranged a luncheon for them in London on October 15. It lasted till 4 P.M.; and when Pawling left, Crane and Conrad strolled around London until late into the evening, deep in conversation. Wanting to show his familiarity with *The Red Badge,* Conrad shyly said, "I like your General." At first silent, Crane then quietly responded: "I like your young man—I can just see him." Curiously, this was the only exchange they had about their novels that day. For Conrad, "nothing could have been more characteristic of the depth" of their instinctive understanding of each other than that each had "selected for praise the merest by-the-way vignette of a minor character." Brief snippets of conversation about their pasts and their interests were punctuated with periods of silence, and the silences conveyed as much as the words. Neither author believed in idle chatter. At dinner, Crane became animated, insisting that Conrad tell him everything he knew about Balzac's *Comédie Humaine*—a surprising request, given that Crane typically avoided literary talk. Crane was charmed by Conrad's sense of culture and social decorum; Conrad, by Crane's brilliance and youthful spontaneity.[21]

Just as Conrad admired Crane's ability to render the meaning beneath "the surface of things," he was struck with how Crane's own appearance conveyed the depths of his soul: the "very steady, penetrating blue eyes, the eyes of a man who not only sees visions but can brood over them to some purpose," and "the smile of a being who knows that his time will not be long on this earth." Crane appreciated Frederic as a friend, but he was closer emotionally and artistically to Conrad. Whereas Harold was the father offering unasked-for advice, Joseph was the older brother from whom Stephen could seek help. Joseph, like Stephen, had been psychologically and emotionally orphaned at an early age. Stephen had lost his father and his surrogate mother, Agnes, by age twelve; Joseph, whose father had been exiled to a remote Russian province for his political views, had lost both parents by age eleven. Both writers could be self-destructive; both had rejected institutionalized religion, had experienced poverty and sickness, and had survived a disaster at sea. Their bleak vision of humanity adrift in a hostile universe contrasted starkly with Frederic's more optimistic view of society's ability to improve and to shape its own destiny.[22]

Though fourteen years older, Conrad saw in Crane a version of his own heart of darkness. The "intense earnestness," "delicacy of senti-ment," and freedom from "affectation" that marked Crane were also characteristic of Conrad. When Jessie Conrad first met Crane, she no-ticed immediately "the easy terms of complete understanding" between the two writers. Their correspondence bespeaks intimacy and trust. "Did we not have a good pow-wow in London," asked Crane rhetorically; and Conrad agreed, adding that because of their time together "the world looks different to me now." It was "as though we had been born together before the beginning of things." Yet privately, Conrad was concerned about his new friend and could be ambivalent about his work. "He is strangely hopeless about himself," he confided to Edward Garnett in De-cember, at the same time admiring Crane's extraordinary vision and im-pressionistic techniques. He felt that Crane's thought was "never very deep—yet often startling. He is *the only* impressionist and *only* an impres-sionist." Conrad sensed something missing in Crane's writing: "While one reads, of course, he is not to be questioned. He is the master of his reader to the very last line—then—apparently for no reason at all—he seems to let go his hold. It is as if he had gripped you with greased fin-gers. His grip is strong but while you feel the pressure on your flesh you slip out from his hand—much to your own surprise. That is my stupid impression and I give it to you in confidence." Years later, Conrad re-vised his opinion of Crane's technique, perceiving that it "went really deeper than the surface."[23]

Immediately following their meeting in October, Crane and Conrad saw each other rarely because Jessie was pregnant with her first child and Conrad was suffering from one of his frequent bouts of depression, most likely precipitated by anxiety over impending fatherhood. "I hate ba-bies," he confided to Edward Garnett. Yet Crane and Conrad shared their work with each other; and later, Conrad kept his friend's photo on his desk as a reminder of their friendship. After reading "The Open Boat" and "A Man and Some Others," Conrad declared, "Your temperament makes old things new and new things amazing." After reading page proofs for the book publication of *The Nigger of the "Narcissus,"* Crane called it "simply great" and tried (unsuccessfully) to get it serialized in America. In reading the death scene of the tubercular James Wait, Crane acknowledged his own mortality: the description "is too good, too terrible. I wanted to forget it at once. It caught me very hard. I felt ill over that red thread lining from the corner of the man's mouth to his chin. It was frightful with the weight of a real and present death." By February, the Conrads were ready to travel; and Joseph and Jessie, their five-week-old baby, Borys, and Jessie's younger sister, Dorothy ("Dolly") George, spent ten days at Ravensbrook, where the two authors worked daily in Crane's study. Conrad was amused by Crane's devotion to his dogs, who repeatedly scratched at the door. Crane would immediately let them in, close the door, and return to his work; then get up again minutes later when they wanted to go out. Though Conrad hid his annoyance at the constant interruption, he admired Crane's dedication to his loyal companions.[24]

In December 1897, shortly after Conrad's book was published in England, a perceptive review by W. L. Courtney appeared in the *Daily Telegraph*. He suggested that Conrad had been influenced by *The Red Badge of Courage* but was a better writer than Crane. Conrad wrote a gracious letter to Courtney, expressing "my high appreciation of your luminous and flattering notice," responding calmly to Courtney's criticisms of the novel, and saying nothing about the comparison between Crane and himself.[25]

Conrad worried that the review might wound his new friend's ego and make him defensive the next time they met. Two years earlier, the same reviewer had criticized *The Red Badge of Courage* for what he saw as its weak plot and crude style and was now saying that Conrad had a better technique. In an attempt to preserve their friendship, Conrad sent holiday greetings to the Cranes on December 24 with a friendly note. He discounted the value of book reviews—"Criticisms (!) are coming in. Some praise, some blame, both very stupid"—and commented on the recent review "by that ass Courtney":

He does not understand you—and he does not understand me either. That's a feather in our caps anyhow. It is the most mean-minded criticism I've read in my life. Do you think I tried to imitate you? No Sir! I may be a little fool but I know better than to try to imitate the inimitable. But here it is. Courtney says it: You are a lost sinner and you have lead [*sic*] me astray. If it was true I would be well content to follow you but it isn't true and the perfidious ass tried to damage us both. Three cheers for the Press!

Conrad's tone contrasts sharply with that of the gracious letter he had written to Courtney. Even for the occasionally mercurial Conrad, the tone is so harsh as to suggest that he was exaggerating to soothe Crane. Yet it raises the question of whether Crane did indeed influence Conrad. In his preface to Thomas Beer's biography of Crane (1923), Conrad implied that he had written his book before he had read *The Red Badge of Courage,* but he acknowledged similarities between the novels.[26]

Although Crane's reaction to the review was never recorded, it must not have offended him because he twice proposed that Conrad collaborate with him on a play. On one occasion, he passionately described a theatrically unworkable plot about a shipwreck on an island; on another, in early January 1898, he concocted a story about the American West tentatively titled "The Predecessor."[27] Crane's far-fetched plot involved a man who, in order to win a girl's heart, pretends to be someone deceased. In one scene, the two characters stand next to their lifeless horses after riding them to death on the prairie. From the outset, Conrad was cool toward the project because he felt his lack of dramatic skills would hinder it, and he suspected that no theater manager could be persuaded to put two stuffed horses on stage. Crane persisted, however, and on March 19 after dinner at the Savage Club they went to Gatti's café, where Crane sketched out the plot. Energized by Crane's insistence on the success of "a dead sure thing," Conrad began contributing ideas for the play. Nothing came of the project. Conrad was already involved in writing *Lord Jim,* and Crane, ever the dreamer, needed to write short stories for quick money. The fate of the project revealed how serious his financial problems had become. In April, he showed a prospectus for "The Predecessor," now recast as a novel, to C. Arthur Pearson, publisher of *Pearson's Weekly* and other magazines. Unsurprisingly, no contract or advance was forthcoming for a ridiculous love story with silly characters and an improbable plot.

Conrad may have proposed that the two authors write a novel about the Franco-Prussian War based on notes he had gathered about the siege of Paris in 1870–1871. They never managed to collaborate on a writing project—but Crane's work and personality did inspire Conrad.[28] Crane himself may have been a model for the protagonist in *Lord Jim;* and years later, Conrad recalled that "The Predecessor" had influenced one of his stories, probably "Freya of the Seven Isles" (1912), serialized in *Metro-*

politan Magazine.[29] Equally striking was the influence of "The Open Boat": Conrad admired the story and would often describe things— using Crane's striking description of the sea—as "barbarously abrupt." The story triggered memories for Conrad, who in 1883 had endured a twelve-hour ordeal in a fourteen-foot rowboat with three other men after abandoning a sinking ship. By June, he had finished his autobiographical account of the experience, "Youth: A Narrative."[30]

Crane's friendships with Conrad and Frederic, in turn, fueled his own creativity and made his period of residence at Ravensbrook among the most productive of his life. During the summer and winter of 1897, he wrote four masterpieces—"The Monster," "Death and the Child," "The Bride Comes to Yellow Sky," and "The Blue Hotel"—all of which are worth considering in detail because of their biographical significance. Crane planned to take control of his literary career and redefine himself as a respectable family man. In late June he compiled a list of the stories he had written, the word count for each, and the place of publication or the location of the manuscript. The list forced him to impose a structure on a hectic literary career that had blossomed very quickly, and the word counts reminded him of the monetary value of his written work. He also decided that England, with its artist colony in Surrey and Sussex, would be his temporary home. *The Third Violet* was being well reviewed in England. Although a number of American reviewers dismissed it—"an experiment in inanity," asserted one critic—respected English journals praised it. "For psychological insight, for dramatic intensity, and for potency of phrase," declared the *Academy,* "he is already in the front rank of English and American writers." And the *Athenaeum* announced: "If he continues in his present line of writing he may be the author who will introduce the United States to the ordinary English world."[31]

21

Creative Outburst

OCTOBER 1897–APRIL 1898

CRANE WAS OPTIMISTIC about his professional career during his early months in England, but he soon became ambivalent about Cora. According to Corwin Knapp Linson, Stephen wanted to marry her; but his three book inscriptions to her, written shortly after they had met, project an ephemeral relationship. His uncertainty grew as a result of his lifelong wanderlust; by the summer of 1897, he was considering traveling as a foreign correspondent to South Africa, the Sudan, India, or the Klondike. "The Bride Comes to Yellow Sky," a story about a Texas marshal named Jack Potter who returns home nervously after secretly getting married, captured Crane's anxiety about his relationship with Cora and his public image in America.

On October 29, 1897, Crane sent a letter to William that revealed guilt, apprehension, and restlessness. After mentioning that friends considered "The Bride Comes to Yellow Sky" the "very best thing" he had written, he confessed his fear that rumors about his reputation would damage his family: "There seem so many of them in America who want to kill, bury and forget me purely out of unkindness and envy and—my unworthiness, if you choose. All the hard things they say of me effect me principally because I think of mine own people—you and Teddie and the families." He admitted that he had managed his "success like a fool and a child," then said he was thinking of traveling as a foreign correspondent to report on the gold rush in the Klondike or the clash between tribesmen and British troops on British India's northwest frontier. Beyond that, he looked forward to returning home to America: "I am learning every day. I am slowly becoming a man. My idea is to come finally to live at Port Jervis or Hartwood. I am a wanderer now and I must see enough but—afterwards—I think of P. J. & Hartwood." The two locations gave him clear choices. Rural Hartwood consisted of little more than a pond, Edmund's home, and a small train station; nearby was the Hartwood Club. In contrast, Port Jervis was a growing metropolis, which Crane fictionalized in "The Bride Comes to Yellow Sky." Just as Yellow Sky is situated at the convergence of the railroad and the Rio Grande, which "circled near the town," Port Jervis, known as the "River City," was marked by two rivers, the Delaware and the Neversink, that curved around the town and that met the railroad at an angle. Likewise, both towns were already showing signs of cosmopolitanism. Potter's marriage is not the first one in Yellow Sky, and the town has a band, neatly kept lawns, a new hotel, and burgeoning commercial activity. Similarly, by the latter part of the nineteenth century the one-time rural canal community of Port Jervis had become a thriving railroad and business center.[1]

In short, the letter to William depicted a restless youth who was yearning for frontier adventures and who hoped that eventually, after growing up, he would return home to family and respectability. Besides being unusually long for Stephen, the letter was especially striking for two bits of missing information. First, Crane hid his specific location in England. Even though he had stationery with Ravensbrook letterhead, he used plain paper and listed William Heinemann in London as his return address.[2] Second, he said nothing about Cora, knowing that had he done so, it would have led to questions about who she was. Like his character Jack Potter, who is apprehensive about society's response to his marriage, Crane was anxious about the dilemma posed by his new "bride." How could the free-roaming spirit depicted in the letter become a respectable husband in the eyes of his family?

In "Yellow Sky," the stark contrast between Potter and Scratchy Wilson, an aging gunfighter, dramatizes Crane's ambivalence. Crane resembled Scratchy, "a simple child of the earlier plains" who chants "Apache scalp-music"; he loved riding his horse in the Sullivan County wilderness near Port Jervis and used the word "Indians" to refer to the artists, illustrators, and medical students he had roomed with during his literary apprenticeship in New York City. After his first meeting with Conrad, he characterized it as a "good pow-pow in London." Crane never outgrew his penchant for role playing. He was the fraternity brother carousing with the boys at a party or on the playing field; the practical joker banging on a piano for a bemused audience; the seeker of adventure on the battlefield, high seas, and Western plains; an Indian who enjoyed being at a pow-wow with like-minded spirits. Like Scratchy, he was a Peter Pan whose imaginative flights took him to his own Neverland with its gang of Lost Boys.[3]

Potter's anxiety about his bride mirrored Crane's own worries about returning home. Crane must have wondered what it would be like to sail back across the Atlantic from England, take the train from New York City to Port Jervis, and travel westward to his own Yellow Sky. It would have been, as it was for Potter, the "hour of daylight," the start of a new life.[4] One of the most frequently used words in the story is "new," appearing fifteen times. Occasionally Stephen, like Scratchy and Huckleberry Finn, wanted to light out for the territory in order to stay ahead of encroaching civilization; but like Potter, Crane also wanted to return home eventually and settle down. In telling William that he thought of Hartwood or Port Jervis as his final home, Crane wanted to have it both ways: the city of Port Jervis would give him civilization; rural Hartwood, the frontier. But there was one problem: his "bride" had a past and was still married to another man. "The Bride Comes to Yellow Sky" ends without describing how the town responds to Potter's marriage because Crane could not answer the question for himself.

Just as "The Bride Comes to Yellow Sky" reflected Crane's divided self, "The Monster," the first of his Whilomville stories and another of his 1897 masterpieces, was his most complex attempt to reconcile a personal and ancestral past with his own psyche. Crane adapted the archaic word "whilom," meaning "at some past time" or "once upon a time" (a widely accepted literary convention for opening a story), to create the name of a town based on Port Jervis in order to evoke nostalgia in readers about their childhood.[5] But the word also had a private significance for Crane. At family reunions of his maternal ancestors from 1853 to

1874, George Peck and his four brothers would recreate the drum-and-fife corps they had organized as youths. They had named the group the "Whilom drum corps." After Crane's parents had married in 1848, the Crane family had regularly attended reunions until the last one, in 1874. Crane would have heard about the corps and the reunions as a child and had later read about them in a book by his maternal cousin Jonathan Kenyon Peck titled *Luther Peck and His Five Sons,* two copies of which he had with him in England. In naming his imaginary town Whilomville, Crane was creating a childhood world where stories that had taken place "once upon a time" would be told for a general readership. More important, he was also constructing a safe haven in the shadow of family reunions where he could revisit his own distant and recent past in order to address personal anxieties and frustrations.[6]

"The Monster," which Crane began writing during the summer of 1897 and finished in Ireland, portrays the moral smugness and intolerance of small-town America; and it privately addresses his frustration at having his work misunderstood. He had been fired from the *New York Tribune* when readers misread his satirical article about the JOUAM parade in Asbury Park in 1892. After the incident, the *Tribune* had become his enemy and often reviewed his books unfavorably. *Maggie* could be published in 1896 only after it had been expurgated; readers had mocked *The Black Riders;* and *The Red Badge of Courage* had been criticized as an unflattering portrait of American soldiers. More recently, Crane had been misrepresented as an opium addict in New York City. Nowhere in his work is the theme of misreading treated more devastatingly than in "The Monster." The story describes the way nearly everyone in a town misreads the actions of Henry Johnson, a hostler who risks his life to rescue a boy named Jimmie Trescott from a burning house. Initially reported as dead in the local newspaper, Johnson is eulogized for his heroism; yet when he survives his ordeal and is left horribly disfigured by the fire, society labels him a monster. The real monster turns out to be the community of Whilomville, where the *Morning Tribune,* its title reminiscent of the *New York Tribune,* cannot even keep its facts straight as to whether someone is dead or alive.

"The Monster"—a tale of prejudice, fear, and moral blindness—was deeply rooted in Crane's memories of Port Jervis. The setting and architecture of Whilomville were clearly based on those of Stephen's hometown in Orange County, New York. The "Never-Die Hose Company" took its name from one of the eight fire departments in Port Jervis, the Neversink Hose Company. "Bridge Street Hill," in Whilomville, was the nineteenth-century nickname for Main Street in Port Jervis.[7] William Howe Crane's family lived at 19 East Main Street; next door, at 17 East Main, was the prominent Port Jervis physician Dr. Henry B. Swartwout.[8] Both houses had been built in Queen Anne style, and behind the doctor's residence was a carriage house. In "The Monster," Dr. Trescott's house is also a Queen Anne structure; behind it is a carriage house; and the description of the interiors of both buildings roughly matches that of Dr. Swartwout's home and carriage house.[9] Finally, Henry Johnson, Dr. Trescott's hostler, likewise had a counterpart in the real world: the Port Jervis directory for 1893 lists "Henry Johnson, hostler" at 17 Railroad Avenue.[10]

Of all of the childhood memories that Crane incorporated into "The Monster," none was more powerful than the July 4, 1879, cannon explosion that maimed two African Americans in Port Jervis. The fact that the incident occurred on the day commemorating the Declaration of Independence resonated deeply with the young boy, who had grown up believing that one of his namesakes had offered the opening prayer at the First Continental Congress, had signed the Declaration, and had been directly instrumental in the founding of the United States. A wall in the Crane home in Port Jervis featured an engraving—in all likelihood a reproduction of T. H. Matteson's painting *The First Prayer in Congress* (1848) —that depicted the delegates in prayer at the opening of the First Continental Congress in 1774. A key identified each delegate; behind Samuel Chase stood Stephen's namesake. There would have been no better engraving to hang in the parsonage as a reminder of God, country, and the family's ancestry.[11]

An engraving titled *Signing the Declaration* likewise hangs in the Trescott home in "The Monster." Crane's incorporation of a seminal moment in American history gains significance in the light of another powerful historical moment. In 1896, a year before Crane wrote the story, the Supreme Court had settled the controversial case of *Plessy v. Ferguson,* in which Homer Plessy, an octoroon who could pass as white, had challenged Louisiana's law mandating segregation on railroad cars.[12] The court's decision effectively legalized segregation until *Brown v. Board of*

Education overturned it in 1954. The separate-but-equal issue in the 1890s also drew attention to the Declaration of Independence, which was already in the news as a result of its poor physical condition. In 1894, when the State Department withdrew it from exhibition because the text was rapidly fading and the parchment was deteriorating, national magazines and newspapers featured articles about the document. The *Ladies Home Journal* reproduced a facsimile of Thomas Jefferson's first draft of the Declaration, and the *Washington Post* mentioned "all the erasures and alterations that were made before the language was finally agreed upon."[13] As Jefferson recounted in his widely read autobiography, he had criticized the practice of slavery by England and the colonists in his first draft of the Declaration, but had revised it in order to broker a compromise among the delegates. Crane's family had been well aware of Jefferson's desire to condemn slavery in the first draft.[14] His father had quoted from the draft and made it the subject of a college essay, and his maternal grandfather, George Peck, had discussed it in *Our Country: Its Trial and Its Triumph* (1865).[15] Crane's parents had criticized society's racial inequities and had helped to establish the Drew Mission and Industrial School in Port Jervis, to improve the economic condition of African Americans.

Since Crane was so proud of his family's past, it seems odd that in "The Monster" he would destroy the engraving in the fire at the Trescott home. He was not criticizing a document that called for equality among whites yet denied it to blacks. A product of his times, Crane employed racist stereotypes in his fiction and journalism. "Greed Rampant" is an anti-Semitic dramatic skit; *Maggie* presents the clichéd image of the Irish as combative, blustering drunks; "A Man and Some Others" reveals his condescending attitude toward Mexicans, as though they were inferior to other men. Crane patronizes African Americans as well. Before Henry Johnson heroically saves Jimmie Trescott in "The Monster," he dresses like a dandy, shuffles around, and speaks stiltedly as he woos Bella Farragut in Watermelon Alley. Yet the description of the fire reveals Crane's divided mind. Within the context of Crane's ancestry, the Declaration of Independence, and the renewed debate about equality triggered by *Plessy v. Ferguson,* Crane evokes the American Revolution in his description of the fire: with "clan joining clan, gathering to the colors," this "outbreak had been well planned, as if by professional revolutionists"; as the engraving falls off the wall, "it burst with the sound of a bomb"; and as

Henry Johnson tries to rescue Jimmie, he "was submitting, submitting because of his fathers, bending his mind in a most perfect slavery to this conflagration." Henry's attempt to free Jimmie from the bondage of the fire is thus situated within the historical context of America's struggle for freedom and equality; but in order to free Jimmie, this black man must submit to "a most perfect slavery." The price of freedom for all those who are created equal is continued slavery for blacks. As the engraving burns, Crane questions what it means to be black literally and histori-cally—for Henry is figuratively not the only black man who attempts to rescue Jimmie. Hannigan, the Trescotts' white next-door neighbor, his face "black with rage," breaks down the door through which Henry rushes to rescue Jimmie. In a scene dramatizing the colonists' struggle for freedom and equality, Johnson and Hannigan, both with black faces, are indistinguishable as they confront the flames. Despite the vibrant colors of the burning chemicals in Dr. Trescott's laboratory, the dominant color of the scene is black. Against the "blackened sky," a "black crowd" of people runs toward the fire on a road that resembles a "black torrent."[16]

A student of history, Crane debunked the shibboleths of society and often treated historical figures and subjects ironically; yet his pride in his namesakes' role in the formation of America was such that "The Mon-ster" touched his psyche deeply. He saw himself as an outcast following the Dora Clark affair; hence, he identified with Henry Johnson, who is driven out of Whilomville after being labeled a monster, and with Dr. and Mrs. Trescott, who are ostracized when the doctor refuses to institu-tionalize Henry. But Crane's divided self could not cast off society's rac-ism. "The Monster" ends without resolution.

Whatever satisfaction Crane got from writing several masterpieces af-ter settling in at Ravensbrook was offset by financial woes. Living well beyond their means, Stephen and Cora quickly ran into debt by buying furniture and other items for their house and by treating the constant in-flux of visitors—journalists, writers, tourists, some of whom were unin-vited—to fine food and wine, bought on credit. Unable to turn them away, Crane would escape to a London hotel room—yet another ex-pense—seeking a quiet spot where he could write. His inept business dealings exacerbated the matter; and because of the loan he had obtained from McClure in March, Crane had to give him his new work as collat-eral, whether or not McClure published it. By October, more than two thousand dollars in debt, Crane was complaining to John Phillips ("I have delivered to you over 25000 words against my debt but I dont see myself any better off than if I had asked you to wait until I got damned good and ready to pay"), plying Paul Revere Reynolds with elaborate schemes for marketing his material, and beseeching him for any money that could be gotten from a loan, sale, or advance. Crane had been imploring Robert McClure, head of the McClure syndicate's office in London, so often for money that "poor little Robert . . . wails and screams like a mandrake when I mention it."[17]

Burdened by debt, Crane cranked out incidental pieces—"London Impressions," "Irish Notes," "European Letters" (secretly in collaboration with Cora as "Imogene Carter"). He admitted that the "Letters," dashed off in twenty minutes each, were "rotten bad." As Crane became more apprehensive about his plight, his behavior became more erratic. His correspondence with Reynolds in late 1897 and early 1898 revealed Crane's misunderstanding of the workings of the publishing world and jeopardized his agent's credibility within it. After sending Reynolds "Death and the Child" in December, he demanded that the agent "for heaven's sake raise me all the money you can and *cable* it, *cable* it sure between Xmas and New Year's. Sell 'The Monster'! Don't forget that—cable me some money this month." Harper's was willing to publish "The Monster" in *Harper's Magazine,* but only if it could reprint the story in a collected volume. Crane quickly agreed, somehow believing that stories scheduled to appear in Heinemann's *The Open Boat and Other Stories* could also be used in Harper's book. Crane likewise ignored the agreement giving Reynolds exclusive agency-rights to his material and tried marketing his own stories in England. "In all the months I have been in England," he complained to his agent, "I have never received a cent from America which has not been borrowed. Just read that over twice! The consequences of this have lately been that I have been obliged to make arrangements here with English agents of American houses but in all cases your commission will be protected. This is the best I could do. My English expenses have chased me to the wall."[18]

By the end of 1897, Crane had six books in print but little money to show for them. He was still receiving only a 10 percent royalty on American sales of *The Red Badge of Courage;* moreover, Appleton's contract with Heinemann for the British rights did not include a royalty for him. And his modest American royalties would soon stop because of the lawsuit brought by Amy Leslie in January 1898. Feeling abandoned and hearing rumors about Crane's character and possibly about Cora, Amy had written to him complaining about money he owed her. Neither of them knew that Willis Brooks Hawkins had grown weary of being a go-between for them. Crane's response to her in September was a deceptive letter avoiding any mention of Cora or his move to Ravensbrook, giving William Heinemann as his address, and promising his loyalty: "Trust me and it will all turn out right. . . . Dont think too badly of me, dear. Wait, have patience and I will see you through straight. Dont believe anything you hear of me and dont doubt my faith and my honesty."[19] She did, however; when Hawkins received a copy of a warrant of attachment against Crane's property, her lawsuit froze Crane's royalties at Appleton. In February, Crane received a summons to respond to the claim brought against him. With help from William, the case was settled out of court with a financial arrangement, but not before Crane's name once again made headlines in America. He was alarmed at the thought that he could be dragged into court and have his relationship with Cora exposed.

Of the stories Crane wrote at Ravensbrook, none demonstrated more than "The Blue Hotel" his bad luck and his difficulties in dealing with the literary marketplace. According to Cora, Stephen said that the tale was partly based on his experience in Nebraska in February 1895, though he was not inspired to write it until long after his Western trip. When he had visited Conrad in late November, his friend had noted Crane's "strangely hopeless" state of mind. Despite his occasional flights of egotism, Crane's doubts about his career haunted him throughout his life. Heading back to Ravensbrook through a severe storm dispirited him, and a few days later he began writing a story in which stormy winter weather in Nebraska symbolized potential violence among strangely hopeless humans.[20]

Crane had trouble maintaining priorities and being realistic about his financial situation. While working on "The Blue Hotel," he abruptly began writing *Active Service,* a novel about the Greco-Turkish War. He naïvely expected that he could obtain a big advance for it and finish it by the following spring; but when the advance did not come, he returned to his short story, which took more than two months to write. Crane

then assumed that Reynolds could quickly arrange with Harper's for serial and book publication of "The Blue Hotel" in England and America.
He sent him the manuscript on February 7, 1898, then a day later asked
for proofs. *Harper's Magazine,* however, rejected it, as did the *Century* and
Scribner's Magazine. The *Atlantic Monthly* offered to publish it only if
Crane would also submit a novel or a collection of Western stories, but
he could not do this. Reynolds then approached *Collier's Weekly,* which
offered to accept the story only if Crane would shorten it. By this point,
Crane had misplaced the manuscript; and once it was found, he was busy
with other matters. "Cant cut this. Let Collier's do it themselves," he
hastily advised Reynolds.[21] In a continuing comedy of errors, *Collier's*
likewise misplaced its copy of "The Blue Hotel," which eventually appeared, uncut, in two parts in late November and early December 1898
—a year after Crane had started writing a piece he thought would be
quickly and easily published.

Although the story depicts a bleak universe, humans are not simply
amoral creatures controlled by ungovernable forces. Instead, Crane emphasizes what happens when people misread each other, when communication breaks down, and when individuals ignore the natural and ethical consequences of their actions. A character referred to as "the Swede"
misreads the West because of his fondness for dime novels, but other
people in the tale are no better at reading reality than he is. When they
have trouble understanding the Swede, a cowboy dismisses him with
a racist stereotype ("He's some kind of a Dutchman"), prompting the
narrator to mention "a venerable custom of the country": "to entitle as
Swedes all light-haired men who spoke with a heavy tongue." A character named Johnnie dismisses the Swede: "I don't know nothin' about you
. . . and I don't give a damn where you've been."[22]

In the last section of the story, Crane introduces a moral perspective
by asking who is responsible for the Swede's death. Legally, a gambler is
because he has killed the Swede; but morally (as specified in grammatical
terms), the gambler is not "a noun" but "an adverb." He is not the sole
doer of the action; rather, he has modified an action already begun by
others, all of whom contribute to the story's tragic outcome. "Every sin
is the result of a collaboration. We, five of us, have collaborated in the
murder of this Swede," concludes a pipe-smoking "little silent man from

the East" appropriately named Mr. Blanc. His comment reflects Crane's admiration for Tolstoy's view of moral consequences, as popularized in the novels of William Dean Howells. Christianity implies a doctrine of complicity: if someone witnesses an immoral act and does nothing to stop it, he or she shares responsibility for the consequences of the act. In this sense, the Easterner correctly implicates others in the death of the Swede.[23]

But as Crane's persona, the Easterner also addresses the issue of responsibility regarding the Dora Clark incident. Undoubtedly, Crane wanted to have it both ways. He wanted publicly to be the knight rescuing the maiden and privately the rascal who fraternized with prostitutes, but the consequences of his action exposed his double life. When the cowboy, "injured and rebellious," exclaims to the Easterner, "Well, I didn't do anythin', did I?" one hears Crane's own conflicted sense of innocence and guilt.

Frantically searching for ways to raise money, Crane decided once again to head for Cuba to report on the growing conflict there. Accompanied by Joseph Conrad, who opposed the war and sided with Spain, he dashed around London one afternoon during the first week of April, trying to convince publishers to lend him money for passage to America. Rejected time after time, he became distressed, until *Blackwood's* advanced him sixty pounds to be paid off with war stories or articles. Although twenty pounds of the advance went to Cora, this was hardly enough to satisfy their increasingly insistent creditors.[24]

"Nothing could have held him back," recalled Conrad. "He was ready to swim the ocean." Yet Cora had a premonition about Crane's fate. She wrote to Sylvester Scovel and his wife with a request: if they happened to see Stephen on his way to Cuba, would they be so kind as "to look after him a little. He is rather seedy and I am anxious about him, for he does not care to look out for himself." Worried that he might fall ill before sailing, Cora insisted that their Greek servant, Adoni, accompany Crane to the ship.

On April 13, 1898, Crane sailed from Liverpool for New York aboard the *Germanic*. The trip had a dual purpose for him: the writer needed money to pay his creditors, and the boy with wanderlust needed to escape the growing confinement of domesticity with Cora. He had already written a war novel about a youth's desertion during crisis; another youth was now preparing to flee as well. Soon after arriving in New York, he applied for a passport. Nothing he wrote on the preprinted form hinted that he was living in England and planned to return. Swearing that his permanent residence was Hartwood, he said he intended to return to America within a year after his stay in Cuba, "with the purpose," as stated on the application, "of residing and performing the duties of citizenship therein." About a month after applying for the passport, he told Lily Brandon Munroe's sister Dorothy that he would return to England and asked for the address of their sister Stella, who lived there. Crane had sworn that he would return to the United States, primarily to avoid being denied an American passport; but his statement also reflected his ambivalence about Cora.[25]

To escape creditors and to fend off sadness following Crane's departure, Cora—accompanied by Mrs. Charlotte Ruedy, Adoni, and the dogs—stayed with the Frederics at their borrowed estate in the fishing village of Ahakista, on the Irish coast, for two or three weeks in late April and early May. Mrs. Ruedy, Cora's friend from Ohio, had recently arrived in England, apparently to keep Cora company while Stephen was away.[26] The Conrads had also invited Cora to stay with them; but upon her return from Ireland, she chose not to. Thinking of Crane, Conrad wrote, "I trust you will let me know how he fares whenever you hear from him. He is not very likely to write to any one else—if I know the man."[27] He certainly did know the man, who would soon vanish from Cora's life and remain almost completely silent for the next eight months, leaving her with mounting debts.

22

Prelude to War

MINUTES BEFORE MIDNIGHT on April 21, 1898, the *Germanic* crossed the bar of New York Harbor. Early the next day, Crane contracted with Pulitzer's *New York World* for three thousand dollars to report on the Cuban campaign of the Spanish-American War. He confided to *Collier's Weekly* photographer Jimmy Hare that he had signed with the *World* in order to get a military pass so that he could write a book about the war. Crane left New York on April 24 and stopped briefly in Washington to see Lily Brandon Monroe. Since the summer of 1892 in Asbury Park, they had met at least twice—in January 1895, before he had left for the West and Mexico, and in early 1897 (probably January), when he had told her about Cora Taylor and his shipwreck off the Florida coast. Now they met at the Library of Congress, where he asked her one last time to run off with him. She refused, and he never saw her again. A day or two later, he was in Key West. The ensuing months would bring a major transition in his life.[1]

Much has been made about the role of the press in fomenting the Spanish-American War. Sensational accounts of Spanish cruelty against Cuban insurgents stirred sympathy in the United States, but most Americans initially opposed war with Spain. Businessmen feared that it would endanger their investments in Cuba and the economic recovery at home. In his 1897 inaugural address, William McKinley urged America to "avoid the temptation of territorial aggression. War should never be entered upon until every agency of peace has failed." As the last U.S. president to serve in the Civil War, he had witnessed the carnage near Antietam Creek in Maryland on September 17, 1862, the bloodiest single-day battle in American history.[2]

The turning point in the Spanish-American War occurred with the sinking of the battleship *Maine*. In January 1898, tension between Spain and a growing Cuban insurgency demanding self-government precipitated mob riots in Havana. By the end of the month, the *Maine* had arrived in the harbor to protect American lives and property. On February 15, a mysterious explosion blew up the ship, killing 266 crew members. Chanting "Remember the *Maine!* To Hell with Spain!" an outraged American public immediately blamed the incident on Spain and demanded American intervention. "American Women Ready To Give Up Husbands, Sons and Sweethearts to Defend Nation's Honor," clamored the headline in the *New York World*.[3] After Spain ignored President McKinley's insistence in March that Cuba be granted full independence, Congress passed a joint resolution stating that Cuba was free and declared war on Spain in April.

The conflict became the first filmed war. To compensate for lack of footage from Cuba, battle scenes were faked and staged. On the roof of a New York building, toy boats in a bathtub surrounded by cigar smoke depicted maritime battles, and in New Jersey the National Guard patriotically reenacted the Rough Riders in combat. With one journalist for about every 180 soldiers, the war was also the most reported conflict in history until the Grenada expedition in 1982. Newspapers scrambled to increase circulation by hiring famous writers to provide vivid battle descriptions. In addition to the *World's* employment of Crane, the *New York Herald* got Richard Harding Davis; the *New York Journal*, Julian Hawthorne and the writer-illustrator Frederic Remington. Rudyard Kipling was besieged with offers, some inviting him to name his own price, but he declined all of them. Since newspaper editors considered the celebrities inexperienced as reporters, each well-known writer was assigned to a seasoned journalist (Crane was paired with Sylvester Scovel), who ensured that dispatches were written and cabled promptly.[4]

Journalists, volunteers, and hardened war veterans began immediately to head for Florida en route to Cuba. Railroad magnate Henry B. Plant offered his palatial 511-room Tampa Bay Hotel as a base of operations for the U.S. Army. At five stories, it towered above the city, and its lavish accommodations, tropical gardens, and Moorish Revival architecture, distinguished by domes, cupolas, and minarets, reinforced the sensibility of those who viewed the war as a romantic endeavor. Officers lounged on the porch in rockers, drinking iced tea and champagne, while their soldiers camped on the grounds and engaged in training drills. April, May, and June were "the rocking-chair period of the war," wrote Davis. "It was an army of occupation, but it occupied the piazza of a big hotel." Frustrated by the delay, other journalists headed farther south to Key West, hoping to find quicker passage to Cuba, but constant problems hindered the invasion. Tired of waiting for orders to sail for Cuba, one correspondent quipped, "Cube, or not Cube; that is the Key Westion."[5]

On April 22 the Atlantic Squadron, under the command of Admiral William T. Sampson, blockaded the coast of Cuba in order to intercept the Spanish fleet of Admiral Pascual Cervera y Topete and to protect the transport of American troops. It was the first major act of belligerence between Spain and the United States. Crane admired Admiral Sampson, whom he called "the most interesting personality of the war." Though he initially thought that the admiral was bored by the Cuban campaign, he later concluded that "hidden in his indifferent, even apathetic, manner, there was the alert, sure, fine mind" of one of America's greatest sea captains. Crane's admiration for professional, heroic seamen reflected his patriotism, adventurous spirit, and pride in his ancestry. William Montgomery Crane (1776–1846), a grandson of the Revolutionary Stephen Crane, was a naval officer who fought in the First Barbary War and the War of 1812 and became a commodore. As a child, Crane had relished the pioneering, exciting sea fiction of James Fenimore Cooper and English naval officer Captain Frederick Marryat (much admired by Joseph Conrad and Ernest Hemingway); and in May, when a dispatch boat thought it was being chased by a Spanish ship, Crane wrote excitedly: "A stern chase! Shades of Marryat and Cooper!"[6]

Like Tampa, Key West was already teeming with reporters impatiently awaiting passage to Cuba. For Crane, it was a reunion of friends spanning his journalistic career. He had been a cub reporter with Ralph D. Paine

in Asbury Park; Paine had also been with him in Jacksonville, along with
Ernest W. McCready and Edward Marshall, who had opened the doors
of the *New York Press* and *Journal* to him; and he and Sylvester Scovel had
been in Greece.

Crane stayed at the Key West Hotel, which was so crowded that guests
paid five dollars daily for a cot in a hallway. At night, he escaped to the
roulette wheel at the Eagle Bird, a local gambling house named after
a term used in roulette. He would drawl lines from "The Five White
Mice," his Western story about gambling, which two weeks earlier had
appeared, abridged, in the *New York World:*

> Oh, five white mice of chance,
> Shirts of wool and corduroy pants,
> Gold and wine, women and sin,
> All for you if you let me come in—
> Into the house of chance.[7]

Like roulette, throwing the "five white mice" was a game in which the
odds were against the individual. For Crane, however, gambling was
much more than a diversion. In a game of chance, Crane confronted the
universe with each toss of the dice, spin of the wheel, turn of the card.
His almost compulsive need to gamble had nothing to do with a desire
for instant wealth; he and his friends typically bet matchsticks and only
rarely pennies. Once, Crane insisted that they play Hearts for five dollars
a heart, but he did so only to test their courage in a tense, unpredictable
situation. In "The Five White Mice," the "New York Kid" reenacts the
scene, betting fifty dollars on the roll of one die to give him the winning
hand in poker-dice. No one takes him up on his bet, and he still loses the
game; but he has pulled off, as the bartender observes, "the greatest cold
bluff I ever saw worked." For Crane, winning or losing was not the point.
Gambling was his way of admitting uncertainty amid an inscrutable universe in which, as Melville's Ishmael also learns, life is a mixture of
"chance, free will, and necessity." Like the crew searching for the unfath-
omable Moby Dick, the New York Kid is on his own "sea-voyage," on a
Mexico City street "as dark as a whale's throat at deep sea," heading for
a potentially fatal confrontation with three ominous-looking Mexicans.
Yet he learns, as Crane learned, that in the game of life the winners are

those who avoid being imprisoned by their own egos and accept their ultimate insignificance.[8]

The biblical metaphor of life as a sea journey had long attracted Crane. "God fashioned the ship of the world," he wrote in one of the better-known poems in *The Black Riders and Other Lines,* but it has become "rudderless." Growing up on the New Jersey coast, Crane recognized the peril of a ship's running aground on a sandbar or being buried in the Graveyard of the Atlantic, yet these same incidents tested one's courage and validated the comradeship of the four men in "The Open Boat." While Crane began making incursions into the slums of New York City in the fall of 1891, Melville was soon to die in obscurity, on September 28, only blocks away in his home at 104 East 26th Street. Crane never met the greatest writer of sea fiction in American literature, yet he understood Ishmael's quest for what Melville called "the ungraspable phantom of life."[9]

During the first month of the war, Crane sailed in and out of Key West on the *World's* two dispatch boats, the *Triton* and the *Three Friends,* following navy patrols awaiting the arrival of the Spanish fleet of Admiral Pascual Cervera y Topete. At the end of April, he spent two days aboard Admiral Sampson's flagship on a reconnoitering expedition surveying Spanish batteries in the Bay of Mariel. Throughout May, he sailed along the Cuban coast writing news dispatches that he wired from Haiti, Jamaica, and Key West.

On one excursion, Crane met a relatively unknown writer named Frank Norris. Within a few months, Norris would publish a novel, *McTeague* (1899), that would make him a major voice in American literature.[10] He was already familiar with Crane's work. In February 1898, he had become an editorial assistant for S. S. McClure's newspaper syndicate, *McClure's Magazine,* and the Doubleday and McClure Company, which had published *The Open Boat and Other Tales of Adventure* in April. Norris had lampooned *Maggie, The Red Badge,* and "The Open Boat" (as "The Green Stone of Unrest") in his "Perverted Tales," a series of parodies of Crane, Rudyard Kipling, Bret Harte, Ambrose Bierce, and Anthony Hope published in the San Francisco weekly magazine *The Wave* in December 1897.

On May 8, Crane, Norris, and Scovel, head of the *World* staff, sailed from Key West aboard the *Three Friends* for two days, gathering news on the stalled war from American warships blockading the coast. In a post-humously published report on the blockade, Norris characterized Crane as "the Young Personage" whose trousers were "grimed and fouled with all manner of pitch and grease and oil." "His shirt was guiltless of collar or scarf, and was unbuttoned at the throat. His hair hung in ragged fringes over his eyes, his dress suit-case was across his lap and answered him for a desk. Between his heels he held a bottle of beer against the rolling of the boat, and when he drank was royally independent of a glass." Norris was not alone in commenting on Crane's unkempt appearance during the Cuban campaign. To fellow *Journal* reporter Charles Michelson, Crane, "with his ragged overalls and buttonless shirt flapping about his emaciated limbs, . . . was the dirtiest man in an army." Yet Norris's acerbic tone suggested jealousy of a more successful author and correspondent who was almost two years younger. Unlike Crane, who by working for a daily newspaper could immediately report the excitement of a breaking news story, Norris, employed by a monthly magazine, could not expect to see his name in print for some weeks, by which time the story had become old. Three decades later, Norris's widow told Franklin Walker, his first biographer, that Norris had disliked Crane at least partly because he "drank too much and made a fool of himself." Yet it is not simply Norris's fastidious nature that accounted for his criticism. Crane was partly responsible for the way others perceived him. He flaunted his indifference to the daily conventions of news reporting; he cared little about his own appearance and demeanor; he was taciturn, aloof, even arrogant at times toward colleagues. Richard Harding Davis privately confided to his family, "I don't like him."[11]

Life on a dispatch boat was often tense and hazardous for correspondents. Unable to write while in a bunk or at a table during rough seas, they were forced to lie on their stomachs, pen in hand and paper on the floor, sliding around while composing dispatches. At night or during inclement weather, a dispatch boat could easily be mistaken for an enemy ship. The protocol was to fire a round across the bow of a suspicious ship, with the expectation that she would identify herself immediately. In May, the U.S. gunboat *Machias* mistook the *Three Friends* for an enemy ship and accidentally rammed it after the warning shot had nicked the funnel of the tug; later, on board the dispatch boat *Somers N. Smith,* Crane and fellow journalists mistakenly thought that a Spanish gunboat was chasing them.[12] Though it turned out to be the American auxiliary cruiser *St. Paul,* they initially feared being imprisoned and executed because the enemy had announced that journalists would be treated as spies.[13]

Despite the dangers of reporting, Crane found humor in war. On the evening of May 14, the *Three Friends* arrived at Haiti with Crane, Ralph Paine, Ernest McCready of the *New York Herald,* and Harry Brown, chief of the *Herald* staff. They headed for Môle-Saint-Nicolas, the site of a French cable station, but they immediately encountered armed Haitian soldiers who repeatedly confronted them with "Qui vive?" a sentry's challenge that is used to mean "Who goes there?" Wandering around in the dark and unable to understand the local French patois, the frightened correspondents failed to convince the soldiers that they were simply reporters. Only Crane was amused by the confusion. "It is your move, Crane," said McCready. "Fiction is your long suit. Here it is. Things like this don't happen in real life. Let us have a few remarks from the well-known young author of 'The Red Badge of Courage.'" "Me?" grinned Crane. "If I caught myself hatching a plot like this, I wouldn't write another line until I had sobered up. Steady, boys, the night is still young, and I have a hunch that there'll be lots more of it. This opening is good."[14]

Crane was right. When Brown suggested that they return to the boat and wait until morning, Crane quipped, "Stick around, Harry. Age has dulled your feeling for romance. We can beat this game yet." Suddenly a deckhand named Bill, who had come ashore with the correspondents but had wandered away, reappeared with good news. By simply insisting to the armed natives that he was the boss, he had convinced them to defer to his command. "Bill, you are a wonder," declared Crane. "But, darn you, you are too impossible for fiction. I shall have to get good and drunk to do you justice. And you told them you were the boss and got away with it?" The correspondents soon had proof of Bill's scheme. Strutting up to the natives, he proclaimed haughtily, "I-AM-THE-BOSS! Salute, you black sons-of-guns"—to which the four correspondents added, "I-AM-THE-BOSS! Salute, you black sons-of-guns." The sentinels, somehow believing that the command was "Haitian French lingo" for the password, saluted the Americans, who were then greeted by the local governor's chief-of-staff in his pajamas and slippers. When he learned why the correspondents were there, he flaunted his self-importance by donning a military coat decorated with gold lace and epaulets, rounding up an escort of soldiers, and marching off with the correspondents to awaken two operators at the cable station, proudly announcing, "You admire how I speak English, eh? Pretty smooth! I twist her by the tail. Why not? Four years I was a butler in New Rochelle, New York!"[15]

"Hooray for the Chief-of-Staff!" chimed Crane. "He buttled in New Rochelle! My hunch was a winner. This is a purple night with spangled trimmings."[16] Crane appreciated the ludicrous tone of the situation, heightened now by a short colonel who repeatedly tripped over his own sword, other soldiers who were needlessly commanded to stand at attention outside the cable station, and an incongruously dressed Haitian in pajamas who forced sleepy operators at gunpoint to cable dispatches. A lifelong admirer of Lewis Carroll, Crane insisted on calling the chief-of-staff Alice in Wonderland for the rest of the evening.

When the correspondents offered to buy the soldiers a drink, the evening devolved into slapstick. As they headed out, their numbers rapidly increased, as sentinels, overhearing rumors of free liquor, eagerly joined the group. The soldiers had not had a drink for some time because they had not been paid for months. When the marchers got to a nearby grog shop, they battered down the door and startled the drowsy landlady, who, in descending from her sleeping loft, missed the ladder and crashed to the floor. Once she had composed herself, Harry Brown gave her three dollars for two bottles of rum, then learned that rum was merely forty cents a gallon. As the liquor flowed, so did the festivities. The soldiers toasted Haiti, the United States, and their new "eternal" friends, joyously fired salutes from increasingly wobbly rifles, danced on the beach, and sang "There'll Be a Hot Time in the Old Town To-Night." The next morning, the Haitians honored their newfound comrades with a cacophonous marching band and a review of barefoot troops strutting in a cakewalk through a field of cactus bushes and repeatedly stopping to remove thorns from their feet. The following evening, according to McCready, Crane—unshaven, unkempt, and barefoot in soiled pajamas —"went native," "successfully invited a seduction," and considered swimming in shark-infested water to salvage rum hidden in a barque anchored across the harbor.[17]

The Haitian escapade, as recorded by Ralph Paine, was a farce, complete with improbable situations, pratfalls, and wordplay, but it also captured Crane's sense of the instability of reality—a "game" and a "plot" with a good "opening" and characters "too impossible for fiction"—which he had already examined in *The Third Violet* and would soon revisit in his Cuban war stories. Despite jingoistic pronouncements about honor, war could be ludicrous and nonsensical. For Crane, as for Alice in an equally surreal context, Haiti had been a curiouser and curiouser adventure in Wonderland.

While awaiting deployment to Cuba, Crane wrote "His New Mittens," a story about a child in Whilomville. After completing "The Monster" in the summer of 1897, he had stopped thinking about the fictional town and its children. A few weeks later, in October, children had been on his mind again with "Death and the Child"; and they resurfaced in May 1898 with "His New Mittens," in which Crane, Janus-like, looked anxiously backward to his own troubled past and forward to his uncertain future with Cora.

A boy named Horace, torn between the social pressures of his peers and the moral and familial demands of a domineering mother and aunt, runs away from home and heads for California, the farthest place he can go and still maintain his American identity. He immediately encounters a "wild storm": "Panting, stung, half-blinded with the driving flakes, he was now a waif, exiled, friendless, and poor. With a bursting heart, he thought of his home and mother. To his forlorn vision they were as far away as Heaven." The story ends somewhat happily when a friendly butcher, a surrogate father figure who had been friends with Horace's late father, escorts the boy home. But Crane's thinly veiled disguise of himself as the boy left his own anxiety unresolved. A waif like Horace? Crane had considered himself a loner since childhood. Exiled? He was persona non grata in New York City. Friendless? He had a few close friends, but believed he was destined to drift through life by himself. Poor? He had joined the Cuban campaign to defray his mounting debts in England. The story's war imagery, violent "blue snow" (reminiscent of the tumultuous snowstorm in "The Blue Hotel," which he had finished only a few months earlier), and sense of "martyrdom" (an important theme that Crane would revisit in another Whilomville story) attested to a deeply divided psyche.[18]

Though the story dramatizes the consequences of Horace's ruining his mittens during a snowball fight, it contains two seemingly inconsequential details about Horace's mother and his planned escape. Though there seems no reason why she should be wearing "widow's weeds," the conventional dress of a wife in mourning, Crane might have been recalling his mother's dress following Reverend Crane's unexpected death in February 1880. It must surely have been unsettling for young Stephen, who had been forced, along with his family, to leave the parsonage in Port Jervis and live with distant relatives for three months. With the image of widow's weeds in "His New Mittens," Crane was reliving his loss of father, family, home. But as would be the case with later Whilomville stories, this one looked back to a painful experience and captured Crane's current anxiety about his future with a second apparently arbitrary detail. Just as Horace plans to travel three thousand miles to California to escape the authority of his mother and aunt, Crane himself had made a similar decision shortly before writing the story. In April 1898 he left England to travel three thousand miles to America, not only to work as a war correspondent but also to flee female authority.

23

War in Cuba

JUNE–JULY 1898

SINCE NO INFORMATION was available about the location of the Spanish fleet, the U.S. Navy had chosen to blockade what seemed to be Cervera's most likely point of arrival: the northwestern coast of Cuba around Havana, the capital and major port. By the third week in May, Commodore Winfield S. Schley's Flying Squadron confirmed that Cervera had sailed undetected into the harbor of Santiago de Cuba, on the southeastern coast; and by the end of the month, the American blockade had shifted to the Santiago coast to prevent Cervera from escaping.

On June 10, six hundred fifty U.S. Marines landed at Guantánamo Bay to establish a coaling station for the blockading ships, which previously had made the eight-hundred-mile voyage to Key West to recoal in port. Crane, Ernest McCready, and Ralph Paine watched the landing from the *Three Friends,* and in the evening Crane went ashore while the other correspondents took the dispatch boat to Port Antonio, Jamaica, to cable their stories. Crane rarely felt compelled to file dispatches immediately. He abhorred the daily grind of simply churning out factual news reports or cable dispatches, and irritated colleagues and superiors because he preferred to gather personal impressions of an event and filter them through his imagination, however long it took. Once he immersed himself in a setting, a "hawser," wrote Paine, "could not have dragged him away from the show."[1]

As a result, his account of a current news event might not be written and published until months later. His sketch covering the events of mid-June, "Marines Signaling under Fire at Guantanamo," was written in October and published in February 1899. At first there was no resistance to the invasion on June 10; but by the next day, fighting had intensified at Camp McCalla, the provisional headquarters named after the naval captain in charge of the Marines' landing. To an even greater extent than the battles Crane had seen in Greece and Turkey, the Cuban combat revealed the exhilarating experience of war, the selflessness of humans under pressure, and the tragic consequences of the violence. By this time, McCready had returned from Port Antonio and was trying to convince Crane that, for their own safety, they needed to get back to the *Three Friends*. "What the hell's the rush?"[2] Crane asked. He hadn't slept for forty-eight hours, yet he sat calmly on a rock immersing himself in the moment and experiencing vicariously the courage of the Marines. Only when the fighting subsided did he return to the boat, lured by food, drink, cigarettes, and Macready's offer to take dictation while Crane composed a dispatch.

Back on board, Crane dictated notes for a dispatch about the fighting at Guantánamo Bay, deliberating over word choice and often requiring McCready to cross out passages and insert revisions. McCready the ever-practical reporter became impatient—the piece should have been a quickly written objective account of the recent skirmish—and began recording only Crane's factual details. Suspicious, Crane burst out, "Read it aloud, Mac, as far as it goes. I believe you are murdering my stuff." "I dropped out a few adjectives here and there, Steve," responded McCready. "This has to be news, sent at cable rates. You can save your flubdub and shoot it to New York by mail. What I want is the straight story of the fight."[3] McCready got his wish. Crane's dispatch, "In the First Land Fight Four of Our Men Are Killed," was a factual account consisting of short, to-the-point paragraphs. It appeared the next day, June 12, in the *New York World* and carried no byline because Crane and McCready considered it jointly written.

As they assembled the dispatch, Crane chanted, "Accuracy! Terseness! Accuracy!" These were words that Joseph Pulitzer had posted on the

World's newsroom walls to remind his staff of their goal. None of Crane's colleagues would have missed his sarcasm. Originally, Pulitzer had insisted that his newspaper report only facts—who, what, when, where, how—but William Randolph Hearst's purchase of the *New York Journal* in 1895 had precipitated an intense rivalry between the two titans of journalism. In the Dora Clark affair, Crane himself had been a victim of the kind of sensationalized reporting that burgeoned during the Spanish-American War. Hearst did everything he could to challenge the *World*'s status as the most widely read American newspaper. The most famous anecdote is an apocryphal story about Frederic Remington, who had traveled to Cuba in 1897 to record rumored Spanish atrocities against the insurgency and to provide illustrations for the *Journal*. After Remington notified Hearst that there was no war to draw, Hearst supposedly wired back: "You furnish the pictures; I'll furnish the war." And indeed he helped to do so, overstating the Spanish abuse of Cubans and calling Valeriano Weyler y Nicolau, the Spanish general sent to suppress the rebellion, a "butcher" for his brutal treatment of dissidents in concentration camps, cruelty that infuriated Americans. By the time the Spanish-American War broke out, in 1898, Hearst had cruised the Caribbean on his yacht like an adventurous sailor, captured a Spanish vessel and its crew, and bragged with a front-page headline, "How Do You Like the Journal's War?"[4]

Occasionally, the competition over circulation devolved into mutual ridicule. The newspapers stole stories from each other and rewrote them, and this led to trickery. On June 8, 1898, Hearst published a fictitious article in the *Journal* claiming that Colonel Reflipe W. Thenuz, an Austrian artillery officer with the Spanish, had died during combat in Cuba. The next day the *World* also reported his death, even including a dateline: "On board the *World* dispatch boat *Three Friends,* off Santiago de Cuba, via Port Antonio, Jamaica." The *Journal* gleefully exposed the hoax, pointing out that the colonel's name was an anagram for "We Pilfer the News." For more than a month, the *Journal* mocked the *World* for such pilfering. It printed an outlandish cartoon of Colonel Thenuz with a caption reading, "Specially taken for the *World,* by the *World*'s special photographer." It proposed that a monument be built honoring the colonel, published a poem memorializing him, and collected worthless money—Confederate notes, Chinese currency, and repudiated bonds—

for a Thenuz Memorial Fund. The hoax must have caused at least mild consternation among the correspondents aboard the *Three Friends,* since the *World*'s report on Colonel Thenuz had simply been tacked onto a long dispatch from Ralph Paine speculating about the impending battle for Santiago. As one historian wrote about the rivalry between Pulitzer and Hearst, it was a "a battle of gigantic proportions, in which the sufferings of Cuba merely chanced to furnish some of the most convenient ammunition."[5]

Crane did not forget the events of the first land fight—indeed, they led to two of his finer pieces on the war. Among the four men reported killed was Dr. John Blair Gibbs, an assistant surgeon in the U.S. Navy, whose death Crane witnessed. He described the scene in "War Memories," a semifactual account of his Cuban experiences during the spring and summer of 1898 but not written until 1899. The piece dramatized Gibbs's prolonged suffering, during which, "no longer a cynic," Crane became "a child who, in a fit of ignorance, had jumped into the vat of war":

> I heard somebody dying near me. He was dying hard. Hard. It took him a long time to die. He breathed as all noble machinery breathes when it is making its gallant strife against breaking, breaking. But he was going to break. He was going to break. It seemed to me, this breathing, the noise of a heroic pump which strives to subdue a mud which comes upon it in tons. The darkness was impenetrable. The man was lying in some depression within seven feet of me. Every wave, vibration, of his anguish beat upon my senses. He was long past groaning. There was only the bitter strife for air which pulsed out into the night in a clear penetrating whistle with intervals of terrible silence in which I held my own breath in the common unconscious aspiration to help.[6]

In school, Crane had romanticized war and told a friend that his strongest wish was to die in combat.[7] Later, he had depicted death in his war fiction and witnessed it in Greece and Turkey; but now the experience was different. In the short time they had been together, Crane and Gibbs had quickly become friends. They had joked about the dearth of fighting at the outset of the invasion, and they had probably talked about growing up in New Jersey, where Gibbs had attended grammar school and college in New Brunswick, thirty-five miles from Crane's home in Asbury Park. But on the third night, as Dr. Gibbs was standing outside the hospital tent and saying, "Well, I don't want to die in this place," fighting had suddenly erupted and he was shot in the forehead.[8] Crane had dropped to the ground to evade the bullets and listened to the death rattle of his friend. Just as Henry Fleming had stared at a dead soldier in *The Red Badge of Courage,* yielding to "the impulse of the living to try to read in dead eyes the answer to the Question," Crane struggled with the meaning of Gibbs's death but found only darkness. The cynic had been baptized by fire in the "vat of war."[9]

In contrast to the poignant "War Memories" was "Marines Signaling under Fire at Guantanamo." On June 14, 1898, Crane accompanied U.S. Marines and Cuban insurgents led by Captain George F. Elliott on a mission to Cuzco, six miles down the coast from Guantánamo Bay, to destroy a guerrilla outpost guarding the only well in the area. In order to direct artillery from an offshore ship, Sergeant John H. Quick stood with his back to the fighting, exposed and defenseless, and signaled with a flag. Crane was impressed with the bravery of an individual who demonstrated what Ernest Hemingway would later call "grace under pressure": "I watched his face, and it was as grave and serene as that of a man writing in his own library. He was the very embodiment of tranquility in occupation. . . . One need not dwell upon the detail of keeping the mind carefully upon a slow spelling of an important code message."[10]

Having once considered applying to West Point, Crane was attracted to the military and saw the actions of a signalman as being similar to those of an author. He admired the professional soldier who performs his tasks calmly and stoically without expecting praise. In his accounts of the skirmishes at Camp McCalla and Cuzco in "Marines Signaling" and "War Memories," Crane depicted himself as an insecure, frightened individual who, like Henry Fleming, considered running away: "My heart was in my boots and I was cursing the day that saw me landed on the shores of the tragic isle." Unmentioned were his own demonstrations of military valor. He quietly carried supplies, built entrenchments, dragged artillery up hills, and helped to fire guns. When Captain Elliott needed someone to take messages to company commanders during combat, Crane accepted the responsibility and, as Elliott officially reported to his battalion commander, "was of material aid during the action." A year later, Henry Clay Cochrane and other officers were still praising Crane's bravery during combat.[11]

After Crane, Sylvester Scovel, and fellow journalist Alexander Kenealy set up the *New York World*'s headquarters near Santiago on June 17, Crane and Scovel swam two little Jamaican polo ponies ashore from the *Triton*. Escorted by Cuban insurgents to avoid Spanish lines, they labored through "nine infernal miles" of "dodging and badgering and botheration" over barely passable terrain, then trudged through chaparral up a two-thousand-foot mountain overlooking the Santiago Harbor to spy on the Spanish fleet.[12] Three days later, they reported their findings to Admiral Sampson. At daybreak on June 22, sixteen thousand American troops began landing at Daiquirí, eighteen miles east of Santiago; later that morning soldiers also came ashore at Siboney, seven miles farther down the coast. On June 24, Crane, McCready, Edward Marshall of the *New York Journal,* and Burr McIntosh, a correspondent and photographer for *Leslie's Weekly* (later they were joined by Richard Harding Davis) met up with the dismounted First Volunteer Cavalry—the Rough Riders—under the command of Colonel Leonard Wood and Lieutenant Colonel Theodore Roosevelt on the jungle trail from Siboney to Las Guásimas. Crane remained in the rear of the march because Roosevelt, still fuming over Crane's involvement with Dora Clark, ignored him.

At dawn on June 24, the Rough Riders, whom Jimmy Hare denounced as "a superabundance of exhibitionists and egomaniacs," were ambushed and suffered heavy casualties. Among those killed was Sergeant Hamilton Fish, one of the most famous of the prominent Ivy Leaguers who had volunteered for duty with the Rough Riders. Roosevelt had boasted that their athletic prowess—Fish had been captain of his college crew team—qualified them for combat. Also among the casualties was Marshall, shot in the spine and paralyzed permanently from the waist down. Crane and Davis arranged for him to be moved to a field hospital, then Crane trudged six miles round-trip through rugged terrain in hundred-degree heat to cable Marshall's dispatch to the *World*'s rival, the *New York Journal*. Crane was at least partly motivated by their friendship and the important role that Marshall had played in the young journalist's budding career. As Sunday editor of the *New York Press,* he had published several of Crane's New York City tales and sketches, convinced him to show the manuscript of *The Red Badge of Courage* to Irving Bacheller, and praised the novel's literary impressionism in an early review. Crane's selflessness toward Marshall was not an anomaly. When sailors aboard a dispatch boat had quarreled and almost begun fighting, Crane had calmed them and made peace. Shaking hands, they had declared him the "best little fellow alive."[13]

As it turned out, the *World* resented Crane's decision to cable Marshall's dispatch to the *Journal,* and his own reports about Las Guásimas were controversial. Although the battle involved regulars as well as volunteers, newspapers acclaimed it as an honorable rite of passage for the Rough Riders. "Their First Battle Marked by Many Acts of Bravery," announced the *New York Times:* "Rough Riders Prove Heroes." Crane likewise praised the Rough Riders' courage and defended Roosevelt against the charge that he had led them into the ambush; but in "Roosevelt's Rough Riders' Loss Due to a Gallant Blunder" and "Stephen Crane at the Front for the World," he criticized them for talking loudly, marching noisily, and ignoring the Cubans' warnings of an impending attack. Crane and the Rough Riders knew that the supposed cooing of wood doves was actually the sound of the enemy signaling the location of American troops. In 1899, Roosevelt defended his actions during the skirmish and indirectly criticized *The Red Badge of Courage* and Crane's account of the Rough Riders: "I did not see any sign among the fighting men, whether wounded or unwounded, of the very complicated emotions assigned to their kind by some of the realistic modern novelists who have written about battles. . . . But there was doubtless . . . a good deal of panic and confusion in the rear where the wounded, the stragglers, a few of the packers, and two or three newspaper correspondents were, and in consequence the first reports sent back to the coast were of a most alarming character, describing, with minute inaccuracy, how we had run into an ambush, etc."[14] Roosevelt implied that since Crane had been at the rear, he could not have reported the ambush accurately. Three years earlier, Roosevelt had said that *The Red Badge* was his favorite book by the young author and had asked Crane to inscribe his copy. Now he maintained that Crane's depiction of Henry Fleming's "complicated emotions" was false.[15] Unsurprisingly, Roosevelt's own copy is no longer part of his personal library, which is archived at Harvard.

Roosevelt never forgave Crane for the impact of the Dora Clark incident. Four years after the Spanish-American War, Jimmy Hare was traveling by train with now President Roosevelt and his secretary, George B. Cortelyou. After noticing that Cortelyou was reading *Wounds in the Rain,* Crane's posthumous collection of Cuban War stories published in September 1900, Roosevelt confronted Hare. "You knew this fellow Crane rather well, didn't you, Jimmy?" Quite well, Hare replied. "I remember him distinctly myself," retorted Roosevelt. "When I was Police Commissioner of New York I once got him out of serious trouble." When Hare defended Crane for merely doing research for a series of articles on the Tenderloin, Roosevelt bristled: "He wasn't gathering any data! He was a man of bad character and he was simply consorting with loose women."[16]

Before dawn on July 1, 1898, American troops began advancing toward the fortifications of San Juan, on the eastern outskirts of Santiago, and toward the village of El Caney, six miles northeast of the city, where the enemy was entrenched. Crane climbed the hill of El Pozo, about two and a half miles south of El Caney, where he observed the opening of the decisive battle in the Cuban campaign. Joining him on the hill were Frederic Remington, Burr McIntosh, and Henry J. Whigham of the *Chicago Tribune.*

The American army was under the command of Major General William R. Shafter, whose gruff manners, mismanagement of the campaign, and portly three hundred pounds made him the subject of ridicule. "Old fat Shafter," Richard Harding Davis wrote to his mother, "has at last arrived at the front in a buckboard. He is too absurd and silly." Reporters became increasingly frustrated with the general. Though he was typically polite toward them, he revealed little about his plans; and following the collapse of Santiago, he forbade them from entering the city or witnessing the flag-raising ceremony, possibly out of concern for their safety in the newly captured city. Still, he was reviled. "Hanging is too good for him," fumed Davis. Scovel's reaction was more forceful. After sneaking into Santiago and being discovered, he got into a heated argument with Shafter that apparently led to an exchange of blows. Accounts differed as to what actually happened, but Scovel was arrested, and subsequently fired by the *World.* Though the paper briefly rehired him after the end of the war, the incident essentially ended his career as a reporter.[17]

General Shafter had concluded that success lay first in capturing El Caney, then taking San Juan Hill, a high ridgeline overlooking Santiago from the east. Doing so would give the U.S. forces a tactical advantage over the city below. The American offensive repeatedly stalled, however, and resulted in the bloodiest battle of the campaign. After General Shafter became ill, he was confined to his tent at headquarters two miles away at El Pozo and forced to convey orders to mounted staff officers. The prediction that El Caney would fall within two hours soon proved wrong. Soldiers—already suffering from malaria, typhoid, and dysentery —dropped from heat exhaustion; and dense smoke from American artillery, as well as the fact that the Spanish were using smokeless powder, hampered attempts to locate the enemy.[18] One of the most tragic decisions made on that day was the use of an observation balloon by the Signal Corps. Although it provided a clear view of enemy activity, it also revealed the location and movement of Americans to the Spanish, who quickly blanketed the area with deadly artillery fire.

Growing impatient for orders, Roosevelt, who had become a colonel after Leonard Wood was promoted to brigadier general, commanded the Rough Riders to charge up Kettle Hill and provided support fire for troops charging up San Juan Hill about a quarter-mile away. Accompanied by Jimmy Hare and other journalists, Crane headed into the fray in search of a story. An obvious target in his shiny white raincoat and astride his pony, Stephen remained calm as Jimmy urged him to be more cautious. "Nonsense. If they aim at me, so much the better; no Spaniard ever hits the thing he aims at." Ever the fatalist, he was fond of saying, "What is to be is not to be dodged, and let worry go hang." General Wood thought otherwise. Crane, standing on the crest of San Juan Heights to observe the enemy, drew fire on the American soldiers and pretended not to hear Wood's order to lie down. To Richard Harding Davis, Crane, hands in his pockets and pipe in his mouth, "appeared as cool as though he were looking down from a box at a theatre." Thinking that his colleague was feigning a stolid demeanor, Davis yelled, "You're not impressing any one by doing that, Crane!" At first the plan worked. Crane immediately crawled over to Davis. "I knew that would fetch you." Grinning, Crane replied, "Oh, was that it?" But Crane could not resist the visceral need to immerse himself in the moment and soon was on his feet again. Davis jumped up as well; but as he pulled his colleague to the ground, one bullet knocked off Davis's hat, and another dented his binoculars case.[19]

Crane's behavior was not simply a desire to impress people with his courage; he needed to test his own limits under extraordinary stress. Lying flat on the ground next to Crane during fighting at Guantánamo, a colleague asked him how the experience compared to what he had written in *The Red Badge of Courage*. "Oh, hell!" Crane replied. "This isn't half as exciting." On another occasion, he was with a company that was under fire and that badly needed water. Crane collected canteens, then trudged through harsh terrain for the closest water, seven miles away. Returning, he became the object of sniper fire, which barely missed him as it pierced the men's canteens. He reached the parched soldiers, only to faint from exhaustion.[20] A recurring theme in Crane's fiction is the individual in danger of death. Because he wanted to make readers see and feel the plight of his characters, he himself sought the extremes of sensation—whether huddled in a breadline in New York City or standing in the midst of bullet fire in Cuba—so as to experience an intense moment without regard to personal safety. It was a deliberate choice for a man whose tuberculosis constantly reminded him of the frailty of existence. In deeply personal poetry, Crane wrote of his own "weak heart." Willa Cather was convinced that he "had the precocity of those doomed to die in youth" and "a vague premonition of the shortness of his working day. . . . In the heart of the man there was that which said, 'That thou doest, do quickly.'"[21]

As Crane and Hare reached the medical station known as "Bloody Bend" on a ford of the Aguadores River, they were shocked to find doctors treating a hundred wounded men while still under siege. Among them was Crane's Claverack schoolmate Corporal Reuben McNab. Crane had seen corpses and badly wounded men in Greece, but the Cuban experience was different because he knew them. Only days earlier, he had lost his new friend Dr. John Gibbs; and Edward Marshall, who had written his dispatch while bleeding on the ground, was expected to die. Now, the sight of McNab lying in the mud, his body riddled with bullets, traumatized Crane "into stutterings, set me trembling with a sense of terrible intimacy with this war which theretofore I could have believed was a dream—almost." This once "long, lank boy, freckled, sandy-haired," reminded Crane of the carefree days at Claverack. But that was gone—irrevocably gone with the dying man's words, "Well, they got me."

In "War Memories," Crane tried to understand his experience with death in Cuba. In El Caney he had seen a wounded Spanish prisoner on an operating table in the doorway of a church converted into a makeshift hospital: "Framed then in the black archway was the altar-table with the figure of a man upon it. He was naked save for a breech-clout, and so close, so clear was the ecclesiastical suggestion, that one's mind leaped to a phantasy that this thin, pale figure had just been torn down from a cross." Yet the image failed to console Crane; and by the end of "War Memories," one of America's greatest accounts of war, he could only conclude that in his attempt to describe its "overwhelming, crushing, monstrous" horror, "you can depend upon it that I have told you nothing at all, nothing at all, nothing at all." If his time in Greece and Turkey had exposed him to the reality of war, the Cuban campaign revealed the inability of language to articulate its meaninglessness.[22]

Many years later, soldiers in Vietnam, when asked about the American loss of life, responded, "It don't mean nothing," as a way to maintain their sanity. Crane already knew what they sensed: it meant everything.

24

New York City, Adirondacks, Puerto Rico

JULY–AUGUST 1898

OVERWHELMED BY THE intensity of combat, Crane was put aboard the transport *City of Washington* on July 8 at Siboney, headed for Hampton Roads, Virginia. He was suffering from delirium, high fever, and what he described as "a languorous indifference to everything in the world": "The truth is that Cuba libre just about liberated me from this base blue world." When a doctor initially diagnosed the illness as yellow fever, he ordered that Crane be isolated on ship from the more than two hundred sick and wounded soldiers. The "yellow scourge" had devastating consequences, with a mortality rate reaching at times as high as 85 percent. Whereas 968 American soldiers were killed in action following the *Maine* explosion, more than five thousand died from disease. For the next five days, Crane propped himself up against the flagstaff on deck, anguished and alone, suffering from what was later diagnosed as malaria.[1]

The arrival of the *City of Washington* at Old Point Comfort in Hampton Roads on July 13 and the *Breakwater*'s arrival the following day evoked both the pride and the anguish that the war had inspired in America. Crowds wept as tattered, wounded troops marched toward the tented hospital and cheered other soldiers on stretchers who were singing "The Star-Spangled Banner." For a moment, America's deep-rooted racism disappeared. Four white soldiers carried a stretcher with a black trooper shot nine times; two others helping to escort a black amputee conversed with him, reported one newspaper, "with perfect equality."[2] Tearful at the sight of loyal Americans who had risked their lives for honor and country, Crane became once again the patriotic Claverack cadet who took pride in his military ancestry: "I would live and die a good soldier, a true, straight, unkicking American regular soldier."[3] When a woman desperately searching for her wounded husband on the *City of Washington* saw the man from afar, her silent, swift gesture of covering her face with her hands "told us the other part" of the consequences of war: the painful suffering of loved ones left behind. "And in a vision," Crane wrote, "we all saw our own harbor-lights" (images of loved ones) —"that is to say those of us who had harbor-lights."[4] It was a rare, poignant moment for Crane, whose cynicism served as emotional armor that protected a sensitive soul from a crass, insensitive world. The belief that ships passing in the night would find harbor lights to guide them home safely comforted the lonely. But there was in Crane's ambiguous addendum, "those of us who had harbor-lights," a sense that, facing his own mortality, he might not be among those with a safe port.

By the time the ship had reached Old Point Comfort, Crane had recovered enough to visit the Chamberlin, an elegant hotel that catered to tourists and dignitaries, and nearby Fort Monroe, a hexagonal stone structure surrounded by a moat. Crane no doubt reveled in its castle-like setting and historical importance. Edgar Allan Poe had been stationed at the fort in 1828–1829 and had given a memorable poetry reading at Old Point Comfort in September 1849, only a few weeks before his death. The fort had been an important site during the Civil War and became known as "Freedom's Fortress," a refuge for runaway slaves; and Jefferson Davis had been imprisoned there in a casemate for two years after the war. Crane visited the Casemate Club at Fort Monroe, where he probably learned that his ancestor Colonel Ichabod B. Crane had commanded the post briefly in 1842 and in 1853–1854.[5] By late July, he was heading for New York to negotiate with the publisher Frederick A. Stokes for the printing of a collection of his Cuban war stories and to visit the business office of the *New York World*. He needed reimbursement for expenses, including twenty-four dollars for a new suit he had bought after reaching Fort Monroe, to replace his tattered clothing.

To Crane's surprise, he was met with hostility under circumstances that still remain sketchy. Don Carlos Seitz, the *World*'s business manager who had known Crane since their days at the Lantern Club, disliked him. Crane had created an embarrassing situation for the newspaper. His June 12 dispatch, "In the First Land Fight Four of Our Men Are Killed," had reported that the Spanish had mutilated corpses of American soldiers with machetes. Two days later, however, Crane had sent a retraction saying that the presumed mutilation of two of the soldiers had actually been caused by bullets. Although the *World* had wired the correction to other newspapers on June 16, it had withheld publication, ostensibly because it wanted to rely on an official statement rather than Crane's word for verification; however the *World* probably did not publish the correction because it would have undercut the sensationalism of a feature story that had been printed only the day before. A four-column headline on page one of the June 15 *World* read: "Mutilation of Our Marines / Too Horrible for Description / Universal Sentiments of Horror Expressed at / Dastardly Work of the Spanish Butchers of Guantanamo."

The awkward situation that the *World* found itself in would not have been enough for Crane's dismissal. More serious, from Seitz's point of view, were Crane's professional disloyalty and reputed laziness. Seitz must have heard that Crane had filed Edward Marshall's dispatch for the *World*'s rival, the *New York Journal;* and he would also have learned from Henry N. Cary, manager of the *World* field staff in Cuba, that Crane was "a drunken, irresponsible and amusing little cuss. He kept me busy trying to get a little work out of him, but I failed in that respect."[6] Years later, Seitz claimed that Crane had submitted only one significant dispatch while in Cuba (a false charge—he had actually filed two dozen) and that it was causing an uproar in the country. On July 1, the 71st New York Volunteer Regiment, "the Gallant Seventy-first," had come under heavy fire on the Santiago road. In the midst of confusion, more than four hundred men had been killed or wounded. On July 16, the *New York World* printed an unsigned, front-page story sent from Port Antonio charging the regiment's officers with cowardice during the attack. Seitz accused Crane of writing the dispatch, but he clearly could not have, for he had been in Hampton Roads when the dispatch was sent.[7] The author was probably Scovel.[8] For the next three days, the *Journal* condemned the *World* for doubting the honor of the 71st Regiment. Embarrassed, the *World* denied it had censured the regiment, and Joseph Pulitzer quickly tried to raise money for a battlefield memorial commemorating its fallen members as well as the Rough Riders, but the damage had already been done and he soon abandoned the idea.[9] The incident had also harmed Crane. John Norris, the *World*'s financial manager, refused to give him any money even for expenses. "I have just kissed your little friend Stephen Crane good-bye," he gleefully told Seitz. "He came here asking for another advance. Don't you think you have had enough of Mr. Pulitzer's money without earning it?" demanded Norris. "Oh, very well," Crane supposedly replied, "if that is the way you look at it, by-by." "So we're rid of him."[10] Ironically, the *World* later acknowledged in an obituary that Crane's Cuban dispatches "were masterpieces of description. If he had a fault as a war correspondent it was that his enthusiasm took him too deeply into the thick of the fighting."[11]

A curious set of circumstances may offer another reason for Crane's dismissal from the *World*. On June 16, the *New York Herald* published "On a Ridge Fighting an Unseen Foe," its author being identified only as the newspaper's "special correspondent." The dispatch recounts Captain Elliott's mission on June 14 to Cuzco to destroy the guerrilla encampment guarding a well. The *Herald* wired it to the *St. Louis Republic* and the *London Times.* Although the *Times,* apparently, did not print the piece, the *Republic* did. It revised the title and named the correspondent: "Tuesday's Battle as Witnessed at Close Range. / Cubans Were Brave, but Fired Wildly—The Execution Was Done by American Marines. / By Stephen Crane."

Because the *Somers N. Smith* was the dispatch boat for the *World* and the *Herald,* this article might have wound up in the wrong dispatch box and been sent to the wrong newspaper. The *Herald* would have known that Crane worked for the *World,* but may have printed the dispatch anyway and hidden the correspondent's identity. Oddly, his name remained when the dispatch was wired. The newspaper must have realized that someone in the profession would notice the incongruity. But might Crane have been secretly employed by one of Pulitzer's rivals, James Gordon Bennett, publisher of the *Herald?* If he had been, and if Seitz had discovered this fact, it could have contributed to the firing. Richard Harding Davis was Bennett's star reporter; and although there was professional rivalry between Crane and Davis, Crane was friends with other

Herald staff: Frederic Remington, Harry Brown, Poultney Bigelow, and Ernest W. McCready. Crane often engaged in unprofessional behavior regarding publishers and literary agents and might have tried to earn extra money by working for Bennett. If so, the *Herald* would have deleted Crane's name from the byline to avoid upsetting Pulitzer; but it did not delete the name when it wired the dispatch to the *St. Louis Republic.* If Seitz did not discover Crane's ruse, perhaps Sylvester Scovel did. Mrs. Scovel and her family were from St. Louis and would have read the dispatch in the *Republic.*

Shortly after leaving the *World,* Crane signed with the *New York Journal* to report on the Puerto Rico campaign of the Spanish-American War; but before leaving for Pensacola, Florida, at the end of the month, he thought about his health. Despite his chronic physical ailments, Crane was often playful, even fatalistic, about it. Once, when he was ill at Ravensbrook, a doctor had been pleased to learn that his patient's appetite was still keen. When he asked Crane what he had eaten for breakfast, Crane replied, "Double the usual quantity." "Oh, splendid," said the doctor. "I had," Crane continued, "two brandies and soda instead of one!"[12] But his recent bout with malaria and the death of two friends, Gibbs and McNab, prompted him to consult Dr. Edward Livingston Trudeau, an eminent lung specialist who had established a clinic in Saranac Lake, New York: the Adirondack Cottage Sanitarium, the first American facility for the treatment of tuberculosis. Crane had long known of his illness, and his recent bout with malaria had weakened his constitution. Over the years, he had recuperated by escaping to the wilderness of Sullivan County, where fresh air and a jaunt on horseback through the woods would reinvigorate his lungs and spirit.

The cold, clear mountain air of the Adirondacks provided an ideal setting for tubercular patients, but the circumstances surrounding Crane's visit are murky. Instead of formally registering at the sanitarium, he saw Dr. Trudeau, who had a practice in a nearby hamlet, as a private patient. On September 16, the doctor wrote to Cora: "Your husband had a slight evidence of activity in the trouble in his lungs when he came back here this summer but it was not serious and he has improved steadily I understand since he came. I have only examined him once but he looked very well and told me he was much better last time I saw him."[13]

The letter raises a number of questions. First, what prompted it? Had

Cora heard rumors about Stephen's illness, then written to the doctor for information? If so, how did she know that she should contact Dr. Trudeau, as opposed to another specialist? Crane must have told her about his trip to the sanitarium. There is no direct evidence that he was writing her at the time—yet there is circumstantial evidence that they did correspond while he was away.[14] Before Crane left England for Cuba, they had briefly discussed the possibility of moving from Ravensbrook and renting Brede Place, a country manor owned by Moreton Frewen. In the weeks from mid-April, when Crane left England, to early June, Cora had discussed Brede house repairs with an architect and shared the details with Stephen. After getting his approval, she had written to Moreton's wife, Clara, on June 4, formally proposing a rental agreement.

Also, as Trudeau's letter stated, Crane had already seen the doctor before the visit in late July. A month earlier, he had anticipated his trip to the sanitarium in the dispatch "Hunger Has Made Cubans Fatalists." Recounting the arduous journey up a mountain to spot the Spanish fleet, the breeze rustling through the foliage had reminded him of "a brawling, noisy brook like an Adirondack trout stream" and "the kind of country in which commercial physicians love to establish sanitariums." Crane's familiarity with the location of the Adirondack Cottage Sanitarium suggests that he recognized its importance to his health. Finally, Dr. Trudeau's assertion that Crane's illness was "not serious" contradicts the description of him only days later by Charles Michelson: "shambling, with hair too long, usually lacking a shave, dressed like any of the deck hands, hollow-cheeked, sallow, destitute of small talk, critical if not fastidious, marked with ill-health—the very antithesis of the conquering male." His body "revealed the wreck of an athlete's frame—once square shoulders crowded forward by the concavity of a collapsed chest; great hollows where the once smooth pitching muscles had wasted; legs like pipe-stems—he looked like a frayed white ribbon, seen through the veil of green as the seas washed over him." The contrast between Trudeau's description and Michelson's is striking—but Stephen may have urged the doctor to sound optimistic if he received an inquiry from Cora. This would certainly have fit Crane's pattern of behavior: the wayward boy was also the caretaking adult.[15]

At the end of July, Crane sailed from Pensacola to report on the war in Puerto Rico, but the nineteen-day military campaign was uneventful.

Despite occasional resistance, most of the towns greeted American troops, as Richard Harding Davis wrote, "with one hand open and the other presenting either a bouquet, or a bottle."[16] Crane arrived in Ponce on August 1, shortly after it was captured. Immediately, he immersed himself in the back streets and alleys of the city, aligning himself with the social outcasts of Ponce: the gamblers, waifs, prostitutes, and drunkards. The strangers in town, unable to speak one another's language, had a tacit bond and a common plight—the same he had witnessed earlier in the Tenderloin. Crane's attitude was more than a pose. He identified with other loners seeking community.

Richard Harding Davis's reaction toward his chief rival as celebrity correspondent revealed much about Crane's disposition. Davis developed a respect for Crane in Cuba and Puerto Rico that he had not had in Greece and publicly acknowledged his colleague as the best correspondent in Cuba. Privately, he disliked his arrogance and indifference to social decorum and gloated because he, not Crane, had been on board Admiral Sampson's flagship, the *New York,* when it had shelled Matanzas on April 27 during the Santiago campaign. Davis became the literary darling at dinners hosted by military officers. Immaculately dressed in tailored clothing, he charmed them with graceful conversation and rousing ballads, accompanying himself on the banjo. In contrast to Davis—nicknamed "Richard the Lion-Harding" by his contemporaries—was the slovenly dressed Crane, who, if he did attend a dinner, was, according to Michelson, "a social bankrupt." Attempts to get him to talk about his writing drew little response, for though he enjoyed heated literary discussions with fellow authors, he had no patience with idle cocktail chit-chat. He could not have remained anonymous, for at least one soldier was reading his work on the battlefield: a member of the Doubleday family, serving with the troops at Guantánamo Bay, had brought with him a copy of *The Open Boat and Other Tales of Adventure,* just published by Doubleday and McClure in April.[17]

Davis captured the complex, even paradoxical, nature of his rival in his short story "The Derelict" (1901).[18] A disheveled, chain-smoking correspondent named Channing, who has malaria and is accused of being a drunkard and an opium eater, is known for his distinctive style of impressionistic reporting. Among his publications are a series entitled "Tales of the Tenderloin" and dispatches about the Marines at Guantánamo.

Davis's mostly sympathetic portrait of Channing captured Crane's own warring desires. He was caring and generous one moment, thoughtless and inconsiderate the next. When Davis was suffering from sciatica, Crane (along with Jimmy Hare) helped him down from the San Juan Heights and back to the correspondents' camp, where he ensured that Davis could rest comfortably in a tent. Crane was also compassionate toward a thirteen-year-old black boy named Cecil Benjamin Williams, whom he had met in Jamaica or St. Thomas and taken to Cuba as an interpreter. Crane cared for him when he was sick and planned to take him back to England as a servant, but, as one account reported, Williams did "something to bring himself into disgrace with his new master."[19] Yet years later, when he learned that Crane had died, a tearful Williams praised his old friend.[20]

Abandonment versus commitment was a psychological issue that troubled Crane throughout his life and work. He was neglected by his parents while they went about their church work, experienced a deep sense of isolation following the sudden deaths of his father and his sister Agnes, was moved to save—then abandon—Amy and Cora, and felt duty-bound to rescue ailing correspondents and a sickly boy during combat. A major part of his rebellion against institutionalized religion stemmed from his inability to understand how an all-loving God could deprive a child of parental mentors, yet as an adult he was ashamed of being a prodigal son who had forsaken his family. In 1892, Crane started a sketch titled "A Desertion," but never completed it. In 1894, he wrote another story with the same title about a girl named Nell, living in a tenement district, who discovers that her father has unexpectedly died; associated with his death is her sense of guilt over somehow having let him down, for his "eyes, fixed upon hers, were filled with an unspeakable hatred."[21] In *Maggie: A Girl of the Streets,* the central character is abandoned by her family, her church, and her boyfriend; in *The Red Badge of Courage,* Henry Fleming abandons his comrades, in particular a forlorn, tattered soldier; in "The Black Dog," a master abandons a starving dog; in "Death and the Child," parents abandon a child; and in "Manacled," an actor in leg-irons and handcuffs is abandoned on stage during a fire. Crane's unresolved issues about self-worth and identity surfaced in conflicted depictions of himself. Trying to impress Nellie Crouse, he made much of his virtue; writing to an admirer, he confessed he was a rascal.

The title of Davis's tale "The Derelict" succinctly captures Crane's state of mind: a derelict is not only a drifter but also something abandoned, especially a ship at sea. Since childhood, Crane had been drifting alone, rudderless, ever searching for clear direction.

In contrast to Crane's tangled psyche, his behavior was often simple, playful, even naïve. As soon as he disembarked from the ship at Old Point Comfort in July, he went to a soda fountain for an orange ice-cream soda; he had loved the drink as a child, and the horror of war made him thirst for the comforting memories of childhood. On another occasion, Crane and Davis had heard that the local inhabitants in Puerto Rico were eager to surrender to American troops. One town gave itself up to an officer who had gotten lost and wandered in by mistake; another surrendered to the leader of a pack train who had come to town trying to steal ponies. The two correspondents wanted to try their luck. They decided to get up early on August 3 and sneak off to Juana Díaz, ten miles from Ponce. Crane was supposed to wake Davis; but after Michelson learned of their plan, he convinced Crane that there was no reason a reporter for a rival newspaper should accompany a *Journal* correspondent on a possibly important story. Perhaps Crane was selfish or impulsive in not waking Davis, but evidently Davis didn't mind. What happened next depends on whose account one accepts. As Crane strolled into Juana Díaz, according to Davis, he was immediately accepted as a conqueror and given the keys to the town. Whimsically dividing the male residents into "suspects" and "good fellows" simply based on appearance, he sent the former home, then celebrated throughout the night with the others. The next morning, while having coffee outside the local café, Crane saw a regiment of eight hundred soldiers approaching. The colonel in charge, recognizing the famous author, was disappointed to learn that Crane had not been marching with the men in order to write a dispatch about them and thus immortalize their conquest of the town. "I am sorry," said the colonel. "I should like you to have seen us take this town." "*This* town!" an amused Crane replied. "I'm really very sorry, Colonel, but I took this town myself before breakfast yesterday morning."[22]

Davis's account of the way Crane captured Juana Díaz differed from that of Charles Michelson, in which Crane was one of several hungry correspondents heading to the town in advance of the troops. The correspondents expected that if everyone arrived at the same time, hungry officers would preempt them. Crane then concocted a scheme. He would ride alone into the town, announce that the American governor of Puerto Rico and his entourage were coming for breakfast, and claim that they did not want to be disturbed. The scheme worked, according to Michelson: when the American officers arrived, Crane peeked out the window and gleefully described to his colleagues a befuddled general and his aides, who were barred from entering the inn. A short while later, Crane told the general a fib, claiming that the residents had misunderstood the correspondents.[23]

However the events actually occurred, Crane was the merry prankster enjoying harmless, imaginary games with friends. As a child, Stephen had played at cowboys and Indians, cops and robbers, and hunts for buried treasure; as an adult, he recreated these games with his nieces, lived with "Indians" in the Art Students League, and headed west in January 1895 "en route to kill Indians."[24] His division of Juana Díaz's residents into good guys and bad guys and his assigning roles to fellow correspondents were the imaginative constructions of an archetypal Peter Pan, a mischievous boy who refused to grow up. Not surprisingly, Crane would soon return to writing children's stories after arriving back in England in 1899.

With the signing of the peace protocol in Washington on August 12, 1898, fighting ceased between Spain and the United States. Crane prepared for departure, but found himself struggling once again with the tension between loyalty and abandonment. Several correspondents had bought horses for transportation around Puerto Rico. Crane ended up with what Michelson called "a hammer-headed, spur-scarred, hairy-hoofed white beast hardly bigger than a goat, with all the bad habits that could be grafted on original sin by ignorance and bad treatment." Christened "El Dog" by Crane, it had been separated from the other horses because it constantly bit and kicked. Unlike the other correspondents, however, Crane never exchanged his horse for a better mount when the opportunity arose—for in its rebellion, irresponsible behavior, and feisty independence, Crane recognized himself. On his last day on the island, a tear-stained Crane put his arm around the horse's bowed neck and reluctantly said goodbye. On board the steamer, Crane took one last look at the shoreline, and there stood his companion. For as long as El Dog stayed visible, Crane kept waving his handkerchief.[25]

25

Havana

SEPTEMBER–DECEMBER 1898

THOUGH THE WAR BETWEEN Spain and the United States ended in August 1898, the peace treaty was not signed until December 10. Spanish troops were still in Havana because American forces were not scheduled to assume formal control until January 1, 1899. As the city was suffering from scarce supplies, inflated prices, and unsanitary conditions, the Spanish were attempting to control entry. Crane estimated in a dispatch to the *New York Journal* that, in addition to the U.S. peace team, only thirty or so American civilians—Red Cross workers, tobacco buyers, and correspondents, whose dispatches were screened by a censor—were initially allowed to enter Havana.[1]

In the third week of August, Crane, pretending to be a tobacco buyer, returned to Cuba, sneaked into Havana without permission, and registered at the luxurious Grand Hotel Pasaje, where other journalists were staying. His action was risky because he had no passport, and the Spanish government had already arrested nine correspondents for trying to wire uncensored reports.[2] Though little is known about Crane's daily whereabouts and state of mind while he was in Cuba, in an unfinished, untitled dispatch written on the back of Hotel Pasaje stationery, he characterized the Americans in Havana as "an unregenerate and abandoned collection of newspaper correspondents, cattle men, gamblers, speculators and drummers [salesmen] who have lived practically as they pleased, without care or restraint, going—most of them—wherever interest or whim led, with no regard for yellow fever or any other terror of the tropics."[3] In many ways, the description is a self-portrait. The presumed tobacco buyer was also an unregenerate, iconoclastic journalist who rebelled against traditional ways of reporting, a risk taker who lived on the edge, and a lover of wilderness where one could roam freely.

The Café Inglaterra became the daily center of operations for the journalists, from 10 A.M. to 10 P.M.—or, as Walter Parker of the *New Orleans Times Democrat* remarked, "until a riot broke out."[4] Though Cuban revolutionaries were prevented under the peace protocol from entering Havana until January 1, they often wandered into local cafés frequented by Spanish officers, occasionally scuffling with them. The correspondents were often on the scene of a breaking news story because a local revolutionary—a man whose life Crane had saved during the sinking of the *Commodore*—was secretly guiding them past Spanish guards to forbidden Cuban activities. Forever grateful, the Cuban would kneel and kiss Crane's hand or the hem of his coat whenever he saw him. Indeed, among all the correspondents, only Crane was respected by the Cubans, who knew that his experience on the *Commodore* had proved his dedication to their cause.

More than once Crane acted selflessly as an intermediary between the Cubans and the correspondents during tense moments. One night, during a fundraiser for the Cuban cause, a drunken correspondent behaved rudely toward a woman. When her boyfriend (Crane's Cuban friend) attacked him with a knife, Crane grabbed the blade, prevented the man from stabbing the correspondent, and calmed rattled nerves. The accidental wound he received from the blade left him seriously ill for days. On another occasion, Crane, Parker, and a Cuban officer in civilian clothes were joined by a Spanish officer in a café. When the Spaniard denigrated the recent fight for freedom, the Cuban reached for his pistol. Tension was already high because on the previous night a bloody riot had erupted in the Hotel Inglaterra, and Crane feared that another one would lead to killings. Crane intervened and, realizing that the Spaniard spoke only his native tongue, calmed the Cuban in French.[5] Crane might have learned elementary French from his friends in the Art Students

League who, like Corwin Knapp Linson, had studied painting at the Académie Julian and the Ecole des Beaux-Arts in Paris. Writing to Linson from New Orleans in 1895, he had once jokingly displayed his limited knowledge of the language: "Mardi gras tres grande. . . . Ce matin I write un article sur le railways du South which were all made in hell." This time, his language skills saved the day. Just as Crane, while at Claverack, had identified with Cuban students who were marginalized by snobbish classmates, his native friends in Havana sensed his loyalty to them.[6]

Before beginning to cable dispatches from Havana in late August, Crane visited the Cementerio de Cristóbal Colón and paid his respects to the sailors buried there who had died during the destruction of the *Maine*. In September, he witnessed the disinterment of Columbus's remains, which were shipped back to Spain.[7] For the next three months, Crane closeted himself with his writing in an unsuccessful attempt to pay off mounting debts back in England—an arduous task, because he had misunderstood his financial arrangement with the *New York Journal*. He still thought that an expense account would cover his bills and that payment for dispatches would be forwarded to Cora in England. With hostilities over, however, the newspaper removed him from the payroll in September, stopped payments to Cora, and paid him only twenty dollars for each dispatch—money he never saw, because his account with the newspaper was already in arrears. Aware that English creditors were hounding Cora during his time in Havana, he cranked out seventeen newspaper dispatches, four Cuban war stories for the collection he had proposed to Frederick Stokes in July, five poems for a sequence titled "Intrigue," and possibly a portion of *Active Service*.[8] Convinced that the *New York Journal* was exploiting him, he insisted that the paper allow him to copyright his dispatches, and he proposed writing a weekly column that his agent Paul Revere Reynolds could syndicate. Beyond a few dispatches, nothing came of the idea.[9] Curt and impatient, Crane fired off letters to Reynolds, expecting immediate answers to his queries and requesting money for work mailed only days earlier, in order to keep him from being "ruined": "I am working like a dog. When—oh, when,—am I to have some money? If you could only witness my poverty!"[10]

Unable to afford a room at the Hotel Pasaje for long, he moved to Mary Horan's lodging house, where he lived almost as secretly as the

American spy Charles H. Thrall, who had sneaked in and out of Havana earlier in the spring, ostensibly as a *New York World* reporter, and whom Crane had interviewed for an article. Mary was a surrogate mother, tough yet compassionate, who coddled her lodgers. She cared for them when they were ill or hungry, and let them stay when they could not pay the rent.[11]

In September, Crane was traumatized again by what Walter Parker called "a personal shock." Crane happened upon a woman he had previously known and most likely become involved with in Havana, but was stunned when he noticed the photograph of a rival in her room. Following the incident, Crane avoided his friends, ate little, and remained cloistered in his room, laboring to write six hundred words a day. His gaunt face, yellowish complexion, and weary aspect revealed a man ravaged by life; only when Mary Horan insisted did he eat occasional meals and take evening walks. It is unknown who the woman was and why he was so disturbed, though his writing in the fall of 1898 suggests he might have been still reeling from rejection by a lover in Florida or Cuba and indicates his characteristic ability to present shifting points of view on the same subject, in this case courtship. In the largely unknown comic jewel "How They Court in Cuba," a young man misinterprets as love his infatuation for "a fair face seen through a grated window," when in fact she may be "dragging her mother up and down the stairs by the hair and beating her father daily with the cooking instruments." The man begins an elaborate courting ritual "full of circumlocution and bulwarks and clever football interferences and trouble and delay and protracted agony and duennas. There is no holding hands in it at all, you bet. It is all barbed wire entanglements." Clever courtship stratagems, however, "count for nothing against the tides of human life, which are in Cuba or Omaha controlled by the same moon."[12]

In contrast, "How They Leave Cuba" is a sentimental sketch about the grief of a woman and her son, who have been abandoned by her Spanish lover as he sails home after the war. Similarly, in "The Clan of No-Name," Crane's bitter, most complex Cuban war story, a young belle in Tampa named Margharita is encouraging the attentions of an American, Mr. Smith, while secretly having a romance with Manolo Prat, an officer with the Cuban insurgents. Manolo and Margharita exchange photographs; but when she learns of his death, she destroys his photo and accepts Mr. Smith's marriage proposal. Though it is unclear whether the theme is the importance of duty and self-denial or a parody of these principles, the story clearly deals with betrayal by a crass Margharita, whose avarice is matched only by that of her American fiancé. The story captured Crane's own conflicted emotions. Like Manolo, he had a stoic devotion to duty, helping to save lives on the *Commodore* and aiding marines in Cuba; but like Margharita, he was duplicitous, betraying the confidence of Amy Leslie by simultaneously wooing Cora.

As perplexing as "The Clan of No-Name" is the sequence of ten poems titled "Intrigue," which concludes *War Is Kind,* Crane's second book of verse. The first five were apparently completed in December 1896 and early 1897, and the remainder were written or revised in September 1898 in Havana. They reveal the tormented mind of a man whose lover has betrayed him: "Thou art my love / And thou art the ashes of other men's love." Disillusioned and embittered, the man vows to "use the happy cruel one cruelly / And make her mourn with my mourning." In the last poem, he hastily concludes that although she no longer loves him, she has given him "an eternal privilege / For I can think of thee." The sequence consists of mawkish, tedious outbursts of self-pity: the first poem repeats the refrain "Woe is me" in each of the first eleven stanzas and expands it in the twelfth and last stanza. The title "Intrigue" suggests that the poems are not simply about love but about a complex liaison involving deception and manipulation. Equally puzzling is the identity of the woman in the series. The first five poems might have been composed shortly after Crane met Cora, who had already been "the ashes of other men's love," though his failed relationships with Nellie Crouse and Lily Brandon Munroe (he had written at least one letter to Lily while in Cuba) could also have inspired him. Conceivably, the woman is a composite of Cora, Nellie, Lily, and the woman who caused Crane's "personal shock." Whatever the case, "Intrigue" is a maze of yearning, disappointment, and betrayal that he struggled to escape. Crane never fully reconciled his divided sensibility about women. He thought of romantic love, he told Nellie, as one of the "ingenious traps for the imagination," but romanticized his relationships and projected what Frederic M. Lawrence called "a curious trace of chivalry" that attracted women to him. After he failed to get to Cuba on the *Commodore,* women around the country wrote him, urging that he take them on his next attempt.[13]

During the Spanish–American War, Crane supported military intervention in the Caribbean and the Pacific because he believed it was justified and idealistically motivated. During an interview in January 1899, he was asked about the future of Cuba. "That is a large question to ask a small man," responded the ever-ironic Crane, then denied that the United States had imperialistic intentions.[14] His first dispatch, "The Terrible Captain of the Captured Panama," was filled with hyperbole and boastful jingoism, and other dispatches proclaimed American patriotism; but he soon began criticizing the management of the war itself and exposed inefficiency and corruption on both sides. American troops were dying unnecessarily, he reported, because they were forced to use outdated rifles that fired black-powder ammunition. Unlike the smokeless powder used by the Spanish, black powder betrayed the location of the shooter. Crane also exposed grocers in Havana who hoarded food and pretended there was a shortage in order to raise prices; castigated an inefficient American military commission supervising the Spanish evacuation; and criticized a Spanish member of the commission who demanded that 25 percent of the profits from a fundraiser to help sick American soldiers be remitted to his government. Later, in a letter to the editor of a London newspaper, he chastised the American commander in the Philippines, General Elwell Otis, for failing to understand the nature of guerrilla warfare. Moreover, Crane became increasingly upset with the public's thirst for yellow journalism. Newspapers, he complained, cared little about accurate reporting and wanted sensationalized accounts of deeds and battles.

One expert purveyor of the sensational was the journalist Elbert Hubbard. His hyperbolic piece "A Message to Garcia" immortalized Captain Andrew Summers Rowan, who had delivered a message from President William McKinley to the Cuban revolutionary General Calixto García in the spring of 1898. "By the Eternal! there is a man whose form should be cast in deathless bronze and the statue placed in every college of the land," proclaimed Hubbard, who invented details to dramatize a story that was only incidentally about Rowan. His essay glorified Rowan's obedience and perseverance as an example of the Gospel of Work. Leaders in business, government, and the military quickly distributed the article to their staffs. More than forty million copies were sold by 1913, earning Hubbard more than a quarter of a million dollars in royalties; it was translated into thirty-seven languages and made into two films (1916, 1936). The later version romanticized the incident and included, among other concoctions, a renegade Marine and a Cuban señorita who guides Rowan through the jungle. Fact and fiction had become so entwined that even Rowan joked about his original mission. "Colonel, what *was* this message to Garcia, anyway?" he was asked late in life. "It was, madam, an invitation from President McKinley to an old-fashioned New England boiled dinner at the White House."[15]

Soon after "A Message to Garcia" first appeared in Hubbard's monthly *The Philistine: A Periodical of Protest* in March 1899, Crane wrote to him:

> I have been working up some grievances against you. I object strongly to your paragraphs about Rowan. You are more wrong than is even common on our humble incompetant globe. He didn't do anything worthy at all. He received the praise of the general of the army and got to be made a lieutenant col. for a feat which about forty newspaper correspondents had already performed at the usual price of fifty dollars a week and expenses. Besides he is personally a chump and in Porto Rico where I met him he wore a yachting cap as part of his uniform which was damnable. When you want to monkey with some of our national heroes you had better ask me, because I know and your perspective is almost out of sight.[16]

Ever sensitive to military decorum, Crane objected to Rowan's disregard for a proper uniform; and although Crane admired valor, he knew how storytelling could twist historical fact. Years earlier, in his Sullivan County sketch "Not Much of a Hero," he had observed how folktales about "Tom" Quick, a famous Indian slayer idolized by children, belied his merciless slaughter of Native Americans. With Quick and Rowan, legend had trumped historical reality.

Over the next few months, Crane reshaped his dispatches into *Wounds in the Rain,* a collection of eleven war stories that explored the complex nature of courage and sacrifice. Unlike his earlier war stories, these were more firmly grounded in current social and political issues. In "The Price of the Harness," which dramatizes the American attack upon the fortifications of San Juan on July 1, 1898, Crane criticized the constant attention paid in the American press to colorful volunteer regiments such as Roosevelt's Rough Riders, at the expense of the regular-army soldier. Crane had already recorded a diatribe against the press in his dispatch "Regulars Get No Glory." Instead of gloating over "the gallantry of Reginald Marmaduke Maurice Montmorenci Sturtevant, and for goodness sake how the poor old chappy endures that dreadful hard-tack and bacon," the press should discuss the common soldier, whom Crane typifies as "Michael Nolan": "the sweating, swearing, overloaded, hungry, thirsty, sleepless Nolan, tearing his breeches on the barbed wire entanglements, wallowing through the muddy fords, pursuing his way through the stiletto-pointed thickets, climbing the fire-crowned hill." Shortly after the dispatch appeared in newspapers on July 19 and 20, a regular-army artillery unit sent Crane a gold medal with his name inscribed on it, in appreciation of his support for their efforts. In "The Price of the Harness," Crane continued his praise for regular, unsung soldiers, who, rather than expecting glory for their actions, do their jobs quietly and responsibly. Despite his admiration for common army privates during combat, his tone never becomes chauvinistic, and the story ends sardonically with a delirious soldier singing "The Star-Spangled Banner" to dying and fever-stricken comrades. Similarly, in "Marines Signaling under Fire at Guantanamo," regular-army signalmen calmly stand up in the line of fire to call in artillery shells from nearby ships. In contrast to the stoicism of regular-army troops is the unrealistic view of volunteers who see war as a game or heroic adventure. In "The Second Generation," Crane criticizes nepotism and class privilege as the basis for a military commission. The fictional Senator Cadogan manipulates the political system to secure a position as army captain and commissary officer for his pampered son, Caspar, who is "resolved to go to the tropic wars and do something." To the narrator, however, appointing an inexperienced blueblood like Caspar as an officer has "all the logic of going to sea in a bathing-machine." When the troops land at Siboney, this "selfish young pig" spends much of his time looking for his missing saddle bags and eating other people's rations.[17]

Other stories debunk the attempt by newspapers to sensationalize commonplace events during the Cuban War. In "God Rest Ye, Merry Gentlemen," a correspondent is sent home for not producing yellow journalism. In "This Majestic Lie," Cuban and Spanish newspapers proclaim that the American fleet was defeated at Manila Bay, that "the inhabitants of Philadelphia had fled to the forests," that "Boston was besieged by the Apaches," and that "Chicago millionaires were giving away their palaces for two or three loaves of bread." American journalism is not much better: "If the news arrived at Key West as a mouse, it was often enough cabled north as an elephant." In "The Lone Charge of William B. Perkins," Crane satirizes incompetent correspondents who have "no information of war and no particular rapidity of mind for acquiring it," and who "could not distinguish between a 5-inch quick-firing gun and a nickel-plated ice-pick." When a correspondent named Perkins thinks he sees a Spanish soldier behind a bush, he grabs a rifle and foolishly runs like "an almshouse idiot plunging through hot crackling thickets," only to discover that the supposed enemy is actually a palm branch.[18]

While Stephen was incommunicado in Havana, Cora was growing increasingly distraught back in England. She transformed her anxiety about him into two short fables about lost love and disillusionment: "The Poor Soul" and "What Hell Might Be Like."[19] An already serious financial crisis worsened when she received two summonses for unpaid butcher and grocery bills and was sued by a furniture dealer.[20] She then began a barrage of letters and cablegrams that she called "one long inky howl!"[21] She begged Crane's agent Reynolds for money, fearing that she might be evicted from Ravensbrook. Rumors about Stephen also began surfacing—Spanish authorities had imprisoned him, he was hiding out in Havana, he was planning on deserting her—but attempts to get additional information from James Creelman, London chief of the *New York Journal* office, failed, though he was convinced that Crane had received at least some of her communications. Overwhelmed by the silence from Cuba and fearing for Crane's safety, she sent cables to government authorities and to his brother William, asking if they knew anything about her missing husband.[22] The message from an unknown woman must have startled William—indeed the whole family—for it was the first time he had heard that his youngest brother had not only disappeared but was also supposedly married. Cora also wrote to John M. Hay, U.S. ambassador to England and secretary of state, and to Russell A. Alger, secretary of war, at the end of September, in an attempt to locate Crane. Her request for information did not reach Major General J. F. Wade, head of the American Evacuation Commission in Cuba, until two weeks later. Crane was alerted that he had two London cablegrams, and he ignored them because he assumed they were bills; pressured to retrieve them, he apologized to authorities for having caused a problem. He did not, however, break his almost complete silence. Throughout the fall, Crane communicated regularly only with Reynolds. On August 16, Crane cabled Cora to say that he was now back in Key West. It would apparently be the last time she would hear from him for three months.

In Crane's defense, he had arranged in June for Reynolds to forward payments to Cora through John Scott Stokes at the Savage Club in London, and he told Dorothy Brandon, one of Lily's two sisters, that he was planning on returning to England as soon as the war ended. During and after the Cuban campaign, mail delivery was difficult. Crane's letter to Dorothy was written on a dispatch boat on May 19 but not postmarked in New York City until June 19, and William's letters to his brother were returned as "uncalled for"—evidence of unreliable mail delivery, for Stephen had no reason to avoid his brother's correspondence, which over the years referred to loans. Yet despite his awareness of Cora's worries and economic plight, he was not eager to return to her. His arrangement that money go to an intermediary rather than directly to Cora suggests that he wanted to keep his relationship with her out of the public eye in America. His assumption in October that recent cablegrams from London were from creditors was most likely willful ignorance. Around the same time that he apologized for not picking them up, he told Reynolds that he might stay in Havana throughout the winter if the proposed weekly syndication of articles worked out. In short, Crane was once again disappearing—this time from Cora.[23]

Distraught, Cora sought help from friends. In October the Conrads invited her to their home, Ivy Walls, where Jessie tried to allay her anxieties about Stephen's safety and loyalty; but Joseph, like Harold Frederic, questioned Crane's motive for staying in Cuba. "His future is here—I firmly believe," he told Cora, "but will he see it?" Conrad asked David Meldrum, head of Blackwood's London office, to lend Cora fifty pounds, with Crane's future work, Cora's furniture, or his own work as security. William Blackwood, however, was angry with Crane. The previous April he had advanced him sixty pounds for articles from Cuba, apparently assuming that he had first refusal of Crane's war stories; but as of the fall, Crane had submitted only "The Price of the Harness" to *Blackwood's Magazine*. As Conrad told Cora, had Crane simply written a note apologizing for the delay in submitting copy but promising to do so, Blackwood would have been satisfied—but Crane was often unprofessional and self-centered in personal dealings. Though Meldrum admired "The Price of the Harness," he advised Blackwood not to advance another loan to Crane: "I fancy he is far more foolish than you know. I can find no justification for the man, though I can [find] many excuses for one with such a strange and all-on-edge temperament as his."[24]

Like Conrad, their neighbor Robert Barr helped Cora to manage her finances, but also criticized Crane's irresponsibility: "The only person at fault is Stephen Crane, & as he is not within cursing distance there is no use in swearing." When Cora decided to sail from England to Cuba and rescue Stephen herself, Barr helped her to arrange deferred payment for transport on the SS *Mohegan* of the Atlantic Transport Line. Barr told Atlantic Transport that Crane had been captured by the Spanish; but once he was released and back in New York, Barr assured the company, Crane would pay for the ticket. The ship planned to sail on October 6, but was delayed until October 13, the scheduled departure date of the *Manitou,* another Atlantic Transport ship. At the last minute, the company transferred passengers from one ship to the other and, for unknown reasons, Cora did not sail. This proved fortuitous for her. A day after leaving port, the *Mohegan* struck a reef and sank.[25]

Meanwhile, Cora's torment intensified because of her relationship with Kate Lyon and Harold Frederic. After he suffered a stroke in August, Cora sent Adoni Ptolemy to help Kate Lyon care for him and took their three children—Helen, Héloïse, and Barry—to live with her at Ravensbrook.[26] As Harold became increasingly ill, Kate called in Mrs. Athalie Mills, a Christian Science faith healer, to treat him; but he died at Homefield on October 19. The *New York Times* tried to protect the reputation of its former London bureau chief by reporting that the death had occurred at his official residence with his wife in London, but a coroner's inquest two days after the death led to charges of medical neglect and an indictment against Kate Lyon and Mrs. Mills for manslaughter. Both were eventually acquitted, but not until they had been denounced in the press and Kate's illicit relationship with Harold had been exposed. Cora, beset with her own problems, nonetheless reached out to help.

Cora recognized the similarity between her situation and Kate's. Like Kate, Cora had no legal rights to her lover's income or property, but she did not wallow in self-pity and understood the frailty of human relationships. She had been married twice and had been the mistress of two wealthy lovers; as hostess of a gambling house and proprietor of the Hotel de Dreme, she had no illusions about the opposite sex. During the trial, Cora testified on behalf of Kate and Mrs. Mills, and later worked with John Scott Stokes, Frederic's secretary and English executor, to raise money to support Kate's children. Most contributions were small.[27] Henry James and George Bernard Shaw could afford only five pounds, and Conrad regretted he had barely enough to pay his own bills. Others were hostile to the idea of helping Kate Lyon. When Mrs. Alice Creelman, wife of James Creelman, self-righteously denounced her as evil, Cora castigated "the supreme egotism of women who . . . set themselves upon their pedestals of self-conceit and conscious virtue, judging their unfortunate sisters alike."[28] At least some of Mrs. Creelman's anger may have been directed at Cora. Crane and James Creelman had worked for William Randolph Hearst in Greece and Cuba, but were never close. When Cora implored Creelman as Hearst's representative in London to give her money for a trip to Havana in search of Crane, he gave her a mere two pounds, then ignored her.

Desperate for money, Cora attempted to sell Crane's work without understanding the literary market. In a confusing series of events, the magazine *Illustrated Bits* plagiarized "The Bride Comes to Yellow Sky" after she transferred copyright to Heinemann, leading to a lawsuit by Heinemann and distress for Cora. Unaware that she needed power of attorney to negotiate for Stephen, she also tried to convince James B. Pinker, a London literary agent who would later be acknowledged as the greatest agent of his time, to market unpublished New York City sketches she had found among Crane's papers at Ravensbrook.[29] Ironically, Pinker had written Crane in August offering to represent him, but the letter did not reach Cuba until November. Pinker worried that marketing Crane's earlier, minor work might hurt his literary reputation. Cora also embarrassed Pinker by trying to market Crane's work on her own. When he proposed to Grant Richards's London publishing house that it advance Crane a hundred pounds for an unwritten novel, he was surprised to learn that Cora had, on her own, tried to negotiate a contract with Richards for the same book for seventy-five pounds.

Meanwhile Crane, now exhausted, realized the futility of staying in Cuba. From a distance of more than fifteen hundred miles, he was responding to magazines and publishers through Reynolds, with little success. Penniless, he asked William one more time for a loan. Whether William sent it is unclear, but Stokes arranged a fifty-pound advance from Heinemann to bring Crane home. If for no other reason, Crane decided to return to England because he had a reliable publisher in Heinemann. From 1896 to 1900, the firm published nine of his books, more than any American publisher. On December 24, Crane sailed from Havana aboard the SS *City of Washington* and arrived in New York four days later, ravaged by disease and disheartened about his future, though he hoped that America would inspire his writing more than "those damned stinking Latin-American islands." He was too embarrassed to visit his family, whom he had not seen since early February 1897, until he could sort out his relationship with Cora. Instead, he cabled Edmund to come to New York to see him, just as he had asked him to do before sailing for England in March 1897. Accepting and nonjudgmental, Edmund empathized with his brother. He feared, however, that Stephen's constant coughing signaled a more serious condition. Howells and Garland concurred; both of them also sensed his restlessness. "We were getting at each other less than ever," Howells noted when Crane stopped by to see him before sailing for England, and Garland felt snubbed when they ran into each other in the offices of S. S. McClure. Gaunt and disheveled, Crane seemed to Garland an "unwholesome type." Crane could express his appreciation of someone in writing—as he had done with his two "literary fathers"—but he found it difficult to reveal himself emotionally in person, especially toward Garland. Having just returned from the Yukon searching for adventure and literary inspiration, Garland was the principled representative "of the great honest West" whom Crane emulated, the surrogate brother who guided him, and the father he wanted to please. Yet Crane, the wayward son "of the false East," felt he had somehow let Garland down. Fearing for his own safety in Cuba, Crane had asked his boyhood friend Louis C. Senger to tell Garland how indebted he was to him, in case he died during the war. When Garland came to England in 1899 and ignored the Cranes' invitation to visit them, Cora later told him how this had saddened Stephen, who feared that Garland thought Crane was ungrateful for his guidance over the years.[30]

In a letter filled with deep concern for Stephen, Cora pleaded with Reynolds to persuade Crane to return to England. On December 31,

Crane sailed aboard the *Manitou*. "It is the opinion of all the men who know," she insisted, "that Stephen's future is in England. No matter what he writes, there is *always* favorable notices in every English paper. He has a great vogue here and sure he must return if he is ever going to do more great work. A man must have pure wholesome air if he wishes to succeed in art. I beg you will advise Mr. Crane to return to England. He has a great future and a wonderful home awaiting him."[31]

That was her plan—an ideal setting insulated from the stress of daily life. Before their separation in April, Stephen and Cora had already begun talking about moving to a new home. Uncomfortable at Ravensbrook, they had heard from Edward Garnett about an ancient manor in the village of Northiam, Sussex, called Brede Place. The thought of a five-hundred-year-old house steeped in legend, lore, and history fascinated a history buff like Crane, proud of his ancestry and heritage. Back in July he had excitedly told fellow correspondents about his new home, and in a playful moment they had imagined him as Lord Tholepin, an East Indian British squire about to inherit an ancestral manor named Mango Chutney.[32] While he was in Cuba, Cora negotiated with Moreton and Clara Frewen to lease the place; and in December, Cora—wanting the sort of Victorian rose garden that was so much in vogue—planted more than three hundred roses in front of the house. It was a bouquet of love for her sallow knight that could not wait till spring. Living in the manor were two of Kate's children—a family that he and "Auntie" Cora could provide for.[33]

Cora's insistence that Crane needed wholesome air to flourish as a writer was more than metaphorical. She knew that his time in Cuba had coincided with the island's tropical rainy season (May to October), the most damaging weather for a tubercular condition. Unfortunately, the home she had found for him would prove to be the worst possible place. "The horror of the last few months is almost at an end," a relieved Cora told Moreton Frewen.[34] She was right—but she had little notion of how much Crane's health had deteriorated since he had left England.

Part V

SEARCH FOR RESPECTABILITY,
COUNTRY SQUIRE

26

Brede Place, Return to Childhood, Another Potboiler

JANUARY–JUNE 1899

"THE WORLD, ACCORDING to the best geographers, is divided into Europe, Asia, Africa, America, and Romney Marsh," proclaimed the Reverend Richard Harris Barham in 1840. Romney Marsh, a wetland area in the counties of Kent and East Sussex in England, was the site of Brede Place. It was also home to a literary colony that included Crane, Conrad, H. G. Wells, Ford Madox Ford, and Henry James—"a ring of foreign conspirators plotting against British letters," as Wells wryly described them.[1]

After Stephen and Cora mentioned to Edward Garnett that they were uncomfortable at Ravensbrook, he told them about Brede Place, a nearby manor house that he assumed could be rented, along with its hundred-acre game park. Even before seeing the house, Crane was fascinated with the idea of being a country squire surveying his estate on horseback; and while he was in Cuba, Cora began negotiations with the owner, Moreton Frewen.[2] For Stephen and Cora, it would be an escape from the problems they faced in New York City and Jacksonville and the start of a new life of respectability.

Located in Northiam, East Sussex, near the site where the Battle of Hastings had been fought in 1066, Brede Place was a dilapidated manor built partly in the fourteenth century that had been restored in Tudor and Elizabethan times but had since fallen into disrepair. It lacked gas, electricity, and plumbing, relying on a rudimentary earth closet for sanitation; rushes were strewn on the floor of the entrance hall to serve as insulation (a practice common in the Middle Ages); and most of the rooms were uninhabitable. Yet it was steeped in British history and folklore.[3] The Oxenbridge family, its owner for two hundred fifty years, had had close family ties to Elizabeth I and had added two wings to form an E-shaped house, a design that had been fashionable at the time, in honor of the queen. Its most famous owner was Sir Goddard Oxenbridge, a sixteenth-century knight who, it was rumored, had hanged his wives from an oak beam in the gallows room above a private dungeon. According to local lore, he had also been a giant ogre who ate a child for dinner each night. In retaliation, local children had killed him by drugging his liquor and sawing him in half while he lay drunk and unconscious. The spirit of Sir Goddard was said to be among the ghosts that haunted the house, a rumor probably started by smugglers to discourage anyone from living at Brede Place; they could hide contraband in a nearby cavern, reached by a secret underground passageway connected to the Brede River a mile away. Guests who slept in a circular room in the tower at one end of the house reported hearing footsteps on a winding staircase and seeing doors mysteriously opened; one visitor, the writer Robert Barr, piled furniture against one of the doors to keep out the ghost. (Wind and a worn-out door latch were the culprits.) At Brede Place, Stephen—whom Cora affectionately called "the Duke"— enjoyed telling tales about a ghostly ogre and about phantom women who haunted a kitchen in which a former tenant had hanged unsatisfactory cooks from a crane mounted high on a two-story wall.[4]

Soon after his arrival in England on January 11, 1899, Crane was greeted with heartening news. His Cuban war story "The Price of the Harness," which had just been published in December in *Blackwood's Edinburgh Magazine* and in the American monthly illustrated magazine *Cosmopolitan,* was the talk of English literati. Conrad said it was Crane's best piece of writing since *The Red Badge of Courage.* Just a few weeks earlier, in England's influential journal *Academy,* Edward Garnett had declared Crane unequaled in his ability as an impressionist; and soon thereafter, in the equally powerful American *Saturday Evening Post,* Robert

Barr had proclaimed him "probably the greatest genius America has produced since Edgar Allan Poe." Now that he planned to settle down, Crane "will write the great American novel we have all been waiting for."[5]

Several days after Stephen's return, he and Cora visited the village of Brede. "A solemn feeling of work came to him," and they decided "to move Heaven and Earth" to live at Brede Place.[6] They could not have found a more understanding landlord than Moreton Frewen. A friend of Teddy Roosevelt and a lover of the American West, Frewen was much like Stephen. He had lived as a cowboy in Wyoming in the 1870s and 1880s and had fought the Sioux. His wife was Clarita "Clara" Jerome, daughter of New York millionaire Leonard Jerome, and his father was an aristocrat. Frewen befriended literary writers and lived a life of intrigue and adventure, but he squandered money and was often in debt, earning the nicknames "Mortal Ruin" and "the splendid pauper." Obviously, he and Stephen were kindred spirits.

Although the Frewens were planning on renovating Brede Place and eventually occupying it themselves, they offered it rent free to Stephen and Cora, but Stephen insisted on paying something. The agreed-upon figure, forty pounds a year, was a symbolic gesture rather than a realistic amount. As part of the arrangement, they were supposed to make a number of repairs, but they never could afford to do so. They also could not move in immediately because a year's rent on Ravensbrook was still due, and merchants were demanding payment on items purchased months earlier. A week after Crane's arrival in England, a magistrate issued a writ ordering him to settle one of the accounts right away. Overwhelmed, the Cranes sought assistance. Moreton Frewen's solicitor, Alfred T. Plant, helped them to manage their finances; James B. Pinker acted as guarantor for their debts; and a Mr. Dominick, head of the London office of Frederick A. Stokes and Company, gave them a loan for back rent on Ravensbrook in exchange for a lien on future royalties from Crane's Appleton books: *The Red Badge, Maggie, The Little Regiment,* and *The Third Violet.* Thinking that their financial situation had improved, they began moving to Brede Place on February 12.[7]

The move marked a new beginning for Stephen and Cora. To confront his past, clear his record, and find respectability, Crane impulsively wrote to Reverend Charles J. Little, his former professor of history at

Syracuse University. Crane recalled a dramatic moment between them. Following an examination on the French Revolution, Professor Little had warned him that he needed to become a more serious student if he wanted to succeed in life. Crane had never forgotten his teacher's concern for his future and remembered those words with gratitude. He alluded in the letter to his international success as an author, but minimized his "silly talent." He was concerned that Reverend Little might have been misled by rumors about his former student's behavior: "It has stuck in my mind for years that some of the information you had recieved of me was quite false. Candidly, I was worse than I should have been but I always had a singular faculty of having it said that I was engaged in crimes which are not of my accomplishments. Indeed, this singular faculty has followed me out of college into real life."[8] Crane's letter to Reverend Little is puzzling. What prompted him to write to his teacher so suddenly, eight years after the fact, and why was he trying to correct the record about his behavior at Syracuse?

Adopting a confessional yet defensive tone, Crane acknowledged that he had been a poor student, but maintained that Little had once scolded him in error, when Stephen had been wrongly accused of committing misdeeds at Syracuse. Yet in his letter Crane was doing more than confessing to sins past, downplaying his skill as a writer, and defending himself against erroneous charges. Beneath the surface was insecurity born of the need for affirmation from a surrogate father—someone who was, like Reverend Crane, a highly respected Methodist minister, author, and teacher. Hoping for a reply "even if it is only three lines," Crane concluded, "Remember there is one who will always be grateful to you"— words also addressed tacitly to his own deceased father.[9] The reply from Reverend Little was satisfyingly long and detailed. He seemed familiar with some of Stephen's writings, but had apparently forgotten much about the incident of misbehavior. He implied that Stephen had misinterpreted what he had said. The rest of his letter was full of paternal comments and advice.

Crane's hopes for a fresh start in England were soon dashed. After meeting with Morrisons and Nightingale, solicitors for the Ravensbrook landlord, he had wrongly concluded that they would let him move to Brede Place solely on James Pinker's promise that Crane's debts would eventually be paid. Within hours after hearing that Stephen and Cora had begun moving on February 12, the law firm demanded that Pinker immediately pay the back rent on Ravensbrook and fund the repairs they had agreed to make at Brede Place. More than four decades after Crane's death, the firm still kept a file of his bank statements, his overdrafts, and merchants' pleas for payment.[10]

Crane was determined "to borrow money from pretty near every body in the world." "I must have every pennie that you can wrest from the enemy," he told his agent Paul Revere Reynolds, and pleaded with him to insist that Harper and Brothers pay the remaining twenty-five pounds owed as an advance on the book publication of "The Monster" and on previously unpublished stories.[11] In March 1898, Crane had settled for a hundred twenty-five dollars (about twenty-five pounds), half of the advance, and in May he submitted "His New Mittens" for the book. When Harper's decided that the two Whilomville stories and "The Blue Hotel" (which *Harper's Magazine* had already rejected) would not make a sufficiently long volume, they withheld the rest of the advance. Not until March 1899 did Reynolds receive the second half of the advance. Cora likewise tried to raise money, by writing articles about her experience as a war correspondent in the Greco-Turkish War. Though the editor of *Wide World Magazine* was interested in the idea, Pinker could not convince him to offer her an advance until she had submitted a sample of her work.

Crane—for whom a penny earned was never a penny saved—found it impossible to manage funds wisely and turned to William repeatedly as a last resort. A little more than a year earlier, Crane had poked fun at himself in a letter to his brother: "I am just thinking how easy it would be in my present financial extremity to cable you for a hundred dollars but then by the time this reaches you I will probably be all right again. I believe the sum I usually borrowed was fifteen dollars, wasnt it? Fifteen dollars—fifteen dollars—fifteen dollars. I can remember an interminable row of fifteen dollar requests."[12] This time, the request for money strained their relationship. From November 1898 to March 1899, a period during which Stephen had continually asked him for money to pay expenses, William must have been wondering about his brother's behavior. When Stephen telegraphed him for a loan in November, William's letters to Havana were returned because Stephen had not picked them up. Shortly thereafter, William received a cable from Cora, desperate for information about her "husband." The cable startled him, for he had heard nothing to indicate that Stephen was married. William was reconsidering a brother who had a history of turning to him only when in need and who had not even shared news about his "wife."

William undoubtedly shared the news with his brother Edmund, who probably asked Stephen about it before the latter sailed for England. Crane would have been shocked to learn that his secret had been exposed. Upon returning to Ravensbrook, his first letter was to William, saying that he was married. Shortly thereafter, Crane composed "The Lover and the Tell-Tale," a story about the exposure of a boy's secret love for a girl named Cora. Crane's need for secrecy was obsessive. The entire time he had been living at Ravensbrook, he had not even given his family his home address.

Now back in England, Crane confessed to having been the "wayward brother," but couched his request for a five-hundred-dollar loan in several letters to William in January–March, depicting himself as a responsible family man who wanted to ease his family's doubts about him. He included photos and a guidebook description of his new home at Brede Place, talked of a possible month-long visit to America so that his relatives could meet Cora, and invited William's daughter Helen to visit them in England. Crane acknowledged his current financial difficulties and projected the persona of a hardworking writer sensitive to the feelings of others. Upon learning that "The Monster" had generated considerable gossip in Port Jervis among townsfolk who wondered whether the story was based on their community, he stated that although he had probably been influenced by his childhood experiences in the town, he was not trying to criticize anyone there. He also admitted to occasional moments of depression, but claimed that "if the month of March dont wipe me off the earth I hope by this time next year to be fairly rich so much confidence have I in the different life I am now leading."[13]

Despite its occasionally deferential tone, Crane's correspondence requesting a loan was misleading. Although he was still living at Ravensbrook in January and February, when he wrote William twice, Crane used Brede Place stationery to impress him. (When he wrote to Reynolds and Pinker during the same period, he used Ravensbrook as his address; both knew the truth about his financial problems.) He also claimed that his wife was "an English lady" whose connections allowed them to live in a "beautiful old manor," thus implying that he had married into British aristocracy; and his assertion that they were almost bankrupt only because of his "long illness" ignored their extravagant spending. William did not know that his youngest brother could be dishonest about financial affairs.[14]

Ever the gracious hosts, the Cranes supported a household that included Mrs. Ruedy, Héloïse and Barry Frederic (ages six and four), their governess (Mrs. Lily Burke), two horses (Glenroy and Gloster, a.k.a. Gloucester), and three dogs (Sponge, Flannel, and Ruby).[15] Their already strained resources were stretched even tighter because the rental agreement with Frewen required that they retain the current help: a half-dozen or so occasionally tipsy, often complaining staff members, most of whom refused to sleep in a haunted manor. One night, the drunken butler knocked over a lamp that started a fire in Crane's study; on another, during a dinner party the cook refused to work until bribed with a bottle of brandy.[16] Stephen and Cora's increasingly careless lifestyle worsened their plight. Their debts included almost a hundred pounds for Cora's piano, purchased nearly two years earlier; and before they were even sure they could move into Brede Place, Cora had bought expensive embossed stationery and planted a rose garden. Stephen was equally unrealistic about finances. When a maid rescued a number of manuscripts after another fire broke out in his study, he and Cora rewarded her with an all-expenses-paid month's vacation at a seaside resort, in addition to her wages.[17] He also believed that he could live on half of what he was used to spending, be debt free within months, and earn the enormous sum of fifteen hundred pounds in 1899.[18]

Cora had initially feared that Crane lacked the "machine-like application which makes a man work steadily"; but over the next sixteen months he worked harder than he ever had in his life, never letting a fleeting thought escape. Outdoors or on a train, he often asked, "Anyone got a pencil & paper? I've just thought of something." He would then dictate his ideas to a companion, rarely altering the words for fear of losing valuable time. From January 1899 to April 1900, he completed one novel, finished two-thirds of another, and wrote more than fifty stories, sketches, and newspaper articles, some of which were hackwork.[19]

Conditions at Brede Place were harsh for a consumptive. Storm winds screeched through leaky casements and forced chimney smoke back into

Crane's already chilly, damp study. To avoid interruption, he would lock himself in—another example of his habitual need to vanish—for as long as three days, cranking out one story after another and sliding each one under the door for Cora to type. Shortly after his return to England, Crane had bought a typewriter to avoid the cost of a typist and to speed up production of copy for a publisher. Only his dogs were allowed entry. "They come each morning," Crane said, "to let me know things are all right." He was incredibly devoted to them, though they occasionally caused problems. When they killed sheep and lambs, a local shepherd demanded reimbursement. After Crane said he could not (or would not) pay for the loss of animals, he was startled to find five sheep carcasses hanging from trees on his land. In April 1900, he was fined thirty-five shillings for not having dog licenses.[20]

Among Crane's many projects was a return to his own personal past in a series of Whilomville stories about children, written in January–November 1899, published in *Harper's Monthly* starting in August 1899, and continuing for the next thirteen months. The presence of children in his life—baby Borys Conrad, and Héloïse and Barry Frederic—renewed his sense of family, and he and Cora explored the possibility of adopting Barry under American adoption laws.[21]

Throughout the stories, Crane's playfulness with puns and names is evident. The name of the gang leader Willie Dalzel raises the question: Will he dazzle anyone with his exploits? That of the tattle-tale Rose Goldege makes the reader wonder whether there was ever a rosy "Golden Age" in childhood. The phrase was well-known at the time because of Kenneth Grahame's enormously popular volume *The Golden Age* (1895). Like Crane's Whilomville stories, Grahame's book was a collection of stories that satirized the myth of the innocent, admiring child and the thoroughly benevolent adult. As with his two previous Whilomville stories, "The Monster" and "His New Mittens," Crane encoded names with people, places, and events from his own life. He had always been sensitive about his own name. As a child, he had been "bitterly ashamed of it" and as an adult, when asked if it was a pseudonym, would declare it "the homliest name in created things." In the story "Shame," girls refuse to call Jimmie Trescott by name and simply use the label "Him"; and in "The Angel Child," a barber is treated as an outsider because he has a foreign-sounding and difficult-to-pronounce surname.

A retainer known as Clarence took his name from two of Crane's school friends at Syracuse, Clarence Loomis Peaslee and Clarence Goodwin, whose name was also used for the character Martha Goodwin. The name of Crane's closest friend at Claverack, Earl T. Reeves, lives on in the fictional Earl family and in Reeves Margate, whose last name is associated with two popular seaside resorts: Margate, New Jersey, which was just south of Asbury Park, where Crane lived after Port Jervis, and Margate in the county of Kent, in southeastern England, not far from where he was while writing the Whilomville stories. The most obvious example of a name association is Cora the "angel child," whose character was apparently based on anecdotes that Cora told Stephen about her childhood.[22]

Like "The Monster," the new Whilomville stories recreated the setting of Crane's Port Jervis childhood. In "Lynx-Hunting," the "grey cliffs" that "sprang towards the sky" and that are seen in a lithograph—*A Bird's Eye View of Whilomville, N.Y.*—are the same sheer cliffs that tower above Port Jervis and that are depicted in a popular local nineteenth-century lithograph, *A Bird's Eye View of Port Jervis, N.Y.* In "Showin' Off," the Whilomville suburb of Oakland Park (as well as Oakhurst in "The Monster") was based on Oakland, New York; and in "The Carriage-Lamps," the carriage house depicted was the one next to William Howe Crane's home on East Main Street.

Once again, Crane's return to his past affected him deeply and resulted in stories that reflected his concerns both as a child and as an adult. In "The Fight," a new boy, Johnnie Hedge, moves to Whilomville from Jersey City, New Jersey. Crane, who was born near Jersey City, in Newark, was as much an outsider as Johnnie Hedge and likewise had lived throughout New Jersey, making him a Jersey city boy. In "Making an Orator," Jimmie's trauma regarding declamation was rooted in Crane's lifelong fear of public speaking. At Claverack College, Stephen had been excused from declaiming, even though the school considered it essential to a good education; later, when he had been asked to read his poetry in front of the Uncut Leaves Society in New York in 1894, he could not do it. In "The City Urchin and the Chaste Villagers," Crane was the urban waif revisiting his own childhood sense of abandonment; and when children decide to reenact a story from "a certain half-dime blood-and-thunder pamphlet"—"a dramatization that would gain no royalties for the author"—Crane was venting his frustration. While composing the

Whilomville stories, he had heard that someone was planning to dramatize one of his parodies of "half-dime" stories, "The Bride Comes to Yellow Sky," without paying a royalty.[23] In the last Whilomville story, "A Little Pilgrim" (a.k.a. "A Little Pilgrimage"), which was finished either on
his birthday or just a day or so away and which begins "One November . . . ," he identified with his biblical namesake—Saint Stephen, the
first Christian martyr—and returned to an issue that had disturbed him
while writing "The Monster." Hanging on a Sunday-school wall is a
"lithograph of the Martyrdom of St. Stephen."[24] In the Book of Acts,
people chastise Saint Stephen for "blasphemous words" because "they
could not withstand the wisdom and the spirit with which he spoke"
(Acts 6:10–11). With a council of false accusers misreading him and focusing on "his face," Saint Stephen is driven out of the city and stoned to
death.[25] His fate is similar to that of Henry Johnson, Dr. Trescott, and
Crane himself. An angry crowd throws stones at Johnson because of his
disfigurement; and when Trescott tries to visit the sickly Sadie Winter,
her mother stares at him with "stony surprise" and her father "hurl[s]"
his "fiery rage" at him. For Crane himself, the identification with Saint
Stephen was even deeper. Crane, too, had been criticized for blasphemous words. The *Atlantic Monthly* had criticized *The Black Riders* for
being "blasphemous to a degree which even cleverness will not reconcile to a liberal taste"; and when Ripley Hitchcock had requested that
Crane delete blasphemous remarks from *Maggie* in 1896, Crane had excised "the words which hurt."[26] Later that year, his motives for protecting
Dora Clark had been misread, and he had been driven out of New York
City by police accusations. Writing about the lithograph, he was focusing on an image that mirrored his own troubles.

Crane's most sustained literary effort in 1899 was his longest completed novel, *Active Service.* In October 1897, he had considered writing a
long novel based on his experiences in Greece. He hoped that it would
be serialized and bring him a large advance. Though he was pressed for
money, his financial situation seemed manageable at the time, and he felt
confident that he could finish the book by April or May 1898; but as he
sank further into debt, he turned to writing short stories, which gar-
nered money more quickly. If he did any work on the book in Havana,
he never mentioned this in his letters to Reynolds.

Upon returning from Cuba, Crane began "working like a galley slave" on *Active Service,* and the loan he had received from Dominick at Stokes for the Ravensbrook rent became an advance on the novel. His negotiation with the publisher was yet another example of his willful ignorance about the literary marketplace. By contacting Dominick directly, he was bypassing Reynolds, who, as Crane's American agent, should have been handling the negotiations with the firm and collecting a commission. Similarly, a month later Crane bypassed Stokes, ignoring the firm's wish and probable expectation that the novel not be serialized in newspapers before book publication. He encouraged Reynolds to arrange American serial rights.

Crane's dealings with James B. Pinker, his English agent, were just as problematic. Since Crane's return from Cuba, Pinker had saved him from financial ruin. He had industriously sold Crane's stories, arranged for advances, and paid creditors; and like Reynolds, he promoted Crane in the literary marketplace. Yet Crane, his financial situation becoming ever more desperate, deluded himself into believing that whatever he wrote could easily be sold. Convinced that his English agent could serialize *Active Service* in England, he was annoyed when this did not happen; and when Pinker had trouble selling the Whilomville stories there, Crane, in letters to Reynolds in March, privately blamed Pinker for being "ass enough to think them not good enough." "I only wish I could get my English Agent to imitate your success," he told Reynolds; and, in an apparent attempt to pit one agent against the other, remarked, "I may say for your edification that you have one bitter enemy in England, Pinker by name." In the third week of July, Reynolds either quit as Crane's American agent or was fired, and Pinker became Crane's literary agent in England and America. Their relationship likewise became strained. By October, Pinker had already advanced Crane two hundred thirty pounds on stories for which he himself had not yet received payment. When Crane demanded more, an exasperated Pinker retorted, "I confess that you are becoming most alarming. You telegraphed on Friday for £20; Mrs. Crane, on Monday, makes it £50; today comes your letter making it £150, and I very much fear that your agent must be a millionaire if he is to satisfy your necessities a week hence, at this rate. Seriously, you pinch me rather tightly." The following January, Crane said that if Pinker could not send fifty pounds immediately, he would find another agent who could. "I know this is abrupt and unfair but self-preservation forces my game with you precisely as it did with Reynolds."[27]

By March 1899, Crane was telling Pinker and Reynolds that all his friends agreed with him: *Active Service* would be his "most successful book." But the assertion was self-puffery.[28] Dashing off as many as ten thousand words a week, he relied on contrived plotting and stock characterization and knew that the book was devolving into a potboiler. Crane never fully resolved what Willa Cather had termed his "double literary life" as a serious author and hack writer, a struggle he had already dramatized in *The Third Violet* and was reliving in *Active Service*.[29] When Cora suggested he could make a lot of money with a potboiler that appealed to a wide audience, he banged his fist on the table and angrily retorted, "I will write for one man" and "that man shall be myself."[30] He ended up writing a novel marred by clichés, in which the hero is victorious in a love battle and marries the heroine. After it was finished in May 1899, it was syndicated in America and published in the fall by Stokes in New York and Heinemann in London.[31]

Disappointed by the quality of the book, Crane confided to Clara Frewen "that on Saturday morning [May 13] at 11.15—after dismal sorrow and travail—there was born into an unsuspecting world a certain novel called 'Active Service,' full and complete in all its shame—79000 words.—which same is now being sent forth to the world to undermine whatever reputation for excellence I may have achieved up to this time and may heaven forgive it for being so bad." Although several reviewers appreciated the novel, H. G. Wells and others recognized that Crane was wasting his time on romantic fiction. Willa Cather derided "a book so coarse and dull and charmless": "Every page is like the next morning taste of a champagne supper, and is heavy with the smell of stale cigarettes."[32]

Active Service is at times a sentimental romance; at others, a realistic depiction of war in Greece. It begins as a parody of popular, romantic adventure fiction, such as Rudyard Kipling's novel *The Light That Failed* (1890) and Richard Harding Davis's *Soldiers of Fortune* (1897), yet ends up becoming just that sort of fiction. Its contradictions mirrored Crane's anxieties about his life and career. Whereas *The Third Violet* charted his personal and professional struggles on the verge of fame, his Greek war

novel considered them again from the perspective of an already successful writer. Like Crane, the character Rufus Coleman is a successful journalist who smokes, drinks, and gambles, whose work gets him into trouble with the police, and whose first experience of combat tempers his
cynicism as a reporter. He has, however, the financial stability that Crane
lacked. As Sunday editor of the *New York Eclipse,* with a comfortable annual salary of fifteen thousand dollars, Coleman also easily gets an unlimited expense account—starting at a thousand dollars—to report on
the Greco-Turkish War. Crane, having recently struggled with his own
expense accounts in Havana, could only wish for the economic security
of his fictional counterpart. Coleman's publisher, Sturgeon, is a stand-in
for William Randolph Hearst. In both men, egotism and tyrannical behavior were offset by brilliance and generosity; both became involved
in fomenting the Spanish-American War; and both reveled in yellow
journalism. Indeed, the fictional *Eclipse* regularly publishes sensationalized accounts of scandals, disasters, and medical oddities.

Beyond its treatment of contemporary journalism, *Active Service* also
dramatized Crane's unresolved conflicts regarding women. Like Grace
Fanhall in *The Third Violet,* Marjory Wainwright is the thoroughly conventional all-American girl that Crane courted in his correspondence
with Nellie Crouse; and like Florinda O'Connor in *The Third Violet,*
Nora Black, an actress who is also a war correspondent in Greece for the
fictional *New York Daylight* and whose name conveniently rhymes with
Cora's, represents the alluring dark figure of romance, the woman with a
"past." Crane never reconciled these contrasting views of women. The
chivalrous knight who had wooed the maidenly Nellie rushed to the
Hotel de Dreme as soon as he arrived in Jacksonville, seeking a sexually
experienced woman. Despite Mrs. Wainwright's accusation that Rufus is
merely a scoundrel chasing after Nora, rather than a worthy companion
for Marjory, Professor Wainwright is dazed by how "one man could play
two such divergent parts." Those impulses in part accounted for Crane's
incessant need to vanish when he felt pressured. His attempts to win over
Nellie ended abruptly when she finally rejected him; but given his wanderlust and her conventionality, he could not have stayed with her even if
she had accepted him. The same was true with Cora and his disappearance into Havana, which was as much an escape from her as it was an
attempt to ward off distractions in order to write. He was, as she affec-

tionately nicknamed him, her "mouse," and he extended the image in
"The Cat's March," a story written in Cuba and destroyed before publication. In the tale, Florinda O'Connor marries an artist (who likewise
figures in *The Third Violet*) and moves to a small town, where respectable
women ostracize her. The story reflected Crane's anxiety about introducing Cora to his family. The fear of entrapment in a cat-and-mouse
game, whether by a fair-haired maiden or a worldly temptress, was overwhelming for him.[33]

Active Service is also a story of escape and rescue. Professor Wainwright
flees abruptly to Greece with his family and students in order to prevent
Marjory from marrying Rufus. After the Wainwright party is trapped
behind enemy lines, Coleman envisions newspaper accounts of his rescue of Marjory and her companions "as a sort of sensational novel, to
those who would work up a gentle sympathy for the woe of others
around the table in the evenings. He saw bar-keepers and policemen taking a high gallery thrill out of this kind of romance. He saw even the
emotion among American colleges over the tragedy of a professor and
some students." "No knight ever went out to recover a lost love" as dili-
gently as Coleman: "He was on active service, an active service of the
heart, and he felt that he was a strong man ready to conquer difficulty
even as the olden heroes conquered difficulty. He imagined himself in a
way like them. He, too, had come out to fight for love with giants, drag-
ons and witches. He had never known that he could be so pleased with
that kind of a parallel."[34]

Clearly, Coleman envisions his own version of *Active Service* in which
he is a reporter of, and participant in, an adventurous love story. Yet
encoded within his psyche is Crane's own immediate past. The State
Department's involvement in the search for the Wainwright party and
Coleman's failure to retrieve cablegrams from his publisher reflect
Crane's guilt regarding attempts by Cora, friends in England, and the
American government to locate him in Havana. Similarly, Coleman's
cryptic sense of "the God whom he had in no wise heeded" and "the
most incredible tyranny of circumstance," resulting from a clash with
"the police of a most proper metropolis," alludes to Crane's rejection of
institutionalized religion, his sense of being adrift in a universe controlled by fate and circumstance, and his defense of a fallen maiden
against New York police. No well-plotted romance could have asked for

a better trio of names for three dark women: "Dora," "Cora," and "Nora." But Crane could not ultimately resolve the moral dilemma that his view created. At the end of *Active Service,* the professor supports his daughter's marriage to Coleman, the two lovers are in an idyllic setting by the sea, and Nora—the "witch" who had "bound him helpless with the power of her femininity"—is nowhere to be found. If Nora in any way represented Cora, Crane apparently wanted to drive both of them away, a situation that would have made for tense bedtime conversation in Brede Place when Cora read the novel.[35]

When Crane told Reynolds, "For business reasons I think it should be announced that Coleman simply drowns all opposition and marries Marjory," he was appealing to the kind of book that he hoped would sell: a romance ending happily for the hero and heroine. At the same time, Crane the ironist encoded an alternate story into his potboiler with two literary allusions that privately acknowledged his relationship with Cora. When Nora calls Coleman "Lochinvar," she alludes to the gallant knight in Canto 5 of Sir Walter Scott's enormously popular narrative poem *Marmion* (1808). Lochinvar rescues the maiden on her wedding day after she has been coerced by her parents into an unwanted marriage, and the two lovers escape into the unknown. Similarly, Coleman overcomes the recalcitrance of Marjory's parents after rescuing her. Crane himself had been a sort of Lochinvar who rescued Cora, stuck in an unhappy marriage to Captain Stewart, and escaped with her to what they hoped would be an idyllic home in England. In *Active Service,* the American minister to Greece, the Honorable Thomas M. Gordner of Nebraska, praises Coleman: "The rescuer! Perseus! What more fitting?" In Greek myth, Perseus rescues Andromeda from her doomed existence and marries her.[36]

Much of Crane's work had two audiences, the buying public and the private self. The act of writing became a way for Crane to explore anxieties about his own career and relationships. There are striking instances of self-portraiture in "God Rest Ye, Merry Gentlemen," a short story he was writing in February while composing *Active Service.* The story satirizes attempts to sensationalize ordinary events of the recent war in Cuba. When a reporter nicknamed "Little Nell, sometimes called the Blessed Damosel," becomes disillusioned with yellow journalism, he is berated for his inactivity and ordered back to New York. Crane satirized the profession of journalism in other Cuban war stories—"The Lone Charge of William B. Perkins," "The Revenge of the Adolphus," "Virtue in War"—and criticized correspondents who easily became distracted by trivial matters and inflated with their own self-importance.[37] Only one correspondent in the Cuban stories, Little Nell, is treated sensitively. As with Lochinvar and Perseus, Crane is alluding to two famous literary figures—Charles Dickens's Little Nell in *The Old Curiosity Shop* and the titular character in Dante Gabriel Rossetti's poem "The Blessed Damozel" (1850; revised 1856)—in order to portray his own situation. Nell, a thirteen-year-old orphan with almost no friends her age, rescues her grandfather following his mental breakdown and their eviction from his shop and escapes with him to the Midlands of England. Nell reminds one of Stephen, who at twelve was left an orphan after the death of his sister Agnes, and who years later rescued Cora and escaped with her to England.[38] Cora grieved during their separation while Stephen was in Cuba, just as the Damozel is saddened by her separation from the man she loves. Both pairs of lovers are ultimately reunited. *Active Service* was a sentimental potboiler catering to popular tastes, but it also revealed Crane's affection for Cora. The last scene of the novel, where Rufus and Marjory sit in a secluded seaside cove once inhabited by sea-maids, captures as well as anything else in Crane's writing the impassable gulf between the sexes. Marjory stares at the ocean "with woman's mystic gaze, a gaze which men at once reverence and fear since it seems to look into the deep simple heart of nature and men begin to feel that their petty wisdoms are futile to control these strange spirits, as wayward as nature and as pure as nature, wild as the play of waves, sometimes as unalterable as the mountain amid the winds; and to measure them, man must perforce use a mathematical formula."[39] The antinomies of fear versus reverence, of wayward dark woman versus pure maiden, of momentary impulse versus fixed resolve: these were a result of woman's nature, which man—or at least Stephen—simply could not fathom.

27

Brede Place Visitors, Return to Ancestry

JUNE–AUGUST 1899

WHILE CRANE WAS finishing *Active Service,* his second collection of poetry, *War Is Kind,* was published by Frederick A. Stokes in April. Heinemann deposited an advance copy of the Stokes edition in the British Museum to secure copyright, but it was not published in England. Unlike *The Black Riders and Other Lines,* it is more a collection of diverse poems than a stylistically and thematically coherent work, and more than half of them had already appeared in print. The topics include humanity's spiritual isolation in an indifferent world, best exemplified in one of Crane's most famous poems:

> A man said to the universe:
> "Sir, I exist!"
> "However," replied the universe,
> "The fact has not created in me
> "A sense of obligation."

Other poems contain some of Crane's most explicit social commentary. "A newspaper is a collection of half-injustices" reflected his distaste for yellow journalism; "The impact of a dollar upon the heart" and "The successful man has thrust himself/Through the waters of the years" satirized the worship of wealth and power in the Gilded Age. With fame as a novelist and war correspondent had come a heightened awareness of greed and injustice.

Like *Active Service, War Is Kind* failed to generate funds to offset Stephen and Cora's mounting debt and was received unfavorably. Reviewers criticized the lavish Art Nouveau illustrations accompanying the poems, as well as the publisher's choice of gray cartridge paper for the interior. One of the reviews, titled "Mr. Crane's Crazyquilting," dismissed the volume as a confusing mess: "What manner of joke Stephen Crane and his illustrator, Will Bradley, had in mind when they got up their new book has not leaked out." Willa Cather considered it an embarrassment: "This truly remarkable book is printed on dirty gray blotting paper, on each page of which is a mere dot of print over a large I of vacancy. There are seldom more than ten lines on a page, and it would be better if most of those lines were not there at all. Either Mr. Crane is insulting the public or insulting himself, or he has developed a case of atavism and is chattering the primeval nonsense of the apes. His *Black Riders,* uneven as it was, was a casket of polished masterpieces when compared with *War Is Kind.*"[1]

Crane realized that his poetry was controversial. When *The Black Riders* was published, he privately admitted that he "was getting very ably laughed at"; yet a little more than a decade after his death, critics began viewing his poetry as a forerunner of the Imagist movement led by Hilda Doolittle, Ezra Pound, and Amy Lowell in the early part of the twentieth century. Like Crane, they rebelled against the traditional conventions of prosody and wrote poetry that relied on a specific image at a particular moment, that used everyday language but avoided clichés, and that suggested rather than articulated the meaning of the poem. Years later, the poet John Berryman called "War Is Kind," the title poem in Crane's second collection, "one of the major lyrics of the century in America" and described Crane as "the important American poet between Walt Whitman and Emily Dickinson on one side, and his tardy-developing contemporaries Edwin Arlington Robinson and Robert Frost with Ezra Pound on the other." Crane wanted to be remembered as a poet and considered his "lines" more significant than *The Red Badge of Courage,* so it is fitting that posterity has granted his wish. His tombstone in Hillside,

New Jersey, reads "Stephen Crane / Poet—Author / 1871–1900," and in 1993 a memorial stone for him was added to the Poets' Corner in New York City's Cathedral of St. John the Divine.[2]

Cora had hoped that "the perfect quiet of Brede Place and the freedom from a lot of dear good people, who take his mind from his work," would allow him to work peacefully; but her actions were inconsistent, and he was plagued with constant visitors. Believing that they would inspire Stephen and increase his popularity, Cora arranged for a horse-drawn wagon to pick them up at the Rye train station, and wined and dined them lavishly—a sign that she deluded herself into believing that wealth was imminent. The result was that they gossiped about the couple upon returning home and spread the rumor that Stephen could write only when drunk. Normally he said little during literary discussions, preferring to listen to the opinions of others. But one evening a number of writers, including Robert Barr and actor and novelist A. E. W. Mason, heatedly discussed the use of intricate action in the plot of a novel. A Londoner who had made "a small fortune from his adventurous pen" boorishly exclaimed that American novelists failed to write good stories because they were "too contemplative. Without plot, nothing." Agitated, Crane retorted, "You fellows make me tired. You chatter a lot and occasionally write a book that is forgotten to-morrow. But over in little New York there sits the man with the gray bangs who can let you have a plot handicap half-way round the track and will then trot past the judges an easy quarter-mile ahead of you." When the surprised Londoner asked the name of the writer Crane was describing, he proudly replied: William Dean Howells.[3]

On another occasion, Crane, Conrad, Mason, and Karl Edwin Harriman, a correspondent from the *Detroit Free Press,* were gathered at Brede Place. They sat around the kitchen table, drinking whiskey and discussing methods of composition.[4] A violent thunderstorm foreshadowed a spirited exchange. Crane recalled Harold Frederic's "adverb screen," a window shade on which Frederic had written a long list of adverbs that could modify the verb *said.* "He was a stickler for adverbs and adjectives," he explained. "And it was his custom to go over the first draft of a manuscript and underline each adjective in red and each adverb in blue, so that with one blow of the eye he could determine whether the nuance he sought had been achieved." Conrad laughed and thought it might work, but Mason doubted its effectiveness: "The only way is to know exactly what you're going to do before you attempt anything. . . . I always make a complete outline, the frame first, so to speak, and then I paint my picture." As if energized by a sudden crack of thunder from the storm, Crane exploded, "Can't agree with you at all. . . . My belief has always been that the whole business is a matter of technique. If a man is master of his particular technique he can write a story about anything." "If that is true," snapped Mason, "write a story about those hay-cocks out there. I challenge you!" Crane accepted with a smile, then disappeared.

The next day, he arrived at dinner with a manuscript rolled up and tied with a blue ribbon. "You see," Cora joked, "Stevie has just graduated and he's brought his diploma to show you. Haven't you, Stevie?" But Crane was serious—he was determined to prove a point. After dinner, he read "Siege," the story he had written in response to the challenge. Set at Brede Place during the English Civil War (1642–1651), it depicted Oliver Cromwell's soldiers concealed behind the haystacks and awaiting the order to attack the house. Inside, terrified monks hid in the underground passageways. As soon as Crane finished, Conrad nodded in approval and Mason reached out to shake hands with Crane: "I stand corrected." Always alert to the monetary value of Stephen's writing, Cora grabbed the manuscript; but Crane, perhaps thinking that it was even worse than his hackwork, apparently destroyed it. His colleagues never doubted his brilliance. Among the new American writers, said Arthur Conan Doyle, only Crane had the "touch of true genius . . . the boy with the aspen-like nature, his big heart and little frailties."[5]

Edward Garnett vilified the interlopers at Brede Place as "the offensively vulgar set of journalists who hugged him to their Bohemian bosoms, invaded his house, and ate and drank at his expense." In September, Crane readily admitted: "I have had a lot of idiotic company all summer." Among the visitors was an acquaintance who upset Cora with talk about Stephen's health problems, prompting him to lash out uncharacteristically: "Please have the kindness to keep your mouth shut about my health in front of Mrs. Crane hereafter. She can do nothing for me and I am too old to be nursed. It is all up with me but I will not have her scared. For some funny woman's reason, she likes me. Mind this." Equally insensitive was Karl Harriman, who overstayed his welcome by spending several weeks at Brede Place, forcing Crane to escape to Brown's Hotel in London, where he could work without interruption. "You are too good-natured, Stephen," declared a protective Conrad, who was convinced that many guests were jealous of, and intimidated by, Crane's talent. Crane smiled back: he had no illusions about fame and fair-weather friends in a world in which all is vanity.[6]

Though socializing interfered with his work, Crane welcomed friends and family—"many charming people," he wrote in the Visitor's Book at Brede Place. Walter Howard, who had been with him in Cuba as a war correspondent for the *New York Journal* and who had likewise sought treatment for tuberculosis in the Adirondacks, visited in March and was treated to a tea party at the "Crown and Thistle" in nearby Northiam. In May came Elizabeth Robins, an American-born actress, playwright, and novelist living in London. Her acclaimed performances in Henrik Ibsen's plays won her the sobriquet "Ibsen's High Priestess" from one reviewer and the name "Miss Hedda Hilda Gabler Wangel Robins, christened Elizabeth" from George Bernard Shaw.[7] After Crane read her short story "A Lucky Sixpence," Cora invited her to Brede Place.[8] Later in the month, when Commander J. C. Colwell, naval attaché of the U.S. Embassy in London, was a weekend guest along with his wife, Crane asked him for help with the naval terminology in the manuscript of "The Revenge of the *Adolphus*." Elbert Hubbard was planning to visit in July, though he did not make it. Others guests included novelist Edith Evelyn Bigelow and her husband, Poultney, whom Crane may have first met at the Authors Club in New York City in 1896 and who served as a war correspondent in Cuba in 1898; and Mr. and Mrs. Lafayette Hoyt De Friese. A well-known American lawyer working in London, De Friese admired Crane's work and had been introduced to him by Harold Frederic. The Cranes occasionally visited the De Frieses at their flat in Queen Anne's Mansions.

Henry James, who lived nearby at Lamb House in Rye, Sussex, also visited Brede Place. Little is known about his relationship with Stephen, and much of what has been written about it comes from Ford Madox Ford and Thomas Beer, two unreliable sources. Ford's assertion that Crane referred to James as "Henrietta Maria" and "the old man" is doubtful, as is Beer's claim that James sent Crane five manuscripts for evaluation. Beer also says that while they were discussing literary style at a London party, a woman named Madame Zipango poured champagne into James's top hat, which Crane later salvaged; there's no evidence that this incident occurred. During the summer of 1899, Stephen and Cora occasionally went to Lamb House for tea, and James would cycle the eight miles from his home to Brede Place to visit them. The get-togethers could become occasions for amusement, as when Cora arranged a recital involving singers and five howling puppies, or for pranks and wry humor. Crane enjoyed dressing like a stable boy, in riding breeches and puttees, because he knew it would startle James; and once he asked Mark Barr (no relation to Robert Barr), a scientist whose wife was the niece of Kate Lyon, to secretly treat common firewood chemically so that when it burned in the fireplace, James would be horrified thinking that it was valuable ship timber. On another occasion, during a discussion in which Crane "was getting the better of the argument," James asked, "How old are you?" Crane said he was twenty-seven. "Humph," replied James (who was in his fifties), "prattling babe!"⁹

James was a member of the Mermaid Club at the Mermaid Inn in Rye; he sponsored Crane's admission to the club, as well as Cora's to the club's "woman's corner." The relationship between James and Crane was never close, however, because of their contrasting dispositions. The patrician James disliked vulgarity and maintained a Victorian sensibility. Although he liked Crane, he seemed uncomfortable with his bohemianism. Crane, in turn, occasionally disapproved of James's behavior. James had claimed to like Harold Frederic; but when the scandal about his two households was made public following his death, James's lack of support annoyed Crane. "He professed to be er, er, er much attached to H. and now he has shut up like a clam," Stephen confided to his brother William. Yet James admired *The Red Badge of Courage* and told Mark Barr: "We love Stephen for what he is; we admire him for what he is going to be," implying that he would become one of America's greatest writers. Crane appreciated James's fiction; and in "Concerning the English 'Academy,'" an essay published in March 1898 that satirized the attempt by the London journal *Academy* to evaluate literary merit, he had praised James's novel *What Maisie Knew* as "alive with all the art which is at the command of that great workman."¹⁰

James may have captured his feelings about the Cranes—especially his occasional discomfort around Cora—in his own fiction. He wrote *The*

Sacred Fount, a novel about an older wife who thrives to the detriment of her husband, in 1900 while Crane was slowly dying.[11] More striking is "The Great Condition," which appeared in the June 1899 issue of the *Anglo-Saxon Review.* In March 1900, James gave Crane a copy of the issue. The story is about a woman with a "past": "something or other in her life; some awkward passage, some beastly episode or accident . . . some chapter in the book difficult to read aloud—some unlucky page she'd liked to tear out."[12] Someone—most certainly Cora, after Stephen had died—excised the story from Crane's copy of the journal. James was known to have considered Cora a woman with a past, and developed "so vivid, or rather so dark, a view of her" that he ignored her pleas for financial help following Stephen's death and disregarded her when she returned to England in 1907.[13]

Another visitor whose stay at Brede Place created an intriguing possibility was Sir J. M. Barrie. He and Crane had remained friends since meeting in 1897. Apparently, it was at Brede Place that Barrie heard the story about Reverend John Williams Maher, former rector of the Church of St. George in Brede, who, unbeknownst to his congregation, had been a pirate, had lost his hand while swashbuckling, and had replaced it with a hook. Several years later, he would be transformed into Captain Hook in Barrie's most famous play, *Peter Pan; or, The Boy Who Wouldn't Grow Up* (1904).[14] Although Peter Pan was partly based on the sons of Barrie's friends Arthur and Sylvia Llewelyn Davies, Barrie might also have been inspired by his American friend. Crane never lost his love of children, mischievous pranks, and sense of play, delighting in blindman's buff in the great hall at Brede Place.[15] "You are the greatest of the boys," remarked Conrad.[16] Now, with the Whilomville stories, Stephen was imagining his own Neverland and gang of Lost Boys playing as pirates, cowboys, and Indians. His flights of imagination took him to war, the frontier, the open sea, the greatest cities, and the poorest ghettoes, and he never fully grew up. "To die will be an awfully big adventure," says Peter. Stephen would have agreed.

Of all the visitors to Brede Place, none were more welcome than Joseph Conrad and his family, who stayed more than two weeks on their first visit, in June 1899. Jessie noticed that the ravages of war in Cuba had made Stephen even more frail, but that he found comfort in strumming on his guitar and serenading his guests with an Italian love song.[17] The

Conrads' son, Borys, became infatuated with Stephen and Cora, jabbering about "the 'nice man' and the 'Annann' (which means aunties)," his father wrote, "and generally behaving like a man in the first stages of lunacy." Crane was equally amused; he delighted in watching Borys take his first steps at Brede Place. Now that he and Cora were helping to raise Barry and Héloïse Frederic, Crane had become a surrogate parent planning for the children's future. "I shall teach your boy to ride," he told Conrad, "and he must have a dog, a boy ought to have a dog." Later, he gave Borys a puppy named Soap.[18]

During the summer of 1899, Conrad and Crane bought a twenty-two-foot sailboat, *La Reine,* from Conrad's friend Captain G. F. W. Hope. The plan was that half of the time it would be kept in Folkestone for the Conrads; the other half, in Rye for the Crane household. Financial problems delayed Stephen's paying his share until late August, though Jessie, prone to bitter distortions, later claimed that he never paid his share. According to her, Cora wanted to use Stephen's half-share in the boat as payment for a supply of wood.[19]

Just as Mrs. Ruedy was leaving England in June to return to the United States, William's eldest daughter, eighteen-year-old (Mary) Helen Crane, arrived at Brede Place. Because Stephen had always liked Helen, he had invited her for an extended stay. They had corresponded while he was in England, and he had proposed that she maintain his stamp collection, stored at Asbury Park, so that they could be "partners." Yet the timing of the invitation—it was accompanied by a desperate plea to William for five hundred dollars—suggests that it might have been partly an inducement to provide a loan. William struggled with indecision about the matter. His hesitation was not meant to be punitive, for he did send the money at the end of March. A thoughtful conservative, he simply wanted to ensure that he was acting wisely before lending such a large sum to Stephen, who had already joked about his frequent borrowing of money and who had a reputation for not paying back loans.[20]

William actually came to see the invitation as a "god-send" because Helen had become rebellious at home and school, and he was convinced that she had acquired a tendency toward irresponsible behavior from her mother.[21] Separating mother and daughter and sending Helen to live with an uncle she adored, as well as with her new "aunt" Cora, seemed a feasible solution. Kate Lyon's niece Edith Richie, then nineteen, arrived in July to be a companion for Helen and stayed until January 1900. Unfortunately, problems developed quickly with Helen. Cora, who had long been drawn to the rituals and moral depth of Catholicism, asked advice from her friend Father Roe. William was willing to follow Cora's suggestion that his daughter be raised as a Catholic; but when Helen continued to misbehave, tension developed between her and Stephen. Though the details are murky, by August Helen had apparently stolen something. Soon thereafter, her father, aunt, and uncle concluded that she needed the cultivation, guidance, and regimentation of a boarding school. In September, Stephen took Helen to the Rosemont-Dézaley School in Lausanne, Switzerland, a facility that Edith Richie had attended. Further trouble developed when Helen borrowed money from schoolmates and apparently extorted more from the schoolmistress, under the pretext that it was a loan for her uncle Stephen. Though she showed modest improvement, she was back at Brede Place by April of the following year and remained there until she accompanied Cora back to America in June.

In January 1899, Crane had signed a contract with Methuen for an unspecified novel and had received an advance of one hundred pounds, but he could not start on the project because of several other writing commitments, most notably the completion of *Active Service,* which had taken longer than expected. Hoping to work quickly and make a considerable amount of money, he envisioned a story about the American Revolution. Historical novels, especially those about the war, were popular at the time. *Hugh Wynne, Free Quaker* (1897), by S. Weir Mitchell; *Janice Meredith: A Story of the American Revolution* (1899), by Paul Leicester Ford; and *Richard Carvel* (1899), by the American writer Winston Churchill, had sold several hundred thousand copies each.[22]

Crane apparently considered modeling his story on the first American war novel—*The Spy: A Tale of the Neutral Ground* (1821), by James Fenimore Cooper—and on George Bernard Shaw's play *The Man of Destiny* (1897), a parody of Napoleon's life, with intrigue, comedy, and romance. He also planned to draw on a now-lost essay by his father, "The History of an Old House," written in 1874. It is unclear whether "house" referred to a physical structure or a lineage or both, as in Edgar Allan Poe's use of the word in "The Fall of the House of Usher"; but Reverend Crane, with his intense interest in genealogy, had previously used "house" to connote "family," and the Crane family had a long tradition of using first and middle names to highlight their ancestry. When Mrs. Crane gave birth to a girl in 1865 (the baby died a year later), Reverend Crane told his father-in-law that the "house"—the family—was considering naming her after a relative in a nearby town: "[The] question of a name for her has been before the house several times, but nothing is fixed. The most prominent candidate for the honor is Mrs. Blanche, of Haverstraw. Her name is Almira B. It is proposed to omit the first syllable, & call the baby Mira Blanche, which will make the whole name signify 'Wonderful White Crane,' which is a very appropriate title, & moreover sounds like an aboriginal Indian name."[23]

Crane's notes for the projected novel reveal his interest in the essay by his father. He wanted to incorporate their ancestors into the story by "showing great influence of Crane family in carrying the revolution through." The main characters would be his Revolutionary namesake and a grandfather of Henry Fleming, the central figure in *The Red Badge of Courage.* The diction would rely on what Crane called "biblical phraseology," and the setting would be New Jersey, with some reference to Elizabethtown, where his other namesake had settled in 1665. The major dramatic scene would be the Battle of Monmouth (1778), which, like the Battle of Chancellorsville in *The Red Badge,* was fraught with irony. Although it had been a tactical victory for the British, it had been a draw strategically and proved that the Continental Army could withstand the enemy. The battle was also the source of the tale of Molly Pitcher, who risked her life to carry water to soldiers under fire. Crane had already described such bravery in his tale "A Mystery of Heroism" and had displayed it himself in Cuba. Certainly he was at least partly motivated to write the novel for money, yet the incorporation of his own lineage—especially one, if not both, of his namesakes—as well as the inclusion of a grandfather of his most famous fictional character, suggests that he conceived of the book as more than just a potboiler. With the Whilomville stories he was currently writing, he had already begun exploring his own past; and in the first one, "Lynx-Hunting" (1899), he had resurrected Henry Fleming as a character. Now, with his planned novel, he was prepared to explore his ancestral past. Just as he had tried to convince a former Syracuse professor that he had mended his ways, Crane used his return to England, the birthplace of his ancestors, to reinvent himself as a respectable citizen with a noble pedigree that would be celebrated in his next novel. He had already asserted his pride in ancestry by joining the Sons of the American Revolution in 1896; with this novel, he intended to align himself publicly with other noble folk, as well as search his family tree for psychological and ethical affinities in order to identify his place within the lineage. In *The Black Riders and Other Lines,* a defiant Crane had railed against a world in which "the sins of the fathers shall be visited upon the heads of the children, even unto the third and fourth generation of them that hate me." In his new novel, he would celebrate a family line in which the duty and honor of the fathers had been passed on to later generations. "In those old times," Crane had proudly proclaimed in 1896, "the family did it's duty."[24]

Crane requested books on the war from William, the New Jersey Historical Society, and the Frederick A. Stokes Company, with whom he signed a contract in September for the American edition of the projected historical novel. But he had overextended himself while trying to complete other projects. The contract with Methuen in January stipulated that the manuscript be at least seventy thousand words and be delivered by August 1. When he had done nothing substantial on the book by July, Methuen drew up a new contract, but Crane refused to sign it because there was no advance. Despite his initial enthusiasm for the book, he found the research too laborious and time-consuming. By autumn he had abandoned it, having written only a few brief notes.

Crane kept up a frantic pace of writing throughout 1899, but he and Cora managed to socialize away from Brede Place. At the beginning of July, along with Helen, Edith, Karl Harriman, and Mark and Mabel Barr, they attended the three-day Henley Royal Regatta, an annual rowing event on the River Thames that was one of the highlights of the social season. With its strict dress code and royal patronage, it allowed the Cranes to show their respectability and their determination to rise above daily exigencies. Determined never to let near-poverty destroy the gaiety of the moment, they insisted on paying all the expenses of their friends and arranged for a special picnic to be delivered daily by train. As extravagant as Stephen, Cora always ensured that the delivery included a surprise for him, such as baked beans. Knowing that he loved the dish, she had earlier traveled to London to the flagship of England's Army & Navy department stores simply to teach the head chef how to prepare it to Stephen's satisfaction. Stephen lost his temper only once, when a servant accidentally knocked his last box of cigarettes into the river. Calmly, Cora arranged for the shipment of another supply.[25]

Time stopped and worries disappeared for the vacationers, as they floated lazily on the river in punts gently propelled by a long pole. For Crane, though, the frailty of existence was always apparent. Passing by the ruins of the once-mighty twelfth-century Cistercian abbey in nearby Medmenham, he was reminded of his own mortality. "I've long known I shan't live to be thirty-one," he prophesied to Harriman one evening. When asked why this number, he replied, "Oh, I don't know . . . unless it's because thirty-one is thirteen, tail-end foremost, and thirteen has always really been my unlucky number." Crane the fatalist knew that life was a gamble in which the cards are stacked against you, and in the chance roll of dice you ultimately lose. He had learned this in the forests of Sullivan County and the slums of New York City, on the frontier of the West and the coasts off Florida and New Jersey, and on the battlefields of Greece and Cuba. Yet he never surrendered to his fate but continually pushed himself to the limit, living his life as he played his favorite sport of baseball: "with a sort of wild-cat fury."[26]

On July 3, Cora went to London to attend the monthly meeting of the Society of American Women, established in 1899 to promote social and cultural activities. According to its bylaws, the society admitted only "the right kind of people." An honorary member, Cora, who helped to raise money and increase membership, hoped that her participation would lead to her formally being presented at court to Queen Victoria.[27] The most prominent member was Lady Randolph Churchill, sister of Clara Frewen and mother of a future prime minister, Winston Leonard Spencer Churchill. On July 4, the Cranes attended receptions hosted by the Honorable and Mrs. Joseph H. Choate, U.S. ambassador to England, at the American Embassy and their home. Later in the month, they invited their friends from the regatta—along with A. E. W. Mason and George Lynch, a war correspondent for the *London Chronicle* whom Crane had met in Cuba—to a party at Brede Place, which was followed by tea at Henry James's house in Rye. At the end of August, Stephen and Cora helped to raise money for the District Nursing Association and the Brede village church at a party in the rectory garden. They sold knick-knacks and potted plants at a booth; George Lynch snapped photos at sixpence each; and Edith Richie, dressed as a gypsy, told fortunes and sold love potions to the "local yokels" (as Stephen called them), while a bemused James, enjoying a doughnut from the Brede Place kitchen, kept her company.[28]

By the end of summer 1899, Crane's financial and physical problems had exhausted him. Cora pleaded with Pinker for thirty-five pounds to reimburse a local wine dealer threatening a lawsuit for an unpaid bill and, worried that a beleaguered Crane might "break down," renewed a request for twenty pounds so that he could take Helen to Lausanne and rest on the Continent for a few days. His health declining rapidly, Crane confided to George Wyndham: "The clockwork is juggling badly." Having heard of sanatoriums in Germany, he asked, "What do you know about the Black Forest there?" An anal fistula, which was driving him "mad" and making him "feel like hell," confirmed that his tuberculosis was much worse.[29]

28

Trips to Europe, Final Celebration, Badenweiler

SEPTEMBER 1899–JUNE 1900

IN MID-SEPTEMBER Stephen, Cora, Helen Crane, Edith Richie, and George Lynch left for Paris. On the way, they spent the night at the home of H. G. and Catherine Wells in Folkestone, where they played the popular Victorian card game "Animal Grab." Noisy and fast-paced, it involved making the correct animal sound as pictures of animals were shown. Thoughts of financial woes disappeared as Stephen roared like a lion, Cora twittered like a canary, and H. G. barked like a dog. Self-deprecating humor was a tonic that reinvigorated their souls. Once, after a late-night snack in the Brede Place kitchen, Crane, toasting fork in hand, conducted an orchestra made up of the Wellses and other guests playing tissue-covered combs. On another occasion, Wells mentioned that he and his wife had recently discovered a new delight, American corn, which they had grown themselves. "How did you cook it," inquired Crane. "Cook it! We didn't cook it," replied Wells. "We cut it when it was six inches high, and ate it for salad. Wasn't that right?"[1]

On the train to Paris, Lynch angered Crane when he popped the cork of a bottle of soda water into a sleeping Frenchman's open mouth. And late on the first night, at the Hôtel Louis le Grand, Crane was awakened by the delivery of a note: the "Wild Irishman" (Edith's epithet for Lynch) was asking Crane to be his second in a duel. Thinking that this was simply another of Lynch's pranks, Stephen ignored the request. The next morning he discovered that there had indeed been a duel: Lynch had wounded his opponent in the arm—and had then become his friend.[2]

While Cora and Edith stayed in Paris and Lynch went off on his own, Stephen took Helen to her boarding school in Lausanne. On his return, an energized Crane began writing stories and, along with Cora and Edith, dined with friends and shared the Parisians' *joie de vivre;* but a longing for their dogs, which had been regularly receiving penny candy mailed to them from Paris, drove Stephen and Cora back to Brede Place. Their problems were waiting for them, along with their dogs. Stephen came down with "a slight attack of Cuban fever" that left him feeling "seedy" (he'd had a bout of the same fever only a few days before in Paris), and he continued to have difficulties with Stokes regarding the manuscript for *Wounds in the Rain,* a collection of Cuban war stories. While in New York City in July 1898, he had signed a contract for the book, and had later announced that publication would take place in the spring of 1899; but he overestimated how quickly he could work, for the volume was not published until September 1900.[3]

Crane attempted to cancel the contract when Stokes refused to send him an advance on royalties. In September 1899 he told the publisher that he had completed the manuscript and that he believed he was then entitled to the agreed-upon advance of one thousand dollars; but Stokes reiterated that the sum would be paid only upon receipt of the manuscript. Crane's constant barrage of letters and cablegrams demanding advance payments prompted a stern rebuke from his publisher in September:

> We note your reference to our distrustfulness.
>
> This is hardly just. The difficulty is not one of confidence or trust, but one of adhering to an agreement already made. . . .
>
> You do not quite seem to appreciate, also, the fact that we have no easy task before us in trying to rehabilitate the commercial standing of your work in book form.
>
> If we should show you quotations from the letters of our traveling salesmen, showing that for some reason or other the leading houses in the trade throughout the country have a strong prejudice against you and your work, you would we think have a little more consideration for us.
>
> We do not care to discuss the reasons for this prejudice, and whether it

is just or unjust, except that it is probably due to the comparative failure of your books since "The Red Badge of Courage" and to newspaper attacks on you, with which the writer certainly has no sympathy.

The "prejudice" was clear in a bit of doggerel that had appeared in the *Chicago Daily Tribune:* "The gayety of the nations / Would suffer not a whit / And life would be worth living still / If Stephen Crane would quit."[4]

When Crane complained to Robert Barr about Stokes's admonition, he expected him to listen supportively; but after studying the correspondence between author and publisher, Barr was candid:

> I have read both your letter and Stokes' over three or four times to get the hang of the thing, and this is my understanding of it.
>
> 1. Crane and Stokes. (Mutually agreeing.) £100 paid on receipt of copy.
> 2. Crane. (Cabling.) "Book finished. Will you cable money."
> 3. Stokes. (Cabling.) "Yes on receipt of completed Ms."
> 4. S Crane. (Cabling.) "I withdraw the book."
> 5. Stokes (Writing.) "We stand by the London convention of 1884" [This was a treaty that governed relations between Great Britain and the South African Republic until 1899].
> 6. BLOODY WAR.

Barr knew that Crane was being unreasonable: "You are all right when you stick to the pen, and are apt to be all wrong when you meddle with business." He then urged Crane to let James Pinker handle all of his business communications. "Write, write, write, anything but business letters." After Crane entrusted his negotiations to his literary agent, Stokes yielded on the question of an advance for *Wounds in the Rain;* but the decision did not solve Crane's problems. By moving to England, Crane had hoped to start a new life, but, as Stokes had cautioned him, his personal affairs and his failure to repeat the commercial success of *The Red Badge* were plaguing his career. An increasingly frenetic pace of writing also left him, as Wells had remarked, "altogether out of control." He misplaced manuscripts, forgot about stories he had already written, and desperately turned to anything for "sure quick money." Deceiving himself, he boasted to Pinker, "I can go all over the place and write fiction about almost anything."[5]

In September–October 1899, he heavily mined a book by his maternal grandfather, George Peck—*Wyoming: Its History, Stirring Incidents, and Romantic Adventures* (1858)—and cranked out three stories about a Revolutionary battle that had taken place in Pennsylvania's Wyoming Valley on July 3, 1778, when several hundred patriots had been massacred. By early November, he had also finished four stories about an infantry regiment in a war between imaginary countries called Spitzbergen and Rostina. Crane named the fictional Colonel Sponge after one of his dogs, and Major General Richie after Edith Richie, who had transcribed at least one of the stories from Crane's dictation. In the fall, Crane also began working on a series of eight articles about famous battles—a series that the editor of *Lippincott's Magazine* had requested in April. Crane had at first declined; he did not consider himself a historian and lacked the time to do research. But his financial problems forced him to reconsider, and in July he had agreed to write the articles, which would be published in the magazine from March to November 1900, then later in the collected volume *Great Battles of the World*. Unknown to Lippincott, Kate Lyon, ever indebted to the Cranes for their aid following Harold Frederic's death, helped with the project. She researched particular battles and transcribed lengthy quotations from history texts; Crane would then write connecting paragraphs for the extracts. As his health declined, she became increasingly involved in writing the articles.

Amid all the hackwork, Crane produced two masterpieces that fall. When Lady Randolph Churchill asked for a contribution to her new quarterly, the *Anglo-Saxon Review,* he sent "War Memories," a semi-autobiographical account of his experiences in Cuba during the spring and summer of 1898. He initially wrote it without expecting a fee, but she paid him after learning of his financial problems. Unlike other accounts of the war, which focused on factual summaries of military details and major events, Crane presented impressionistic accounts of his own experience of combat. As experimental stylistically as *The Red Badge of Courage,* "War Memories" blurs the line between fact and fiction. It dramatizes an author's efforts to make sense of himself and his struggles with ontological and linguistic questions about the nature of reality.

Equally stunning is one of the Spitzbergen stories, "The Upturned Face." With lean, understated prose and a reliance on aural and tactile imagery rather than on plot, setting, and visual imagery, the tale, like "War Memories," demonstrates that Crane could still be innovative stylistically. He knew it was a gem. "I will not disguise from you that I am wonderfully keen on this small bit of 1500 words," he told Pinker. "It is so good—for me—that I would almost sacrifice it to the best magazine in England rather than see it appear in the best paying magazine."[6]

In the midst of incessant writing, Crane felt the urge to become a war correspondent again. In early October 1899, tension between British South Africa and two independent Boer republics, the South African Republic (Transvaal Republic) and the Orange Free State, erupted into the Second Boer War (1899–1902). As a gesture of friendship between England and America, the Society of American Women in London, under the leadership of Lady Churchill, funded the hospital ship *Maine,* named after the American battleship sunk during the Spanish-American War, to aid sick and wounded soldiers and refugees in South Africa. Though financial problems prevented the Cranes from contributing money to the project, they supported the British cause. The following February, they lent their gramophone for a concert at the Brede village school aimed at raising money for a hospital fund for the Imperial Yeomanry, a British voluntary cavalry regiment that fought in the war. At the end of September, Crane applied for a visa as a correspondent. The *New York Journal* was interested in his proposal to write political sketches about the war from Saint Helena, the barren island in the South Atlantic to which Napoleon had been exiled after Waterloo and that was now the site of a Boer prison. He also considered going to Gibraltar in February and staying till summer.

Cora, however, was worried about Stephen's frail health and probably feared that he might once again disappear, as he had in Havana. In a photo of Crane taken around the time he was considering leaving for South Africa, a snapshot of Cora on his desk has been turned—perhaps by her—toward the camera, as though to ward off potential rival lovers (see Figure 18). After Pinker convinced him to stay in England, Cora privately expressed her relief: "I am so glad that you wrote him not to go to the Transvaal. His health is not fit for it." In a postscript, she added: "Please dont let Mr. Crane know I've said a word against the Transvaal."[7]

But the following April, after doctors recommended that Stephen take a sea voyage for his health, Cora asked Pinker to get an English newspaper to finance a month-long stay on Saint Helena for her and Stephen, so that he could write articles and interview the South African Republic's General Piet Cronjé, who was incarcerated there. Crane's declining health, however, prevented any departure from England.

International support for the Boers encouraged a growing Anglophobia, and from January to March 1900, Crane wrote a series of articles about the war for the *New York Journal*. He was characteristically ambivalent about British imperialism. Typically apolitical, he tended to avoid partisan issues, but he could be cynical about the European powers and their expansionist policies, as he had been about Great Britain in "A Foreign Policy in Three Glimpses" (1891 or 1892) and about Germany in "The Blood of the Martyr" (1898). When the poet William Watson was accused by the British press of being unpatriotic for opposing British imperialism in South Africa, Crane publicly defended him. One can love one's country, Crane argued, yet not support all of its policies. In his defense of Watson, Crane hinted that actions by the American Anti-Imperialist League might have contributed to the death of American soldiers in the Philippines, but he opposed the Anglo-Saxon Christian imperialism popularized by American clergyman Josiah Strong in his influential book *Our Country: Its Possible Future and Its Present Crisis* (1885).

Crane's decision to race off as a Boer correspondent in the midst of various projects typified his impulsive nature. When the assignment did not immediately materialize in early October, he announced at breakfast: "Edith has never been to Ireland. Let's go to Ireland."[8] Ostensibly, he wanted to gather local color for his next novel, *The O'Ruddy*, but only its opening paragraphs are set there. After three days in London being fêted by friends, Stephen, Cora, and Edith traveled from Cork to Ballydehob, Skibbereen, Schull, Bantry, and Glengariff, staying at quaint country inns and getting to know the local residents, until they started to miss the dogs and decided to head back to Brede Place.

Despite the constant pressures of penury and frail health, Crane never lost his sense of play. With the turn of the century at hand, he began planning an elaborate three-day Christmas party for fifty to sixty people, featuring a new play to be premiered at the Brede schoolhouse.[9] Envisioning it as a musical farce about the ghost of Sir Goddard Oxenbridge,

Crane asked literary friends—Robert Barr, Joseph Conrad, George Gissing, H. Rider Haggard, Henry James, H. B. Marriott Watson, A. E. W. Mason, Edwin Pugh, and H. G. Wells—to participate in its creation by contributing a scene, a sentence, a phrase, or just a word. Among the contributions that this "distinguished rabble" made to "this crime" were an epigram by Conrad ("This is a jolly cold world"); a joke by Gissing ("He died of an indignity caught in running after his hat down Piccadilly"); and a puzzle by Marriott Watson consisting of five words that were written on individual pieces of paper pasted on his letter and that, when deciphered, read, "Most publishers are d—d fools."[10]

Crane incorporated the passages into his own "awful rubbish" and, with Cora's aid, composed a scenario that included "music frankly stolen from very venerable comic operas such as 'The Mikado' and 'Pinafore.'" Blurring the fictional worlds of his friends, Crane also borrowed characters from their novels. From Wells's *Island of Doctor Moreau* came Dr. Moreau; his son, Peter Quint Prodmore Moreau, combined Peter Quint from James's *The Turn of the Screw* and Prodmore from James's tale "Covering End," as well as possibly a character from Conrad's *Nigger of the "Narcissus."* Suburbia was inspired by Edwin Pugh's *Street in Suburbia,* and Tony Drunn was taken from Pugh's *Tony Drum: A Cockney Boy.* Miranda was derived from Mason's *Miranda of the Balcony* and Marriott Watson's *Heart of Miranda.* Even Rufus Coleman from *Active Service* made a guest appearance.[11]

While Stephen hastily completed the script and arranged for a carpenter to remodel the stage, Edith painted scenery. Cora mailed invitations, engaged extra servants, hired a three-piece orchestra, rented sleeping cots, and leased an omnibus to transport guests between the train station and Brede Place. Once the script was finished, Cora and Edith quickly typed up copies, then helped to decorate the manor's large hall with holly, greenery, and dozens of candles in iron sconces made just for the formal ball that would culminate the festivities. Refusing to let frail health and near-bankruptcy put a damper on the celebration, the ever-impractical Stephen and Cora convinced themselves that the twentieth century would be the dawn of a happier era in their lives. He set his play in the bound-to-be-brighter year 1950. Cora investigated whether their ancestry was related to British royalty; establishing a lineage would erase their past and ease their acceptance into high society, especially for a bohemian turned lord of the manor. "Wealth makes less difference here than in any country in the world," Cora later wrote. "But *class* distinction makes a difference."[12]

On December 25, they hosted a traditional American Christmas dinner for Edith, her parents, the Mark Barrs, and A. E. W. Mason, Stephen's chief collaborator in the farce as well as its lead actor, director, and stage manager. Crane was fascinated by the monocle that Mason wore and seemingly never removed from morning to night. "If I could wear a monocle the way Mason does," joked Crane, "I'd wear *two.*" Mason must have told the others about an incident that had occurred only hours earlier. While passing through Rye, he had informed Henry James that he was headed for the holiday festivities at Brede Place, and James had drolly warned him to be wary of falling prey to any actresses there: "Some of those poor wantons have a certain haggard grace."[13]

Guests and cast members began arriving on December 26. The next day, the cast rehearsed briefly in the morning, then in the evening held a dress rehearsal for the village children in the Brede schoolhouse. The principal, and only, performance of the play—titled *The Ghost*—took place there on the evening of December 28. Newspaper reviews suggesting that it was an original musical comedy written by distinguished authors prompted Sir Herbert Beerbohm Tree, a leading actor-manager in English theater, to inquire whether it could be performed after *A Midsummer Night's Dream* at Her Majesty's Theatre in London. Mason quickly told him no.

On the evening of December 29, the three-day celebration climaxed with a gala ball replete with elegant waltzes, a "quadrille of the Lancers," a country barn dance, and a game devised by H. G. Wells that consisted of racing on broomsticks. The guests reveled late every night throughout their stay, then would feast the next morning on a brunch of bacon, eggs, sweet potatoes, and beer. The weather, unfortunately, was not cooperative. Snow, severe thunderstorms, and icy roads prevented many local residents from seeing *The Ghost* and made travel to Brede Place hazardous. The omnibus transporting guests often got stuck in the mud, forcing them to get out and push. Crane himself seemed out of sorts. When he tried to teach some of the men poker, they chatted idly instead of paying close attention to the rules. "In any decent saloon in America," he complained, "you'd be shot for talking like that at poker." Abruptly he left, sulking. During the ball, he sat silently in a corner of the huge fireplace in the hall, bewildered by the frenetic pace of his life. He knew he was dying. After everyone had gone to bed, he tried unsuccessfully to hide from Cora the fact that he had just had a severe lung hemorrhage. Distraught, she awakened Wells, who, having once been diagnosed with tuberculosis, understood the gravity of the situation and cycled seven miles in freezing rain to bring the local physician, Dr. Ernest B. Skinner.[14]

Bedridden, Crane began the new year by wishing Hugh Frewen (Moreton and Clara's son) "a very shining 1900."[15] Crane was now in print more than at any other time in his life. *Active Service* and *The Monster and Other Stories* had come out in late 1899. Early in the new year, he published a series of newspaper articles about South Africa and some shorter magazine pieces that included the start of the Spitzbergen tales, the "Great Battles of the World" series, and additional Whilomville stories. Crane returned to working on his untitled Irish romance (which would eventually become *The O'Ruddy*) and agreed to write another series of short stories, set in New York City and featuring little Cora, the resourceful, mischievous child in the Whilomville stories. Cora herself was excited about planning a hedge maze, planting trees and shrubs, and recording future guests in a new Visitor's Book. At the beginning of February, Thomas Parkin, a local county magistrate and bibliophile, hosted a luncheon honoring the Cranes at his home. In short, Stephen and Cora yearned for a fresh start.

But with the new year came old worries. Crane sat quietly at the luncheon. He had, one guest observed, "that white, worn-out, restless look betokening complete nervous exhaustion" and "moved about uneasily as if in search of something he could not find." Debts from their recent Christmas celebration had impoverished them even more, checks had bounced at their Oxted bank, and their account at a London bank was overdrawn. According to Ford Madox Ford, when Stephen knew that the tax collector was coming on January 1, he hid in a nearby house because he mistakenly thought that failure to pay one's taxes on New Year's Day would result in a prison sentence. Cora insisted to Pinker that they needed at least one hundred fifty pounds to prevent them from "going smash." Could he not, she implored, immediately get a hundred-pound advance from Methuen on the Irish romance and another two hundred on the next book? She was being completely unrealistic. Stephen had not completed his Irish romance, and she was already expecting an advance on a book he hadn't even conceived yet. She also convinced herself that Pinker could easily sell a thousand of Crane's short stories if he had them. Though an ever-resourceful Pinker arranged for some payment, there was never enough to ward off creditors.[16]

Nothing more dramatically embodies the misfortune that the couple experienced than three short stories written during their last few months together—one by Cora, one by Stephen, and one a joint effort. Cora's "Cowardice" is a gothic story based on the Brede ghost and set at the fictional Shene Place, a fourteenth-century house in Sussex. Clearly modeled after Brede Place, it takes its name from the royal residence of Sheen in Surrey, where Edward III died in 1377. Construction on Brede Place had begun during his reign six years earlier. "Cowardice" also expresses Cora's deeply felt anxieties about her relationship with Stephen. A penniless artist, overwhelmed by hectic city life, escapes to rural Sussex to ease his "load of ill health and despondency" and meets at Shene Place a widow and her son, who is suffering from tropical fever. The artist cannot ultimately avoid "the misery of heartbreak" and "that great human cry of loneliness," and finds "only desolation" there.[17] It is unclear when Cora composed the story—perhaps in late 1899—but it is disturbingly autobiographical. Like the impoverished artist, Stephen and Cora had fled to Brede Place for a new beginning. They had hoped to cure their insolvency and Crane's ill health. Three years earlier, in Jacksonville, Crane had reminded her that relationships, like encounters between ships that pass in the night, are fleeting. "Cowardice" was her acknowledgment of this fact.

Crane's obsession with rescue and entrapment had long haunted him. In his sketch "When Every One Is Panic Stricken" (1894), a graphic account of an imaginary fire, a policeman runs into a New York City tenement building to rescue a baby. There is no mention of whether he succeeds. The scene is repeated in "The Veteran" (1896), when a character known only as "the Swede" loses his life trying to rescue colts from a burning barn, and in "The Monster" (1897), when Henry Johnson is disfigured in the act of saving Jimmie Trescott from a blazing house. Nowhere is the sense of confinement more hauntingly captured than in "Manacled," a short story written in late 1899 and based on a nightmare Crane had had several months earlier. An actor in prison garb, handcuffs, and leg irons is abandoned onstage after a fire breaks out in a theater. The story parodies melodrama and blurs reality and fantasy; but the actor's futile attempt to escape, the chaotic flight of the audience, and a policeman's frantic sounding of the alarm are depicted graphically. No image in Crane's writing is more frequent than that of fire. Lamps, stoves, campfires, and burning buildings, as well as metaphorical renderings of a blaze, can intensify a setting and dramatize a scene; but they also convey Crane's long-standing awareness that he was burning out and powerless to change his fate. In "A Man and Some Others," a story that Crane wrote during the summer of 1896 and that he considered one of his best works, the flames of a campfire "capered merrily through its mesquit branches, filling the silence with the fire chorus, an ancient melody which surely bears the message of the inconsequence of individual tragedy." He was writing about the insignificance of humankind. The central figure in "Manacled" was actually himself, nameless because of his own inconsequentiality in the face of fate and chance. On one occasion, he deliberately evoked the feeling of imprisonment by having Cora and Edith tie up his ankles and wrists as he struggled to escape. It is no coincidence that he arranged to have a scarlet carpet, walls, and ceiling in his study at Brede Place: they mirrored the fiery intensity of his genius.[18]

Crane's sense of imprisonment resurfaced in the early spring of 1900 with "The Squire's Madness." After ten years of "incomprehensible wandering," a poet settles down in "a manor-house in Sussex" named "Oldrestham" (as in "old rest home"). He closets himself in his study, available only to his wife and dogs, and becomes obsessed with death and insanity as he struggles, and fails, to complete a poem about a woman who poisons her lover. After his wife convinces him to see a brain specialist, the doctor (named "Redmond," a reminder of Crane's passion for scarlet) concludes that the wife, not the husband, is mad: "Mad as a Hatter!"[19]

Although the story parodies gothic fiction, it was chillingly autobiographical, with its obvious references to Brede Place and its description of a sickly, emaciated squire with "burning" eyes. For about ten years— the length of Crane's professional career, starting with his work for Townley in Asbury Park—he, too, had been wandering through life. He realized that his attempt to start life anew at Brede Place had failed. Ill health had finally beaten him. His increasing weakness forced him to dictate part of "The Squire's Madness," which Cora completed following his death. He had instructed her on how to finish it, and she composed almost the entire second half. Was she merely following his outline, or was she tacitly acknowledging that the strong personality that had initially drawn Crane to her might have ultimately poisoned his psyche? In the part of the story written by Cora, Grace Linton is the "antithesis" of her husband. In a moment of denial, Cora hid the truth. She and Stephen were much alike. Both were creative, caring, and playful, as well as rebellious, impulsive, and irresponsible. Just as she had fled Jacksonville without paying all her bills, he had likewise fled Havana leaving an unpaid bill. Both had conflicted personalities; they rejected the norms of society, yet wanted to be part of it. Crane was the bohemian squire; she, the lavish hostess and "Auntie" Cora. Each was attracted to the other's rebellious, even reckless lifestyle, but it strained their relationship. Crane had fled to Cuba partly to escape the confinement he felt Cora imposed on him, and had hidden in Havana because he feared she was threatening his literary output and his double life. As much as Clara and Moreton Frewen liked Cora, they occasionally became exasperated with her extreme behavior. "She was what my father called 'a terror'—the worst type of bossing American woman," their daughter Clare remembered in later years. "She overpowered & overshadowed and overlaid Crane and every one else in her vicinity!! How Crane could stand her . . ."[20]

On March 31, Cora left for Paris to meet Helen, who, against her parents' wishes, had dropped out of school in Lausanne. Two hours after Cora's departure, Stephen suffered the first of two massive hemorrhages. He wanted to protect her from the distressing news; but Vernall, the housekeeper and cook, secretly wired her on April 3. As soon as Cora received the telegram, she and Helen immediately caught the night boat across the English Channel. With the help of the American Embassy, friends arranged for medical experts to come immediately to Brede Place: Dr. Thomas J. Maclagan, a well-known lung specialist in London, and a nurse. Maclagan's guarded optimism about Crane's condition momentarily cheered Cora, but she implored Pinker to deposit fifty pounds for the bill in Stephen's bank account in order to prevent another overdraft.[21]

During the next two months, they attempted to salvage Crane's career and health and to fend off bankruptcy from growing medical bills. Despite the earlier break with Reynolds, Crane had begun sending him manuscripts again, hoping that he could place them in the American market. Reynolds had no luck trying to sell an unfinished and untitled two-act comic play set on a sugar plantation toward the close of the Cuban War, but he eventually sold Crane's article "The Great Boer Trek" for a hundred dollars, twice the amount Crane had requested, and offered to make an advance payment on stories or articles before they were sold. Crane was less fortunate with Methuen, who declined to pay any further advance on *The O'Ruddy*. After Pinker failed to persuade Tillotson's, an English newspaper syndicate, to serialize the romance, he approached *McClure's Magazine;* but when *McClure's* learned that Stokes already had book rights to it, they offered only two hundred fifty pounds, which Pinker rejected because the amount was so small, and the novel did not appear serially in America. Attempts at getting advances from other publishers or newspapers proved futile. Crane, the most innovative American writer of the 1890s, was now destitute in pocket and spirit.

By the time Edwin Pugh came to stay at Brede Place, Stephen was already quite ill. Yet he had not lost his wry sense of humor. Greeting his guest at the train station, Crane remarked, "This looks like Edwin Pugh." And on the ride back in the carriage, he hummed a refrain:

I'll be there, I'll be there!
When the Hully Gee is calling I'll be there—
Sure as you're born!

This was a paraphrase of a typical Methodist hymn, such as Sunday-school teacher James M. Black's popular "When the Roll Is Called Up Yonder" (1893), in which, on Judgment Day, when Hully Gee (slang for "Holy Jesus") is calling, the singer says, "I'll be there." A rebel against religious indoctrination who recognized humanity's insignificance in the universe, Crane longed to believe that life was ultimately meaningful. In 1899, he began collecting his ancestors' theological volumes, which he proudly showed to visitors. He enjoyed reading at least two of them: his cousin Jonathan K. Peck's *Luther Peck and His Five Sons* (1897) and their great-uncle J. T. Peck's *The Seven Wonders of the New World* (1885), which appealed to his current longing for family and cosmic order.[22] "Eternity's an entr'acte," he wrote to Pugh, an entr'acte being the musical interval between two acts of a play or opera. Crane anticipated that eternity might simply be an interval before the next phase of his existence.[23]

Even with his philosophical musings, Crane remained playfully ironic. In the refrain, he was also identifying with Richard Outcault's Yellow Kid, whose ghetto argot included the expression "Hully Gee." Like the Kid, Crane affected slang for comic effect and viewed himself as an outcast victimized by newspapers. Just as the Kid's fate was shaped by the crass commercialism that Outcault originally lampooned, Crane's journalistic career suffered from the fallout after he had rescued a fellow pariah, Dora Clark, and from the actions of insensitive editors, one of whom had fired him in response to false accusations of shoddy reporting in Cuba.

As spring approached, Crane rested outside on sunny days. Though he had stopped hemorrhaging, he grew weaker and suffered miserably from a rectal abscess. Most likely at his request, doctors periodically gave Cora slightly encouraging reports about his condition in order to keep her from worrying. She protected him by handling all of his correspondence and by shielding him from distressing realities—such as the lack of advances on his unwritten work and her plan to sublet Brede Place to ease their financial burden. As sleepless nights, anxiety, and the fear of losing Stephen drained Cora emotionally and physically, her letters expressed a range of emotions, from panic to hope; they were variously coherent, then rambling. "*What* is the matter with Stephen?" a concerned Kate Lyon asked. "I could not tell from your letter." Cora convinced herself that he was getting along well and clung to what turned out to be tenuous diagnoses of his condition. According to her, one doctor announced that Crane's right lung was "entirely unaffected"; another, that he could be back to work again in three weeks if he did not hemorrhage for another ten days: "The trouble seems only superficial; not deeply rooted." Ocean air would strengthen him, pronounced one doctor, while another urged that he not be moved from Brede Place for at least two months.[24]

Crane knew that death was imminent and agreed to travel to a sanatorium only to ease Cora's anguish. He also agreed to her proposal that a bazaar be held at Brede Place in August to raise money for the families of Boer War soldiers—and to give her something to do. In the meantime, he revised the will he had sent to William in 1896 from Jacksonville, making his "dear wife Cora Howorth Crane" sole beneficiary of his estate until her death or remarriage.[25] If the latter, one-half of the estate would go to Stephen's namesake, Edmund's son, born a few weeks earlier, and the other half would be divided equally between Edmund and William.

Crane may have had anxieties about Cora in their relationship, but he expressed his loyalty to her in *The O'Ruddy*. He chose to draw on a popular genre, the historical romance, at least partly to make money to pay his debts. Though he completed only about two-thirds of the book, he was still dictating portions to Cora two days before his death, and his manuscript and notes suggested a final solution to his uncertainty about her. Crane recreated the free-roaming frontier spirit of his youth in Thomas O'Ruddy, who, after his adventures, marries his sweetheart in the chapel at "Brede Place" and raises a family. Along the way, he defeats the villain, "black Forister," in a duel, a hopeful prediction that Crane would conquer his own illness in the Black Forest of Germany. Robert Barr eventually agreed to write the last eight of the twenty-five chapters in the romance, and Crane, days before his death, instructed him on how to do this. No record exists of precisely what Crane said, but he did tell Barr that the story should end at Brede Place. Family life at the actual manor suggested more. With a household that included two of Kate Lyon's children, Helen Crane, and Edith Richie (who stayed there until January 1900), Stephen and Cora were raising a family as husband and wife while he was writing *The O'Ruddy*. If the romance, his first extended piece of fiction using a first-person point of view, expressed a wish for domesticity following a life of adventure, then his dedication for the book implied that he was ready to acknowledge Cora as his spouse: "May—1900 / Brede   Place / Sussex / England / To / My   Wife / Stephen Crane."[26] In an example of life imitating art, Crane, like Jack Potter in "The Bride Comes to Yellow Sky," had gone away to find a bride but was finally ready to cast off his boyhood ways and bring her home. Barr fulfilled Crane's wish at the end of the romance. After Father Donovan presides over the marriage of Thomas O'Ruddy and Lady Mary in the Brede Place chapel, the couple raise seven children. It "is difficult to write with Patrick and little Mary and Terence and Kathleen and Michael and Bridget and Donovan playing about me and asking questions," the O'Ruddy acknowledges, "but I would not have the darlings sent from the room for all the writings there is in the world."[27]

At the end of April, Cora convinced herself that Crane was out of serious danger. Despite recurring problems with the abscess and fever (brought on by his bout with malaria in Cuba), she rejoiced to H. G. Wells that the "lung trouble seems over!" After Stephen suffered a relapse a few days later, however, the doctors insisted he needed to leave England's damp climate immediately. William could not help him financially anymore; instead, he proposed that Cora and his brother come to Port Jervis and let family care for them. Upon hearing of Crane's physical and financial problems, Eben Alexander, U.S. ambassador to Greece, who had befriended the couple in 1897 and to whom Crane had dedicated *Active Service,* invited them to live with his family at the University of North Carolina, Chapel Hill, where he had returned as a professor of Greek: "There is absolutely nothing that either of you will have to spend a cent for. . . . We shall be as glad to have you as if you were our own children." Sadly, the letter did not arrive until after Crane's death. The offer would have been difficult to accept, in any case. Given his condition, a long sea voyage was impractical. Cora found an alternative: she hurriedly arranged a trip to Badenweiler, in the Black Forest. Beatrice Harraden's *Ships That Pass in the Night* had pointed the way. The character Robert Allitsen travels from England to die in the sanatorium in Petershof, Switzerland, where he and Bernardine met; similarly, Stephen and Cora were headed to nearby Badenweiler. Cora must have felt betrayed by fate: when she was six years old, her father, at the age of thirty-five, had likewise died from tuberculosis.[28]

Moreton Frewen, to whom Crane had dedicated *Wounds in the Rain* two weeks earlier, appealed to wealthy friends like J. P. Morgan, Sr., and Joseph Pulitzer. Frewen, who raised most of the funds for Crane's trip (and for the return of his body to the United States), established a Stephen Crane Testimonial Fund, the proceeds of which were collected by Lady Randolph Churchill. Among others, Andrew Carnegie immediately donated fifty pounds. On May 8, Cora wrote to James Pinker with details about the trip and an impossible plea for around two hundred pounds to finance it. She still hoped that the trip would allow Stephen "to get well & live for years." Yet her telegram on the same day to John

Hay at the War Department in Washington revealed the chilling reality: "Last hope Stephen Cranes life Blackforest immediately few hundreds need can you help."[29]

The hastily assembled travel plans involved transporting Crane on an air bed and taking a special train car to Dover. After Stephen had rested there for a week, he and Cora would take a steamer to Calais en route to Badenweiler. Dr. Otto Walther, a lung specialist from nearby Nordrach, had developed the "Nordrach cure," a treatment of rest coordinated with mild exercise, overfeeding, and fresh air. On May 15, Stephen and Cora with their entourage—a servant, Richard Heather; Dr. Skinner; two nurses; Helen Crane; and the dog Sponge, to comfort Stephen—arrived at the Lord Warden Hotel in Dover. Unable to afford the amenities at the hotel, Cora skipped meals so that others could eat.

During the next few days, friends came to pay Stephen what they resisted admitting would be their last respects. The Conrads arrived on May 16; and while Jessie and Borys comforted Cora, Joseph visited his beloved friend. The next day came Wells. Like Conrad, he struggled to remain positive while silently being shocked by Crane's emaciated condition. Stephen was too wasted to say more than a passing word. The physical description on his four passports reveals how quickly he had deteriorated. In November 1896 his complexion had been "light"; two months later, it had been "clear"; by April 1898, it had been "medium"; scarcely more than a year later, it was "dark." On May 19, Robert Barr and aspiring novelist Stewart Edward White arrived; but because Stephen was too sick to see them, they spent the evening reading the manuscript of *The O'Ruddy*. The following day, a slightly improved Crane joked with his visitors in a whisper. Berating his physician for the injunction against smoking, Crane delighted in caressing the bowl of his pipe and smelling the fragrance of Barr's cigarette, which Crane had urged him to light. Before their visit, Cora and Dr. Skinner had implored them to agree to anything that Crane requested. Thus, when he asked Barr to finish the manuscript, Barr was not surprised. Shortly before coming to Dover, Barr had received a letter and a telegram from Cora urging him to complete it. Now, he agreed; though when Crane inferred his hesitancy about finishing someone else's work, he playfully suggested that Barr split the last sentence in the manuscript in half, then start there: "They'll all think you began with a new chapter, so you can defy them to point out the junction."[30] (After Crane's death, Barr would reconsider his promise and suggest that White or Cora herself complete the manuscript. Both would decline; likewise H. B. Marriott Watson and Rudyard Kipling. A. E. W. Mason would hold the manuscript for two years without working on it. At last, feeling a sense of obligation to his late friend, Barr would finish it in 1903.)

Barr promised to visit Crane in the Black Forest in a few weeks, but Crane knew the assurance was intended simply to cheer him up. Wrapped in blankets and sitting before an open window, as he had been since arriving at the hotel, he stared wistfully at the tranquil sea, the calm evening sky, and the occasional ship passing in the night. He was aware that he, too, would soon be crossing from one port of life to the next. He whispered to Barr: "Robert, when you come to the hedge—that we must all go over—it isn't bad. You feel sleepy—and—you don't care. Just a little dreamy curiosity—which world you're really in—that's all." And to Conrad: "I am tired. Give my love to your wife and child." Alone with his wife, Joseph lamented, "It is the end, Jess. He knows it is all useless. He goes only to please Cora, and he would rather have died at home!"[31]

The Crane party crossed the English Channel to Calais on May 24. They stopped to rest for two or three days in Basel, Switzerland, at Les Trois Rois, one of Europe's oldest and most elegant hotels, overlooking the Rhine. The cost was enormous, but Cora convinced herself that anything less than the best would impede Stephen's recovery. On May 28, they reached Badenweiler and moved into Haus Luisenstrasse 44, on the corner of Bergstrasse. Owned by Herr Albert Eberhardt, it was also called Villa Eberhardt. Here Crane was attended by Dr. Albert Fraenkel, who had established a sanatorium for tuberculosis in Badenweiler and who rented nearby homes for his patients. The doctor was distressed to find that Crane had been misdiagnosed in England. Although at least one consultant, Dr. Mitchel Bruce, had recommended the Nordrach treatment in the Black Forest, he had declared that only one of Crane's lungs was infected and had underestimated the severity of his patient's yellow fever.

Growing increasingly weak, Crane alternated between dictating fragmentary episodes of *The O'Ruddy* to Cora and hallucinating about his open-boat ordeal. Crane had never fully recovered emotionally from the most traumatic part of the *Commodore* crisis: the failure to rescue crew members left on board or on rafts. Cora was distressed by what he said. "It is too awful to hear him try to change places in the *'open boat'!*" He might have been alluding to a shift in seating in the dinghy as someone else rowed, but Crane the caretaker might also have been trying to rescue a comrade by changing places with him before the ship and rafts "were suddenly swallowed by this frightful maw of the ocean." Crane himself had always felt on the verge of being sucked into the maelstrom of fate, chance, and nothingness. His feverish nightmares confirmed this.[32]

When anxiety about mounting debts continued to beleaguer Stephen, Cora comforted him by saying they had three hundred pounds, surely an exaggeration to protect him from the truth. The trip from Brede Place to Badenweiler had cost one hundred fifty pounds; they had had to pay an additional lodging fee in Basel because they had not taken meals at the hotel, and their rent at Villa Eberhardt was ninety marks weekly, in addition to the wages of a helper who cooked, cleaned, and washed Stephen's bedsheets three times a day. "It seems awful!" Cora lamented. In an incoherent letter on May 29, she demanded that Pinker send her money and explain what had been done about the sale of serial rights to *The O'Ruddy* and the Wyoming Valley stories: "I simply must have money for Mr. Crane." On June 1, she tried to forget her own anguish by sketching the surroundings at Badenweiler, but the oppressively dark house, woods, hills, and sky she envisioned revealed only impending disaster. After she "nearly went mad" from sleeplessness and worry, a nurse medicated her, bringing only momentary relief. "It is too dreadful to have to think or write that if God takes my husband from me I shall not know what to do," she confided to Moreton Frewen on June 3. "What shall I do! I can't write more about it."[33]

Crane fell into a coma the following day. The end came at 3 A.M. on June 5, under peculiar circumstances. Fearing that an inappropriate medical procedure had hastened Crane's death, a distressed Cora scribbled incoherently in her notebook:

Write to Dr Skinner about Morphine—
—"Thats what strayed him"—
"You can cut them she cant."
"Little Butcher, I will tell Skinner how he came to Bali & stole me"—

To nurse: "Did you know Dr Bruce never heard of him?" Dr called June 4th 8 P.M.—Gave morphine injection—went at once to heart, I could see by muscular contraction Dr. saw too, tried to give champhor injection to revive action of heart. Dr said next day: "Can you forgive me?" What did he mean? don't dare to think.[34]

Upon hearing the news of his friend's death, Henry James, who had just mailed the Cranes fifty pounds to ease their financial burden, expressed what would soon be the grief-stricken sentiments of others: "What a brutal, needless extinction—what an unmitigated unredeemed catastrophe! I think of him with such a sense of possibilities and powers!"[35]

Crane had blazed across the literary sky as the most innovative writer of his generation and had become front-page news for his exploits. And now the life of fire was burned out, extinguished by the intensity of his passion, which refused compromise. In one sense, Crane died incomplete. He never resolved the oppositions of his double-sided literary life, balancing hackwork with serious art, and he never reconciled his conflicted persona: bohemian rebel and irresponsible lover, chivalric knight and country squire. Yet he died with the certainty that he had lived in the moment. Hours before his death, his final breath imminent, Crane had whispered peacefully to Cora: "I leave here gentle, seeking to do good, firm, resolute, impregnable." He was comforted by knowing he had fought his own good fight, had finished his own race, had kept to his own faith, and would be granted his dying wish: to be buried with his mother and father. The prodigal son, once adrift on the sea of life, had found his port and was coming home.[36]

Abbreviations

Beer Thomas Beer, *Stephen Crane: A Study in American Letters* (New York: Knopf, 1923)

C Stanley Wertheim and Paul Sorrentino, eds., *The Correspondence of Stephen Crane,* 2 vols. (New York: Columbia University Press, 1988)

Columbia Stephen Crane Papers, Rare Book and Manuscript Library, Butler Library, Columbia University

EFC Edith F. Crane

"Flagon" "Flagon of Despair," incomplete manuscript of Melvin H. Schoberlin's biography of Stephen Crane, MHSC Files

Gilkes Lillian Gilkes, *Cora Crane: A Biography of Mrs. Stephen Crane* (Bloomington: Indiana University Press, 1960)

GP Reverend George Peck

GP Papers George Peck Papers, Special Collections Research Center, Syracuse University Library

JTC Reverend Jonathan Townley Crane

JTC, Jr. Jonathan Townley Crane, Jr.

LHS Lackawanna Historical Society

Linson Corwin K. Linson, *My Stephen Crane,* ed. Edwin H. Cady (Syracuse: Syracuse University Press, 1958)

Log Stanley Wertheim and Paul Sorrentino, *The Crane Log: A Documentary Life of Stephen Crane, 1871–1900* (New York: G. K. Hall, 1994)

MHC Mary Helen Crane

MHS Melvin H. Schoberlin

MHSC Files Melvin H. Schoberlin Research Files (part of the Stephen Crane Collection), Special Collections Research Center, Syracuse University Library

SCRem Paul Sorrentino, ed., *Stephen Crane Remembered* (Tuscaloosa: University of Alabama Press, 2006)

Stallman and Gilkes R. W. Stallman and Lillian Gilkes, eds., *Stephen Crane: Letters* (New York: New York University Press, 1960)

Syracuse   Stephen Crane Collection, Special Collections Research Center, Syracuse University Library

TB   Thomas Beer

Virginia   Stephen Crane Collection, Special Collections, University of Virginia Library

WFP   Wilbur Fisk Peck

Yale   Thomas Beer Papers, Beer Family Papers, Sterling Library, Yale University

Weatherford   Richard M. Weatherford, *Stephen Crane: The Critical Heritage* (London: Routledge and Kegan Paul, 1973)

Works   Fredson Bowers, ed., *The Works of Stephen Crane,* 10 vols. (Charlottesville: University Press of Virginia, 1969–1976)

Notes

Introduction

1. "Be certain of anything": John Berryman, *Stephen Crane* (1950; rpt. Cleveland: World-Meridian, 1962), xvi; "crushing me flat": Thomas Beer, letter to "The Literary Lobby," *Literary Review*, 17 December 1921, 296; "would I tackle it again": transcript titled "fragment of letter BEER to HONCE ab 1923," R. W. Stallman Collection, Special Collections, University of Connecticut (Beer asked Honce to destroy the letter; Honce did this, with the exception of the last paragraph and Beer's signature, which he kept with his copy of the biography); "my foremost trait": *C*, 213.

2. Stanley Wertheim and Paul Sorrentino, "Thomas Beer: The Clay Feet of Stephen Crane Biography," *American Literary Realism, 1870–1910*, 22 (Spring 1990), 2–16. See also John Clendenning, "Thomas Beer's *Stephen Crane: The Eye of His Imagination*," *Prose Studies*, 14 (1991), 68–80; Clendenning, "Stephen Crane and His Biographers: Beer, Berryman, Schoberlin, and Stallman," *American Literary Realism, 1870–1910*, 28 (1995), 23–57; and Paul Sorrentino, "The Legacy of Thomas Beer in the Study of Stephen Crane and American Literary History," *American Literary Realism, 1870–1910*, 35 (2003), 187–211.

3. "It were his own story": Ernest Boyd, *Portraits: Real and Imaginary* (1924; rpt. New York: AMS, 1970), 214, 216; "if he were challenged": Wilson Follett to E. R. Hagemann, 12 April 1962, Virginia; "in the lives of others": Thomas Wolfe, *The Web and the Rock* (New York: Harper, 1939), 476.

4. Beer, 140, 233, 143.

5. *C*, 191, 69.

6. *Works*, 8: 287.

7. "Sought a new road": *Works*, 10: 11; "solitude of his own heart": Alexis de Tocqueville, *Democracy in America*, vol. 2, trans. H. C. Mansfield (Chicago: University of Chicago Press, 2002), 483; "unwritten responsibilities": *Works*, 2: 25; "brotherhood of men": *Works*, 5: 73.

8. "Making biography for himself " : Stallman and Gilkes, 331; "world unexplained": *C*, 163; "sense of annoyance": *C*, 213.

Prologue

1. *C*, 590. Sadly, Crane's namesake, like his uncle, died young, at the age of twenty-one, from flu (EFC to TB, 19 November 1922, Virginia).
2. Almost precisely four years later, on 3 June 1904, another masterful ironist, Anton Chekhov, arrived in Badenweiler to be treated for tuberculosis. He died there on July 15.
3. "Admirers paid homage": *C*, 545; "courage and faith": Frank J. Prial, "Littered Lot His Memorial," *Newark Evening News*, 5 June 1960, 41; "the landmark": Kathryn Hilt, "Changes at Crane Birth Site," *Stephen Crane Studies*, 6 (Fall 1997), 15–16. Elsewhere in Newark are Stephen Crane Plaza and Stephen Crane Village, a housing development built in 1940.
4. Frederick R. Karl and Laurence Davies, eds., *The Collected Letters of Joseph Conrad*, vol. 5: 1912–1916 (Cambridge: Cambridge University Press, 1996), 546–547.

1. Roots and Beginnings

1. "Hours of anxiety": JTC to GP, 14 July 1868, Virginia; "need not comment": JTC to GP, 14 July 1868, Virginia. (These are two separate letters.)
2. "A Jerseyman as you can find": *C*, 227; "later renamed Montclair": Max Herzberg, "New and Old Data on Stephen Crane," *Torch*, 4 (April 1931), 37; R. W. Stallman, *Stephen Crane: A Critical Bibliography* (Ames: Iowa State University Press, 1972), 1–2; "in New Jersey, in 1665–1666": according to Ellery Bicknell Crane, *Genealogy of the Crane Family*, vol. 1 (Worcester, MA: Press of Charles Hamilton, 1895), 45 (no relationship has been established between Jasper Crane and the first Stephen Crane); see also G. Archer Crane, *The Family of Stephen Crane of Elizabethtown, N.J.: The First Five Generations in America* (Rutherford, NJ: privately printed, 1934); "two Colonial Assemblies in New York": *C*, 166; "Continental Congress": Lynn Montross, *The Reluctant Rebels: The Story of the Continental Congress, 1774–1789* (New York: Harper, 1950), 428. Regarding the influence of Crane's ancestry on his writing, see Peaslee in *SCRem* 87, 319, n. 63.
3. "General Washington's army to the enemy": family members differed on how Jonathan had died. William Howe Crane told Max Herzberg that Jonathan had first misled the enemy regarding the location of colonial troops. After the deception was discovered, Jonathan was shot by a firing squad (Herzberg, "Old and New Data," 37). "Ultimately promoted to major general": *C*, 166, 227; "New York harbor during the Revolution" and "gentle Britisher": EFC, signed biographical statement ("Though usually very

quiet . . ."), 28 February 1931, Virginia. Because EFC ended letters with a complimentary close, this was probably a document prepared for a future biographer.

4. *C,* 166.

5. "Crane's portrait": Lawrence in *SCRem,* 121; "created things": *C,* 201.

6. Robert K. Crane, "Stephen Crane's Family Heritage," *Stephen Crane Studies,* 4 (Spring 1995), 13, 37, lists two different birthdates: June 18 and 19.

7. "Trunks he had made": R. K. Crane, "Family Heritage," 14; "in 1841": for information on JTC's time at Princeton, see Thomas A. Gullason, "A Legacy for Stephen Crane: The Princeton Writings of the Reverend Jonathan Townley Crane," *Courier* [Syracuse University Library], 25 (Fall 1990), 55–79.

8. "A horse and a few religious texts": JTC (1866), 17; "à la mode de Virgil": JTC to GP, 30 August 1847, Virginia. JTC is probably alluding to Virgil's disappearance in Dante's *Purgatorio,* Canto 30, or to characters in the *Aeneid* who occasionally vanish, such as Aeneas's mother, Venus, in Book 1, Mercury in Book 4, or Turnus, who is whisked away from battle by the gods in Book 11. "Piece of nonsense": JTC to GP, 1 December 1848, Virginia; "do with another text": Price in *SCRem,* 20; on JTC's wit, see Sidbury and Peaslee in *SCRem,* 51, 87; "troubled dream": JTC to GP, 25 January 1849, 9 February 1867, Virginia.

9. "Expediency of the performance": JTC, *An Essay on Dancing* (New York: Carlton and Porter, 1849), 4; "good reason for the portrayal": JTC, *Popular Amusements* (Cincinnati: Jennings and Pye; NY: Eaton and Mains, 1869), 121. The novella *A Temperance Story for Youth* was never published, most likely because of problems with plot and character development; see Thomas A. Gullason, ed., *A Garland of Writings: Stephen Crane's Literary Family* (Syracuse: Syracuse University Press, 2002), 56–70, for an excerpt. "*The best works of fiction*": JTC, *Popular Amusements,* 126; "secular list": untitled article, *Christian Union,* 4 November 1874, 352.

10. Jesse Truesdell Peck condemned novel reading as a crime because "it murders the heart, the intellect, and the body"; see J. T. Peck, *The True Woman; or, Life and Happiness at Home and Abroad* (New York: Carleton and Porter, 1857), 154. Ironically, Syracuse University now has an endowed chair titled the Jesse Truesdell Peck Professor of Literature. "Female Institute in 1847": R. Vanhorne, "Mary Helen Peck Crane," *Minutes of the Thirty-Fifth Session of the Newark Conference of the Methodist Episcopal Church* (New York: Hunt and Eaton, 1892). Although Edna Crane Sidbury stated that Mary Helen Peck had graduated from the College of the City of New York (*SCRem,* 51), see R. K. Crane, from Rutgers Female Institute ("Family Heritage," 17); and Gullason, from Young Ladies Institute (*A Garland,* 1).

11. "Memories and political leanings": For a selection of Mrs. Crane's writing, see Thomas A. Gullason, ed., *Stephen Crane's Career: Perspectives and Evaluations* (New York: New York University Press, 1972); and Gullason, *A Garland*. "Divine prerogytives of men folks": Gullason, *A Garland*, 166; "home with her children": Price in *SCRem*, 20; "devoted to Stephen": W. F. Crane in *SCRem*, 18; "in those days": Helen R. Crane in *SCRem*, 45–46.

12. "From *the city*": MHC to GP and Mrs. Peck, 14 March 1848, Virginia; "lonely when left alone": MHC to GP and Mrs. Peck, 14 March 1848, Virginia. "Unpack years later": On 18 January 1893, on what would have been the Cranes' forty-fifth wedding anniversary, their son George sent each of his siblings a piece of the cake in honor of their parents.

13. MHC to GP and Mrs. Peck, 14 March 1848, Virginia. The family tradition was to shorten the name of the father and son, "Jonathan Townley," and to pronounce it in various ways. For example, Reverend Crane called his son Jonathan "Jon. T." in his diary (Wertheim [1993], 45), and family members occasionally pronounced the diphthong "ow" in "Townley" "oo," as in "tooth." For the phonetic spelling used by Stephen and his brother William, see *C*, 58, 265, 302, 546. Mrs. Crane's "Jounty" combines the oral "oo" with the written "Jon. T." "Darby and Joan": MHC to GP and Mrs. Peck, 20 November 1864, Virginia.

14. "Student was gone": Gullason, *Stephen Crane's Career*, 31; "do the deed": Gullason, *A Garland*, 136.

15. Gullason, *Stephen Crane's Career*, 31; JTC to GP, 13 June 1855, Virginia. During Reverend Crane's tenure, the school's name changed to Pennington Seminary and Female Collegiate Institute; today it is the Pennington School. Decades after Crane's departure, his impact on the school was still being memorialized. An 1890 program celebrating the history of the school included the address "Reminiscences of Dr. Crane," and in 1900 a stained-glass window in the school's chapel was dedicated to his memory. See Thomas A. Gullason, "The Cranes at Pennington Seminary," *American Literature*, 39 (1968), 533.

16. "Morristown": In 1864 Reverend Crane declined when offered the presidency of Genesee College in Lima, New York. The college moved to Syracuse in 1870 and became the basis for Syracuse University in 1872. Had he accepted the position, he would have been president of the college that his son Stephen would attend years later. "Perpetual whirl": JTC to GP, 3 December 1863, Virginia.

17. Paul Sorrentino, "Newly Discovered Writings of Mary Helen Peck Crane and Agnes Elizabeth Crane," *Courier* [Syracuse University Library], 21 (Spring 1986), 121. Though Agnes eventually became "reconciled to B.B." (127), her anxiety about the move was not unique for her: "I haven't felt so

ugly and despairing since I was homesick at Wyoming Seminary," a school in the Wyoming Valley of Pennsylvania founded by her maternal grandfather that she and her mother attended.

Although the family lived in Bound Brook, Reverend Crane was minister at the Methodist church in Bloomington. From 1869 to 1891 South Bound Brook was called Bloomington.

18. Crane's signed copy is at Columbia.

19. Daniel T. Atwood, *Atwood's Country and Suburban Houses* (1871; New York: Orange Judd, 1883), 7.

20. "Not in the 'Ring'": JTC to GP, 3 December 1863; "ride over the rest of the preachers": JTC to GP, 20 January 1862. Despite Reverend Crane's feeling of being an outsider, in a 27 December 1867 letter to his father-in-law, his call for "a change in the *Advocate*" and his mention of the "very fine" "prospects of my success" regarding the "Adv[ocate] business" imply that he was being seriously considered for the editorship in late 1867. "Disliking perpetual moving": JTC to GP, 3 December 1863, Virginia. "They had once had at Pennington": While at Hackettstown, Reverend Crane also served as Professor Extraordinary in Greek and New Testament Exegesis at Drew Theological Seminary, which had been founded in 1867 in Madison, New Jersey; see *Drew Theological Seminary: Alumni Record, 1869–1895* (New York: Wilbur B. Ketcham, 1895), 9. "Presiding Elder of the Newark District": MHC to GP and Mrs. Peck, 25 March 1868, Virginia; "preaching three times daily": JTC to GP, 4 December 1868, Virginia; "all unstrung from the anxiety": MHC to GP and Mrs. Peck, 25 March 1868, Virginia.

21. "Simple, practical truths": Gullason, *A Garland*, 121. JTC's publication of a series of articles on childrearing in *The Sunday-School Times* (Gullason, *A Garland*, 120–136) drew considerable attention to his suggestion. "Treat them fairly": Gullason, *A Garland*, 128, 129.

22. Ibid., 130.

23. Ibid., 131. See also JTC, *The True Man: A Discourse Delivered before the Belles Lettres Society of Dickinson College, June 26, 1851, by Rev. J. Townley Crane, A.M., an Honorary Member* (Philadelphia: T. K. and P. G. Collins, 1851), 6: "To be a man, then, in the worthy sense of the term is to be something noble and brave, and honorable. It is to be strong in intellect, strong in generous emotions, and large-hearted sympathies. . . . Strong in the power to will, and the power to do. It is the reverse of all that is cowardly, or weak, or mean in mind and in soul."

24. Stephen's boyhood friend (George) Post Wheeler recalled in an interview with MHS that because Stephen was not physically strong and was sensitive regarding his health, he would prove his endurance to others by boxing until completely exhausted ("Post Wheeler Interview," MHSC Files). De-

spite his father's admonition against fighting, it would have been difficult
for a small child like Stephen to avoid being picked on. He later recounted
this difficulty in "The Fight."

The extent of Stephen's fighting as a child typifies the problem of separating truth from legend in his life. According to one account, neighbors
recalled that as a child in Newark he was "a good deal of a torment" who
had "a genius for getting into scrapes" (Clara S. Littledale, "Newark Discovers a Little Brick Shrine," *New York Herald Tribune*, 15 November 1925, 4).
Stephen, however, lived there only until he was two and a half, hardly the
age of someone getting into neighborhood "scrapes."

25. "Doings of the race": Jesse T. Peck, *God in Education: A Discourse to the Graduating Class of Dickinson College, July 1852* (Washington: Robt. A. Waters,
1852), 11; "rather than formal education": *C,* 99. See also GP, *Formation of a
Manly Character: A Series of Lectures to Young Men* (New York: Carlton and
Phillips, 1854), 38: "You should make every man, woman, and child around
you a *book,* from which you make it your daily business to derive lessons of
instruction." Ironically, although Reverend Peck was convinced "the idea
that human character is more truthfully developed in works of fiction than
in veritable history, is an absurdity too monstrous to be entertained for a
moment" (37), his grandson would demonstrate that fiction could be as
"veritable" as reality. Peck did, however, admire what he considered serious fiction—such as Jonathan Swift's *Gulliver's Travels* and Samuel Johnson's
Rasselas—because of its moral enrichment.

26. GP, *Formation of a Manly Character,* 61.

27. *Works,* 5: 85.

2. Childhood

1. "An only child": During Stephen's early years, the family had a Swedish
maid whose son was near Stephen's age. When Mrs. Crane was away on
church business, Stephen occasionally stayed with his sister Nellie (JTC to
GP, 24 September 1874, Virginia). "Thriving in September 1873": *Log,* 6;
"his well-being": Thomas A. Gullason, ed., *Stephen Crane's Career: Perspectives and Evaluations* (New York: New York University Press, 1972), 21.

2. "Ganma": *Log,* 6; "James Fenimore Cooper": *Works,* 10: 343, 345; "sewing
and reading": JTC to GP, 10 and 21 February 1853, 30 January 1854, Virginia; "certain baby witticisms": JTC to GP, 28 December 1855, Virginia;
"any of her siblings": JTC to GP and Mrs. Peck, 18 September 1856, Virginia; "would impair her health": JTC to GP, 4 and 21 December 1868,
Virginia.

3. "Pe-pop-ty": "Stephen Crane and Asbury Park," *Asbury Park Sunday Press,*
31 May 1931, 15; *Works,* 10: 343; "on this side": JTC to GP, 19 November

1874, LHS; "spell 'O'?": E. B. Crane in *SCRem*, 11; "spent hours enacting": *Works*, 10: 345. See also E. B. Crane and Elizabeth (Archer) Crane in *SCRem*, 12, 16; "hunters shooting ducks": Mrs. Alice (Crane) Ludwig and EFC, interview with MHS, Poughkeepsie, NY, 15 May 1948, MHSC Files.

4. Thomas A. Gullason, ed., *A Garland of Writings: Stephen Crane's Literary Family* (Syracuse: Syracuse University Press, 2002), 134. Reverend Crane's comment appeared in his article "Christ and the Painters," published in July 1877, in which he alludes to having attended Children's Day in Brooklyn in May and having visited the tenement district of Manhattan. Though he could have visited the tenements at any time, the specificity of his contrast between two types of children suggests that he saw both groups on the same day.

5. "Delighted with his grit": E. B. Crane in *SCRem*, 11–12; "doctor could cauterize it": Price in *SCRem*, 21. Whereas Price suggests that the incident occurred in 1882, MHS (*Log*, 21) implies that it happened in 1879. The latter date seems more likely. Following Reverend Crane's death in 1880, the Cranes led an unsettled life until Mrs. Crane moved to Asbury Park. There would have been little time simply to go on a vacation in the wilderness. "Of his race, of his kind": *Works*, 8: 66.

6. Post Wheeler and Hallie Erminie Rives, *Dome of Many-Coloured Glass* (Garden City, NY: Doubleday, 1955), 20–22. An edited version of Wheeler's reminiscence appears in *SCRem*, 22–29. Because of space limitations, part of it was deleted.

   In notes taken during an interview with Wheeler, MHS implies that Crane and Wheeler first met in 1876 when they were dining with their mothers and Bishop Padock in Kingston, Pennsylvania. If MHS is correct in saying that Stephen was five at the time, the event occurred after November 1 in 1876. Though the year may be inaccurate, Wheeler recalled an anecdote from the event. When the bishop talked at length on Rome, Roman history, and gladiators, an inquisitive Stephen asked, "What is a gladiator?" Unsure of how to reply, the bishop responded, "A gladiator—is a man—who indulges in gladiatorial exploits." Though the circular definition bewildered Stephen, the question showed his fascination with words ("Post Wheeler Interview," MHSC Files).

7. Wheeler in *SCRem*, 23–24.

8. "Infant's undershirt": Sidbury in *SCRem*, 51; "here in the dirt": Mary Peck to GP, undated letter, GP Papers.

9. "Sixteen-year-old Townley": Robert K. Crane, "Stephen Crane's Family Heritage," *Stephen Crane Studies*, 4 (Spring 1995), 37, incorrectly lists JTC, Jr., as being born in April 1853; the correct date is 29 April 1852 (JTC to GP, 1 May 1852, Virginia). "Writing the letter during school": JTC, Jr.,

to Mrs. GP, 2 April 1868, Virginia; "would like to be pope": Though Townley wrote 23 April 1874 on his answers, the dating is problematic. To the question asking him to name his favorite character in a romance, he answered, "'Jan.' Vedder," who appears in Amelia E. Barr's 1885 popular romance *Jan Vedder's Wife.* If he responded in 1874, he would have been a few days shy of twenty-two years old; if in 1885, he would have been thirty-three. Either age suggests that Townley had unresolved anger toward his father even as an adult. Townley's complete response to the questionnaire is in MHSC Files.

10. "Boiling a Corpse," *Jersey City Evening Journal,* 3 April 1883, 4. The article lists the student and letter writer as E. B. Crane, not Wilbur Crane.

11. "With the collar turned up": Wheeler in *SCRem,* 25; "two sizes too large": "Stephen Crane and Asbury Park," 15; "Cyprus": "Stephen Crane and Asbury Park," 15; "'crazy' quilt": *Log,* 33; "'Crane' backwards": Enarc, "A Trip to Canada," *Asbury Park Shore Press,* 5 January 1883 [for 1884], 1; "gift from him and his wife": Untitled transcript, *Asbury Park Shore Press,* 8 August 1890, 1; "'tumbling' to numerous 'hot balls'": "Local Items," *Asbury Park Shore Press,* 21 July 1883, 3. Though the news item is unsigned, Townley in all likelihood wrote it. As editor of a newspaper with a small staff, he would have been the primary person to write editorial commentary. "All in a fitting manner": "Heirs to the Townley Estate," *Asbury Park Shore Press,* 3 April 1885, 3. There is no evidence that Townley received any part of the inheritance.

12. "To elect the woman": Untitled transcript, *Asbury Park Shore Press,* 23 March 1888, 1, MHSC Files; "divorced in 1900": "Mrs. J. Townley Crane Divorced," *New York Times,* 14 November 1900, 2; "certificate or tombstone": R. W. Stallman, *Stephen Crane: A Critical Bibliography* (Ames: Iowa State University Press, 1972), 361; "Ancient Mariner": Wheeler in *SCRem,* 25. See also Post Wheeler to MHS, 25 December 1947, MHSC Files.

13. "Self-doubt, and spiritual anguish": WFP to GP and Mrs. Peck, 20 July 1853, Syracuse; "my weakness and many failings": WFP to GP and Mrs. Peck, 20 July 1853, GP Papers; "father upset him as well": WFP to GP, 13 June 1849, GP Papers; "in body and mind": WFP to GP, 11 June 1850, GP Papers.

14. "178th Pennsylvania Infantry": Newton Allen Strait, *Roster of All Regimental Surgeons and Assistant Surgeons in the Late War, with Their Service, and Last-Known Post-Office Address* (Washington: n.p., 1882), 256; "allude to the past again": WFP to GP, 24 June 1863, GP Papers.

15. "Separated from a loved one": WFP to GP, 27 January 1854, GP Papers; "good may come out of it": JTC to WFP, 29 May 1874, Virginia; "listed as 'a

physician'":"George Peck, D.D.: Interesting Biographical Sketch," p. [1] in scrapbook compiled by Stephen's brother George and his wife. In my possession.

16. My statement about the sword is based on two sources: *C,* 301, and Greene in *SCRem,* 128, n. 150. Of Crane's two swords, Greene believed that at least one of them belonged either to Stephen's father or to an uncle; the uncle would have been Wilbur. As a military officer, he had a sword as standard issue; a minister was not given one. After Crane's death, Cora gave the swords to Lafayette College, where they once hung over the fireplace in Brainerd Hall ("Swords in Brainerd Are Not Lafayette's," *The Lafayette,* 17 November 1926, 5).

17. *C,* 221.

18. Paul Sorrentino, "Newly Discovered Writings of Mary Helen Peck Crane and Agnes Elizabeth Crane," *Courier* [Syracuse University Library], 21 (Spring 1986), 126. Written sporadically during the years 1873–1880, the diary occasionally is addressed to an imaginary character named Samantha. Starting in 1873, American humorist Marietta Holley began writing a popular series of books about the adventures of Samantha, a sensible country woman who comments on the follies of society and politics. In all likelihood, Agnes is talking to her.

   Agnes's independence resulted at least partly from family upbringing. Jesse Peck's insistence on equality for women—"there is nothing . . . which she may not learn, no practicable conquest which she cannot achieve"—would have empowered her. See Jesse T. Peck, *The True Woman; or, Life and Happiness at Home and Abroad* (New York: Carleton and Porter, 1857), 353–354.

19. "Burning passion to write": Sorrentino, "Newly Discovered Writings," 127. "Advocate of women's rights": Agnes closes her essay "A Helpless Person" (Gullason, *A Garland,* 189) with a quotation from Carrie Chapman Catt, the activist for women's rights who founded the League of Women Voters in 1919. "Sad shipwreck of life": Gullason, *A Garland,* 186; "trusting glasses of ignorant youth": Sorrentino, "Newly Discovered Writings," 129; "you look at roses": *Works,* 10: 49.

20. "Maintaining a sense of propriety": Sorrentino, "Newly Discovered Writings," 128; "School in Port Jervis, New York": Thomas Gullason, "Stephen Crane's Sister: New Biographical Facts," *American Literature,* 49 (1977), 235; "persuade her to remain": Gullason, "Stephen Crane's Sister," 235. "Frequently away on church business": In the December 11 entry in her diary, Agnes wrote "Looked for Ma all day." On December 13, Agnes had to come "home early" from a friend's house because "Ma and Pa went away for over Sunday" (Sorrentino, "Newly Discovered Writings," 117). "A reward for weekly attendance": "Flagon," II-3; "Solomon the dog":

"Flagon," II-4. "From the anxiety of loneliness": The typescript portion of Agnes's diary for 12 December 1873 contains this entry: "Left Nellie's early with my ?baby?" The transcriber probably wrote the two question marks because of difficulty reading Agnes's handwriting. If the word is "baby," it suggests that she considered herself a surrogate mother (Sorrentino, "Newly Discovered Writings," 117). "Anything but an unpleasant experience": Price in *SCRem,* 21.

21. "Ugly duckling": Price in *SCRem,* 21. "Much of his work": It may also be coincidental that Edmund's wife's maiden name was Fleming.

22. Crane recalled that when he was eight, he "became very much interested in a child character called, I think, Little Goodie Brighteyes, and I wrote a story then which I called after this fascinating little person" (*C,* 232). The story does not survive. He may have been influenced by the classic children's story with a similar title, *Little Goodie Two-Shoes* (1765), in all likelihood written by Oliver Goldsmith.

23. The story's language, dialect, and local color reveal Stephen's precocity. The complete title, "Sketches from Life: Uncle Jake and the Bell-Handle," implies that he considered it part of a series of sketches, and his use of printer's symbols with the story's punctuation suggests that he intended it for publication.

24. "At the age of twenty-eight": For additional information on Agnes Crane, see Gullason, *A Garland;* Gullason, "Stephen Crane's Sister"; and Sorrentino, "Newly Discovered Writings." "Abruptly ended his innocence": Marston LaFrance, *A Reading of Stephen Crane* (London: Oxford University Press, 1971), 5–8; "grim hatred of nature": *Works,* 10: 47.

3. The *Holiness* Controversy

1. "A Remarkable Family Reunion," *Christian Advocate,* 49 (5 November 1874), 357.

2. "Methodist bulldog": Peter Cartwright, *Autobiography of Peter Cartwright,* introd. Charles L. Wallis (Nashville: Abingdon Press, 1984), 73; "consciences of the people": Cartwright, *Autobiography,* 61, 12, 236; "religious denomination in America": Sydney E. Ahlstrom, *A Religious History of the American People* (New Haven: Yale University Press, 1972), 436, 437; "lighting their matches": Cartwright, *Autobiography,* 64.

3. "Every working day for a year": Jesse T. Peck, *The History of the Great Republic, from a Christian Stand-Point* (New York: Broughton and Wyman, 1869), 538, 453; "the vine grew": JTC, *The Fruitful Bough: The Centenary Sermon Preached before the Newark Conference, at Washington, Warren County, New Jersey, March 23, 1866* (New York: John W. Oliver, 1866), 9; "great nu-

merical strength": JTC, *The Fruitful Bough*, 12; "cease to be safe": JTC, *The Fruitful Bough*, 23; "battlegrounds at camp revivals": Christopher Benfey, *The Double Life of Stephen Crane: A Biography* (New York: Knopf, 1992), 29.

4. "Church membership": MHC in Thomas A. Gullason, ed., *Stephen Crane's Career: Perspectives and Evaluations* (New York: New York University Press, 1972), 33; "Morristown": Julia Keese Colles, *Authors and Writers Associated with Morristown* (Morristown, NJ: Vogt Brothers, 1893), 332.

5. MHS was the first scholar to suggest a connection between the controversy surrounding *Holiness* and JTC's forced reassignment. In *The Double Life* and "Stephen Crane's Father and the Holiness Movement," *Courier* [Syracuse University Library], 25 (Spring 1990), 27–36, Benfey explored the extent of the connection. See also Daniel Hoffman, *The Poetry of Stephen Crane* (New York: Columbia University Press, 1956), ch. 3.

6. "Read aright": Gullason, *Stephen Crane's Career*, 21; "George Peck for comments": JTC to GP, 11 October 1873, Virginia. "Sanctification for total conversion": see GP, *The Scripture Doctrine of Christian Perfection Stated and Defended: With a Critical and Historical Examination of the Controversy, Both Ancient and Modern* (New York: Lane and Sanford, 1842). Jesse T. Peck, Reverend Crane's uncle-in-law, also advocated the more orthodox view; see Peck, *The Central Idea of Christianity*, rev. ed. (New York: Nelson and Phillips, 1876).

7. "Methodist literature in America": *New York Methodist*, quoted in *Christian Advocate*, 50 (July 1875), 232. The controversy regarding Holiness neither started nor ended with JTC's book. See John Leland Peters, *Christian Perfection and American Methodism* (New York: Abingdon Press, 1956), 170–176; "books we have ever read": Reviews, *Christian Advocate*, 49 (23 July 1874), 240, and *Christian Advocate*, 50 (17 June 1875), 190; "general and annual conferences": Rev. Charles Blakeslee, "Christian Holiness: The New Theory," *Christian Advocate*, 49 (24 September 1874), 306; "prevent future 'outrages'": comment from "Advocate of Holiness," quoted in "Publisher's Department," *Christian Advocate*, 49 (30 July 1874), 248; "it would do no harm": comment from "Guide to Holiness," quoted in "Publisher's Department," *Christian Advocate*, 49 (30 July 1874), 248.

8. Reverend Anthony Atwood, *The Abiding Comforter: A Necessity to Joyful Piety and Eminent Usefulness*, rev. ed. (Philadelphia: Published by the Author, 1874), 42, 41, 68. Atwood quickly revised his book after it sold out in six months. He deleted gratuitous charges that Crane had been influenced by "educational prejudices" (39) while attending a Presbyterian school, Princeton; that his "talents" were "fair, but by no means brilliant or attractive" (40); that his preaching style was "dry and devoid of sympathy or feel-

ing" (40); and that his years as an academic at Pennington had "prevented him more or less from ever being a popular and attractive preacher" (40). Atwood's anti-intellectual position distinguished between the first generation of Methodist preachers with their "warm and gushing" piety and academics like Crane who evinced "average piety" and who buried themselves in "text-books" (40). Nonetheless, the attack in the revised edition was still devastating, and Atwood added an appendix with excerpts from book reviews praising his position and denouncing Crane's.

9. "Deep things of God": Atwood, *The Abiding Comforter,* 68; "presiding elder of a district": ibid., 61–62; "the world and the church": ibid., 70, 114. Correspondence between JTC and GP reveals no tension between them. On 19 November 1874 (LHS), Crane praised his father-in-law's autobiography, saying that "the notices of your book were very fine" and that "all the remarks I have heard, or heard of, are decidedly favorable." The publishers of the autobiography were apparently not threatened by Crane's criticism of the Movement, for they advertised *Holiness the Birthright of All God's Children* and two of Crane's other books in the back of Peck's autobiography.

10. "Carcass into the street": Rev. Dr. Asbury Lowrey, "Dr. Crane's Book and the *Quarterly Review,*" *Christian Standard and Home Journal,* 5 September 1874, quoted in "Quarterly Book-Table," *Methodist Quarterly Review,* 56 (1874), 677; "hopes of ecclesiastical preferment": "Quarterly Book-Table," *Methodist Quarterly Review,* 56 (1874), 663; "a scheme of proscription": "Quarterly Book-Table," *Methodist Quarterly Review,* 56 (1874), 663; "church orthodoxy": advertisement for *Holiness* in JTC, *Methodism and Its Methods* (1875; rpt. New York: Nelson and Phillips, 1876).

11. "Learn all I can": JTC to GP, 19 November 1874, LHS; "had been painful": MHC in Gullason, *Stephen Crane's Career,* 34; "reaffirming his position": JTC, *Holiness the Birthright of All God's Children,* 2nd ed. (New York: Nelson and Phillips, 1875), Preface.

12. JTC, *Holiness the Birthright,* 54. Crane's general comments on disagreement within the church had appeared three years earlier in a slightly modified form, but he would definitely have seen their specific application to him three years later. See his article "The Organization of the Methodist Episcopal Church," *Methodist Quarterly Review,* 4th series, 24 (1872), 199; "for decades": Frederick A. Norwood, *The Story of American Methodism* (Nashville: Abingdon Press, 1974), 175.

13. "Supernumerary minister": C. R. Barnes, ed., *Minutes of the 19th Session of the Newark Conference of the Methodist Episcopal Church, Held at Halsey Street ME Church, Newark, March 29–April 5, 1876* (New York: Nelson and Phillips, 1876), 8; "difficult for Reverend Crane to fulfill": Paul Sorrentino, "Newly

Discovered Writings of Mary Helen Peck Crane and Agnes Elizabeth Crane," *Courier* [Syracuse University Library], 21 (Spring 1986), 115, n. 12; "more by maneuvering than by merit": JTC, *Holiness*, 370, 371; "their own conversion experience": "Flagon," II-9, II-10.

4. Onward to Port Jervis

1. Peter Osborne, *The Gilded Age of Port Jervis* (Port Jervis, NY: Port Jervis Area Heritage Commission, 1992), 24–25.
2. Stanley Wertheim, "Another Diary of the Reverend Jonathan Townley Crane," *Resources for American Literary Study*, 19 (1993), 43.
3. "The accursed system": Thomas A. Gullason, ed., *A Garland of Writings: Stephen Crane's Literary Family* (Syracuse: Syracuse University Press, 2002), 35; "condition of African Americans": *Log*, 20. Mrs. Crane had been devoted to social causes for decades. In a letter to GP, JTC spoke of his wife's making garments for the "destitute" (1 December 1848, Virginia). "Rich in complacence": *Works*, 7: 185.
4. "Trashy literature": *Log*, 19.
5. "Pete and Bill": Linson, 4–5; "variously titled": *Works*, 10: 219, 263; "ten-pin to it": *C*, 172; "unworthiness": *C*, 301; "but with myself": *C*, 187. For brilliant analyses of Crane's dual perspective, see James B. Colvert, "Structure and Theme in Stephen Crane's Fiction," *Modern Fiction Studies*, 5 (1959), 199–208; and Colvert, "Stephen Crane's Magic Mountain," in *Stephen Crane: A Collection of Critical Essays*, ed. Maurice Bassan (Englewood Cliffs: Prentice-Hall, 1967), 95–105.
6. "Historic in the family": Wilbur F. Crane in *SCRem*, 18; "felt for him": *Works*, 7: 220–221; "jungles of childhood": *Works*, 7: 170, 167, 168; "to their children": *Log*, 31–32; "raising her family": Price in *SCRem*, 20.
7. "Exercises in oratory": JTC to GP, 20 January 1862, Virginia; "Bingen on the Rhine": on Crane's use of the poem in "The Open Boat," see David A. Jackson, "Textual Questions Raised by Crane's 'Soldier of the Legion,'" *American Literature*, 55 (1983), 77–80; "his school-fellows": *Works*, 5: 85; "his until he died": *Works*, 7: 158, 163. When Stephen was a student at Claverack College and Hudson River Institute, Mrs. Crane wrote to Reverend A. H. Flack, principal of the school, about her son's anxiety regarding declamation. Reluctantly, Reverend Flack excused Stephen from the exercise (*Log*, 43).
8. *Works*, 8: 224.
9. The events surrounding the July 4 tragedy are reconstructed from the following newspaper articles: "To-Morrow's Exercises," *Port Jervis Evening Gazette*, 3 July 1879, 1; "Our Nation's Natal Day" and "The Shooting Acci-

dent," *Port Jervis Evening Gazette,* 5 July 1879, [3?]; "Casualties," *Tri-States Union* [Port Jervis], 8 July 1879, 1; [Brief Notes], *Port Jervis Evening Gazette,* 16 August 1879, 1; "Obituary," *Port Jervis Union,* 3 October 1913, 3.

10. Wertheim, "Another Diary," 47, 48.

11. Ibid., 48.

12. "Port Jervis had ever seen": obituary of JTC, *Newark Daily Advertiser,* 21 February 1880, 2; MHC in Gullason (1972), 34–35; "dedicated to him": *Port Jervis Evening Gazette,* 13 March 1880, 1.

13. E. B. Crane in *SCRem,* 12. On the way in which Reverend Crane's death shaped Stephen's outlook, see Joseph Katz, "Stephen Crane's Concept of Death," *Kentucky Review,* 4 (Winter 1983), 49–55.

14. "Fatherless children": Paul Sorrentino, "Newly Discovered Writings of Mary Helen Peck Crane and Agnes Elizabeth Crane," *Courier* [Syracuse University Library], 21 (Spring 1986), 128, 129; "simple mind": *C,* 166.

5. Schooling at Asbury Park, Pennington, Claverack

1. "Its fulness": quoted in Victor A. Elconin, "Stephen Crane at Asbury Park," *American Literature,* 20 (1948), 275; "until 1977": *A Brief History of Ocean Grove: A National Historic Site* (Ocean Grove, N.J.: Ocean Grove Camp Meeting Association, ca. 1991), n.p.

2. "Loss of property": "Mr. Bradley of Asbury Park: Eccentric, Perhaps, but a Man of Sterling Integrity," *New York Times,* 22 October 1893, 19; "for whiskey": "War on Beer at Asbury Park," *New York Times,* 6 August 1895, 9; "use as directed": untitled transcript, *Philadelphia Press,* 7 July 1888, 8; 15 July 1888, 5, MHSC Files.

3. "Beach at 10 P.M.": "Mr. Bradley of Asbury Park"; "nor the other": *Works,* 8: 519.

4. An obituary of Mrs. Crane stated that she was the Ocean Grove correspondent for the *New York Tribune;* see R. Vanhorne, "Mary Helen Peck Crane," *Minutes of the Thirty-Fifth Session of the Newark Conference of the Methodist Episcopal Church* (New York: Hunt and Eaton, 1892), 91. And Thomas A. Gullason, ed., *A Garland of Writings: Stephen Crane's Literary Family* (Syracuse: Syracuse University Press, 2002), 152, 153, reprints the WCTU minutes about her work as a correspondent. Unfortunately the minutes are ambiguous concerning the precise number of dispatches and columns that Mrs. Crane wrote for the Associated Press and the New York papers. Although she typically did not sign these pieces, two examples she sent from Ocean Grove are "Entertained by Mrs. Grant" and "Temperance Women in Convention."

5. *Log,* 47.

6. Ibid., 33, 34, 38, 52, 66; George Monteiro, *Stephen Crane's Blue Badge of Courage* (Baton Rouge: Louisiana State University Press, 2000), 9, 38, 125.

7. "A Minister Exonerated," *New York Times,* 1 April 1884, 5; "The Rev. Mr. Peck's Case," *New York Times,* 4 April 1884, 1; and "The Rev. Mr. Peck Vindicated," *New York Times,* 9 April 1884, 2.

8. "Did well in his first year":Thomas Gullason,"Stephen Crane's Sister: New Biographical Facts," *American Literature,* 49 (1977), 236, n. 15;"Philomathean Society":"Jottings through Jersey," *Philadelphia Inquirer,* 10 June 1900, 4; "on Sunday were prohibited":Thomas A. Gullason,"The Cranes at Pennington Seminary," *American Literature,* 39 (1968), 534–535. On Crane's time at Pennington, see also Jean Cazemajou, "Stephen Crane: Pennington Seminary: Etape d'une éducation Méthodiste," *Etudes Anglaises,* 20, no. 2 (1967), 140–148;"I came home":W. F. Crane in *SCRem* (2006), 18.

9. "Columbia County, New York": on Crane's time at Claverack, see Travis in *SCRem,* 61–62, and Wickham in *SCRem,* 62–70; Lyndon Upson Pratt, "The Formal Education of Stephen Crane," *American Literature,* 10 (1939), 460–471;Thomas F. O'Donnell, "John B.Van Petten: Stephen Crane's History Teacher," *American Literature,* 27 (1955), 196–202; O'Donnell,"DeForest,Van Petten, and Stephen Crane," *American Literature,* 27 (1956), 578–580; Vincent Starrett, "Stephen Crane at Claverack," *Stephen Crane Newsletter,* 2 (Fall 1967), 4; Stanley Wertheim,"Why Stephen Crane Left Claverack," *Stephen Crane Newsletter,* 2 (Fall 1967), 5; Joseph Katz,"Stephen Crane at Claverack College and Hudson River Institute," *Stephen Crane Newsletter,* 2 (Summer 1968), 1–5; and Thomas A. Gullason, "Stephen Crane at Claverack College: A New Reading," *Courier* [Syracuse University Library], 27 (Fall 1992), 33–46. According to one alumnus, Harvey Wickham, by the time Crane arrived at Claverack, the once highly respected academic institution had devolved into "a mere boarding-school, quartered like an octopus in the college dormitories, taught by the college faculty and drawing much of its patronage from parents cursed with backward or semi-incorrigible offspring" who "roamed as in a terrestrial paradise like packs of cheerful wolves out of bounds, out of hours and very much out of hand" (Wickham in *SCRem,* 63).Wickham, however, is the only source for a negative view of the school. See Gullason, "Stephen Crane at Claverack College," 46, n. 26.

Among Crane's teachers at Claverack was John B.Van Petten, professor of history and elocution. As chaplain of the 34th New York Volunteers, a number that suggests the fictional 304th Regiment in *The Red Badge of Courage,* and as commander of another regiment, he witnessed at the battles of Antietam and Winchester the terror and confusion during the Civil War depicted in the novel; however, he probably did not directly influence *The Red Badge*. As a minister, professor, and veteran, he wanted to instill courage and patriotism in his students rather than illustrate the cowardice of soldiers.

10. "Structured academic program": Katz, "Stephen Crane at Claverack College and Hudson River Institute," 2; "might lead students astray": E. B. Crane in *SCRem*, 12; Katz, "Stephen Crane at Claverack College and Hudson River Institute," 4; Gullason, "Stephen Crane at Claverack College," 36, n. 6. Beer claimed that Townley found the pony in May 1884, then gave it to his brother (48). Stallman believed that the pony's name was "Pudgy"; see *Stephen Crane*, rev. ed. (New York: Braziller, 1973), 9.

11. "Flack Alley": In "Flagon," V-5, Schoberlin writes that Crane was assigned at Claverack "to cubicle 117 'Flack Alley,' as the third-floor corridor of the boys' dormitory was commonly called." "Tough devils": *C*, 36; "collection of tobacco": Wickham in *SCRem*, 62.

12. "Opinion be damned": Wickham in *SCRem*, 63.

13. "American flag": Gullason, "Stephen Crane at Claverack College," 40–41; "very miserable": *C*, 212; "very Harrying": Wickham in *SCRem*, 64; "before she dies": Wickham in *SCRem*, 69; Wickham in *SCRem*, 64. Wickham speculated that "S. S. T." stood for "*sic semper tyrannis.*"

14. "Damn you, Wickham": Wickham in *SCRem*, 65; "seduction from him": *Log*, 44–45; "my after-life": *C*, 212.

15. "Hen-like attitude": Wickham in *SCRem*, 66; "means to drop your gun": Wickham in *SCRem*, 6; "That is it": Wickham in *SCRem*, 67.

16. "Stephen cranium": Wickham in *SCRem*, 64; "social outcasts": Wickham in *SCRem*, 67. Founded in 1838, Pennington began accepting international students by the late 1800s, introduced to the school by businessmen and Methodist missionaries; "March 27, 1888": *C*, 31. "Stood for 'Townley'": Stanley Wertheim, "Stephen Crane's Middle Name," *Stephen Crane Newsletter* 3, no. 4 (Summer 1969), 2, 4.

17. "Rainless blue": *Works*, 6: 247; "classics and contemporary literature": Crane said that he read "a great deal" while "gradually acquiring a style" (*C*, 232). In an interview conducted with a Syracuse University classmate, Mansfield J. French recalled that "Steve read newspapers greedily and he always looked first to the sports pages, then to international news. He certainly talked about those foreign explosions." See Thomas Arthur Gullason, "Stephen Crane: Anti-Imperialist," *American Literature*, 30 (1958), 238. On Crane's reading interests, see the listings in *SCRem*, 379.

18. "Academy graduates": Gullason, "Stephen Crane at Claverack College," 37–38, n. 9; "farmers of Columbia Co.": *C*, 35.

6. College at Lafayette and Syracuse

1. David E. E. Sloane, "Stephen Crane at Lafayette," *Resources for American Literary Study,* 2 (1972), 104.

2. MHS interview with Dr. William Hall, Lafayette College, 17 April 1948, MHSC Files. See also Thomas Gullason, "Stephen Crane at Lafayette College: New Perspectives," *Stephen Crane Studies,* 3 (Fall 1994), 2–12; Lyndon Upson Pratt, "The Formal Education of Stephen Crane," *American Literature,* 10 (1939), 460–471; and Michael Robertson, *Stephen Crane at Lafayette* (Easton, PA: Friends of the Skillman Library, 1990).

3. Crane maintained his ties with Delta Upsilon and, according to a newspaper report, was scheduled to give a five-minute talk in Philadelphia at the fraternity's annual convention on 21 October 1898 ("Greek Letter Men," *Philadelphia Inquirer,* 17 October 1898, 14). But he was in Havana, Cuba, at the time.

4. Frederick Webb Hodge, ed., *Handbook of American Indians North of Mexico: N–Z* (Washington: Government Printing Office, 1910), 217. There are variant spellings for Paxinosa's name.

5. Sloane, "Stephen Crane at Lafayette," 104.

6. "Explosion in another": David Bishop Skillman, *The Biography of a College: Being the History of the First Century of the Life of Lafayette College,* vol. 2 (Easton, PA: Lafayette College, 1932), 65–66; "resigned in 1852": Charles Colman Sellers, *Dickinson College: A History* (Middletown, CT: Wesleyan University Press, 1973), 231–234.

7. "Defended the banner": *C,* 35. Crane's letter is vague concerning the specific cause of his injuries. Instead of the banner scrap, it may have been another annual rivalry such as the tug-of-war between freshmen and sophomores. "In the classroom": *Works,* 3; 118, 121; "any college in the country": *C,* 35.

8. "Had been suspended": Skillman, *The Biography of a College,* 55; "spoke about the incident": E. G. Smith in *SCRem,* 71, "Prof. Hunt Tells of Stephen Crane, '94," *The Lafayette,* 20 October 1931, 1; "in his honor": Skillman, *The Biography of a College,* 84.

9. *C,* 166.

10. "Worthy passages": F. W. March, "English at Lafayette," *The Dial,* 16 (1894), 294; "Homeric experts": *Works,* 8: 420; "education elsewhere": *Commercial Advertiser* [New York], 13 June 1896, 10.

11. *Log,* 56.

12. *Illustrated Bulletin, Syracuse University* [1900], 1, transcript (typos corrected), MHSC Files. Though the bulletin is from 1900, the wording makes clear that the message had not changed since the school's inception in 1871. For

information on Crane at Syracuse, see Thomas Gullason, "Stephen Crane at Syracuse University: New Findings," *Courier* [Syracuse University Library], 29 (Spring 1994b), 127–140; Claude Jones, "Stephen Crane at Syracuse," *American Literature*, 7 (1935), 82–85; Pratt, "The Formal Education of Stephen Crane"; Paul Sorrentino, "New Evidence on Stephen Crane at Syracuse," *Resources for American Literary Study*, 15 (1985), 179–185; and Lester J. Wells, "The Syracuse Days of Stephen Crane," *Syracuse*, 10.2 (1959), 12–14, 40–42.

13. "Preparatory studies": *Annual of the Syracuse University for the Collegiate Year, 1889–90* (Syracuse, 1889), 49; "tobacco smoke": Peaslee in *SCRem*, 84.

14. Goodwin, Lawrence, and Noxon were DU fraternity brothers. Although Mansfield and Peaslee attended Syracuse, they were not members of the fraternity.

15. "Bawdy drinking songs": Lawrence in *SCRem*, 112–113; "fell in the fire": Goodwin in *SCRem*, 80.

16. Crane may also have attended a psychology course. See John N. Hilliard, "Stephen Crane," *New York Times*, 14 July 1900, BR2.

17. "Long-dead scholars": *Works*, 3: 113; "St. Paul": *Log*, 59; "grindstone for anybody": Peaslee in *SCRem*, 86; "the un-Godly": Lawrence in *SCRem*, 110.

18. "He did not care for": Stallman and Gilkes, 307; "conic sections": Herford in *SCRem*, 157; "despised academic tradition": Lawrence in *SCRem*, 113; "gilds the mine": *Log*, 60; "among his peers": Sorrentino, "New Evidence on Stephen Crane at Syracuse," 182.

19. *C*, 231–232; "Lived a Strenuous Life," *Sunday Oregonian* [Portland], 17 June 1900, 2. Though the article is unsigned, the author is either Clarence Loomis Peaslee or someone familiar with Peaslee's article "Stephen Crane's College Days" (in *SCRem*, 84–87). "Lived a Strenuous Life" contains verbal echoes of Peaslee's article. Hilliard's "Stephen Crane" also has verbal echoes of "Lived a Strenuous Life."

20. "Patent-leather shoes": Peaslee and French in *SCRem*, 84, 77; "American college baseball": E. B. Crane in *SCRem*, 13; "played tenaciously": French and Peaslee in *SCRem*, 77, 84.

21. John Montgomery Ward, *Base-Ball: How to Become a Player, With the Origin, History and Explanation of the Game* (1888; rpt. Cleveland: Society for American Baseball Research, 1993), 30.

22. "Jan 18th / 91": *The Poetical Works of John Keats, with a Life*, biographical introd. James Russell Lowell, vii–xxxvi (1854; rpt. Boston: Little, Brown, 1863). The inscribed copy is catalogued as 811.6 / K / Rare Books at the Monmouth County [New Jersey] Historical Association.

23. While in college, Crane inscribed his name in Frances L. Mace, *Under Pine*

and Palm (Boston: Ticknor and Company, 1888) and twice in Bertha Meriton Gardiner, *The French Revolution, 1789–1795,* 4th ed., Epochs of Modern History (London: Longmans, Green, 1889), once at the Delta Upsilon House at Lafayette, and another time on 13 January 1891 at Syracuse. See Joseph Katz, "Ex Libris Stephen Crane: *Under Pine and Palm,*" *Stephen Crane Newsletter,* 3 (Summer 1969), 8; and James E., Kibler, Jr., "The Library of Stephen and Cora Crane," in *Proof: The Yearbook of American Bibliographical and Textual Studies,* vol. 1, ed. Joseph Katz (Columbia: University of South Carolina Press, 1971), 218. *The French Revolution* was the textbook for Dr. Charles J. Little's history course at Syracuse, which Crane attended without enrolling in; see Thomas A. Gullason, ed., *A Garland of Writings: Stephen Crane's Literary Family* (Syracuse: Syracuse University Press, 2002), 5.

24. "Startling Facts," *Utica Observer,* 15 April 1896, 4. *Le Ventre de Paris* was translated by Henry Vizetelly and published in 1888 as *Fat and Thin.* After Vizetelly's imprisonment for obscene libel, his son revised and expurgated the translation. The new version, *The Fat and the Thin,* appeared in 1896.

25. "His own individual style": J. D. Barry, "Plain Talks," *New York Evening Telegram,* 18 December 1917, 8; "with a loud whoop": "Stephen Crane's Boyhood Literature," *Rochester Democrat and Chronicle,* 14 May 1902, 6; "hint of self-deprecation": William F. Hills, "The Personality of Stephen Crane," *Success,* August 1900, 286.

26. "Some fun here": *C,* 36; "singers and dancers": McMahon in *SCRem,* 81; "But dead": McMahon acknowledged that although the lines were not exactly what Crane had written, they were "a fairish copy of one verse" (*SCRem,* 81).

27. *SCRem,* 81–83. John Northern Hilliard also observed that Crane "was bubbling over with fun and . . . was always playing" (Stallman and Gilkes, 326).

28. Mrs. Alice [Crane] Ludwig and Edith F. Crane, interview with MHS, Poughkeepsie, NY, 15 May 1948, MHSC Files. See also Thomas A. Gullason, "Stephen Crane at Claverack College: A New Reading," *Courier* [Syracuse University Library], 27 (Fall 1992), 39.

29. "American Episcopal churches": S. B. Whitney, "Surpliced Boy Choirs in America," *New England Magazine,* April 1892, 139–164; "sing along with the choir": Noxon in *SCRem,* 76; "hearts of the children": Gullason, *A Garland,* 122.

30. "One Thousand Copies of St. Nicholas To Be Given Away," *Syracuse Standard,* 7 March 1891, 3.

31. "Textbook was inaccurate": Sorrentino, "New Evidence," 181; "at the university": Charles G. Little to Ames Williams, 28 October 1941, MHSC Files. The professor told this account to his son, Charles G. Little.

32. "Journalism and literature": *C,* 429–430; "deserted streets": Thomas E. Martin, "Stephen Crane: Athlete and Author," *Argot* [Syracuse University], 3 (March 1935), 2; "crazy stuff": *SCRem,* 316, n. 32. Further evidence that Crane wrote a draft of *Maggie* at Syracuse is in another reminiscence from a classmate: "Characteristics of Stephen Crane," *Syracuse Journal,* 6 June 1900, 9.

33. "Changed his attitude": Chancellor Day to JTC, Jr., 18 November 1899, GP Papers; "recover from college": Chandler in *SCRem,* 88, *C,* 99. "Steph Crane": The earliest known reference to the inscription is in a 1906 Syracuse newspaper article, where Crane's first name is spelled out and the wording rearranged; see Lew Collings, "Carved Name and Date Are Reminder of Stephen Crane," *Syracuse Post-Standard,* 13 October 1906, 12. The inscription is reproduced in Thomas E. Martin, "Stephen Crane: Athlete and Author," *Argot* [Syracuse University], 3 (March 1935), 1–2, though by 1935 paint partly covered it.

7. Fledgling Writer

1. "January 1891": For a groundbreaking analysis of Kipling's influence on Crane, see James B. Colvert, "The Origins of Stephen Crane's Literary Creed," *University of Texas Studies in English* 34 (1955), 179–188, reprinted in Gullason, *Stephen Crane's Career: Perspectives and Evaluations* (New York: New York University Press, 1972), 170–180. The novel exists in at least four different versions. *Lippincott's* published a twelve-chapter story with a happy ending. There are also versions with eleven chapters (happy ending), fourteen chapters (sad), and fifteen chapters (sad).

2. "The artist's own experience of it": *C,* 230; "live more comfortably with siblings": Sidbury in *SCRem,* 53; "their work would be better": Rudyard Kipling, *The Light That Failed* (Garden City, NY: Doubleday, 1899), 34; *C,* 231. For similar comments from Crane, see also *C,* 232 and 323. "Glib humor and contrived prose": *C,* 63; "1896, in New York": Thomas Pinney, ed., *The Letters of Rudyard Kipling,* vol. 3: 1900–1910 (Iowa City: University of Iowa Press), 1996, 21, n. 2.

3. "'Desire' to write": *C,* 97; "writers of fiction": Michael Robertson, *Stephen Crane, Journalism, and the Making of Modern American Literature* (New York: Columbia University Press, 1997), ch. 1.

4. "Middle class expanded": David W. Francis, "Cedar Point and the Characteristics of American Summer Resorts during the Gilded Age," *Hayes Historical Journal,* 7 (Winter 1988), 5–27; "Sunday gabble": *Log,* 80; "folks everywhere": "Asbury's New Move," *Philadelphia Press,* 12 July 1887, 7.

5. "Employing him": Johnson in *SCRem,* 38. "Barnegat Bay": Another cub reporter, Edgar C. Snyder, was treasurer. Later he became Washington cor-

respondent for the *Omaha Bee* and president of the Gridiron Club of correspondents in Washington.

6. The details concerning the relationship between Garland and Crane are
   confusing because in later years Garland gave conflicting accounts of it.
   Nonetheless, one can reconstruct a plausible scenario.

7. *Works,* 8: 507. Years after the event, Garland claimed that when he had read
   Crane's account, he was immediately impressed with its "unusual precision
   of expression" (Garland in *SCRem,* 91); he was forgetting that much of the
   account was a transcription of his own words.

8. "Rebellious art": Hamlin Garland, *Crumbling Idols: Twelve Essays on Art and
   Literature* (Gainesville, FL: Scholars' Facsimiles and Reprints, 1957), iii, 185,
   192; "true to your time": Hamlin Garland, "The West in Literature," *Arena,*
   6 (November 1892), 676.

9. "New York Topics," *Boston Daily Advertiser,* 2 April 1894, 4.

10. "Late into the night": Lawrence in *SCRem,* 114; "forty nights": Lawrence
    in *SCRem,* 115.

11. "Father was a lawyer": Joseph Katz, "Friends Were Basis of Four Men," *Port
    Jervis Union-Gazette,* 19 August 1982, 2. "Of all professions": typed excerpt
    from an undated letter from Louis C. Senger, Jr., to Rees Frescoln, MHSC
    Files. Senger says that Crane was no more than seventeen years old dur-
    ing the conversation about careers, which would put it in 1888–1889; but
    Crane did not meet Lawrence until January 1891, when they began attend-
    ing Syracuse University. The conversation must have occurred during one
    of the summer camping trips in 1891–1895/1896.

12. "First work in fiction": *C,* 167; "creating the county": *Works,* 8: 207, 208,
    203; "impassable gulfs": *Works,* 8: 232; "hymns of abandonment": *Works,* 8:
    240.

13. "For the night": *Log,* 66; "Asylum in New Jersey": *Log,* 65.

14. "1885–1886": MHC to GP and Mrs. George Peck, 21 January 1868, LHS,
    Log, 34; "members at her side": EFC to TB, 19 November 1922, Yale; "sixty-
    four": Mrs. Crane's age is incorrectly listed as sixty-eight in the *Log* (67).

15. Transcript of will, MHSC Files; Thomas A. Gullason, "The Last Will and
    Testament of Mrs. Mary Helen Peck Crane," *American Literature,* 40 (1968),
    234.

16. "February 1892": Johnson in *SCRem,* 39; "clever school": *C,* 63.

8. Satirist in Asbury Park

1. "May 28": "Briefs," *Port Jervis Morning Index,* 28 May 1892, 3; "the inquest":
   Log, 71–74.

2. "Waste basket": "Methods of Stephen Crane," *Boston Herald,* 7 June 1896,
   32; "Be yourself": Oliver in *SCRem,* 30.

3. "He actually disliked it": Linson (1958), 19. For a summary of details about Lily Brandon Munroe, see Stanley Wertheim, *A Stephen Crane Encyclopedia* (Westport, CT: Greenwood, 1997), 231–232. See also EFC to MHS, 24 July 1948; Frederick B. Smillie to MHS, 23 March 1949; MHS to Ames Williams, 26 June 1949; Frederick B. Smillie to Lillian Gilkes, 7 March 1955; Mrs. Frederick B. Smillie to Miss Mary Benjamin, 15 February 1963; Ames Williams's interviews with Mrs. George F. Smillie (Lily Brandon Munroe), 1 and 30 January 1948 (source of Mr. Brandon's remark). Copies of the letters and interviews are in MHSC Files.

4. *C*, 58; John Berryman, *Stephen Crane* (1950; rpt. Cleveland: World-Meridian), 1962, 45. After Townley's first two wives died, he married his third wife on July 20, 1893. Townley's third marriage helps to date Letter 27 in *C* as being after 20 July 1893. Berryman's source for information is at least partly based on his interview with Mrs. Smillie.

5. EFC to TB, 30 December 1933, Yale.

6. "Those young men": *Works*, 8: 13; "hope of dreams": *Works*, 5: 3–12.

7. *C*, 55, 58, 63.

8. "Features libelled": *Works*, 8: 512; "sombre hued waves": *Works*, 8: 518; "false hues": *Works*, 8: 517; "possession of nickels": *Works*, 8: 512; "moral machine": *Works*, 8: 510; "warm nights": *Works*, 8: 521, 520.

9. "Men shrunk": *Works*, 8: 513; "diapason snore": *Works*, 8: 527–528.

10. "Crowded tenements": *Works*, 8: 514; "the unfortunates": *Works*, 8: 514.

11. "In their eyes": *Works*, 8: 508; "of the world": *Works*, 8: 525, 514; "be surprised": *Works*, 8: 503.

12. "Three thousand JOUAM members": "Round about New Jersey," *Philadelphia Press*, 18 August 1892, 6, transcript in MHSC Files; "Stevie Crane famous": Oliver in *SCRem*, 32; "a kaleidoscope": Oliver in *SCRem*, 33; "mulcted by him": *Works*, 8: 521–522.

13. "Midwest campaigning": editorial page, *New York Tribune*, 28 August 1892, 6; "condemning him": "Reid Must Explain," *Asbury Park Daily Spray*, 23 August 1892, 1.

14. "Parade story": untitled article, *The Daily Inter Ocean* [Chicago], 19 April 1896, 32; "Death of Stephen Crane," *Boston Daily Globe*, 6 June 1900, 2. "A boomerang": Oliver in *SCRem*, 36; "discharge them": J. Townley Crane, "Asbury Park," in Thomas Gullason, ed., *Stephen Crane's Career: Perspectives and Evaluations* (New York: New York University Press, 1972), 38; "die young": *Log*, 80.

15. "For the season": Johnson in *SCRem*, 42; "things anyway": Garland in *SCRem*, 92; "the opportunity": Oliver in *SCRem*, 34. Post Wheeler recalled in 1947 that at some point Crane did not want to talk about the incident (MHSC Files).

16. "What I said": Oliver in *SCRem,* 34; "newspapers for years": *C,* 45.

17. "*Asbury Park Shore Press*": "The Passing Throng," *Asbury Park Journal,* 5 November 1892, 1, transcript in MHSC Files; "literary and journalistic skills": "Stephen Crane and Asbury Park," *Asbury Park Sunday Press,* 31 May 1931, 15. Though this article relies heavily on Beer, it cites Mrs. W. S. Sees as the source for several important details about Townley, whom she knew. Her aunt, Elizabeth Richards, was his third wife, and she lived with the Cranes.

18. "Newspaper Men Eat," *Asbury Park Daily Spray,* 25 August 1898, 1, transcript in MHSC Files.

19. "Had the article not appeared": *SCRem,* 309, n. 50; "he owed him": Max Herzberg, "New and Old Data on Stephen Crane," *Torch,* 4 (April 1931), 37.

20. "Stephen Crane Dies in Germany," *Newark Daily Advertiser,* 5 June 1900, 4, transcript in MHSC Files; "Stephen Crane's Roast," *Asbury Park Press,* 8 June 1900, 1.

21. *Works,* 8: 654.

9. *Maggie*

1. "Printed in New York City": Gerald R. Wolfe, *New York: A Guide to the Metropolis—Walking Tours of the Architecture and History* (New York: New York University Press, 1975), 52; "to the world": James L. Ford, *The Literary Shop and Other Tales* (New York: Geo. R. Richmond, 1894), 69, 127–128.

2. "*Newark Daily Advertiser*": *Log,* 80. "Life and society": For evidence that Crane named the house, see *SCRem,* 327, n. 96. A well-known private gentleman's club in Louisville, Kentucky, founded in 1881, was also named the Pendennis Club, but Crane was more likely alluding to Thackeray's novel.

3. Although Lawrence (*SCRem,* 116) stated that he and Crane explored the Bowery, it is unclear how well Crane knew the area before he began writing about it for the *New York Press* in 1894. In *Maggie,* the dime museum and the first beer hall, which is based on the Atlantic Garden, were in the Bowery district; but the novella is, as the subtitle states, "a story of New York." Besides the Bowery, the setting includes the Tenderloin district, the theater district, and the midtown East Side in the upper 50s and the 60s, the neighborhood where Maggie lives. *George's Mother* is also primarily set in midtown on the East Side. The confusion regarding the setting of the two novellas stems from the decision of Heinemann to publish them together in 1900 under the title *Bowery Tales.* When Fredson Bowers published them together in 1969 as the first volume of the Virginia edition of Crane, he used the same title. For an important analysis of the setting of the two novellas, see Stanley Wertheim, "The New York City Topography of *Maggie* and *George's Mother,*" *Stephen Crane Studies,* 17 (Spring 2008), 2–12.

    "The size of Dublin": Vincent P. DeSantis, "The Gilded Age in American

History," *Hayes Historical Journal,* 7, ii (Winter 1988), 51; "on the Lower East Side": Jacob Riis, *How the Other Half Lives: Studies among the Tenements of New York,* introd. by Donald N. Bigelow (New York: Hill and Wang, 1957), 229; "have had a church on it": Luc Sante, *Low Life: Lures and Snares of Old New York* (New York: Farrar Straus Giroux, 1991), 10; "a street comparable": Julian Ralph, "The Bowery," *Century Illustrated Magazine,* December 1891, 227.

4. "Guiltless of crime": Roy L. McCardell, "When the Bowery Was in Bloom," *Saturday Evening Post,* 19 December 1925, 87.

5. Lawrence in *SCRem,* 116–117.

6. There has been much discussion about the meaning of Garland's note to Gilder and Crane's penciled comment on it. According to the normally reliable Post Wheeler, Crane told him that Garland had sent Gilder the manuscript of *Maggie,* although Garland recalled seeing it only in book form; however, Wheeler was writing more than fifty years after the fact and was influenced by Beer (Wheeler in *SCRem,* 27; *Log,* 80). A biographer is thus forced to infer a version of the events: After Crane showed Garland a manuscript of *Maggie* in late August 1892, Garland wrote the note of introduction to Gilder about a manuscript. The question is which manuscript was he referring to. If one assumes that it was *Maggie,* then instead of immediately taking it to Gilder, Crane must have revised it and then written his comment. Although "different one" could refer to a totally different manuscript, it was apparently a revision of what Garland had first seen. It would have been confusing, perhaps even embarrassing, if Garland asked Gilder about the manuscript of *Maggie,* only to discover that Gilder did not know what he meant.

7. "Stuff in him": Johnson in *SCRem,* 40; "men talk": Sidbury in *SCRem,* 56.

8. "Mob of Smiths": Linson, 21. "On the title page": J. D. Barry, "Plain Talks," *New York Evening Telegram,* 18 December 1917, 8; *New York Tribune,* 16 June 1900. "Under His Arm": G. A. Cevasco, *The 1890s: An Encyclopedia of British Literature, Art, and Culture* (New York: Garland, 1993), 691.

9. *Works,* 1: 12, 67. Although I am citing the University of Virginia edition of Stephen Crane to be consistent with citations of Crane's work in other endnotes, scholars consider the text of *Maggie* in Volume 1 unreliable because of the controversial method used by the editor to prepare the text; however, the passages I quote are accurate. The preferred, 1893 version of *Maggie* is widely available in paperback.

10. *Works,* 1: 77.

11. Ibid., 7, 29.

12. "Slang for a warning": Ralph, "The Bowery," 35. "Cages at once": Linson, 27; Lawrence in *SCRem,* 118–119; *Log,* 86–87; *C,* 46, 59, n. 1.

13. "*Maggie*-mad": Noxon in *SCRem,* 73; "but I manage to live": Stallman and Gilkes, 301; "The Author": *C,* 53; "good that story is": Stallman and Gilkes, 300.

14. "Approaching genius": quoted in Van Wyck Brooks, *Howells: His Life and World* (New York: Dutton, 1959), 10; "a wretched thing": *C,* 51; "sympathy and truth": *Works,* 8: 507; "his meeting with Howells": Lawrence and Greene in *SCRem,* 120, 125; "literary skill": *C,* 54; "important writers": Johnson in *SCRem,* 40. On the relationship between Howells and Crane, see Paul Sorrentino, "A Re-Examination of the Relationship between Stephen Crane and W. D. Howells," *American Literary Realism,* 34 (Fall 2001), 47–65.

15. "Hopeless hardship": Weatherford, 38; "public from him": Stallman and Gilkes, 306; "I *know* it": Weatherford, 61.

16. "To be dangerous": *C,* 50; "reform work": *C,* 50; "lightens narrative": Linson, 33; "Mellins-food": Wheeler in *SCRem,* 29; "firing her": Post Wheeler and Hallie Ermine Rives, *Dome of Many-Coloured Glass* (Garden City, NY: Doubleday, 1955), 107.

17. Though the book generated almost no critical response, other authors responded in fiction to what they perceived as Crane's inaccurate portrayal of slum life. Among the influential critics that Garland encouraged Crane to mail a copy of the book to was Brander Matthews, professor of drama at Columbia University and a staunch supporter of literary realism, whose *Vignettes of Manhattan* (1894) reflected his outspoken advocacy of accurate portrayals of New York City life. There is no record of a direct response from him to Crane about *Maggie,* but Matthews's melodramatic short story "Before the Break of Day" (1894) revised the plot and theme of *Maggie.* Though Maggie O'Donnel faces repeated hardships in her slum setting, she ultimately achieves the American dream in the kind of romanticized world that Crane satirizes in his book. See Lawrence J. Oliver, "Brander Matthews' Re-visioning of Crane's *Maggie,*" *American Literature,* 60 (1988), 654–658.

18. "They smelled the smoke": Linson, 21; "one of my first loves": *C,* 232. Crane was rumored to have begun a novel about a boy prostitute, "Flowers in [or 'of'] Asphalt," but no reliable evidence exists to support the assertion. See *Log,* 105–106; and Wertheim, *A Stephen Crane Encyclopedia* (Westport, CT: Greenwood, 1997), 110; "thirty years ago": Weatherford, 326. In *Stephen Crane* (1950; rpt. Cleveland: World-Meridian, 1962), 52, John Berryman reiterated the assertion.

19. "From your fire": McBride in *SCRem,* 161; "Phil Crane": *C,* 47; "resale value": EFC to MHS, 10 April 1949, MHSC Files; *SCRem,* 311, n. 88. "Burning the book": Mrs. P. M. Murray-Hamilton to Mr. Ralph Allan,

9 September 1927, Virginia; Elmer Adler, *An Informal Talk at the University of Kansas, April 17, 1953* (Los Angeles: Plantin Press, 1953), 15–17.

20. Jean Holloway, *Hamlin Garland: A Biography* (Austin: University of Texas Press, 1960), 74, 291.

10. Genesis of *The Red Badge of Courage*

1. "To be true": Edson Brace, "Stories and Studies of Stephen Crane," *St. Louis Republic,* 17 June 1900, part II, 6; "open house": Linson, 7.

2. "Leading illustrators": "'Girl of To-day' Jury Famous for American Types," *New York Times,* 7 December 1913, SM6; "an aquarium": "Mme. Branchard of 'Village' Dead," *New York Times,* 10 January 1937, 48; William H. Honan, *The Greenwich Village Guide* (New York: Bryan Publications, 1959), 21–23.

3. "Ten thousand devils": *Works,* 8: 683; "entering the harbor": Vosburgh in *SCRem,* 134; "City Is War": Linson, 37; "like a bomb": *Works,* 1: 19, 48, 49.

4. "Days on end": Stallman and Gilkes, 319–320; "Town Tonight": Linson, 16–17; "working this side": "An Anecdote of Stephen Crane," *Watertown* [N.Y.] *Daily Times,* 9 February 1905, 10; "friend's meal": Ericson in *SCRem,* 137; "leaving a trace": Lawrence in *SCRem,* 119; "champagne dinner": Lawrence in *SCRem,* 119; "again penniless": Gordon in *SCRem,* 140; "rescued by Linson": "An Artist in His Hilltop Aerie," *Asbury Park Sunday Press,* 27 March 1932, feature section, 1.

5. Linson, 28, 29.

6. "Lamented to Linson": Linson, 36; "Astor House": Linson, 13; "I believe I will": Herford in *SCRem,* 156.

7. "Know the kind": *Log,* 91–92; "That's like war": Vosburgh in *SCRem,* 134.

8. "Emotionless as rocks": Linson in *SCRem,* 105, requoted with slight variation in Linson, 37 (see also Herford in *SCRem,* 156); "on the floor": Linson, 38; "ample generosities": Corwin K. Linson to B. J. R. Stolper, 5 April 1933, Columbia.

9. *Log,* 81.

10. EFC to TB, 19 November 1922, Yale.

11. *Works,* 8: 313.

12. "He had no shoes": Vosburgh in *SCRem,* 134; "almost cadaverous": Marshall in *SCRem,* 227; "coal box": Greene in *SCRem,* 125–126; "bed for a week": Gordon in *SCRem,* 139.

13. "Commercial movie theater": Brian Clegg. *The Man Who Stopped Time: The Illuminating Story of Eadweard Muybridge—Pioneering Photographer, Father of the Motion Picture, Murderer* (Washington: Joseph Henry Press, 2007), ix; "spirit is with us": Lynn Sherr, *America the Beautiful: The Stirring True Story behind Our Nation's Favorite Song* (New York: Public Affairs, 2001), 25; "America the Beautiful": Sherr, *America the Beautiful,* 78; "this fair": Hamlin

Garland, *A Son of the Middle Border* (New York: Collier, 1917), 458; "had failed": Peter Lyon, *Success Story: The Life and Times of S. S. McClure* (New York: Scribner's, 1963), 125; "higher wages": Ellen Moers, *Two Dreisers* (New York: Viking, 1969), 4.

14. Linson, 58.

15. "In the race": *Works,* 8: 317; "nature and truth": *C,* 63.

16. "Next two years" and "come to this": Linson, 59.

17. "Fire fighter": Michael Robertson, *Stephen Crane, Journalism, and the Making of Modern American Literature* (New York: Columbia University Press, 1997), 95–96; "pneumoniac novel": quoted in William R. Linneman, "Satires of American Realism, 1880–1900," *American Literature,* 34 (1962), 91–92.

18. "My own way": *Log,* 92; "That is great": Ericson in *SCRem,* 137.

11. Struggling Artist, Poet at Work

1. "At the moment": Hawkins in *SCRem,* 166; "ten dollar bills": Hawkins in *SCRem,* 166; "that's all": Linson, 49–50.

2. "A man is he": Linson, 50.

3. "With an ax": Linson, 51–52, and Linson in *SCRem,* 105–106; "in a book": Linson, 51–52. "Indian" was the affectionately scornful term Crane often used to describe good friends. Later in England he used the term more derisively to characterize freeloaders who stayed at Brede Place and made it difficult for him to work.

4. Linson, 81, quotes only part of the inscription. The complete inscription reads "To Stephen Crane / A genius. / from his friend. / Hamlin Garland / Jan. 24 94." See Brick Row Book Shop (San Francisco), Miscellany 52: Recent Acquisitions (2010).

5. "From his family": Garland in *SCRem,* 94.

6. "On paper": Garland in *SCRem,* 94.

7. "Five weeks": Keith Newlin, *Hamlin Garland: A Life* (Lincoln: University of Nebraska Press, 2008), 185.

8. "So superbly": *C,* 62, 75.

9. "Die than do it": *Log,* 99; "hear 'em roar": Linson, 55.

10. "Iced cucumbers": *C,* 184, 185; "slow speaking style": *Works,* 10: 345; "free himself from it": Amy Lowell, Introduction, *The Black Riders and Other Lines,* vol. 6 of *The Work of Stephen Crane,* ed. Wilson Follett (New York: Knopf, 1926), xix; "attract attention": Wickham in *SCRem,* 70.

11. Linson, 54–56; *Log,* 107; Marston LaFrance, "A Few Facts about Stephen Crane and 'Holland,'" *American Literature,* 37 (1965), 200.

12. "Shoe trade": *Log,* 102–103. Crane clipped Edwards's article, which is a commentary on Maggie, and pasted it in a scrapbook. Crane wrote next to the article, "This is a fake—not only a fake but a wretched, unartistic fake

written by a very stupid man. But it was a great benefit." Crane's attitude is confusing because the article is generally positive. Like Howells and Garland, Edwards was ambivalent about *Maggie*. He found it "shocking," yet acknowledged its "cold, awful, brutal realism" and recognized that Crane could become as great as Tolstoy. In the spring Crane asked Edwards to read the manuscript of *The Red Badge*. Later in the year, after it was serialized, Crane thought enough of Edwards's editorial commentary on the novel to make a handwritten copy of it.

13. "Book covers before": *Log*, 99, 100; "make a book": *C*, 65.

14. "Formidable for them": *C*, 63.

15. "Most likely Lily": Linson, 17; "in her head": Linson, 17–18.

16. "Social condition": *Works*, 8: 297; "kill 'em": *Works*, 8: 282.

17. "Avowed Socialist": Greene in *SCRem*, 126. In a letter to TB (19 November 1922, Yale), EFC quoted Crane as saying, "I was once a Socialist for as much as two weeks." TB embellished the comment. According to him, Crane said: "I was a Socialist for two weeks but when a couple of Socialists assured me I had no right to think differently from any other Socialist and then quarrelled with each other about what Socialism meant, I ran away" (Beer, 205–206).

18. "Monkey about politics": *C*, 125–126; "writing a political novel": *Log*, 177.

19. "Out of ten": Michelson in *SCRem*, 216 "race or color": Hilliard in *SCRem*, 162; "yellow and young": *C*, 44; "Some of her": E. G. Smith in *SCRem*, 165; "mind and speech": Greene in *SCRem*, 128; "the way out": Robert H. Davis in *SCRem*, 154–155.

20. "Outa sight": *Works*, 1: 27; "from something": *Works*, 1: 138, 139.

21. "Gertrude Selene": Greene in *SCRem*, 128.

22. "Building on West 57th Street": John Clendenning, "Crane and Hemingway: A Possible Biographical Connection," *Stephen Crane Studies*, 5 (Fall 1996), 4; "*Il Trovatore* throughout *The Third Violet*": Paul Sorrentino, "Stephen Crane's Struggle with Romance in *The Third Violet*," *American Literature*, 70 (June 1998), 265–291; "Crane's children's stories in *Harper's*": James D. Brasch and Joseph Sigman, *Hemingway's Library: A Composite Record* (1981; Boston: Electronic edition, John F. Kennedy Library, 2000), 10; www.jfklibrary.org/Research/The-Ernest-Hemingway-Collection/~/media/C107EFE32F9C446A8A30B7C46C4B035F.pdf (accessed 6/23/2013); "*The Red Badge of Courage*": Peter Griffin, *Along with Youth: Hemingway, the Early Years* (New York: Oxford University Press, 1985), 13; "similar to those of Crane": Philip Young, *Ernest Hemingway: A Reconsideration* (University Park: Pennsylvania State University Press, 1966), 191–196; Jeffrey Meyers, *Hemingway: A Biography* (New York: Harper, 1985), 134–135; "good writers": Ernest Hemingway, *Green Hills of Africa* (New York: Scribner's, 1935), 22;

"one of the finest books in our literature": Ernest Hemingway, ed., *Men at War* (New York: Crown, 1942), xvii. "Fallen in love with": John Clendenning initially mentioned to me the possible connection between Crane and Grace Hall and offered convincing internal evidence that TB's fictional creation Helen Trent is based on Hall. Clendenning later published his explanation for the connection (Clendenning, "Crane and Hemingway"). Edward Roger Stephenson had earlier suggested the connection in a footnote in his dissertation; see Edward Roger Stephenson, "Stephen Crane and Ernest Hemingway: A Study in Literary Continuity" (Ph.D. diss., Brown University, 1972), 13, n. 4.

12. Frustrated Artist

1. "Self-derisive smile": Garland in *SCRem*, 95; "enemy tribe": Garland in *SCRem*, 96; "football field": *C*, 228.

2. One of Garland's reminiscences is the only source for what is a confusing detail about a lost typescript. Whereas Garland states that Crane gave him the first half of the manuscript, Crane's statement that the typist had the second half raises the question of whether or not the first half had already been typed. If so, why did Crane give Garland a manuscript rather than a typescript? Here is one possible explanation: Crane took the complete manuscript to a typist, who might have started typing after Crane paid him a set amount. When Crane heard that Garland would soon be leaving for Chicago, Crane asked the typist for the manuscript so that he could show it to Garland. To make sure that Crane returned, the typist gave him just the first half. After Crane got fifteen dollars from Garland, he retrieved the second half and gave it to Garland on April 24, the day before Garland left for Chicago. While Garland was reading the second half, the typist might have been working on the first half.

3. "His Uncle Wilbur": Greene in *SCRem*, 128; "dollars in cash": Garland in *SCRem*, 97.

4. "Benjamin Orange Flower": *SCRem*, 321, n. 25; "is hungry": Garland in *SCRem*, 96; "make money": Joseph Katz, "Stephen Crane: Muckraker," *Columbia Library Columns*, 17 (February 1968), 3.

5. Years later, Linson was delighted to learn that Crane "repaid" the debt by giving a wounded soldier in Tampa fifty dollars to enable him to get home; but unknown to Linson, Beer is the only source for the anecdote (Linson, 70; Beer, 182).

6. Helen R. Crane in *SCRem*, 46.

7. "At the post": *C*, 79.

8. Crane's friends offered other sources for the novella. Harvey Wickham stated that George and his mother were based on two of his relatives

(*SCRem*, 68). Frederic Lawrence stated that *Maggie* and *George's Mother* were based on his and Crane's "own observations and adventures" (Stallman and Gilkes, 331) and that the wild party in March 1893 at the Pendennis Club to commemorate the publication of *Maggie* inspired the party in Chapters 8–9 of *George's Mother* (Lawrence in *SCRem*, 118–119).

9. "Shame and humiliation": *Works,* 1: 156, 157; "wild son": *Works,* 1: 161; "run by William B. Kelsey": "Local Items," *Asbury Park Shore Press,* 12 January 1884, 3.

10. R. W. Stallman (*Stephen Crane: A Critical Bibliography* [Ames: Iowa State University Press, 1972], 212) states that "Crane told Edward Garnett that George's mother was an exaggerated portrait of his own mother's characteristics," and Thomas Gullason (ed., *Stephen Crane's Career: Perspectives and Evaluations* [New York: New York University Press, 1972], 399), quotes Crane's "well-known statement" that "'George's mother was an exaggerated portrait' of his own mother's characteristics." Neither, however, cites a source. The source is an unsubstantiated claim in a letter from TB to E. B. Crane, 30 October 1922, Yale.

11. John Julian, *A Dictionary of Hymnology* (New York: Dover, 1957), 55; Frances E. Willard, *Woman and Temperance: or, The Work and Workers of the Woman's Christian Temperance Union* (Hartford, CT: Park Publishing, 1883), 312, 350. See also George Monteiro, *Stephen Crane's Blue Badge of Courage* (Baton Rouge: Louisiana State University Press, 2000), 54–55.

12. *Works,* 1: 178.

13. "Of the bar": *Works,* 1: 116; "pride in himself": *Works,* 1: 135.

14. "I now forget": *C,* 130; "furniture at Edmund's home": EFC to TB, 19 November 1922, Yale; "hills of Hartwood": *C,* 181; "sailing alone on Hartwood Lake": Mrs. Alice (Crane) Ludwig and Edith F. Crane, interview with MHS, Poughkeepsie, NY, 15 May 1948, MHSC Files. "Stephen Crane's Pond": This phrase comes from an unpublished fragment of a letter by E. B. Crane: "My brother and I think that the little lake that has never up to now been dignified on any map by a name should henceforth be called 'Stephen Crane's Pond.'" Quoted in Doug Hay, "For Judge, Stephen Crane Is a Personal Memory," *Port Jervis Union-Gazette,* 4 July 1976, 10.

15. Linson, 75.

16. "Account of the camping trip": Joseph Katz, "Solving Stephen Crane's *Pike County Puzzle,*" *American Literature,* 55 (1983), 174; "*Pike County Puzzle*": *Works,* 8: 608–635. See also Katz, "Solving," 171–182. "Cider presses": Crane alludes to one of the major industries in northeastern Pennsylvania–southeastern New York, the quarrying and fabricating of bluestone.

17. "Proportionately so little": *Works,* 8: 606; "boiled shirt-fronts": Linson, 70. A comparison of the manuscript and magazine versions of "In the Depths of

a Coal Mine" reveals a number of stylistic and substantive changes, most notably the removal of editorial commentary in the published version; but scholars disagree on who actually made the revisions. There are also differences between the newspaper and magazine versions of the article. For an analysis of the issue, see *Works,* 8: 923–932. For arguments in favor of the view that McClure edited the text, see Bernard Weinstein, "Stephen Crane, Journalist," in *Stephen Crane in Transition: Centenary Essays,* ed. Joseph Katz (De Kalb: Northern Illinois University Press, 1972), 3–34; Katz, "Stephen Crane: Muckraker," 3–7; and Katz, "Stephen Crane: The Humanist in the Making," in *William Carlos Williams, Stephen Crane, Philip Freneau: Papers and Poems Celebrating New Jersey's Literary Heritage,* ed. W. John Bauer (Trenton: New Jersey Historical Commission, 1989), 75–85. For the view that Crane revised at least part of it, see Edwin H. Cady in *Works,* 8: xxxvi–xxxiii; Patrick K. Dooley, *The Pluralistic Philosophy of Stephen Crane* (Urbana: University of Illinois Press, 1993); and Dooley, "Openness to Experience in Stephen Crane's 'In the Depths of a Coal Mine,'" in *Caverns of Night: Coal Mines in Art, Literature, and Film,* ed. William B. Thesin (Columbia: University of South Carolina Press, 2000), 186–198.

18. "Enclosed address": *C,* 73–74; "literary prejudices": *C,* 75.

19. Quoted in James B. Colvert, "Fred Holland Day, Louise Imogen Guiney, and the Text of Stephen Crane's *The Black Riders,*" *American Literary Realism: 1870–1910,* 28 (Winter 1996), 22.

20. "Use it but": *C,* 79; "pen for culprits": *Log,* 155.

21. "Financial panic": Peter Lyon, *Success Story: The Life and Times of S. S. McClure* (New York: Scribner's, 1963), 125; "November 1894": ibid., 126–134.

22. "Turned down one more time": Hawkins in *SCRem,* 167; "serial rights": for the amount, see Herford (158), Cather (176), and Harriman (272) in *SCRem.*

23. *C,* 81.

24. "Tellers of tales": Marston LaFrance, "A Few Facts about Stephen Crane and 'Holland,'" *American Literature,* 37 (1965), 201–202. On "Stevey" as the name used by Bacheller and other journalists, see Stallman and Gilkes, 298. "Power of genius": Bacheller in *SCRem,* 149–150; "Gawd like a soldier": Irving Bacheller, *From Stores of Memory* (New York: Farrar and Rinehart, 1933), 111: "before then": Stallman and Gilkes, 298; "rejected it": Stallman and Gilkes, 298–299.

25. Linson, 89–90.

13. On the Verge of Celebrity

1. "Newspaper trip": *C,* 93; "letter of introduction": "The Author of *The Red Badge,*" *The Critic,* n.s., 25 (1896), 163.

2. For the best summary and analysis of the relationship between Crane and Hitchcock during the preparation of the manuscript of *The Red Badge,* see James Colvert, "Crane, Hitchcock, and the Binder Edition of *The Red Badge of Courage,*" in *Critical Essays on Stephen Crane's "The Red Badge of Courage,"* ed. Donald Pizer (Boston: G. K. Hall, 1990), 238–263.

3. "Book-doctor of his time": Post Wheeler to MHS, 25 December 1947, MHSC Files; "deleting the word 'red'": *C,* 100; "*Saturday Evening Post*": *Log,* 215; Stanley Wertheim, "Stephen Crane Balks: Two New Letters," *American Literary Realism,* 29 (Winter 1997): 76–80; "any changes in them": *Log,* 215.

4. *C,* 96.

5. "The Modern Ship of the Plains" is the title of an illustration depicting immigrants traveling westward on a train, in *Harper's Weekly,* 13 November 1880, 728; the illustration is reprinted as plate 21 in Henry Nash Smith's *Popular Culture and Industrialism, 1865–1890* (New York: New York University Press, 1967). For two examples of the sea image in dime novels, see Edward S. Ellis, *Seth Jones; or, The Captives of the Frontier;* and Anonymous, *Frank Reade, the Inventor: Chasing the James Boys with His Steam Team,* in Bill Brown, *Reading the West: An Anthology of Dime Novels* (Boston: Bedford Books, 1997). From *Seth Jones:* "As the tide of emigration has rolled westward, it has ever met that fiery counter-surge, and only overcome it by incessant battling and effort. And even now, as the distant shores of the Pacific are well-nigh reached, that resisting wave still gives forth its lurid flashes of conflict" (176). From *Frank Read:* A mechanical wagon, the "steam team," "went skimming over the prairie as a swift sailing yacht might over a smooth sea with a favorable breeze" (393).

6. *Works,* 8: 82.

7. Ibid., 415, 420.

8. "University of Nebraska": Cather in *SCRem,* 174 (in her reminiscence, Cather says she was a junior); "Moping, are you": Cather in *SCRem,* 174; "stuff that would sell": Cather in *SCRem,* 177; "takes forever": Cather in *SCRem,* 177; "your fingers": Cather in *SCRem,* 175. In 1899, a year before her article on Crane, Cather condemned *War Is Kind* and *Active Service* in reviews. Regarding the former: "Either Mr. Crane is insulting the public or insulting himself, or he has developed a case of atavism and is chattering the primeval nonsense of the apes." In 1926, however, she wrote an appreciative introduction to Crane's *Wounds in the Rain,* volume nine in *The Work of Stephen Crane,* ed. Wilson Follett, 12 vols. (New York: Knopf, 1925–1927).

9. Cather in *SCRem,* 175.

10. "Innocent hair": *Works,* 8: 423; "expensive gems": Linson stated that Crane got the opals from an engineer named Charles Gardner and gave them to

his friends in New York City upon his return (Linson, 89); Beer, 119, however, is Linson's source for the reference to Gardner. "Street vendors": *Works,* 8: 442.

11. "Dans New Orleans": *C,* 98; "Eastern and Western life": *Works,* 8: 474; "Atlantic Ocean": *Works,* 8: 475; "handsome business blocks": *Works,* 8: 468.

12. "Allowed to stand": *Works,* 8: 471; "then they live": *C,* 136; "false East": *C,* 242.

13. "From hades": *Works,* 8: 47; "a rose on his coat": Frank H. Bushick, *Glamorous Days: In Old San Antonio* (San Antonio: Naylor, 1934), 98–100.

14. "Capitalist from Chicago": *Works,* 8: 446; "strange life": *Works,* 8: 451; "bragged about his children": *Works,* 8: 451; "Doubled my money": *Works,* 8: 449; "matter of speculation": *C,* 102; "moral assassin": *Works,* 8: 431.

15. "Men of another": *Works,* 8: 436; "New York City sketches": *Works,* 8: 437; "pity them": *Works,* 8: 439; "manner of the people": *Works,* 8: 436; "new point of view": *Works,* 8: 435.

16. Stanley Wertheim, "Stephen Crane Remembered," *Studies in American Fiction,* 4 (1976), 52.

17. *C,* 104.

18. "Magnificent": EFC to Louis Zara, 14 December 1958, Special Collections, Louis Zara Papers, Ohio State University; "found freedom": Linson, 87. Crane's allusion to writing a story about his "personal troubles in Mexico" (*C,* 123) has led biographers to speculate about whether "One Dash— Horses" was based on fact. A Mexican robber and his gang try to rob and threaten to kill an Easterner and his guide until the latter are rescued by the Mexican army. In a 1903 reminiscence, Linson hinted vaguely that the events in "One Dash—Horses" occurred to Crane (*SCRem,* 107, 326, n. 72), and EFC told MHS that she recalled hearing her uncle talk about the toughness of Mexican bandits (MHSC Files). Beer is the only source for the name of the bandit, Ramón Colorado, and that of the guide, Miguel Itorbide, and most likely got the name "Itorbide" from the Hotel Iturbide, where Crane stayed in Mexico City.

19. "Fourteen newspaper dispatches": Greene in *SCRem,* 129; "considered 'vivid'": Irving Bacheller, *From Stores of Memory* (New York: Farrar and Rinehart, 1933), 111.

20. "A puzzle": *C,* 77, 80; "paragraphed": *C,* 81.

21. "Form of insult": *C,* 162; "his most autobiographical work": "Methods of Stephen Crane," *Boston Herald,* 7 June 1896, 32; "You are a toad": *Works,* 10: 28; "Wicked image, I hate Thee": *Works,* 10: 8; "My poor child": *Works,* 10: 31; "in the heart / So softly": *Works,* 10: 23; "original relation to the universe": Ralph Waldo Emerson, *Emerson's Prose and Poetry,* ed. Joel Porte and Saundra Morris (New York: Norton, 2001), 27.

22. "An amplification": *C*, 231.

23. "So too is Existence": Crane's search for God was ongoing. Later in the year, he and a friend, Harry P. Taber, were hiking in snowy woods near East Aurora, New York. They stopped beside a stream, where Crane, crouched on the bank, began digging with his stick. "What have you found," asked Taber. With a tiny crawfish in his hand, Crane replied philosophically, "This—and God." When frozen branches creaked in a gust of wind, he added, "The Death-Demon in the Tree Tops again," alluding to his poem "The chatter of a death-demon from a tree-top," which had appeared in the *Philistine* in August. See Harry P. Taber to TB, 19 December 1923, R. W. Stallman Collection, Archives and Special Collections, Thomas J. Dodd Research Center, University of Connecticut; also quoted in Stallman, *Stephen Crane: A Critical Bibliography* (Ames: Iowa State University Press, 1972), 311. *The Black Riders and Other Lines* had indeed been a search for God; and though "The chatter of a death-demon from a tree-top" was written later, it, too, captured "the rise of his agony" during moments of spiritual doubt and despair forcefully depicted in *The Black Riders* (*Works*, 10: 56).

24. "Slovenly work": Weatherford, 66; "poetic lunacy": Marc Ferrara and Gordon Dossett, "A Sheaf of Contemporary American Reviews of Stephen Crane," *Studies in the Novel*, 10 (1978), 168; "given birth": Weatherford, 63, 65; "stephencranelets": Wheeler in *SCRem*, 27; "the lobsters": *Log*, 158; "Steamin' Stork": *Log*, 136–137; "parodies of *The Black Riders*": Hawkins in *SCRem*, 166; "think it great": *C*, 111; "a review": Abraham Cahan, *Bletter fun Mein Leben*, vol. 4 (New York: Forward Publishing, 1928), 63. A slightly different translation of the Yiddish text appears in Rudolf and Clara M. Kirk, "Abraham Cahan and William Dean Howells," *American Jewish Historical Quarterly*, 52 (September 1962): 38–40.

25. Earle Labor, Robert C. Leitz III, and I. Milo Shepard, eds., *The Letters of Jack London*, vol. 1: 1896–1905 (Stanford, CA: Stanford University Press, 1988), 79, 82. London was also familiar with Crane's "Flanagan and His Short Filibustering Adventure" (Labor, Leitz, and Shepard, *Letters of Jack London*, 97).

26. Herbert Mitgang, ed., *The Letters of Carl Sandburg* (New York: Harcourt, 1968), 92; Carl Sandburg, *The Complete Poetry of Carl Sandburg*, rev. ed. (New York: Harcourt, 1970), 73.

27. Carl Sandburg, *Ever the Winds of Chance* (Urbana: University of Illinois Press, 1983), 130.

28. Irving Bacheller fictionalized club members in two novels, *Eben Holden: A Tale of the North Country* (1900) and *The Master: Being in Part Copied from the Minutes of the School for Novelists, a Round Table of Good Fellows Who, Long Since, Dined Every Saturday at the Sign o' the Lanthorne, on Golden Hill, in New*

York City (1909). In *The Master,* Crane, as the character Ben Lovel, is the "lately elected president of the Mechanics' Union"—an ironic twist, given that the Junior Order of United American Mechanics denounced Crane in 1892. Lovel is arrested when he has "a row with patrolman Conley at one o'clock in the morning over the arrest of a disreputable young woman of the Ninth Ward." When the incident makes the headlines in the newspapers, a friend, who knows the "great kindness" of Lovel's heart, fears that it will sully his career: "I fear it will do you harm. . . . One must look out for his reputation." To which Lovel replies, "Some will despise me, but I cannot help it. . . . Some who are dear to me will turn away, but I put justice above them" (*The Master* [New York: Doubleday, Page, 1909], 106, 107, 108). Bacheller was alluding to a notorious incident in 1896 in which Crane publicly defended a prostitute wrongfully arrested.

29. Many of my details about the club come from "The Sign o' the Lanthorn," *New York Daily Tribune,* 26 April 1896, 32; Post Wheeler to MHS, 25 December 1947, MHSC Files; transcript of Post Wheeler's diary, MHSC Files.

30. Arthur Barlett Maurice, *New York in Fiction* (1899; Port Washington, Long Island, NY: Ira J. Friedmann, 1969), 44.

31. "Old Friends Chat of Stephen Crane," *Newark Evening News,* 8 November 1921, 10, transcript in MHSC Files.

32. "Grow high": *Log,* 132; "the title 'Mr.'": Post Wheeler's diary; "weaknesses, not its strengths": Thomas L. Masson, "Literary Memories: Writers and Publishers of Yesterday," *Dearborn Independent Magazine,* 26 December 1925, 16; "said little at the gatherings": ibid., p. 16; "better told": cited in Thomas Gullason, ed., *Stephen Crane's Career: Perspectives and Evaluations* (New York: New York University Press, 1972), 131; "financial problems in 1898": Post Wheeler's diary.

33. [No first name] Wiggins, "Mostly about People: Albert Bigelow Paine on the Bread Line," *Brooklyn Daily Eagle,* 14 January 1925, section 1, 1. Although the title of the newspaper proposed by Bacheller is unknown, it is called *The Whole Family* in Paine's novel. In *The New York of the Novelists* (New York: Dodd, Mead, 1917), 192–195, Arthur Bartlett Maurice does not suggest that any of the characters are based on Crane, and states that the actual events occurred in 1897, during which Crane was in New York City only intermittently from January to March; however, a character in the novel's one illustration resembles Crane.

34. "Lines by a prose writer": "The Sign o' the Lanthorn," *New York Daily Tribune,* 26 April 1896, 32; "but Mark Twain": Linson, 31.

35. "One letter to him": The Hartford (Connecticut) Public Library once reported that it had a letter from Clemens to Crane, but a librarian told me that it is missing. "July 1895": Willis Brooks Hawkins, "All in a Lifetime,"

no. 2, 1–2, Willis Brooks Hawkins Collection, Virginia. Internal and external evidence in "Lifetime" helps to date the luncheon. When Twain's publishing company went bankrupt in 1894, he arranged the most ambitious
lecture tour of his life and left for it on July 14, 1895. On July 12, Twain was
on Randall's Island in Manhattan to give a talk at the New York House of
Refuge, a reform school for juvenile delinquents. During his visit to the
club, he told the members that he would soon be leaving on this trip; thus
the visit occurred on July 13 or 14. Hawkins stated that Twain was sixty-
two at the time, which would put the visit after 30 November (Twain's
birthdate) 1897; however, he was fifty-nine when he took the trip.

36. Post Wheeler's diary.

37. See letters 233 and 602 in C.

38. Carl Dolmetsch (1992) inspired my thoughts on the connection between
Twain's story and Crane's novel; see Dolmetsch, "Cowardice and Courage:
Mark Twain, Stephen Crane and the Civil War," *Profils Américains,* 3 (1992):
39–50. Although "The Private History" was excluded when the *Century*
reprinted the series as a four-volume edition, both of Linson's accounts
above make clear that Crane read the series when it first appeared in the
magazine. If he missed the story there, he could have found it in Twain's
Merry Tales (1892).

39. *C,* 111.

40. "Tired of the project": *C,* 116; "Feel great": *C,* 118; "between him and
me": *C,* 127; "in New York": *C,* 126; "for some time": *C,* 127; "things are
yours": *C,* 124.

41. Roy Macbeth Pitkin, *Whom the Gods Love Die Young: A Modern Medical Perspective on Illnesses That Caused the Early Death of Famous People* (Pittsburgh:
RoseDog Books, 2008), 83–84.

42. "Looks in dying": Diane Yancey, *Tuberculosis,* rev. ed. (Minneapolis: Twenty-
First Century Books, 2008), 17–18; "I haven't time": Cather in *SCRem,*
177; "spent wisely": Amy Lowell, introd. to *The Black Riders and Other Lines*
(1926), vol. 6, *The Work of Stephen Crane,* ed. Wilson Follett, 12 vols. (New
York: Knopf, 1925–1927), 7.

14. International Fame

1. Peter Osborne, *The Gilded Age of Port Jervis* (Port Jervis, NY: Port Jervis Area
Heritage Commission, 1992), 7.

2. *Works,* 2: 11.

3. Donald Pease, "Fear, Rage, and the Mistrials of Representation in *The Red
Badge of Courage,*" in *American Realism: New Essays,* ed. Eric J. Sundquist
(Baltimore: Johns Hopkins University Press, 1982), 155–175; Amy Kaplan,

"The Spectacle of War in Crane's Revision of History," in *New Essays on "The Red Badge of Courage,"* ed. Lee Clark Mitchell (New York: Cambridge University Press, 1986), 77–108; Harold R. Hungerford, "'That Was Chancellorsville': The Factual Framework for *The Red Badge of Courage*," *American Literature,* 34 (1963): 520–531.

4. *Works,* 2: 40, 47, 6.

5. "Quiet man-hood": *Works,* 2: 135; "rain clouds": *Works,* 2: 135.

6. "Stammered": *Works,* 2: 5; "blubbering": *Works,* 2: 36; "babbling": *Works,* 2: 35; "bundles": *Works,* 2: 36; "spoiled child": *Works,* 2: 31; "bawling": *Works,* 2: 31; "tragedy": *Works,* 2: 46; "enamelled sky": *Works,* 2: 98; "between nature and humanity": *Works,* 2: 46, 47.

7. On the difficulty in establishing the printing history of *The Red Badge,* see Joseph Katz, "*The Red Badge of Courage:* A Preliminary History of the Appleton Printings," *Stephen Crane Newsletter,* 4 (Spring 1970), 5–7.

8. Marion Elizabeth Rodgers, *Mencken: The American Iconoclast* (New York: Oxford University Press, 2005), 38.

9. Ernest Hemingway, ed., *Men at War* (New York: Crown, 1942), xvii; Joseph Blotner, ed., *Selected Letters of William Faulkner* (New York: Random House, 1977), 69; Andrew Turnbull, ed., *The Letters of F. Scott Fitzgerald* (New York: Scribner's, 1963), 597.

10. "Warring emotions": Weatherford, 108, 109, 107; "average reviewer": *C,* 181; "in my head": *C,* 190.

11. "American soldiers and American armies": Weatherford, 140; "to nature and to life": Weatherford, 142. Criticism was not limited to whether the book was satirical or realistic. A local committee in Watertown, New York, proposed removing *The Red Badge* (along with *Uncle Tom's Cabin*) from the library because "it has more swear words in it than any book" and is "one long, livid wall of blood and woe" ("Watertown Schools," *Watertown Daily Times,* 16 February 1897, 5); "bad criticism": Weatherford, 147.

12. "Use of dialect": *Log,* 134–135; "but strenuously": *Log,* 146.

13. "Admire most of all": *C,* 232; "*Sebastopol*": J. C. Levenson, introd. to *The Red Badge of Courage,* in *The Works of Stephen Crane,* vol. 2, ed. Fredson Bowers (Charlottesville: University Press of Virginia, 1975), xli–xlii; "validity of the inscription," *C,* 247; "pursuit of truth": *C,* 192.

14. "In my work": *C,* 165; "purpose-novel": F. Marion Crawford, *The Novel: What It Is* (1893; rpt. Westport, CT: Greenwood, 1970), 11; "divorce laws": Crawford, *The Novel,* 12, 13; "political intrigue": Romantic novels were frequently serialized in major newspapers and magazines, as was the case with *Trilby* in *Harper's Monthly Magazine.*

15. *Works,* 8: 637.

16. Ibid., 635–638.

17. "Style for the story": *C,* 128; "pretty rotten work": *C,* 161; "trousers with": *C,* 144; "serious work": *C,* 191; "vacuous trifle": Weatherford, 206.

18. "In the marketplace": Paul Sorrentino, "Stephen Crane's Struggle with Romance in *The Third Violet,*" *American Literature,* 70 (June 1998), 265–291; "ordinary thing": *Works,* 3: 18; "some pot-boiler": *Works,* 3: 80; "who is killing": *Works,* 3: 60; "with the easel": *Works,* 3: 60, 61; "comic paragraphs": *Works,* 3: 16.

19. "Pursuit of truth": *C,* 144, 192; "should be lived": *C,* 233, 186, 187.

20. "Inspector of the Universe": "Elbert Hubbard: An American Original," www.pbs.org/wned/elbert-hubbard/timeline.php (accessed 6/14/2013). "During the 1890s": Harry Taber later contended that Hubbard claimed credit for things he had not done. According to Taber, he started the *Philistine* alone, and the author of Hubbard's inspirational essay "A Message to Garcia" was actually William Mackintosh, managing editor of the *Buffalo* [*New York*] *Evening News.* After tension between Taber and Hubbard developed, they severed their relationship in February 1896. Crane was interested in Taber's proposal to publish his next book, but nothing came of the plan. For additional details about Hubbard, the *Philistine,* and the banquet as they relate to Crane, see R. W. Stallman, *Stephen Crane: A Critical Bibliography* (Ames: Iowa State University Press, 1972), 298–301, 310–312, 356–358.

21. "Presumably Hubbard": Albert Lane, *Elbert Hubbard and His Work: A Biography, a Sketch, and a Bibliography* (Worcester, MA: Blanchard Press, 1901), 84; "prejudice against royalties": Noxon in *SCRem,* 76; "aegis of the Roycrofters": Amy Lowell, introd. to *The Black Riders and Other Lines* (1926), vol. 6 of *The Work of Stephen Crane,* Wilson Follett, ed., 12 vols. (New York: Knopf, 1925–1927), xxiii, xxvi; "two names apiece": *Philistine,* November 1895, 200.

22. *Log,* 148. Once news got out that Hubbard was planning a banquet for Crane, two organizations in Buffalo—the Saturn Club (a private men's club) and the Browning Club (a women's club for the study of Robert Browning and other writers)—also planned dinners for him, though at least the latter was probably not held, for Stephen told Nellie Crouse that he had gone "dashing through the back streets of Buffalo to escape the Browning Club" (*C,* 154, 171).

23. "Decline the offer": *C,* 140; "with my woods": *C,* 135; "Love and Himself": Harry P. Taber to TB, 19 December 1923, R. W. Stallman Collection, Archives and Special Collections, Thomas J. Dodd Research Center, University of Connecticut; also quoted in Stallman's *Stephen Crane: A Critical Bibliography* (Ames: Iowa State University Press, 1972), 311.

24. "Now I would": *C,* 140, 155; "recognize that cause": *C,* 142; "the slaughter": Bragdon in *SCRem,* 169; "characterized them": Noxon in *SCRem,* 75; "what happened": *C,* 162.

25. "No doubt about that": Elbert Hubbard to Julia Ditto Young, 30 July 1900, quoted in Paul Sorrentino, "The Philistine Society's Banquet for Stephen Crane," *American Literary Realism,* 15 (1982), 235; "his protégé": Stallman, *Stephen Crane: A Critical Bibliography,* 246; "be damned": *Philistine,* January 1897, 61–62; "Justice may be done": EFC to MHS, 8 December 1948, MHSC Files.

26. "Blue funk": Hawkins in *SCRem,* 169. "Akron, Ohio": Nellie attended school in Washington, D.C., traveled to England, and married Samuel E. Carpenter in 1897. When they divorced in 1914, she apparently relinquished custody of her six children, who were raised in the Carpenter family home in Philadelphia. After living in Paris, Nellie moved to Philadelphia, where she died in 1943.

27. *C,* 181.

28. George Washington Crouse served as a schoolteacher, civil servant, member of Congress from Ohio, and successful businessman who helped to finance the Goodyear Rubber Company and the Diamond Match Company.

29. Nellie was apparently amusing herself by writing to a London barrister and a Belgian count, as well as to Crane. When the barrister and the count proposed marriage, she stopped writing to them (George Monteiro, "Crane's Letters to Nellie Crouse: An Unpublished Essay," *Stephen Crane Studies,* 13 [Spring 2004], 6). However, after receiving Crane's fourth letter, according to Karl Medcalf, "she realized that she had come to mean something to the man and was very anxious to renew the acquaintance but the various plans for a visit to Akron never materialized" (Karl Medcalf to Elmer Adler, 11 February 1930, enclosure, Elmer Adler Collection, Special Collections, Princeton University Library). Although one of her children asserted that Crane did visit Nellie in Akron (Edwin H. Cady and Lester G. Wells, eds., *Stephen Crane's Love Letters to Nellie Crouse* [Syracuse: Syracuse University Press, 1954], 74), Nellie told a news reporter that she had seen Crane only once (Paul E. Tanner, "New Stephen Crane Letters Found Here Reveal Despair," *Rochester* [*New York*] *Democrat Chronicle,* 29 December 1929, 1).

30. "If he does it well": *C,* 198, 200; "his 'dusty' uniform": *Works,* 6: 71, 68; "from his Western trip": Lawrence in *SCRem,* 120; "I'm through": Greene in *SCRem,* 130; "they will be reunited": *Works,* 6: 80, 81; "charming": *C,* 171, 180.

31. "Crane's love for her": Cady and Wells, *Stephen Crane's Love Letters to Nellie Crouse,* 74; "came off decently": *C,* 164; "to so think": *C,* 186.

32. *C*, 182, 187.

33. Ibid., 208, 207, 186.

34. Ibid., 209.

15. Price of Fame

1. "Found myself famous": R. E. Prothero, ed., *The Works of Lord Byron: Letters and Journals,* vol. 2 (London: John Murray, 1898), 106; "discover himself famous": Thomas L. Masson, "Literary Memories: Writers and Publishers of Yesterday," *Dearborn Independent Magazine,* 26 December 1925, 16; "mighty proportions": *C*, 130; "new hero": *C*, 209; "accursed tumult": *C*, 189; "to my hills": *C*, 191.

2. "Out of sight": *C*, 230, 231; "that interests me": Weatherford, 156; "forcible way": *Log,* 192. According to another observer, although Crane accepted honest criticism, he was hurt by vitriolic attacks on his work (John N. Hilliard, "Stephen Crane," *New York Times,* 14 July 1900, BR2).

3. Crane, however, remained ambivalent about clubs. Post Wheeler recalled that in Crane's letters from Brede Place, occasionally there was "a line or so flinging at the older 'literary darks' as he used to dub them, or railing at the Authors Club in old Carnegie Hall. . . . Personally he had only jibes for the crowd there." Crane supported Wheeler's application for membership in the club, but wrote him: "What the hell your reasons were for joining the club I can't see!" (Post Wheeler to MHS, 28 August 1948, MHSC Files; *C*, 591).

4. *C*, 175.

5. There is confusion about the actual date of the dinner at the Authors Club. According to the *Bookman,* 3, no. 2 (April 1896), 112, it occurred on March 7; however, a deposit recorded in Crane's bank book states that he was in Washington on March 6 (*Log,* 174). It is possible that he returned to New York City for the dinner, then immediately went back to Washington until April 2, when he returned to New York. The matter is complicated by the fact that the *Bookman* states March 7 was a Friday; it was actually a Saturday. And the dinner could not have been held on Friday, February 7, because Crane was in Hartwood.

6. "In regard to war": *C*, 175; "busy at them": *C*, 161; "battle was fought": *C*, 177; "associate color with sound": Willis Brooks [Hawkins], "Eagle Quills," *Brooklyn Daily Eagle,* 18 April 1907, 4.

7. "How it happened": *C*, 161; "internal despair": *C*, 198, 175; "dull and uncreative": *C*, 192; "cannot be sustained": *C*, 161, 191.

8. "Careless work": *C*, 245, 241; "dealing with battle": *C*, 205.

9. "Greatest diffidence": *C*, 174; "let it go": *C*, 191.

10. "Words which hurt": *C*, 200; "if they suit": *C*, 206; "chapter titles": *C*, 224; "able to see it": *C*, 224; "hate the book": *C*, 207.

11. "Very short": *C*, 200; "75-cent series": *C*, 174. For a valuable analysis of the relationship between Crane and Hitchcock during the revision of *Maggie*, see Fritz Oehlschlaeger, "Stephen Crane, Ripley Hitchcock, and *Maggie*: A Reconsideration," *Journal of English and Germanic Philology*, 97 (1998), 34–50; "ill-advised": Weatherford, 162.

12. "My foremost trait": *C*, 213; "next novella, *George's Mother*": George Monteiro, "Stephen Crane's 'Dan Emmonds': A Case Reargued," *Serif*, 6 (1969), 32–36; "business courtesies": *C*, 217.

13. "Artist's hand": *Log*, 188; "means nothing": *Log*, 191, 186.

14. "Extraordinary insight": Weatherford, 47, 48; "has been said of me": *C*, 245; "September 22": incorrectly listed as September 26 in *Log*, 208; "his companion had been": Abraham Cahan, *Bletter fun Mein Leben*, vol. 4 (New York: Forward Publishing, 1928), 63. Cahan also observed Crane's "intelligent appearance. Rarely does the talent of a gifted person mirror itself in his face. Crane's talent was indeed seen in his gestalt." A slightly different translation of the Yiddish text appears in Rudolf Kirk and Clara M. Kirk, "Abraham Cahan and William Dean Howells," *American Jewish Historical Quarterly*, 52 (September 1962), 38–40.

15. "From the West": *C*, 214; "knowing them": *C*, 218; "fifteen languages": biography.yourdictionary.com/matthew-stanley-quay (accessed 6/19/2013).

16. "Death of Brisbane," *Time*, 4 January 1937, 10.

17. "Sensational Fiction": Ferdinand Lundberg, *Imperial Hearst: A Social Biography* (New York: Modern Library, 1936), 56; "run the *New York Journal*": Lundberg, *Imperial Hearst*, 59.

18. Edmund Morris, *The Rise of Theodore Roosevelt*, rev. ed. (New York: Modern Library, 2001), 500.

19. Different versions of Williams's statement exist. For a discussion of the term "Tenderloin" and its derivation, see Herbert Asbury, *The Gangs of New York: An Informal History of the Underworld* (Garden City, NY: Garden City Publishing, 1928), 177; and B. A. Botkin, ed., *New York City Folklore: Legends, Tall Tales, Anecdotes, Stories, Sagas, Heroes and Characters, Customs, Traditions, and Sayings* (1956; rpt. Westport, CT: Greenwood Press, 1976), 331–333.

20. Asbury, *The Gangs of New York*, 248–250; James Lardner and Thomas Reppetto, *NYPD: A City and Its Police* (New York: Holt, 2000), 97.

21. Aloysius A. Norton, *Theodore Roosevelt* (Boston: G. K. Hall, 1980), 32.

22. On September 20, 1896, the *New York Journal* announced a forthcoming series of articles by Crane dealing with the life of the metropolitan policeman. The September 1896 issue of *Book News* also reported that Crane was

writing a story or group of stories about the police; but he had been hired
to write about the Tenderloin district. Hearst cabled him on August 11, asking how much money he wanted for the job. Crane's response does not
survive. A month later, he was hired to write "novelettes based upon real
incidents of New York life" (*C*, 244, 255), yet he never wrote them. He
published sketches about the Tenderloin in the *Journal* and *Town Topics,* but
none about the police.

23. Crane was already familiar with Bryan's oratory, having used the phrase
"crown of thorns," another famous image from the "Cross of Gold" speech,
in his short story "A Man and Some Others." After the Democratic National Convention in July, Crane wrote the story; but when Paul Revere
Reynolds submitted it on October 2 to the *Century Magazine* for publication, its editor, Richard Watson Gilder, requested that the phrase be deleted
because it was "hackneyed." See *Log,* 209; *Works,* 5: clxv.

24. "Great Night: New York Sizzles with Heat but Roots Loudly for Bryan,"
Minneapolis Journal, 13 August 1896, 1, 3, 7. There are various reports on the
specific details surrounding Bryan's speech at Madison Square Garden—for
instance, how high the temperature rose and how many people and police
were inside and outside the Garden. What is important is that people became increasingly restless and impatient in the sweltering heat on the night
of August 12.

25. Morris, *The Rise of Theodore Roosevelt,* 569. See also 858, n. 23. Morris
points out that "it would be unfair to accuse Roosevelt of deliberately allowing the Bryan meeting to degenerate into a noisy, embarrassing sham-
bles" (569). Yet the fact remains that Roosevelt did not attend the speech
and supervise police activity; the task was left to a Republican sympathizer.
Roosevelt was opposed to Bryan's radical financial reform advocating the
free coinage of silver and was convinced that a Bryan presidency would be
a disaster, but it is uncertain if Roosevelt's political views influenced his
handling of events that evening.

26. "Article about the police force": Peter Lyon, *Success Story: The Life and Times
of S. S. McClure* (New York: Scribner's, 1963), 140; "about 'Madge'": *C*, 241.
"On the short story": Crane's letter to Roosevelt and the inscribed copy of
George's Mother are no longer extant, but Roosevelt's comments about "A
Man and Some Others" survive. "Some day I want you to write another
story of the frontiersman and the Mexican Greaser in which the frontiersman shall come out on top; it is more normal that way!" (*C*, 249). Although
Joseph Conrad stated that "A Man and Some Others" was "an amazing bit
of biography" (*C*, 315), there is no evidence that it was based on an actual
incident in Crane's life.

27. "Simply shameful": Joseph Katz, "Stephen Crane: Metropolitan Corre-

spondent," *Kentucky Review,* 4 (Spring 1983), 43; "incapacity and inexperience": Katz, "Stephen Crane: Metropolitan Correspondent," 44; "systematic police persecution": Katz, "Stephen Crane: Metropolitan Correspondent," 46.

28. Hamlin Garland, *Roadside Meetings* (New York: Macmillan, 1930), 330. An attempt to date the luncheon is complicated by the fact that Garland confused the timing with that of another luncheon. According to Garland, sometime in October 1896 he attended an earlier luncheon honoring Roosevelt, who was planning on resigning as New York City Police Commissioner to become Assistant Secretary of the Navy. This luncheon, however, could not have occurred in 1896, because Roosevelt did not leave his post as police commissioner and become the assistant secretary until April 1897. Nor could it have occurred in October 1897, for Crane was in England at the time. The luncheon honoring Roosevelt had to have occurred sometime just before April 1897.

Though Garland suggests that this luncheon and the one at which Crane sat silently and "looked like a man in trouble" occurred close together, the latter must have occurred months earlier, sometime after July 1896, when Garland returned to New York City. In all likelihood, it did not occur between July and mid-August, for most, if not all, of that time Crane was at his brother's home in Hartwood or at the summer camp he frequented in Pike County, Pennsylvania. When he returned to New York City in August, he stayed only briefly, left again on "a business journey" (*C,* 245), then returned on August 19. It could not have occurred for three weeks after this date, however, because Roosevelt left for his three-week trip to the West on August 21; and it did not occur just before his departure, since he wrote Crane on August 18, "I wish I could have seen Hamlin Garland" (*C,* 249) before leaving. If Roosevelt did not see Garland before the trip West, Garland could not, of course, have reported being at a luncheon with him.

In short, the luncheon with Roosevelt attended by Crane, Garland, Riis, and Chanler must have taken place three weeks after Roosevelt had left for the West, which would put it sometime around September 11 and most likely before September 16, the date that marks the beginning of the Dora Clark incident.

29. Katz, "Stephen Crane: Metropolitan Correspondent," 47.

16. The Dora Clark Incident

1. *Works,* 8: 938. Crane's sketch "An Eloquence of Grief" evolved from one of his court visits. For detailed accounts of the consequences of Crane's exploration of the Tenderloin district, see Olov W. Fryckstedt, "Stephen Crane in the Tenderloin," *Studia Neophilologica,* 34 (1962), 135–163; Christopher P.

Wilson, "Stephen Crane and the Police," *American Quarterly,* 48 (June 1996), 273–315; and Wilson, *Cop Knowledge: Police Power and Cultural Narrative in Twentieth-Century America* (Chicago: University of Chicago Press, 2000).

2. "Not be seen with her": *Works,* 8: 657. "Charged with solicitation": In *The Double Life of Stephen Crane: A Biography* (New York: Knopf, 1992), 176–179, Christopher Benfey suggested that Crane was attempting to entrap Becker on September 16 as part of an exposé of police corruption and that Crane encouraged Dora Clark to press charges against Becker. See also Mike Dash, *Satan's Circus: Murder, Vice, Police Corruption, and New York's Trial of the Century* (New York: Crown, 2007), 1–20.

3. "That sort of thing": *Works,* 8: 658; "completely at their mercy": *Works,* 8: 659; "to their own affairs": *Works,* 8: 659.

4. "Mud all over you": *Works,* 8: 660; "Suicidal Purpose": *Works,* 8: 384–387. "Defense of Dora Clark": The dating of "In the Tenderloin: A Duel between an Alarm Clock and a Suicidal Purpose" is uncertain. Because a few lines of dialogue in it are similar to a brief passage of dialogue in Crane's notebook (*Works,* 8: 880) apparently written from 1892 to 1894, Fredson Bowers has suggested that Crane may have begun thinking about the story during this time, perhaps in 1894. In 1892–1894, however, Crane was primarily exploring Park Row and the Bowery, not the Tenderloin district. Most likely, he jotted down dialogue in his notebook for possible use later. As the title "In the Tenderloin" makes clear, Crane was writing about the Tenderloin district, which he was exploring in the fall of 1896. Moreover, Swift Doyer reappears in another Tenderloin story, "Yen-Hock Bill and His Sweetheart," which was published in the *New York Journal* on November 29, 1896. "In the Tenderloin: A Duel between an Alarm Clock and a Suicidal Purpose" had to have been written by October 1, 1896, its date of publication. If he had written it in August, when Hearst assigned him to explore the Tenderloin, Crane would have submitted it to the *Journal* rather than withhold it from publication. Given the similarities in character, image, and theme between the story and Crane's situation, it was probably written shortly after September 15.

5. R. W. Stallman and E. R. Hagemann, eds., *The New York City Sketches of Stephen Crane and Related Pieces* (New York: New York University Press, 1966), 225.

6. For a sample of headlines, see Fryckstedt, "Stephen Crane in the Tenderloin," 147–148; and R. W. Stallman, *Stephen Crane: A Critical Bibliography* (Ames: Iowa State University Press, 1972), 253–254.

7. *Works,* 8: 392.

8. "Rarely leave alone": *New York World,* 20 January 1897 (clipping in Cora Crane's green scrapbook, p. 16, Columbia); "*Port Jervis Evening Gazette*":

Works, 8: 657; Joseph Katz, "Stephen Crane: Metropolitan Correspondent," *Kentucky Review,* 4 (Spring 1983), 47; "information on that subject": *Works,* 8: 663.

9. Fryckstedt, "Stephen Crane in the Tenderloin," 151, 154.

10. Stallman and Hagemann, *The New York City Sketches,* 232.

11. Lawrence in *SCRem,* 123.

12. Although Crane felt comfortable enough to be in Hartwood by November 3 (*C,* 258), he might have hesitated to be there or in Port Jervis in October. He probably felt that he would have less explaining to do to one person, his close friend Lawrence, than he would have had to do amid a large family.

13. "Treat everyone fairly": Lawrence in *SCRem,* 12; "at Becker's trial": The details regarding Crane's flight to Philadelphia are complicated by his statement in the *New York Journal* on October 11. When asked about rumors that he wanted to distance himself from Dora Clark, he replied, "There is not an atom of truth in any report that I shall fail to appear against Becker. I have not tried to avoid subpoena servers, and I have not left town. My address is with a lawyer, who will notify me when the time arrives to appear. I have not received any intimations from the police that I would be 'shown up' if I appeared against Becker, either. It wouldn't make the slightest difference to me if I had. I have never, since I testified in the police court, had any idea of refusing to proceed further in the case" (Stallman and Hagemann, *The New York City Sketches,* 234–235). If Crane had not left town yet, it means that he traveled to Philadelphia sometime between October 11 and October 15, the date of the trial. The self-confident tone of the statement belies Lawrence's statement that Crane fled New York "in order to escape interviewers and let the noise die down." A less plausible explanation is that Crane had lied about not having left the city, for his telegram to Roosevelt would clearly have identified his location. In all likelihood, Crane made his statement a day or two before it was printed on October 11, then decided to get away.

   The circumstances concerning his actions were further complicated by the rumor that he was avoiding cooperating with the police. The *New York Tribune* reported on September 29 that Crane had failed to respond to the police request for an official statement about Clark and Becker (Stallman and Hagemann, *The New York City Sketches,* 231). But Crane never got the request, because it was mistakenly sent to the wrong person: "S. Crane, journalist, 29 Park Row." When Samuel Crane, president of the Atlantic Baseball League and author of *The Rough Slide of Kelly,* received the letter, he was stunned and waited almost two weeks before telling the police of the mistake. See "Conlin's Dora Clark Letter," *New York Sun,* 29 September 1896, 1, typescript in MHSC Files; "No Reply from Mr. Crane," *New York*

Tribune, 29 September 1896, 16, typescript in MHSC Files; "The Letter Reached the Wrong Crane," *New York Tribune,* 30 September 1896, 11, typescript in MHSC Files.

14. "Accuracy of Crane's testimony": Fryckstedt, "Stephen Crane in the Tenderloin," 152, citing *Harper's Weekly,* 10 October 1896, 998. "Damage Crane's reputation": Hamlin Garland recalled his and Roosevelt's response to the Dora Clark affair. "I saw Crane several times during his troubles with the New York police, and while I sympathized with him in his loyalty to a woman whom he considered had been unjustly accused of soliciting, his stubborn resolve to go on the stand in her defense was quixotic. Roosevelt discussed the case with me and said, 'I tried to save Crane from press comment, but as he insisted on testifying, I could only let the law take its course'" (Garland in *SCRem,* 100).

Even if Roosevelt had supported Crane more readily, the timing was bad. Though Roosevelt, as chairman of the Board of Commissioners, had begun enthusiastically in April 1895 to reform the New York police and had amassed an impressive record, by 1896 his work was becoming, as he frequently called it, "grimy," and his conflict with police chief Peter Conlin and another board commissioner, Andrew D. Parker, over the power of the police force was intensifying. In the fall he was campaigning in the Midwest for the Republican ticket; and by the time McKinley was elected president in November, Roosevelt had already been thinking about his own political future and would resign as police commissioner in April 1897 to become assistant secretary of the U.S. Navy. To a politician with national aspirations, the Dora Clark affair was a hindrance.

"Put an end to their relationship": Fryckstedt, "Stephen Crane in the Tenderloin," 152, citing *Harper's Weekly,* 10 October 1896, 998.

15. Stallman and Hagemann, *The New York City Sketches,* 246.

16. Fryckstedt, "Stephen Crane in the Tenderloin," 155.

17. Stallman and Hagemann, *The New York City Sketches,* 250.

18. There has been much confusion in Crane scholarship regarding Amy Leslie's identity. For years it was wrongly assumed that she was the Chicago drama critic Amy Leslie (pseudonym of Lillie West). How they first met is unclear, but she was invited to attend the Society of the Philistines banquet honoring Crane in December 1895, and was already on warm terms with him. In a letter written most likely in early January 1896, he began, "My dear Indian, did you really like the stuff?"—presumably alluding to his work—and wished her "a long, flaming '96" (George Monteiro, "Amy Leslie on Stephen Crane's *Maggie,*" *Journal of Modern Literature,* 9 [1981–1982], 147). At the party for her seventy-fifth birthday, Amy showed Philip R. Davis, a Chicago attorney and fellow journalist, a parcel of now-missing

letters that Crane had written her and that, according to Davis, threw "interesting light on Crane's struggles as a writer before 'The Red Badge' made him famous" (Philardee [Philip R. Davis], "Letters from a Genius," *Chicago Daily Tribune,* 20 July 1939, 14). Yet when journalist and writer Vincent Starrett asked whether she had any letters that he could use in his Crane research, "she almost bit my head off as she turned me down. 'Certainly not!' she snapped" (Vincent Starrett, *Born in a Bookshop: Chapters from the Chicago Renascence* [Norman: University of Oklahoma Press, 1965], 93). Another journalist, Ashton Stevens, did not fare any better. A question about the letters, when he was at dinner with Leslie, prompted her to threaten him with a wine bottle (Starrett, *Born in a Bookshop,* 93). The complex connection between Crane and Leslie was exacerbated by the Dora Clark trial, during which he admitted that he had lived with Amy. Later, when she brought a warrant of attachment against him to get money she claimed he owed her, newspapers across the country reported that a nationally known drama critic was suing Crane. Although she immediately denied that identification, the assertion has confused scholars, biographers, and journalists and remained uncorrected for decades after her death in 1939. How could such a public figure as Amy Leslie, they wondered, have also been a streetwalker living secretly with Crane? Not until 2000 was the question answered. Crane knew two people with the same name: a Chicago critic and a New York City prostitute named Amy Traphagen, one of whose pseudonyms was Amy Leslie (Kathryn Hilt and Stanley Wertheim, "Stephen Crane and Amy Leslie: A Rereading of the Evidence," *American Literary Realism,* 32 [2000], 256–269).

19. Timothy J. Gilfoyle, *City of Eros: New York City, Prostitution, and the Commercialization of Sex, 1790–1920* (New York: Norton, 1992), 205.

20. Andy Logan, *Against the Evidence: The Becker-Rosenthal Affair* (New York: McCall, 1970), 110.

21. "Woman's Arrest Justifiable": Fryckstedt, "Stephen Crane in the Tenderloin," 157, 158; "organizations in the world": *Log,* 213; "protect an unfortunate woman": Stallman and Hagemann, *The New York City Sketches,* 255. "Scheme of police intimidation": On the same page as the editorial, the *Journal* published a thinly veiled, scathing satire of the court proceedings by James L. Ford, editor of the humor magazine *Truth.* When Mr. Benjamin Cherryble witnesses two men robbing a drunken man, he races into a saloon to alert Officer Nightstick of the crime. Annoyed that he has been interrupted while playing pinochle, the officer refuses to arrest anyone, because he had not seen the crime. When Cherryble testifies against Nightstick in court, two commissioners, Guff and Stuff, turn the case into a character assassination of Cherryble with irrelevant questions. Didn't he know

that the house he had lived in more than fifteen years ago on "West Steenth street" was now occupied by an opium smoker? Wasn't it true that his wife's uncle Henry Piler was once imprisoned for grand larceny? And hadn't his sister been a typist on Wall Street, before she married "a well-to-do hardware dealer"? See Stallman and Hagemann, *The New York City Sketches,* 256–258.

22. "Marshall supported him": Edward Marshall, "Loss of Stephen Crane: A Real Misfortune to All of Us," *New York Herald,* 10 June 1900, section 6, 8; "the law take its course": Garland in *SCRem,* 10; "turned to the light": Garland in *SCRem,* 100; "I'll do it": Garland in *SCRem,* 100.

23. *C,* 266.

24. "City's chief of police": James Lardner and Thomas Reppetto, *NYPD: A City and Its Police* (New York: Holt, 2000), 120. "Harvard football games": Crane wrote another Tenderloin sketch, "Stephen Crane in Minetta Lane," that was not published in the *New York Journal;* it was syndicated on December 20, 1896, most likely by Bacheller, and appeared in several newspapers, including the *New York Herald.* He probably gave the sketch to Bacheller because he was now working for him.

25. "Dora Clark's Soft Voice," *New York Sun,* 2 January 1897, 2; transcript in MHSC Files.

26. "Sallow prince": *Works,* 8: 665, 666. "On the throne of death": F. Scott Fitzgerald alluded to the incident in *The Great Gatsby,* in the passage where Meyer Wolfsheim reminisces about the shooting of Becker's gambling partner, Herman Rosenthal: "Four of them were electrocuted," Nick Carraway recalls. "Five," replies Wolfsheim, "with Becker."

The Dora Clark affair may also have been dramatized by John Galsworthy. The MHSC Files contain a typescript of a newspaper article identifying the affair with Galsworthy's play *Escape:*

*

Stephen Crane Is Model of Hero in Galsworthy Play

Philip Hale, in his column called "As the World Wags," in the *Boston Herald,* contributes this information about John Galsworthy's *Escape,* which Winthrop Ames has produced and Leslie Howard acts.

"There is a play in Boston that is not only interesting, unusually interesting in these days of tailor-made comedies and 'thrilling' melodramas, but one that is remarkably well acted. Perhaps it is needless to say that we are speaking of John Galsworthy's *Escape,* which should be seen by all Bostonians who have a respect for fine plays and admirable performances. Those who have seen *Escape,* and many who should see it, will find strange matter in a letter sent to the Herald by D.S. [Don Seitz?].

"The Captain Denant of Galsworthy was Stephen Crane, a literary lion of his day who gained fame overnight by writing *The Red Badge of Courage.* The woman in the case was named Dora Clark. The policeman's name was Becker. The place was Sixth Avenue and Thirtieth street, New York, directly opposite the old Haymarket dance hall, a notorious resort. The only difference between the prologue of *Escape* and this incident was that Galsworthy's prologue is located in Hyde Park, London, and Crane did not injure the policeman.

"Crane and the girl were arrested. There was a great fuss over the affair, but Crane stuck to his guns and defended the girl. I think he was reprimanded in court. Everyone interested in personal liberty rushed to his defense and he came out of it rather a hero, with the girl a close second. Becker, the policeman—Charles Becker was his name—was the same man who, as Lieutenant Becker, was executed at Sing-Sing for the Rosenthal murder.

"Now this is what sticks in my crop. Crane was feted in London afterwards as a literary man. Isn't it possible that he met Galsworthy and told him of the incident in New York? I know about the New York affair because, as a reporter, I wrote the story of Crane's arrest."

★

MHS typed marginal comments: "From an unidentified newspaper in Mrs. Lucius L. Button's papers. / Use with discretion. / Paper may be *The Public Ledger.*" He then wrote "Unproved" at the beginning of the article. If Crane knew Galsworthy, it might have been through their mutual friend, Joseph Conrad.

17. Jacksonville

1. "Shining star": Bacheller in *SCRem,* 150; "if he did not return": EFC to Edith E. Greenberg (an editor for Indiana University Press), 30 December 1959, Lillian Gilkes Collection, Syracuse. Unfortunately, EFC did not supply a date for what she described as Crane's last trip to Hartwood, and in other correspondence she contradicted herself regarding the matter. He may have visited there shortly after the *Commodore* experience and just before his departure for England in March 1897, but in correspondence in 1933 and 1934 she strongly denied this (*Log,* 240–241). In 1948, she did allude to unidentified "records" that supposedly showed Crane had visited Hartwood after being in Florida (EFC to MHS 24 July 1948, MHSC Files). If he did so in January, February, or March, it would have been only briefly,

for much of that time Crane was stuck in New York City, writing to work off his debt to McClure. It is also highly unlikely that Crane visited Hartwood in 1898. After sailing from England en route to Cuba, he crossed the bar of New York Harbor at 11:53 P.M. on April 21. For the next two days, he was busy contracting with Pulitzer's *New York World* and applying for a passport. By April 24, he was on a train heading for Key West. He arrived back in New York on December 28. Realizing he had no time to get to Hartwood before his December 31 departure for England, he cabled Edmund to come to New York to say goodbye. It would have been the last time he had a chance to visit his family. It seems more likely that he tentatively gave away his possessions to Edmund's wife around the time that he was in Port Jervis preparing his will. EFC also thought that Crane told Edmund to keep his horse, Peanuts, if he did not return. The letter to Edith E. Greenberg also offers details involving William and Cora regarding the subsequent life of the horse, as does EFC's letter to TB, 14 January 1934 (Yale).

2. "Shipment to Cuban insurgents": Walter LaFeber, *New Empire: An Interpretation of American Expansion, 1860–1898* (1963; Ithaca: Cornell University Press, 1998), 284–300. "*Dauntless* and the *Three Friends*": The expression "Cuban fleet" or "Cuban navy" was used by south Florida newspapers to describe filibusters that sailed from Jacksonville, but other ships were also involved in filibustering activity. "Twenty-seven reached Cuba": R. W. Stallman, "Journalist Crane in That Dinghy," *Bulletin of the New York Public Library*, 72 (1968), 261.

3. *Log*, 229.

4. "Trips to the Cuban coast": *Works*, 9: 97; "mail is uncertain": C, 159.

5. Will Carleton, *Song of Two Centuries* (New York: Harper, 1902), 118–119. For information on Crane in Jacksonville, see William Randel, "Stephen Crane's Jacksonville," *South Atlantic Quarterly*, 62 (1963), 268–274.

6. "Human flotsam": Michelson in *SCRem*, 215; "seem very harmless": C, 271.

7. Nine of Crane's New York City sketches were grouped under this title in *The Open Boat and Other Stories* (London: Heinemann, 1898). They are not present in the American edition of the book, titled *The Open Boat and Other Tales of Adventure* (New York: Doubleday and McClure, 1898).

8. "Riding gear": Hawkins in *SCRem*, 167–168; "blessing of life": C, 205.

9. "Never forget them": C, 268; "temporary separation": C, 268, 269.

10. "Really a great trouble": C, 267; "a man named Isidor Siesfeld": A note by Marlene Zara in the library at Ohio State University reads, "Mrs. Anthony told me that Hawkins told her that Amy Leslie had 'framed' Crane, saying she was pregnant, in an effort to get Crane to marry her." In *Dark Rider: A Novel Based on the Life of Stephen Crane*, Zara's husband, Louis Zara, used the

note to speculate on Crane's reaction: "His thoughts drifted to Amy. Had there been a child? Would he ever know? Was it alive or dead? Was it somewhere, in Chicago perhaps, being reared in obscurity, a child who would one day curse its father?" Louis Zara, *Dark Rider: A Novel Based on the Life of Stephen Crane* (Cleveland: World, 1961), 435.

11. "About the story itself": *Works,* 8: 677. See 677–678 for the quotations from the review, "Ouida's Masterpiece." "Asked him to review it": The *Book Buyer* may have thought of asking Crane because the journal was planning to review *The Little Regiment* in the same issue (January 1897).

12. [Richmond Barrett], "Correspondence," *American Mercury,* June 1934, xxi.

13. Edith Richie Jones in *SCRem,* 289, 360–361, n. 123.

14. "Served more than one purpose": Luc Sante, *Low Life: Lures and Snares of Old New York* (New York: Farrar Straus Giroux, 1991). "Her own establishment in Jacksonville": Stanley Wertheim has suggested to me that Cora must have established a reputation as a successful madam while running the Hotel de Dreme. Her safe-deposit box in the Stephen Crane Collection at Columbia University contains checks showing that when she returned to Jacksonville after Crane's death to build an elegant brothel named the Court, local banks lent her an inordinate amount of money, despite her lack of collateral and her existing debts.

15. McCready in *SCRem,* 205. Because McCready says that it was a book of short stories, it would have been *The Little Regiment;* but McCready's confusion regarding the chronology of events suggests that he can be an unreliable source. It is also possible that Cora was reading *George's Mother,* which Crane had given her. Hours before leaving for Jacksonville, he had requested that the publisher give him an extra copy of the book (*C,* 259). Cora may also have read *The Red Badge of Courage,* for an 1895 edition signed by her is at Columbia.

McCready is also the only source for the assertion that Cora renamed the house the "Hotel de Dream" (McCready in *SCRem,* 205).

16. "Monmouth Park racetrack": Elizabeth Friedmann, "Cora before Crane: The Prologue," 5, unpublished paper delivered at "Stephen Crane: A Revaluation," 28–30 September 1989, Blacksburg, VA; "popularized Long Branch": *Works,* 8: 423.

17. Cora later wrote in the book, "The first thing my mouse ever gave me was this book / 1896" (Matthew Bruccoli, "Cora's Mouse," *PBSA* [Papers of the Bibliographical Society of America], 59 [1965], 188). "Mouse" was Cora's nickname for Stephen. Though Cora dated the inscription 1896, she included her English address in South Kensington, where she was living in 1901, after Crane's death. Bruccoli's comments about the copy of Kipling's book strongly suggest Cora's personality. Besides the inscription and ad-

dress, the book also contained pieces of paper pasted onto the front free endpaper. One contained Kipling's signature; the other, his address. When the paper with the signature was steamed off, it revealed the following inscription in what appeared to be Cora's handwriting: "Cora / Jacksonvill [*sic*] 1896." According to Bruccoli, "the only explanation for Mrs. Stephen Crane's attempt to conceal this inscription is that it connected her with Jacksonville and the Cora Taylor who was proprietor of the Hotel dé Dream [i.e., Dreme], a disreputable house. She eventually returned to Jacksonville and housekeeping, but in 1901 she was the respectable widow of Stephen Crane" (189).

18. *C,* 270.

19. "Nov [for December] 4th, 1896": *C,* 269–270. The book cannot be identified, because the flyleaf with the inscription was separated from it. Only the flyleaf has been located. Unfortunately, Cora removed inscribed flyleaves from books for easy storage.

20. Additional evidence that Crane knew Cora was already married when they met exists in a May 19, 1897, letter from Sylvester Scovel to his wife, in which he told her that Captain Stewart refused to divorce Cora. If Scovel knew about the marriage, Crane most certainly would have as well (*Log,* 260–261). Cora, Crane, and Scovel were together in Athens when he wrote the letter.

21. Though the poem was written earlier, sometime in 1895–1896, its publication in the October issue of *Bookman* certainly would have reminded Crane of it.

22. "Junta Is Full of Joy," *Florida Times-Union,* 31 December 1896, 5.

23. "May be for the Spanish army": ibid.; "potatoes for the Spanish army": ibid.

24. "Crew of twenty-seven or twenty-eight men": *Log,* 237 (explanation regarding the confusion over the number of people on the *Commodore*); "earning twenty dollars a month": *Log,* 232.

25. *Works,* 9: 89.

18. The *Commodore* Incident

1. Crane had already written about irrational behavior. In his sketch "When Every One Is Panic Stricken," a woman flees a burning building while carrying a bamboo easel worth about thirty cents, but forgets that her baby is still inside.

2. "On his head": R. W. Stallman, "Journalist Crane in That Dinghy," *Bulletin of the New York Public Library,* 72 (1968), 264; "binoculars": "Praise for Crane," *New York Press,* 4 January 1897, 1, 2; "have to swim": *Log,* 238.

3. "Body washed ashore": "Stephen Crane, Now Dying, Is a Strange Char-

acter," *New York Morning Telegraph,* 13 April 1900, 6; "large as a hotel": *Works,* 9: 90; "in the lifeboat": *Log,* 237–238.

4. Montgomery later criticized Rojo for not sending the sailboat to look for survivors on the other rafts (Stallman, "Journalist Crane in That Dinghy," 266).

5. "Filibuster Sunk—Crane Missing," *New York Press,* 3 January 1897, 1, 2; "Twelve Men Lost through Treachery," *Florida Times-Union,* 4 January 1897, 1; "The *Commodore* Was Scuttled," *New York Journal,* 4 January 1897, 1–2. Given the traumatic nature of a shipwreck, it is not surprising that the survivors gave inconsistent accounts and that newspapers reported conflicting and contradictory stories. For an analysis of the events, see Cyrus Day, "Stephen Crane and the Ten-Foot Dinghy," *Boston University Studies in English,* 3 (Winter 1957), 193–213; Stallman, "Journalist Crane in That Dinghy"; and *Log,* 236–237.

6. R. W. Stallman, *Stephen Crane: A Critical Bibliography* (Ames: Iowa State University Press, 1972), 258–259.

7. *C,* 273.

8. Ibid., 274, 276.

9. Shortly after the burial, the body was exhumed at the request of Higgins's relatives and shipped to Salem, Massachusetts, for burial ("One of the Dead," *Florida Times-Union,* 8 January 1897, 5).

Crane spent the night at the residence of Mr. and Mrs. Laurence Thompson, which is today called Lilian Place, while Murphy and Montgomery stayed at nearby Surfcrest cottage. In 1897, Daytona and Daytona Beach were separate towns. The Silver Beach area, where Lilian Place is now located, was formerly called Goodall. To the South was the area called Seabreeze—the location of Surfcrest cottage and the place where Crane and the others came ashore. Daytona, Daytona Beach, and Seabreeze merged in 1926.

As a token of thanks for their kindness, Crane sent the Thompsons an autographed copy of *The Red Badge of Courage.* Patricia T. Bennett, granddaughter of the Thompsons and later the owner of Lilian Place, recounted details about the survivors' stay in Daytona Beach. Unfortunately, the autographed copy of *The Red Badge* was lost before its inscription could be recorded (Patricia T. Bennett, "Family Reminiscences of Stephen Crane's 'The Open Boat,'" unpublished presentation given at Daytona Beach Community College, 27 February 1989, typescript, Halifax Historical Museum, Daytona Beach, Florida).

Crane apparently stayed at more than one place. According to a typed transcription of a reminiscence written by one of the children of a Mr.

Lathrop, Crane was at their house following his rescue. Later Crane sent Mr. Lathrop an inscribed copy of *The Open Boat* (Berryman Papers, untitled transcript "I learned that he had been carried . . . ," University of Minnesota).

10. Berryman Papers, untitled transcript "I learned that he had been carried . . . ," University of Minnesota.

11. There is a question regarding how Cora got to Daytona. According to Richmond Barrett, whose family was staying at the St. James Hotel while Crane was there, his parents stated that she "chartered a private car, rushed to the scene and carried him back to Jacksonville in state" (Richmond Barrett, "Correspondence," *American Mercury,* June 1934, xxi).

12. "Embraced": Charles LaPointe, "The Day That Stephen Crane Was Shipwrecked," *Daytona Beach Sunday News-Journal,* 22 April 1962, 7A; "babies all nude": Barrett, "Correspondence," xx; "January 4, 1897": Barrett, "Correspondence," xxi. Typical of Crane, he misdated the inscription as 1896, then wrote a 7 over the 6.

13. Stallman, "Journalist Crane in That Dinghy," 265. For the argument against treachery, see Stallman, "Journalist Crane in That Dinghy," 274, appendix 1, reprinted in R. W. Stallman, *Stephen Crane,* rev. ed. (New York: Braziller, 1973), 548–549, appendix 5. Although Stallman notes that the Junta inspected the ship and monitored the selection of its crew, a spy could still have infiltrated the crew. It was safer for the Junta to blame the disaster on a natural cause rather than the possibility that the enemy had penetrated its ranks.

14. *Log,* 238. While recuperating, Crane wrote his brother William to describe the *Commodore* ordeal and thank him for having taught his younger brother how to swim. Though this letter is lost, I have inferred its contents from its description in Helen R. Crane's reminiscence in *SCRem,* 48.

15. "To the Bacheller syndicate": *C,* 277, *Log,* 239; "far beyond words": *Works,* 9: 93–94; "told here and now": *Works,* 9: 94.

16. "At the Lantern Club": *C,* 279; "before writing it down": E. B. Crane in *SCRem,* 14; Linson, 88, n. 1; "how we felt": Paine in *SCRem,* 191; "brotherhood of men": *Works,* 5: 73.

17. "Damn good oiler": Paine in *SCRem,* 191; "Sunk Steamer Commodore": The English edition of the book, retitled *The Open Boat and Other Stories* (1898), changed the first line to "To the Memory of."

18. "Penetrating observation": Weatherford, 217; "crown of all his work": Weatherford, 271; "just for fun, mostly": *Works,* 5: 95; "wind-crossed void": *Works,* 5: 108; "weight and complexion": *Works,* 5: 107; "political significance": *Works,* 9: 98 (in "Some Curious Lessons from the Transvaal" [*Works,* 9: 240–243], Crane explores a correspondent's dilemma in reporting truthfully when military engagements are censored); "bottom of the sea": *Works,*

5: 133, 121, 129; "slant of a rough sea": *Works,* 5: 140; "the moving sea, the sea": *Works,* 10: 83. Based on the kind of paper that Crane wrote this poem on, Bowers argues convincingly that it was composed in England after Crane returned from Greece, probably around June 1897 (*Works,* 10: 232, n. 24). The poem was not published until 1929.

19. "At night./Stephen Crane": *C,* 279–280. Only the book's flyleaf with the inscription survives.

20. Richard Senger to "the Stephen Crane Collections of Syracuse University," 24 August 1958, Rare Books Folder, Syracuse. Internal evidence suggests when Crane read Harraden's novel. Senger also recalled that Crane considered Sarah Grand's novel *The Heavenly Twins* (1893) romantic nonsense.

21. Cora copied the epigraph and passages in her "memorandum book" (36–37) and "manuscript book" (29–30), with slight changes in the transcription (Columbia). See Beatrice Harraden, *Ships That Pass in the Night* (New York: G. P. Putnam's Sons, 1894), vii, 113, 154, for the quoted material. Cora also copied a number of other passages from the memorandum book into the manuscript book. Although Harraden's novel first appeared in 1893, Stephen and Cora most likely read the "authorized American edition," published in 1894. When the novel first appeared, it lacked the epigraph because Harraden could not remember the source for her title. After readers told her about Longfellow's lines, she added the epigraph and wrote a preface acknowledging him in the 1894 reprinting.

19. The Greco-Turkish War

1. *C,* 281.

2. "Financially indebted": For another reading of Crane's initial involvement with Reynolds, see *Works,* 3: xxxviii. "Any way changed": *Log,* 231.

3. *C,* 280.

4. Ibid., 305, 301.

5. "Dance on champagne bottles": "Rows at the French Ball," *New York Times,* 21 January 1891, 8; "French Ball Opens Sedately," *New York Times,* 22 January 1902, 6; "kiss the young women": "Very Slow French Ball," *New York World,* 20 January 1897, news clipping in Cora Crane's green scrapbook, 16, Columbia.

6. "I can see": "Very Slow French Ball"; "trumped-up charges": "Flagon," XIII-29.

7. "Mental condition": *C,* 72; "stormy interviews": "Amy Leslie vs. Stephen Crane," *Chicago Daily Tribune,* 5 January 1898, 1; "at Appleton's": *C,* 337.

8. "Faith and . . . honesty": *C,* 298; "desire of mine": *C,* 297.

9. "Their lingo": Linson, 99; "Dora Clark affair": Stallman and Gilkes, 327; "blood anyhow": Linson, 101; "chivalry itself": Stallman and Gilkes, 327.

10. An entry in the *Log* (246) states that it was uncertain whether Cora was

aboard the *Etruria* with Crane. I am indebted to Elizabeth Friedmann for sharing with me her copy of the ship's manifest for the March 20 sailing, which lists Cora as a passenger.

11. "America possesses": quoted in "People Talked About," *Leslie's Illustrated Weekly,* 4 February 1897, 67; "British public": *C,* 151; "self-promotion": Arthur Waugh, "London Letter," *The Critic,* 17 April 1897, 277.

12. "Fighting is concerned": Scott C. Osborn, "The 'Rivalry-Chivalry' of Richard Harding Davis and Stephen Crane," *American Literature,* 28 (1956), 53; "average saw-log": *C,* 186 (in writing to his brother William, Stephen dismissed Davis as "a fool" [*C,* 301]); "adventure-seeking hero": Sinclair Lewis, *Dodsworth* (New York: Harcourt, 1929), 5, 173; "better writer than Davis": Weatherford, 38, and Vosburgh in *SCRem,* 135–136.

13. "Unlike I imagined": Osborn, "The 'Rivalry-Chivalry' of Richard Harding Davis and Stephen Crane," 53 (Davis misspelled "Quite" as "Quiet"); "War Office": Charles Belmont Davis, ed., *Adventures and Letters of Richard Harding Davis* (New York: Scribner's, 1917), 115–116.

14. "I and God": *C,* 285; "journalists an interview": *Works,* 9: 18.

15. *Works,* 9: 71, 72.

16. Cora also used the pseudonym for a series of London columns on topics of interest to women. The columns were unsigned and appeared in the *New York Press* from August 15 to October 10, 1897. There is evidence that Stephen and Cora collaborated on pieces "written by" Imogene Carter. See *C,* 306, n. 5.

17. Osborn, "The 'Rivalry-Chivalry' of Richard Harding Davis and Stephen Crane," 54 (Davis misspelled "Stewart" as "Stuart").

18. Ibid.

19. Davis's treatment of the correspondent is partly sympathetic. For accounts of whether or not the story is based on Crane, see James L. Ford, "The Father of Ragtime," *Bookman,* 43 (1916), 616–618; "The Story of 'The Derelict,'" *Bookman,* 14 (1902), 17; and *C,* 303, n. 2.

20. *Log,* 260.

21. "Mysterious force": ibid., 254; "who died there": *Works,* 9: 20.

22. *Works,* 9: 27.

23. Ibid., 9: 45.

24. *C,* 285.

25. "Changed Front and Advanced," *Boston Daily Globe,* 7 August 1904, 2.

26. "Mere episode": *C,* 233; "as an artist": *C,* 232.

27. "All right": Beer, 11.

28. "Adequate to describe": *Works,* 9: 54; "shouting and victory": *Works,* 9: 56; "own egotism": *C,* 172.

29. "The Dogs of War," Crane's amusing anecdote about finding the puppy

on the battlefield of Velestino, was published in the *New York Journal*, 30 May 1897. For the possibility that Cora rescued the dog, see *Log*, 254.

30. Gilkes, 110, 394; Lillian Gilkes, "Stephen and Cora Crane: Some Corrections, and a 'Millionaire' Named Sharefe," *American Literature*, 41 (1969), 277, n. 12.

31. *C*, 295.

20. Ravensbrook, Harold Frederic, Joseph Conrad

1. *"The Black Riders"*: John N. Hilliard, "Stephen Crane," *New York Times*, 14 July 1900, BR2; "make a new start": EFC to TB, 19 November 1922, Yale.

2. Quoted in Lillian B. Gilkes, "Stephen Crane and the Harold Frederics," *Serif*, 6 (December 1969), 23, n. 7.

3. Legend had it that Roman soldiers looking for water followed ravens to a brook near the house; hence its name. The Cranes' residency is still remembered today. Many years later, Ravensbrook was converted into apartments, and in its garden were built small villas, one of which was named "Cranes." See Robert M. Cooper, *The Literary Guide and Companion to Southern England* (Athens: Ohio University Press, 1985), 199.

4. "Other's affairs": Ford Madox Ford, *Mightier Than the Sword: Memories and Criticisms* (London: George Allen and Unwin, 1938), 155; "pick up a pea": cited in Reginald Bliss [H. G. Wells], *Boon, the Mind of the Race, the Wild Asses of the Devil, and the Last Trump: Being a First Selection from the Literary Remains of George Boon, Appropriate to the Times* (London: T. Fisher Unwin, 1915), 108.

5. *C*, 323.

6. Crane visited the Pease house to be shaved by Constantin, one of the Ptolemy twins, who worked there as a servant and whom Crane called "a butler in shirt sleeves." Because Pease regularly shaved himself, he commented "unfavorably on Crane's defection from English middle-class standards in this matter!" Michael Pease to MHS, 27 November 1948, MHSC Files.

7. David Garnett, *The Golden Echo* (London: Chatto and Windus, 1954), 18.

8. Ford in *SCRem*, 353, nn. 35, 36. Ford admitted privately to his literary agent, Ruth Hamilton Kerr, that he had fictionalized Crane's comments in *Return to Yesterday:* "All the slang words I put into Stephen Crane's mouth I took straight from O. Henry's stories of 1897." Ford Madox Ford to Ruth Hamilton Kerr, 25 November 1933, Kerr Mss., Lilly Library, Indiana University, Bloomington.

9. Ford in *SCRem*, 262. Helen R. Crane also recalled Crane's use of dialect: "His sisters-in-law never knew what he was going to do. There were instances when he behaved very nicely, but there were more when he did not. Sometimes, on being introduced to a socialite, he would assume an

East Side accent (which he could do perfectly) and blare forth yarns he had picked up in the night-courts." H. R. Crane in *SCRem*, 46.

10. Ford in *SCRem*, 256. See also the headnote to the Ford section in *SCRem*, 256–257, as well as 352, n. 32, and 356, n. 60.

11. "Fighting line": Despite this statement, Crane saw action in Epirus and Velestino during the Greco-Turkish War. "Like rabbits": Pugh in *SCRem*, 297. The dating of Pugh's reminiscence is uncertain. He recalled playing handball with Crane in a garden, which Stallman ([1972], 456–457) identified as being at Ravensbrook. Although it is conceivable that Crane and Pugh knew each other before 1899, no evidence exists to support this. In most of Pugh's reminiscence, Crane was already ill at Brede Place. For Crane's use of "Hully Gee," see also H. G. Wells in Stallman and Gilkes, 316.

12. Weatherford, 115.

13. "Mohawk Valley": *Works*, 8: 729; "*Theron Ware*": Thomas F. O'Donnell and Hoyt C. Franchere, *Harold Frederic* (New York: Twayne, 1961), 33; "Here is a writer": *Works*, 8: 731.

14. "Two Anecdotes," *New York Times*, 11 February 1906, 3.

15. Gilkes, 118; Gilkes, "Stephen Crane and the Harold Frederics," 36; "The Claim by Mr. Stephen Crane," *Pall Mall Gazette*, 9 June 1898, 2.

16. Gilkes, 118.

17. "As well as loaf": *C*, 334; "monopolize attention": *C*, 339; "come to grief": *C*, 339. In "Stephen Crane and the Harold Frederics," Gilkes has suggested that the "changed conditions" referred to "Crane's accelerating drive for respectability" (37).

18. "November 19": George Fortenberry et al., eds., *The Correspondence of Harold Frederic*, vol. 1 of the Harold Frederic Edition, 1977–1986 (Fort Worth: Texas Christian University Press, 1977), 463; "a set sneer": "Literary Notes," *The Star* [Canterbury, New Zealand], 17 February 1898, 4; "emotion of mankind": *C*, 515.

19. Robert M. Myers has suggested that Frederic's notes for his novel *Gloria Mundi* under the heading "Man at 40" may describe Crane: "Attitude toward younger men just coming into life. Tenderly anxious [to] be kind, yet impelled to advise, censure. Their passion for arguing on abstractions wearies him." Robert M. Myers, *Reluctant Expatriate: The Life of Harold Frederic* (Westport, CT: Greenwood Press, 1995), 146.

20. "Himself considered it": *Works*, 10: 344; "annoyed people": *C*, 213; "British subjects in his fiction": *Works*, 8: 731–732.

21. "Can just see him": *Log*, 275; "minor character": Beer, 12.

22. "To some purpose": Joseph Conrad in *SCRem*, 249; "on this earth": Beer, 5.

23. "Affectation": Beer, 6, 7; "complete understanding": Jessie Conrad in *SCRem*, 251; "beginning of things": *C*, 310, 312, 313; "to you in confi-

dence": Edward Garnett, ed., *Letters from Joseph Conrad, 1895–1914* (Indianapolis: Bobbs-Merrill, 1928), 118, 119; "than the surface": Joseph Conrad in *SCRem*, 250.

24. "Hate babies": Frederick R. Karl and Laurence Davies, eds., *The Collected Letters of Joseph Conrad*, vol. 2: 1898–1902 (Cambridge: Cambridge University Press, 1986), 33; "reminder of their friendship": *Log*, 332; "things amazing": *C*, 315; "simply great": *C*, 310; "present death": *C*, 310.

25. Frederick R. Karl and Laurence Davies, eds., *The Collected Letters of Joseph Conrad*, vol. 1: 1861–1897 (Cambridge: Cambridge University Press, 1983), 421.

26. "Weak plot and crude style": Eric Solomon, *Stephen Crane in England: A Portrait of the Artist* (Columbus: Ohio State University Press, 1964), 107; "cheers for the Press": *C*, 319. See also Donald W. Rude, "Joseph Conrad and W. L. Courtney's Review of *The Nigger of the 'Narcissus,'*" *English Literature in Translation, 1880–1920*, 21 (1978), 188–197.

27. Garnett in *SCRem*, 267.

28. Norman Sherry, "A Conrad Manuscript," *Times Literary Supplement*, 25 June 1970, 691.

29. "Protagonist in *Lord Jim*": Nina Galen, "Stephen Crane as a Source for Conrad's Jim," *Nineteenth-Century Fiction*, 38 (1983), 78–96. Also on the possibility that Crane inspired Conrad, see Elsa Nettels, "Conrad and Stephen Crane," *Conradiana*, 10 (1978), 267–283; and Nettels, "'Amy Foster' and Stephen Crane's 'The Monster,'" *Conradiana*, 15 (1983), 181–190. On a related note, in *Joseph Conrad: A Biography* (New York: Scribner's, 1991), 161, Jeffrey Meyers suggests that Cora influenced Conrad's depiction of Lena in *Victory*. "Serialized in *Metropolitan Magazine*": Joseph Conrad, *Last Essays* (London: J. M. Dent and Sons, 1926), 118. In *A Stephen Crane Encyclopedia* (Westport, CT: Greenwood, 1997), 61, Stanley Wertheim states that the story is "The Planter of Malta." In "Stephen Crane's 'The Predecessor': Unwritten Play, Unwritten Novel," *American Literary Realism*, 13 (1980), 99, Stanton Garner suggests that it is "Freya of the Seven Isles."

30. "Barbarously abrupt": *C*, 315, and Beer, 13; "abandoning a sinking ship": Meyers, *Joseph Conrad*, 57. "Youth: A Narrative": In "'The Open Boat' and Conrad's 'Youth,'" *Modern Language Notes*, 73, no. 2 (1958), 100–102, Guy Owen, Jr., notes similarities between the two stories.

31. "Experiment in inanity": Weatherford, 206; "English world": Weatherford 201, 202.

21. Creative Outburst

1. "P. J. & Hartwood": *C*, 301; "circled near the town": *Works*, 5: 114.

2. When Crane wrote his Port Jervis friend Louis Senger, who knew the

Crane family, on November 8 (*C,* 309), he was again careful to use blank paper rather than Ravensbrook letterhead. But when it was important that someone know his location—e.g., his American literary agent, Paul Revere Reynolds—he used the letterhead (*C,* 305–306, 308).

3. "Scalp-music": *Works,* 5: 120, 118; "pow-pow in London": *C,* 310.

4. *Works,* 5: 111.

5. J. C. Levenson suggests that Crane uses a word meaning "once upon a time" to evoke a sense that the town "exists outside of time, exempt from progress." See Levenson, introduction to *The Red Badge of Courage,* in *The Works of Stephen Crane,* vol. 2, ed. Fredson Bowers, xiii–xcii (Charlottesville: University Press of Virginia, 1975), xiii.

6. "Drum corps": Ellen A. Brown and Patricia Hernlund, "The Source for the Title of Stephen Crane's Whilomville Stories," *American Literature,* 50 (1978), 116–118. "He had with him in England": two years later, Peck sent Crane additional copies of books written by their ancestors. See *C,* 470–472.

7. *Directory of Port Jervis, Monticello, Matamoras, Milford and Stations on the Line of the Port Jervis, Monticello & New York Railroad, from Port Jervis to Monticello, 1893* (Newburgh, NY: Breed Publishing, 1893), 10.

8. The law offices of Cuddeback and Onofry are currently in the house.

9. The carriage house is also a major setting in the Whilomville story titled "The Carriage-Lamps."

10. *Directory of Port Jervis,* 67. According to Edna Crane Sidbury, another man was the model: "A certain man there had his face eaten by cancer. He used to haul ashes, and we children often met him with his cart, as we drove around town with our pony. He was an object of horror to us, for it could truthfully be said of him, 'He had no face.' One day I mentioned him to my father, and he told me that there is where the idea of 'The Monster' originated." (Sidbury in *SCRem,* 52. See also *SCRem,* 313, n. 106.)

11. EFC recalled that the engraving was of the Second Continental Congress, but it was of the First Continental Congress (EFC to MHS, 11 July 1948, MHSC Files).

12. Crane may be alluding to the Supreme Court case in a later Whilomville story, "The Trial, Execution, and Burial of Homer Phelps." A boy named Homer is put on trial because he will not follow the rules created by the other neighborhood children, who ostracize him for refusing "to play it the right [white?] way."

13. "Finally agreed upon": "The Declaration of Independence as It Is To-day," *Ladies Home Journal,* July 1898, 3; "*Washington Post*": cited in "Federal Constitution Photographed," *New York Times,* 13 July 1895, 13.

14. Jefferson's views on slavery and African Americans are complex. His oppo-

sition to slavery was based on his hostility to England, which controlled the slave trade, and on his belief that everyone had an inherent right to freedom; yet he feared that emancipation would cause additional problems. Of the hundreds of slaves that he owned, he freed only two in his lifetime and five in his will. As Joseph J. Ellis has said, the problem of slavery created for Jefferson "a moral chasm between what he knew to be right and what he could not do without." See Ellis, *American Sphinx: The Character of Thomas Jefferson* (New York: Knopf, 1997), 145.

15. *"Our Country: Its Trial and Its Triumph"*: Reverend Crane's point in "English Strictures on American Slavery"—and in a sermon titled "Christian Duty in Regard to Slavery"—was that African Americans were being treated inhumanely in a country professing equality. This, he said, was one of our "national sins." (Thomas A. Gullason, ed., *A Garland of Writings: Stephen Crane's Literary Family* [Syracuse: Syracuse University Press, 2002], 35, 37.) Similarly, Crane's maternal grandfather, the Reverend George Peck, discussed the first draft of the Declaration in *Our Country: Its Trial and Its Triumph* (New York: Carlton and Porter, 1865), 146, 143: "The hand which the parent government had in bringing to her colonies such a vast mass of slaves is made matter of complaint in Jefferson's original draft of the Declaration of Independence. . . . Our statesmen, at the formation of the federal Constitution, did not allow the word *slave* or *slavery* to be incorporated in that instrument, supposing that the institution would gradually die out." Concerning the issue of equality in America, Reverend Peck wrote: "If all men are created equal, as we have a right to assume that they are, and as that immortal bill of rights, the Declaration of Independence, asserts, no human being can be born a slave."

16. "Employed racist stereotypes": Stanley Wertheim, "Unveiling the Humanist: Stephen Crane and Ethnic Minorities," *American Literary Realism*, 30, no. 3 (1998), 65–75; "black torrent": *Works*, 7: 19–23.

17. "Ready to pay": *C*, 307; "I mention it": *C*, 307.

18. "Rotten bad": *C*, 306; "money this month": *C*, 321; "to the wall": *C*, 327.

19. *C*, 298.

20. "February 1895": "The Literary Week," *Academy*, 60 (2 March 1901), 177 (Cora did not offer details about the experience); "'strangely hopeless' state of mind": Frederick R. Karl and Laurence Davies, eds., *The Collected Letters of Joseph Conrad*, vol. 1: 1861–1897 (Cambridge: Cambridge University Press, 1983), 416.

21. *C*, 359.

22. "A heavy tongue": *Works*, 5: 152; "where you've been": *Works*, 5: 146.

23. "Murder of this Swede": *Works*, 5: 170; "from the East": *Works*, 5: 143.

24. "Sided with Spain": Zdzislaw Najder, *Joseph Conrad: A Chronicle* (New

Brunswick: Rutgers University Press, 1983), 226; "advance went to Cora": *Log,* 296.

25. "Swim the ocean": Beer, 32–33; "citizenship therein": "Stephen Crane's Passport Applications: Part III," *Stephen Crane Newsletter,* 3 (Summer 1969), 6; "Stella, who lived there": *C,* 60.

26. Mrs. Ruedy has often been mistakenly cited as having known Cora at the Hotel de Dreme and as having been with the Cranes in Greece. Conrad's description of her as "the good Auntie Ruedy" suggests that she was Cora's friend rather than her maid. See Frederick R. Karl and Laurence Davies, eds., *The Collected Letters of Joseph Conrad,* vol. 2: 1898–1902 (Cambridge: Cambridge University Press, 1986), 135.

27. *C,* 357.

22. Prelude to War

1. "Book about the war": Carnes in *SCRem,* 221; "Florida coast": Ames Williams, interview with Mrs. George F. Smillie (Lily Brandon Munroe), 1 January 1948, Lillian Gilkes Research Files, Syracuse.

2. "Opposed war with Spain": Albert A. Nofi, *The Spanish-American War, 1898* (Conshohocken, PA: Combined Books, 1996), 261; "peace has failed": *Speeches and Addresses of William McKinley: From March 1, 1897, to May 30, 1900* (New York: Doubleday, 1900), 12.

3. *New York World,* 6 March 1898, 8.

4. "Expedition in 1982": Nofi, *The Spanish-American War,* 261; "he declined all of them": F. Lauriston Bullard, *Famous War Correspondents* (Boston: Little, Brown, 1914), 412–413; "cabled promptly": Arthur Brisbane, "Great Problems in Organization: The Modern Newspaper in War Time," *Cosmopolitan Magazine,* September 1898, 550; Arthur Brisbane, "Some Men Who Have Reported the War," *Cosmopolitan Magazine,* September 1898, 556.

5. "Big hotel": Richard Harding Davis, *The Cuban and Porto Rican Campaigns* (New York: Scribner's, 1898), 50; "Key Westion": Jefferson Beale Browne, *Key West: The Old and the New* (St. Augustine: Record Company, 1912), 146.

6. "Personality of the war": *Works,* 6: 239; "greatest sea captains": *Works,* 6: 239; "Marryat and Cooper": *Works,* 9: 126.

7. "Cot in a hallway": Joyce Milton, *The Yellow Kids: Foreign Correspondents in the Heyday of Yellow Journalism* (New York: Harper, 1989), 245. Crane's lines paraphrased a verse popular among American dice players: "Little white mice of chance, / Coats of wool and corduroy pants, / Gold and wine, women and sin, / I'll give to you, if you let me in / To the glittering house of chance." The verse is also the epigraph to the fourth chapter in Lady Sarah Wilson, *South African Memories: Social, Warlike and Sporting, from Diaries Written at the Time* (London: Edward Arnold, 1909).

8. "Only rarely pennies": Greene in *SCRem,* 127. See also McBride in

SCRem, 160. "Tense, unpredictable situation": Carmichael in *SCRem,* 243; "ever saw worked": *Works,* 5: 43; "free will, and necessity": Herman Melville, *Moby-Dick,* ed. Harrison Hayford and Hershel Parker (New York: Norton, 1967), 185; "at deep sea": *Works,* 5: 46.

9. Melville, *Moby-Dick,* 14.

10. Crane and Norris may have also met in a Key West bar. In a tantalizing assertion that unfortunately lacks verification, Crane and Norris discussed women's fashion after Crane read a brief notice in *Leslie's Weekly* about the growing interest in Princess Gowns and Corsets. See Gregory Mason, *Remember the Maine* (New York: Holt, 1939), 130–131.

11. "On May 8": Joseph R. McElrath, Jr., and Jesse Crisler, *Frank Norris: A Life* (Urbana: University of Illinois Press, 2006), 268; "independent of a glass": *Log,* 302; "man in an army": Edson Brace, "Stories and Studies of Stephen Crane," *St. Louis Republic,* 17 June 1900, part II, 6; "fool of himself": for evidence that Norris was not jealous of Crane, see McElrath and Crisler, *Frank Norris,* 273–276; "like him": Scott C. Osborn, "The 'Rivalry-Chivalry' of Richard Harding Davis and Stephen Crane," *American Literature,* 28 (1956), 55.

12. *Works,* 9: 118–120. In *Roads of Adventure* (Boston: Houghton Mifflin, 1922), 215, Ralph D. Paine remembered only that the shot nicked the funnel. Rather than infer that Crane and Paine were alluding to two separate incidents involving the two ships, I have assumed that there was just one.

13. Crane was not interested in what appeared to be a Spanish gunboat, because he was "polishing a poem on Cuban insurgents." To break his concentration and alert him to the possible danger of the moment, Paine "poured a carafe of water over him" (Walter Scott Meriwether, "Queer Adventures of War Correspondents Recalled by 30th Anniversary Outbreak Spanish-American War," clipping, Rare Books Folder, Syracuse, 2). Once Crane realized that he might be captured and executed, he washed the coal dust from his hair so that he would look presentable ("War's Comic Side," *West Australian* [Perth], 22 February 1905, 9).

14. Paine in *SCRem,* 193.

15. Ibid., 194–195.

16. Ibid., 196.

17. "Thorns from their feet": Paine in *SCRem,* 196–199; "across the harbor": McCready in *SCRem* 211.

18. "Far away as Heaven": *Works,* 7: 91; "sense of 'martyrdom'": *Works,* 7: 90.

23. War in Cuba

1. "Recoil in port": G. J. A. O'Toole, *The Spanish War: An American Epic, 1898* (New York: Norton, 1984), 248; "from the show": Paine in *SCRem,* 201.

2. McCready in *SCRem,* 209.

3. Paine in *SCRem,* 203.

4. "Accuracy": McCready in *SCRem,* 210; "butcher": Jerry Keenan, *Encyclopedia of the Spanish-American and Philippine-American Wars* (Santa Barbara, CA: ABC-CLIO, 2001), 405; "Journal's War": David Nasaw, *The Chief: The Life of William Randolph Hearst* (Boston: Houghton Mifflin, 2000), 132.

5. "Memorial Fund": W. A. Swanberg, *Citizen Hearst* (New York: Scribner's, 1961), 149. For the suggestion that Hearst wanted to personally entrap Pulitzer with the hoax, see Charles H. Brown, *The Correspondents' War: Journalists in the Spanish-American War* (New York: Scribner's, 1967), 268–269; "battle for Santiago": Brown, *The Correspondents' War,* 268; "convenient ammunition": Walter Millis, *The Martial Spirit: A Study of Our War with Spain* (Cambridge, MA: Riverside Press, 1931), 68.

6. *Works,* 6: 226–227.

7. "Lived a Strenuous Life," *Sunday Oregonian* [Portland], 17 June 1900, 2. The friend may have been Clarence Loomis Peaslee, the possible author of "Lived a Strenuous Life." In "Stephen Crane," *New York Times,* 14 July 1900, BR2, John N. Hilliard also stated that Crane told him of his wish to die in combat.

8. Larry Daley, "The Taking of Guantanamo," www.spanamwar.com/Guanta namo.htm (accessed 6/26/2013). Dr. Gibbs died not on the third night but on the second night, June 12, at 1 A.M., but Crane expanded their time together to three days in order to suggest their deepening acquaintance.

9. When Crane saw another soldier horribly wounded, he was also apparently reminded of his own description of combat in *The Red Badge* (H. J. Whigham, "One of the Glorious Deeds of the World," *Chicago Tribune,* 13 July 1898, 1).

10. *Works,* 6: 199–200. Sergeant Quick was awarded the Congressional Medal of Honor for his bravery during the Cuban campaign.

11. "Tragic isle": *Works,* 6: 232; "helped to fire guns": H. J. Whigham, "Sixty Spaniards Fall in Battle," *Chicago Tribune,* 16 June 1898, 1; "during the action": *Log,* 313; "bravery during combat": *C,* 478–479. See also Carmichael in *SCRem,* 242.

12. *Works,* 9: 150.

13. "Exhibitionists and egomaniacs": Cecil Carnes, *Jimmy Hare, News Photographer: Half a Century with a Camera* (New York: Macmillan, 1940), 61; "fellow alive": *Log,* 319.

14. Theodore Roosevelt, *The Rough Riders* (New York: Scribner's, 1899), 107–108. According to a study of Roosevelt in Cuba, one evening Crane "walked back along the trail to look for his baggage. Passing El Poso Hill, he stumbled over the sleeping form of an intemperate Roosevelt who awakened for a moment to insult Crane vigorously." See Peggy Samuels

and Harold Samuels, *Teddy Roosevelt at San Juan: The Making of a President* (College Station: Texas A&M University Press, 1997), 202.

15. *C,* 249.

16. Carnes in *SCRem,* 225.

17. "Absurd and silly": quoted in Mary S. Mander, "Pen and Sword: Problems of Reporting the Spanish-American War," *Journalism History,* 9 (Spring 1982), 7; "good for him": Mander, "Pen and Sword," 7; "career as a reporter": For various accounts of the altercation between Shafter and Scovel, see Darien Elizabeth Andreu, "Sylvester H. Scovel, Journalist, and the Spanish-American War" (Ph.D. diss., Florida State University, 2003), 23–25.

18. Soldiers were also ill from eating rancid canned meat supplied by the army's quartermaster. After the war, a political scandal erupted after it was discovered that a quickly arranged contract at the lowest possible price had led the Chicago meatpacking industry to cut corners.

19. "He aims at": Carnes in *SCRem,* 223; "go hang": Hilliard, "Stephen Crane," BR2 (see also "Lived a Strenuous Life," 2); "was that it": R. H. Davis in *SCRem,* 347, n. 37; "binoculars case": Fairfax Downey, *Richard Harding Davis and His Day* (New York: Scribner's, 1933), 161.

20. *SCRem,* 348, n. 37. Cora, too, realized that Crane immersed himself in the conflict "to see what it is really like I suppose" (*Log,* 314). In the *Log,* the source for Cora's letter is listed as "CtU" (University of Connecticut; the original is in the Manuscript Division of the Library of Congress). For other explanations for Crane's behavior on the battlefield, see C. H. Brown, *The Correspondents' War,* 363, note.

21. "Weak heart": *Works,* 10: 14, 65; "do quickly": Cather in *SCRem,* 178.

22. "They got me": *Works,* 6: 247, 248; "from a cross": *Works,* 6: 254; "crushing, monstrous": *Works,* 6: 254; "nothing at all": *Works,* 6: 263.

24. New York City, Adirondacks, Puerto Rico

1. "In the world": *Works,* 6: 259; "blue world": *C,* 515; "died from the disease": "The Yellow Scourge in Cuba," http://www.hsl.virginia.edu/historical/medical_history/yellow_fever/cuba.cfm (accessed 6/14/2013).

2. This scene is a composite of *Works,* 6: 262–263; "Transport City of Washington Arrived Old Point," *Richmond Times,* 14 July 1898, 7, "Transport Breakwater Arrived at Old Point," *Richmond Times,* 15 July 1898, 7; "Animated Scenes," *Norfolk Dispatch,* 14 July 1898, 1; "Pitiful Scenes at Old Point," *Norfolk Dispatch,* 14 July 1898, 4; "Sick and Wounded," *Daily Press* [Newport News, VA], 14 July 1898, 1; "Wounded in Battle," *Daily Press* [Newport News, VA], 14 July 1898, 1.

3. *Works,* 9: 198. "The Private's Story," the source of the quotation, is cast as an account of Crane's archetypal regular-army soldier but is based on his ex-

perience at Old Point Comfort. The account is repeated almost verbatim in "War Memories."

4. *Works,* 6: 262.

5. Robert Arthur, *History of Fort Monroe* (n.p.: n.p., 1930), 74, 75. The inference that Crane stayed in the area for more than a day comes from a reminiscence by Captain Samuel Riggs, who introduced him to the mint julep and who "saw him often during his stay at Old Point Comfort (Fort Monroe)." Riggs's statement that he "carried him" from the Chamberlin to the Casemate Club suggests Crane's weakened condition (Paul Sorrentino, "A Reminiscence of Stephen Crane," *Courier* [Syracuse University Library], 19 [Fall 1984], 111). Unfortunately, it is difficult to establish how long Crane stayed at Old Point Comfort. The records of the Chamberlin Hotel were destroyed by fire in 1920; those of Fort Monroe for the period no longer exist; and the local papers did not record Crane's presence in the area.

6. *Log,* 321. Although Cary did not make this statement until 1922, he must have said something comparable to Seitz's remark.

7. Crane did not witness the rout of the 71st, but probably first heard about it from his friend Captain L. S. Linson, Corwin's brother, who was captain of Company D in the regiment.

8. For internal evidence that Scovel wrote the article, see Darien Elizabeth Andreu, "Sylvester H. Scovel, Journalist, and the Spanish-American War" (Ph.D. diss., Florida State University, 2003), 21–22.

9. Roosevelt, however, accepted the charges in the article and insisted that no Rough Rider would be buried with cowards (R. W. Stallman and E. R. Hagemann, eds., *The War Dispatches of Stephen Crane* [New York: New York University Press, 1964], 109). Later, after he became governor of New York, he demanded that the officers of the 71st resign. They did.

10. *Log,* 331–332. The circumstances surrounding Crane's departure from the newspaper are vague, but a letter from Robert H. Lyman of the *New York World* to B. J. R. Stolper, 25 February 1933, states, "Norris' incredible performance severed his connection" (Columbia). The statement suggests that Crane was fired. Additional evidence comes from Samuel Riggs, whom Crane had met at Old Point Comfort. Riggs later wrote that Crane "lost his job" at the *World.* After being fired, Crane must have told Riggs what had happened.

11. "Madcap Genius: Stephen Crane," *New York World,* 10 June 1900, E3.

12. Ridge in *SCRem,* 299.

13. *C,* 370.

14. For evidence of correspondence between Stephen and Cora, see four of her letters: to Clara Frewen, 4 June 1898, about Brede Place (*Log,* 307–308);

to Moreton Frewen and to an unknown recipient, both 16 June 1898, saying that Cora had received a cable from Stephen from Port Antonio (*Log,* 314, *C,* 364); and to Paul Revere Reynolds, 25 September 1898, saying that Cora had heard from Stephen (*C,* 371). Because Cora saved practically all the letters to her, however inconsequential they were, the question is what happened to the letters from Crane. Although no evidence exists to answer it, she may have destroyed them. Rather than come back to England, he apparently wanted to return to America, where he could continue leading a double life, maintaining outward respectability while disappearing into the seamy part of society; but he knew he could not do that if Cora came back with him. If their correspondence discussed the matter, she would most likely have destroyed it once he was back with her.

15. "Establish sanitariums": *Works,* 9: 149; "washed over him": Michelson in *SCRem,* 216.

16. Stallman and Hagemann, *The War Dispatches,* 196.

17. "Santiago campaign": R. H. Davis in *SCRem,* 230; *Log,* 299–300; "by his contemporaries": Philip Littell, *Books and Things* (New York: Harcourt, 1919), 230–236; "social bankrupt": Michelson in *SCRem,* 219; "Guantánamo Bay": Joseph Katz, "The Unmistakable Stephen Crane," *Antioch Review,* 25 (1965), 341. It was published simultaneously in England as *The Open Boat and Other Stories,* an expanded edition containing nine additional stories. Carl Sandburg may have read *The Black Riders* in Puerto Rico and met Crane there. Michael J. Quigley stated that he interviewed Carl Sandburg for his dissertation at Ohio State University: "A Study of Carl Sandburg: A Major Writer for the Secondary School of Today" (1970). In Quigley's transcription of the interview, Sandburg said: "I read Stephen Crane in Puerto Rico in a leaky poncho tent by a penny candle when the lantern wouldn't light. I saw him down there, too—he was about the best writer there was. I read two of his books of poetry—*Black Riders* and *War Is Kind.* He sure knew a lot about war for a young fellow who'd never been close to one except with a notebook in his hand" (62). He admired Crane, whose poetry "is the most underrated and unknown of any major American writer. It was genuine and cut of the fabric of emotional alienation with the world around him. Anyone who read Steve Crane was influenced by his stuff. There's another one the critics don't like, too" (232). Unfortunately there is no way to verify the accuracy of Quigley's transcription.

18. Although Davis denied that he modeled the main character of the story after Crane, Robert Emmet MacAlarney, a fledgling journalist at the time, stated that Crane's colleagues told him Davis's portrayal accurately reflected Crane (two letters from Robert Emmet MacAlarney to B. J. R. Stolper, both dated "Friday morning," Columbia). In *Richard Harding Davis and His*

Day (New York: Scribner's, 1933), 162, n. 9, Fairfax Downey cites a letter from Franklin Clarkin, war correspondent for the *New York Times,* to Downey: "Some of Davis' fellow-correspondents in Cuba were critical of 'The Derelict.' They found in it 'misleading allusions,' 'inexact references to persons,' not allowing for the circumstances that it was fiction and that, while it integrated and generalized to present a total picture, it did not pretend to be history. His characters in the tale are composites. One recalls that there was on the blockade of Havana and Santiago and the push through the Siboney chaparral a correspondent who was brilliant, one who drank hard, one who was caddish, one who saw the battle of Santiago and wrote the earliest description and one who was sunstruck in a land battle and whose account had to be written from his lips by a comrade who signed and got credit for it, while the sun-smitten man received a harsh cablegram from his office for a supposed dereliction that had been really heroic devotion to duty. The true Harding Davis, the expression of a gentlemanliness of heart, which one remembers as his characteristic, came out in the climax where the derelict sees the man he had made being dined and celebrated and would not spoil the party." Much of what Clarkin says applies to Crane.

19. Walter F. Clowes, *The Detroit Light Guard: A Complete Record of This Organization, from Its Foundation to the Present Day; with Full Account of Riot and Complimentary Duty, and the Campaigns in the Civil and Spanish-American Wars, a Complete Roster of Members at the Time of Muster-Out of the United States Service, as well as a Roster of All Classes of Members* (Detroit: J. F. Eby, 1900), 168. See also Edson Brace, "Stories and Studies of Stephen Crane," *St. Louis Republic,* 17 June 1900, part II, 6. Unless Crane had another black attendant, the person with the nautical nickname "the Bosun" in Stallman (1972), 283, is Cecil.

20. Winfield W. Dudley to Cora Crane, 5 May 1901, Columbia. An undated clipping, presumably from a Baltimore newspaper, of Charles Michelson's "Estimate of Stephen Crane" tells slightly the same story (MHSC Files).

21. *Works,* 8: 81.

22. "Ice-cream soda": *Works,* 6: 262; "steal ponies": Stallman and Hagemann, *The War Dispatches,* 197; "yesterday morning": Davis in *SCRem,* 232–233.

23. Michelson in *SCRem,* 219–220.

24. *C,* 96.

25. "Bad treatment": Michelson in *SCRem,* 220; "waving his handkerchief": Michelson in *SCRem,* 220, 345, n. 11.

25. Havana

1. *Works,* 9: 188.

2. Because information about correspondents in Havana at this time is almost

nonexistent, I have inferred their activity from Crane's Havana dispatches and Walter Parker's reminiscence in *SCRem,* 236–240. See also Charles H. Brown, *The Correspondents' War: Journalists in the Spanish-American War* (New York: Scribner's, 1967), 439–440.

3. *Works,* 9: 188.

4. Parker in *SCRem,* 236.

5. "Stephen Crane and the Cubans," *Washington Post,* 22 July 1900, 17. The syndicated story later appeared in modified form in column 29 as "The Ashes of Love," in Walter Parker, "Reminiscences of Life in New Orleans during the Gay Nineties" (Walter Parker, "New Orleans Reminiscences, 1894–1940," bound clippings from *New Orleans Official Daily Court Reporter,* January 22–May 19, 1941, Special Collections, Tulane University Library). Though Crane initially showed little regard for Cuban insurgents in his dispatches, as he spent more time with them in Havana he came to empathize with their plight. See "'You Must!'—'We Can't!'" in *Works,* 9: 209–212.

6. *C,* 98. Crane had enrolled in French classes at Lafayette, but his poor attendance suggests he did not learn the language there.

7. Emerson in *SCRem,* 245. The bodies of those who died on the *Maine* were disinterred in December 1899 and reburied in Arlington National Cemetery.

8. According to Vincent Starrett, Crane began, but then destroyed, a story titled "The Cat's March" (*Stephen Crane: A Bibliography* [Philadelphia: Centaur, 1923], 10). Lillian Gilkes likewise states that Crane began a love story about an aristocratic Spanish woman and a stranded American sailor, but destroyed it; her source seems to be Beer (Gilkes, 155; Beer, 199).

9. *Works,* 9: 506–507.

10. *C,* 383, 385.

11. H. R. Crane in *SCRem,* 49–50. In "This Majestic Lie," Crane depicted Mary Horan as Martha Clancy, "born in Ireland, bred in New York, fifteen years married to a Spanish captain, and now a widow, keeping Cuban lodgers who had no money with which to pay her" (*Works,* 6: 206–207). A Mrs. Clancy also appears in Crane's playlet "At Clancy's Wake."

12. "Personal shock": Parker in *SCRem,* 239; "cooking instruments": *Works,* 9: 203; "same moon": *Works,* 9: 203, 205.

13. "Second book of verse": "Intrigue" was going to be the original title of *War Is Kind* (*C,* 368); "September 1898 in Havana": according to a friend of his, Crane had said that he put more thought and attention into writing *War Is Kind* than almost anything else he had written ("Books and Their Makers," *Utica* [New York] *Sunday Tribune,* 12 August 1900, 12); "I can think of thee": *Works,* 10: 62, 66, 69; "deception and manipulation": for an astute

argument that "Intrigue" parodies nineteenth-century English Decadent poetry, see George Monteiro, *Stephen Crane's Blue Badge of Courage* (Baton Rouge: Louisiana State University Press, 2000), 103–114; "one letter to Lily while in Cuba": Ames Williams to MHS, 27 December 1948, MHSC Files; "for the imagination": *C,* 208; "trace of chivalry": Lawrence in *SCRem,* 327, n. 84; "his next attempt": "Stephen Crane Bothered by Women," *Chicago Daily Tribune,* 10 January 1897, 3.

14. *Works,* 9: 225.

15. David Wallechinksy and Irving Wallace, eds., *The People's Almanac 2* (New York: Morrow, 1978), 564.

16. *C,* 475–476. Although Crane rarely commented on contemporary political issues, there is another example of a diatribe against mock heroism in "France's Would-Be Hero" (*Works,* 8: 751–755).

17. "Fire-crowned hill": *Works,* 9: 171; "appreciation of his support": "Medal for Stephen Crane," *Albany* [New York] *Evening Journal,* 2 September 1898, 2; "do something": *Works,* 6: 264; "bathing-machine": *Works,* 6: 265; "young pig": *Works,* 6: 269.

18. "Loaves of bread": *Works,* 6: 201–202; "an elephant": *Works,* 6: 204; "ice-pick": *Works,* 6: 114; "palm branch": *Works,* 6: 116, 117.

19. "The Poor Soul" was unpublished; "What Hell Might Be Like" appeared in *The Smart Set* in November 1901, p. 48. It is uncertain when Cora wrote the two fables, but their tone and content suggest that they deal with her relationship with Crane.

20. The lawsuit was dropped when Cora explained that Crane had been called to Cuba suddenly and promised the court that the bill for furniture would be paid immediately upon his return ("Mrs. Crane Sued," *New York Times,* 21 October 1898, 1).

21. *Log,* 353.

22. Gilkes, 153.

23. "Club in London": *C,* 361; "uncalled for": *C,* 390; "articles worked out": *Works,* 5: cx–cxi.

24. "Will he see it": *C,* 388; "submitted only 'The Price of the Harness'": *Log,* 296; "temperament as his": *Log,* 353.

25. "Use in swearing": *C,* 377. "Atlantic Transport Line": Details about payment for the ticket are uncertain. Instead of a deferred payment, Barr may have helped Cora to get loans from friends and Heinemann. "Did not sail": "Friends Fear the Worst," *Chicago Daily Tribune,* 16 October 1898, 5.

26. Paul Mattheisen et al., eds., *The Collected Letters of George Gissing, 1897–1899,* vol. 7 (Athens: Ohio University Press, 1995), 262.

27. A number of prominent figures—including Sir Henry Irving, Henry James, Arthur Conan Doyle, James M. Barrie, A. Quiller Couch, William Heine-

mann, and W. E. Henley—signed a letter published in several London newspapers appealing for donations for Mrs. Frederic and her children, but no
provisions were made for Kate Lyon and her children. See C. W. E. Bigsby,
"The 'Christian Science Case': An Account of the Death of Harold Frederic and the Subsequent Inquest and Court Proceedings," *American Literary
Realism, 1870–1910,* 2 (Spring 1968), 80.

28. *C,* 402–403.

29. Fredson Bowers suggests that Cora may have offered the Sullivan County
    tales and sketches to Pinker for republication (*Works,* 8: 850).

30. "Latin-American islands": Frederick Lewis Allen, *Paul Revere Reynolds*
    (New York: privately printed, 1944), 62; "constant coughing": EFC to TB,
    19 November 1922, Yale; "offices of S. S. McClure": Stallman and Gilkes,
    307; James B. Stronks, "Garland's Private View of Crane in 1898 (with a
    Postscript)," *American Literary Realism,* 6 (1993), 249; "unwholesome type":
    Donald Pizer, ed., *Hamlin Garland's Diaries* (San Marino: Huntington Li-
    brary, 1968), 120; "literary fathers": *C,* 63; "over the years": Stallman and
    Gilkes, 308.

31. *C,* 388–389.

32. *Log,* 333.

33. After Harold Frederic's death in October, Kate Lyon and her three children
    lived with Cora at Ravensbrook. The younger two children continued to
    live with the Cranes after they moved to Brede Place.

34. *C,* 405.

26. Brede Place, Return to Childhood, Another Potboiler

1. "Best geographers": Thomas Ingoldsby, *The Ingoldsby Legends* (London:
   Richard Bentley and Son, 1882), 363–364; "against British letters": Ford
   Madox Ford, *Return to Yesterday* (London: Gollancz, 1931), 20.

2. A. E. W. Mason wrote, "It has always surprised me how Stephen Crane, who
   came over to England perhaps a little contemptuous of English ways (although that may have been a mere façade as self-defense) was taken by ancient England" (Mason in *SCRem,* 362–363, n. 147). The *Delta Upsilon
   Quarterly* (Crane kept in touch with his fraternity) reported that he was
   considering running for Parliament. See "Literary Notes," *Delta Upsilon
   Quarterly,* 17, no. 1 (1 December 1898), 159–160.

3. Allen Andrews, *The Splendid Pauper* (Philadelphia: Lippincott, 1968), 194–
   195; M. Barr in *SCRem,* 292. For a brief history of Brede Place, see Sheila
   Kaye-Smith, *Weald of Kent and Sussex* (London: Robert Hale, Limited,
   1953), 208–209. The Peases commented on the rushes and were privately
   amused by "the Americans aping the Elizabethans in the old country" (Michael Pease to MHS, 27 November 1948, MHSC Files). According to Ford

Madox Ford, Crane while at Brede Place led "the life of an Elizabethan baron," with Cora in medieval dress and a banquet hall strewn with rushes, where their dogs gnawed on bones that guests threw on the floor (*SCRem*, 260). Ford's description of Crane as a baron may be the source for Beer's claim that Sanford Bennett called him "Baron Brede" (Beer, 210).

4. "Private dungeon": Robert M. Cooper, *The Literary Guide and Companion to Southern England* (Athens: Ohio University Press, 1985), 81; "were the culprits": M. Barr in *SCRem*, 292. Stephen and Cora also told the story to Curtis Brown (Curtis Brown, *Contacts* [London: Cassell, 1935], 224–225); "the Duke": Stallman and Gilkes, 320, Linson, 109; "two-story wall": Brown, *Contacts*, 225.

5. "Illustrated magazine": The editor of *Cosmopolitan* published "The Price of the Harness" under the title "The Woof of Thin Red Threads," adapted from a phrase in the story. Crane objected to the revision (*C*, 387). "As an impressionist": *Log*, 356; "been waiting for": Robert Barr, "American Brains in London: The Men Who Have Succeeded," *Saturday Evening Post*, 8 April 1899, 649.

6. *C*, 420.

7. "Insisted on paying something": Mark Barr, letter to the editor, *New York Herald Tribune*, 7 January 1940, section 2, 9. "*The Third Violet*": The loan apparently became an advance. See *C*, 466.

8. *C*, 429–430.

9. Ibid., 430.

10. Ames W. Williams, "On Collecting the Writings of Stephen Crane," *Courier* [Syracuse University Library], 2 (December 1962), 7.

11. *C*, 419. Throughout his career, Crane never made more than five cents a word, a respectable rate but not enough to make him successful financially. See R. W. Stallman, *Stephen Crane*, rev. ed. (New York: Braziller, 1973), 599–600, n. 9; James B. Stronks, "Stephen Crane's English Years: The Legend Corrected," *Papers of the Bibliographical Society of America*, 57 (1963), 340–349; and Matthew Bruccoli and Joseph Katz, "Scholarship and Mere Artifacts: The British and Empire Publications of Stephen Crane," *Studies in Bibliography*, 22 (1969), 277–287.

12. *C*, 302.

13. "Wayward brother": *C*, 416; "am now leading": *C*, 446–447.

14. "Financial problems": for other examples of Crane's use of Brede Place stationery to impress someone, see *C*, 459, 464, 465; "extravagant spending": *C*, 416.

15. Kate Lyon stayed in London and Liverpool with her seven-year-old daughter, Helen Frederic. The Cranes eventually had more dogs, including Pow-

der Puff. Crane renamed the horses Hengist and Horsa because, as he told Mark Barr, they were temperamental horses that "were true 'Kentishmen!'" (Barr in *SCRem*, 291). Hengist and Horsa are the legendary leaders of the German (Anglo-Saxon) invasion of Britain. In Germanic myth, Hengist was the name of Siegfried's horse.

16. Jessie Conrad in *SCRem*, 255. In a letter to Moreton Frewen, Crane alluded to a fire that had been started by tipsy help, in conjunction with "lamps and the open fire," and that had caused him "anxiety for the safety of your old house" (*C*, 524). William MacVittie (known as Mack)—the valet, groom, coachman, gardener, and head of staff—eventually resigned because Stephen and Cora locked up their liquor.

17. "Seaside resort": "An Experience Resurrected," *Detroit Free Press*, 17 September 1899, A4.

18. "Fifteen hundred pounds": *C*, 419.

19. "Work steadily": *C*, 413; "valuable time": *Works*, 7: 126.

20. "Cora to type": Harriman in *SCRem*, 270; "things are all right": Harriman in *SCRem*, 278 (see also Jessie Conrad in *SCRem*, 254); "dog licenses": Jessie Conrad in *SCRem*, 254.

21. According to a report in the *Saturday Evening Post*, one of the Frederic children "had been regularly adopted" by the Cranes ("Stephen Crane's Good Heart," *Saturday Evening Post*, 21 July 1900, 20), but there is no evidence to support the assertion.

22. "In created things": *C*, 166. "Clarence Loomis Peaslee": Peaslee's name reappears as Peasley, the Marine sergeant in "The Sergeant's Private Madhouse," which was written in 1899, at the time of the Whilomville stories. "About her childhood": Jones in *SCRem*, 289. In a letter to TB (14 January 1934, Yale), EFC reported that when Cora visited the Crane family, she told them that she was the "angel child." Though it is uncertain how much of Cora's childhood influenced the writing of the stories, Crane's childhood certainly did.

23. When Harper and Brothers wanted Crane to surrender dramatization rights as part of the contract for *The Monster and Other Stories*, he immediately wrote to Paul Revere Reynolds on March 31, 1899, saying that he would "not consent to their having any claim at all upon a possible dramatizeation of the stories. If there is possibility of good drama in 'The Monster' for instance it is there because I made it and Harper and Bro's. had nothing to do with it" (*C*, 463).

24. For the conjectured dating of the story, see *C*, 543, n. 3.

25. In "Mr. Stephen Crane on the New America," Crane again identified with Saint Stephen. Attempting to preserve peace following a war can be risky:

"The art of war is applied mechanics. It only needs one goading, two asides, and three insults. Thereupon we become a military people. If an apostle of peace does appear with true spirit and with true eloquence, he will . . . be some poor devil, and will probably be stoned to death for talking beyond his audience" (*Works,* 9: 228).

26. "Liberal taste": *Log,* 168; "words which hurt": *C,* 200.

27. "Not good enough": *C,* 448; "your success": *C,* 459; "Pinker by name": *C,* 464; "rather tightly": *C,* 539; "did with Reynolds": *C,* 575.

28. Ibid., 457.

29. Cather in *SCRem,* 177.

30. *Works,* 10: 344. Although Cora's recollection of this incident does not specifically mention *Active Service,* the only other novel that she could be alluding to is *The O'Ruddy.* By the time he was writing it, however, Crane had little strength for angry outbursts and knew his career was nearly finished. With his Greek novel, he was writing frantically, and constantly besieging agents and publishers for money; with his Irish romance, Cora had to handle the correspondence of her dying companion.

31. McClure syndicated *Active Service* in the United States, but it is unclear whether Reynolds or Stokes sold it. For the likelihood that Stokes did, see *Works,* 3: 351–358.

32. "Being so bad": *C,* 480–481; "on romantic fiction": Weatherford, 249, 273; "stale cigarettes": *Log,* 406.

33. "Divergent parts": *Works,* 3: 237. "Overwhelming for him": Vincent Starrett is the only source of information about "The Cat's March" (*Stephen Crane: A Bibliography* [Philadelphia: Centaur, 1923], 10). Although I am suggesting that Crane's depiction of Cora as a cat alludes to her description of him as a mouse, he might also have been thinking of the title of a popular humorous song, "Our Old Tom Cat; or, The Cat's March Out of the Ash Hole" (1836).

34. "Professor and some students": *Works,* 3: 179; "lost love": *Works,* 3: 166; "of a parallel": *Works,* 3: 187–188.

35. "Proper metropolis": *Works,* 3: 191, 192; "of her femininity": *Works,* 3: 222.

36. "Marries Marjory": *C,* 459; "Lochinvar who rescued Cora": *Works,* 3: 220; "What more fitting": *Works,* 3: 306.

37. See also Crane's cynical poem "There exists the eternal fact of conflict," which criticizes jingoistic patriotism.

38. Crane extended the self-portrait of himself as Little Nell, who works for the *New York Eclipse* and wears pajamas while on a dispatch boat. The *Eclipse* is a stand-in for the *New York World,* and either Sylvester Scovel or his wife took the photos of a disheveled Crane dressed in pajamas aboard the dispatch boat *Three Friends.*

An American version of Nell as a dime novel heroine appears in Agile
Penne (pseudonym of Albert W. Aiken), *Orphan Nell, the Orange Girl; or, The
Lost Heir,* serialized in 1870–1871 in a magazine and published as a book
in 1880.

39. "Mathematical formula": *Works,* 3: 328.

27. Brede Place Visitors, Return to Ancestry

1. "Leaked out": Weatherford, 232; "*War Is Kind*": William M. Curtin, ed., *The
World and the Parish: Willa Cather's Articles and Reviews, 1893–1902* (Lincoln:
University of Nebraska Press, 1970), 700.

2. "Laughed at": *C,* 187; "Pound on the other": John Berryman, *Stephen Crane*
(1950; rpt. Cleveland: World-Meridian, 1962), 271, 269.

3. "Mind from his work": *C,* 413; "William Dean Howells": "Literary Folk:
Their Ways and Their Work," *Saturday Evening Post,* 16 December 1905, 19.
For another version of this anecdote, in which Crane also praises Garland,
see Harriman in *SCRem,* 279.

4. Scholars have always thought that Karl Edwin Harriman and Kenneth
Herford, another journalist who knew Crane, were separate people, as did
I when I edited *SCRem;* but a newspaper article reporting Harriman's
marriage states that "Kenneth Herford" was his pen name ("Quiet Home
Wedding," *Detroit Free Press,* 19 October 1899, 7). In hindsight, one can see
the similarity between the title of Herford's article "Young Blood—Stephen Crane" and that of Harriman's first piece about Crane, "A Romantic
Idealist—Mr. Stephen Crane" (*SCRem,* 156–158, 270–271). The revelation
about the names creates a problem. Whereas Harriman makes clear that
he did not meet Crane until 1899, Herford recounts a conversation with
Crane about *The Red Badge of Courage* that must have occurred in 1893. If
Crane told Herford/Harriman about the conversation in 1899, it suggests
that "they" might have fictionalized events in their reminiscences.

5. "Apparently destroyed it": Harriman in *SCRem,* 278–280. If Vincent Starrett (*Stephen Crane: A Bibliography* [Philadelphia: Centaur, 1923], 121) is correct regarding the dating of the composition of "Siege," then the anecdote
occurred in August 1899. "Little frailties": James Walter Smith, "Literary
Letter," *Literary Era,* 7 (July 1900), 201.

6. "At his expense": Edward Garnett, review of Thomas Beer, *Stephen Crane,
The Nation and the Athenaeum,* 11 October 1924, 58; "all summer": *C,* 515;
"Mind this": *C,* 504. "All is vanity": Much of what is known about the extravagant hospitality at Brede Place comes from Joseph and Jessie Conrad's
reminiscences (*SCRem,* 249–256), in which Jessie occasionally has harsh
words to say about Cora.

7. Angela V. John, *Elizabeth Robins: Staging a Life, 1862–1952* (London: Routledge, 1995), 64; [George] Bernard Shaw, *Dramatic Opinions and Essays: With an Apology,* vol. 2 (London: Archibald Constable, 1907), 92.

8. Circumstances surrounding the story are confusing. It was published anonymously, so someone must have told Stephen and Cora that Robins was the author; yet Robins denied having written it (Joanne E. Gates, *Elizabeth Robins, 1862–1952: Actress, Novelist, Feminist* [Tuscaloosa: University of Alabama Press, 1994], 59–60). Cora's assertion to Elizabeth that Stephen had "never read a story which pointed a stronger moral lesson" (*C,* 480) is unlikely. The conventional tale about a master who seduces and abandons his servant girl breaks one of Crane's cardinal tenets: "Preaching is fatal to art in literature" (*C,* 230).

9. "The old man": Ford in *SCRem,* 260, 262. Ford claimed that when James realized Crane was dying, he ordered New England delicacies from the U.S.-based Wanamaker's in London (*SCRem,* 263). Although the incident may have occurred, Ford, as with many of his assertions, is the only source. "Crane later salvaged": Beer, 236, 169–170; "to visit them": Edith Richie Jones states that James visited the Cranes three or four times weekly, though the number may be an exaggeration based on a faulty memory of events almost twenty-five years later (Edith Richie Jones to TB, 6 February 1923, MHSC Files); "would startle James": Harriman in *SCRem,* 273. In *Henry James: The Master, 1901–1916,* vol. 5 of *The Life of Henry James* (Philadelphia: Lippincott, 1972), 61–62, Leon Edel says Ford Madox Hueffer likewise stated that the costume shocked James, but Edel knew that Hueffer could be an unreliable source. "Valuable ship timber": M. Barr in *SCRem,* 291; "prattling babe": Jones in *SCRem,* 284. Ford Madox Ford (*SCRem,* 260) claimed that he rarely saw Crane and James, but Edith Richie Jones is probably more reliable, for she lived with the Cranes from July 1899 to January 1900.

10. "Woman's corner": Robert M. Cooper, *The Literary Guide and Companion to Southern England* (Athens: Ohio University Press, 1985), 73; Lillian Gilkes, *Cora Crane: A Biography of Mrs. Stephen Crane* (Bloomington: Indiana University Press, 1960), 204; "like a clam": *C,* 496; "*The Red Badge of Courage*": Edel, *Henry James: The Master,* 59–60; "America's greatest writers": Mark Barr, letter to the editor, *New York Herald Tribune,* 7 January 1940, section 2, 9; "great workman": *Works,* 8: 734.

11. Nicholas Delbanco has suggested that the country-house party in the novel is based on the Christmas celebration at Brede Place in December 1899; see Delbanco, *Group Portrait: Joseph Conrad, Stephen Crane, Ford Madox Ford, Henry James, H. G. Wells* (New York: Carroll and Graf, 1982), 51. Leon Edel has suggested that the story "may have derived some of its poignancy from

his vision of Crane visibly dying in the damp old house while Cora thrived unaware"; see Edel, *Henry James: A Life* (New York: Harper, 1985), 532.

12. Quoted in Adeline R. Tintner, "Cora Crane and James's 'The Great Condition': A Biblio-Biographical Note," *Henry James Review,* 13 (Spring 1992), 193; and in Stanley Wertheim, "New Stephen Crane Letters and Inscriptions," *Stephen Crane Studies,* 1 (Spring 1992), 19, with slight variations. Both authors elaborate on the significance of the story's excision from the journal.

13. "A view of her": Leon Edel, ed., *Henry James: Letters,* vol. 4: *1895–1916* (Cambridge, MA: Harvard University Press, 1984), 162. "England in 1907": For a helpful analysis of James's attitude toward Cora following Stephen's death, see Edel, *Henry James: The Master,* 66–68.

14. "*Peter Pan*": J. R. Glorney Bolton, "Real Captain Hook," *West Australian* [Perth], 5 January 1952, 12. Lovers of the play have long discussed the inspiration for Captain Hook. When Barrie published *Peter and Wendy* (1911), the novelization of the play, he wrote: "Hook was not his true name. To reveal who he really was would even at this date set the country in a blaze." J. M. Barrie, *Peter and Wendy* (New York: Scribner's, 1911), 203.

15. "Hall at Brede Place": Edith Richie Jones to TB, 6 February 1923, Yale.

16. "Greatest of the boys": *C,* 516.

17. "Italian love song": I have inferred that Crane was singing in this particular style because Jessie Conrad labeled the song "some haunting Neapolitan air" (*SCRem,* 252), which suggests that he was singing a "canzone Napoletana" (a Neapolitan song), a traditional form of Italian music for male soloists that became popular in the nineteenth century. Among the most popular songs was "O sole mio," which had just been published in 1898. But Jessie Conrad's assertion that Crane also occasionally accompanied himself on the violin (255) is most likely wrong. Her source seems to be Beer, 234.

18. "Stages of lunacy": *C,* 486; "ought to have a dog": Jessie Conrad in *SCRem,* 252. Conrad renamed the dog "Escamillo" (often shortened to "Millo"), after the toreador in Bizet's opera *Carmen.* According to Edith Richie Jones's letter to TB on February 6, 1923 (Yale), the dog that was given this name was Pizanner. Regardless of which it was, Crane revealed his love of horses by apparently naming one of his dogs after the famous Lipizzaner stallions.

19. Jessie Conrad in *SCRem,* 256.

20. "Be 'partners'": *C,* 302; "paying back loans": For an extended discussion of the loan and invitation, see Paul Sorrentino, "Stephen and William Howe Crane: A Loan and Its Aftermath," *Resources for American Literary Study,* 11, no. 1 (1981), 101–108.

21. "God-send": *C,* 62.

22. "Thousand copies each": Jay Martin, *Harvests of Change: American Literature, 1865–1914* (Englewood Cliffs, NJ: Prentice-Hall, 1967), 83, n. 8.

23. JTC to GP, 26 September 1865, Virginia.

24. "Revolution through": *Works,* 10: 160; "biblical phraseology": *Works,* 10: 160. "Settled in 1665": Crane's notes on the book, "Plans for New Novel" and "Plans for Story," are in *Works,* 10: 158–160. For his interest in Elizabethtown, see *C,* 505. "Them that hate me": This quotation, which is from Exodus 20:5, is the epigraph to poem 12 in *The Black Riders.* "Did it's duty": *C,* 166.

25. "Of the social season": http://www.hrr.co.uk/?pid?1 (accessed 6/14/2013); "another supply": Harriman in *SCRem,* 281–282.

26. "Unlucky number": Harriman in *SCRem,* 282; "wild-cat fury": Pugh in *SCRem,* 297.

27. "Kind of people": Gilkes, *Cora Crane,* 195. If one of the "European Letters" is based on personal experience, Stephen and probably Cora were among the six thousand attendees at a garden party at Buckingham Palace on June 2, 1897, as part of the Queen's Diamond Jubilee celebration. Although Queen Victoria talked with attendees, it is uncertain whether the Cranes were among the fortunate few (*Works,* 8: 696).

28. "Kept her company": Edith Richie Jones in *SCRem,* 286.

29. "Break down": *C,* 508; "feel like hell": *C,* 515.

28. Trips to Europe, Final Celebration, Badenweiler

1. "Tissue-covered combs": Edith Richie Jones in *SCRem,* 284; "Wasn't that right": Brown in *SCRem,* 141–142. Although Brown does not date the anecdote, the harvested corn suggests early fall.

2. Edith Richie Jones in *SCRem,* 287.

3. "Seedy": *C,* 524; "spring of 1899": *C,* 385.

4. "Has no sympathy": *C,* 522, 523; "would quit": "In a Minor Key," *Chicago Daily Tribune,* 15 June 1899, 6.

5. "Business letters": *C,* 529–530, 531–532; "out of control": Wells in *SCRem,* 268; "misplaced manuscripts": Edith Richie Jones in *SCRem,* 287; "had already written": *C,* 519; "quick money": *C,* 605; "fiction about almost anything": *C,* 544.

6. *C,* 543–544.

7. Ibid., 527, 528.

8. Edith Richie Jones in *SCRem,* 287.

9. Only fragments of *The Ghost* survive. For a detailed discussion about the play, see Jesse S. Crisler, "'Christmas Must Be Gay': Stephen Crane's *The Ghost*—A Play by Divers Hands," *Proof,* 3 (1973), 69–120; John D. Gordan, "*The Ghost* at Brede Place," *Bulletin of the New York Public Library,* 56 (1952), 591–595; and *Works,* 8: 162–179, 835–839.

10. "This crime": *C,* 549; "d—d fools": *Log,* 408; *C,* 554, 552.

11. "Awful rubbish": *C,* 548; "Pinafore": *C,* 569.

12. "Related to British royalty": *C,* 559–561, n. 1; "makes a difference": Cora Crane to Agnes Crane, 16 December 1900, typescript in MHSC Files.

13. "I'd wear *two*": Harriman in *SCRem,* 278, 280; "haggard grace": Mason to MHS, 21 January 1948, MHSC Files. There is disagreement regarding whether James attended the farce. Lillian Gilkes states that he did not (*Cora Crane: A Biography of Mrs. Stephen Crane* [Bloomington: Indiana University Press, 1960], 222), and Leon Edel says that he was at least not at the party (*Henry James: The Master, 1901–1916,* vol. 5 of *The Life of Henry James* [Philadelphia: Lippincott, 1972], 65). Clare Sheridan, Mr. and Mrs. Frewen's daughter, recalled that H. G. Wells told her James was there, but "went home, unable to stand the discomfort" (Clare [Frewen] Sheridan to Mr. [Ames] Williams, 7 June 1945, Syracuse).

14. "Racing on broomsticks": Mason in *SCRem,* 295; Gilkes, 226; "like that at poker": Wells in *SCRem,* 268; "pace of his life": Hind in *SCRem,* 298.

15. *C,* 569.

16. "Old worries": *C,* 572; "he could not find": *Log,* 424; "prison sentence": Ford in *SCRem,* 263; "going smash": *C,* 572; "two hundred on the next book": *C,* 583; "stories if he had them": *C,* 541.

17. "Only desolation": Mrs. Stephen Crane, "Cowardice," *Evening Post* [Wellington, New Zealand] *Supplement,* 1 November 1902, 1.

18. "Individual tragedy": *Works,* 5: 60; "struggled to escape": Edith Richie Jones in *SCRem,* 285; "his study at Brede Place": M. Barr in *SCRem,* 291.

19. *Works,* 8: 187–196.

20. "Fled Havana": *C,* 465–466. Reynolds learned about the bill unexpectedly when a creditor from a Cuban company showed up at his office demanding payment. It is unknown whether or not the bill was paid. "Could stand her": Clare [Frewen] Sheridan to Mr. [Ames] Williams.

21. English Channel": Stallman and Gilkes, 318; "Dr. Thomas J. Maclagan": The name is incorrectly given as Dr. J. T. Maclagen in *C* and as Dr. Thomas J. Maclagen in *Log.*

22. "Sure as you're born": Pugh in *SCRem,* 297. H. G. Wells recalled Crane's showing him a shelf of books written by his relatives (Stallman and Gilkes, 316). On April 21, 1899, Jonathan K. Peck sent his cousin a list of available books by the Pecks and thanked him for his "very kind words and timely check" (*C,* 470–472). Though Crane's letter is not extant, a local newspaper alluded to it on April 22, implying that the check was for *Luther Peck and His Five Sons* and *The Seven Wonders of the New World;* the article stated that Crane was "expressing pleasure at having read them, and saying that he wished to add them to his library" ("Stephen Crane," *Wilkes-Barre Times,* 22 April 1899, 8). The newspaper reprinted the article in a slightly

different version on October 20, 1899. Crane had two copies of his cousin's book at Brede Place.

23. "An entr'acte": Pugh in *SCRem*, 297.

24. "From your letter": *C*, 617; "deeply rooted": *C*, 632, 624.

25. Although Stephen and Cora were never married, Cora used his last name and people referred to them as the Cranes.

26. "First-person point of view": Fewer than a dozen of Crane's stories use the first-person point of view, and rarely does he explore the narrative implications of this technique. A notable exception is the Poe-like "A Tale of Mere Chance." J. C. Levenson has suggested that as Crane dictated notes to Cora regarding the ending of *The O'Ruddy*, he may have identified with the hero (*Works*, 4: l–lii, 360–362); "My Wife / Stephen Crane": *C*, 648. Cora enclosed the dedication, written in Crane's hand, with a letter to James B. Pinker on May 20, 1900. When *The O'Ruddy* was published in 1903, however, neither the American nor the English edition contained it. The dedication may have been temporarily misplaced, given that it had been written only on a small piece of paper three years earlier.

27. "In the world": *Works*, 4: 267.

28. "Trouble seems over": *C*, 632; "our own children": Eben Alexander to Cora Crane, 17 May 1900, Columbia.

29. "Lady Randolph Churchill": Frewen may have helped to pay some of Stephen and Cora's outstanding debts (Gilkes, 252). "Live for years": *C*, 642; "can you help": *C*, 641.

30. *Log*, 440.

31. "That's all": Conrad in *SCRem*, 251; "died at home": Jessie Conrad in *SCRem*, 255.

32. "*Open boat*": *C*, 655–656; "of the ocean": *Works*, 9: 94.

33. "Seems awful": *C*, 656; "money for Mr. Crane": *C*, 654. In February, Stokes had agreed to accept *The O'Ruddy* in place of the Revolutionary War novel, and Methuen was willing to take it as the unstipulated novel Crane had been contracted to write for them (*Log*, 425, 426). "Impending disaster": Helen Crane Sketchbook, Columbia, *Works*, 4: l–li, n. 85; "medicated her": *C*, 656; "can't write more about it": *C*, 657.

34. "Don't dare to think": *Works*, 10: 343.

35. "Possibilities and powers": Leon Edel, ed., *Henry James: Letters*, vol. 4: *1895–1916* (Cambridge, MA: Harvard University Press, 1984), 145.

36. "Impregnable": *Works*, 10: 343; "buried with his mother and father": *Port Jervis Union*, 13 June 1900, 3.

Acknowledgments

I would like to thank John Clendenning, Michael Squires, and Stanley Wertheim for reading an early draft of my biography; thanks, as well, to the outside readers for Harvard University Press. Elizabeth Friedmann, Jerome Loving, and Keith Newlin graciously read specific sections. All of them offered excellent advice and suggestions for revision. Susan Belasco, Larry Berkove, John Bird, Jackson R. Bryer, Donna Campbell, James Colvert, Sarah Daugherty, Patrick K. Dooley, Robert Dowling, John Dudley, Dennis Eddings, Benjamin F. Fisher, Steven Frye, Kevin J. Hayes, Kathryn Hilt, Daniel Hoffman, Charles Johanningsmeier, Richard Kopley, Linck Johnson, J. C. Levenson, Eric Carl Link, Sanford E. Marovitz, James Meredith, George Monteiro, Roark Mulligan, Joel Myerson, James Nagel, Hershel Parker, Donald Pizer, Jeanne Reesman, Michael Robertson, Michael Schaefer, Gary Scharnhorst, Sandra Spanier, Donald Vanouse, and Edmund White shared their insights on Crane and American literature with me. I learned much about biography from N. John Hall, as well as from Jesse Crisler, Carl Dawson, Scott Donaldson, Ed Folsom, Susan Goodman, Joseph McElrath, Kenneth Silverman, and Linda Wagner-Martin, all of whom participated in one of the two roundtables on literary biography that I organized for the American Literature Association. Colleagues of mine at Virginia Tech—Linda Arnold, Andrew Becker, Glenn Bugh, Roger Ekirch, Sam Riley, Donald Rude, Michael Saffle, John and June Stubbs, and Bailey Van Hook—patiently answered my questions about American art, music, journalism, and history, as well as about Virgil, Joseph Conrad, and two of Crane's poems translated into Italian. Lynn Talbot answered questions about Spanish, and Peter Osborne shared with me the Minisink Valley Historical Society's resources and his extensive knowledge of New York's Orange and Sullivan counties. Robert K. Crane gave me, as a gift, a Crane family scrapbook compiled by Stephen's brother George and his wife. Charles Alaimo, Colleen Bain, Marisa Bourgoin, Jules Chametzky, Frank D'Alessandro, Alan Davies, Carl G. and Brearley B. Karsch, A. Melissa Kiser, Madeline Morrow, Julian Munby, Linda Briscoe Myers, Steve Peck, Nicholas Siekierski, Linda Siwarski, Tony Splendore, and Bonnie Taylor-Blake kindly answered questions about Crane from a stranger. The interlibrary staff of Newman Library at Virginia Tech promptly responded to my ongoing requests for material. Over the years, I have been fortunate to receive funding for my research from Virginia Tech, the National Endowment for the Humanities, and the John Simon Guggenheim Memorial Foundation.

It has been a pleasure to work with the staff at Harvard University Press. I am indebted to Heather Hughes and Graciela Galup for their help in the production of the book, as well as to Tom Broughton-Willett, who created the index, and Kathryn Blatt, who did the proofreading. Two people have greatly improved my manuscript. Maria Ascher's keen eyes spotted many errors and infelicities. She strengthened the sound and the sense of my prose. I could not have asked for a better editor than John Kulka, whose sage advice and detailed commentary helped shape the contours of the narrative. I have the highest admiration for both of them.

Finally, I am above all indebted to my wife, Peg, to whom I dedicate this book. Her profound understanding of human nature has improved every page, and her love and counsel have long guided me. She has been the rudder steering my own open boat into port.

Index